Taxation: Policy and Practice

25th Edition

2018/19

Taxation
Policy and Practice

25th edition
2018/2019

Andy Lymer
Professor of Accounting & Taxation
University of Birmingham

Lynne Oats
Professor of Taxation & Accounting
University of Exeter

Taxation: Policy and Practice – 25th Edition 2018/2019

Copyright © Andy Lymer & Lynne Oats

For more information, contact Fiscal Publications, Unit 100, The Guildhall, Edgbaston Park Road, Birmingham, B15 2TU, UK or visit: http://www.fiscalpublications.com

ISBN 9781906201401

First edition	1993	Fourteenth edition	2007
Second edition	1994	Fifteenth edition	2008
Third edition	1995	Sixteenth edition	2009
Fourth edition	1996	Seventeenth edition	2010
Fifth edition	1997	Eighteenth edition	2011
Sixth edition	1999	Nineteenth edition	2012
Seventh edition	2000	Twentieth edition	2013
Eighth edition	2001	Twenty first edition	2014
Ninth edition	2002	Twenty second edition	2015
Tenth edition	2003	Twenty third edition	2016
Eleventh edition	2004	Twenty fourth edition	2017
Twelfth edition	2005	Twenty fifth edition	2018
Thirteenth edition	2006		

Cover design by Filter Design Ltd
Printed and bound by CPI Group (UK) Ltd, Croydon, CR0 4YY

Typesetting and production by Mac Bride, Southampton.

Contents

P Preface to the 25th Edition

Philosophy and history of the book

This book was initially created at a time when there was a significant gap in the market for tax textbooks. Excellent material already existed which covered a legal approach to tax, an economic/public sector approach and very detailed technical materials. What was missing, however, was an introductory level text that took a combined, interdisciplinary view on the subject, written in a readable style. Dora Hancock (Birmingham City University) produced the first six editions of the text until Andy Lymer (University of Birmingham) took over producing the text. Since the eleventh edition, authorship has rested entirely with Andy and Lynne Oats (University of Exeter).

In attempting to continue to provide a complete, but readable, general UK tax textbook we have also tried to provide as wide coverage as possible of professional level introductory UK tax courses. This book is therefore suitable as a supplement to the UK accounting and business professional examinations, particularly in providing greater depth to the courses you may be undertaking towards professional exams to enhance your understanding of this topic.

A number of key changes were made in this edition including:

1. Updating the book fully for the various changes brought about this year in the November 2017 Budget and the various Finance and other Acts in 2017 and 2018 including:
    - Changes to personal tax allowances;
    - Increase in the capital gains tax annual exemption;
    - Removal of CGT indexation allowance for companies;
    - Increase in rate of research and development tax credit;
    - Stamp duty relief for first time home buyers;
    - Corporate interest deductibility restriction rules;
    - Reform to corporate loss rules;
    - Freezing of VAT threshold;
    - Outline details of important changes that were announced in the November Budget 2017 but will not apply until at least April 2019.

2. Further development of the Quick Quiz questions for all computational chapters. These allow students to practice their skills on short questions before tackling the more difficult ones that then we provide (some of which have answers only available through the course lecturer).

3. A significant number of new computational questions in all chapters for use by both students and lecturers both in the book and on the website. Many of these questions are based on recent professional examination questions.

4. Updating and widening of the range of Fiscal Facts added throughout the text to contextualise further the material being discussed.

5. Review and updating of the tax glossary.

Other well liked features of the book have been updated and developed where necessary based on user feedback received and reviews of how tax is taught in the UK at present.

How to use this text

This textbook is not written as a reference text, although the detailed indices and glossary it contains will help direct you to specific areas of material when you need this help. It is instead written to be read. To gain the most from this text we would advise you to read chapters in their entirety, preferably starting at the beginning of the chapter!

Regular activities are included in the text to illustrate the important points you will need to understand and to give you a chance to practice what you are learning as you go through the book. Although there may be a significant 'urge' to jump straight from the activity to the feedback provided, you will miss much of the benefit of the activities if you do not first attempt them yourself.

You will also find a number of quick quizzes, longer self-test and full exam level questions at the end of each chapter that cover the material explained in the chapter. Some of these have answers provided in the back of the book but for others you will have to obtain the answers from your lecturer or teacher, as they will only be provided to them via their section of the website.

As you read the text you will regularly meet new tax terms. You will find all the terms you will need to be familiar with in the glossary at the back of the book. Use this resource as you come across the terms so you can gradually build up your tax vocabulary as you learn new tax ideas and techniques. To help you in this process we put words in italics when we introduce new terms that so you can easily spot you need to take special note and make sure you are aware of their meaning.

Website

A comprehensive website is available to all purchasers of this book to support your use of this text (**http://www.taxstudent.com/uk**). This site is enhanced each year and you should consider it as a direct extension to the book. It contains a range of materials and resources that will help you gain the most from your studying of the UK's taxation system. The site includes:

- extensive multiple choice based self-test questions for each chapter,
- extensions to many areas of the text to allow you to go deeper into particular topics if you need to (watch out for the pointers to this as you work through the text – these are marked with the computer symbol in the left hand margin), and
- a range of links and other resources to help with your wider reading for this subject and any assignments/dissertations you may need to undertake associated with a course you may be taking.

The website is frequently updated throughout the year so check it from time to time for changes.

Acknowledgements

We acknowledge the permission granted us by CIMA, ICAS and ACCA to use past examination questions in this text, and on the website.

CIMA, the Chartered Institute of Management Accountants, is the world's leading and largest professional body of management accountants, with 172,000 members and students operating in 168 countries, working at the heart of business.

The Institute of Chartered Accountants of Scotland (ICAS) is the world's first professional accountancy body. It was the first to adopt the designation 'Chartered Accountant', and the letters 'CA' can only be used in the UK by ICAS members. ICAS has been training CAs for over 150 years and is highly regarded throughout the world for the high calibre of its members.

ACCA (the Association of Chartered Certified Accountants) is the global body for professional accountants. They aim to offer business-relevant, first-choice qualifications to people of application, ability and ambition around the world who seek a rewarding career in accountancy, finance and management.

You can find out more about these bodies at the following links:
- CIMA at www.cimaglobal.com or www.cimaglobal.com/Students/
- ICAS at www.icas.org.uk or www.icas.org.uk/Becomea CA/ and
- ACCA at www.accaglobal.com or
  www.accaglobal.com/en/qualifications.html

The Fiscal Facts notes added throughout the text were sourced from various public online resources including the Institute for Fiscal Studies, HM Treasury and HMRC websites.

We would particularly like to thank Nicky Thomas (Senior Lecturer in Tax and Accounting, University of Exeter) for her continued technical assistance in the development of this year's text and various others, particularly our students, who have provided helpful suggestions and ideas included in this edition.

Please note, however, that whilst every attempt has been made in writing this text to be accurate and true to the current UK tax system it should not be solely relied upon as a definitive source of information on current tax rules. Readers are advised to seek specific professional advice in their tax planning affairs. Neither the authors nor the publishers accepts any legal responsibility for any loss related to actions taken based on material contained in this book.

This book is improved year on year in part on the basis of feedback people provide to us as the authors. We are most grateful for this and very much welcome comments you wish to make about the book or suggestions for future development of the book, or the associated website. The authors can be contacted for this purpose at:

lymer&oats@taxstudent.com

Andrew Lymer and Lynne Oats
July 2018

W Taxation: Policy & Practice – website

http://www.taxstudent.com/uk

Fiscal Publications, and the authors of this text, have created a website to be used in conjunction with this text book.

Visit the above address to find:

1   Answers to questions at the end of each chapter (note – some are reserved for lecturer use only as teaching aids – if you want copies of these please ask your lecturer).
2   Extension materials for many parts of the text allowing you to go deeper into these topics than are covered in the book.
3   Multiple choice questions – self test questions for each chapter.
4   Large extra question and answer bank for self or classroom managed extra practice and illustration of tax computations.
5   A large list of tax related links for further reading, dissertation etc.
6   Easy to print rates and allowance pages.

Whilst the lecturer area of the website is only available to bona fide teachers, the student area is open to all purchasers of this book. Basic registration will be required for this access.

Please use your unique user ID and password, as listed below, to gain access to this part of the site.

User ID: 2018student689912
Password: 2018tywg32!

Do not provide these details to others. Fiscal Publications reserves the right to block your access to the site if it suspects this has occurred.

Fiscal Publications

Other useful books to aid your study of UK and international taxation

This text is produced by a UK-based publishing house that specialises in taxation and public economics texts. See below for some of their other books that will enhance your understanding of UK and international taxation.

Taxation: incorporating the 2018 Finance Act

by Alan Combs, Ricky Tutin and Peter Rowes

ISBN 9781906201418

This is the companion text for Taxation: Policy and Practice. It provides many further examples and 100s of questions and answers for additional explanation and practice of all the topics covered in this book.

Economics of Taxation – 18th edition

by Simon James and Christopher Nobes

ISBN 9781906201425

For approaching 40 years this textbook has been the leader in its field. Updated annually, the 18th edition provides a clear and authoritative introduction to the economic theory of taxation and to its practical operations in the UK. It also highlights useful international comparisons throughout.

Comparative Taxation: Why tax systems differ

by Chris Evans, John Hasseldine, Andy Lymer, Robert Ricketts & Cedric Sandford

ISBN 9781906201364

This book analyses and compares taxation in different countries. It looks at what tax systems have in common, how they differ and seeks to explain the similarities and the differences. The book provides answers to questions such as: why has VAT become the dominant sales tax world-wide?, why are there so many differences in the way countries tax corporate income and capital gains?, and why is income tax the dominant tax in advanced countries?

For further details see **http://www.fiscalpublications.com**

Student discounts available for many titles – see website for details.

1 The framework of UK taxation

Introduction

1.1 Taxation has played an important role in civilised societies since their birth thousands of years ago. The earliest written records of how such societies formed and were organised illustrate the importance of taxation in their successes, but also some of their downfalls. Taxation continues to play an important role in modern societies, as we will see throughout this chapter.

Ever since people began to gather together in groups and share resources as communities, taxes have had to be raised to pay for services that can be used by the community as a whole, rather than just to the benefit of specific individuals or groups. This included, for example, provision of defence for the group. In the early part of the 21st century taxes are now used to achieve a number of government objectives as well as to raise revenue to fund its public spending and to repay its rapidly rising borrowing. In modern Britain taxation has become completely embedded in our society. Without taxation, the country would cease to operate. Whilst few people would say they like to pay taxes, their presence provides the foundation for an orderly, well managed, country.

At the end of this chapter you will be able to:

- outline the need for tax in a civilised society;
- discuss the historical background of taxation, particularly in the UK;
- describe the main features of UK tax policy making; and
- understand the structure of the current UK tax system.

Objectives of taxation

1.2 Taxation is used as a tool by the UK government to support and pay for its basic functions. These basic functions include:

- Managing the economy – including employment levels, the nature, type and location of business activity, levels of inflation, the balance of payments and relationships with our trading partners overseas;
- Regulation – protection of the environment, the public generally or of groups within society who might otherwise be exploited;
- Developing society – providing a social welfare and health system to improve the standards of living for the whole society;
- Providing public goods – provision of products and services for common consumption that would be unlikely to be adequately provided by the market. These include defence and education systems for example.

The primary purpose of imposing a tax on society is to raise money to pay for public (government) spending in performing the basic functions listed above. However, taxes are also used to influence the behaviour of taxpayers directly in ways that will support achieving these functions for society's benefit. For example, taxes are charged on petrol, alcohol and tobacco (in part at least) to increase their cost in the attempt to discourage their consumption in order to improve the environment and health of the country.

Tax reliefs can also be offered by a government to encourage activity that might not otherwise occur but that is considered beneficial for society in some way. For example, creating enterprise zones which have lower than normal taxes to persuade businesses to locate in particular areas. We will look at these tax reliefs, or tax expenditures, more closely in Chapter 14.

Taxation, therefore, is a very important feature of a modern society and the nature of a particular tax system reflects the views of its society, and government, at a point in time. Tax systems change regularly as society modifies its views on how best to balance the various aspects of the basic functions of government listed above. They also change as society's views of the balance of the importance of particular issues in the society, such as environmental protection, change over time. Key changes in the tax system often therefore occur when government philosophies change, such as when power in the Government shifts from one political party, or several parties in coalition, to another after an election, as we saw in the UK following the 2015 General Election. This produced a second budget in that year to implement some of these changes.

What is a tax?

1.3   Before we study the history of tax and examine the current UK rules for taxation in detail, we must understand what a tax is. All taxes have some features in common. They are a compulsory levy, imposed by government or other tax raising body, on income, expenditure, wealth or people, for which the taxpayer receives nothing specific in return.

Not all payments to a government are taxes however. Charges, fees for services, costs for provision of goods supplied by a government entity (e.g. electricity if the supply if state owned), tolls and other levies could be paid to a government, but where they are paid simply to cover the cost of providing something specific in return then they are not strictly taxes.

The collection of all the taxes in operation in an economy at a specific point in time, and the rules related to these taxes, is called a 'tax system'.

A brief history of taxation

1.4   Before we look at how the UK tax system operates at present, it is important to look back at history. As tax systems usual evolve slowly over time, with often fairly small changes and tweaks made each year rather than big swings from one approach to another, understanding the tax system of today requires at least some appreciation of the tax system of the past. Only by understanding a little of the past, and why particularly taxes were created as they were when they were, will you be able to appreciate some of the complexities of the current system you are learning about. Most taxes made sense at the time they were introduced, even if they sometimes make less obvious sense later!

Throughout history tax has been a sensitive issue between rulers or governments and their subjects or citizens. Significant civil unrest and even wars, have resulted from tax disputes. This section reviews some of these events both in ancient history, and more recent British history, illustrating the dynamic nature of tax systems over time and how methods and mechanisms for taxing people have changed. As you will see in this section, governments and rulers have used a wide variety of methods to raise money from their citizens and subjects. These include taxes on purchases and sales of goods and services, ownership and transfers of property and on receipts of income and wealth. As you read this section, note how the complexity of the tax system generally can be said to be developing over time but at the same time, many of the basic features of taxation have actually remained fairly constant.

Taxation in ancient times

1.5 Taxes have been levied on societies for just about as far back in history as we have records (e.g. taxes feature in ancient Egyptian, Chinese and Central American societies). We will use the example of taxes in the Roman Republic (and then Empire) to illustrate how many taxes raised now have their roots in ancient tax practices.

Taxation in the Roman Republic and Empire

1.6 In the times of Julius Caesar (c100 – 44BC) Roman citizens did not pay tax. All the revenue required by the Empire, including the cost of the military operations, was requisitioned from the people who lived in territories which had been occupied by the Romans. Only *indirect taxes** such as taxes on the sale of goods were raised in Rome itself, as direct taxes were seen to be humiliating and undignified because of the need to reveal details of personal circumstances (e.g. income levels) to enable such taxes to be levied.

Whilst the requisition system raised resources for the state, it had a number of serious disadvantages as a source of funding public expenditure, principally its lack of certainty. This led to tax demands being levied in an unpredictable and arbitrary way (which taxpayers did not like) and made planning for state expenditures difficult.

Occasionally (e.g. to fund a larger than usual war) it was considered necessary to raise a *direct tax*, called a tributum, on the citizens of Rome and its dependent, controlled territories, leading to the necessity of a census. Often the tributum was repaid by the state after the need for it passed. In addition, some indirect taxes were raised by charging import and export duties.

The Romans introduced a system of collective responsibility so that members of the taxpayer's family, neighbours and community could be called upon to pay any taxes which the taxpayer could not pay. Tax collection was undertaken by publicani (tax gatherers) under contract to the Republic (referred to as 'tax farming') and there was a considerable amount of corruption by both the various rulers of the Republic and the publicani.

When he became Rome's first Emperor, Augustus (Julius Caesar's great nephew 63BC – AD14 and First Citizen of Rome 27BC – AD14) realised that a fairer system of tax would have to be introduced to improve the stability of the newly

---

* Where you meet a technical tax term like this for the first time you may want to check its meaning in the glossary at the back. All the technical terms you need throughout this book are defined for you there so you can refer back to their definitions as you need them.

created Empire, and created a civil service to administer the tax. He introduced a 5% inheritance tax, which was payable on the death of a taxpayer from their estate, a 1% sales tax on public auctions and a 4% tax on the sale of slaves.

Tiberius (42BC – AD37 and Roman Emperor AD14 – 37), when encouraged to increase the direct taxation from the provinces, refused saying 'A good shepherd should shear his flock, not skin it.'

Fiscal Fact

This offered wisdom from Tiberius is hung prominently inside No 11 Downing Street (the official residence of the UK's Chancellor of the Exchequer – the person ultimately responsible for tax policy and its implementation in the UK). Chancellors today could be said to agree with Tiberius, operating with rates of income tax between 0 – 45%, but in the 1970s some taxpayers paid tax at rates as high as 98% on some income types – which most people would consider to be skinning and not shearing!

The Romans also introduced a rudimentary system of social security as part of their public expenditure return to society. This was in the form of a type of family allowance.

Between the 2nd and 3rd centuries AD inflation was extremely high and many of the taxes described above were allowed to lapse. Instead taxes were raised in the form of goods rather than money.

At the beginning of the 4th century AD, Diocletian introduced *capitatio*, (a poll tax), and *jugatio*, (a tax on land). The land was divided into four classes: vines, olive trees, arable land and pasture land, each class with further sub-classes. Land of a higher quality fell into a higher class leading to higher taxes than land of a lower quality, regardless of the way in which the land was actually used. This is an early example of taxing the capacity to generate wealth, rather than taxing the wealth generated, a trend used in some taxes today as we will see later.

An individual paid poll tax for himself and all his employees. The fraction to be paid varied across the Empire. A man was taken as being a unit of tax with all taxes, including land taxes, expressed as a fraction of a man. Rome decided how much tax should be raised in total and allocated this to regions, which then calculated the tax which must be levied on a 'man'.

From this process all tax liabilities were calculated and collected from the citizens. Taxes were still largely based on payment in kind rather than cash and the majority of the taxes were collected at their source. Hence landowners with tenants were required to pay taxes for themselves and their tenants. Individuals, who were not wealthy landowners or tenants, paid their taxes directly to the local municipal council. In practice the land tax system tied citizens to their land, limiting prospects for advancement, and was extremely progressive.

Under a *progressive tax system* a taxpayer who is better off pays a higher proportion of his or her income or wealth in tax than a less well off individual. In contrast, in a *regressive tax system* the 'burden of tax' falls more heavily on the poorest, who pay higher proportions of their incomes or wealth in tax.

The income tax system in operation in the UK now is largely progressive because taxpayers on lower incomes pay a relatively smaller proportion of their income in income tax while better off taxpayers pay a higher proportion (0% or 20% compared to up to 45% as we will see in Chapter 4). For a tax system to be progressive, better off taxpayers do not just pay more tax than the less well off: the better off must pay *proportionately* more (i.e. a higher proportion) in tax than the less well off.

Parts of the tax system in Diocletian's time in Rome were so progressive that the tax paid on an extra 'unit' of income was greater than 100%. This tax system was blamed for the decline in both economic prosperity and personal freedom and ultimately contributed significantly to the downfall of the Roman Empire by undermining its ongoing stability.

The development of taxation in the UK

1.7   What about the history of the UK tax system? England was, of course, part of the Roman Empire and some traces of Roman tax principles remain in the UK's tax system. In this section we review some of the key parts of UK tax history after the Norman Conquest (1066), to help you understand further how the current tax system evolved.

Medieval taxation

1.8   In medieval times kings (via their Treasuries) had access to revenue from three sources. Firstly, they received income from Crown property – that is property owned by the ruling King rather than personal property owned before becoming King – and secondly from feudal rights where kings received income in various form) from the land owners, who in turn extracted it from their tenants. These together were considered to provide the kings with sufficient revenue to meet their normal expenditure. In addition, kings could raise customs duties and other levies in times of emergency, provided that King's Counsel or Parliament approved this extra levy being charged.

Feudal services, or payments made in lieu of such services called scutage, are examples of direct taxes, while customs duties are indirect taxes. Indirect taxes prove to be both easier and more economical to collect while the direct taxes were generally more difficult and expensive to collect. For example, citizens were able to challenge an assessment of a direct tax in the courts which often delayed payment and therefore also increased the cost of collecting taxes. There were, (and still are) a number of advantages of customs duties as a means of raising revenue for the Government compared to direct taxes. Firstly, during this time there was a large volume of overseas trade, primarily with Europe, so that a relatively large amount of tax could be raised from a relatively low rate of tax. Secondly, the tax was relatively cheap and easy to collect via customs officials at the docks (although tax evasion, through smuggling, was widespread).

Fiscal Fact

King John levied scutage, the payment in lieu of feudal knight's service, eleven times in his sixteen year reign at rates varying from 2 marks (26s 8d.) to 3 marks (40s.) per knight.

Taxation in the Middle Ages

1.9   In times of war the King was often unable to raise enough revenue from his usual sources to fund the military effort. The King had no absolute right to raise additional funds and so had to negotiate with his wealthier subjects to raise extra sums if needed. These subjects usually insisted that the King follow the formal procedures which meant that Parliament had to be convened for the King to request either increases in customs duties or to raise a 'lay subsidy', such as the system of the 'fifteenths and tenths', which was a tax on all movable property and some income. This system operated by taxing a fraction of the assessed value of goods such as livestock, corn and other produce, household goods and stock-in-trade. The tax fraction applied was one fifteenth in country areas and one tenth in cities and boroughs. Some personal goods however, such as clothes and armour, were exempt from this tax.

The members of Parliament at the time were the country's wealthiest citizens, and were therefore the people most likely to be affected by an increase in the King's tax raising power. The role of Parliament was to act as a brake on public expenditure. (Today, it is more likely to be Parliament which is restrained by the Treasury than the other way around). On the other hand, these members were also the people with the most to lose if the King was unsuccessful in the war, and so Parliament usually granted the King his request, in part, if not in its entirety.

Perhaps ironically, increases in these taxes raised to fight wars had the effect of redistributing wealth from the King's wealthier subjects (who paid the taxes) to the peasants who became soldiers (and therefore received wages and other 'benefits' like food and clothing from the taxes paid). Taxes are still regularly used to produce economic redistribution in this way.

In 1377, Parliament gave the new King permission to levy a poll tax of four old pence on all his adult male subjects. Two years later the King was granted permission to raise a graduated poll tax. Peasants still paid four old pence but subjects with positions were taxed at higher rates depending on their status: up to £4 for barons, earls and mayors. In real terms the poll tax represented about 2% of the King's income. On both occasions when this poll tax was used, the general populace rebelled and evasion was widespread.

Two years later Parliament once again, and with reluctance, granted the King the right to levy a poll tax, this time at one shilling (12 old pennies) a head. Because the tax was not graduated by reference to the taxpayer's wealth it was effective regressive, that is the burden of tax fell most heavily on the poorest members of society, and was once again widely evaded. Once again the peasants revolted and nearly brought about the downfall of the King and the feudal rights system, by then increasingly outmoded. (Perhaps if Margaret Thatcher had taken more notice of tax history she might have survived the challenge to her leadership in 1990 which was due, in part, to the unpopular poll tax, called the community charge, she had reintroduced in the UK in the late 1980s and that followed similar principles to these earlier taxes!).

By Henry VIII's reign (1509-1547) a mixture of the two systems of taxing the population was operating. Individuals whose income could easily be ascertained, such as the clergy, wage-earners and landowners, were subject to a form of income tax while individuals whose income fluctuated, such as merchants, professionals and tenant farmers, were subject to tax on their movable property.

During the reign of Elizabeth I (1558-1603) the income tax rate was 20% while movables were taxed at a rate of two-fifteenths. Movables included coins, plate, merchandise, household goods and debts owing less debts owed to the taxpayer. Even the poor were subject to these taxes as exemption limits were set very low. As before both these taxes were only raised during times of financial urgency. By the middle of the 16th century the exemption limits had been raised somewhat so that only the upper classes paid taxes.

The struggle between King and Parliament

1.10   Taxation became a particularly contentious issue between the King and Parliament during the first reign of the Stuarts (1603–1649) primarily because, as is now generally agreed by historians, the Stuarts had insufficient revenue to fulfil their royal functions. This led to King James (1603–1625) applying to Parliament for further financing for the ordinary expenses of government causing bitter quarrels. King Charles I (1625–1649), James's son, also suffered from this problem (although by the later 1630s the King's income had risen to £1,000,000 a year) and Parliament refused to grant him the right to raise revenue through customs duties for life, as had been done in the past, but granted the duties for only 12 months at a time. As customs duties at this time made up the bulk of Charles' revenue (only 8% of his income came from direct tax sources), eventually in 1629, Charles began levying the duties without the consent of Parliament.

The differences (both tax related and others) between the monarch and Parliament became insurmountable and finally there was a civil war which ended with Charles' execution in 1649. From that day until the present, Parliament has effectively ruled in the UK, although a limited monarchy, as we have it today, was restored with Charles II in 1660.

One interesting result of this struggle is that the Board of Her Majesty's Revenue and Customs (HMRC) receive their commission to act from the Crown rather than from Parliament. Thus the Board is deemed to have inherited some of the qualities of the Crown, in particular justice, equity and mercy. (We will not have the opportunity to evaluate the performance of HMRC against these criteria in this book, but you might like to consider this question during your working life of dealing with the Revenue).

Excise duties on food, drink and other essentials were introduced by Parliament in 1643 during the English Civil Wars. They were unpopular because the burden of the tax fell on everyone including the poor, but they had the administrative advantage of being easy to collect. Like the poll taxes before them, excise duties on the necessities of life are often regressive, that is, the poor pay a larger proportion of their income in duty than the better off (because a large percentage of their incomes have to be spent on these excise bearing necessities).

Parliament attempted to reform the personal tax system after Charles' execution in 1649 but was largely unsuccessful. The country was divided into regions which were each then required to raise a set amount of revenue, with little guidance about the way in which the tax should be levied, and little central supervision. The tax system under this structure became dominated by taxes on land rather than on income or other assets.

Unusual taxes

1.11 Over the UK's history some unusual things have been taxed. In 1662 for example, a hearth tax was introduced (a tax charge on the number of hearths/fireplaces in a house). This was a crude attempt at a progressive tax on the basis that people who have more fireplaces probably have bigger houses (and therefore probably are richer), would have to pay more of this tax than those with fewer hearths (and therefore probably poorer). This was a relatively easy tax to avoid, however, by the simple practice of blocking up hearths.

A similar attempt at developing progressivity by using taxes linked to property was made in 1696 when a window tax was introduced. In a similar way to the hearth tax it was argued that the rich had larger houses and therefore more windows and so would pay more tax than poorer citizens. Like the hearth tax before, it was fairly simple to avoid the tax by bricking up a window. Also lying about the number of windows in the house was widespread. In 1851 the window tax was abolished on the grounds of public health.

Fiscal Fact

In 1792-3 the Government earned 23% of its total taxation revenue from direct taxes on land and property, 53% from excise duties on food, drink and tobacco, 18% from excise duties on other items such as coal, iron, cloth, soap, candles and 6% from stamp duties.

The modern era of taxation

1.12 Modern-day income tax has its roots in 1799 in the tax introduced by William Pitt (The Younger), the UK Prime Minister at the time. When the Napoleonic Wars started Pitt borrowed money against future excise revenue in order to finance the war, a practice first developed at the start of the eighteenth century (a system called 'deficit financing'). However, it became apparent that the war was going to last too long to enable this method of financing to be sustained. Pitt needed to find a new way to raise taxes. He introduced an income tax at a rate of 10% which was targeted on the rich middle and upper classes, the people with the most to lose if the war was lost. However, there was widespread evasion of the tax and only £6m was raised in the first year, rather than the £10m anticipated.

Although the poorest people were not subject to direct tax in the form of income tax, it is estimated that by 1810 a labourer earning £22 a year paid £11 in indirect tax. Given how high indirect tax already was, it did not seem possible to fund the war by further increasing this form of taxation. Instead taxpayers earning over £60 per annum were required to make a return listing all their sources of income and calculating the amount of tax which was due on it.

The law bringing this new tax into force did not allow for any control over enforcing the correctness of the return. In an attempt to reduce the widespread evasion that this brought about, *withholding taxes* were introduced by the Bank of England, by paying its dividends net of tax.

Pitt resigned in 1801 and his income tax was repealed in 1802 by Henry Addington (Prime Minister after Pitt) because it was seen as a wartime tax only. In 1803 however, Addington re-introduced a new income tax based on five Schedules, named using the first five letters of the alphabet, which largely continue to be used as the structure for the UK's income tax rules today, although as we will see later, the names of these Schedules have been changed in recent years to be more descriptive of the forms of income to which they relate.

Addington was also responsible for more widespread taxation at the source. This means that the payer of certain amounts, such as rent, salaries, pensions and interest had to deduct tax and pay the recipient net of a suitable rate of tax. This helped reduce the levels of non-compliance and also improved the efficiency of the tax collection system.

Because of these innovations it is probably fair to say that Addington is the true father of UK income tax rather than Pitt, who has generally been awarded the dubious honour of this title. Addington's income tax was progressive and ranged from 1% on an income of £60 to 10% on an income of over £200. Income tax was repealed once again in 1816.

Income tax reintroduced

1.13 In 1842 Sir Robert Peel (Prime Minister from 1841–1846) reintroduced income tax, again as a temporary measure, at a very low level, this time to try to deal with the budget deficit the country faced at the time of £5million. Peel drew on Addington's Act of 1803 for his legislation, making only minor amendments. Peel rejected proposals to impose high rates of tax on the wealthy, arguing that it would lead to them closing their businesses or even leaving the country. A major criticism of any income tax is the need to undertake an annual investigation of income, or as Peel put it: 'A certain degree of inquisitorial scrutiny is, therefore, inseparable from an income tax.' As in Roman times, it was this need to disclose their income, rather than the actual rate of the tax, which was generally opposed by those who disliked this form of taxation.

Under Peel's income tax system, income below £150 was exempted. Income above this figure was taxed at 3% regardless of the amount of the income. This fairly high minimum threshold level excluded a large proportion of the population from needing to pay the tax.

At the same time indirect taxes were reduced as part of the free trade movement in order to help the country's manufacturing, trading and commercial sectors. The appropriate balance between the use of direct taxes, like income tax, and indirect tax is a key decision for any government now, just as it was in Peel's time.

Peel's income tax was supported, despite its drawbacks, because it was seen to be a temporary solution to resolve a particular public finance problem, and set at a relatively low level. In addition, industrialists were supportive of this tax as they believed that if the Government were to raise all the revenue they needed by means of further indirect taxation, it would cut consumer spending and increase inflation.

Fiscal Fact

The administration of the new income tax, like many existing taxes, was largely in the hands of Commissioners who 'ought to be persons of a respectable situation in life, as far as possible removed from any suspicion of partiality or any kind of undue influence, men of integrity and independence.' In 1798, however, (the famous 'Coventry scandal') the list of Land Tax Commissioners was found to include journeymen, weavers, scavengers, dealers in dead horse flesh and cat meat, dealers in dung, paupers receiving parish relief, two fiddlers and two idiots.

Under Peel's rules, income was not all taxed in full, for example, farmers were taxed on the rental value of their land rather than their farming profits. Farmers were not taxed on their income until 1941.

In order to ease the concerns of taxpayers about making personal income declarations, Peel created a system of Special Commissioners, (who were experts in taxation), with whom businessmen could deal rather than the General Commissioners (who were local businessmen), from whom the taxpayer might want privacy. In addition, if the taxpayer disputed the amount of tax which was deemed to be payable he could choose to appeal to either the Special Commissioners or the General Commissioners. Like much of the rest of Peel's system, this process of appeals to expert Special Commissioners remained in operation for many years and only ceased to operate like this in April 2009 when a new tribunals system was introduced in the tax area as we will see in the next Chapter.

Peel also introduced penalties into his income tax system. For example, a fixed penalty of £50 was created for any taxpayer who was found to be 'neglectful' in connection with his return of income. This specific penalty was abolished in 1923 but today penalties are still a key part of the administration of the tax system and HMRC can impose interest charges as well as penalties on taxpayers who fail to pay the full amount of tax due and provide their tax returns on time, as we will see in the next chapter.

William Gladstone, UK Chancellor who became Prime Minister from 1868-74 (and again at various points between 1880 and 1894), introduced 13 budgets during the last half of the 19th century. At the time of his first in 1853 public expenditure was over £50 million a year and nearly £30 million of the total was used to pay interest on the National Debt. Gladstone claimed that the cause of the deficit was the prevailing level of income tax. Less tax was raised in 1853 from income tax than was collected in each of the years from 1806 to 1815.

Gladstone was aware of the limitations of the system of income tax, especially self-assessment, which led to widespread fraud. To start to redress the balance Gladstone extended the legacy duty so that land and also businesses were subject to tax on the death of their owner. He reduced the rates of indirect taxation, believing that this would stimulate consumption and thus not actually reduce the net receipts to the Government. This, together with the reforms introduced by Peel, helped to free the restrictions on trade by encouraging imports and enabling exports to be sold as cheaply as possible.

Gladstone intended to phase income tax out by 1860, but for a number of reasons this did not prove to be possible and instead the rate of income tax actually rose. Public expenditure was growing rapidly, much to Gladstone's regret, and this made it impossible ever again to consider abolishing income tax.

William Vernon Harcourt, as UK Chancellor of the Exchequer at the time, introduced Estate Duty, referred to as Death Duties, in 1894. The Estate Duty removed many of the injustices of the old legacy duties which had evolved over many centuries and so suffered from many inconsistencies. The origin of the present-day inheritance tax can in fact be traced back to at least 1694 and the development of probate duties. This new Estate Duty fell most heavily on the landowners. Harcourt justified this bias by claiming that property values had been greatly increased since the railways were built. The duty was at the rate of 1% on estates worth between £100 and £500, with estates worth more than £1 million taxed at 8%.

The new tax was highly unpopular with the families who were affected by it. They argued that an individual who chose to spend his money during his life could avoid paying the tax which would be levied on the estate of the careful person who accumulated assets to pass on to the next generation. The question of tax avoidance was also raised by commentators at the time who argued that by simply giving the estate away during the lifetime of the testator the tax could be completely avoided. Harcourt defended his tax, arguing that estate duty was the only viable opportunity to tax non-income-generating assets such as the taxpayer's main residence. This debate about the fairness of inheritance taxation continues today.

Fiscal Fact

In 1855 the tax on newspapers, which had been introduced in 1712, was finally repealed. At its highest rate in 1815, the tax was 4d per sheet of paper so that most newspapers were printed on a single sheet folded in half and sold for 7d. This is why 'broad sheets' began to be printed as they are today – to get as much text on as little paper as possible to minimise the tax to be paid.

Harcourt next turned his attention to income tax, in particular seeking to make it more progressive. Harcourt was strongly in favour of the system of deduction of tax at source, which could be applied to about three-quarters of all income tax collected, arguing that it meant that there was limited inquisitorial prying into the affairs of individuals this way (one of the key problems of using income tax if you remember from earlier in this chapter). The Revenue supported this strongly and argued that if the system of deduction at source was not widened, the investigations that they would have to make and the penalties which they would have to impose for misdeclarations as the income tax system continued to grow would render the collection of the income tax so 'odious' as to 'imperil' its existence and in all probability make it impossible to maintain the tax.

Taxation in the 20th century

1.14   At the beginning of the 20th century tax was paid on earned income by fewer than a million people. Hence income tax was a tax paid only by the better off in UK society. However, during the 20th century (and of course particularly now in the 21st century as a result of the financial crisis) public expenditure increased phenomenally and today income tax in the UK is paid by the majority of working adults.

In 1907 Herbert Henry Asquith, the UK Chancellor at the time, introduced a system of personal allowances, which exempted a proportion of earned income from income tax. In 1908 old-age pensions were introduced. This, together with a need to increase spending on the Navy, necessitated an increase in taxation to pay for this increased public expenditure.

In 1909 David Lloyd George introduced the first progressive tax on income in the so-called 'People's Budget'. The budget was not generally accepted and was rejected by the House of Lords in November 1909, but it eventually became law in 1910. As a result of this problem, the power of the House of Lords to veto budgets was removed in 1911 (and is still the case in the UK now). Lloyd George believed that the tax system should ensure that everyone contributes taxes to the country no matter how poor they were. He also believed that taxes should be so constructed that they did not inflict injury on trade and commerce – a concept called *tax neutrality*. This is an idea which we will consider later in this chapter and in more detail in Chapters 3 and 14.

The First World War led to increases in income tax including a top rate of 15%. However, the tax raised was insufficient to fund the war and the deficit was funded by borrowing from the population at large, using War Bonds, etc. The new top rate of income tax was called 'supertax' and its introduction doubled the rate of tax on incomes. In 1928 supertax was renamed surtax and income over £5,000 (around £150,000 in today's values) was taxed at 8%. In addition, car licences were introduced, a new tax on petrol was imposed and an excess profits duty introduced. The excess profits duty was designed to tax the additional profits that many businesses made during the war, partly because of public concerns about 'profiteering', that is businesses taking advantage of wartime conditions to make huge profits. The excess profits duty was repealed after the close of the First World War, and during the Second World War, a slightly different version of the tax, excess profits tax, was implemented.

Fiscal Fact

By 1939 fewer than one in five of the working population were liable to income tax and so people on average earnings did not pay tax. However, the Second World War tripled the number of taxpayers to 12 million as well as tripling the amount of tax raised. One of the reasons for this increase was a substantial rise in inflation during the Second World War.

A new income tax payment system called *pay-as-you-earn* (PAYE) was introduced in 1944, where tax is deducted from individuals' wages and salaries before they received it. Until the introduction of PAYE only individuals paid by central or local government had tax deducted at source from their salaries. Everyone else paid any income tax due by *direct assessment* that is, were billed for the tax owed on their income at some stage after they received it, and after declaring it to the tax authority.

The PAYE system had a number of advantages over the direct assessment system. Primarily, the Government's cash flow was improved as they no longer had to wait until the end of the tax year for the collection of tax. Their bad debts were also reduced as the Government made themselves the ultimate preferential creditor both in the case of business failures and personal bankruptcy. This meant they received a cut of any remaining business assets even before the individual employees got their final wages. It also meant requiring bankrupt individuals to pay of sums owed to the Government before paying off other creditors. It was also believed that it was easier for individuals to pay tax weekly or monthly collected directly from their salary rather than facing a large bill at the end of the tax year.

After the Second World War ended there was an explosion in government expenditure and this was inevitably matched by the increase in taxes raised to pay for this, with the top rate of tax on incomes of over £20,000 per annum standing at 52.5% in 1946.

By 1946 the exemption limit for estate duty purposes had increased from £100 to £3,000, the first increase in this area of taxation for 50 years. The increase had the effect of exempting many smaller estates from the duty. However, the highest rates of tax to be paid on non-exempted estates were also increased to a maximum of 75% on estates of over £2 million.

After the Second World War, the National Health Service was formed and national insurance contributions were introduced (although their history really starts in the National Insurance Act of 1911) to provide for health care, retirement pensions and sickness benefit. Although these payments are not strictly taxes because of their association with specific returns received for their payment (remember the definition of 'tax' at the start of this chapter), some of the returns earned on national insurance contributions are now added to the general taxation 'pot' that the Government receives. They are no longer all earmarked (called in tax terms *hypothecated*) specifically for expenditure in the areas they are traditionally paying for, and therefore are effectively an additional tax on income, in part at least.

A purchase tax was used to tax spending for a large part of the 20th century. There were a large number of rates of tax and many inconsistencies in the rates applied to various expenditure. For example, pianos and organs were exempt but other musical instruments were taxed at 27.5%; records were taxed at 50% while books were exempt from the tax. Purchase tax was replaced in 1973 by Value Added Tax (VAT), as a precursor to Britain becoming part of the European Economic Community (now the European Union), and which is now the primary tax on consumption in the UK (we will discuss UK VAT in Chapter 10).

In 1965 two new taxes were introduced, corporation tax and capital gains tax. Until 1965 companies were subject to income tax as if they were individuals and there are still many similarities between the two systems because of this common history they share (we will discuss corporation tax in Chapter 9). Capital gains tax was originally intended to reduce tax avoidance and increase the equity of the tax system rather than primarily to raise significant revenue. This tax helps reduce the opportunities for people to earn capital growth untaxed instead of receiving income which is taxed (we will discuss capital gains tax in Chapter 8).

In 1975 capital transfer tax was introduced as a new tax on estates but was itself replaced by inheritance tax in 1984 (we will discuss inheritance tax in Chapter 8). The pre-1975 estate duty only taxed the value of the taxpayer's estate at death. Lifetime gifts were completely exempt. Capital transfer tax introduced tax on lifetime transfers of wealth for the first time.

In 1979 the top rate of tax on earned income in the UK was 83% and unearned income over £5,500pa, such as rents received and dividends, was subject to an investment income surcharge of 15%, giving a top rate of tax of 98% for some taxpayers receiving these types of income.

Taxation in the 21st century

1.15 As we have moved into the 21st century various key changes face the UK's tax system. This includes possible changes that will come from leaving Europe and also from new ways of administering the tax system that digitalisation enables.

In the first case, as Europe has various powers over how our tax system operates, including the rates we can use for VAT as we will explore in Chapter 10, our departure from Europe will enable the UK to revisit rules it previously had no power to change. We will have to wait and see how this translates into specific tax system changes, although currently most commentators suggest the chances of dramatic changes occurring initially will be low.

Changes related to the greater use of technology are likely to affect more of us sooner however. HMRC are keen to be one of, if not the, most technologically advanced tax authorities in the world. The increased use of technology in dealing with our tax affairs started some years ago with greater use of electronic filing and changes to back-office data processing to improve the auditing capabilities of HMRC on data they received. Technology based interactions with HMRC will become much more of a feature for all tax filers in the next few years with the roll out of a scheme entitled 'Making Taxes Digital' starting in earnest from April 2019, this will see many of those who have to file tax returns move completely online for their interactions with HMRC. This will affect all aspects of how taxpayers keep their business or personal accounting records, and how they send and receive information from the tax authority.

Income and corporation tax categories and schedules

1.16 Income was for many years taxed according to a number of different Schedules and Cases. These were the same broad categories as introduced by Addington in 1803 and in recent times directly refer to parts of the Income and Corporation Taxes Act 1988. These classifications disappeared for individual taxpayers however, in April 2005 (although continued for corporate taxpayers until 2009, as we will see in Chapter 9) and, although the tax rules themselves haven't changed, their names have. Previously each source of income received by a taxpayer was assessed under a Schedule and some of these Schedules were further sub-divided into "Cases". Income from a trade or profession was taxed under Schedule D Case I and II. Schedule A was used to describe the rules for taxing income from UK property. Schedule F outlined the rules for taxing dividends from UK companies (having been introduced in 1965 in conjunction with the introduction of corporation tax). Schedule D Case VI was used to tax annual profits or gains not falling under any other Case of Schedule D and not charged under either Schedule A or Schedule E.

Income from employment, including pensions, used to be taxed under rules outlined in Schedule E. In March 2003 however, Schedule E rules were replaced by the Income Tax (Earnings and Pensions) Act 2003 (ITEPA 2003), and subsequent amendments to this Act found in places such as various Finance Acts resulting from Budget changes over the years since 1988. This process consolidates the rules in this area into one place.

The other schedules of the 1988 Act still applied for both individuals and companies until 5 April 2005 when a new Act came into force, the Income Tax (Trading and Other Income) Act (ITTOIA) 2005 which re-classified Schedules A, D and F into new headings for income tax. Each category of income has its own rules which determine how much income should be assessed, what deductions are allowed and when the tax should be paid. The final Act needed to rewrite all the relevant income tax rules into new legislation came into force on 6 April, 2007 as the Income Tax Act (ITA) 2007. For corporation tax, the Corporation Tax Act (CTA) 2009 removed the Schedule names and corporation tax is now largely consistent with income tax in the categories. We will study the rules for each category in detail in later chapters.

Current tax legislation and regulation

1.17 Tax rules are currently created in the UK by a combination of law, regulation and cases, and to a lesser degree rulings and best practice guidance from HMRC. There are a number of sources of tax law today. Table 1.1 below lists the key tax laws that contain the rules we will examine in this book.

In each of these cases the rules may subsequently be changed or amended by the annual Finance Acts that bring into UK law the plans of the Chancellor announced in the Budget each year). In most years only one Finance Act is passed and it is given the date of that year – i.e. this year it will become the Finance Act 2018. However, in some years there can be more than one Finance Act if this proves necessary. The different Acts in the same year are given a number to differentiate them from each other i.e. the second Finance Act in 2017 became Finance (No. 2) Act 2017 and in some years (the last was in 2010) there was even a third (No. 3) Act. Other regulations and laws (such as Statutory Instruments) can also be used by the Government to amend or extend these various Acts as thought necessary.

Some tax aspects can also be found in more general, non-tax specific, Acts. For example, in November 2006 an Act on charity regulation came into force. This Act included various details about the taxation of charities.

Table 1.1: UK Tax Legislation

Source	Key Relevant Act
Income Tax	
Earned income/pensions	Income Tax (Earnings and Pensions) Act 2003 (ITEPA)
Other sources	Income Tax (Trading and Other Income) Act 2005 (ITTOI) and Income Tax Act 2007 (ITA)
Corporation tax	Income and Corporation Taxes Act 1998 (ICTA), Corporation Tax Act 2009 (CTA), Corporation Tax Act 2010 and Corporation Tax (Northern Ireland) Act 2015.
Capital Allowances	Capital Allowances Act 2001 (CAA)
National Insurance Contributions	Social Security & Benefits Act 1992, National Insurance Contributions Act 2011 and 2015
Capital Gains	Taxation of Chargeable Gains Act 1992 (TCGA)
Value Added Tax	Value Added Tax Act 1994 (VATA)
Inheritance Tax	Inheritance Tax Act 1984 (IHTA)
Stamp Duty	Stamp Act 1891 and Electronic Communications Act 2000 (ECA),
Land Tax	Stamp Duty Land Tax Act 2015 and Land and Buildings Transactions Tax 2015 (LBTT – applicable in Scotland only)
Administration of direct tax	Taxes Management Act 1970 (TMA) and Commissioners for Revenue and Customs Act 2005 (CRCA)

Whilst we look at the current law as we examine each tax issue, this text does not include a detailed consideration of these laws and therefore does not make reference to particular parts of these Acts or regulations. This is a deliberate policy to reduce the complexity of our explanation. However, it is very important that you remember that law underpins all the detail we describe and you may need to refer to this at some point to fully understand how the tax rules work for a particular issue.

In addition to UK tax law, the UK's tax system is shaped by a number of other laws, cases and guidance statements from HMRC. This can make for a complex web of rules in many areas of tax but is a feature of the UK's detailed tax system.

Because the UK is a currently a member of the European Union, EU law must also be adhered to in the UK, and in fact takes priority over UK law where they disagree. This will change once the UK has completed its exit of the EU in 2019 after the vote in June 2016 began this process.

The UK's tax system is a case law system. This means that specific tax related laws created by Parliament are interpreted by judges in courts as disputes are brought before them to be settled. Throughout this book you will meet a number of legal cases that determine how legal principles should be applied to specific circumstances.

The UK's tax authority (HMRC) also periodically issues guidance of various types for taxpayers and their advisors. Whilst this is not legally binding on taxpayers and can be challenged, it does provide useful advice on the tax authority's view on how specific tax issues should be handled. Taking a look at HMRC's website for example, you will find guidance in the form of Statements of Practice (their interpretation of the law), Extra statutory concessions (specific relaxations of the law allowed by HMRC), Press Releases (various statements on tax issues), Internal Manuals (publicly published internal manuals to illustrate how tax issues are to be handled) and leaflets (general advice that usually provides overviews for taxpayers). However, the boundaries between these forms of guidance are disappearing with the growth of the Internet where technologies, such as search engines, make it easier for taxpayers to discover information they need in a timely fashion.

National v local taxation

1.18   Like many other countries, the UK suffers from 'vertical fiscal imbalance'. This means that lower levels of government, which in the UK is local (e.g. city, district or county councils) or regional government (e.g. Welsh or Northern Irish Assemblies and the Scottish Parliament), don't raise enough money of their own to meet their spending obligations and instead need to rely on central government for extra funds, usually paid in the form of grants. In the UK, local government currently only raises about 25% of its own revenue needs and has to get the rest from central government. This balance of funding between the two levels of government hasn't always been this way. Before 1992, local government used to raise between 45% and 60% of its own revenue, mainly from taxes. After this date however, capping systems imposed on local governments by central government have prevented local governments raising higher percentages of their spending from taxation.

The current degree of vertical fiscal imbalance is considered to be a problem, and the Government set up a Balance of Funding Review in 2003 to consider options for change. Following on from this Review, which concluded that further research was needed, in 2004 the Government commissioned Sir Michael Lyons to examine the issue. He produced an interim report, and a consultation paper in December 2005 and his final report was published with the 2007 Budget. No changes were made following this report, however the current government set up a review of local government resources in March 2011 to look into ways of giving local government in England more control over their money. From 2013 local councils are able to decide how their grants from central government should be spent in their area.

Fiscal Fact

Despite local government having legal powers to use council tax to raise some of their funding, historically the only regional government with legal rights to raise taxes in the UK was the Scottish Parliament. They have the power to vary income tax by increasing or decreasing it up to 3% in either direction from the national levels for taxpayers in Scotland, and now have a different rate scale from the rest of the UK.

However, greater tax raising powers were granted to Scotland as part of the Scotland Act (2012). These cover areas such as land taxation (instead of the use of Stamp Duty, Scotland now operates a Land and Buildings Transaction Tax (LBTT) effective from April 2015), and a separate Scottish Landfill Tax (SLfT). They are collected by a body called *Revenue Scotland* (http://www.revenue.scot). The income tax varying powers were also formalised at the same time to enable a *Scottish Rate of Income Tax* (SRIT) to be created. This came into force in April 2016. Other taxes will also become more directly under the Scottish Parliament's control as part of the devolution process currently underway following the Independence vote at the end of 2014.

Also in 2014 Northern Ireland was given powers to set its own Corporation tax (this was due to commence in April 2018 but has been delayed). This was to enable it to compete more effectively in this area with the Republic of Ireland that operates a much lower rate of this tax.

Wales did not historically have any of these same powers, however, from April 2018 it has been allowed to collect its own Land Transaction Taxes, paid via a new body entitled the *Welsh Revenue Authority* (http://www.beta.gov.wales/welsh-revenue-authority). Now, much like the situation in Scotland, land transactions-based taxes are different in this region to other parts of the UK. The Welsh government also has the power to vary income tax for Welsh residents, but has yet to do so.

The main tax levied by local government is *council tax*, which was introduced in 1993. Before considering how this tax works, we will briefly review the local taxes that existed before 1993.

For many years, the main local tax in the UK was *domestic rates*. This was based on a percentage of the value of property (both residential and non-residential) located in the area of control of the local government. In the 1980s there was growing concern that rates were unfair. In part this was because the people who had to pay them were not always the same people who voted for, and benefited from, local government spending; only property owning members of the community paid rates, but everyone who lived in the area, whether they owned property or not there, voted for local government plans.

In 1990, the rates system was abolished and replaced with a new tax, the *community charge*, sometimes referred to as the *poll tax*. The community charge was organised very differently to domestic rates because it wasn't linked to property values and ownership, but rather paid by all adults resident in the area irrespective of whether they owned property or not. The community charge was extremely unpopular (as we will see in Chapter 2) and so in 1993 the Government was forced to abolish it and replace it with yet another form of local tax, the *council tax*.

The council tax is made up of two elements, which makes it a 'hybrid tax'. Half of the tax bill relates to the value of the property, and the other half is based on a charge of 25% for each of the first two adults living in the property. This means that a single adult household will only pay 75% of the usual bill, although a three or more adult household won't pay more than the usual bill.

Council tax is set locally and therefore it was, until recent new powers given to the regions, the only personal tax in the UK that varied according to where you lived. Property values are placed into 8 bands and the local government sets the rate for one of them, the others then are a proportion of that rate.

Large increases in the rate of council tax cause a lot of dissatisfaction, which is one of the reasons why local government funding is regularly under review.

Tax policy making in the UK

1.19 The most critical event of the annual taxation calendar in the UK (most years) is the annual Budget Statement made by the Chancellor of the Exchequer. Until 2017 this was usually made during March, but from 2017 this switched to November each year. This statement outlines the Government's budget plans for the year, which correspondingly have to be balanced with how they will raise the money to finance these plans. It is in this statement each year that most tax changes for the year are therefore to be found.

The Treasury is in fact legally bound to provide two economic forecasts each year. Between 1993 and 1997 this was done in the Budget in November and the Summer Economic Forecast (given late June or early July). However, under the Labour Government, elected in May 1997, the system changed back to a Spring Budget with the addition of a Pre-Budget report in the previous autumn. This Pre-Budget statement gave an update on the state of the economy. It also outlines ideas and plans for the main Budget the next year. The pre-1997 system is therefore being returned to from this year with Budget statement being made in November each year. (Summary details of this year's Budgets, and summaries of those of the last few years, can be found in Appendix B.)

In June 2010, the then newly elected Coalition Government issued a document alongside an emergency budget, called *Tax Policy Making: A new approach.* This document discussed several proposals for improving the policy making process for the UK, which had long been criticised for a lack of consultation and ad hoc changes without sufficient warning. Following a period of discussion, the Government published a Draft Consultation Framework in December 2010 in which it set out five concrete improvements:

1. In the case of major areas of reform, the Government will set out its rationale and policy objectives;
2. Tax policies are to be developed over a longer policy cycle, giving more time for consultation and reflection;
3. In relation to consultation, the aim is to publish more legislation in draft form, so that it can be exposed to greater scrutiny at least three months before the relevant Bill is introduced;
4. The Government will adopt a more strategic approach to tax avoidance (see Chapter 11), balancing the need to protect the system from avoidance, against the desire to keep the system stable and predictable;
5. Changes in tax law will be accompanied by Tax Information and Impact notes that will explain the changes and their expected impact.

The Institute for Fiscal Studies, in its 2011 *Green Budget* was generally supportive of these developments but also noted that tax policy is subject to less scrutiny in Parliament than other areas of public policy and that the split of policy making responsibility between HM Treasury and HMRC is not ideal.

Three further important developments in tax administration were created in the early days of the Coalition Government in 2010. First, was the creation of an Office of Tax Simplification. This is an independent body, attached to the Treasury, charged with trying to find ways to simplify the UK tax system. We will consider why simplicity is considered to be important in a tax system in Chapter 3. This body has proven effective in getting a range of tax simplifications made to the UK tax system – including changes to the way tax is computed on employee expenses and benefits in kind as we show in Chapter 5.

Second, the Coalition Government created the Office for Budget Responsibility. This body provides independent economic forecasting and analysis for the Government in an attempt to take political pressure out of important judgements of the state of the UK economy, and to ensure the Treasury is held to better account by independent expertise.

Third, the new approach to policy making introduced a new process for undertaking impact assessments for policy changes. From Budget 2011 onwards, the Government publishes Tax Information and Impact Notes (TIINs) for policy changes, once they become final, or nearly final. They are supposed to provide a clear statement of the policy objective of the legislative change, the impact on the Exchequer, the economy, individuals, businesses and civil society.

In January 2017 a further review of the process of tax policy setting was published by the Chartered Institute of Tax (CIOT) the Institute of Fiscal Students (IFS) and the Institute for Government entitled 'Better Budgets: making tax policy better'. This report welcomed the shift to a single budget in the year and also recommended:

- Publishing by Government of clear principles and priorities for tax policy;
- Improvements to be made to the consultation process, making sure that consultation happens before key change decisions (not afterwards); and
- The use of external, public, reviews of aspects of the tax systems as a means of encouraging more public debate on the shape of the tax system.

The report argued that these measures, if adopted, would result in more challenges to the Treasury in their role as tax policy makers. The report also called for more scrutiny of outcomes once tax changes were implemented. At present this is not routinely undertaken and made public. You will note many of these proposals reflect those found in the Coalition Government's document 10 years before, as detailed above. Time will tell if any of them are adopted to any greater degree this time around.

Money raised and spent by the UK Government

1.20 Income tax has for a long time been the biggest revenue raiser for the UK government, as it is for many other similar countries. To give some idea of how many people pay income tax, Table 1.2 gives details of the number of UK income tax payers over the last thirty years.

Table 1.2: Number of individual income taxpayers (in thousands)

Year	Number of individuals paying tax	Number of lower[1], starting[2] or savers[3] rate taxpayers	Number of basic[4] rate taxpayers	Number of higher[5] rate taxpayers	Number of additional[6] rate taxpayers
1990/91	26,100		24,400	1,700	
1994/95	25,300	5,180	18,200	2,000	
1999/00	27,200	3,234	21,400	2,510	
2004/05	30,300	4,403	22,500	3,330	
2005/06	31,100	4,356	23,100	3,590	
2006/07	31,800	4,377	23,700	3,770	
2007/08	32,500	4,510	24,100	3,870	
2008/09[7]	*	*	*	*	
2009/10	30,600	765	26,600	3,190	
2010/11	31,300	899	27,100	3,020	236
2011/12	30,800	939	26,000	3,570	262
2012/13	30,600	900	25,700	3,720	273
2013/14	30,400	975	24,900	4,200	311
2014/15	30,700	971	25,100	4,300	328
2015/16	31,000	806	25,300	4,510	362
2016/17[8]	30,800	650	25,400	4,420	341
2017/18[8,9]	30,800	677	25,500	4,260	368
2018/19[8,9,10]	31,000	779	25,600	4,280	393

Notes:

[1] Taxpayers with total taxable income below the lower rate limit and some taxpayers whose savings and dividend incomes took them above the lower rate limit. From 1993-94 until 1998-99 a number of taxpayers with taxable income in excess of the lower rate limit only paid tax at the lower rate. This was because it was only their dividend income and (from 1996-97) their savings income which took their taxable income above the lower rate limit, and as such income was chargeable to tax at the lower rate and not the basic rate.

[2] In 1999-2000 the starting rate replaced the lower rate. Between 1999-2000 and 2007-08 taxpayers with total taxable income below the starting rate limit. From 2008-09 taxpayers with no taxable earnings and total taxable income from savings below the starting rate limit. From

2015/16 the starting rate of tax for savings income has been reduced to 0% and the starting rate limit to £5,000.

[3] Before 2016-17 taxpayers with no taxable earnings and total taxable income from savings between the starting/lower rate limit and the basic rate limit and/or dividends at the 10p ordinary rate. From 2016-17 taxpayers with no taxable earnings and total taxable income from savings charged at 20% and/or dividends at 7.5%. Before 1999-2000 these taxpayers would have been classified as lower rate taxpayers.

[4] Between 1999-2000 and 2007-08 taxpayers whose total taxable income is between the starting rate limit and basic rate limit and includes income from earnings or income taxed as earnings. From 2008-09 taxpayers whose income includes earnings or other income taxed as earnings and with total taxable income below the basic rate limit.

[5] Before 2010-11 taxpayers with total taxable income above the basic ate limit. From 2010-11 taxpayers with total taxable income between the basic rate limit and the higher rate limit.

[6] Taxpayers with total taxable income above the higher rate limit.

[7] Figures for 2008-09 tax year are not available

[8] Projected estimates based upon 2015/16 Survey of Personal Incomes, using economic assumptions consistent with the OBR's March 2018 economic and fiscal outlook.

[9] From 2017/18, individuals who are classified as resident in Scotland and have their total taxable incomes above the Scottish Basic Rate Limit (BRL) but below the UK government's BRL have their marginal rate classification based on their income within this notional band. For these taxpayers, non-savings non-dividend (NSND) income within this band is taxed at the higher rate, whereas savings and dividends income is taxed at the basic rate. A Scottish taxpayer with any taxable NSND income within this band (but no total taxable income above the UK BL) is classified as a Higher Rate taxpayer, as this is the top rate they are paying. A Scottish taxpayer with only savings and/or dividend income within this band (and no total taxable income above the UK BRL) is classified as a Basic Rate taxpayer.

[10] From 2018-19 individuals who are classified as resident in Scotland and have total taxable income in the Scottish starter rate or Scottish intermediate rate have their marginal rate classified based on their income within this notional band. For these taxpayers, non-saving non-dividend (NSND) income within this band is taxed at 19% or 21% respectively, whereas savings and dividends income is taxed at the basic rate. A Scottish taxpayer with any taxable NSND income within these bands (but no total taxable income above the UK BRL) is classified as a basic rate taxpayer, as this is the top rate they are paying. A Scottish taxpayer with only savings and/or dividend income within this band (and no total taxable income above the UK BRL) is classified as a basic rate taxpayer.

Table 1.3 shows the current taxes in operation in the UK for 2018/19 and how much each tax contributes to the total revenue raised by the Government each year. You will see that the most important UK taxes, in terms of the revenue they raise for the Government, are income tax, VAT, corporation tax and social security contributions.

Table 1.3: UK Tax Receipts

From Table 4.6: Current Receipts, Autumn Budget 2018, Office of Budget Responsibility Forecast, November 2017. Crown copyright is produced with the permission of the Controller of Her Majesty's Stationery Office (for full notes to this table please see the full report available on the HM Treasury website).

	£ billion		
	Outturn 2016/17	Forecast 2017/18	Forecast 2018/19
Income tax (gross of tax credits)	177.2	177.2	184.7
of which: Pay as you earn	146.7	154.5	158.0
Self assessment	28.5	25.5	29.9
National insurance contributions	125.9	131.0	134.4
Value added tax	121.6	125.8	130.3
Corporation tax	54.1	52.8	55.5
of which : Onshore	53.5	51.5	54.4
Offshore	0.6	1.3	1.0
Petroleum revenue tax	−0.7	−0.6	−0.5
Fuel duties	27.9	27.9	28.0
Business (non-domestic) rates	29.2	29.3	30.5
Council tax	30.4	32.2	33.8
VAT refunds	13.8	14.1	14.5
Capital gains tax	8.4	8.8	9.9
Inheritance tax	4.8	5.3	5.4
Stamp duty land tax[2]	11.9	13.2	13.2
Stamp taxes on shares	3.7	3.4	3.5
Tobacco duties	8.7	9.4	9.2
Spirits duties	3.3	3.5	3.5
Wine duties	4.2	4.3	4.3
Beer and cider duties	3.6	3.7	3.7
Air passenger duty	3.2	3.3	3.5
Insurance premium tax	4.9	5.8	6.0
Climate Change Levy	1.9	1.8	1.9
Other HMRC taxes[1]	7.4	7.3	7.3
Vehicle excise duties	5.8	6.0	6.2
Bank levy and surcharge	4.6	4.4	4.3
Apprenticeship levy	0.0	2.7	2.7
Licence fee receipts	3.2	3.2	3.3
Environmental levies	5.2	8.9	10.5
EU ETS auction receipts	0.4	0.4	0.6
Scottish and Welsh taxes[3]	0.6	0.7	1.0
Diverted profits tax	0.1	0.2	0.3
Soft drinks industry levy	0.0	0.0	0.3
Other taxes	7.2	7.0	6.8
National Accounts taxes	672.7	692.8	718.6
less own resources contribution to EC budget	−3.4	−3.5	−3.5
Interest and dividends	6.5	7.1	8.1
Gross operating surplus	47.2	45.5	43.1
Other receipts	3.7	3.5	3.4
Current receipts	726.7	745.4	769.8
Memo:			
UK oil and gas revenues[4]	0.0	0.7	0.5

[1] consists of landfill tax (excluding Scotland and Wales from 2018-19), aggregates levy, betting and gaming duties and customs duties
[2] includes SDLT for England, Wales (up to 2018-19) and Northern Ireland
[3] consists of devolved property transaction taxes and landfill tax but not the Scottish rate of income tax or aggregates levy
[4] consists of offshore corporation tax and petroleum revenue tax

How does the UK Government spend its money?

1.21 The next table shows how the Government is planning to spend the revenue it raises in 2018/19. To give you a comparison we have also given you the figures for 2017/18's estimated expenditure. We have not shown all the expenditure plans of the Government here, but all the key costs are given.

Table 1.4: UK Government Expenditure

Selected from Table 1.7 – Departmental Expenditure Limits – resource and capital budgets, Autumn Budget 2017 Report, November 2017. Selected resource budgets only. (Detailed capital budgets not shown). Crown copyright is reproduced with the permission of the Controller of Her Majesty's Stationery Office. (for the full table and associated notes to this table please see the full report).

	£ billion	
	2017/18 (Plans)	2018/19 (Plans)
Education	61.3	62.4
Health (including NHS)	119.1	121.9
Transport	2.0	2.1
Business, Energy and Industrial Strategy	1.7	1.8
DCLG Local Government & Communities	9.5	7.1
Home Office	10.6	10.7
Justice	6.6	6.2
Defence	27.5	28.2
Foreign and Commonwealth Office	2.0	1.2
International Development	7.6	8.7
Environment, Food & Rural Affairs	1.6	1.5
Digital, Culture, Media & Sport	1.4	1.5
Work and Pensions	6.2	6.0
HMRC	3.6	3.4
Exiting the European Union	0.1	0.1
Scotland	14.3	13.8
Wales	13.4	13.2
Northern Ireland	10.0	10.0
:		
:		
Total Resource Budget	304.0	309.6
Total Capital Budget	48.2	52.6

Summary

In this chapter we have laid the foundations that you will need to study taxation from this textbook, and beyond. We have drawn on the lessons of history to try to illustrate how taxation affects all of us today. You are now able to trace the history of taxation over more than 2,000 years. The difficulties facing Parliament today have been faced by leaders throughout the centuries. Governments must raise revenues in ways which are seen by the electorate as being fair and equitable if they can reasonably expect them to be paid.

A modern Chancellor has to consider many conflicting objectives when setting out tax proposals in the annual budget. He (or she – although there is yet to be a female Chancellor in the UK) must decide how much tax he wishes to raise and then determine exactly how that tax should be raised from the different taxes available. To do this a Chancellor must be aware of the potential consequences of the legislation on individuals and businesses.

In this chapter we have been able to introduce the complex relationship between legislation and case law and understand the limitations of each and we illustrated how the Government uses the current tax system to raise revenue, and briefly how they spend this revenue.

In Chapters 2 and 3 we will consider in more detail the UK tax system and the nature of a 'good' tax. We will look at the administration of the UK tax system in Chapter 2, then the general principles of the design of tax systems in Chapter 3.

Project areas

There are a number of areas covered in this chapter which would provide good material for projects. These include the following:

- a comparison of the progressive nature of the tax systems of a number of countries,
- exploring the history of UK taxation,
- examining the implications of Brexit on UK tax policy,
- assessing the relative use of different taxes in the UK tax system and the corresponding spending activity of the UK government,
- comparing the balance of local v national (federal) taxation in the UK with other countries. Why might these balances be different?
- discussing the impact of the devolving of more tax powers to regional governments in Scotland and Northern Island (and Wales in due course?)

Discussion questions

1   Do you think that people will be more likely to work if they receive support through the tax system rather than the benefits system?

2   Is it right (and fair) that the UK is so dependent on income taxation? What risks are involved in such a policy? Why might these risks be acceptable to assume?

3   What other unusual taxes can you discover that have existed in some point in history? How effective are they?

4   How is Lady Godiva connected with taxation? What other interesting events in history have been influenced by tax policy issues?

Further reading

History

HMRC website on the history of income tax and current administration procedures; http://www.hmrc.gov.uk

Beckett, J.V., Land Tax & Excise: The levying of taxation in seventeenth and eighteenth-century England *100 English Historical Review*, 285, 1985.

Daunton, M. J., *Trusting Leviathan: the politics of taxation in Britain*, 1799 – 1914, Cambridge University Press: Cambridge, 2001.

Daunton, M. J., *Just Taxes: the politics of taxation in Britain 1914 – 1979*, Cambridge University Press: Cambridge, 2002.

Dowell, S., *A History of Taxation in England* (4 volumes), Frank Cass & Co. Ltd: London, (1965 - 3rd Edition, first published in 1884).

Ezzamel, M., Accounting Working for the State: Tax Assessment and Collection During the New Kingdom, Ancient Egypt *Accounting and Business Research*, 32/1:17-39, 2002.

Farnsworth, A., *Addington: Author of the Modern Income Tax*, Stevens & Sons Ltd: London 1951.

Harris, P., *Income Tax in Common Law Jurisdictions: from the origins to 1820*, Cambridge University Press, Cambridge, 2006.

Kennedy, W., *English Taxation 1640-1799*, G. Bell & Sons Ltd: London, 1913.

Monroe, H.H., *Intolerable Inquisition? Reflections on the Law of Tax*, Stevens & Sons: London, 1981.

Sabine, B.E.V., *A History of Income Tax*, George Allen & Unwin: London, 1966.

Soos, P., *The Origins of Taxation at Source in England*. IBFD Publications: Amsterdam, 1997.

Tax Reform

Sandford, C., *Successful Tax Reform: Lessons from an analysis of Tax Reform in six countries.* Fiscal Publications: Birmingham, 1993.

Steinmo, S., The Politics of Tax Reform, in Sandford, C. (ed.) *More Key Issues in Tax Reform*, Fiscal Publications: Birmingham, 1995.

Progressivity

James, S. and Nobes, C., *The Economics of Taxation: 18th Edition*, Chapter 2, Fiscal Publications: Birmingham, 2018.

Dilnot, A., The Income Tax Rate Structure, in Sandford, C., (ed.) *Key Issues in Tax Reform*, Fiscal Publications: Birmingham, 1993.

Scottish Taxation

Cooper, C., Danson, M., Whittam, G. & Sheridan, T. "The neoliberal project—Local taxation intervention in Scotland" *Critical Perspectives on Accounting,* Volume 21, Issue 3, March 2010, Pages 195-210.

Institute of Chartered Accountants of Scotland (ICAS), *Guide to Scottish Taxes*, https://www.icas.com/__data/assets/pdf_file/0005/340889/20180419-ICAS-Guide-to-Scottish-Taxes.pdf

Comparative Taxation

Evans, C., Hasseldine, J., Lymer, A., Ricketts, R. & Sandford, C. *Comparative Taxation: Why tax systems differ*, Fiscal Publications, Birmingham 2017.

For more information about local taxation see the Ministry of Housing, Communities and Local Government's website:

https://www.gov.uk/government/organisations/ministry-of-housing-communities-and-local-government

which also contains a section on local government finance:

https://www.gov.uk/government/collections/local-government-finance-reports.

For further details on the Office for Budget Responsibility see their website: *http://obr.uk/*

For further details on the Office of Tax Simplification see:

https://www.gov.uk/government/organisations/office-of-tax-simplification

For further details on Revenue Scotland see:

https://www.revenue.scot

For further details on the Welsh Revenue Authority see:

https://beta.gov.wales/welsh-revenue-authority

---

2 Tax administration and compliance

Introduction

2.1   In the previous chapter we considered the historical development of the UK tax system and looked briefly at the current tax structure and tax policy making process. This chapter extends our understanding of the UK tax system by looking more closely at how it is administered by HMRC.

At the end of this chapter you will be able to:
- describe the main administrative features of the UK tax system today, including the systems for collecting taxes, penalties and dispute procedures;
- understand how HMRC operates to encourage taxpayers to voluntarily comply with their tax obligations; and
- discuss the issues that affect whether or not taxpayers comply with the tax rules.

Tax administration

2.2   Until April 2005 the UK tax system was mostly managed by two Government departments, the Inland Revenue and H.M. Customs and Excise.

The Inland Revenue administered all of the following parts of the tax system:
- Income tax
- Corporation tax
- Capital gains tax
- Inheritance tax
- National insurance contributions
- Stamp duties
- Working tax credit and child tax credit
- Child benefit
- Other smaller duties including overseeing the national minimum wage rules and student loan repayments.

HM Customs and Excise were tasked with managing customs duties and excise charges (such as on petrol), and other taxes not managed by the Inland Revenue, including the landfill tax, the climate change levy, and insurance and air passenger duties. They also looked after the VAT system.

Customs and Excise was in fact one of the oldest Government departments (although they were only combined into one department in 1909) with a history dating back to the 13th century as a formal body working for the King to collect duties and prevent smuggling.

Following a lengthy consultation process, the Inland Revenue and H.M Customs and Excise merged into one body with effect from 18 April 2005 and are now called Her Majesty's Revenue and Customs (HMRC). While the two former departments continue to operate in part independently of one another, they now have a common management structure and some joint or merged HMRC departments (e.g. research). This was an important development in UK tax administration as it brought the UK into line with most other developed countries in having one main government department in charge of the tax system. It remains however, one of the non-Ministerial departments of the UK Government in that it has no dedicated Minister to oversee its operation. There are 21 Non-Ministerial departments currently compared with 25 Ministerial departments.

The tax year

2.3 Until the mid-18th century the Government used an accounting year which ended on Lady Day, 25 March, the first quarter day in the calendar year (and the date of the start of the church year, i.e. it was the old New Year's Day for most purposes, as the Feast of the Annunciation of the Virgin Mary – exactly nine months before Christmas Day). In 1752 the Government adopted the Gregorian calendar which required the loss of 11 days between the 2 and 14 of September to bring the calendar year back into line with the solar year. However, the Government was unwilling to have an accounting period which did not run for 365 days and so moved their year-end forward by 11 days to 5 April. Hence today a tax year (for an individual) runs from 6 April to the following 5 April: the tax year 2018/19 runs from 6 April 2018 to 5 April 2019. This is the year we will use for most of the examples in later chapters although for companies the tax year differs. It is 1 April – 30 March (we will cover corporation tax in Chapter 9) and is called a 'financial year' to differentiate it from an individual's tax year.

The self assessment system

2.4   Self assessment is a system under which the taxpayer is responsible for working out his or her own tax liability and reporting it to the revenue authority – the HMRC in the UK's case. During the 1990's the Government switched a number of UK taxes over from an official (direct) assessment system, where the revenue authority works out the tax liability, to self assessment. For example, individual taxpayers are now required to use self assessment in the case of income tax and capital gains tax, as are companies for corporation tax.

The key advantage of self assessment from the Government's point of view is that the tax authority doesn't have to produce assessments for taxpayers. By putting the responsibility on the taxpayer to work out his or her own tax liability (i.e. to 'self' assess), HMRC can devote more of its resources to following up cases that might be inaccurate, providing more advice and offering other services to help taxpayers rather than having to check every tax return that is filed to assess the tax liability, as previously was the case. So self assessment may reduce the cost to the Government of administering the tax system, but on the other hand, increases the cost to the taxpayer of complying with the system as they can no longer rely on the tax authority to do some of the work for them.

Time limits apply to the operation of various parts of the tax system and penalties are possible if those time limits are not adhered to. For example, a taxpayer may find that they have forgotten to include something in their self assessment for income tax, perhaps an expense that qualifies as an allowable deduction, and need to ask for an amendment to be made. Another possibility is that HMRC may discover something about the taxpayer's affairs, perhaps some omitted income, that means that the self assessment is incorrect, and need to issue a new assessment. From 2008, the time limits have been harmonised across the different taxes and they are as follows:

For taxpayer claims	4 years
For ordinary assessments	4 years
Assessments where the loss of tax is due to carelessness	6 years
Assessments where the loss of tax is deliberate	20 years

This is a change from the previous regime where, for example, income taxpayers used to have up to 6 years to go back with claims they had missed, but now as you can see, it is only 4.

Another important feature of the UK's self assessment system is online filing. The Government have for some years been encouraging taxpayers to file their annual tax returns online and provides free software to allow many taxpayers to do so. Online filing, or e-filing, has a number of advantages for both HMRC and taxpayers. For example, the online filing system has a number of checks automatically built in to its operation so that as a taxpayer completes his or her return form online, the system ensures that figures are put in the correct place and calculates the amount of tax due. For both parties the key advantage is speeding up the filing process. This includes for taxpayers getting any tax refunds due to them as soon as possible.

Fiscal Fact

HMRC predict that there will be 31 million individual income taxpayers in 2018-19. More than 85% of all self assessment tax returns are now filed online. This will move to almost 100% by April 2021 after the rollout of the *Making Tax Digital* strategy is complete.

In early 2014, HMRC announced a new pilot project that will allow a small number of self assessed taxpayers to use a secure, personalised portal to view messages from HMRC, and receive email alerts.

In the first Budget 2015 the Government announced this pilot was to be dramatically extended to eventually cover all individual and small business taxpayers. The proposed scheme, promoted under the banner of 'Making Tax Digital', will be arranged to remove the need for many to file a tax return in the future. This will be possible because data HMRC holds on the taxpayer will be linked to their new *Personal Tax Account* so that many taxpayers will just need to check and validate or correct this information, without needing to provide most data the tax return normally asks for. Only those who receive income, or incur tax deductible expenses, that HMRC do not know about from other sources will need to provide additional information (as at present). Taxpayers will be able to do this at any point in the year to update their account.

It is proposed that this new approach will enable taxpayers to be able to pay their tax bill as they go – on a month by month basis if they wish.

The roll out of this new online account approach commenced in 2015/16. By early 2016 the Government predicted all five million small businesses currently operating in the UK, and the first ten million individual taxpayers would have accounts under this new scheme. According to HMRC's 2017 Annual Report, 9.4 million people have been given access to their personal tax account by March 2017 and by the same point every small business customer had access to their own equivalent online account – called their *Business Tax Account*.

The plan proposes complete roll out country wide to all taxpayers by 2020. The extension of this project beyond the pilot has been delayed for small businesses but all businesses that pay VAT will have to use this process from April 2019, and all other businesses that pay income or corporation tax will be included from 2020. Detailed legislation to enact this requirement was included in the Finance Act (No. 2) 2017.

More information on HMRC's plans for digital tax management can be found in their 'Making Tax Digital' strategy paper at:

https://www.gov.uk/government/publications/making-tax-digital

Table 2.1: Estimated number of UK taxpayers

(Source: HMRC website - Number of taxpayers and registered traders, Numbers: thousands)

	Income Tax	Corporation Tax	Capital Gains Tax[2]	Inheritance Tax[3]
2017/18	30,800[1,4]	NA	NA	28[1,4,5]
2016/17	30,800[1,4]	NA	NA	34[1,4]
2015/16	31,000	1,375	258[4]	30[4]
2014/15	30,700	1,235	245[4]	27
2013/14	30,400	1,120	215[4]	23
2012/13	30,600	1,040	171	22
2011/12	30,800	965	163	19
2010/11	31,300	910	188	19
2009/10	30,600	870	168	18
2008/09	NA	890	146	19[5]
2007/08	32,500	925	272	29
2006/07	31,800	885	264	37
2005/06	31,100	895	225	35
:				
2000/01	29,300	520	200	24
:	:	:	:	:
1988/99	25,200	355	150	29
:	: :	:	:	
1983/84	24,000	230	115	30
:	: :	:	:	
1978/79	25,900	185	225	43
:	: :	:	:	
1973/74	23,100	175	285	47

[1] Projected estimates based upon using economic assumptions consistent with the OBR's March 2018 Economic and Fiscal Outlook.

[2] After 1990/91 married couples count as two if both have CGT liabilities as a result of independent taxation. Prior to this they only counted as one.

[3] Figures show the number of death estates paying inheritance tax, capital transfer tax or estate duty and the number of lifetime transfers paying tax.

[4] Provisional

[5] The transferable nil rate band introduced in October 2007 led to a significant reduction in the number of inheritance tax payers during 2007-08 and 2008-09. The introduction of the residence nil rate band in 2017-18 is expected to reduce the number of estates liable to inheritance tax.

Table 2.1 summarises details of the number of UK taxpayers over the last 35 years. It shows the number of people or entities paying the key four UK taxes assessed by self assessment. It illustrates how, after a steady rise for much of this period, the economic problems of the period following the 2007/2008 financial crisis reduced the number of those paying all of the taxes (dramatically in the case of capital gains tax). This is now largely recovered back to the pre-crisis levels. Inheritance tax payer numbers will fall dramatically it is expected in the next few years though because of a large extra exemption that came into effect from April 2018 (the residence nil rate band).

Tax payments

2.5 Whilst the new digital account system announced by the Government in the first Budget 2015 proposes to eventually bring tax payments for different taxes together into one single bill, the current process for paying taxes due varies for the different types of taxes. For income tax, as we will see in more detail in Chapter 4, tax that is not collected throughout the year through deductions at source, or from your employer via PAYE, is paid in instalments with an interim payment on 31 July during the tax year and a final payment on 31 January following the end of the relevant tax year. Capital gains tax is also payable on 31 January following the end of the tax year. Companies' tax payments vary depending on their size; large companies pay tax in quarterly instalments (two during the course of the tax year and two after it has ended) whereas small companies pay their entire tax bill 9 months after the end of their tax year (see Chapter 9 for more details). VAT for most traders is payable on a quarterly basis, although there are some variations for both very small and very large taxpayers (see Chapter 10).

Compliance checks

2.6 The merger of the former two revenue departments into HMRC led to a number of procedures that now apply to all the different types of tax that they administer. Under the self assessment system, taxpayers file their tax returns and do their own tax computation. HMRC accepts this information (and the payment of tax) at face value in the first instance, but then has the right to check that the information and calculations provided are correct.

Compliance checks were introduced in 2008 and apply to income tax, capital gains tax, national insurance contributions, VAT and PAYE, as well as student loans. HMRC provide online guidance explaining how the system of compliance checks works. HMRC can ask for information or documents by sending what is known as an 'information notice'. There are penalties for not supplying the information requested in such a notice. HMRC can also ask for information about a taxpayer's affairs from other people and if necessary, can visit the taxpayer either with a pre-arranged visit or sometimes unannounced.

If the result of a check is that the taxpayer has to pay additional tax, he or she will also have to pay interest on the additional tax not paid at the right time and may be subject to penalties.

HMRC have recently been carrying out a greater number of compliance checks and make use of a number of digital channels to gather information. In particular, the *Connect* tool allows HMRC to pull together a vast array of information about taxpayers with the aim of detecting undeclared income.

Penalties

2.7 The UK also has a penalty regime that applies to all the taxes under the control of HMRC. The penalty regime applies to tax periods commencing on or after 1 April 2008 for returns that are due to be filed on or after 1 April 2009. Penalties are charged as an additional percentage of the tax involved (i.e. in addition to paying the tax due) and are linked to taxpayer behaviour. There are three levels of culpability as follows:

- *Careless* – where the taxpayer has failed to take 'reasonable care' (maximum penalty 30%).
- *Deliberate but not concealed* – where the inaccuracy is deliberate but the taxpayer has not tried to hide it from HMRC (maximum penalty 70%);
- *Deliberate and concealed* – where the taxpayer has made a deliberate mistake, and made arrangements to hide it from HMRC (maximum penalty 100%).

In deciding whether a taxpayer has taken reasonable care, the penalty system considers their particular situation, so, for example, HMRC expects a different standard of care from a large company than from a low income wage earner.

There is provision for the penalty to be discounted if the taxpayer tells HMRC about the mistake before they find out, i.e. unprompted disclosure. In this situation the three levels of penalty become 0%, 20% and 30% for the three levels of culpability listed above. Even where the disclosure of the mistake is prompted by HMRC, the maximum penalty may also be reduced under some circumstances, but not as much as for an unprompted disclosure.

Under self assessment, taxpayers have a duty to make enquiries if their tax position is not clear. In a 2013 case, *Timothy Harding v HMRC* [FTC 56/2013], the taxpayer received a payment when his employment was terminated early, and although he did try to check his tax situation using an article published on a reputable website, the Upper Tribunal held that the penalty for carelessness imposed by HMRC should stand.

A consultation on possible changes to the penalty regime was released in January 2017 in light of the 'Making Tax Digital' programme. The results of this consultation are due in the summer 2018.

Disputing tax liabilities

2.8   What happens if the taxpayer and HMRC disagree about the amount of tax payable? Prior to 2009, there were four tax tribunals that handled tax disputes. There were separate tribunals which dealt with VAT and stamp duty appeals.

For income tax and corporation tax the Lord Chancellor appointed Special and General Commissioner to hear taxpayers' appeals against HMRC's assessments. General Commissioners were part of the income tax system since its inception in 1799, and were part time and unpaid. They were appointed for a division with a focus on a particular area of the tax system. They were aided by a clerk, usually an accountant or a lawyer, who were paid by the Board of Revenue and Customs. There were around 2,000 General Commissioners in the UK at the point they ceased to exist in April 2009.

Special Commissioners were full time and were paid for their services. They had to have been legally qualified for at least ten years. Generally, they heard more complex appeals than those reviewed by the General Commissioners.

Fiscal Fact

A number of famous historical figures have worked for Customs and Excise including Geoffrey Chaucer (Controller of Customs, London 1374-1380), Robert Burns (joined Excise in 1789) and Adam Smith (appointed a Commissioner in 1778 and whose picture is now on the back of £20 notes!).

This situation changed from April 2009 as part of a new tribunals system that applies across many areas of the tax system (and more widely) in the UK. It has its own specialist judiciary and rules of procedure. The tax chamber is overseen up by Lord Justice (Ernest) Ryder as Senior President of Tribunals. Judge Greg Sinfield is the current President of the First-tier Tribunal tax chamber itself. Importantly the tribunal system is independent of HMRC and appeal notices are sent directly to the Tribunals Service (they used to be sent to HMRC under the previous system). If a taxpayer disputes an assessment of tax, he or she has 30 days in which to appeal. There are two tiers of tax tribunal; a first tier tribunal that will hear the less complex cases, and an upper tribunal that will hear more complex cases, and also appeals from decisions of the first tier tribunal.

The upper tribunal can hear appeals from the first tier tribunal. Appeals from the upper tribunal are to the Court of Appeal and then to the Supreme Court (formerly the House of Lords until October 2009), but only on points of law, not questions of fact (as was also the case under the old system). In a number of other countries, there is a dedicated tax court, and there is some suggestion that in the longer term, the new tribunal system may evolve into such a court.

In 2007, HMRC introduced a Litigation and Settlement Strategy which describes the circumstances under which disputes can be settled, that is a tax liability agreed, without having to go to court.

On 3 April 2012, HMRC published a commentary on how it would apply the Litigation and Settlement strategy, together with guidance on Alternative Dispute Resolution (ADR). ADR is common in the commercial world, but was a new development for tax administration in the UK. ADR became HMRC's normal practice from 2013/14 onwards. The ADR guidance suggests that mediation might be appropriate, for example, where both HMRC and the taxpayer want to work collaboratively, but it is difficult to 'pin down the essential points of disagreement', or where a previously collaborative relationship has broken down. HMRC has issued supporting documentation that contains a number of examples of cases that HMRC considers are suitable for mediation as a first step, rather than moving straight to litigation which is costly for both parties.

In August 2012, a new Tax Assurance Commissioner was appointed, not to engage directly with taxpayers, but to oversee HMRC's decision making processes. In September 2012, a new Tax Decision Review Board was established and in November of the same year, a Code of Governance for resolving disputes was published. These developments were partly in response to the criticism of HMRC's settlements with large business taxpayers by the National Audit Office and the Public Accounts Committee.

The Tax Commissioner produces a report each year on their activities. After a number of years of separately produced reports, they now (from July 2017) report as part of the HMRC Annual Report. The latest report outlines the number of disputes and settlements handled over the year and provides several case studies to show how the new systems are working.

Fiscal Fact

According to the Assurance Commissioner's fifth report, now contained within HMRC's Annual Report 2017, in 2016-17 6,559 (5,161 in 2015-16) appeals were made via the tribunal system, of which 4,462 or 68% (3,917 or 76% in 2015-16) were settled either by formal hearing or before a hearing was required. Of the remainder, the outcome of appeal hearings (at first tier tribunal level) was:

Decided in HMRC's favour:	867 (77%)
Decided partially in HMRC's favour	79 (7%)
Decided in the taxpayer's favour	184 (16%)

At the upper tribunal 78 tax appeal cases were heard in the year (62 found in HMRC's favour, with 3 more partially), 15 cases at the High Court (10 found in HMRC's favour and 1 partially), 28 cases at the Court of Appeal (19 found in HMRC's favour and 3 more partially so) and 4 cases at the Supreme Court (2 found in HRMC's favour).

Tax compliance

2.9   One of the key tasks of any revenue authority is to try to encourage taxpayers to comply with the tax rules and regulations. In an ideal world, the rules would be very clear, taxpayers would understand how much they have to pay, and would willingly pay the right amount of tax at the right time. Unfortunately our world is not ideal, and the level of compliance among taxpayers is variable, to say the least.

There are many interesting research studies of tax compliance that try to understand what drives taxpayers to comply, or not comply, with the tax rules, and also what types of taxpayers are more likely not to comply. In November 2010, the OECD released a helpful information note *Understanding and Influencing Taxpayer's Compliance Behaviour* which includes a review of some recent studies (OECD, 2010).

A number of factors are found to influence taxpayers' compliance behaviour:

- *Deterrence* – this means that taxpayers will be deterred from not complying because they are worried about being caught and punished. Not all taxpayers are equally affected by this factor, however, and the relationship between deterrence and compliance is very complex.
- *Personal norms* – these are related to values and ethics and is sometimes referred to as tax mentality or tax morale. In the tax context, a personal norm is the belief that one is morally obliged to comply with tax rules, and is related to personality characteristics.
- *Social norms* – are the behaviours and ideas among social groups that affect the behaviour of people belonging to that group. As human beings we tend to be influenced by what other people do.
- *Opportunities* – some forms of tax are easier to get around than others, so the way a tax is designed can have an effect on whether or not people do comply.
- *Fairness and trust* – if taxpayers believe the tax system, and the tax authority, is fair, and they have trust in both, they are more likely to comply with the tax rules.
- *Economic factors* – which can include loss aversion and liquidity problems.

These factors interact with each other, and we are only beginning to understand them better. There has been a significant increase in the amount of research into taxpayer compliance in the past decade, and increasingly tax authorities around the world are sharing their experiences and ideas through fora such as the OECD.

Compliance costs

2.10 Compliance costs are the costs resulting from the need to comply with the tax rules such as paying for tax advice, employing someone to keep records for tax computations, time spent completing tax forms if you do it yourself or costs for paying someone else to do it for you, and so on. Such costs would not have been incurred if there was no tax to pay and so should be considered as part of the effective incidence of taxation. In 2005 the accounting firm KPMG undertook a study of compliance costs in the UK tax system. They discovered that these costs amount to around 0.45% of UK GDP (i.e. approximately £5 billion!). While this is a large amount of money, the situation in the UK is comparable to other developed countries where these costs are of a similar scale.

While all tax systems will produce some compliance costs, keeping them to a reasonable sum is a problem for any tax system and there are regular calls for these costs to be reduced. One possible way to do this is to make the tax system less complicated; therefore, hopefully, costing people less to comply with it. The KPMG report highlighted around 2,600 obligations in the UK tax system in force at the time, most of which only impact on a small number of businesses but, they argued, could be rationalised, or even done away with, to reduce the extra complexity in the tax system. HMRC responded to this KPMG study, and other calls, in the 2006 Budget by suggesting they have an aim to reduce the compliance cost burden on businesses of the current UK tax system by 10% over the following five years. In the 2009 Budget, HMRC reported that they had reduced the burden by £540million since the KPMG study as evidence they were taking these promises seriously. To achieve this they created a new Board within HMRC, called the Administrative Burden Advisory Board, to look at, then implement, the best ways of achieving these cost savings.

The Office of Tax Simplification (OTS) has also been targeting this issue since its creation in 2010. They produced a report in February 2012 providing suggestions to remove burdens that added significantly to tax compliance costs for small businesses where they thought these were unnecessary (OTS, 2012). At Budget 2012 the Treasury published a report, entitled 'Making tax easier, simpler and quicker for small businesses' on its planned responses to the initial suggestions of the OTS targeted at smaller businesses. It committed to a number of changes to the UK's tax system over the following three years. A key proposal in this paper was to allow small businesses to use cash accounting, instead of the usual accrual accounting, principles to compute their profits on which tax has to be paid. This was introduced for these businesses in Budget 2013 and the OTS claims more than 1 million self-employed individuals have benefited from a switch to these rules since their introduction (see Chapter 6 for further details on these rules).

Changes to the way employee benefits and expenses are handled were introduced with the Budget 2015 (see Chapter 5 for more details on these changes). These also had been highlighted by the work of the OTS (OTS 2014).

An update on the first five years of the OTS's work on complexity was released in March 2017 (OTS 2017). Amongst other issues it addressed the issues of the length of tax legislation that was being produced each year and how legislation related to tax could be drafted differently to make it less complex.

Tax agents

2.11   In the UK, as in other countries, tax agents play an important role in the tax system. Tax agents are people who help taxpayers fulfil their tax obligations, and are sometimes referred to as tax intermediaries, because they operate between the taxpayer and HMRC. In recent years we have seen increasing attention being given to tax agents and how they operate. In the UK there is no formal requirement for tax agents to be registered with HMRC, but they are usually professionally qualified accountants or lawyers.

As members of professional bodies, most tax agents will adhere to a code of professional conduct. The Chartered Institute of Taxation (CIOT) regularly updates its published guidance for members for professional conduct in relation to taxation (CIOT, 2016). The guidance is prepared jointly with a number of other professional bodies including ICAEW, ICAS and ACCA. It states that the fundamental principles are as follows:

- Integrity;
- Objectivity;
- Professional competence and due care;
- Confidentiality; and
- Professional Behaviour.

Fiscal Fact

According to the National Audit Office (2010), eight million UK taxpayers receive help from third parties in completing and filing their income and corporation tax returns each year. Around 43,000 professional tax agent firms, from international corporations to sole traders, help taxpayers to manage their tax affairs.

In October 2010, the National Audit Office released a report into the way HMRC engages with tax agents (NAO 2010). According to the report, eight million taxpayers in the UK get help from third parties to fill in their income and corporation tax returns each year. HMRC had announced a number of initiatives in 2008 to improve its dealings with tax agents, including dedicated telephone lines and improved online support (with a new system promised by March 2015 and launched in the Budget 2015 as part of the new online digital accounts programme). A new Tax Agent Strategy, and related programme of activity, is also currently under development to further enhance this relationship.

One finding from the NAO report is that HMRC does not keep records of whether tax agents helping taxpayers with their returns are professionally qualified or not, which makes analysis of compliance rates difficult. Nonetheless, HMRC is developing a strategy for developing better relations with tax agents and there is some suggestion that we may see a registration regime introduced in the not too distant future.

Encouraging tax compliance

2.12   In recent years, HMRC have changed their approach to encouraging tax compliance using 'responsive regulation'; an approach seeking to understand the different types of taxpayers in the population and creating different strategies for dealing with each type. Part of this process is referring to taxpayers as 'customers'. In November 2008, HMRC launched a departmental vision statement which is available on the HMRC website and is reproduced below:

Our Purpose

- We make sure that the money is available to fund the UK's public services
- We also help families and individuals with targeted financial support

Our Vision

- We will close the tax gap, our customers will feel that the tax system is simple for them and even-handed, and we will be seen as highly professional and efficient organisation.

Our Way
- We understand our customers and their needs
- We make it easy for our customers to get things right
- We believe that most of our customers are honest and we treat everyone with respect
- We are passionate in helping those who need it and relentless in pursuing those who bend or break the rules
- We recognise that we have privileged access to information and we will protect it
- We behave professionally and with integrity
- We do our own jobs well and take pride in helping our colleagues to succeed
- We develop the skills and tools we need to do our jobs well
- We drive continuous improvement in everything we do.

There are a few aspects of this vision statement that are worthy of further comment. The language that is used is quite informal, suggesting that HMRC are an approachable department, in keeping with the view of taxpayers as being 'customers'. The reference to 'targeted financial support' is in recognition that the department is responsible not only for collecting taxes, but also for giving tax credits as benefits to those entitled to them. There is also mention of the 'tax gap' as something that HMRC are trying to close.

Recently, HMRC have begun to measure the tax gap (for the latest report see HMRC 2017). The tax gap is the difference between the tax actually collected and the tax that should be collected (the theoretical liability). According to the 2017 report, the total tax gap is estimated to be £34bn in 2015/16 (6% of total tax liabilities), although it is admitted that all of the tax gap estimates for the different taxes are subject to error, and so need to be treated with some caution.

The good news is that this gap is coming down from a peak f 7.9% of total tax liabilities in 2005/6 to this last report which is the equal lowest figure achieved in the period since then (a 6% figure was also obtained in 2011/12).

For the VAT tax gap (estimated to be approximately £12.6bn or 9.8% of the theoretical VAT liability in 2015/16), and excise duty gap (estimated to be £3bn or 5.5% of theoretical excise tax liability in 2015/16), HMRC draws on national statistics such as household consumption figures, as well as internal data collected within HMRC. For other taxes (estimated to be approximately £13.7bn or 4.5% of theoretical liability for personal income tax, national insurance contributions and capital gains tax, and £3.3bn or 6.4% of theoretical liability for corporation tax), HMRC can only use its own data, and uses a number of techniques to arrive at the tax gap estimates, including random enquiries and data matching, which involves using data supplied by third parties such as banks to try to estimate undeclared income. This is difficult to do fully in the UK, however, because not everyone has to fill in a tax return.

HMRC uses a risk based compliance strategy which means it tries to focus on areas of highest risk. This means identifying tax avoidance and evasion and the types of taxpayers who are most likely to engage in these activities. Tax evasion (where taxpayers deliberate omit or misrepresent information to reduce their tax liabilities), the hidden economy and criminal attacks, accounts for approximately 45% of the net tax gap according to HMRC estimates.

HMRC are trying to organise their operations to minimise the tax gap, but at the same time to encourage as many taxpayers as possible to comply voluntarily with their tax obligations. As part of the process of trying to understand taxpayers better in order to make sure they are dealt with appropriately, HMRC is broken down into a number of specialist areas, including a high net worth individuals area, that focuses on very wealthy taxpayers, and a large business service that focuses on very large companies. It also 'segments' individual taxpayers into groups, recognising that not all taxpayers are out to avoid or evade their tax obligations. Details of the operations of these specialist areas was provided in a report published with Budget 2013 entitled, 'Levelling the tax playing field' (HMRC 2013).

Tax transparency for individuals

2.13 In November 2011, HMRC launched a consultation on the modernisation of the personal tax system, trying to find out more about taxpayers' awareness of their personal tax responsibilities and payments. A research report published in 2012 (see https://www.gov.uk/government/publications/personal-tax-transparency-customer-survey) suggests that UK adults are more engaged with their personal financial affairs than with their tax affairs; indeed 50% of the people interviewed said that they didn't check their income tax and national insurance payments, and 57% said they did not know how much they paid. There was interest among interviewees in learning more about how their income tax and national insurance contributes to different areas of Government spending.

In Budget 2012, the Chancellor announced plans for income taxpayers to receive a personal statement from 2014 with a detailed breakdown of how Government spends the revenue. Currently around 30 million people receive these statements annually in the UK via their new digital Personal Tax Accounts.

The move is part of the previous Coalition Government's commitment to making the tax system more simple and transparent. For more details on these statements see:

https://www.gov.uk/guidance/annual-tax-summary

or for examples of the new tax statements, see:

https://www.flickr.com/photos/hmtreasury/sets/72157643350598405

Summary

In this chapter, we have extended our understanding of how the UK tax system works by looking at how it is administered by HMRC. As an organisation, HMRC has undergone considerable change in recent years, and continues to evolve to keep pace with modern developments not just in the UK, but overseas as well. Some of the administrative policies adopted by HMRC have been borrowed from other countries or from the research of supra national bodies such as the OECD, such as the segmentation of the taxpayer population so as to provide a different type of service or enforcement strategy to each category.

Before we move on to the detail of the individual taxes that make up the UK tax system, in Chapters 3 we will first consider the nature of a good tax – if indeed any tax can be considered to be good – addressing firstly the principles of the design of tax systems. This means that you will be in a position to evaluate each of the UK's taxes according to these design principles.

Project areas

There are a number of areas covered in this chapter which would provide good material for projects. These include the following:

- exploring the effectiveness of a self-assessment system for income tax assessment, and the impact the new digital accounts may have on taxpayer compliance and taxpaying behaviour,
- assessing the effectiveness of the new Tribunals Service compared to the previous dual roles of the General and Special Commissioners,
- exploring what motivates taxpayers to comply, or not, with the tax rules and regulations,
- there has been significant work done over the last twenty years on assessing (as accurately as we can) the compliance costs of taxation. An exploration of how this can be done in practice by looking at this research would be an interesting project or dissertation.
- reviewing the performance of HMRC in its task of administering the UK tax system.

Discussion questions

1 What are the advantages and disadvantages of a system of self assessment under which taxpayers are responsible for working out their own tax liabilities?

2 What demographic characteristics play a role in tax compliance, for example, are women more or less likely to cheat on their taxes than men, or better educated taxpayers than uneducated taxpayers?

3 HMRC now refer to taxpayers a 'customers'. What are the benefits for the department and for taxpayers of doing this?

4 What can be done in practice to address the tax gap?

5 What are the implications for taxpayers of being moved online for the management of their tax affairs and tax filing as part of the 'Making Tax Digital' processes?

Further reading

Dates in UK Tax System

J. Jeffrey-Cook, (2001), A year beginning on 6 April, *Taxation*, 5 April, p8.

Tax Administration

Sandford, C., M. Godwin & P. Hardwick, (1989), *Administrative and Compliance Costs of Taxation*. Fiscal Publications: Birmingham.

For more details of the administration of UK tax see the HMRC website (https://www.gov.uk/government/organisations/hm-revenue-customs).

Penalties

For the HMRC 2015 discussion document and other information – see https://www.gov.uk/government/consultations/hmrc-penalties-a-discussion-document

For a discussion of penalties in light of the introduction of 'Making Tax Digital' see: https://www.gov.uk/government/consultations/making-tax-digital-sanctions-for-late-submission-and-late-payment

Tax Compliance

Braithwaite, V., (2009), *Defiance in Taxation and Governance*, Edward Elgar: Cheltenham.

HMRC (2017), *Measuring Tax Gaps 2017 edition: Tax gap estimates for 2015-16*, available at https://www.gov.uk/government/statistics/measuring-tax-gaps

HMRC (2013), *Levelling the playing field: Compliance progress report – March 2013*, available at http://www.hmrc.gov.uk/budget2013/level-tax-playing-field.pdf

Kirchler, E., (2007), *The Economic Psychology of Tax Behaviour*, Cambridge University Press: Cambridge.

OECD (2010), Forum on Tax Administration: SME Compliance Sub-group *Understanding and Influencing Taxpayers' Compliance Behaviour*, available at http://www.oecd.org/dataoecd/58/38/46274793.pdf

Compliance Costs

European Union (2013), A *Review and Evaluation of Methodologies to calculate tax compliance*, TAXUD Taxation Paper

Evans, C., Hasseldine, J., Lymer, A., Ricketts, R. & Sandford, C. (2017) *Compliance Costs (Chapter 11)* in Comparative Taxation: Why tax systems differ, Fiscal Publications: Birmingham.

HMRC (2013), *Making tax easier, simpler and quicker for small businesses*, available at https://www.gov.uk/government/publications/supporting-small-business-making-tax-easier-quicker-and-simpler

Office of Tax Simplification (2012), Small business tax review – final report, available at:
https://www.gov.uk/government/publications/small-business-tax-review

Office of Tax Simplification (2014), Review of employee benefits and expenses – final report, available at:
https://www.gov.uk/government/publications/review-of-employee-benefits-and-expenses-final-report

Office of Tax Simplification (2017), Focus Paper – The OTS Complexity Project, – report available at:
https://www.gov.uk/government/uploads/system/uploads/attachment_dat a/file/603469/OTS_Focus_paper_on_complexity_final.pdf

Pope, J. (2002), *Administrative and compliance costs of international taxation*, in The International Tax System, Lymer, A. & J. Hasseldine (eds), Springer: Heidelberg.

Sandford, C. (1995), *Tax compliance costs measurement and policy*, Fiscal Publications: Birmingham.

Making Tax Digital

Overview of Making Tax Digital - Policy Paper (July 2017):

> https://www.gov.uk/government/publications/making-tax-digital/overview-of-making-tax-digital

Taxpayers' Charter

Taxpayers' Charter: available at:
http://www.gov.uk/government/publications/your-charter

Tax Agents/Intermediaries

CIOT (2016), *Professional Conduct in Relation to Taxation*, available at:
http://www.tax.org.uk/professional-standards/professional-rules/professional-conduct-relation-taxation

HMRC (2013), *Tax Agent Strategy*, available at :
https://www.gov.uk/government/publications/agents-strategy-an-overview

National Audit Office (2010), HMRC: *Engaging with Tax Agents*, HC Report 486.

OECD (2008), *Study into the Role of Tax Intermediaries*, available at:
http://www.oecd.org/tax/administration/39882938.pdf

3 Principles of tax system design

Introduction

3.1 In Chapter 1 we considered the objectives of a tax system and determined that taxation is a tool used by government to manage the economy, regulate and develop society and provide public goods. We also noted that the nature of any particular tax system, which consists of a number of different types of tax, is constantly changing with the changing views of society as a whole.

In this chapter we will first discuss a number of ideas and concepts which are relevant to understanding how to design a tax system. We will then identify and explore the desirable characteristics of a tax system that underpin its design. These principles apply to any tax system – not just the UK's. Once we have done this we will evaluate various bases of taxation to illustrate the application of this theory in practice.

At the end of this chapter you will be able to:

- outline the key issues of tax system design;
- state and discuss the five desirable characteristics of a tax system;
- state the range of tax bases from which a tax system may be built; and
- discuss the merits and limitations of each of these tax bases.

Key issues in taxation design

3.2 In this section we will explore the key issues of tax system design that all tax systems must keep in balance to function properly:

- What to tax?
- Who to tax?
- What kind of rate structure?
- How should the tax burden be distributed? and
- What effect do taxes have on taxpayer behaviour?

What to tax?

3.3   We saw in the historical review of taxation in Chapter 1 that taxes have been imposed on all kinds of activities, goods and services throughout history.

The classification of taxes, however, comes down to three broad groups:

Income Taxes	taxes on a taxpayer's income earned or received between specific points in time;
Wealth/Capital Taxes	taxes on a taxpayer's accumulated wealth, its transfer or on its changing value;
Consumption Taxes	taxes on a taxpayer's spending.

The rules used to decide what is taxed, and what is not, under each of these categories is called the *tax base*. For example, what categories of income a taxpayer is taxed on will form the income tax base, and so on. For each of these bases, decisions must be made about what, if any, individual elements of the base should be taxed, exempted from tax, or relived from tax in some other way.

In the case of income tax, the Government may choose to make income from particular activities, or for particular types of potential taxpayers, exempt from tax, thereby removing it from the tax base. For example, if an economic objective the Government set itself was to encourage people to save more, interest income could be exempted from tax or be relived in part so a lower tax rate was paid on it than might otherwise be the case. As taxpayers earning interest would then keep more of it for themselves they are likely to be incentivised to save more than they may have before the tax rule change.

The Government may also allow reductions in tax liability for particular types of expenditure. In some countries, (but not the UK) taxpayers are allowed to deduct mortgage interest in calculating their income tax base, to encourage home ownership.

Wealth taxes can be difficult for Governments to manage, in part because finding a correct value for assets can sometimes be hard. Some countries choose not to tax wealth ownership at all, and some do so using an annual wealth tax at a low rate. Many countries only tax wealth at the time it is transferred from one person to another, for example when a taxpayer dies, or when an asset is sold and a profit (gain) is made. Governments that impose wealth taxes may choose not to tax particular types of asset, for example taxpayers' homes.

Consumption taxes may be comprehensive, which means they are imposed on the full range of goods and services that people buy. In most countries, however, there are certain items of consumption that are taxed differently or not at all. For example, it is common to exempt necessities such as basic food items from the tax base.

Tax bases also change over time as their rules of application are developed in response to a variety of factors including economic and social change.

Balancing the rules of the three tax bases to form the whole tax system is an important task carried out by the Government. Later in this chapter we will look at how the Government goes about deciding how this balance should be set, and how it changes over time. We look at the theoretical arguments for each of these three tax bases later in the chapter.

The primary current UK taxes under each of the bases are:

Income Taxes	For individuals: Income Tax
	For companies: Corporation Tax
Wealth/Capital Taxes	Capital Gains Tax
	Inheritance Tax
	Stamp Duty
	Council Tax
Consumption Taxes	Value Added Tax
	Excise Duties (e.g. on alcohol, petrol or tobacco)

Who to tax?

3.4 In addition to deciding what to tax, Governments also have to decide who should be responsible for paying a tax, i.e., who should the taxpayer be for any particular tax? For income tax, the taxpayer could be an individual or a family. If the Government chooses to tax a family unit, decisions then have to be made about what 'family' means for this purpose. Decisions are also required about whether to impose a tax on legal entities, such as companies and partnerships.

Tax rate structure

3.5 Let's now think about the way in which the tax rate structure might work. A tax rate structure will either be:

- *proportional* – the rate of tax to be paid increases directly in line with increases in the tax base;
- *progressive* – the rate of tax to be paid increases faster than the increase in the tax base; or
- *regressive* – the rate of tax to be paid increases more slowly than increases in the tax base.

In most tax systems, including the UK's, there is a generally accepted principle that income tax should be progressive, i.e. taxpayers with larger incomes should pay a higher rate of tax than taxpayers with smaller incomes.

To be a progressive tax there doesn't necessarily have to be a steadily rising tax rate as the tax base rises. A tax can still be progressive even if it only has two rates of tax. To illustrate this, consider a tax on income for two taxpayers, one earning £10,000 per annum and the other earning twice that, i.e. £20,000 per annum. Assume both taxpayers have a personal allowance (tax free threshold) for income tax of £5,000. This means that the first £5,000 of income is not subject to income tax. The rest of the income is taxed at 20%. The taxpayer earning £10,000 per annum will pay £1,000 ((£10,000 – 5,000) × 20%) tax. This equates to 10% of their income. The higher earning taxpayer will pay £3,000 ((£20,000 – 5,000) × 20%) tax or 15% of their income. The higher income earner pays a higher overall percentage of their income in tax because both have a fixed level of tax-free income (£5,000) before starting to pay tax. In this case the tax they have to pay increases three times when the income only doubles (i.e. the tax rate is rising faster than the income). This simple tax system is therefore a progressive one even with only two rates (0% and 20%).

A good rule of thumb for assessing whether a tax rate is progressive, proportionate or regressive is to compare the *average rate of tax (ART)* with the *marginal rate of tax (MRT)* faced by the taxpayer. The average rate is found by dividing the amount of tax payable by the amount of the tax base. The marginal rate of tax is the rate the taxpayer would have to pay on an extra £1 of the tax base.

If the average rate of tax is less than the marginal rate of tax the system is progressive (for that taxpayer at that point). If the average rate of tax equals the marginal rate of tax the tax system is proportional, and if the average rate of tax is greater than the marginal rate of tax it is regressive.

In this case, for the first taxpayer (with £1,000 income), the average rate of tax is 10%, and the marginal rate of tax is 20% (as they would pay 20p extra in tax if they earned £1 more in income) so the system is progressive for them (10% < 20%) at the point they are currently. The same applies for the second taxpayer (15% < 20%).

An exercise illustrating the relationship between personal allowances and progressivity can be found on the website. You could now attempt it to further develop this idea of tax burdens.

Distribution of the tax burden

3.6   The example of progressivity above is simplified by only looking at the rate of tax, to illustrate the point about how progressive tax rates work. When other tax factors are taken into account, for example tax relief on particular payments made by the taxpayer, or when combined with the effects of other taxes, a fuller analysis of a tax system may not give the same results. It may also vary from taxpayer to taxpayer even though the rules are the same for all.

The tax burden is the degree to which a tax, specific collection of taxes, or a tax system viewed in its entirety, affects a taxpayer or group of taxpayers. It is a question of who in society bears the impact, or *incidence*, of tax. Governments may try to spread this burden evenly throughout society, or may instead decide that it is fairer if the wealthy in society are asked to bear a higher burden than those who are poorer (or vice versa).

Regressivity

3.7   A regressive tax is one that places a heavier burden on poorer taxpayers than wealthy taxpayers. For example, unlike most income taxes that are usually designed to be progressive, VAT is generally considered to be a regressive tax because everybody pays the same rate (most items have been taxed at 20% since 4 January 2011). This means that poorer taxpayers will spend a higher proportion of their total income on VAT than richer people (who are usually able to save a higher percentage of their income and therefore pay less VAT as a proportion of their total income). In the UK, this problem is balanced to some extent by policies to reduce VAT on some essential goods, such as applying a zero rate (i.e. 0%) of VAT on most food. However, this zero-rate taxing does not apply to all basic items and therefore VAT is generally considered to be a regressive tax.

Taxpayer behaviour

3.8   It might seem strange, but we actually know very little about how taxpayers behave in response to the introduction of new taxes, or changes to the tax system. There are academic studies that attempt to match taxpayer behaviour with tax changes, but few are conclusive. This is perhaps to be expected because modern society is so complex. Creating even a moderately complex tax system within such a society will then make it very difficult to map the impact of changes in taxes and taxpayer responses, and even harder to predict this in advance as changes are designed.

A good example of the use of the tax system to influence taxpayers' behaviour in a positive way is the switch to taxing company cars by reference to their level of CO_2 emissions (rather than business miles driven as was previously the case). This made it more expensive to drive higher polluting cars relative to lower polluting cars for the same mileage.

When the Government introduced this new approach in 2002, it hoped that companies providing cars for their employees to drive would switch to using lower emission cars, which would be beneficial for the environment. Recent statistics suggest that this has been successful to some extent. In 2007 the average new car CO_2 emissions was 164.9g/km compared to 181g/km in 2000. By 2017 average emissions for new cars were down further to 121g/km and huge 33% on the 2000 levels. It certainly seems that the change in rules, working along with opinion changes in the wider society in this case, has produced the desired impact of encouraging employers to provide greener vehicles for their employees. It has contributed effectively, with other initiatives, to make the whole sector more conscious of emission levels of cars. (You can find out more detail on company car taxation in Chapter 5)

The newly introduced 'sugar tax' (or Soft Drinks Industry Levy to give it its proper title) on added sugar in drinks, commenced in April 2018. This is another example of how the Government is proposing to use a tax to try to change people's behaviour. The levy is initially set at 18p/litre for drinks with more than 5g/ml of added sugar, rising to 24p/litre where there is more than 8g/ml of added sugar. The Government hopes that this extra tax applied, increasing the price of these drinks compared to others, will mean fewer people will consume them. Further, it is hoped this will then motivate the drinks industry to lower the sugar content in their drinks. Together these effects should, it is hoped, lower the overall levels of sugar consumed in the UK. Whether this will have the desired affect we will have to wait and see.

Unfortunately, taxpayers don't always behave in the way the Government expects them to. An example in the UK of an unexpected change in taxpayer behaviour was the increased use of companies as the trading structure chosen for operating a business to take advantage of the lower tax rates that apply to corporations as compared to individuals. Following the introduction of a new 10% rate (later reduced to 0%) for companies with low profits, there was a significant increase in the number of businesses that switched to trading as companies. In the 2006 Budget the then Chancellor, Gordon Brown, reacted by increasing the rate of tax on corporations with taxable profits of less than £50,000 to the full tax rate that companies earning between £50,000 and £300,000 previously paid. In the 2007 Budget he went further and announced future rate rises for these low profit companies, again citing tax avoidance as his excuse for hitting these smaller companies hard. This action was assumed to make the use of corporate structures solely for tax avoidance somewhat less attractive.

Also, as we saw in the discussion of tax history in Chapter 1, people have found imaginative ways of circumventing a liability to tax for as long as taxes have been used. Some evade tax, for instance by smuggling goods into the country from abroad rather than paying the correct import tax on those goods. Others will under-declare their incomes, or overstate their expenses, to reduce their income tax bill.

Fiscal Fact

The number of higher rate income taxpayers increased from 1.7 million in 1990/91 to 2.1 million in 1996/97. It is estimated this number will rise to 4.28 million in 2018/19 and they will be paying an average total income tax bill of £15,700 each at an average rate of tax of 21.9.%. This rises dramatically to average income tax bills of £143,000 and 37.9% for the 393,000 estimated additional rate taxpayers. [Source: HMRC Statistics – Tables 2.1 and 2.6]

Tax evasion is illegal and is punishable by fines and/or imprisonment. Tax avoidance on the other hand is legal and involves arranging your activities in ways that will reduce your tax bill. Some acceptable tax avoidance, or tax planning, is simple. For instance, saving money in an ISA rather than an ordinary building society account has the result that income from the account is always paid without being subject to tax (subject to certain limits as we will see later) and therefore even needing to be reported to HMRC on tax returns. This, therefore, is a sensible, and fully Government supported, arrangement which enables taxpayers to avoid paying tax on investment interest received.

Attitudes to tax avoidance have changed over the years and vary even at the same point in time depending on the perspective from which the question is considered. Indeed, the boundary between acceptable and (what to some will be) unacceptable tax avoidance is an issue of constant debate (we will explore this further in Chapter 11). Some tax avoidance schemes are highly artificial and involve changing the nature of transactions or creating artificial transactions so as to take advantage of concessions in the tax law. These are generally considered to fall into the unacceptable tax avoidance category (i.e. are likely to be proven not to be legal if challenged in the courts – HMRC has a very good track record in defeating these in court, although not with 100% success). Others are not so clearly on the wrong side of the boundary and may be viewed differently as to whether or not they are acceptable by taxpayers and the tax administrators.

Another topical example is exploiting the different tax rules that apply to employees and consultants (who are self-employed or use a small company structure with themselves as the main/only employee). This use of what are called 'personal service' companies, continues to be a tax avoidance issue of concern to HMRC, which we look at in more detail in Chapter 11.

In the next section we will review in more detail the foundation principles of tax system design that help us to find solutions to some of the problems faced in creating a working tax system.

The desirable characteristics of a tax system

3.9   Prior to the late eighteenth century, taxation was used mainly to raise revenue to fund military campaigns and defend the nation state against their enemies, whoever they happened to be at the time. Taxation was viewed as being the price paid for the protection of the state. Thomas Hobbes wrote in his famous book *Leviathan* in 1651:

> "For the impositions that are laid on the people by the sovereign power are nothing else but the wages due to them that hold the public sword, to defend private men in the exercise of their several trades and callings."

By the late eighteenth century, at the start of the industrial revolution, more consideration was being given to the ways in which taxes were raised and the most appropriate forms of tax to create effective tax systems.

Adam Smith was one of a number of early thinkers on this topic who considered the principles of how to design an effective tax system, and in his book, *The Wealth of Nations*, published in 1776, he outlined four desirable characteristics for a tax system:

1. "The subjects of every state ought to contribute to the support of the Government, in proportion to their respective abilities; that is in proportion to the revenue which they respectively enjoy under the protection of the state.

2. The tax which each individual is bound to pay ought to be certain, and not arbitrary.

3. Every tax ought to be levied at the time, or in the manner, most convenient for the contributor to pay it."

4. Every tax ought to be so contrived as both to take out, and keep out, of the pockets of the people, as little as possible over and above what it brings in to the public treasury of the state. A tax may either take out or keep out of the pockets of the people a great deal more than it brings into the public treasury, and in four ways: a) by the number of officers who levy it; b) by obstructing the industry of the people; c) by penalties incurred in attempting to evade the tax; d) by subjecting the people to the frequent visits and examinations of the tax-gatherers."

It must be remembered, however, that at the time Adam Smith was writing, there was no income tax in Britain, indeed the idea of a tax on income was considered to be abhorrent so his comments are largely made in the context of a tax system made up predominately of capital/wealth and consumption/ expenditure taxes. In more modern terms these 'Canons of Taxation', as they became known, can be re-stated as:

1. *Equity*: a tax should be seen to be fair in its impact on all individuals. Taxes should be levied according to people's taxable capacity.

2. *Certainty*: taxes should not be arbitrary, the taxpayer should know his or her tax liability and when and where to pay it.

3. *Convenience*: it should be easy for the taxpayer to pay what they owe.

4. *Efficiency*: the tax system should not have an impact on the allocation of resources and it should be cheap to administer. Taxes which are too costly for the tax authority to administer should be avoided as much as possible. Costs to governments include administration costs, the cost of chasing up delinquent taxpayers through audits and the like, and the costs of considering disputes with taxpayers over the way in which the tax laws operate.

Other writers have subsequently proposed further characteristics to add to this list. Two common additions are *simplicity* and *flexibility*. Designing for simplicity would suggest that, where possible, the tax system should have as little complexity as possible (e.g. not having either elaborate nor large numbers of exceptions for particular activities or personal characteristics of the taxpayer). It is important for a tax to be simple to understand so that a taxpayer can easily calculate his or her liability.

Aiming for flexibility suggests that a tax system should be established in such a way as to be able to cope with changing economic circumstances over time without requiring substantial changes.

A problem with desirable characteristic lists, as given above, is that their authors usually do not order them in any practically useful way. Should each of the characteristics be allocated equal weight in the design of the tax system, or are some more important than others? Are some of the characteristics so important that any successful system of tax must have them? What happens when two desirable characteristics conflict with each other? We need to consider each of these characteristics in more detail before attempting to answer these questions.

Equity

3.10 A tax which is not seen to be equitable, or fair, is usually resented by the individuals asked to pay it and therefore equity is an important constituent of any tax system – as a government clearly needs people to pay the taxes they charge them with or the whole system will grind to a halt.

There are two aspects to the fairness of a tax system – *horizontal equity* and *vertical equity*:

- a tax system is horizontally equitable if taxpayers with equal taxable capacity bear the same tax burden;
- a tax system has vertical equity if those with greater capacity to pay tax bear a higher tax burden.

Horizontal equity

3.11 We have two problems of definition when considering horizontal equity. Firstly, how will we identify taxpayers with equal taxable capacity? Two individuals doing the same job for the same money with the same personal circumstances are likely to have the same taxable capacity in most tax systems, but how do you compare the taxable capacity of an individual who has earned income with another, who is not working but has substantial wealth? Equally, an individual who prefers to spend his leisure time drinking alcohol incurs a greater tax liability (because alcohol attracts VAT and excise duty) than an individual who spends the same amount of money on trips to the theatre, as this isn't as heavily taxed (only VAT, not excise duty, is charged on theatre tickets), regardless of their relative taxable capacities.

The second problem of definition relates to ensuring that in practice equal amounts of tax are paid by individuals with the same taxable capacity. Suppose we consider two individuals with the same lifetime income, one of whom earns the average UK income for each year of his working life of 40 years while the other earns 20 times as much as the average for only two years of her working life (i.e. both earn the same income in total). Under a progressive income tax system, like the one in operation in the UK at present, the first taxpayer will pay less tax than the second as the second taxpayer will pay a higher rate of tax on their income on average. For a tax to have full horizontal equity it would therefore need to be based on the lifetime income of the taxpayer not on incomes from year to year. This approach is likely to prove difficult, if not impossible, to operate in practice. Even if this could be arranged it would, in turn, raise further knock-on difficulties. For example, how should individuals with different life spans be taxed? Women generally have a longer life expectancy than men. If income is to be spread over a taxpayer's lifetime should women pay less tax than men on their taxable capacity because they will need to support themselves for more years?

Vertical equity

3.12 What about vertical equity? Achieving this is also difficult in practice. There are at least three layers to this problem. To implement a tax system with vertical equity we must first decide who, in principle, should pay tax at higher rates. Then we must decide how much higher that rate should be than the rates paid by other taxpayers, and finally we must devise a tax system which achieves these objectives for the full variety of taxpayers.

Taxable capacity

3.13 An individual may be considered to have a greater taxable capacity or to have a higher level of economic well-being or to receive more benefits from government spending. Any of these criteria might be used to identify individuals who should pay the higher rate of taxation. However, which, or which combination, of these criteria should be used? So far, we have assumed that it is easy to determine what a person's taxable capacity is, so that we can make judgements about horizontal and vertical equity. In practice, however, it is extremely difficult to decide what factors should be taken into account in working out a person's taxable capacity. Most often we use the notion of 'ability to pay', which links directly to Adam Smith's notion of 'respective abilities'.

Ability to pay

3.14 There are a number of practical difficulties involved in measuring ability to pay.

Activity

What factors should be taken into account when measuring a person's ability to pay taxes?

Feedback

The first factor you probably thought of is the person's income level. But using this then raises further questions about how people earn their income. For example, suppose two individuals undertake the same job but the first chooses to work only the basic required hours, and spends more leisure time in their garden, while the second chooses to work overtime each week instead. If income alone is used to determine 'ability to pay' then the second individual will pay more tax than the first. But both employees had the same opportunity to earn extra money so is it really fair that one of them should pay more tax than the other? If we could assess the ability to earn an income, instead of simply taxing what is actually earned, then both could be made to pay the same amount of tax.

If we want to use the ability to pay as our criteria for assessing how much tax someone should pay we must therefore first decide whether we will use actual income or some measure of potential income. In practice, of course, it is actual income that is taxed because of the practical difficulties of reliably determining potential income. But even if we settle for only being able to tax the actual income of taxpayers we will have still further problems with achieving vertical equity. Suppose two individuals have the same income but the first saves money in order to provide for retirement while the second spends money as it is earned and depends on the state for support in their old age. The first individual will probably pay tax on the returns earned on their savings, and so could well pay more tax in total than the second individual, while the second receives more benefits from the state if given extra help in their old age. Can this be considered to be equitable? It is unlikely that, put this way, the first individual will agree!

In answering the above Activity question, you may also have considered a person's stock of wealth as part of their ability to pay. Some people are known to be "asset rich, but income poor" (for example, a person who may own and live in a large house with no mortgage, but whose only source of income may be government benefits), which raises the question of whether wealth holdings should be counted in deciding what ability to pay is.

What about family circumstances? There is an argument that a single person with no dependents has a larger capacity to pay tax than one who has numerous dependents, maybe a non-working partner and several children for example. There may be an argument that this should be factored into decisions about how much tax burden he or she should bear.

As a result of these difficulties in working out how to assess people's taxable capacity using a concept of ability to pay, both horizontal and vertical equity are therefore difficult to achieve in practice – even if in theory they sound appropriate.

Fiscal Fact

According to the Taxpayers' Alliance (using 2013/2014 data), the bottom 10% of households paid an average of 45.1% of their gross income in taxes and pay an average of £28,685 more in tax than they receive in benefits. The top 10% of households paid an average of 34% of their gross income in taxes.

The benefit principle

3.15   An alternative approach to the use of 'ability to pay' to achieve equity is to try to relate tax charged to the benefit received from the state. This implies creating a tax system where those who benefit most from the services provided by a government should pay the most tax. This might sound fair in principle but proves difficult to achieve practically.

In practice there are relatively few activities which can be effectively taxed using the benefit approach. For example, many services provided by a government cannot be opted out of if someone does not want to receive the benefit. Defence or law and order are, for example, benefits which are impossible for a citizen to choose whether to consume or not (these types of services or goods are referred to as *public goods*).

On the other hand, it may be undesirable for some services to be withheld from citizens who do not contribute to their cost, even if it were feasible. For example, there was a time when homeowners and businesses could subscribe to the fire service in the same way as a motorist can choose to join the roadside assistance agencies (like the AA or the RAC) today. While on the surface it seems this could work - the fire service would only show up for subscribers - however, if a non-subscriber suffered a fire and the fire services did not put the fire out it was possible that the fire would spread to neighbours who had paid to have their property protected. A public service to put out fires that is common for all makes more sense practically. In addition, it is likely to be unacceptable to the community as a whole that some members of society are not helped by the fire services when they are in need, for example, those who cannot otherwise afford to make a private contribution. Nowadays, this service is therefore provided largely as a public good.

Another example of this situation is education. The imposition by the Government of minimum education standards for all citizens produces a benefit for the whole of society whether the individual would want to, or be able to, pay for these benefits directly or not. Therefore, education to at least the age of 16 is provided free of charge to all children in the UK.

Further problems with achieving equity via a benefit approach includes issues with how to value benefits received, over what time scale do you try to measure the benefit (e.g. over their whole life or only part of it?) and also what does this do to the redistribution objective of a government (an important element of the objectives for a tax system as we discussed in Chapter 1).

It therefore seems difficult to imagine that a significant part of the tax system could be organised on the basis of assessing, and taxing, benefit received. Taxes which are raised to pay for specific (usually predefined) activities are termed *earmarked* or *hypothecated* taxes. In the past they have been unpopular with the Treasury as it limits how they can use tax revenues received. We therefore have seen little use of such taxes in recent tax history.

However, there are a number of examples of hypothecated taxes that have been raised in the UK. For example, Vehicle Excise Duties (VED) were originally intended to fund highway construction and maintenance. In practice, the receipts from these duties are now used for general expenditure from which highway construction and maintenance will come, but not in a way that is directly related to the revenue raised from these taxes (i.e. they are no longer really hypothecated - although VED increases proposed in the Summer Budget 2015 are to be hypothecated to infrastructure projects it is promised).

Another example is the TV licence fee. Only those individuals who have a television, or who watch live broadcasts on a computer using the BBC's iPlayer, are required to contribute to the cost of the BBC by way of the licence fee - a sort of tax as it is a compulsory levy on owning a TV or watching the BBC on a computer (and not really directly related to the benefit received as the tax must be paid even if you never actually turn the TV on or actually watch anything in iPlayer). However, this is a crude measure of benefit. There is no way of evaluating how much benefit a taxpayer derives from watching BBC programmes. In addition, the tax is difficult to collect and necessitates the use of a database of all addresses in the UK and detector vans to ensure compliance with the tax to collect a relatively small sum per taxpayer. The charge also is levied on the unit of a 'household' with no differentiation as to how many people share the benefit of the single licence just because they happen to live in the same house.

The television licence fee, however, is still used exclusively to finance the BBC as a hypothecated tax, although there are increasing calls for this to change too, so that the licence fee can be shared more widely (e.g. shared with commercial TV channels and online providers of TV style content).

In the past proposals have been outlined for the National Health Service (NHS) to be funded by way of a hypothecated tax on the basis that taxpayers would be willing to pay more taxes if a clear link between the tax and health care could be established. A new hypothecated tax of this kind was proposed by the then Chancellor, Kenneth Clarke, in his November 1993 budget but this was never implemented. The 2002 Budget, however, picked up on this idea, and announced a rise from April 2003 in National Insurance Contributions to pay for some of the growth in the NHS. This may be an indication that we will see more hypothecation of this type in the future - although the subsequent budgets since this change have not brought any further substantial hypothecation promises despite the ever greater financial pressure on the NHS we have seen in the last few years.

The congestion charge now in operation in London is yet another example of a hypothecated tax as money raised from car users in the centre of London from this charge, over and above the cost of providing the collection service itself, is spent directly on improvements to the city's infrastructure and public transport system rather than paying for other services the Greater London Authority is responsible for.

The concept of equity is complex and we have done little more than introduce the subject in this section, however, you should now be able to see that it is an important concept that should be considered when examining the effectiveness of any tax system.

Certainty

3.16 Having explored the desirable characteristic of equity, and the difficulties that arise in putting it into practice, we will next examine the nature of certainty as a feature of good tax system design.

A country's citizens need to be fully informed about who will have to pay the taxes in the tax system and when they will have to be paid (called the *incidence of tax*). Taxes where the incidence is clear are to be preferred over taxes where there is disagreement and uncertainty over the ultimate payer of the tax and when the tax must be paid.

Under this criterion, as we will see in Chapter 9, corporation tax could be considered to be a poor tax, for example, because it is unclear whether the shareholders, employees, customers or others bear the ultimate burden of the tax. It is also argued by some that individuals are more aware of how much income tax they pay than how much VAT they pay, making income tax more certain than VAT. We can use the term 'salience' to describe awareness of the tax burden, and say that income tax is more salient than VAT.

To achieve full certainty in designing a tax, the complete tax consequences of any financial transaction should be known in advance of the transaction being undertaken. It is difficult to achieve this in practice. This is due to both problems with interpreting the rules (particularly grey areas of the law), but also as rules need to change from time to time (e.g. because the ideas develop of how best to tax or economic conditions alter and so on) so perfect certainty can't be assured.

This characteristic has an important impact on how tax systems evolve over time. In part, because of the need to consider certainty when designing tax systems, tax rule changes are only rarely made retrospectively. Tax policy makers typically only change how the tax system will be applied in the future, not how it was applied to past events or activities that have already been undertaken. They will very rarely seek to collect different taxes on past events to those that have already been paid.

If imposing taxes retrospectively regularly occurred in a tax system then a taxpayer's certainty would be significantly decreased. When they made a particular choice that affected how much tax they pay (e.g. accepting a new job or taking out a particular investment) they could not be certain the tax cost of doing this would not change. A good example of how retrospective taxes can upset taxpayers was the suggestion to increase Vehicle Excise Duties on the most polluting cars that was announced in the 2007 Pre-Budget. As these plans were to impose increased duties on all cars over a certain engine capacity obviously people who have already made the choice to own such cars were going to have to pay extra taxes they were not expecting to have to pay when they bought them. This rarely meets with taxpayer approval.

As another example, in recent years there has been growing unrest among large corporate taxpayers about the uncertainty surrounding the way the UK taxes foreign income earned by companies. Several years ago, some large companies threatened to leave the UK and move to other jurisdictions because of the uncertainty about how new rules might operate. We look at some of these changes in Chapter 12.

Certainty is therefore an important characteristic that affects how tax system changes are usually brought about. However, no tax system can remain the same forever or it will negatively affect its other characteristics. Tax systems do have to change from time to time and will often affect at least some previous decisions people have made (e.g. income tax rates may go up meaning you have to pay more tax on the same job you do for the same wages). A government therefore has a difficult task balancing these often conflicting characteristics.

We will consider the question of incidence more fully in Chapter 14, once you have learned more about how the UK tax system works in practice.

Convenience

3.17   The third 'Canon of taxation' is convenience, which relates to how people pay their taxes, or otherwise engage with the tax system. For example, it is usually more convenient for people to have tax deducted at source (i.e. withheld by the payer before payment is made, and paid directly to the Government on behalf of the taxpayer, like income tax), or at the time they pay for something (like VAT)

than having to pay a lump sum periodically on something already received.

This raises the question of whether tax should be paid at source (as you receive it) rather than directly assessed (paid some time after receipt). This has historically been a particularly important feature of the income tax part of the UK's tax system.

Tax deducted at source is normally calculated independently of the taxpayer's personal circumstances and so does not always represent the correct amount of tax due. An individual who is not liable to income tax can often reclaim any tax deducted at its source by contacting HMRC, or can even prevent its automatic deduction in the first place.

An individual may also sometimes need to pay more tax on income they receive than is deducted at source. We will review how this extra payment is collected in practice in Chapter 4.

Taxpayers who are employed pay income tax on their earnings from employment under the Pay As You Earn (PAYE) scheme. Although this tax is deducted at its source (i.e. withheld by the employer on behalf of their employees) it is different to the other examples of income taxed at source because the amount of tax deducted is partially dependent on the taxpayer's personal circumstances to try and improve the accuracy of the tax deducted. This, however, involves a complex process that is difficult to administer to get right. We'll review further how PAYE works in practice in Chapter 4.

Income tax collected via the self assessment system is an example of direct assessment – the alternative to taxing at source. In the UK, any income subject to taxation which has not been fully taxed at source already will need to be directly assessed. Each year, if you have any such income, you are required to declare it to HMRC (i.e. self-assess – hence the name) by filling out a tax return. Tax due on this income can then be paid directly to the Government. Capital taxes are mostly paid by direct declaration and assessment in this way, and some categories of income are also taxed in this way for some taxpayers. Look back to Chapter 1 to be reminded of who has to file tax returns as they need to be directly assessed.

You can see that the way in which tax is collected is an important consideration and taxation at source would seem to meet the criteria of 'convenience', at least for the taxpayer. It is not so convenient, however, for the person having to deduct the tax, for example in the case of PAYE, the employer incurs considerable cost in making sure the correct amount of tax is deducted from employees' wages and paid to HMRC on time.

In Chapter 2 we saw that the costs of administering a tax system include not only the direct costs incurred by government in operating the system itself, but also the difficulties the tax rules create for the taxpayer (i.e. how inconvenient they are). These difficulties are given a numeric value to give what is known as the *compliance costs* of the taxpayer. Compliance costs are the costs which are imposed on a taxpayer when he or she attempts to comply with a given tax or set of taxes. These will include any costs related to the need to keep records for tax purposes, costs of employing tax related staff, costs of collating data to complete the tax returns and so on. Compliance costs can be significant as part of the total cost of taxation.

There is a welcome current trend from the UK Government towards measuring and planning for the full costs of tax imposition (direct and indirect) as they review new taxes or changes to the tax system. This includes changes to tax rules in the last few years directly aiming to reduce some of the compliance costs on sole traders and partnerships. As we saw in Chapter 2, these measurements of impact costs are called Tax Information and Impact Notes (TIINs) (previously called Regulatory Impact Assessments or RIAs). A TIIN will be created for each non-minor change to the tax system and they are usually published on the HMRC website to make them easy to access.

The burden of complying with rules for PAYE, VAT and capital gains tax should not be underestimated when you are thinking about ways in which a tax system could be developed. This is captured by the Canon of convenience.

Efficiency

3.18   There are two separate aspects to efficiency derived from Adam Smith's Canons of taxation: economic efficiency and administrative efficiency.

Economic efficiency

3.19   A tax system is seen to be *economically efficient* if it does not distort the economic and commercial decisions which are made by individuals. Economic efficiency is sometimes referred to as *fiscal neutrality*, and the key idea is that taxes should, as far as possible, not interfere with the workings of the market including the decisions taxpayers make about their various activities. We will be considering economic efficiency in more detail in the Chapter 14 where we discuss the impact of the UK tax system on decision making. Here, however, we will consider the way in which the tax system affects people's behaviour more generally, referred to as "distortions", and therefore the extent to which a tax system is economically efficient by its design.

As we noted earlier in this chapter, tax can affect peoples' behaviour in many ways. For example, take planning for retirement. An individual who invests funds in an approved pension fund obtains tax relief on contributions and the pension fund itself is exempt from both income and capital gains tax. This contrasts with an individual who proposes to finance retirement in some other way, perhaps by investing in a valuable asset such as a painting or perhaps property – with the aim of selling the items for a profit in the future to provide a source of wealth to fund their retirement. For these assets, the tax situation may be very different to the approved pension fund asset. No relief is available in the current UK tax system for funds initially invested in the valuable asset that is being purchased to fund retirement and capital gains tax will probably be levied when the asset is sold. This means the tax system may well distort how people choose to invest to provide for their retirement by making investment of retirement savings taxable and the other not. This means there is not full economic efficiency between these choices.

Sometimes distortions resulting from particular taxes are deliberately intended by a government in order to affect individuals' behaviour. Such taxes are termed *corrective taxes*. The example above of giving tax advantages to pension funds may be considered a corrective tax as investing in a pension, rather than other assets, will encourage people to save for their old age where they might not otherwise make such arrangements, or may spend the money they would have otherwise invested before they reach retirement age.

Other examples of planned distortions might include a *tax break* or *tax concession* (a reduction in taxes normally due, sometimes also referred to as a *tax expenditure*) given to employers who provide jobs to individuals who have been unemployed for a long time, or the tax reductions given to businesses for locating in a particular area the Government is seeking to regenerate or develop.

There are also numerous examples of the impact that tax related announcements have on people's behaviour. For example, if people believe that the duty on cigarettes will be increased in the Budget they may purchase more cigarettes in the days before the Budget in anticipation of an increase in tax.

In addition to the immediate effect of a tax change on taxpayer behaviour, there is also the problem of subsequent 'knock-on' effects that are even more difficult to control.

Activity

Road pricing has been proposed for motorways to discourage their use for environmental and congestion-reducing purposes. What 'knock-on' effects could arise from such a measure?

Feedback

A problem of direct pricing for the use of some roads and not others is that some drivers might just reduce their total miles driven, but instead will just change to use different roads to avoid paying the taxes. The accident rate per mile driven is higher on roads which are not motorways, leading to fears of an overall increase in road traffic accidents if such a scheme was introduced. It also seems likely that congestion will increase on roads which do not carry a charge as road users switch to them more. This might increase journey times and fuel consumption for all road users and the accident rate might rise still further. To minimise these effects the Chancellor would have to set carefully the cost per mile travelled to a level that would deter enough road users from motorways but not simply to transfer too many journeys onto other roads or the effect may be to worsen the overall situation.

Knock-on effects like this, caused by the presence of taxes or resulting from changes in the tax system, are a common feature of many taxes and a constant headache for tax policy creators. Tax system changes which do not have a knock-on effect will not distort the decisions made by individuals and companies and are therefore referred to as 'fiscally neutral'.

The extent to which tax changes create behavioural changes depends in part on how heavy the tax burden is to start with. The 1980s and early 1990s was an active period of tax reform throughout many parts of the world. In particular, the major trend was a move to limit (usually meaning *reduce*) the level of public expenditure (and hence the amount of tax revenue needed to sustain this expenditure was able to fall). This was followed by the reform of the assessment of taxation. Many tax rates were reduced throughout the world but correspondingly the tax base was broadened in many countries. That is, a wider range of taxpayer's income sources were taxed but the tax rate applied per pound was lower. In 1979 the highest rate of tax in the UK was 98% (on some types of income from investments). This was (probably rightly) seen as undesirable, if only because the incentives to avoid (legal) or even evade (illegal) tax were so large given that the potential savings that could be made were such a large percentage of the income. Today the highest rate of personal income tax in the UK is 45%, and in other countries can be even less, for example, in the US it is only 39.6%. The lower the rate of tax, the more the taxpayer keeps of their income and so (theoretically at least) the less incentive there is to avoid or evade tax. This makes further changes to the tax system relatively more fiscally neutral – i.e. have less effect on changing people's behaviour due to the tax change.

Since the 1980s, although the rates of tax in many countries have generally fallen, the tax base has been broadened by decreasing the range of allowances which taxpayers can use to reduce their taxable income and adding taxes to more things that previously were not taxed. The removal of a tax deduction (generally termed a *tax relief*) available for interest paid on mortgages and the benefit of the married couple's allowances are examples of this practice.

While the goal of fiscal neutrality can be important in tax policy development, it would not be right to say that any government is committed to fiscal neutrality to the extent of never introducing policies which are intended to distort the economic decisions made by individuals and businesses. As we discussed in Chapter 1, taxation is an important tool for a government to use explicitly to affect how people make decisions. A government will therefore sometimes use non-fiscally neutral taxes in a targeted way where they consider the knock-on impacts to be desirable (and manageable). For example, tax advantageous treatment has been given to some forms of investments, particularly pensions, but also ISAs (Individual Savings Accounts) and items of expenditure like the reduction in the vehicle licence fee for the cleanest and smallest cars. These were done deliberately to affect taxpayers' behaviour towards using these saving schemes, or buying these cars, over alternative choices.

The reverse can also, of course, be true. Taxes can be explicitly used in a non-fiscally neutral way to dissuade particular behaviour. For example, heavy increases to the Vehicle Excise Duty on the most polluting cars in the 2007 Budget was an attempt by the Government to use the tax system to reduce the environmental impacts of cars by making it more expensive to use some cars (the more polluting ones) compared to others (less polluting ones).

Taxes therefore regularly have distortionary effects on peoples' decisions – some planned and some not. Examining economic efficiency, or fiscal neutrality, provides a measure of the extent to which these distortions are created by the tax system, or changes to the tax system. Some distortions improve the system, but controlling these impacts can prove difficult in practice. The use of taxation as a behaviour influencing tool by governments is one of the key reasons the tax system is constantly changing. We will return to the subject of fiscal neutrality again in Chapter 14, once you have learned more about the detail of how the UK tax system works.

Administrative efficiency

3.20 A second aspect of efficiency as a characteristic of a good tax system relates to the administration of taxation. The more a tax costs to administer (creating and checking returns, chasing non-payment etc.) the less of the money raised by the tax is available to the Government for their expenditure plans as the administrative costs have to be paid for out of tax revenues. It is not possible to have a 100% efficient collection system where some non-compliance is likely to occur (to achieve the equity aim at least – some administrative effort must be incurred to ensure everyone pays who should pay) but this administration cost should be as small as possible to achieve the desired economic efficiency.

Most tax authorities are constantly seeking new ways to increase the administrative efficiency of their tax systems. An example of seeking to apply this characteristic in practice is the move to a self-assessment system for income and corporation taxes. This move aims, in part, to reduce administrative costs of these taxes for the tax authority as under this system taxpayers do their own assessment of their taxes due. Prior to this the tax authority had to determine this from returns supplied by taxpayers and other sources and 'raise' (create) an assessment (a tax bill) that the taxpayer then paid. Unfortunately the move to self-assessment shifts the burden of some of the costs no longer incurred by the tax authority on to taxpayers in the form of higher compliance costs so that the net gains for society associated with self-assessment (i.e. both the direct government costs savings plus the extra 'cost' placed on taxpayers) are difficult to measure.

Simplicity

3.21   Simplicity was not specifically mentioned as one of Adam Smith's Canons of taxation, but this is perhaps not surprising since, at the time he was writing, the tax system was relatively simple. There was no income tax for example, only a variety of wealth and consumption taxes. The idea of simplicity as a goal for tax and tax system design is linked to certainty and convenience, and really only began to become popular as an explicit goal in the last part of the twentieth century.

The rationale for stating that a good tax is a simple tax is that the more complex a tax or tax system is, the more difficult it is for everyone concerned, both taxpayers and tax administrators, to operate and use it. It is also a commonly held view that too much complexity allows opportunities for more unacceptable tax avoidance activity and that if the system were more simple and easy to understand, tax avoidance opportunities would be reduced.

The aim of simplifying the tax system has quite a long history in the UK, and the previous Conservative government initiated a rewrite of the direct tax legislation trying to make it easier to understand. This rewrite completed its main goal of rewriting the direct tax legislation in 2010 in the process producing several pieces of rewritten tax legislation, as we noted in Chapter 1. Arguably, however, rewriting the legislation is not enough by itself, because the legislation still has to deal with the underlying complexity of the detailed rules governing the different types of taxes levied in the UK.

The Brown Government reiterated a commitment to simplification of the tax laws in the Pre-Budget Report of 2007 and announced several reviews aiming to simplify specific aspects of the tax system. Some progress has been made, for example with capital gains tax, where a complex system to remove the inflation component of capital gains so that it is not taxed has been replaced by a low flat rate of tax, at least for individual taxpayers.

In July 2008, the Conservative party, then in opposition, published proposals designed to lead not only to simplification of the tax system but also a reduction in the size of tax legislation. One recommendation was to establish an Office of Tax Simplification (OTS) to examine the existing rules and make proposals for simplification. The Coalition Government implemented this when they came to power in 2010 and the OTS was created that year. It has already produced a number of reports and saw some of its recommendations for simplification implemented in the 2011 Budget. Reports released in 2012 include proposals to simplify small business taxation, pensioner taxation and tax advantaged employee share schemes. In February 2013 the OTS also released a complexity 'index' aimed at showing which areas of the tax code are considered to be excessively complex. This work continues with further emphasis recently on tax complexity and the growing length of the annual additional tax legislation.

Simplification is therefore becoming a more prominent issue, as concerns about the costs of complexity, including lack of certainty, increase. One of the difficulties, however, is that in order to simplify the tax system, or individual taxes within the tax system, policy makers have not only to be able to identify the causes of the complexity that need to be removed, but also to have the political and public will to address it. Often this is not sufficiently present to allow simplification to occur in practice at the pace that might otherwise be desirable.

Flexibility

3.22   A flexible tax is one which changes, or can be changed, easily in response to changes in the economic environment. A key aim of government is to reduce the fluctuations in economic activities caused by the economic cycle (the so called 'boom/bust' cycle) as this is often seem as good for an economy in the longer term. A flexible tax, designed properly, can have a stabilising effect on the economy to assist with this goal. For example, it can cause money to be taken out of a growing economy to keep its growth at a manageable level, and reduce the amount of money that is taken out of the economy when it enters a 'slow down' or a recession to soften any downward spiral effect.

Therefore, in times of recession a government might be content to see its tax receipts fall and increase its borrowing (as an alternative way to fund its expenditure plans) in order to give the economy a boost while during boom years a government might be happy to see its tax receipts increase, thus moderating the boom.

The modern income and corporation tax systems are good examples of relatively flexible tax systems. When incomes and business profits rise, the amount of tax raised increases without any direct action from government and equally when income or business profits fall, the amount of tax collected also falls. Because of the stepped progressive nature of most income tax systems the percentage change in the tax collected is greater than the percentage change in wages or profits. If wages increase by, say, 10% in a year income taxes will increase by more than 10% over the same period without a need for a change in the legislation. Taxes will increase by a greater percentage than wages because marginal rates of tax (the amount of tax you must pay if you earn an extra pound of income) are higher than average rates of tax for most income taxpayers in a progressive tax system).

Another example of a tax which changes automatically and flexibly is stamp duty on houses. In the UK, all house purchases (not buy-to-let) over £125,000 attract stamp duty land tax. The rates range from 2% to 12%, so this is a progressive tax rate, and importantly, the amount of this tax that is collected increases both as the number and the value of houses sold increase.

Fiscal Fact

In 2012/13, total revenue from stamp duty land tax on property and land was around £6.4 billion. By 2016/17 this had risen to £10.4 billion. This has grown from a total of only £2.1 billion in 1998/99. [Source: HMRC Stamp Duty receipts]

In practice, there is often a time lag between the decision by the Government to take some fiscal action, the implementation of the policy and the full impact of the tax on the economy. For example, during the 1980s there was great pressure from environmentalists to reduce the lead emissions from petrol. In the late 1980s the duty on unleaded petrol was reduced to make it more attractive to use than leaded petrol. Demand for unleaded petrol increased as a result of the changes but there was a time delay while information about unleaded petrol was disseminated throughout the population and car owners arranged to have their engines modified or changed the type of car they drove. Ultimately, however, this has now resulted in almost no new petrol cars being sold which do not use unleaded fuel.

This same trend is being seen in the gradual move to more environmentally friendly bio-fuels as extra tax concessions are again being used by the Government to encourage, albeit slowly, their wider use.

Smith's Canons revisited

3.23 Now that we have spent some time discussing each of Smith's desirable tax system characteristics (plus simplicity and flexibility) we can return to the question we asked at the start of this section – can we rank the factors by importance to make them more useful for tax system designers to use in practice? To do this we can use the examples of two particular taxes proposed and supported by the Government at the time, to illustrate the importance of understanding the different characteristics and considering their relative ranking: first the community charge (or poll tax) and then the proposed increase in VAT on domestic fuel from 8% to the then full rate of 17.5%.

Community Charge (Poll Tax)

3.24 As was introduced in Chapter 1, the Community Charge replaced Domestic Rates in April 1990. The Rates had been a long–established, but unpopular, tax used as the primary form of local taxation for provision of many local services (like schools, roads, police, fire service etc.). Rather than levy local tax solely on homeowners as the rates system did, the Community Charge was instead levied on virtually all individuals over 18 years of age i.e. changed from being a property tax to an individual, personal, tax. The supporters of the Community Charge argued that it increased certainty (at least political accountability) by making the individuals who were eligible to vote in local government elections responsible for paying for their elected council's expenditure proposals – not just those individuals in the community who owned property there.

Opponents of the Community Charge, however, claimed that the tax was unfair because the majority of individuals were required to pay the same amount of tax regardless of their personal circumstances (i.e. it was regressive) It was considered vertically inequitable as it was less 'ability to pay' focused than the rates system had been and instead tried to focus more on a benefits approach to tax setting – i.e. followed the argument that everyone benefited from good local services so all should contribute to their cost. Some individuals, including students and the unemployed, were able to pay a reduced amount but little relief was available for the majority of individuals.

In practice the tax proved to be difficult to collect (i.e. administrative inefficient) with significant numbers of people simply disappearing from official records, like electoral rolls, to avoid having to pay the tax. With many missing taxpayers equity was therefore compromised. In addition to the administrative problems, protests about the unfairness of the Community Charge (leading ultimately to the Poll Tax riots in March 1990) escalated until the Government backed down on the tax's imposition and it was replaced with the current system of Council Tax which, ironically, took us back to a property related, 'ability to pay' style, local tax system as the previous Rates system had been, despite its apparent faults and flaws.

VAT on domestic fuel

3.25 An increase in VAT on domestic fuel was proposed in the Spring Budget of 1993. In April 1994 VAT was levied on domestic fuel at 8% and towards the end of 1994 the then Chancellor attempted to introduce the legislation needed to increase the rate from 8% to 17.5%. In the event the House of Commons defeated the motion and the Chancellor was forced to abandon his proposal. The defeat occurred despite measures announced in the Budget to protect many of the less well off in society from the increase in VAT. These measures included substantial increases in the state pension as well as increases above inflation to a number of other state benefits.

The opponents of this proposed tax argued that heating and lighting were essential for everybody, and not a luxury, and so should not be taxed at the full rate despite the presence of any compensatory benefits. They successfully argued that, in general, people on lower incomes spend proportionately more of their income on gas and electricity and so the increase in price would affect the poorest people in society disproportionately (again an issue of equity as this was seen to increase the regressivity of VAT).

The importance of equity

3.26 It would appear then that the Community Charge failed because it was difficult to collect once taxpayers considered it to be unfair (i.e was regressive). The increase in VAT on domestic fuel was also seen to be regressive and therefore unfair. While only two taxes are used here to illustrate the case, there is also other evidence that the most important characteristic of a good tax system, (in the UK at least), is that it should be seen to be (and ideally should actually be) fair, making equity important to get right in planning tax reform. These two cases illustrate that the most effective way of achieving acceptable equity is likely to be to use an ability to pay approach. They also illustrate the importance of perceptions of equity, taxpayers will be unhappy if they think a tax is unfair, even if a closer analysis shows that it is, in fact, equitable.

However, other characteristics should not entirely be ignored just to improve equity. Some consideration must at least be given to these other characteristics if the tax system is not to become unbalanced. What is clear from our examination of the desirable characteristics of the tax system is that there are overlaps between them, but also considerable tensions, or even conflicts, between them and it is not possible to design a system that addresses all characteristics at the same time. Over time, priorities change, and also different countries will have different priorities depending on social, cultural and economic conditions. The design of the tax system is likely therefore to evolve over time and the need will remain to continually review the desirable characteristics present in the planned changes.

The Mirrlees Review

3.27 In 2006, the Institute for Fiscal Studies embarked on a major review of the UK tax system to explore more options for the development for the tax base mix in the UK 30 years on from the creation of the Meade Committee. This review was chaired by Sir James Mirrlees and included various eminent economists who examined the UK system and recommended improvements and alterations to the core principles of the use of the all three tax bases in the UK. Its findings were released at the end of 2010. There are a number of recommendations including:

- Refining VAT to remove zero rating and low rates;
- Exempting savings income, i.e. interest, from income tax;
- Merging income tax and national insurance contributions;
- Merging welfare benefits with income tax; and
- Having the same tax burden regardless of whether you are employed, self-employed or operating through a company.

These recommendations clearly give priority to the criteria of economic efficiency (fiscal neutrality), based on the idea that tax should not influence decision making unless absolutely necessary. Implementing these ideas will create both winners and losers in society and therefore likely to affect the balance of equity that has previously dominated the design of the UK tax system, and it and to date little change has resulted from this analysis.

Alternative tax bases

3.28   We started this chapter by asking the question what should be taxed? We now return to that question with a more detailed look at the three main possible tax bases. A considerable amount of debate has been generated by the question of the tax base, or other method, which should be used to determine an individual's contribution to public funds. The above discussion of six desirable characteristics of a good tax system should now equip you to evaluate the relative merits of each of these tax bases. We have already discussed two ways of allocating the tax burden; the ability to pay and the benefit approaches. In this section we will consider the nature of the three possible tax bases to which these approaches can then be applied i.e.:

- wealth (or capital)
- income
- consumption.

   In particular, we need to ask ourselves, if we were designing a tax system, should we use one, two or three tax bases in our tax system design to enable the six desirable characteristics of good tax system design to be delivered optimally? We conclude this section with a summary of some of the latest thinking on changes to the use of different tax bases.

Wealth

3.29   First, could we create a tax system just using a wealth tax (or taxes)? Wealth can be held in various forms so a tax system only using wealth taxes would need to include a focus on different forms of wealth to work effectively. These would include probably both what you have earned yourself (your accumulated income) and what you have been given (inheritances or gifts).

   Chapter 1 provided a history of wealth taxes. These types of taxes are among the oldest forms of taxation. This is because wealth can, under some circumstances, be easier to tax than income, where wealth is held in forms you can see (e.g. tangible property).

   A comprehensive wealth tax could perhaps therefore be used to replace separate wealth related taxes such as those on unearned income (savings or dividends) and capital gains and could be a tax based on wealth ownership, which reflects the ability to pay of the taxpayer. At present, the few wealth taxes in the UK are imposed on a 'realisations' basis, that is they are applied when the taxpayer disposes of the wealth, not throughout the period of ownership.

3.30 A tax on wealth is also useful as a tool for redistributing wealth, often a key goal of a government. However, there are a number of difficulties which arise when trying to fairly value wealth which can make wealth taxes costly to administer.

Activity

List some of the things that may contribute to an individual's wealth.

Feedback

3.31 You have probably included some tangible assets in your list like land and buildings. Other assets include shares and securities and the market value of a business run by the individual. However, for many people the present value of their future earnings and the present value of their pension fund are probably their most valuable assets. Did you include these? Wouldn't these need to be included in any comprehensive wealth tax?

The present value of an individual's future earnings is the estimated positive cash flows arising from employment throughout their working life, restated in present value terms. However, we live in a rapidly changing world in which an individual may be faced with redundancy, retraining and second or even third careers during his or her working life. In practice it does not seem feasible to value the future earnings of every citizen for taxation purposes. Since future pension rights are generally dependent on earned income it would also be difficult to value the future pension of every citizen regularly – at least in a way that taxpayers are likely to accept as appropriate given it would then affect how much tax they have to pay.

In practice where a wealth tax is used it is usually a tax on (capital) assets. However, individuals who do not use a pension fund, for whatever reason, may accumulate other assets in order to provide for old age (e.g. property) and a wealth tax which is levied on these assets but not pension rights will therefore be inequitable to some people.

In addition, some capital assets may provide additional benefits to their owner such as power and influence. For example, a wealthy individual is likely to be able to borrow money at a lower rate than is available to other people because they can influence the lending decision in ways others may not be able to. However, it would be extremely difficult to ascribe a value to these economic benefits to determine a comprehensive measure of wealth.

3.32 So, while some wealth taxes (for example, property based taxes like Council tax) have proven relatively cheap to collect in practice, a general wealth tax as the primary tax base for the country is likely to be expensive to administer compared to other tax bases because of the difficulties of assessing current values of assets not currently available for sale (i.e. for which there is no market that will reveal their true value reliably and consistently). The difficulties of a general wealth tax are probably too great to enable it to be used as the main national tax base in the more developed economies, where people's wealth can be held in complex forms. They could, however, be useful as a key tax in less developed countries where more wealth is held in assets that can be more easily valued (land, buildings, physical property etc.).

Although a full wealth tax may be impractical as the primary tax base for the reasons we have just examined it is probably a good idea to have at least some way of taxing wealth in a tax system. In the UK at present, there are three main taxes which fit into the category of wealth taxes; capital gains tax, inheritance tax and stamp duties. Together these taxes provide the Exchequer with only slightly more than 5% of its total tax revenue and are expected to contribute only around £29.6 billion in 2017/18. This is only about two-thirds of the average proportion of total revenue which is raised by wealth taxes in other OECD countries (at approximately 8%), suggesting the UK makes proportionally less use of wealth taxes in its tax system when compared to other similar countries.

Fiscal Fact

 For 2017/18 approximately £7.9 billion of capital gains tax is expected to be collected; the second highest sum raised with this tax in recent years. In the previous peak year, in 2008/09 (the year in which the most recent financial crisis became publicly very visible), around 2,000 individuals realised gains of more than £1,000,000 on which they paid tax totalling almost £3 billion. [Source: HMRC receipts & Table B.5, Budget 2016]

Do wealth taxes then have any place in a tax system? One of the purposes of wealth taxes in a tax system, such as a capital gains tax, is to reduce tax avoidance. Without some kind of wealth tax as part of the system some tax otherwise due could be avoided if taxpayers were able to increase their total wealth in a form that is not then captured by the other tax bases, for example, by owning shares or owning property either of which may grow in value over time, but aren't easily captured by income or expenditure taxes.

To illustrate this idea, imagine you owned your own company. To take money out of the business you could either pay yourself a wage from its profits or you could instead issue new shares to yourself each year and then sell them periodically to achieve the same increase in your total wealth but in a different form – wealth gains rather than income. Without a tax on the sale of shares, you would be able to keep more of the increase in value of the company than if you pay yourself a wage, on which an income tax would probably have to be paid. This would provide an incentive (i.e. create a tax induced distortion and not be tax neutral) to receive capital (new shares) instead of income (wages). In the UK until 2008/09, taxpayers had to pay tax on their realised capital gains at the same rates of tax as for income (i.e. at their marginal rate of income tax). As a result of having both an income tax and a similar wealth tax therefore, there was relatively little incentive to realise capital gains in the UK rather than taxable income. Between April 2008 and June 2010 however, the capital gains tax system changed, in the interests of simplicity as we noted earlier. Capital gains tax was charged at a flat rate of 18% (for individuals) irrespective of their income level. Even a very basic analysis suggests that, as the marginal rate of income tax for many people was 20% in that period (with others paying a marginal rate of income tax at either 40% or 45% for the last 3 months of that period), this is likely to create a tax incentive to receive wealth gains in capital forms rather than as income if taxpayers can (as 18% is less than 20%, 40% or 45% obviously).

This incentive to receive gains via the capital tax base instead of the income tax base was partly reduced in the Emergency Budget in June 2010. From that point higher (40%) and additional rate (45%) tax payers had to pay 28% on any gains over their allowance instead of 18%. However, this isn't a full return to the use of marginal income tax rates as in the pre-April 2008 system, which could be argued to be a more equitable rate perhaps, and many were expecting. From April 2016, the rates on gains were dropped to 10% and 20% respectively, which once again increases the gap between tax rates on capital gains and those on income.

Other measures may now have to be introduced to restrict the scope for converting income into capital gains in order to limit the potential loss of income tax revenues or to create inequity between different citizens who earn wealth gains in different ways.

Inheritance tax, although a form of wealth tax, does not serve the same purpose as a capital gains tax as it is currently used in the UK. This is because it is almost entirely avoidable by taxpayers who can afford to undertake effective tax planning and are not unfortunate enough to die unexpectedly. However, there are a number of other arguments in favour of keeping inheritance tax as a part of the UK's tax system even though it affects relatively few people. Firstly there is no

3 Principles of tax system design

evidence that a tax on inheritance affects individuals' incentives to work so its distortive effects in this area are less of an issue than other taxes (we'll talk about this more in Chapter 14). Second, it is argued that one role of the tax system is to facilitate a fair balance of wealth between the better off and the poorer in society (see Chapter 1's discussion of redistribution). An inheritance tax is probably one of the best ways of achieving a redistribution of wealth, as at least once in a lifetime, money is taken from relatively richer people so that the Government can pass it on to others.

We will explore the details of the current system of capital gains tax and inheritance tax further in Chapter 8.

Activity

Could a comprehensive wealth tax be used to replace all other taxes? What would be the advantages or disadvantages of such an approach to taxation?

Feedback

3.33 It could be argued that a comprehensive wealth tax is most in keeping with the concept of using ability to pay to design a tax system and is therefore likely to lead to a more equitable tax system overall than other taxes alone may be able to achieve. On the other hand, it is unlikely to raise enough revenue alone because of the levels of the UK Government's expenditure plans. It would need a rate so high that it would force taxpayers to sell off assets each time it is due in order to pay the tax, which may not be in the best interests of either the taxpayer concerned, or the wider society. There are also considerable measurement and assessment problems. For example, it is relatively easy for some items of wealth to be concealed from the tax authorities. Finally, as we have discussed, wealth is difficult to accurately value.

Income

3.34 If wealth isn't a perfect tax base to use by itself, what about just taxing income? Income is used as a major tax base throughout the world and in many countries, including the UK, is the most important tax base in the tax system (at least in terms of revenue raised for the Government). However, this does not mean that the application of an income tax is without difficulties or that it is the best tax base to use in all cases. Our first problem arises when we try to define what we mean by 'income'.

Problem of definition

3.35   On the surface income might seem an easy concept – isn't it just what we earn between two dates? In reality it isn't as simple as that, at least when it comes to writing rules for a workable tax system. If you have studied any accounting, for example, you will know that profit for a business (their 'income') can be measured in various ways resulting in different 'profit' figures. Which one should we pick for tax purposes? The same applies to individuals' income measures. How comprehensive should it be? Should it include more than wages or salary? What if you aren't just paid in cash but also receive goods or services as part payment for your labour? Should they also be included in your taxable income? If so, at what value? Also, when should they be included? When you are given them or when you use them? Writing a set of rules that will work out the income to be taxed for a period of time is therefore not easy.

Hicks (1939) defined income as the maximum value which "a man can consume during a period and still expect to be as well off at the end of the period as he was at the beginning". Hence, if a tax system which taxes income is to be equitable it must allow for the inflation impacts i.e. some value will be lost from the tax base each year just because of price increases. In times of inflation some of the income generated therefore must be retained within a business just in order to cover the loss in value of assets over the year due to inflation. Perhaps this inflation component shouldn't be included in income for tax purposes therefore? This sounds very reasonable but there are a number of difficulties which have probably deterred the Government from implementing such a system. These problems include:

- Determining how the value of the capital base should be measured.
- The use of the word 'expect' in Hick's definition. It does not tell us how much an individual can consume with certainty, only what he can consume and expect to maintain his capital base. It does not help us, therefore, to determine how to tax unpredicted profits, or losses.

Governments are generally reluctant to allow inflation to become an integral part of the tax system. One area of the tax system you will find this, however, is for some personal allowances and tax limits which are usually increased in line with the increase in inflation (from 2012 using the Consumer Prices Index – CPI), unless the Chancellor elects to either freeze them (as was done for the basic personal allowance between 2002/03 and 2003/04, again between 2009/10 and 2010/11) or increase them by some other amount (as was the case for age allowances in 2011/12 with an extra £1,000 added to basic personal allowances). Governments are perhaps reluctant to cater for inflation impacts for fear that it will itself then fuel further inflation.

Comprehensive Income Tax

3.36 At the same time as Hicks was coming up with a definition of income, in the US, the economists Simons (1938) and Haig (1921) were considering this same issue in relation to income tax. Concerned with equity, they recommended a broad tax base. Simons' classic book *Personal Income Taxation* (Simons 1938) recommended accrual taxation with a definition of income that didn't contain any exceptions and deductions. Under this system, income is the sum of the increases in a person's net wealth over a period of time plus the amount of that person's consumption during the period. This can be restated in terms of real events so that comprehensive income would be equal to the amount which is consumed plus/(less) any increase/(decrease) in the value of the individual's wealth. By using such a definition for the tax base, we have a clear picture of a person's taxable capacity, but don't need to be concerned with how that capacity came into being.

Like many theoretical approaches to tax, however, the idea of a comprehensive income tax sounds good, but is almost impossible to put into practice. The use of this type of comprehensive income tax would result in creating all the difficulties described in the section on a wealth tax above, as it links income measures to measures of wealth.

In 1978 a group of tax experts, called the Meade Committee, was set up to evaluate the UK's tax system. The report they produced was entitled *The Structure and Reform of Direct Taxation*. Among the assessments and proposals for change they examined, the Committee considered the possibility of using a comprehensive income tax – i.e. one that could exist as the only form of taxation in the UK removing the need for capital and expenditure taxes.

The Meade Committee rejected the possibility of using a comprehensive income tax of this kind, claiming that it was impracticable to introduce all the measures which would be necessary to adjust for inflation. Instead they supported the introduction of an extended expenditure tax, which we consider in the next section.

Other more recent efforts have revisited this idea however, attempting to address these limitations in different ways. For example, the Taxpayers' Alliance's Single Income Tax proposal published in 2012 as the result of its 2020 Tax Commission. A more comprehensive income tax was also a central element of the Institute for Fiscal Studies' Mirrlees Review of the UK tax system published in November 2010.

Activity

Explain why the use of a comprehensive income tax might result in undesirable impacts on the economy of the country that introduces it.

Flat taxes

3.37 Many of the problems with income tax arise because of the use of a progressive tax rate, in the interests of vertical equity. There is currently considerable debate around the world, however, about the benefits of using a 'flat tax'. The premise for this tax is that a progressive system of income tax rates is a disincentive to extra work, savings and reinvestment, whereas if a tax was imposed at a low, flat rate, people would have more incentive to work and invest which would then benefit the whole economy. This can be demonstrated using the so called 'Laffer Curve', proposed (although he argued not created) by Arthur Laffer in the US (see Laffer 2004), which shows the relationship between tax revenue and the tax rate as follows:

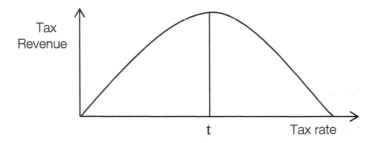

The graph proposes that tax revenues would be zero if the tax rate was 0% or 100%, but will increase at a steeper rate when the tax rate is low as the low rates encourage growth of economic activities. A point is then reached (tax rate t) where a government is obtaining the maximum possible revenue. After this point, if the tax rate increases, a government gets a decreasing amount of revenue because there is less incentive to work harder or invest, and more incentive to avoid paying taxes – to the point at a tax rate of 100% when, it is argued, no-one would have any incentive to work or invest. The difficult question therefore, is determining in reality where the point t might be both for individual taxes and for the tax system as a whole.

Much tax policy has looked to build on this basic principle to create optimal tax revenues. At one extreme, in a 1985 book by Hall and Rabushka called *The Flat Tax*, published in the US, a new system of flat taxes was proposed that looked to build on this idea. Under this system, wages and salaries would be taxed at a low flat rate after a personal allowance to seek to motivative economic activity. Business income would be taxed on:

- Total revenue from sales
- Less inputs purchased from other businesses (which are taxed in the hands of those other businesses)
- Less wages and pensions paid to workers (which are taxed in the hands of the employees)
- Less purchases of plant and equipment (so that investment is not discouraged by the tax system)

Notice that under this model it was proposed that savings and investment income would not be taxed at all.

There is some evidence that a flat tax works well as an incentive to economic activity, but so far it has only been tried in either tax haven countries such as Hong Kong and Jersey, or transitional economies such as Estonia. No other developed country has yet tried such a flat tax, despite its potential attractions.

Taxes are also used for other economy adjusting, market correcting and behaviour changing purposes than simply to maximise revenue at any point in time (see our discussion on the objectives of taxation in Chapter 1). Even with the use of a single tax within a tax system, such as a comprehensive income tax, these different motivations and purposes for taxation would make it very difficult to optimise all at the same point.

Consumption

3.38 Having illustrated important limitations with taxes on wealth and income as sole tax bases, we finally consider the possible use of consumption taxes as the key tax base in a tax system. A consumption tax taxes what an individual takes out of the economy, unlike an income tax which can really be said to tax what is contributed to society. If we only had a consumption tax there would no need to value wealth, which we have already concluded is difficult to do equitably in all circumstances. This problem is avoided as consumption tax is only levied when the taxpayer spends money, not on the wealth they hold on to in whatever form.

If we only taxed consumption, income receipts would also be free of tax. Importantly, not only would wages, salaries and profits be tax free on receipt, but since a consumption tax does not tax the return on an investment until it is spent, there is a significant encouragement to save rather than spend with this type of tax system. As governments often see increasing savings as good for the long-term health of their economy, this would arguably be a good feature of this kind of tax system (and where spending rather than saving is needed, consumption tax can be adjusted to encourage more spending).

Theoretically, a consumption tax can be designed to incorporate personal allowances and varying rates of tax exactly as an income tax typically does. This would probably require some kind of tax return being filed to obtain refunds of overpaid tax, but could be possible to achieve with reasonable administrative efficiency. Hence, a consumption tax could be progressive and take account of a taxpayer's personal circumstances – if that is considered desirable.

However, because income and savings are not taxed directly under a consumption tax, the tax base will be narrower than for income tax and so the consumption tax rate will have to be set at a suitably higher rate to compensate for this narrowing in order to raise the same revenue for the Government.

One radical form of consumption tax was recommended by the Meade Committee in 1978, which suggested four alternative ways of operating a comprehensive expenditure tax system. In each case the main problem is how to approximate actual expenditure. The Committee proposed that this was to be resolved largely by measuring expenditure as a residual from gains in income or wealth (i.e. expenditure in a period = income received in that period +/- changes in wealth in that period) to avoid the impracticality of needing to track actual expenditure.

The Committee considered two forms of expenditure tax: a universal expenditure tax which is described below, and a two-tier expenditure tax which would collect a basic rate of tax through a system of VAT at the point of purchase and higher rates of tax directly from taxpayers periodically under a separate collection/repayment system such as an annual return detailing what the taxpayer spends in a period.

Under a universal expenditure tax, a taxpayer's consumption expenditure would be calculated by adding the taxpayer's total realised income to any capital receipts, including the sale of capital assets and any amounts borrowed, and deducting any expenditure which is not for the purposes of consumption, including expenditure on capital assets and amounts repaid. Then tax could be levied on consumption expenditure at a number of rates if desired.

Expenditure taxes, particularly in the form of value added taxes as the first of the Meade Committee's options above, have become popular with governments everywhere in recent years (albeit combining a VAT system with an income tax system rather than any form of more direct way of taxing expenditure as the second element of the system) but only a few countries have used this tax as their primary tax base. We'll review why this might be the case in the next section.

Growth of the consumption tax base

3.39   Income is used as a tax base in almost all countries around the world but taxes on consumption (even if not fuller expenditure taxes as discussed above) have become more popular as a way of raising revenue in recent years. There are a number of reasons for preferring a consumption tax to an income tax as a way of increasing tax revenue or as part of a general reform of a tax system which may explain this trend towards consumption taxes and away from income taxes as the core of a tax system design:

- It can be argued that it is fairer to tax consumption, that is, the value of goods and services which an individual takes out of society, than to tax the contribution that he or she makes to a society in the form of either work effort or capital supplied (i.e. consumption tax tries to take a greater account of benefits received as a motivation for the tax system design). The difference between income and consumption is equal to savings. However, even the individual who saves will eventually use savings for consumption and therefore has just really deferred the consumption tax rather than avoided it. Of course, it may be that the beneficiaries of an individual's estate who use these savings for consumption at a later stage pay the tax rather than the individual who earned the income in the first place, but eventually the consumption tax will be paid by someone.

- A consumption tax does not discriminate against individuals who defer their expenditure by saving, as savings (and their returns) would be exempt from any consumption tax until they are consumed. An income tax, however, discriminates against individuals who save in order to undertake consumption in the future by having already taxed the money saved once when it was received as income and then also taxing the return on savings (i.e. saved income is already invested net of tax providing a smaller base for the return than would otherwise be the case) A consumption tax on the other hand only taxes income once; when it is spent, and so larger sums can be invested producing larger returns, other things being equal.

- There would be no need for capital gains tax to address tax avoidance of personal income taxation. A consumption tax would treat all expenditure equally irrespective of whether it comes from someone's stock of wealth or income.

- The evidence suggests that savings returns are not directly affected by savings activity. That is, the returns to savings are not entirely dependent on the level of savings instead they are influenced by other economic, accounting and market factors. This implies that a consumption tax would perhaps not seriously distort the savings decision whereas income taxes probably do given they affect the sums that can be saved directly.

- Income tax computations mostly relate to an (often artificial) annual cycle. This is necessary to make personal income tax assessment work but is unfair to those on uneven incomes as it often means they pay more tax on average (e.g. some years they may pay more in higher tax bands than they would if earnings were evenly distributed over longer periods). With a consumption tax it is instead in the hands of the taxpayer to decide when it is paid (i.e. when they decide to spend their income or accumulated stock of wealth and on what) they control when tax falls due and in what period it is calculated.
- Consumption taxes cope better with the impact of inflation (i.e. are inherently more flexible) than income taxes, particularly for capital income (e.g. where some adjustment is needed for the return required on the capital value just to maintain its value as prices rise).

However, there are a number of potential disadvantages of consumption taxes which make an income tax look more attractive in practice than may otherwise be the case. For example:

- Taxpayers who save in order to consume later are subject to higher levels of uncertainty than those who spend their income immediately because they cannot be sure of the tax they must pay when they spend their savings.
- Taxpayers usually have a changing pattern of income and expenditure over their lifetime. Many individuals spend more than they earn in the early years of their adult life and save in the middle years in order for expenditure to exceed income once again in retirement. This pattern may mean that individuals incur the greatest tax burden in years when their income is least able to provide for their needs. This means that their wealth will have to be drawn on to pay for consumption, with the associated problems of having to realise assets, as we discussed above.
- Because the return made on savings would not be subject to a consumption tax it seems likely that the level of a consumption tax would have to be higher than its equivalent income tax to raise the same amount of tax revenue. This may prove to be a disincentive to work. People are generally better at valuing their work effort in terms of goods and services rather than money. This is important in times of inflation when people know that a certain increase in salary is necessary simply to maintain a given standard of living (and hence why workers ask for at least inflation levels of salary increases every year). Prices can be thought of in terms of how many hours an individual on average wages must work in order to earn enough to buy the goods or services they want. If this is indeed how individuals think about the relationship between work and consumption then an increase in a consumption tax will have a similar effect to an increase in an income tax. Hence a consumption tax can still distort the decision to undertake extra work and does not resolve this distortion.

Mixture of bases?

3.40 Therefore, as none of the tax bases are adequate in their own right to form the sole tax base for a balanced tax system, it is more commonly found that a combination of the bases is used. In most cases these will usually involve all three bases being used to enable the advantages and limitations of each base to offset each other to the extent this is possible. This doesn't have to always be the case however, and some countries will sacrifice a rounded tax system design to focus on one or two tax bases. This may be seen, for example, in a tax haven where tax is used as a competitive tool to attract activity to the country. Lowering, or removing, taxes on one tax base can be used to achieve this although this must be applied carefully to ensure government spending needs can be fulfilled with the other tax bases, or alternative means, if a key tax base is not to be subjected to taxation.

The UK taxation system

3.41 To conclude this chapter we will briefly review how the theory of tax bases that we have just discussed in the previous section is directly translated into the UK's current tax system. In reality, because the use of any one tax base alone creates practical difficulties for the effectiveness of tax systems (as we have seen) a mixture of income, wealth and expenditure taxes are often used to try and minimise their individual limitations, create maximum flexibility in the system and address each of the other desirable characteristics of a good tax system, (to the degree this is possible in practice).

As we saw in the section on how the UK raises its revenue in Chapter 1, the key taxes in operation in the UK at present are:

1. Income tax – direct tax on income base payable by individuals

2. Corporation tax – direct tax on income base payable by companies

3. VAT – indirect tax on consumption base payable by all

4. Capital Gains tax – direct tax on capital asset disposals/wealth payable by individuals

5. Inheritance tax – direct tax on wealth/capital asset transfers on death payable by individuals

6. Stamp Duty – direct tax on certain capital/wealth transfers payable by all

7. Customs and Excise Duties (Various) – indirect taxes on consumption payable either by all or on a selective basis on some purchases.

The rest of this book, in conjunction with the web site, presents a review of most of the above taxes in detail. It illustrates how the detailed rules for each, and the interaction of these taxes, are applied in practice at the present time.

As we examine the detail of the current rules for each tax, consider what we have learned so far about the desirable characteristics of a good tax system and ask yourself to what degree the UK's current tax system is effective in achieving these goals. You will see we are good in some areas and not so good in others, and hence the need for constant reappraisal of the tax system and regular adjustments to its operation even perhaps some radical changes (as has been proposed in the Mirrlees Review discussed at the end of the previous section).

Summary

In this chapter we explored what to tax and how to design a suitable tax system to tax it. This included thinking about issues such as: whether we should tax at source or to directly assess tax due, the role of hypothecated taxes, tax neutrality, distribution of the tax burden and issues of tax avoidance and evasion in tax system design.

We have also spent some time discussing desirable characteristics of taxation as the foundation principles for how a tax system should be designed. We then evaluated the feasibility of using wealth, income and consumption as a dominant tax base for the tax system before concluding with a brief summary of how the theory of tax bases is applied in current UK practice.

In this chapter we may have raised as many questions for you as we have given answers. We will attempt to answer many of these questions as we review the detail of the current UK tax system throughout the remainder of this book.

Project areas

There are many interesting questions which are inspired by the material dealt with in this chapter. For example,

- the potential role for hypothecated taxes;
- the impact on the UK economy of avoidance activity and corresponding anti- avoidance strategies;
- is progressivity always desirable in a tax?
- what is the appropriate mix of tax bases for the UK's tax system?

You may consider for a project the extent to which a particular tax, or tax system more generally, achieves one or more of Adam Smith's desirable characteristics, or how some countries can operate without a balance of income, wealth and expenditure taxes.

The question of the funding of higher education is topical. An interesting question is 'Should a graduate tax be used to fund higher education?' Would this comply with the characteristics of a good tax system?

Using the tax system as a way of influencing transport policy has been a recent focus of the current UK Government. For example:

- congestion charges have been introduced for vehicle traffic in London (and proposed for other UK cities),

- a number of new roads have been built in a way that allows for them to pay for themselves using tolls,

- the Government is considering replacing the Vehicle Excise Duty (VED) with a charge based on road use (and the 2006 Budget introduced more graduation to the levels of this duty in favour of low emissions producing vehicles and in 2008 increased Vehicle Excise Duty on higher polluting cars).

Why do you think taxes, and related charges, have become some popular as a way of influencing transport policy?

Discussion questions

1 Road fund licences were originally introduced to pay for road building and maintenance. This is a tax based not on an ability to pay but according to use. In practice much of the road fund licence is now used for other purposes. Is this a good way to raise taxes?

2 Would increased hypothecation be a better way to organise the Government's revenue and expenditure systems?

3 What corrective taxes, if any, might you introduce in the UK at present?

4 Do you think parents should pay more or less tax than childless individuals?

5 If a government wished to provide funding to increase the level of fitness of the population would it be better to provide subsidised facilities such as leisure centres or to give tax relief on the cost of getting and keeping fit, such as health club memberships?

6 Will a sugar tax produce the desired effect to reduce sugary drink consumption?

7 To what degree does the current UK tax system fulfil the characteristics of a desirable tax system?

8 Is an expenditure, income or wealth tax inherently fairer than the others?

9 Not all countries use all tax bases. Why might this be the case and what features of a country allow different mixes of tax bases to operate?

10 Have the Mirrlees Review or the Taxpayer's Alliance Single Income Tax proposals provided useful and practical suggestions for improving the UK's tax system?

Further reading

ACCA, (2008), Discussion Paper: *Perspectives on Fair Tax*, available at http://www.accaglobal.com/uk/en/technical-activities/technical-resources-search/2008/june/perspectives-on-fair-tax.html.

Haig, R., (1921), The concept of income – Economic and legal aspects, *The Federal Income Tax*. New York: Columbia University Press, pp. 1-28.

Hall, R. and Rabushka, A., (1985), *The Flat Tax*, Hoover Institution Press: Stanford, California, USA.

Hicks, J.R., (1939), *Value and Capital*, Oxford University Press: Oxford, UK (2nd Edition, 1974).

Laffer, A., (2004), *The Laffer Curve: Past, present and future*, https://www.heritage.org/taxes/report/the-laffer-curve-past-present-and-future

James, S. and Nobes, C., (2017), *The Economics of Taxation, 17th edition*, Fiscal Publications, Birmingham, UK.

Meade Committee Report (1978), *The Structure and Reform of Direct Taxation*, IFS/Allen and Unwin: London, UK.

Mutén, L., (1998), "Minimising the Tax Effects of Inflation" in Sandford, C., (ed) *Further Key Issues in Tax Reform*, Fiscal Publications: Birmingham, UK.

O'Connell, J., (2012), *Total Lifetime Tax*, Report for the Taxpayers' Alliance, see http://www.taxpayersalliance.com/total_lifetime_tax .

Smith, A., (1776), *An Inquiry in the Nature and Causes of the Wealth of Nations*, Ward, Lock & Co. Ltd: London, UK. (The World Library 1812 reprint).

Sandford, C., (1995), "Taxing Wealth", in *More Key Issues in Tax Reform*, Fiscal Publications: Birmingham, UK.

Sandford, C., (1995), "Minimising Administrative and Compliance Costs", in *More Key Issues in Tax Reform*, Fiscal Publications: Birmingham, UK.

Simons, H., (1938), *Personal Income Taxation: The Definition of Income as a Problem of Fiscal Policy*, University of Chicago Press: Chicago, USA.

Taxpayers' Alliance, (2012), *The Single Income Tax*, Final report of the 2020 Tax Commission, see http://2020tax.org/2020tc.pdf .

For detailed discussions of alternative tax bases and their application see:

Evans, C., Hasseldine, J., Lymer, A., Ricketts, R. and Sandford, C., (2017), *Comparative Taxation: Why Tax Systems Differ*, Fiscal Publications: Birmingham, UK.

For the Mirrlees Review publications, see:
http://www.ifs.org.uk/mirrleesReview

Details on the work of the Office of Tax Simplification can be found at:
https://www.gov.uk/government/organisations/office-of-tax-simplification

Personal income taxation

4

Introduction

4.1 In Section 1 of this book we examined the history of the UK tax system, outlined its administration and looked at the principles of tax system design. This foundation provides us with the background we need to now begin to examine the current UK tax system in detail.

This chapter introduces you to the personal income tax computation and explains the various elements that go into its make-up. Chapters 5, 6 and 7 review the sources of taxable income in more detail and show you how to calculate the correct values to enter into the respective parts of the income tax computation. Chapter 8 then introduces you to capital taxes particularly focusing on capital gains tax, a different tax to income tax, but one that is also paid by individuals. Throughout the chapters in this section the focus is on income taxation of the individual, either as an employed person, or as a self-employed person (as a sole trader). We will examine how the direct tax system operates for companies in Chapter 9.

Fiscal Fact

In 1938/39 there were only 3.8 million taxpayers liable for income tax (with married couples counting as one taxpayer, as that was how income taxpayers were assessed then) of 47.4 million people in the UK at that point i.e. approx.15% of the population were income taxpayers (on the basis that around 50% of the total population were married then). By 2018/19 the number is expected to reach 31 million (of est. approximately 66 million people, i.e. 47%). Of these, 24.6 million are expected to be aged 65 or less, with 6.4 million therefore aged over 65; 18 million are male and 13 million are female. (Source: HMRC Income tax statistics and distributions - Table 2.1. ONS Historical UK Population Estimates)

In the UK, individuals pay tax on their income for a *tax year*. The tax year runs from 6 April to the following 5 April (the reason for these odd dates was described in Chapter 1).

A tax system rarely remains the same for long and in recent years there have been a number of major changes to the way in which individuals are taxed in the UK. For example, key changes in the last 30 years have included the introduction of independent taxation in the 1990/91 tax year (separate taxation of men and women whether they are married or not) while self-assessment for personal taxation was introduced from 6 April, 1996. A more recent key change is the renaming in 2007 of the different income components from names that were largely meaningless to the average taxpayer (Schedule A, Schedule D Case 1, Schedule E etc.) to more obvious names (property income, trading income, employment income etc.) as part of the process of clarifying the tax rules. We will consider the effects of these important changes to the UK tax system in more detail later in this chapter.

In this chapter you will learn how to calculate the amount of an individual's income that is subject to income tax and learn how to determine the amount of any reliefs and allowances that are available to reduce the tax due. Once you have deducted the allowances and reliefs from the taxable income you will learn how to compute a taxpayer's tax liability.

At the end of this chapter you will be able to:

- differentiate between income that is taxable and that which is exempt;
- describe the tax rules for the different categories under which individuals pay income tax;
- calculate the allowances and reliefs available to an individual;
- describe the system of national insurance and calculate any national insurance contributions payable by both employers and employees;
- prepare a personal tax computation for an individual;
- outline the system of self-assessment for individuals; and
- offer basic income tax planning advice to individuals and members of a family unit.

The tax computation

4.2 A tax computation for an individual can be set out in the following way. This structure is identical to the one used by HMRC when calculating income tax due and follows the computation steps of the Income Tax Act 2007. Laying out your computation this way therefore helps with real tax filing processes. It will also help ensure you include all the necessary stages in your computations and put things in the correct order. You are strongly advised to follow this proforma each time you do a personal tax computation.

We will outline the seven steps in this computation briefly for you first in this section before providing further details on each step of the calculation.

Thomas Lester's income tax computation for 2018/19:

	Non-savings £	Savings £	Dividends £	Total £
Income:				
Property Income	1,500			1,500
Trading Income	21,000			21,000
Employment Income	28,850			28,850
Savings Income:				
Bank interest received		3,500		3,500
Building Society interest		3,000		3,000
Dividend Income			1,500	1,500
Total Income	51,350	6,500	1,500	59,350
Less reliefs	(500)			(500)
Net Income	50,850	6,500	1,500	58,850
Less Personal Allowance	(11,850)			(11,850)
Total Taxable Income	39,000	6,500	1,500	47,000

Tax Due:			
Non savings income	34,500	@ 20%	6,900.00
	4,500	@ 40%	1,800.00
Savings income	500	@ 0%	
	6,000 (6,500 –500))	@ 40%	2,400.00
Dividend income	1,500	@ 0%	–
	47,000		
Tax Borne			11,100.00
Less:			
Tax reductions	(none apply for Thomas this year)		(0.00)
Add:			
Additional tax	(none applies for Thomas this year)		0.00
Tax Liability			11,100.00
Less tax already paid:			
PAYE			(3,400.00)
Tax Payable			7,700.00

In this section of the book you will find out how to produce a tax computation like this one, given basic facts about a taxpayer's situation.

You can see that Thomas receives his income from a number of sources (*components*) of income. This includes income from owning property in the UK, income from being partly self-employed, income from employment and some interest and dividends. It is not uncommon to see multiple income sources like this in a tax computation although it is probably more common to see either income from employment or from self-employment (trading income) rather than from both sources in the same tax year.

The income tax computation is split into seven 'steps'. The first three aggregate a taxpayer's taxable income from all sources and then deducts any reliefs and allowances that are applicable to produce "taxable income". The remaining four steps then calculate the tax due on this taxable income. The way in which a particular component of income is taxed depends on the tax rules under which it is assessed. We'll look at the key elements of this computation briefly before going into more detail about the current tax rules.

Computing taxable income

Step 1 – Aggregating the components of income

4.3   All the taxable income Thomas has received or earned in the year, from all sources, is listed in his tax computation. A few sources of income are exempt from income tax, as we will see later, but most have to be taxed and so must be listed here. For most components of income we include what is due to Thomas, even though he hasn't actually received it yet (i.e. we use an *accruals basis*).

Note that we split up Thomas' income sources into different components by using different rows and into different types by using four columns. This is important to help us calculate the correct rate of tax at step 4 of the tax computation; note how each of the three (non-total) columns in the first part of the computation becomes a row when computing tax borne – the fourth step.

Property, trading and employment income
4.4   Income from owning property, from being self-employed or from employment is listed in Thomas's tax computation first. Usually property and trading income have not had tax deducted at source so can just be listed here at the value the rules for each category determine (we'll show you how these rules work in Chapter 5, 6 and 7). Income from employment, however, usually has PAYE deducted by the taxpayer's employer so you'll see that Thomas shows the total (gross) he has received from employment during this year (£19,850) in step 1, but he is able to later deduct the PAYE already paid via his employee (£1,600) at the end of the computation when determining what tax may still be payable. PAYE can be thought of as an advance payment of income tax due.

Savings and investment income
4.5   Bank deposit interest and the building society interest used to be received after tax was deducted at the basic rate of tax, however from 6 April 2016 this is no longer the case. All such income will be received gross and no tax will ordinarily be withheld.

The tax return must always include the gross amount of income in the top part of the tax computation to make sure that the correct tax rate is applied. This depends on the taxpayer's taxable income, which will include other sources of income. Where a payer is required to deduct tax at source when making payments to a taxpayer (e.g. patent royalties), the tax is deducted (or withheld) at a flat rate that doesn't take into account what other income that taxpayer might have. This is efficient for the Government because it enables some tax to be collected without having to disclose a taxpayer's personal circumstances to everyone who pays the taxpayer any income. The tax withheld from the payment is then allowed as a credit in reaching the net tax payable. This might mean the taxpayer has more tax to pay (if the actual tax rate for this income is higher than the rate of tax withheld) or receive a refund (if the actual tax rate is lower). You will find some examples of this in section 4.5.

Exempt income

4.6   All income which is not specifically exempt is potentially subject to income tax under the UK's tax system. You should be aware of the most significant exemptions, which are:

- the increase in the value of National Savings & Investments savings certificates,
- premium bond prizes, betting and lottery winnings and other competition prizes,
- gifts,
- interest from Individual Savings Accounts (ISAs) or Junior ISAs,
- interest from Child Trust funds,
- some social security benefits, including child benefit and housing benefit,
- shares allotted to employees under approved profit sharing schemes,
- educational grants and scholarships (for the recipient),
- statutory redundancy pay, pay in lieu of notice and some other payments up to a maximum of £30,000 made when an employment is terminated.
- payments made by employers to employees for death in service or in respect of disability sustained at work (e.g. personal injury payments),
- lump sums received from approved pension schemes,
- qualifying care relief (fostering and shared lives carer income) – qualifying income up to an annual sum is exempt from income tax (the excess is taxable). Currently this sum is £10,000 per residence, plus £200 per week (for a child under 11 years of age) and £250 per week (for a child/adult older than 11).

Whether or not tax has to be paid on specific sources of income, and how much, is detailed in the tax legislation. We will review the rules for calculating these amounts throughout the remaining chapters of the book.

Fiscal Fact

Exempting income from tax, of course, costs the UK Government in foregone tax revenue (this is called 'tax expenditure'). For example, for 2017/18, the forecasted cost of exempting ISAs from income tax was £2.9 billion. For the same year the cost of allowing redundancy pay up to £30,000 to be tax free is estimated to be £1 billion, exempting interest on National Savings Certificates £250 million and exempting premium bond winnings could cost £130 million. (See the table 'Estimated costs of principal tax reliefs' on the HMRC website for further examples.)

Step 2 – Dealing with reliefs

4.7 After you have computed the total income received by aggregating all components of taxable income, any reliefs that are applicable can be deducted as step 2. In our example, Thomas made £500 of payments that can be treated as reliefs. An example of a relief is a trading loss, which we will cover in Chapter 7. Tax deductions available for any pension contributions paid gross are another example dealt with at this step (see further details in Chapter 5.3).

Total income minus reliefs produces *net income.*

Step 3 – Personal allowances

4.8 Most individuals are entitled to certain amount of income each year free from income tax. This is called a personal allowance and is deducted from the net income figure to arrive at total taxable income. If a blind person's allowance is applicable it is also deducted at this stage. Thomas does not appear to qualify for a blind person's allowance so no deduction is made in his case.

Net income minus personal allowances produces *taxable income.*

Having completed steps 1-3 and determined the taxable income of the taxpayer, you are now ready for the computation of tax liability using steps 4 -7.

Computing tax liability

Step 4 - Income tax rates

4.9 The next stage of the tax computation is to calculate what rates of tax apply to the total taxable income. As part of step 1, the income components were classified into one of three types – non-savings, savings income, and dividend income. This is necessary as each of these income types has its own tax rates. Later in the chapter we will examine exactly how these different rates are applied to a taxpayer's total income.

Step 5 - Tax borne

4.10 Tax borne is the outcome from applying the tax rates to the taxable income, and represents the amount of tax that the taxpayer is liable for on his or her taxable income before any tax reductions (which can reduce the tax borne) or additional tax on their income (that may increase it).

Step 6 – Tax reductions

4.11 At this step there is a deduction from the amount calculated at step 5 for any entitlements the taxpayer has for tax reductions. These are a limited range of special reductions that include married couples' and civil partners' reduction for elderly taxpayers, qualifying maintenance payments and some special schemes for tax deductible investments. Tax relief for any foreign taxes paid at sources (double tax relief) is also given at this point in the computation – see Chapter 12 for more on this topic.

Step 7 – Additional tax

4.12 The final step in computing *tax liability* for the taxpayer is to add in any extra tax that may be due. These are fairly rare events but include for example, extra tax where gift aid is claimed but insufficient tax has been paid to cover the claim. We will discuss charitable donations, and where this situation may arise, later in this chapter at 4.9. Pension related surcharges are also applied here. We will talk about these in Chapter 5.

Tax payable

4.13 The result of completing all seven steps is the computation of the taxpayer's tax liability for the tax year. This is the sum that the taxpayer needs to pay to HMRC to settle their income tax bill for the year. In Chapter 2 we explained that some of this tax may have already been deducted at source, paid via the taxpayer's employer, or otherwise credited to the taxpayer directly, before this computation is done. The final (eighth) stage in the full computation therefore is to deduct from the tax liability any sums already paid (or deemed paid) to HMRC during the tax year. This most commonly will include PAYE withheld by the taxpayer's employer but occasionally may include other things, such as tax paid at source on patent royalties.

If the taxpayer still owes any tax, it must then be paid to HMRC directly. As outlined in Chapter 2, this is likely to be due by 31 January following the end of the tax year (this is also the latest date by which the tax return for the current year should be received by HMRC). However, sometimes sums are due during the tax year, as we will see in Chapter 6.

If the taxpayer has paid more tax during the year than the final tax liability, the taxpayer will receive a refund (repayment) from HMRC of the tax overpaid.

Important: Note that the *taxable income* part of the calculation (steps 1 to 3) is always rounded down to the nearest pound (i.e. you can effectively chop off the pence at each step in your final computation). For the *tax due* part of the calculation (steps 4 to 7), you should always round down your figures to the *whole penny*. This is important to ensure you do not get rounding errors in your tax computation.

Basis of assessment

4.14   The *basis of assessment* is the way in which income is allocated to tax years for taxation purposes. The different components of income have different ways of working out what amount has to be included in any particular tax year. We can distinguish several different general bases of assessment as follows:

Cash or Accruals basis – a cash basis is sometimes called a *receipts* basis, and is where the amount included in the tax computation for a particular tax year is the amount received during the year. An *accruals* basis on the other hand, includes the amount accrued during the tax year, regardless of whether it is actually received by the taxpayer or not. While the cash basis is what is most commonly used for employment income, the accruals basis has historically been mainly used for trading (business) income, in line with the method used for accounting purposes. From April 2013, however, small businesses have had the option to use the cash basis for this source of income too, as we will see in Chapters 5 and 6.

Arising or remittance basis – where taxpayers have income or profit from other countries, we need to decide when it will be taxed in the UK. An arising basis means that the overseas income or profit is taxed when it accrues, even if the money is not brought into the UK. The remittance basis means that it is not subject to UK tax until it is actually brought in, or remitted, to the UK. We will look at this more closely in Chapter 12.

Current year or preceding year basis – this difference relates to trading or business profits. For many years in the past, businesses were taxed on the profit the business earned during the previous tax year. Now, however, business profits are taxed on a current year basis i.e. what is accrued in the current tax year. For self-employed people this is linked to their business year (i.e. the period for which they produce accounts). We will see how this operates in practice in Chapter 6.

Whether the basis of assessment is cash or accruals can make a difference to the taxpayer. For example, employees are normally taxed on income paid to them during the tax year, i.e. the basis of assessment is income received during the tax year (the cash basis). It would be theoretically possible, however, to tax employment income using an accruals basis. For most employees this would make little or no difference to their tax bills each year, but for those who receive performance-related bonuses, which are often paid in the tax year after the one in which they were earned, the tax on the bonus would then be payable before the bonus was actually received. Most people would not like this idea!

The system of income tax rules

4.15   There are four primary Acts that contain the main rules for income tax: the Income and Corporation Taxes Act (ICTA) 1988, the Income Tax (Earnings and Pensions) Act (ITEPA) 2003, the Income Tax (Trading and Other Income) Act (ITTOIA) 2005 and the Income Tax Act (ITA) 2007. The Finance Acts produced each year from the annual UK Budget amend these Acts. In this book we will look at the combined rules of the various tax Acts and any changes that have occurred to them as a result of any subsequent Finance Acts.

It is important to identify which set of tax rules any particular income stream is taxed under because each has its own specific rules for:

- the income to be taxed;
- allowable deductions, if any, from the income;
- the basis of assessment; and
- how the tax is collected.

We saw in Chapter 1, section 1.3, that ever since we started using income tax, the rules used a series of discrete categories to classify different income sources. There were referred to as 'Schedules', sometimes divided into subsections called 'Cases'. With a recent re-write of the income tax legislation, we no longer refer to these Schedules and Cases, although you may come across references to them when reading older case law, for example.

The current system for determining UK income tax liability is structured as follows:

Employment income	Income from employment or office holding - Part 2 ITEPA 2003 (was Schedule E ICTA 1988);
Pension income	Income received from a pension - Part 9 ITEPA 2003;

Property income	Income, such as rent, from UK property - Part 3 ITTOIA 2005 (was Schedule A ICTA 1988);
Trading income	Income from a trade or profession - Part 2 ITTOIA 2005 (was Schedule D Cases I & II ICTA 1988);
Savings income	Interest income for example from banks and building societies - Part 4 ITTOIA 2005 (was Schedule D Case III ICTA 1988);
Dividend income	Income from UK dividends and other distributions from UK companies - Part 3 & 4 ITTOIA 2005 (was Schedule F ICTA 1988);
Miscellaneous income	Income not dealt with under any of the above categories Part 5 ITTOIA 2005 (was Schedule D case VI ICTA 1988).

As we go through this section of the book we will look in detail at the most important tax rules for calculating what income is taxable. In this chapter we will determine the aggregated income which is subject to tax, the allowances and reliefs which can be set against the income for tax purposes and the date on which tax must be paid. Chapter 5 will look at income from employment and pensions. In Chapter 6 and Chapter 7 we will examine trading income and deductions for taxpayers who are carrying on business as sole traders, as well as property income.

Throughout this chapter we only discuss income from UK sources. The general rules for income tax change when the source of the income comes from outside the UK. We will examine these differences in Chapter 12.

Rates of tax

4.16   Having looked in outline at how we aggregate the components of income in the top part of the individual taxpayer's tax computation (steps 1 – 3), let us jump ahead and examine the *tax due* part of the computation before we return to the top part for a more detailed examination in the following section.

Income tax bands

4.17   As we noted in the previous section, to determine the rate of tax to be paid on the taxable income (i.e. step 4 of the computation), we need to classify the taxable income into three broad types i.e. non-savings, savings and dividend income. This classification is important as each type of income has a different set of rates that will apply to it. Which rate is used will vary from person to person based on the band into which the income type falls. Someone receiving an additional £1 could therefore be taxed on it at different rates depending on the income type it is, and how much other income of that type, and other types, the taxpayer receives. Remember as we discussed in Chapter 3, section 3.5, this is called the *marginal* tax rate.

While this might sound confusing initially, it is fairly simple to apply in practice once understood – particularly if you follow the proforma we illustrated in Thomas Lester's income tax computation.

There are three bands (sometimes called brackets) that currently apply across the various income types: basic rate band, higher rate band and additional rate band. There is also a special starting rate for savings, but first we will deal with the three bands that apply to all income categories.

 From April 2017 several differences exist between the income tax computations for taxpayers living in Scotland and those in the rest of the UK. If you need to know these rules you can find on the website a supplement covering the differences between the Scottish tax system and that of the rest of the UK.

The size of these bands is fixed each year. For 2018/19 this is set as:

	Tax Band
Basic rate	0 – 34,500
Higher rate	34,501 – 150,000
Additional rate	>150,000

All taxable income needs to be allocated to these bands to determine which rate to use to calculate the tax payable. The following sections show how this is done.

Fiscal Fact

 HMRC believe there will be approximately 393,000 UK taxpayers who will have earned £150,000 or more in 2018/19 and 19,000 of these are expected to earn £1m of more. (Source: HMRC Statistics - Table 2.5: Income tax liabilities by income range)

Non-savings income

4.18 Let's look at how these tax bands apply to non-savings income first. This includes any employment, property, trading, foreign and miscellaneous incomes. For most people this is will be their main income type.

For the current tax year rates of tax for non-savings income are:

	Tax Band	Rate	Maximum amount payable in band
Basic rate	0 – 34,500	20%	£ 6,900.00
Higher rate	34,501– 150,000	40%	£ 46,200.00
Additional rate	>150,000	45%	

Before April 2008, non–savings income was taxed at three different rates; a starting rate of 10%, a basic rate of 22% and a higher rate of 40%. Between April 2008 and April 2010 only two rates applied; a basic rate of 20% and a higher rate of 40%. In April 2010, an additional rate was introduced, initially at 50%, then reduced to 45% from April 2013.

Activity

Calculate the income tax due on taxable incomes of:
(a)   £2,500
(b)   £10,000
(c)   £45,000
(d)   £175,000
(Assume all income is non-savings income and after personal allowance.)

Feedback

		£
(a)	2,500 @ 20%	500.00
(b)	10,000 @ 20%	2,000.00
(c)	34,500 @ 20%	6,900.00
	(45,000 – 34,500) @ 40%	4,200.00
		11,100.00
(d)	34,500 @ 20%	6,900.00
	(150,000 – 34,500) @ 40%	46,200.00
	(175,000 – 150,000) @ 45%	11,250.00
		64,350.00

Note what happened in (c). Initially the basic rate band (first £34,500 of taxable income) was 'filled up' and taxed at 20%. Any amount falling into the higher rate band (taxable income between £34,500 and £150,000) is then taxed at 40%. In (d) the 45% rate applied to taxable income over £150,000 as the 40% band (between £34,500 and £150,000) was also filled up.

Fiscal Fact

In 2018/19 income tax of £89.5 billion is expected to be paid by taxpayers with non-savings income taxable within the basic rate band. A further £50.6 billion will be collected from those who have non-savings earnings falling into the higher rate band and £30.9 billion from those with these earnings falling in the additional rate band (a total from non-savings income of £171bn). (Source: HMRC Table 2.6).

Savings income

4.19 Since 1996/97 a distinction has been drawn between savings and non-savings income for calculating tax due and a lower rate of tax used for some savings income to encourage people to save more. Savings income is treated as being the middle part of taxable income for the purposes of determining rates of tax to be applied, so you allocate this income to the tax bands only after you have allocated all the non-savings income to the bands as part of your computation.

Savings income includes:

- interest from a bank account (including from National Savings & Investments accounts);
- interest from a building society;
- interest from gilt edged securities (i.e. British Government stock);
- interest from debentures; and
- income from an annuity.

Under Islamic law, receipt or payment of interest is prohibited. Alternative finance arrangements have developed to accommodate this. For tax purposes, the profit element of purchase and resale arrangements, and profit share return arrangements, is treated as if it were interest i.e. eligible for special savings income relief.

For savings income only, there is an initial tax band that may apply – called the *starting rate for savings* band. Savings income in this band is taxed at 0%. For the current tax year rates of tax for savings income are:

Tax Band £	Rate	Maximum amount payable in band* £
Starting rate	0 – 5,000	0%	–
Basic rate	5,001 – 34,500	20%	5,900.00
Higher rate	34,501 – 150,000	40%	46,200.00
Additional rate	>150,000	45%	

* only if all of the taxpayer's income is from savings.

Note that the starting rate for savings of 0% only applies if the non-savings income is less than £5,000. Savings income falling into the starting rate for savings band in this way is tax free.

A new allowance was introduced from 6 April 2016 called a *personal savings allowance* (PSA). This is available to taxpayers **in addition** to the starting rate for savings band and gives an additional zero rate sum of £1,000 to basic rate taxpayers and £500 to higher rate taxpayers. Additional rate taxpayers are not entitled to a personal savings allowance. This means, irrespective of their non-savings income, they can receive the first £1,000 (if basic rate taxpayers) or £500 (if higher rate taxpayers) of any savings income without incurring any tax.

Once the starting rate for savings band is full, and the personal savings allowance (if applicable) has been taken into account, any further savings income which falls within the basic rate band is then taxed at 20%, as for non-savings income. Also, like non-savings income, any savings income falling into the higher rate band is taxed at 40%, and that falling into the additional rate band is taxed at 45%. Note that, although the personal savings allowance carries a zero rate of tax, it is still taken into account to work out how much of each rate band has been used up. In this way it is different to the personal allowance we saw earlier.

Try the following activity to illustrate how the bands, and this time two income types, interact. Note the order in which the taxable income is applied to the bands. Getting the order right is essential (i.e. the non-savings band is used first before savings).

Activity

Calculate the income tax liability for an individual with total taxable income consisting of savings income of £2,500 and employment income of:

(a)   £3,800
(b)   £20,000
(c)   £50,000
(d)   £160,000

Feedback

		£
(a) Non-savings income		
	3,800 @ 20%	760.00
Savings income		
	(5,000 – 3,800) @ 0%	–
	1,000 PSA @ 0%	–
	300 – (£2,500 – 1,200 – 1,000) @ 20%	60.00
		820.00

(b) Non-savings income

20,000 @ 20%	4,000.00
Savings income	
1,000 PSA @ 0%	–
1,500 @ 20%	300.00
	4,300.00

(c) Non-savings income

34,500 @ 20%	6,900.00
(50,000 – 34,500) @ 40%	6,200.00
Savings income	
500 PSA @ 0%	–
2,000 @ 40%	800.00
	13,900.00

(d) Non-savings income

34,500 @ 20%	6,900.00
(150,000 – 34,500) @ 40%	46,200.00
(160,000 – 150,000)@ 45%	4,500.00
Savings income	
2,500 @ 45%	1,125.00
	58,725.00

In (a) £1,200 (i.e. £5,000 – £3,800) of savings income falls into the 0% tax free band as the savings starting rate band (of £5,000) is not used up by non-savings income. The PSA amount (£1,000 as this person is not a higher or additional rate taxpayer) is taxed at 0%. The remainder of the savings income then falls into the basic rate band and is taxed at 20%.

In (b), all of the starting rate for savings, and part of the general basic rate band is used up by non-savings income so the savings income above the PSA all falls into the basic rate band and is therefore taxed at 20%.

In (c) the PSA is only £500, because the taxpayer is higher rate taxpayer. The non-savings income uses all of the starting and basic rate bands so the savings income above the PSA must be taxed at the higher rate of 40%.

In (d) the savings income is pushed into the additional rate band of 45% by the high non-savings earnings. As an additional rate taxpayer, there is no entitlement to the PSA.

Fiscal Fact

Taxpayers paying tax on savings income at the basic rate in 2018/19 are expected to contribute £355 million, at the higher rate £590 million and the additional rate £595 million. This is a total of £1.54 billion from savings income. (Source: HMRC Table 2.6)

Dividend income

4.20   Before 6 April 1999 dividends from UK company shares were treated in the same way as savings income. Since this time however, dividends have been subject to their own tax rules and so must be treated separately in the tax computation. They are treated as the third part of a person's taxable income when determining which rates of tax to apply. If you receive any dividend income it will be taxed at 7.5% if it falls into the basic rate band, 32.5% if it falls into the higher rate band or 38.1% if it falls into the additional rate band.

For the current tax year rates of tax for dividend income are:

Tax Band		Rate	Maximum amount payable in band*
	£		£
Dividend allowance	0 – 2,000		
Basic Rate	2,001 – 34,500	7.5%	2,437.50
Higher Rate	34,501 – 150,000	32.5%	37,537.50
Additional Rate	>150,000	38.1%	
* only if all of the taxpayer's income is from dividends.			

The special 7.5% rate for dividends is sometimes referred to as the *dividend ordinary rate*, the 32.5% rate the *dividend upper rate* and the 38.1% rate the *dividend additional rate*. We will look at the rules that describe how dividends from companies are taxed in more detail later.

Prior to 6 April 2016, dividends were included in tax computations at their gross value. They were treated in the taxpayer's computation as if 10% had been deducted by the company as a tax at source – although no deductions were actually made. From 6 April 2016 onwards, these rules changed. Instead the actual amount of dividend received is included in the taxpayer's income tax computation and a *dividend allowance* was introduced to give all taxpayers (whatever rate of income tax they pay) the first £2,000 (£5,000 in 2017/18) of dividends received tax free. Like the personal savings allowance we saw earlier, the dividend allowance is taken into account when deciding which band the dividends above the allowance will fall into.

Fiscal Fact

Collectively, all taxpayers are expected to pay £2.2 billion in taxes on dividends at the ordinary rate in 2018/19. Higher rate taxpayers however, are expected to pay an extra £5.91 billion in tax on their dividends and additional rate taxpayers an extra £4.63 billion. This represents a total of £12.74 billion from dividend income. [Source: HMRC Statistics Table 2.6]

Activity

Pat (aged 45) has earned the following income for the tax year:

	£
Taxable trading income from her business	20,850
UK Dividends	1,000
Income from UK property	1,000

Calculate Pat's income tax payable.

Feedback

Pat is entitled to a personal allowance of £11,850 which is deducted from her aggregated income before calculating tax due, as we saw in the Thomas Lester example earlier. (Personal allowances are discussed in more detail later in section 4.6). She is also entitled to a dividend allowance in this tax year.

Pat has three components of income to include in her tax computation; trading income (taxable income for her business), dividend income and property income. These three components fall into two categories; non-savings (the trading and property incomes) and dividends. Pat has no savings income for this year.

	Non-savings £	Dividends £	Total £
Trading income	20,850		20,850
Dividend income		1,000	1,000
Property income	1,000		1,000
Net income	21,850	1,000	22,850
Less: Personal allowance	(11,850)		(11,850)
Taxable income	10,000	1,000	11,000

Tax due:

Non-savings income:	
10,000 @ 20%	2,000.00
Dividend income:	
1,000 @ 0%	–
Tax payable	2,000.00

Note that as Pat has a dividend allowance of £2,000 she has no tax to pay on the £1,000 dividends she received. She only has to pay tax on her non-savings income.

Activity

How would your answer to the previous activity differ if Pat had earned £45,350 income from her business and dividends of £6,000?

Feedback

	Non-savings £	Dividends £	Total £
Trading income	45,350		46,350
Dividend income		6,000	6,000
Property income	1,000		1,000
Net income	46,350	6,000	52,350
Less: Personal allowance	(11,850)		(11,850)
Taxable income	34,500	6,000	40,500

Tax due:

Non-savings income:		
34,500 @ 20%		6,900.00
Dividend income		
2,000 @ 0%		–
4,000 (6,000 – 2,000) @ 32.5%		1,300.00
Tax payable		8,200.00

Notice that the first £2,000 of Pat's dividend income is covered by the dividend allowance. The remaining dividend falls in the higher rate band, because the basic band has been fully used up by the non-savings income, and so this is taxed at 32.5%.

We will return to the taxation of dividends in more detail later in this chapter.

Summary

4.21 We have seen that there are seven rates of tax that may apply to an individual taxpayer's income: 0% (for savings and dividends) 7.5% (only for dividends), 20% (non-savings or savings), 32.5% and 38.1% (only dividends may be taxed at these rates), 40% (for non-savings and savings), or 45% (non-savings and savings). The order in which you include the different incomes in the computation can therefore affect the amount of tax paid because of these various tax rates. You are not allowed to pick the order you want to use unfortunately. You must always calculate the tax due in the following order:

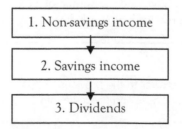

1. Non-savings income

2. Savings income

3. Dividends

Non-savings income must be included in the computation first (if the taxpayer has any), then savings (if they have any) and finally dividends. Dividends can therefore be considered the top part of anyone's income for their income tax computation. As we saw earlier, this means a taxpayer will only be able to use the 0% rate on savings income if there is not more than £5,000 of taxable non-savings income, as non-savings income must come first in the computation.

Note that general reliefs and personal allowances do not necessarily have to be deducted in the same order i.e. from non-savings income first, then if not used up, from savings income and finally from dividends. They should be applied to the taxable income in the way that best suits the circumstances of the taxpayer – i.e. usually the one that minimises the taxpayer's total tax payable. Look back to the example computation at the start of this chapter to review how these rates applied to Thomas' income. In his case, they are both deducted from the non-savings income as neither will use up all of this band of income for this period. We will meet several instances later however, where this approach does not produce the lowest tax payable when applied in a different order to the specific incomes of taxpayers. Do watch out for this.

Liability to UK income tax

4.22 Let's now return to the top part of the personal income tax computation (steps 1 to 3) again to look at how we calculate taxable income in more detail.

The distinctions between the different income tax classifications are important because different rules will apply to a taxpayer having income classified under one category or another. This can have a significant impact on the overall amount of tax they have to pay and when it is paid.

Income taxed at source

4.23 In Chapter 2 we discussed how income can be received in one of two forms:

1. already, at least partly, taxed at source, or
2. not taxed at all yet (to be taxed instead entirely by direct assessment).

Income that is taxed by direct assessment is paid to the recipient gross, while income taxed at source is paid after deduction of some income tax.

We saw in Chapter 1 that the procedure by which some income is paid to the recipient net of tax was introduced at the beginning of the 19th century as an anti-avoidance measure. This is administratively efficient as the payer of the income can then be made partly responsible for the tax due, not just the recipient.

The following income is taxed at source for individual taxpayers (the rules are different for companies as we will see in Chapter 9):

- patent royalties (but not copyright royalties); and
- annuities.

Income taxed at source has tax deducted at the basic rate of 20% (i.e. the recipient only gets 80% of the gross amount due to them).

If individuals who are not liable to income tax (e.g. perhaps because their income is less than the personal allowance) receive income which has been taxed at source, they can usually reclaim the tax which has been deducted directly from the HMRC. However, people who are higher, or additional, rate taxpayers may have to pay more tax at the end of the tax year to make up the full amount they should have paid on this income. The following activities illustrate these situations for you.

Income from earnings and pensions

4.24 Tax on employment income is collected using the PAYE (Pay-As-You-Earn), scheme, which means that the employer deducts the tax due on the income of employees before the payment is made to the employee. Unlike the flat rate of tax at source for patent royalties, PAYE takes into account the taxpayer's personal circumstances. This means that for many employees the correct amount of tax is deducted by their employers so they won't have to complete a tax return each year. This feature of the UK tax system means relatively few people file tax returns in the UK each year compared to many other countries.

Fiscal Fact

Income tax receipts to the UK Government via PAYE were £149.75 billion in 2016/17. This represents 84% of total net receipts from income tax for that year. [Source: HMRC Statistics Table 2.8]

Remember that income from earnings and pensions must be included in the components of income part of an income tax computation (i.e. step 1) as a *gross* amount. If PAYE has been paid on this income already, the amount paid is then deducted from the tax computation at the very end of the tax due calculation (along with any other tax already paid at source) to determine what tax remains still to be paid by the taxpayer.

Property income

4.25 All income from UK land and property is taxed using the property income rules. This includes rental income from furnished lettings and letting caravans and houseboats on permanent moorings. Individuals, whether residents of the UK or not in the tax year, are taxed on any annual profits or gains related to land or property located in the UK. Taxable profits are calculated by deducting total allowable expenses from total income from land and property. The basis of assessment is the accrued income for the tax year for all items other than short lease premiums, although from 6 April 2013 the taxpayer can choose to use a cash basis if they so wish.

We will examine the property income rules in more detail in Chapter 6, section 6.8. The following activity illustrates this for you.

Activity

Mary lets a house that she owns in London. Rent was £9,600 a year until 30 September, 2018 when it was increased to £10,200. Rent is payable a month in advance on the first of the month. The rent due on 1 April, 2019 was not received until 10 April, 2019. Mary incurred allowable expenses of £1,000 during the year to 5 April, 2019.
Determine Mary's property income for 2018/19.

Feedback

Income, using the accruals basis, is:

(6 × £800) + (6 × £850) = £9,900

Notice that it does not matter that one payment due in the tax year was actually paid in the following year – that is the point of the accruals basis.

Hence the property income is £8,900 (£9,900 – £1,000). This is the figure you should put in Mary's tax computation. (Note: strictly the income should be calculated on the daily basis but this monthly basis is usually acceptable to HMRC).

Trading income

4.26 The normal basis of assessment for trading, or business, profit is the *current year* basis. Under this principle the basis period for a year of assessment is normally the 12 months to the accounting date ending in the tax year. However, there are a number of circumstances in which this simple rule cannot be applied, especially in the early years of trading, the final years of trading or years in which a business changes its accounting date. The rules that apply in most of these circumstances will be discussed in Chapter 6, section 6.42. Expenses which are wholly and exclusively for the purpose of the trade are allowable deductions using the *accruals* basis to create a taxable profit figure to be used in the tax computation, although from 6 April 2013, taxpayers can choose to use a cash basis (as we will see in Chapter 6, section 6.40).

We will return to examine trading income computations in more detail in Chapters 6 and 7.

Savings and investment income

4.27   As discussed in the earlier section of this chapter, interest received is taxed as savings income.

The savings income assessable for income tax in a tax year is the interest received within the year of assessment without any deductions, which means either paid to the taxpayer or made available, for example, credited to his or her account. Note therefore, that the accruals basis is not used but instead we use a *cash basis* for savings income.

Activity

Elizabeth opened a savings account in 1991. Interest is credited on 31 December each year, interest in recent years has been:

	£
31 December, 2017	300
31 December, 2018	360
31 December, 2019	310

Determine Elizabeth's savings income for 2018/19.

Feedback

The assessable amount of savings is the interest arising in the tax year (i.e. the cash received basis). Hence the savings income for 2018/19 is £360 as that is what was credited to her bank account in the tax year.

Dividend income

4.28   Dividends and other distributions from companies are taxed under this income category. All non-dividend distributions from companies (which are not specifically excluded from the general rule) are also taxed as if they were a dividend to help reduce an obvious tax avoidance strategy.

Miscellaneous income

4.29 This category is used to tax annual profits or gains not falling under any other category. In particular, income from casual commissions, enterprise allowance payments, some capital sums from the sale of patent rights and business income received after a business has ceased trading (called 'post cessation receipts') are taxed under this heading. The basis of assessment is the *receipts* basis.

Income tax reliefs and allowances

4.30 Individuals may be able to claim tax reliefs and allowances that are deducted from their total income to arrive at their taxable income. Look back at Thomas Lester's tax computation to see where this appears (steps 1 – 3) and the effect it has on his tax computation.

Tax reliefs and allowances serve a number of purposes. They can help particular individuals, products or services or encourage particular activities by making some incomes or activities cheaper than they otherwise would be because they create a tax deduction that can be used to offset other income. When used in this way they are effectively a replacement for direct public expenditure and therefore can be called *tax expenditures*. We will look at the concept of tax expenditures more closely in Chapter 14. HMRC define some reliefs as *structural reliefs*, where they are an integral part of the structure of the tax system, for example, the use of personal allowances to support those on the lowest incomes in a system designed to use an ability to pay principle so that they don't pay income tax. Structural reliefs typically exist year after year rather than appear and then disappear after a period of time. You can get a list of the major tax expenditures and structural reliefs (together called 'principal tax reliefs' by HMRC) from the HMRC website. This also shows how much they cost (in forgone tax revenue).

The way in which tax reliefs and allowances have changed in the latter half of the last century, and the beginning of this one, offers an interesting insight into the history of family life in the UK. Tax allowances for personal circumstances (as a tool for economic welfare and redistribution) and the benefits system have become intertwined throughout recent UK history to support government policies and objectives. The balance between greater use of allowances and greater use of benefits has changed significantly from benefit focus back to allowances and then back again over this period.

Tax reliefs

4.31 An income tax relief is an amount the income tax law allows as a deduction from the payer's total income to calculate their net income (step 2 of the tax computation). The following are eligible to be treated as reliefs:

- pension contributions (for self-employed people or for employed people under net pay arrangements for excess relief – see Chapter 5, section 5.38 for an explanation of these rules)
- loss reliefs that are chargeable against general incomes (these include, for example, trade losses of various types, some property losses if you are running a property business as a landlord – as we will see in Chapter 6, and employment losses)
- payments of eligible interest (see below);
- copyright royalties;
- qualifying annual payments and patent royalties
- relief for patent expenses

Deductions at this step are only possible if there is sufficient income to absorb them. However, where a choice exists, the order that is used for deducting reliefs should be one that gives the greatest reduction in the taxpayer's income tax liability.

Tax relief is given at the taxpayer's marginal rate of tax. To achieve this all reliefs must be shown gross as they are entered into the tax computation and then relief will automatically be given at the taxpayer's marginal rate of tax.

The following activity illustrates how to include reliefs as step 2 in the tax computation:

Activity

Catherine has non-savings income of £15,850 and she makes a pension contribution that is eligible for treatment as a tax relief of £500 (gross). Calculate her tax liability for the tax year.

Feedback

	£
Total income	15,850
Less relief: pension contribution	(500)
Net income	15,350
Less: personal allowance	(11,850)
Taxable income	3,500
Tax due/liability 3,500 @ 20%	700.00

Payments of eligible interest

4.32 Some yearly interest payments can be treated as a relief for tax calculations. The payment of eligible interest is therefore relieved at the taxpayer's marginal rate of tax. Examples of eligible interest that can be treated as tax reliefs are limited but include:

- *Loans to purchase plant and machinery for use in a partnership or as an employee.* The loan must be used to purchase plant and machinery for which capital allowances are available (these rules will be discussed in Chapter 7). The relief is available to partners or employees only (i.e. not to self-employed people or to corporations), for a maximum of three years from the end of the tax year in which the loan was taken out. (Note that interest on loans to purchase plant and machinery is already an allowable deduction for a self-employed person or company for tax purposes, which is why they are not allowed this treatment).

- *Loans to invest in an employee-controlled company.* The loan must be used to acquire ordinary shares either before, or within 12 months of, a company first becoming employee-controlled. The company must be a UK resident, unquoted, trading company or the holding company of a trading group. A company is employee controlled if at least 50% of the issued ordinary share capital and voting power is owned by employees or their spouses. If one employee owns more than 10% of the shares he or she is deemed to own 10% when testing to see if the 50% employee-controlled rule is satisfied (i.e. the rest of their shares will be treated as if not in employee ownership). If any capital is repaid the relief will be reduced.

- *Loans to invest in a partnership.* The loan must be used to either purchase a share in a partnership or introduce capital into a partnership or make a loan to a partnership to be used wholly and exclusively for business purposes. The claimant must be a member of the partnership throughout the time the interest relief is claimed. Limited partners are not eligible for this relief.

Annual payments and patent royalties

4.33 Tax relief is given at step 2 where a taxpayer makes an annual payment eligible for tax relief (such as a life annuity payment) or a patent royalty payment. Where the payment is a commercial payment, it must be made net of basic rate tax (i.e. net of 20%). Tax relief is given at the taxpayer's marginal rate by including the gross sum of the payment at step 2 and adding back the tax actually withheld at step 7 (additional tax stage).

Do note, however, that copyright royalties are not treated in the same way as patent royalties. These payments are always made gross and therefore simply shown at step 2, as illustrated above for other payments eligible for relief.

Activity

How would your answer have differed for Catherine (example above) had the eligible payment she had paid been a patent royalty (i.e. paid net of basic rate tax)?

Feedback

Catherine will have paid to the patent owner during the year £400 (£500 × 80%) this time (i.e. withholding £100 as the relevant tax due on the charge). The payment must be shown gross in the Total Income calculation and then, as tax has been withheld which really forms part of the payment, it must be added back to work out the full tax liability for the year.

	£
Total income	15,850
Less: tax relief for patent royalty	
400 × 100/80	(500)
Net income	15,350
Less: personal allowance	(11,850)
Taxable income	3,500
Tax borne (computation as above)	700.00
Add tax deducted on patent royalty	
500 × 20%	100.00
Tax liability	800.00

In this example, the total of payments eligible for relief actually paid and the income tax liability is £1,200.00 in both cases (i.e. £700.00 + £500 or £800.00 + £400). Hence Catherine's income after tax and payments is the same regardless of whether the eligible payment is paid net or gross.

While this is case for Catherine as she is a basic rate taxpayer, it is not always the case. A taxpayer actually receives relief for the payment at their marginal tax rate even though they only withhold basic rate tax on a net paid payment like a patent royalty. This means they can save money on the payment if they are a higher rate taxpayer, or have to pay extra if they haven't paid enough tax to cover the tax withheld.

More examples can be found on the website to illustrate the impact of tax relief eligible payments on higher rate taxpayers and taxpayers other than those paying at basic rate.

Tax allowances

4.34   Until the Second World War a person on average income did not have to pay income tax because their personal allowances were always greater than their total income. At that time a married man would have been able to claim a married man's allowance, which was substantially higher than the single person's allowance, in order to reflect the costs of supporting a wife who did not work (whether or not she actually worked – a clear tax bias towards marriage). In addition, he received further allowances if he had children.

A married couple was seen as a single tax unit until as recently as 1990, and that unit was focused on the husband. A married woman was not entitled to a personal allowance but her husband could claim his wife's earned income relief, which was of the same value as the single personal allowance, against the married couple's total income. As its name suggests the relief was only available for earned income; a wife's investment income was taxed at her husband's marginal rate of tax even if she did not work. From an equality perspective this was argued to be an unhelpful approach.

Fiscal Fact

It is predicted that for 2018/19 the lowest earning 25% of the UK population will receive 10.3% of the share of total income before tax in the UK and will pay 2.2% of total income tax receipts between them on this income. The highest earning 25% will receive 52.9% of the share of total income received and pay 75.6% of all income tax (i.e. more than thirty-times times that of the lowest 25%). The highest earning 1% are expected to earn 12.2% of all income and will pay between them 27.9% of all income tax (more than twelve times the lowest 25%). There are 6,000 people are expected to earn over £2,000,000 in 2018/19 and will pay an average estimated rate of tax of 39.6% on this income. [Source: HMRC Statistics Tables 2.4 & 2.5]

Until the 1970s fathers also received tax allowances for any children in the family. However, these allowances were withdrawn in 1979/80 and there was a compensatory increase in child benefit – which was paid each week to mothers (usually) instead. This change was welcomed by almost everyone, especially groups concerned with child poverty. It was believed that this way of making payment was more likely to benefit the children as it was paid to the mother rather than the father. Child benefit was also paid regardless of the employment status of either partner, thus providing some much needed income in times of unemployment but also a source of income for mothers independent of the earnings of fathers. However, many people appear to have forgotten the reasons for the transfer from allowances to benefit in the 1970s. Now the benefit is not always increased in line with inflation and in fact it has been frozen since the Coalition's Emergency Budget in June 2010. Further, as part of the austerity measures of the Coalition Government, from January 2013 child benefit is not paid to a family where one or other partner earns more than £60,000 a year. To stagger the impact of this 'cliff edge' where someone would have gone from receiving full benefit to receiving nothing, restrictions were imposed on the full rate after at least one partner earns £50,000 income so that such families get a reduced amount of child benefit.

This produces a cost saving for Government and focuses child benefit payments on families on lower incomes however, it does undo the advantage of a universal, non-means tested, payment focussed on supporting mothers directly that was such an important feature of the system when it was introduced.

During the 20th Century there were various other steps taken that reflected the changing role of women, especially professional women, in society. One of these schemes, introduced in the 1960's, was intended to offer women some measure of privacy in their tax affairs. It enabled women to complete their own tax returns and enter into correspondence with the Revenue themselves (where previously the correspondence had been conducted via their husbands even if it had nothing to do with his tax affairs, only hers). The personal allowances available to the couple were also split between the husband and wife in proportion to their income.

From April 2000 a systematic policy of reforming many of the allowances based on personal circumstances in the tax system (including mortgage interest relief, married couples allowance etc.) has rebalanced the overall impact of this aspect of the tax system on society. As we will see, however, significant growth in the use of tax credits has occurred, particularly under the previous Labour Government, to replace this reduction in allowances. Tax credits have a different impact on taxpayers than tax allowances as they can benefit those without income, or on low income, where allowances may not have been able to assist them until their income was enough to use the allowance against.

In this section we will now review the allowances and reliefs currently available to UK income taxpayers.

Personal allowance (PA)

4.35 The personal allowance operates like a tax free threshold, or zero rate tax band. Most people (whatever age they are) who are UK residents are entitled to this initial sum of income on which no income tax is due. This is called the *basic* personal allowance. For 2018/19 this tax-free sum is at least £11,850 (£11,500 in 2017/18). This includes children, and those who are married as well as single people. However, not everyone gets a basic personal allowance. If a taxpayer's income in the tax year exceeds £100,000 this may be partly, or even fully, lost. We will examine how this occurs below.

Fiscal Fact

In the Queen's Speech laying out the legislation plans of the new Conservative government from May 2015, it was announced that the personal allowance will rise to £12,500 over the following five years. If this is done it will mean no-one earning the national minimum wage for at least 30 hours a week will have to pay any income tax on their earnings. Announcements of rises each year since this date have meant we have kept in line with this promise (so far).

There is provision in statute for the personal allowance to increase at least in line with inflation each year (using the Consumer Prices Index (CPI) to measure this rise since Budget 2011), unless Parliament opts to waive the provision for a particular year (as the Chancellor did, for example, between 2002/03 and 2003/04, and between 2009/10 and 2010/11).

Increases in personal allowances benefit less well off taxpayers proportionately more than better off taxpayers, as these allowances enable a larger percentage of their income to be tax free, lowering their average rate of tax, and are therefore useful as redistribution tools. In 2012/13 and 2013/14 the Government went further by making the extra basic rate personal allowances only beneficial to basic rate taxpayers. They did this by lowering the start of the higher rate band by the same amount it increased the personal allowance. This meant throughout this period higher rate taxpayers were no better off by any increases, even though basic rate taxpayers were. Increases to the higher rate band were, however, given in the past four years – although not as large as the rise in the personal allowance until last year. In 2017/18, the rise in the higher rate band (from £32,000 to £33,500) was three times that of the rise in the personal allowance (£11,000 to £11,500), and again in 2018/19 the rise of £1,000 in the higher rate band starting point (from £33,500 to £34,500) was almost three times that of the rise in the personal allowance (of £350 from £11,500 to £11,850) undoing some of the impact of the previous policy to focus personal allowance increases on the less well off.

Personal allowances are usually only available to be used by the person who is directly entitled to them – they couldn't historically be transferred to anyone else. However, this basic principle changed in 2015/16 with some allowance becoming transferrable under limited circumstances. Between a couple (married or in a civil partnership), one partner can now transfer up to £1,190 (£1,150 in 2017/18) of their un-used personal allowance to the other, providing neither pays tax on their income above the basic rate. This will clearly be beneficial to the combined income they get to keep between them if one is a taxpayer and the other isn't using all their personal allowance, as moving un-used allowance to the taxpaying spouse will enable the couple to have more of their combined income tax-free. The receiving partner's personal allowance is simply increased by the total transferred to them in doing their tax computation (i.e. if the full transfer was made then their personal allowance for 2018/19 would rise to £13,040). This £1,190 limit is called the *Marriage Allowance*.

Fiscal Fact

It is anticipated that up to 4 million households could benefit from the new Marriage Allowance rules. This will include up to 15,000 couples in civil partnerships.

Any personal allowance that is not used (or transferred) in the year is lost if that person's income is insufficient to use the allowance in full in any particular year. They also can't be rolled forward from year to year – but a new allowance can be claimed each year of course.

The 2009 Budget announced an important change to the longstanding philosophy of everyone getting at least some tax-free income, irrespective of their income levels. From April 2010, personal allowances are tapered down to zero for those with an adjusted net income more than £100,000. Adjusted net income starts with "net income", which is the total of the individual's income subject to income tax less certain deductions (for example, trading losses and payments made gross to pension schemes). This is then reduced by the grossed-up amounts of any Gift Aid contributions (charitable donations – see section 4.45 below) and pension contributions which have received tax relief at source. Relief for any payments to trade unions or police organisations that was deducted in arriving at the individual's net income is then added back to arrive at the adjusted net income.

The tapering of personal allowances for those earning over £100,000 is at the rate of £1 for every £2 earned over £100,000 i.e. you will lose all of your personal allowance when you earn over £123,700 (£100,000 + (2 x £11,850)).

Note, you can't end up with a negative personal allowance, so for taxable incomes, after reliefs, above this sum the personal allowance just becomes zero.

For many years the UK tax system had an additional personal allowance for older taxpayers (called age allowances). This has been phased out, and 2016/17 was the first year that it was no longer available.

Activity

Joe's net income for the tax year is £106,728 from various sources (after reliefs but before personal allowances). What will his personal allowance be for 2018/19?

Feedback

Joe's personal allowance will be:

£11,850 – (1/2 x (£106,728 – £100,000) = £8,486

This is the figure you should then use in Joe's tax computation at Step 3 instead of the full £11,850. Had Joe earned over £123,700 his personal allowance would be zero.

Fiscal Fact

The estimated cost to the Treasury in tax revenue foregone of allowing personal allowances was £101.3 billion for 2017/18 – up from £72 billion for 2012/13. [Source: HMRC Statistics – Estimated costs of principal tax reliefs]

A quirk of the reduction in the personal allowances for higher earners is that people falling into this high-earning category suffer a higher than normal effective marginal tax rate on this extra income. The following activity illustrates this.

Activity

Calculate the marginal rate of tax of a single person with net income of £100,000 and compare it with the marginal rate of tax if they earn £8 more in the same period. What is the effective marginal rate on this difference?

Feedback

	£	£
Net income	100,000	100,008
Less personal allowance	(11,850)	
£11,850 – (100,008 – 100,000)/2		(11,846)
Taxable income	88,150	88,162

Hence an increase of £8 in total income leads to an increase of £12 in taxable income. If the marginal rate of tax in both situations is 40% (i.e. assuming the income is non-savings or savings income), the extra £8 of income results in an extra £4.80 (£12 × 40%) of tax, which is an effective marginal rate of tax of 60% (£4.80 ÷ £8).

Therefore, those in the lucky position to be earning between £100,000 and £123,700 are facing an effective 60% marginal tax rate. This falls to 40% again when they reach £123,700 income per annum and their personal allowance is fully used up.

Blind person's allowance (BPA)

4.36 This allowance is given to taxpayers who are registered as blind under local government rules. The allowance is £2,390 for this tax year (£2,320 in 2017/18) and is available in addition to the personal allowance. Unlike the personal allowance however, if the blind person has insufficient income to use the allowance in full the excess may all be transferred to their spouse or civil partner so they get a larger tax-free allowance than they would otherwise.

Trading and property income allowances

4.37 The 2017 Budget proposed the creation of two new allowances of £1,000 each for trading and property income. This is an attempt to save potential taxpayers having to file tax returns for small sums of income tax due on small amounts of income, for example, from selling items on eBay that would otherwise be considered trading, or letting accommodation on AirBnB.

The proposal was structured such that, if an individual taxpayer's (the new allowance is not available to those in partnerships) income received in the tax year from these areas was less than £1,000, then there would be no requirement to declare the income and no tax was therefore considered to be due. However, if the income from these sources exceeded the £1,000 allowance levels, the taxpayer would have to declare this income, as normally, but could either do so as before (by deducting allowable expenses from the income received – as we will see is how this is normally done for trading and property incomes in Chapter 6) or by ignoring expenses actually incurred and just deducting the £1,000 allowance in each case from the income received to determine how much should be declared.

While these new allowances did not make it into the first Finance Act of 2017 when the General Election was announced, they were included in the Finance Act (No. 2) 2017 taking retrospective effect for the 2017/18 year and onwards.

Tax reductions

4.38 After calculating the tax borne (step 5) a taxpayer may be entitled to various tax reductions that must be then taken into account. These include:

- tax reduction for elderly married couples and civil partners;
- venture capital trust (VCT) reduction;
- enterprise investment scheme (EIS) and seed enterprise investment scheme (SEIS) reduction;
- community investment tax (CITR) relief;
- social investment tax (SITR) relief;
- relief for interest on a loan to purchase an annuity; and
- qualifying maintenance payments

Most of the details of computing entitlement to these reductions are beyond the coverage of this book but we will illustrate the first of these for you as one example you may come across. We also discuss VCTs, EIS/SEISs, CITR and SITR briefly. All others are handled in the tax computation in the same way.

Married couples' and civil partners' tax reduction

4.39 A tax reduction for married couples (called the Married Couples' Allowance or MCA), along with a number of other tax reducers, ceased for most people from 6 April 2000. The MCA has now become the Married couples' and civil partners' tax reducer with the addition of the civil partnership legislation (effective from December 2005). This is different to the marriage allowance referred to earlier which allows married couples to transfer part of their personal allowance (see Section 4.35). The only people still able to claim this tax reducer are those where at least one partner was born before 6 April 1935 (i.e. will be at least 84 by 6 April 2019). For anyone in this category the reduction is restricted to 10% of the annual amount available for the reduction of £8,695. This can be limited, however, down to the minimum of £3,360 if the husband's total income exceeds £28,900.

Any entitlement to this tax reducer can be shared between partners in any way they wish. If one partner earns an income and the other does not it can therefore be beneficial for the total tax they have to pay for the earning partner to receive this reduction.

For all other individuals the MCA was replaced by the tax credit system from April 2003 (see section 4.8).

Venture Capital Trusts

4.40   When taxpayers subscribe for newly issued shares in an HMRC approved Venture Capital Trust (VCT), a tax reduction of 30% of the amount invested is available. To be eligible the company will normally need to be less than 12 years old (for investments made after April 2015) and the taxpayer must keep the shares for at least five years to keep the tax savings. Dividends received from these shares are exempt from income tax, and if the taxpayer sells the shares, he or she won't have to pay capital gains tax (see Chapter 8).

Fiscal Fact

Around 3,500 companies raise capital via EISs and 50 via VCTs each year. Since the EIS tax relief scheme was launched in 1993/4 over 26,000 companies have participated in the scheme raising over £16.2 billion of funds between them. Since VCTs were introduced in 1995 they have raised approximately £7 billion of funds.

Enterprise Investment Schemes

4.41   This tax reduction of 30% of the amount invested is available when a taxpayer subscribes for newly issued shares in qualifying Enterprise Investment Scheme (EIS) companies. These are mainly smaller, unlisted companies but can include businesses up to 250 employees and assets of no more than £15 million before the investment and £16 million after. These limits rise to less than 500 employees, and assets of no more £20 million for businesses in knowledge intensive industries (i.e. businesses in industries such as science and engineering that rely on significant investment in research and development and innovation).

An annual limit to tax reductions under this scheme of £1million per investor applies from 6 April 2012. This limit has risen to £2 million from April 2018 provided that any amounts over the £1 million previous limit is invested in one or more so called 'knowledge-intensive' companies. Unlike VCT investments, dividends from EIS shares are not exempt from income tax, although capital gains tax does not apply to the sale of the shares, so long as they are held for at least three years.

From 6 April 2012 a new Seed EIS (SEIS) became available to investors. This applies to new investments made into early stage companies (less than 25 employees and assets less than £200,000). For investments in such businesses tax reliefs of 50% will apply to investors with less than 30% stock in such business (including their directors). A cap of £100,000 per investor applies (unused amounts can be carried back one year). Shares acquired under this scheme are also exempt from capital gains tax – as for the main EIS.

Community Investment Schemes

4.42 Community Investment Tax Relief (CITR) was introduced in 2003 to encourage investments into Community Development Finance Institutions who on lend to SMEs based in disadvantaged communities. Tax relief of up to 25% of money invested is available, spread over 5 years. Maximum relief is available for investors who hold the investment for at least 5 years.

Social Investment Tax Relief

4.43 Budget 2014 introduced a new tax reducer – the social investment tax relief. From July 2014 individuals who subscribe to qualifying shares or who make qualifying debt investments in a social enterprise that meets the rules for the new tax reducer can get a 30% relief of the amount invested, subject to a maximum annual investment of £1 million. The investment must be held for 3 years to keep the relief given.

The investor must have sufficient UK tax liability to offset the relief, although the investor does not have to be a UK resident. The relief can be carried back so it can be treated as having been made in the prior year if sufficient income exists in that year to offset it, but it cannot be carried forward. Therefore, if the taxpayer has not got enough UK tax liability to offset the payment made in the current or prior year then the excess relief is lost.

The social enterprises that can qualify for this investment relief on issuing their shares or receiving loans are carefully defined in the rules. They must have less than 500 employees, not be controlled by another company, must be a charity (or a so-called community interest company or benefit society) and not have more than £16 million in gross assets once the investment has been made. Each qualifying social enterprise can only raise a maximum of £290,000 this way and once they have this money it must be used within 28 months or their investors will lose their relief. It also matters that they are not substantially engaged in a number of restricted activities. These include banking, money-lending, property development, road transport and insurance.

Tax credits

4.44 As part of a swing back to more benefits focussed policies, the last Labour Government systematically removed various tax allowances that used to be given to taxpayers as additional taxable income deductions to reflect their personal circumstance and needs. This has been a policy that was continued by the subsequent governments.

Initially some of these lost allowances were replaced by a series of tax 'reducers' (see section 4.38 above), which were closely related to the tax allowances they replaced (i.e. given to the same people largely) but were used to provide only fixed tax deductions rather than variable deductions. These reducers are deducted from the tax due as a fixed sum, rather than from taxable income, as personal and age allowances are. The effect of deductions from taxable income varies depending on the types of income earned by the taxpayer and their levels of income. Lowering taxable income has the effect of lowering the tax due at the highest marginal rate – which varies for each taxpayer based on their personal income profile. Using tax reducers instead of tax allowances therefore means all taxpayers who are entitled to the reduction get the same amount irrespective of their income level and type.

The last Labour Government opted to focus on giving people tax 'credits' instead of more tax allowances or reducers and so these are becoming less significant over time for many ordinary taxpayers. These credits are not however, treated the same as the tax credits we have already discussed that are associated with dividends from companies (the name 'credit' is used in a different way here, confusingly). These tax credits are direct tax reductions either received as part of your wages or salary, or paid to you directly.

A new system of Universal Credit is currently being rolled out across the country to replace the previous complex system of child tax credits, working tax credits and other entitlements. The new system is based on a single monthly payment.

Details of how the tax credits system works does not form part of most introductory tax courses however, if you wish to know more, see the student section of the website.

Donations to charity

4.45   Since 6 April, 2000 all gifts to charities by individuals, however small and however regular, have been eligible for tax relief at the marginal rate of the taxpayer under the so-called 'Gift Aid' rules.

All that is necessary to operate this scheme is that the donor gives to the charity a Gift Aid declaration (a simple form, or even an oral statement will do) saying that they are giving money to the charity using the Gift Aid rules. The charity can then use this declaration to get back from HMRC at least some of the income tax paid by the taxpayer related to the donation. Charities can reclaim 25p for every £1 you donate (£1 x 100/80 = £1.25, so you pay £1 and HMRC pays 25p). This does not vary however with the marginal tax rate of the donor, i.e. the charity gets 25p for every £1 donated whatever rate the donor pays tax at.

The rules that apply when companies donate to charities are different to the rules for individuals. We will look at the rules for companies in Chapter 9.

Gift relief is also available for donations to community amateur sports clubs (CASCs) as well as to registered charities. The system for receiving the relief is identical to donations to charities. The Budget 2010 extended Gift Aid relief to certain EU based charities for gifts made by UK taxpayers. The same computation rules apply as for donations to UK based charities.

To be eligible for tax relief on charitable donations the donor must have paid at least the amount in tax on their taxable income that HMRC will be asked for by the charity. Either income tax or capital gains tax will suffice to cover the tax (but not others taxes such as VAT). Where a taxpayer does not do this HMRC will ask the taxpayer to pay back the extra money the charity claims from them if gifts are made via Gift Aid rules. Such taxpayers should beware in using these rules therefore when giving to charities or they may get a bill from HMRC they aren't expecting.

Fiscal Fact

In 1990/91, income tax repayments totalling £470 million were made to charities. In 2016/17 total repayments via gift aid totalled £1.27 billion. Between April 2000 and April 2016 a total of £14.4 billion has been reclaimed by charities via the Gift Aid scheme. [Source: HMRC Statistics –Table 10.1]

Tax relief is given to the taxpayer when making Gift Aid donations by increasing their basic rate band by the gross amount of the gift. This process ensures that relief is given at higher or additional rates to taxpayers who are higher or additional rate taxpayers (as their higher rate bands then start at a higher taxable income level). Similarly, basic rate taxpayers will get the deduction at 20% as their marginal rate (increasing their higher rate band start point of course makes no difference as they don't earn at the level at which this limit begins to affect their tax paid).

A charitable gift paid under these Gift Aid rules does not in fact need to appear in the taxpayer's tax computation and so for basic rate taxpayers these can just be ignored when doing their tax computation. However, adjustments to that computation will need to be made under certain circumstances, particularly for higher and additional rate taxpayers. The following activity shows you how this may occur.

Activity

In this tax year Andrew, an employee, makes a Gift Aid donation of £1,000 (net) to his favourite charity. What would his income tax computation be if his only income was non-savings income of:

a) £29,850
b) £11,900
c) £48,850
d) £200,000

Feedback

Andrew's payment, grosses up to £1,250 (£1,000 × 100/80). The charity collects the extra £250 from HMRC via the Gift Aid scheme. What we need to do is to check that Andrew has paid enough basic rate tax to cover the repayment to the charity.

a)

	£
Earnings from employment	29,850
Less personal allowance	(11,850)
	18,000
Tax due: 18,000 @ 20%	3,600.00

Nothing else needs to be done in this case as Andrew's income easily covers the reclaiming of the £250 from HMRC. He also is a basic rate taxpayer so no higher rate band adjustment is needed. In such a situation you would not normally need to list this gift aid payment in Andrew's tax computation as it will have no impact on his calculation.

b)

	£
Earnings from employment	11,900
Less personal allowance	(11,850)
	50
Tax due: 50 @ 20%	10.00

In this case Andrew is not paying enough tax to cover the £250 that the charity would reclaim on his donation. He will therefore need to pay another £240 (£250 – £10) to HMRC as extra income tax or he can inform the charity not to treat this as gift aided if he doesn't want to pay the extra to HMRC.

c)

	£
Earnings from employment	48,850
Less personal allowance	(11,850)
	37,000

Tax due:

(34,500 + 1,250) @ 20%	7,150.00
(37,000 – 35,750) @ 40%	500.00
	7,650.00

In this case as Andrew is a higher rate taxpayer his basic rate band is extended by the gross amount of his charitable donation (£1,250) so that he receives relief for this payment at the higher rate. This means £1,250 extra of his income is taxed at 20% instead of at 40% as would have otherwise been the case, saving him £250 (20% × £1,250) in tax.

d)

	£
Earnings from employment	200,000
Less personal allowance	(nil)
	200,000

Tax due:

(34,500 + 1,250) @ 20%	7,150.00
((150,000 + 1,250) – 35,750) @ 40%	46,200.00
200,000 – 151,250 @ 45%	21,937.50
	75,287.50

In this case both the basic rate band and the higher rate bands are extended by the gross amount of the gift aid payment, so Andrew has saved £312.50 (20% x £1,250)+(5% x £1,250) in tax.

Gift Aid donations do not necessarily have to be dealt with in the tax year in which the payment is actually made. Since 2003, provided a claim is made before the tax return for that year is presented to HMRC, a taxpayer can opt to 'carry back' their payment so that it is treated as if it had been paid in the previous tax year. This will then affect the taxpayer's tax computation for that year, not for the current year.

Another form of tax relief for gifts to charities is the *Payroll Giving Scheme*, set up in the Finance Act 1986. The scheme applies to employees who pay tax under the PAYE scheme and whose employer runs a scheme, which is approved by HMRC, which operates by withholding sums from them. Where this scheme operates the taxpayer can instruct their employer to make the donation to the charity of their choice before PAYE deductions meaning tax relief at their marginal rate is automatically applied then and will not need adjustments to be made via a tax return even if they are higher or additional rate taxpayers.

The Government has been consulting on how to encourage people to make gift aid donations through digital channels. The aim is to simplify the system and therefore increase the volume of charitable donations. The consultation is now closed and the Government is considering what changes need to be made as a result.

In 2013, the National Audit Office undertook a study of the Gift Aid system, to consider the costs and effectiveness of the scheme and also to see if it was being abused for fraud or tax avoidance purposes. The report states (at p11):

"Tax relief on donations reflects a long-held principle... that charitable income should be exempt from taxation where that income is used for charitable purposes. Gift aid and other reliefs on donations are current mechanisms for achieving this. They encompass a wider set of objectives, such as making the tax system simpler for charities and donors to use and encouraging more giving by making donations more tax efficient."

National insurance contributions

4.46 We saw in Chapter 1 that national insurance was introduced in 1948, largely in order to provide for retirement pensions, unemployment and sickness benefit. Much of the UK's social security system continues to be paid for, albeit indirectly now, by these payments made by the working population and by their employers.

Initially national insurance was payable at a flat rate by both employees and employers. The intention was for the payment to represent an insurance payment rather than to tax people on the basis of an ability to pay. Thus the burden of the tax fell heaviest on the lowest paid, i.e. the tax was regressive.

In subsequent years the amount which each contributor had to pay increased as social security expenditure grew. By 1961 the flat rate contribution was seen to be too great a burden on the lowest paid and earnings-related contributions were introduced. By 1975 the entire national insurance contribution was earnings related. Although national insurance is now assessed on a percentage basis there is an upper limit above which employees only pay 2% extra national insurance instead of the full amount. This arrangement means that the tax is still regressive, i.e. taxpayers on low incomes can pay a greater percentage of their income in national insurance contributions than taxpayers on higher incomes.

Until 2000/01 neither employee nor employer national insurance contributions were payable on most benefits in kind (i.e. benefits received by an employee related to their employment but not paid in cash e.g. goods, use of a company car for private purposes and so on), making provisions of benefits in kind a relatively tax efficient form of remuneration. Now employers (but still not employees at present) are required to pay contributions (called Class 1A) on most benefits in kind they provide to their employees. For example, if an employee has a company car and/or fuel for private motoring the employer must pay Class 1A contributions, at 13.8% of the value of the car and fuel benefits. (We will consider how these values are calculated in Chapter 5.)

National insurance contributions are collected by HMRC (http://www.hmrc.gov.uk/nic). The PAYE system is used to collect these payments for employees, but direct payment to HMRC must be made by those who are self-employed, or others not in employment but making contributions.

A record is kept of an individual's national insurance contributions during their lifetime and gaps in contributions can lead to a reduction, or even loss, of benefits in some circumstances, so National Insurance still has some characteristics of an insurance scheme.

Unlike income tax, which is charged on a taxpayer's expected income for the year and collected as income is received under PAYE, national insurance contributions are calculated according to the employee's income for the payment period only. Hence, if a taxpayer works for a number of months during the year and then has no income for the rest of the year, he or she may be able to reclaim some of the income tax already paid so that the correct amount is paid over the whole year, but, no repayment of national insurance contributions already made is possible. UK income tax is termed a cumulative tax system because unused allowances accumulate; national insurance is a non-cumulative tax because payments are only due in periods when payment thresholds are exceeded, irrespective of other earnings in the year.

There are four main classes of national insurance contributions:

- Class 1 are paid by both employees, (called primary contributions), and employers, (called secondary contributions);
- Classes 2 and 4 are paid by the self-employed;
- Class 3 payments are made on a voluntary basis, by those who, while in work and earning money, would otherwise not pay enough contributions via other classes to entitle them to a state pension when they retire.

Various personal circumstances can affect contributions paid; for example, you don't pay if you are under 21 (this was under 16 before April 2015). If you are in full time education between the ages of 16-18, you get credited these years as if you'd paid them. If you are a full-time child carer, and therefore don't work in paid employment, you can claim home responsibilities protection which reduces the number of years of contributions needed to get a full state pension.

Once employees are over national pensionable age they are not required to make further national insurance contributions. However, the employer's contributions, (at the non-contracted out rate) are still payable. The national pensionable age in the UK used to be 60 for women and 65 for men, but this is gradually being increased so that eligibility for pension will be later, and also the rules for men and women will be aligned so that eventually, the state pension age will be 68 for both.

National insurance contributions for the current year are as follows (rates are unchanged from the previous year, but the thresholds have risen after being fixed last year):

Class 1

Employee: Pay per week (per month/per annum)	
£162.00 (£702/£8,424) or less	
– employee primary threshold	0%
£162.01 – £892.00 (£702 – £3,863/£8,424 – £46,350)	
– employee's primary threshold to upper	
earnings limit (UEL) main percentage	12%
Over £892 (£3,863/£46,350)	
– additional primary percentage	2%

Employer: Pay per week (per month/per annum)	
£162.00 (£702/£8,424) or less	
– employer primary threshold	0%
Over £162.00 (£702/£8,424)	13.8%

4.47 From April 2014, an 'Employment Allowance' has been available to offset national insurance contribution liabilities for small employers. This was £3,000 from April 2016 (£2,000 before April 2016). Owner-directors are not able to claim this if they are the only employee of their company. This will mean many small businesses will not have to pay employer national insurance contributions in practice. Employer's also don't have to pay NICs for anyone under the age of 21, or those on approved apprenticeship schemes up to the age of 25, provided their earnings are below the Upper Earnings Limit (if their earnings are above this then the normal 13.8% applies on this excess).

Fiscal Fact

The estimated cost of the Class 1 £2,000 per employer holiday is £1.26 billion in 2014/15. It is expected this will rise to £1.73 billion from 2017/18. It will affect 1.25 million employers and prevent 450,000 employers having to pay any employers' national insurance contributions at all now. (Source: Budget 2014)

Class 1 contributions are based on the employee's gross pay without deducting pension contributions.

Because directors may be able to influence the timing of their remuneration package, their Class 1 national insurance contributions are always calculated on an annual basis for directors (see the numbers in brackets in the table above).

Activity

Calculate the primary and secondary (before employment allowance and assuming all are >25 years old) Class 1 contributions of:

- Matthew, who earns £125 per week.
- Mark, who earns £200 per week.
- Luke who earns £500 per week.
- John, who is a company director, earns £400 per week, receives an annual bonus of £10,000 in the year.
- Paul, earns £920 a week.

Feedback

Matthew

Matthew does not pay primary Class 1 contributions because his earnings are less than the primary threshold of £162. Similarly his employer does not pay secondary Class 1 contributions because his earnings are below the secondary threshold of £162.

Mark

Mark pays ((£200 – £162) × 12%) = £4.56.
His employer pays ((£200 – £162) × 13.8%) = £5.24.

Luke

Luke pays ((£500 – £162) × 12%) = £40.56.
His employer pays ((£500 – £162) × 13.8%) = £46.64.

John

For company directors, the annual earnings threshold is £8,424.

John receives an annual income of £30,800 (£400 × 52 + £10,000) so is below the employee's UEL and only pays annual primary Class 1 contributions of (£30,800 – £8,424) × 12% = £2,685.12.

His employer will pay (£30,800 – £8,424) × 13.8% = £3,087.88.

Paul

Paul's weekly salary exceeds the £892 per week UEL level so he will pay:

+ (£892 – £162) × 12% = £87.60

+ (£920 – £892) × 2% = 56p

total = £88.16.

His employer will pay:

+ (£920 – £162) × 13.8%

= £104.60.

If someone has more than one employment, they are liable to pay primary Class 1 contributions for each job, subject to a maximum annual contribution. This maximum contribution is based on formulae that takes into account how much was earned in each employment (i.e. to balance how much should be paid at the regular rate and how much at the extra 2% rate). Any overpayments made can be reclaimed at the end of the year. To avoid the need for repayment, a taxpayer can also claim for a deferral of payment on some of their contributions. Any extra due at the end of the year will then need to be settled directly with HMRC (usually via completing a tax return in the normal way).

Class 1A

4.48 Benefits in kind (non-cash rewards related to an employment or office) are usually not chargeable to Class 1 contributions for employees; however, they do create a Class 1A contribution for employers (not employees). The value used to determine how much the contribution will be is the same as calculated for the employment income benefit in kind on which the employee pays income tax. We will see how this is determined in the next chapter in more detail. Class 1A contributions are paid at the same rates by employers as normal Class 1 contributions (i.e. 13.8%).

Class 2

4.49 The self-employed pay national insurance contributions of £2.95 (£2.85 in 2017/18) per week for the current tax year provided their annual profits are at least £6,205 (£6,025 in 2017/18). If it is below this level they are exempted from these contributions.

These used to be paid directly to HMRC on a monthly or quarterly basis if due but from April 2015, Class 2 contributions have been paid via the self-employed tax return (as Class 4 are currently) as part of a simplification plan for these contributions.

It was however, announced in Budget 2015 that Class 2 contributions will cease in April 2018. It was confirmed in November 2017 that this will be delayed to April 2019.

Class 3

4.50 Anyone can pay voluntary contributions of £14.65 per week (£14.25 in 2017/18) to maintain rights to some state benefits (particularly the state pension) that they might otherwise lose, for example, because their earnings are too low to pay other contributions.

Class 4

4.51 In addition to Class 2 and maybe Class 3 contributions, the self-employed pay 9.0% (unchanged from some years), of their profits between lower and upper limits, which are £8,424 (£8,164 in 2017/18) and £46,350 (£45,000 for 2017/18) for this tax year. As for employees, profits above the upper limit are subject to a further 2% charge (called the additional Class 4 percentage).

For Class 4 national insurance contribution purposes profits are the taxable profits under the trading income rules less trading losses and any interest or annual payments to do with the business but not already deducted in working out trading profit. Personal allowances are not taken into account for Class 4 contributions. The calculation for this amount due usually forms part of the tax return. Class 4 contributions are normally paid at the same time as the income tax on their business profits (and assessed as part of the tax return process). This normally means it is paid in two instalments (on 31 January in the tax year and on 31 July following it) with a third payment due the following 31 January if any balancing payment is due.

Activity

Simon, who is self-employed, has taxable income from his business of £20,000 for this tax year. Calculate his national insurance contributions for the tax year.

Andrew, who is also self-employed, has taxable business income of £48,000 for this tax year. Calculate his national insurance contributions for the tax year.

Feedback

Simon

Simon will pay Class 2 NI contributions of £153.40 (£2.95 ×52) as his earnings are over the small earnings exception limit for the year, and Class 4 contributions of £1,041.84 (9% × (£20,000 –£8,424)). These will both be collected as part of his self assessment payments.

Andrew

Andrew will pay Class 2 contributions of £153.40. His Class 4 contributions will be £3,446.34 (9% × (£46,350 – £8,424) + 2% × (£48,000 – £46,350)).

Benefits received

4.52 A full basic pension is paid to individuals who, for at least 35 years of their deemed working life, have paid at least the equivalent of the lower earnings limit contribution for the whole year, or 52 Class 2 or Class 3 contributions.

Some credits for contributions are available however, if you are registered as unemployed, are receiving job seekers' allowance, are unable to work through incapacity or disability, are in receipt of a carer's allowance or if you receive maternity allowance. People between 16 and 18 will also automatically receive credits if they do not pay enough contributions but this is not the case for anyone in full time education over the age of 18 (i.e. if you are at University, you only get the years of contribution counted if you actually make national insurance payments to the minimal levels, the same as for everyone else).

Taxpayers making Class 1 national insurance contributions at the higher rate are eligible to receive job seekers' allowance and earnings related (i.e. second) state pension which Class 2 and 4 contributors are not eligible to receive.

Impact of national insurance contributions

4.53 National insurance contributions are levied on earned income in addition to income tax – but not on savings or dividend income. This provides a distortion in the tax system between earned income and savings or investment income. A taxpayer with taxable income of less than £46,350 will have an effective marginal rate of tax (including both income tax and national insurance contributions) of 32% on earned income but either 0%, 7.5% or 20% on unearned income (depending on whether it is dividend or savings income). This anomaly may encourage those who are shareholders of businesses in which they are also employees to draw relatively low salaries and to pay dividends in order to reduce national insurance contributions. This question is discussed more fully in Chapter 11, as it is a common tax planning strategy.

Basic income tax planning points for couples

4.54 If one married partner's marginal rate of tax is lower than the other's it is tax efficient to shift income from the higher rate payer to the lower rate payer as this will reduce their combined tax bill. There are broadly two ways of doing this. First, investments held in the higher rate payer's name could be transferred to the lower rate payer. (No capital gains tax liability arises from a transfer between spouses as we will see in Chapter 8). These might include shares in a family business, in which case dividends on the shares would be taxed at the lower rate.

The second opportunity for shifting income from the high rate taxpayer to the low rate taxpayer is where one or both of the spouses are running a business. For example, it is possible to pay a wage to a spouse who also does work for the business e.g. deals with telephone calls and paperwork (although beware – this must be a fair wage for the work actually done or it may be challenged by HMRC). The alternative is to set up in business as a partnership in which case the other spouse can be allocated a share of the profits. A similar strategy can be adopted with adult children with low marginal rates of tax if they also help run the business. If a partnership is established then it is the responsibility of the partners to agree the profit-sharing ratio and HMRC will not challenge such an agreement. However, if a relative is employed by a sole trader, partnership or company then HMRC may wish to be satisfied that the payment is wholly and exclusively for the purpose of trade. In the case of *Copeman v Flood* (1941) a farmer employed his son and daughter as directors of the company and they each received a salary of £2,600. The son was aged 24 and had some business experience but the daughter was only 17 and unable to carry out the duties of a director. Both did undertake some duties for the company but it was held that the entire salary was not an expense incurred wholly and exclusively for business purposes. The Commissioners were asked to decide how much of the payments should be allowable based on the actual work carried out by the son and daughter. This established the principle still in operation now over 60 years later.

Couples may also wish to transfer part of either of their personal allowances (maximum £1,190) if these are not being fully used up by them as their income is below the personal allowance threshold. This is allowed from April 2015 as long as the person to whom they are transferring it is no more than a basic rate tax payer.

Further discussion of income tax planning can be found in Chapter 11.

Summary

This chapter has provided you with the income tax framework, which will enable you to apply the legislation discussed in later chapters.

In order to calculate an individual's tax liability it is necessary to undertake a number of steps:

1. Identify each source (component) of income for a taxpayer.

2. Use the income tax rules to determine the basis of assessment for each component of income.

3. Determine the income tax rules that are used to calculate the taxable income for each component of income.

4. Calculate the income that is assessable and determine any reliefs and allowances from that income that are allowed for tax purposes. This will enable you to calculate the taxable income from each component.

5. Now you can calculate the tax liability of a taxpayer.

You should now be able to review the example personal tax computation for Thomas we presented at the start of this chapter to check that you understand how the figure of Tax Payable has been reached.

Some possibilities for simple tax planning for families were also briefly discussed in this chapter.

You are now able to progress to the next three chapters, which build on the foundations that have been laid in this chapter to provide you with further details of how to perform personal tax computations. In turn they expand on the rules for taxing property income, income from employment and pensions, and income from self-employment (trading income).

Project areas and discussion questions

1. Until April 2005 the various categories of income tax were called Schedules, each of which had sub-sections to them called cases. These names have disappeared now for individuals as part of a process of re-writing the Income tax laws. Check out the role of the Tax Law Rewrite Committee who undertook this work. What was their motivation for doing this work?

2. The additional 2% extra NIC on earnings of employees over the UEL was controversial as it marked a move away from an upper cap on this charge/tax. Is this a fair way to raise extra money by the Government?

3. Does it make sense to continue to have a separate income tax charge and national insurance contributions payment requirement? Review the Office for Tax Simplification's work on this idea:

(https://assets.publishing.service.gov.uk/government/uploads/system/upl oads/attachment_data/file/567491/OTS_report_web_final.pdf.

4. Should unearned income also be subject to National Insurance contributions?

5. Is the tax credit system a more or less effective way to give targeted income tax reductions than previous methods?

6. Is it fair that Child Benefit is now restricted for higher income earners? What complications arise as a result of this interaction between the benefits and tax systems?

7. Does having a separate unit of taxation (i.e. everyone pays their own tax liability rather than combining this into family tax bills as was the case before the 1990's) make this a fairer (more equitable) system for all? Are there losers from charging income tax this way?

Quick quiz

1   Deirdre has employment income of £36,700. What is her tax liability for the year?

2   Benson has pension income of £28,650 and savings income of £1,500. What is his tax liability?

3   Candice has saving income of £18,850 and received dividend income of £2,500. What is her net tax payable?

4   Angela has non-saving income of £23,850 for the year and pays a patent royalty of £200 (net). What is her tax liability?

5   Dominic has earnings from employment of £21,215 and no other income. He makes a charitable donation of £500 under the Gift Aid scheme during the year. What is his net tax payable?

6   Erica has pension income of £12,350 and savings income of £500 for the year. What is her net tax payable?

7   Frank has net trading income of £33,350 for the year and receives dividends of £3,000. What is his net tax payable? What national insurance contributions are due on this income?

8   Geoffrey earns net income of £110,500 from a business and has no other income. What is his net tax payable?

9   Hillary earns net income of £73,850 from a business and has no other income. During the year she subscribes £50,000 to an eligible Enterprise Investment Scheme. What is her net tax payable?

10 Ivan is a sole trader and has taxable profits of £46,000 for the year ended 5 April 2019 with no other income. What is his NIC liability?

11 Josephine is an employee with a salary of £500 per week. What is her weekly NIC liability?

12 Kamran is an employee and is provided with a computer for his private use which is a benefit in kind and has a value of £400 for NIC purposes. What is the NIC liability in respect of the computer?

Questions

Question 1

Sam has the following income:

	£
Gross salary (PAYE deducted of £3,080)	26,850
Building society interest	2,000
Dividends (from UK company)	3,000
Qualifying charitable donation (gross)	880

Required: Calculate Sam's income tax payable for the tax year.

Question 2

Jasper received the following income for the year ended 5 April 2019:

	£
Salary (before PAYE)	67,500
PAYE deducted	15,000
Dividends	6,000
Bank interest	3,000

Required: Calculate Jasper's income tax payable for the tax year.

Question 3

Janet and Dave have lived together for two years. Janet earned £35,850 during 2018/19 on which she paid £6,500 via PAYE. She also received an annual bonus of £3,000 in August 2018 for the year ended on the previous 31 March. She received income of £5,375 in interest payments from a Building Society account in her own name. She also received £1,000 winnings from her premium bonds. Janet owns a cottage in North Yorkshire which she let from 1 October, 2018 at an annual rent of £8,000 payable quarterly in advance. Her allowable expenses on the property while it was rented were £1,000.

Dave earned a salary of £34,000 in the tax year 2018/19 from which his employer deducted £4,780 in PAYE. He also had some investment income of £3,750 from a bank deposit account and received dividends of £8,760 from UK shares.

Required: Compute Janet and Dave's income tax payable for 2018/19.

Question 4

Calculate the national insurance contributions due by both the employee listed below, and their employer:

a) Peter earns £550 per week.
b) Alan earns £240 per week.
c) Kath's earnings in the year are as follows (all for the same employer and all earned evenly over the periods given).

Jan – April	£1,500 per month
May – Aug	nothing was earned
Sept	£350 only was earned
Oct – Dec	£1,200 per month

d) Chris is self-employed. His adjusted profits for tax purposes (i.e. his trading profit) for 2018/19 were £27,600.

(Answer can be found in the lecturers' section of the website.)

Question 5

Zach is employed and has the following income and expenses:

	£
Employment income	48,350
Building society interest	2,100
National Lottery win	5,000
Qualifying charitable donation (gross)	2,000

Required: If PAYE of £7,300 had been withheld by his employer in the year, calculate Zach's income tax payable for the year.

(Answer can be found in the lecturers' section of the website.)

Question 6 (based on ICAS September 2010)

Mr Byte runs a successful software design business. His taxable trading income for the year was £193,900. In addition, he received the following:

1. During 2018/19 Mr Byte's accounts were credited with this interest:

	£
Building society accounts	17,250
NS&I Easy access savings account	9,800
ISA accounts	4,150

2. Mr Byte received UK dividends of £40,200 from his investment portfolio and £15,200 from Venture Capital Trusts.

3. Mr Byte made monthly donations of £200 cash under the Gift Aid scheme.

Required: Calculate Mr Byte's income tax and national insurance contributions payable for the year.

(Answer can be found in the lecturers' section of the website.)

Further test questions for this chapter to test your knowledge can be found in the student section of the website at:

http://www.taxstudent.com/uk

Further reading and examples

Combs, A., R. Tutin & Rowes, P. (2018), *Taxation: incorporating the 2018 Finance Act,* Fiscal Publications: Birmingham.

    – use this book for many other examples to further develop and test your knowledge of this chapter's contents.

See http://www.fiscalpublications.com/rowes/2018

5 Taxing employment and pension income

Introduction

5.1   In Chapter 4 you read about income tax components and you learnt that to calculate the tax liability on income it is necessary to identify the tax rules under which the receipt is taxed. In Chapters 6 and 7 you will study the trading income rules which are used to tax income from trades (businesses), vocations and professions (i.e. collectively – trading income) as well as the property income rules.

In this chapter you will learn about the detail of another set of key tax rules – namely employment and pension income under Income Tax (Earnings and Pension) Act, 2003 (ITEPA). We will not consider the other categories (i.e. savings and dividends etc.) of the Income Tax (Trading and other Income) Act 2005 (ITTOIA) in any more detail than was given in Chapter 4 which is sufficient for the level of knowledge we are aiming to provide in this book.

At the end of this chapter you will be able to:
- understand the tax treatment of employment income, including benefits in kind, and calculate an individual's taxable income from employment; and
- outline the rules which relate to pensions and pension contributions.

Tax on employment earnings

5.2   This chapter examines the tax rules relating to employees. Since employees form a majority of the UK's working population, the rules which apply to them are clearly very important.

Employment earnings are defined as "any gratuity or other profit or incidental benefit of any kind obtained by the employee if it is in money or money's worth". This will therefore include any bonuses an employee may receive, tips from customers if working in the kind of job where this occurs, and also any non-cash payments received (called *benefits in kind*).

Employment or self-employment

5.3   It is not always clear whether an individual taxpayer working in conjunction with someone else is in fact employed by them (working *for* them) or is self-employed (working *with* them). This distinction is important for tax purposes as it will determine whether the taxpayer is taxed using trading or the employment income rules. The total tax the taxpayer will pay on their earnings will vary, sometimes significantly, based on how they are classified.

To determine this classification an important consideration is the contract that describes the working relationship. If it is a contract *of* service, this indicates employment, and the taxpayer will be taxed under employment income rules as an employee. If it is a contract *for* services then this indicates a self-employed (contract) relationship and the taxpayer will be required to pay tax under trading income rules. As the latter usually results in lower income tax and national insurance bills, taxpayers, and those that hire, them often try to achieve trading status if they can.

A simple examination of the contract title alone is not sufficient and the content of the contract will need to be examined to look for the real relationship that exists between the person doing the work and the person or business paying for it. For example, parts of the contract may indicate:

- who has control in the relationship;
- who provides the equipment;
- whether further work must be accepted by the taxpayer;
- whether the 'employer' must provide further work;
- who is responsible for providing other staff to help the taxpayer;
- who bears the financial risk involved in the contract;
- who benefits from efficient management of the contract; and
- whether the taxpayer can choose when to work on the contract.

This list is illustrative, not exhaustive, and HMRC may be interested in other aspects of a contract in some circumstances. However, these are the key features most used and will give you the idea of how to approach this classification task. If the taxpayer appears to be suitably in control of the relationship, providing their own equipment, hiring their own staff, bearing the risk of the contract but benefiting from managing it well, and so on, then the relationship is a proper self-employed relationship. If the balance favours the grantor of the contract, then it is likely the taxpayer will be classified as an employee instead and taxed as such, irrespective of what those involved might prefer.

In recent years HMRC has examined more closely the range of occupations which are taxed under the employment income rules. For example, many individuals who work in television in the past were able to operate their relationships with their 'employers' as if they were self-employed. In many more cases than used to be so they are now considered to be employees and therefore taxed under employment income rules instead of trading income. The media industry is not unique however. These principles are applied across all industries.

The taxation of so called 'personal service companies' has also been caught in this trap. These are created when individuals set up companies with themselves as the only employee and with their 'employer' as their key client so as to benefit from being taxed as a company rather than as an employee. There are special rules dealing with personal service companies (the IR35 rules), which we consider in Chapter 11.

Activity

While you are reading this chapter and undertaking the activities you might like to try and identify the reasons for HMRC's tactics in wishing to have more people taxed under employment income rules rather than taxed under trading income rules.

In Chapter 11 we will look more closely at the implications for a taxpayer's tax bill of the classification as employee or self-employed.

If you want to explore further the various factors HMRC will consider in determining employment versus self-employment status you can now use an Employment Status Indicator tool on HMRC's website (https://www.gov.uk/employment-status-indicator). This tool asks you various questions, similar to those we have just been discussing, and then it will give you an indication of what the likely employment status is based on the facts you provide. This is a useful guide as to how HMRC are likely to view you.

Basis of assessment

Employees

5.4   As we saw in Chapter 4, in general, employment earnings (including benefits in kind which are non-cash payments related to employment) are taxed on a receipts (i.e. cash) basis, that is, they are taxed in the tax year in which the date of the receipt falls. In contrast, pensions and job-seekers allowance are taxed on the accruals basis (although the new Universal credit now being rolled out across the country will not be taxable).

Fiscal Fact

Excluding all Universal Credit receipts from tax, despite some of the benefits its replaces being taxable currently, is expected to reduce tax receipts to the UK Government by approximately £30 million per annum from 2014-15. Around 300,000 individuals who are moving into Universal Credit during its roll out are estimated to pay tax currently on benefits.

For all employees, other than directors, the date of receipt is deemed to be the earlier of the date on which payment is made and the date on which there is an entitlement to payment. This legislation is intended to prevent employees from transferring earnings, such as bonuses, to a tax year in which their marginal rate of tax is lower.

Activity

When might a taxpayer's marginal rate of tax be likely to fall?

Feedback

There are several possible reasons for a fall in a taxpayer's marginal rate of tax. These are most likely to be related to hours they work, or to changing tax rate bands or allowances. Firstly, he or she might suffer a drop of income, or an increase in allowable deductions, which reduces his or her highest rate of tax by dropping then into a lower income tax band. This might happen if, for example, they change their terms of employment to a part-time basis.

Secondly, since 1979 there has been a downward trend in income tax rates (in fact, when the 50% rate was introduced in Budget 2010 it one of the first increases to rates of personal income tax in many years – and this was itself then cut back to 45% from 6 April 2013 so didn't last long). In years where rates fall, anyone in the bands where rates drop will benefit from a lower marginal rate of tax. This principle applied, for example, from April 2013 for anyone paying tax at 50% on any of their earnings. There was an incentive for these people to move income receipts into the 2013/14 year if they could, as they would then have saved 5% tax on their earnings over £150,000 when the top rate of tax fell to 45%.

The same principle applies if tax bands increase while the taxpayer's income doesn't change as much. If the taxpayer is on the bottom edge of a band, increases in that band starting point could move them into the lower band thus dropping their marginal rate of tax to that of the lower band. This would also occur if tax allowances increase for those whose income then falls within the new limits.

Directors

5.5   There are additional restrictions on the date of a receipt for tax purposes if the employee is a company director who may be in a position to influence when the payment is received. Directors' earnings are taxed in the tax year which contains the earliest of the following dates:

- the date of receipt as determined by the above rules for all employees;
- the date when the payment is charged in the company's accounting records;
- the end of the company's period of account in which the amount arose provided that it had been determined by then; or
- the date on which the amount is determined if it is after the end of the company's period of account.

Allowable expenses

5.6   After determining what income received by a taxpayer should be subject to income tax in a given tax year, the next key question is what allowable expenses can they claim against this income? Allowable expenses are the deductions that a taxpayer can subtract from their income to compute their employment income and therefore reduce the overall tax bill on that income.

There are two basic rules to determine if an expense is allowable:

1. first, the employee must be obliged to incur and pay the expense as the holder of the employment. This means that it is the needs of the job itself that is important, not the preferences of the person doing the job. An expense will therefore only be deductible if every holder of the particular job would have to incur it. As such, it is said to be *necessary* for employment; and,

2. second, only expenses which are also *wholly* and *exclusively* incurred in the performance of the duties of employment will be allowable deductions. 'Wholly and exclusively' means that if an expense has more than one purpose, e.g. partly private, then the private part will not be deductible.

In practice, proving the first part (that it is necessary to do the job) is often difficult. Indeed, one judge in 1953 described the three part wholly, exclusively and necessarily requirement as 'notoriously rigid, narrow and restrictive'.

Some trade unions and associations have negotiated special allowances on behalf of their members to help employees with overcoming this problem in practice. These are typically for specialist equipment, such as safety equipment, that is genuinely necessary to carry out their jobs. For example, if you are in the agricultural trade you can claim a fixed deduction of £100 annually for specialist clothing and upkeep of your tools. If you are in the food industry this is £60 or in healthcare it varies with your job from £80 for laboratory staff or pharmacy workers to £185 for ambulance staff (a full list can be found in the HMRC manual http://www.hmrc.gov.uk/manuals/eimanual/eim32712.htm). These deductions are, of course, only available to workers who have to buy specialist clothing or upkeep tools to do their jobs – they will not be available to other workers in these trades or if the employer provides these items to their employees. However, in other cases you may need to negotiate with HMRC if you wish to get deductions from your employment income.

Key to making this system work in practice is the substantial amount of case law that is used to identify expenditure which is an allowable deduction for the purposes of employment income computations. For example, in *Brown v Bullock* (1961) the employee, a bank manager, was required by his employers to join a London club. Even though a case could perhaps have been made that this expenditure was wholly and exclusively used for business (not private) purposes, his subscription was held not to be an allowable deduction because it was not considered to be necessary for the performance of his duties, despite his employer's wishes. Therefore, all three parts were not satisfied.

In *Lupton v Potts* (1969) a solicitor's articled clerk was not able to claim the costs of his examination fees because the expenditure was held not to be incurred wholly and exclusively in the performance of his duties.

In another case (*Fitzpatrick v CIR*, 1994), the House of Lords disallowed the cost of newspapers bought by journalists arguing that buying and reading the newspapers was preparation for work rather than part of the performance of their duties. There are many other examples of similar case law.

Despite the lack of a specific definition in law of what is allowable in all circumstances, some expenditure is specifically allowed by law as a deduction from employment earnings. This includes:

- contributions to an approved pension scheme;
- subscriptions to professional bodies and learned societies approved by HMRC, provided they are relevant to the duties of the employment;
- payments to charities under a payroll deduction scheme (as we discussed in Chapter 4, Section 4.45);
- expenses incurred in performing duties and reimbursed by the employer (within limits) and
- capital allowances on plant and machinery if owned by the employee – rather than, as is more usual, their employer (see Chapter 7).

In practice, an employer will pay for most of the expenses you incur as an employee that are 'wholly, exclusively and necessarily' for your job. An employer will usually reimburse these costs to the employee and deduct them as an allowable trading expense as part of their own income tax, or corporation tax computation (as we will see in Chapter 6). In this situation the employee will have to declare this reimbursement as income and then seek a deduction for expenses incurred. This prevents abuse of the expenses system through employers reimbursing employees more than actual expenditure incurred.

Fiscal Fact

The estimated cost to the UK Treasury of allowing professional subscriptions to be tax deductible is £140 million for 2017/18. Much more significant however, is the cost of making contributions to approved pension schemes tax deductible – estimated to be £24.05 billion for 2017/18 (Source: 'Estimated costs of principal tax reliefs' – HMRC website)

Following are further details of specific expenses that are not always allowed as deductions.

Travelling expenses

5.7 There are special rules dealing with travel expenses incurred by an employee. These will often be paid for by the employer and where this occurs, the amount of allowance or reimbursement is included as income for the employee and the actual cost of the journey will then be deductible. Travel expenses that are not reimbursed by the employer may be deductible to the employee.

There are two main issues to consider here. The first concerns the nature of the journey. The basic rule is that ordinary commuting (travel to and from your place of work) and private travel (unrelated to your work duties) does not qualify for relief. The second concerns the amount of expense that can be allowed as a deduction. We will now look at these two issues in further detail.

Allowable journeys

5.8 It is important to be able to establish where you work (according to the tax rules) to know when you are travelling to get there (not deductible expenses) and when you are travelling 'for' work (usually deductible expenses).

Examples of travelling 'for' work that qualifies for relief include:

- From a permanent place of work to visit a client and back;
- Where the travel is a normal part of the employee's job, for example a service engineer who moves from place to place throughout the day; and

- Travel to a temporary workplace, such as a client's office, even if from home, but only so long as it is because of the nature of the job and not just for the employee's convenience.

Because of the complexity of travel related costs as tax deductions, and concerns over potential abuses that may occur, the rules on employees' travel and subsistence expenses were changed in 1998 to distinguish 'ordinary commuting' (which is not deductible) from other deductible travel. Ordinary commuting is defined as travel between home and a permanent place of work. So, travel to a temporary place of work will not be ordinary commuting and on the face of it will be eligible for relief.

This raises the question of what is a 'permanent place of work'. As a general rule, it will be somewhere where the employee attends regularly to perform the duties of the job. A temporary place of work on the other hand will be where an employee attends for only a limited amount of time.

However, to prevent abuse of the temporary place of work exemption, a rule is needed describing how long a place of work can be temporary for tax purposes before becoming considered a permanent place of work instead. If an employee is required to work to a significant extent at a place for a continuous period of more than 24 months, this place will be considered to be a permanent place of work. HMRC considers 'significant extent' to be at least 40% of the employee's time. So, if an employee spends at least 40% of his or her time at a particular place over a period of more than 24 months, there is no relief for the cost of the travel to and from that particular place as it then becomes part of ordinary commuting.

An employee may not have a normal place of work but may have a normal *area* in which they work. An example might be a district nurse who is required to cover a particular area but lives outside it. In this case the whole area would be considered to be the normal place of work and so costs of moving around in this area would not be deductible.

What if an employee doesn't have a permanent place of work? For example, 'site-based' employees have no fixed place of work but are required to perform duties at several sites by their employer. These are allowed to set the full costs of travelling to and from sites against their employment income. They can also obtain relief for subsistence expenses when staying at a site if that is required.

As you can see, this area of allowable expenses can be difficult to apply in practice. Attempt the following activity to see if you have grasped the basics.

Activity

Consider the following situations, drawn from HMRC Guidance on employee travel expenses. Will relief for the cost of travel be available?

(a) Dermot's employer sometimes requires him to attend his permanent workplace outside of normal hours, for example, on the weekend.

(b) Doris has worked for 5 years at her employer's head office in Warrington. She is sent by her employer to perform duties at a branch office in Wigan for 18 months.

(c) Ellery is employed as a financial adviser in Brighton. His employer sends him to an office in Bournemouth for one day a week over a 10 months period. He travels to Bournemouth directly from his home in Hastings.

Feedback

(a) No relief is available for Dermot because the journey is classified as 'ordinary commuting' i.e. between home and a permanent workplace, even though his employer requires him to be there after hours.

(b) Relief is available for the full cost of Doris' travel between home and the temporary workplace in Wigan (i.e. because her time there is less than 24 months).

(c) Ellery is entitled to relief for his travel to Bournemouth because he has gone there for a temporary purpose. He does not expect to spend more than 40% of his time there, nor does he expect to be going there for more than 24 months.

The amount of the relief

5.9   Having decided that a journey is eligible for tax relief by deducting the cost from the employee's employment income, the second task is to work out how much is deductible. As a general rule, the full cost of the travel will be deductible, regardless of the amount of allowance or reimbursement the employer pays. The cost of travel includes subsistence costs such as accommodation and meals that are attributable to the travel. It also includes car parking expenses, but not things like private phone calls, newspapers and laundry costs. An exception to this is when employees are required to stay away from home overnight on business. In this case, employers can pay for incidental overnight expenses up to a tax-free limit (currently £5 per night within the UK and £10 per night outside the UK).

Activity

Consider the following situations, also drawn from HMRC Guidance on employee travel expenses. How much will each employee be entitled to deduct?

(a) Mary has to travel on business. Her employer pays a travel allowance to cover the cost of a plane fare. Mary travels by train instead, which is cheaper.

(b) Mathew receives payment from his employer to cover the cost of a hotel, but instead decides to sleep in his car.

(c) Mercy has to travel on business and receives a travel allowance from her employer to cover the cost of a standard rail ticket. She decides to travel first class.

Feedback

(a) Mary is taxable on the full payment from her employer but can only claim relief for the cost of the train ticket.

(b) Mathew is taxable on the full amount received from his employer and cannot claim any relief because he hasn't incurred any expenses.

(c) Mercy is taxable on the full allowance from her employer, and relief is available for the cost of the first-class ticket, even though this is more than the amount paid for by the employer. It is the actual cost of the travel that is allowed as a deduction.

You might think that these rules are a bit complicated. HM Treasury agreed this might be the case and so they announced in Budget 2014 a review of travelling and subsistence expenses, following a report by the Office of Tax Simplification in January 2014. A Discussion Paper was issued in September 2015 but the responses received indicated that the current rules are generally well understood. Budget 2016 therefore announced that no further action would be taken to amend the travel and subsistence rules at that time.

Using your own car

5.10 We have explored the general rules for allowing travelling expenses as tax deductions, but what happens when the employee uses his or her own car? The question of whether the journey qualifies for relief is the same, but there are special rules for working out the cost of the journey, which could be quite complicated. To make the process simpler, the government has set out some rates of tax free allowance so that the employer can pay an amount to the employee to cover the cost of using his or her own car without creating a tax liability. The maximum rates payable before a taxable benefit will arise are given in the table below. These are called 'approved mileage allowance payments' or AMAPs. If they are exceeded both income tax and national insurance contribution liabilities (Class 1) will be created. The miles given are for *business miles* driven in a year (i.e. any private miles paid for by an employer will always be a taxable benefit).

If the rate of allowance paid by an employer does not exceed these amounts, then no tax is due on these payments and neither are any national insurance contributions required.

Type of vehicle	Rate
Car or van	45p per mile on first 10,000 business miles in the year
	25p per mile on excess over 10,000 miles
Motorcycle	24p per mile
Cycle	20p per mile

Employees using their own cars who do not receive any mileage allowance payments from their employers, or who receive less than the prescribed levels, will be able to claim tax relief on the difference as an allowable deduction against their employment income.

A rate of up to 5p per mile can also be paid (tax free) to the driver of the car if they carry a fellow employee as a passenger, provided they are also travelling on business. This rate will apply to passengers in both private cars, as discussed here, but also for company cars used for business travel. From 6 April 2011 this 5p rule also applies to carrying volunteers when reclaiming from volunteer organisations. This allowance, however, cannot be reclaimed as a deduction if the employer does not pay the full amount – unlike the regular mileage rates.

Activity

Fred uses his own car when travelling for his employer. During the tax year he drove 8,600 business miles. How would Fred's tax computation be affected if his employer paid him the following rates for his business miles:

a) 30p per mile

b) 50p per mile.

c) 4p per mile for the 2,000 miles he drove with a fellow employee in his car.

Feedback

a) This payment is below the mileage allowance rate Fred is entitled to. He would receive £2,580 (30p × 8,600 miles) from his employer but could have been paid £3,870 (45p × 8,600 miles) before a taxable benefit arose. He is able to claim a deduction of the difference (£1,290) against his employment income.

b) This payment is above the mileage allowance rate and so a benefit in kind is created. Fred will have to add £430 ((50p × 8,600 miles) – £3,870) to his employment income and pay tax on this at his marginal rate of income tax.

c) This rate is below the tax-free sum allowed and therefore no benefit would arise. He would receive £80 therefore tax-free. He is not able to claim the extra 1p per mile, however, as a deduction against his income.

We consider the situation where the employer provides a car for the employee to use later in the chapter under the heading of Benefits in Kind.

Other allowable expenses

5.11 There are a number of expenses other than travelling and the specific items listed earlier that may be deductible if they meet the *wholly, exclusively and necessarily* requirement. We will look at some of the more commonly occurring expenses in this section.

Phone calls

The cost of business phone calls made using a private phone are deductible, but usually no line rental for that phone can be claimed unless it can be proven to be solely dedicated to work related use.

Work clothing

An employee cannot claim the cost of work clothes, unless they are specialist or protective. In *Hillyer v Leeke*, the High Court denied the taxpayer a deduction for clothing that was 'ordinary civilian clothing...of the sort that is also worn off-duty'. In a 2010 case, the BBC television news presenter Sian Williams attempted to claim the cost of clothing, laundry and hairdressing as a deduction. The Tribunal held that she was not entitled to the claim, even though her work meant that she had to appear well dressed and groomed. The clothing was considered to be 'ordinary civilian clothing'.

Working from home

If you work from home by choice, for your own convenience, then the costs will not be deductible. If you are required or allowed to work from home under flexible working arrangements agreed with your employer you will usually be able to claim a part of your additional domestic bills (e.g. heating, lighting, business calls etc.). Further details on how this works in practice is provided in the exempt benefits in kind section below.

Education and Training

As a general rule, training is considered to be in addition to, rather than part of, the duties of employment and so is not deductible. In *HMRC v Banerjee* [2009] EWHC 62 (Ch) however, the High Court found that the cost of training courses paid for by Dr Banerjee was deductible. This was because it was a condition of her contract of employment with the NHS that she had to undertake continuous training which meant that in this case it was a part of the duties of the job.

There are a number of other examples of allowance expenses. A good place to review some others of these is on the Tax Guide for Students website – see: http://www.taxguideforstudents.org.uk/working/employed/employment-benefits-and-expenses/what-payments-and-benefits-are-non-taxable .
The full official list of the treatment of expenses from an employer's perspective is at: https://www.gov.uk/expenses-and-benefits-a-to-z

The area of allowable deductions from employment income is complex due to a lack of clear guidelines from legislation and case law. The 'necessary' rule causes many problems for employees seeking to claim tax deductions, often probably legitimately, for costs they incur in working for their employers but not fully reimbursed by them. Where many of these may be deductible if the employee was instead self-employed (the 'necessary' rule does not apply for self-employed deduction computations as we will explore further in Chapter 6, section 6.4), it seems a little unfair that they cannot claim the same costs just because their employment status is different. This rule is unlikely to change in the near future however, because of the substantial cost to the Government if it were to be more generous for employee claims for deductions.

Benefits in kind

5.12 In addition to receiving a wage or salary, many employees receive other benefits because of their employment. These so-called *benefits in kind* may include things such as subsidised lunches, non-contributory pensions, private health care, sports facilities, child care, company cars etc. There is an endless list of such benefits in practice, however, tax treatments for them all must be determined to create an equitable tax system. Any taxable benefit received as part of your employment must therefore be given a value that can be included in employment income calculations and either be exempted or be taxed accordingly. When computing a taxpayer's employment income, the value of all taxable benefits must be added to their wages or salaries in the tax computation. You have already briefly met the issue of national insurance contributions, which must also be paid on benefits in kind, in Chapter 4, section 4.10. In this section we will consider the income tax issues.

Fiscal Fact

It is expected that 3.76 million individuals received approximately £7.6 billion of taxable value in benefits in kind between them for 2015/16. In 2014/15 this resulted in a tax liability of £2.66 billion and national insurance contributions of £1.06 billion. Company car benefits made up 52% of the taxable value from benefits in kind in that year (£3.95 billion – producing an income tax liability of £1.37 billion and a national insurance contribution liability of £550 million), although private medical and dental insurance benefits had the largest number of recipients at 2.35 million. [Source: HMRC Statistics Table T4.1]

The tax treatment of some benefits in kind is dependent on the status (income level or office held) of the taxpayer while the tax treatment of other benefits in kind is independent of the status of the taxpayer. A limited number of specific benefits in kind are exempt for taxation, but not many. For most benefits, the general rule is that for status independent benefits, employees are assessed on the *cash equivalent* of the benefit. For status-dependent benefits it is *actual cost of provision* that becomes the benefit. This however, becomes the *marginal cost* if the benefit is provided to non-employees as well.

The cash equivalent is taken to be the amount that the benefit could be sold for once the employee has received it. This rule tends to operate in favour of the employee because benefits in kind may have either no resale value, for example, a travel season ticket, or a low resale value, such as the second-hand value of a suit or uniform.

For many years, the system of taxation of benefits in kind distinguished between 'higher income' employees and others, with the threshold being £8,500. This distinction was removed in April 2016 and all employees are now treated in the same way, in order to simplify the system.

Before considering the rules for determining the value of different types of benefit in kind for income tax purposes, we will first look at some forms of benefit that are specifically exempted.

Exempted benefits in kind

5.13 Not all benefits in kind are taxable. Some are specifically excluded from assessment to tax in the hands of all employees. This section explores some of the most common of these.

Sports facilities

5.14 In-house sports facilities for employees and their families do not have to be treated as a benefit in kind and are not therefore liable to tax.

Gifts

5.15 Employees are also not assessed on the benefit of any small gifts which are provided to them by third parties (i.e. not the employer) so long as the following conditions are met:

- the gift was not provided, or procured, by the employer or persons connected to the employer, (Note: a list of who are *connected persons* can be found in the Glossary); and
- the gift was not provided in recognition of services which have been, or are to be, performed.

If these conditions are met, the most an employee can receive tax-free by way of a gift from a single third party is £250 p.a.

Parties, functions and meals

5.16 Tax free benefits can also be received by employees for annual parties or functions provided by the employer. There is a limit of £150 per head for the exemption to apply. The figure of £150 is not an allowance; if the expenditure exceeds this amount then the full amount will be assessable, not just the excess over £150.

Meals which are provided in the employer's cafe for the staff generally are not an assessable benefit. A special rule provides that meals provided to employees on designated 'cycle to work' days are also exempt.

Long service awards

5.17 Employees are not assessable on non-cash long service awards provided that they have worked for the organisation for at least 20 years, have not received a similar award within the past ten years and the cost to the employer of the award is no more than £50 per year of service. If the award is made in cash, it is taxable.

Suggestions

5.18 Rewards for suggestions are usually taxable, but an exemption exists for awards provided there is a formal suggestions scheme which is open to all employees in a relevant group and all of the following conditions are met:

- the suggestion relates to activities which are outside the scope of the employee's normal duties;
- if the award is more than £25 it is only made after a decision has been taken to implement the suggestion;

- awards over £25 either do not exceed 50% of the expected net financial gain during the first year after implementation or do not exceed 10% of the expected net financial gain during the first five years after implementation; and
- awards over £25 are shared equitably between any employees making the suggestion.

If the award exceeds £5,000 the excess is always taxable.

Relocation costs

5.19 If an employee has to move their only, or main, residence for work reasons, and the new work location is more than a reasonable day's commute from the current residence, the costs of relocation paid for by the employer up to a maximum of £8,000 are not taxed as a benefit in kind. If expenses of more than £8,000 are paid, the employee will be assessed on the excess over £8,000 as a benefit in kind. Note that it is not necessary for a taxpayer to sell a house in order to qualify for this relief.

Child care

5.20 A nursery place at a workplace nursery (crèche) is not a taxable benefit. All other forms of childcare provision, including cash or vouchers, provided by the employer are generally taxable. Since 6 April, 2006, however, employees have been able to receive up to £55 per week (or £243 per month) free of tax and NICs for childcare so long as approved childcare providers are used. This scheme is only available however, where employers offer it and will close in its current form in October 2018 (although you can keep using the scheme once in it until you change employers or take an unpaid career break of longer than a year).

New entrants have not been allowed to join this scheme since April 2011. A new scheme was announced in Budget 2013 that began operation in April 2017. It is called the Tax-free childcare scheme. An eligible working family will get 20p contributed to their childcare account for every 80p they contribute up to £2,000 per child per year (i.e. equivalent to getting the basic rate of 20% tax back). A family will be eligible if one (or if two, both) parents earn less than £100,000 a year each (i.e. £200,000 combined), at least one earns more than £120 a week or is self-employed or on maternity or paternity leave, and do not already receive child tax credit or universal credit. This voucher scheme is available to all eligible parents, whether part of the previous scheme or not. For those in the old scheme they can choose which scheme they wish to continue to use – they cannot use both. It is available for each child they care for up to the age of 12 (or 17 if the child is disabled). The new scheme does not involve employers directly.

Working at home

5.21 Employers are able to pay up to £4 per week, or £18 per month, tax free, towards the additional costs employees incur when working at home (e.g. extra costs of gas, electricity and of business phone calls). These costs do not need to be supported by evidence, as is usually required, as there is a concession from HMRC for up to these amounts to be paid tax-free. If amounts over £4 per week are paid, however, they can still be tax free if evidence is provided of actual incremental expenditure resulting from working at home. If sums of less than £4 per week are paid then you can't get personal tax relief for the difference however.

Trivial benefits

5.22 In addition to the above, benefits in kind that cost the employer less than £50 per individual to provide, also became tax exempt from 6 April 2016 (originally announced in Budget 2014). This excludes therefore small gifts, such as flowers for a retirement or illness, from potentially becoming a taxable charge (for income tax and for Class 1A national insurance contributions) on the employee – although in reality many of these were exempted in practice before and as such this largely formalises a limit for this exemption.

If the recipient is an office holder in a business (e.g. a director) or is a close family member of one, a cap of £300 per individual applies for this exemption however.

Others

5.23 There are several others that are commonly found. These include:

- Free car parking space provided to employees is also a tax-free benefit, provided it is at, or near, the employee's place of work.
- Counselling or welfare services generally provided to employees are tax free.
- Goods sold at a discount to employees are tax free provided they are sold for at least a price that covers the costs incurred by the employer making the goods.
- Costs of providing electricity for electrically propelled company cars and vans, including the cost of providing a charging point at the employee's home.
- Health screening and medical check-ups provided once a year.
- No taxable benefit arises with benefits such as air miles or loyalty points that employees receive from employer's expenditure provided this is part of a publicly available scheme and not just given to them as an incentive, bonus etc.

- Broadband internet access is a tax-free benefit if provided by your employer for work purposes if there is no realistic way of distinguishing any specific private usage of this benefit. (Note, however, the cost of a computer to use this access is a chargeable benefit – as we will discuss further below).

Assessable benefits

5.24 This section reviews benefits in kind that all employees are assessed on when they receive them.

General rule – cash equivalents

5.25 The general rule for benefits in kind received by employees is that if because of their employment, an employee or members of the employee's family or household, receive any benefits, they are to be treated as part of the earnings and are chargeable to income tax under the employment income rules. The amount to be taxed as the benefit is the cash equivalent of the benefit (i.e. an amount equal to the *cost* of the benefit) less any contribution made by the employee to those providing the benefit.

The cost for this purpose is not defined in the tax legislation, but in *Pepper* v *Hart* (1992) the House of Lords found that cost should mean the marginal cost to the provider (i.e. rather than other possible costs such as the average cost) in circumstances where the benefit is also available to the non-employees. In this case the benefit received was school education provided to children of the taxpayer. The taxpayer successfully argued the value of the benefit was only the marginal cost of providing for an extra child and not the full cost of that place. This will usually have the effect of substantially lowering the value of the benefit to be taxed. Of course, if it is not possible to directly attribute any costs to the provision of the benefit to the taxpayer then there will be no assessable benefit.

Vouchers

5.26 Any employee who receives cash vouchers, credit tokens or exchangeable vouchers as part of the reward for their employment will be assessable on the cost to the employer of providing the benefit.

Accommodation

5.27 If an employee is provided with accommodation by an employer, the employee will be assessed for tax on the *annual value* of the property less any contributions made by the employee to the employer for the accommodation. This rule does not apply if the accommodation provided is *job related*, as defined below, or only made available to them 'temporarily', defined as the same period of up to 24 months we saw for travel costs benefit in kind rules above.

The annual value to be used in this computation is taken to be the rent that "might reasonably be expected to be obtained on a letting of the accommodation from year to year". This amount assumes the employee pays all the taxes, rates, bills etc associated with living in the property, but the employer pays to maintain the property. In practice, however, the annual value is typically taken to be the rateable value of the property, if this value is known, or a value estimated by HMRC if the property does not have a rateable value. The rateable value is the value used to compute the 1970s rating valuation for that property (i.e. the old valuation system is used from before Council tax was introduced).

If the property is not owned by the employer but is simply rented by the employer for the employee, the employee will be assessed on the higher of the annual value and the actual rent paid by the employer.

If the accommodation either,

- cost over £75,000 when acquired, or
- if acquired more than six years before it was first provided to the employee, its market value on the date it was first provided to the employee was over £75,000,

then the accommodation is classified as "expensive" and a further benefit is charged to the employee. This is equal to the excess of the cost of providing the accommodation over £75,000 multiplied by the *official rate* of interest. The official rate is the interest rate given by the Treasury for various tax related charges – particularly loans. This rate varies periodically, but the latest rate can be found by looking at the 'Rates and Allowances' section on the HMRC website. For the purpose of this book, for simplicity, we will use 2.5%. The cost of providing the accommodation includes the costs of any improvements undertaken before the start of the tax year as well as the purchase price of the property. If the property is only available for part of the year, the benefit arising is reduced proportionately.

If the accommodation provided is *job related* then there is no assessable benefit in kind on the employee (although if the employee is a company director, then they may still incur a tax liability as the rules for directors can be more stringent). Accommodation is job related if either:

- the employee is required to live in the accommodation for the proper performance of their duties, for example a caretaker; or
- the employment is of the kind where it is customary to provide accommodation or the accommodation is provided to enable the better performance of the employee's duties, for example a clergyman, farm worker, pub manager or policeman; or
- the accommodation is provided for reasons of security.

If living accommodation is provided because of a person's employment, then alterations and additions to the accommodation which are of a structural nature, or repairs which would be required if the property were leased under the Landlord and Tenant Act 1985, are not assessable benefits.

Budget 2017 announced a consultation will be undertaken in this tax year on employer-provided accommodation rules to bring the tax treatment of these benefits in kind 'up to date'. These rules may well therefore change in the next year or two.

Activity

George is provided with the use of a flat in Birmingham as part of his remuneration package for a new job. The flat cost George's employers £150,000 to buy and is brand new. George is a management consultant and the flat allows him to live in the city close to his office. George pays all the bills associated with the flat's running and makes a £200 per month contribution to his employer for the use of the flat. The flat has an annual value of £6,000. What is the accommodation benefit in kind assessable on George, assuming an official interest rate of 2.5%?

Feedback

George's use of the flat would not be considered job-related, it is just a benefit he receives that makes his job easier to perform, but it is not necessary to enable him to do his job (he could live elsewhere and still do the job as well). He will therefore have the value of this benefit added to his employment earnings when his tax bill is calculated. The value to be added is:

	£
Annual value of the property	6,000
Additional value	
(£150,000 – £75,000) @ 2.5%	1,875
Less George's contribution £200 × 12	(2,400)
Benefit in kind	5,475

Accommodation related expenses

5.28 Employees who are provided with living accommodation are assessed on the benefit of the accommodation. In addition, however, they are taxed on any other expenses which are paid by the employer which relate to the accommodation, for example, the cost of heating, lighting and of any repairs that are carried out at the employer's expense. They are also taxed on 20% a year of the cost of any furniture provided to them with the accommodation.

If the accommodation is job related, as we defined earlier in the chapter, a cap on these extras is applied – but some charge will still arise. The maximum assessment of the ancillary services is then set at 10% of the employee's net employment earnings. Net employment earning is the employment income assessment after any allowable expenses and pension contributions but excluding the cost of any ancillary services. If the accommodation is not job related, the taxpayer will be assessed on the full cost to the employer of providing any ancillary services.

A director can only claim to be living in job-related accommodation if, as well as meeting the conditions given above, he or she has an interest in less than 5% of the company and he or she is either a full-time working director or the company is non- profit-making or is a charity, unless the accommodation is provided as part of special security arrangements.

Activity

Alexandra has a house in Yeovil and normally lives there but she has been transferred to London for three years to establish a new branch of the company she works for. Her gross salary for the tax year is £27,000. She has been provided with a flat in Mayfair that has an annual rateable value of £1,000. In this tax year the company paid £5,000 in ancillary services. Alexandra made a contribution of £1,000 to these services. Determine Alexandra's employment income for the tax year.

Feedback

Employment income assessment: Alexandra

	£	£
Salary		27,000
Accommodation benefits:		
Annual value (not job related)	1,000	
Ancillary services – cost:	5,000	
Less employee's contribution	(1,000)	5,000
Employment income		32,000

Note that, had this accommodation been job-related, the annual value charge (£1,000) would not have been applied and the ancillary services total would have been capped at 10% of Alexandra's net employment earnings i.e. £2,700. Her revised assessment would therefore have then totalled £28,700 (i.e. £27,000 + (£2,700 – £1,000)).

Assets used by employees

5.29 If an asset is provided for the private use of a higher paid employee or a director then the assessable benefit is the annual value, which is the greater of:

- 20% of the market value of the asset when first provided as a benefit to an employee, and
- the rent or hire charges paid by the employer if the asset was rented or hired.

If the asset is only available to the employee for part of the year then this cost is pro-rated (reduced) for the proportion of the year they do have the use of it.

If ownership of the asset is transferred to the employee at any point a further assessable benefit may be due equivalent to the difference between the sum (if any) paid for the asset by the employee and the *higher of*:

- the current market value of the asset on the date transferred; or
- the market value of the asset when it was first provided to the employee less the total of the annual benefits assessed on the employee so far for the use of the asset.

Activity

On 6 April 2016, Edward was provided with the use of a computer which cost his employer £1,500. On 5 October 2018 Edward purchased this computer from his employer for its market value at that date of £500. What is the amount of Edward's assessable benefit for 2016/17, 2017/18 and 2018/19?

Feedback

For 2016/17 and 2017/18 Edward had use of this asset for the entirety of both years. His annual charge therefore was 20% x £1,500 = £300 per annum.

[Note – if the asset had been provided part way through the 2016/17 the first year's charge would have been adjusted to cover just the period it was available to him. For example, if it had been provided half way through the year, the £300 for that year would have been halved to £150.]

For 2018/19 – a half year's charge will be due for the period 6 April to 5 October – i.e. £150.

The further assessable benefit is difference between £500 and the *higher of*:

1. The current market value of the asset when transferred to Edward; or
2. The market value when first provided, less assessable benefits to date.

1) This is £nil as Edward paid the market value when the computer was transferred.

2)

	£
Market value when first provided	1,500
Less Assessable benefit (2.5 × 20% × £1,500)	(750)
	750
Less price paid by Edward	(500)
Benefit in kind	250

The benefit in kind Edward will have to add to his employment income in 2018/19 to be taxed therefore is £250. Adding the half year charge for the time before he acquired it personally (£150), this gives a total for the year of £400.

Cars

5.30 One of the most important benefits in kind, in terms of the number of employees receiving it at least, is the company car. All employees and directors are assessed on a benefit if they are provided with a company car.

Company cars became widespread during the 1970s for a number of reasons. The most important was probably the wages legislation in force at the time which attempted to limit increases in wages. Providing cars to some employees was a way of increasing the rewards to employees despite this legislation. Providing company cars to employees was extremely tax efficient at the time. The employer could deduct the full cost of providing the car and the employee suffered relatively little tax on the benefit. At that time the provision of a company car also did not then lead to an increase in the national insurance contributions of either employees or employers.

During the 1980s and 1990s, successive Chancellors amended the rules for the taxation of company cars and over a number of years the tax on this benefit has increased very substantially. While there may still be some limited tax advantages for some employees that encourage the use of company cars, the benefits are lower now than in the past. Employers are now required to pay national insurance contributions on company cars (under Class 1A – as we saw in Chapter 4) although employees are still not currently required to pay national insurance contributions on this benefit.

From 1994/95 all car benefits were assessed on their list price, rather than actual cost. This was to prevent abuse of the benefits in kind systems when car manufacturers quoted a higher retail price and then offered discounts. The actual benefit in kind was then calculated using a formula that was affected by the business miles driven in that tax year, the age of the car and any contributions made to the capital cost of the car by the employee.

Fiscal Fact

Approximately 940,000 taxpayers were recipients of taxable benefits in kind for cars in 2013/14 creating a tax liability of £1.3 billion and national insurance contributions of £530 million. The average taxable value of car benefit received in that year amongst claimants was £4,050. [Source: HMRC Statistics Table 4.1]

A major rule change related to calculating the benefit of using a company car was introduced in April 2002. The rules are based upon the CO_2 emissions of the car, rather than how it is used. The rates for 2018/19 are as follows:

CO2 g/km	Taxable % Petrol	Taxable % Diesel	CO2 g/km	Taxable % Petrol	Taxable % Diesel	CO2 g/km	Taxable % Petrol	Taxable % Diesel
0(EV)	13	17	115	24	28	150	31	35
51	16	20	120	25	29	155	32	36
76	19	23	125	26	30	160	33	37
95	20	24	130	27	31	165	34	37
100	21	25	135	28	32	170	35	37
105	22	26	140	29	33	175	36	37
110	23	27	145	30	34	180+	37	37

To use this table, of course, you need to know the CO_2 emissions level of your company car. For all cars registered after 1 January, 1998 these can be found:

- on the cars registration document (V5)
- from the dealer
- in car magazines (for current models only usually)
- on the Vehicle Certification Agency (VCA) website at http://carfueldata.direct.gov.uk/

Once you have found the emission level of your car you simply look up the percentage rate in the above tables to determine the benefit in kind for the year. The CO_2 level is rounded *down* to find the correct percentage. This percentage is then multiplied by the list price of the car when it was new, to give you the annual benefit in kind that must be added to the car driver's employment income.

You will see from the table above that diesel-powered cars have a 4% supplement over petrol-powered cars up to a maximum charge of 37%. This supplement was 3% to 6 April 2018 but was increased to 4% after that date. This supplement only applies to vehicles that are propelled solely by diesel (i.e. does not apply to hybrid vehicles).

For diesel cars, the rates apply irrespective of registration date of the vehicle, however, for petrol cars registered before 1 January, 1998 these rates apply:

Engine Capacity	Rate
up to 1400 cc	15%
1401 – 2000cc	25%
over 2000cc	35%

If the car is supplied with accessories that were not standard on the car when new then the cost of these must be added to list price of the car in this computation (unless the cost of the accessory is less than £100 in which case it can then be ignored).

The rates calculated by this system produce benefit in kind values for full tax years. If you do not have the company car for the full year these calculated rates are pro-rated proportionately for the part of the year the benefit is actually received. For example, if you only had a company car for 6 months of the tax year then only half of the annual benefit is taxable.

This system is designed to benefit people driving newer, lower emissions cars. It is designed to achieve the opposite of the old system which benefited older, higher business mileage cars. To take this even further, from 2020/21 a new set of rules for so-called 'ultra-low emission' cars will be introduced that will offer them a lower benefit charge than other cars.

Fiscal Fact

According to a Revenue press release, the reform of company car tax in April 2002 has saved between 0.15 and 0.2 million tonnes of carbon, which is equivalent to around 0.5% of the CO_2 emissions from all road transport. These reforms continue to have an impact on CO_2 emissions levels of cars. In 2017 the average UK new car was emitting less than 121g/km of CO_2 according to a report produced by the Society of Motor Manufacturers and Traders (SMMT). Today's new cars are 30% more efficient than the average car on the road. Approximately 75% of company cars are diesel and 23% are petrol (but only 46% of all new car purchases currently). While diesel cars produce less CO_2 emissions than petrol cars, they are now considered to be less environmentally friendly as they produce other harmful emissions.

If an employee must make a contribution to the employer towards the running costs of the car (not including insurance costs) this is deducted from the annual charge. Be careful however, as the payment will only count if made in the tax year in which the private usage occurred. If payment is made too late it will count against the next year's computation instead.

If an employee makes a contribution towards the capital cost of the car, this is deducted from the list price for the purposes of this computation (i.e. affects each subsequent year's benefit computation then as long as the employee has use of that car). The maximum capital contribution that be used in this way however, is capped at £5,000 even if the actual contribution made by the employee was higher than this.

Fuel benefit

5.31 If the employee receives any fuel for private use as part of their company car package, he or she is taxed on the benefit of the fuel in addition to the car charge.

If the employee makes a contribution to the cost of the fuel used for private purposes, but does not reimburse the entire cost, the assessable benefit is not reduced. Hence, if the employee is going to make a partial contribution it is more tax efficient if he or she contributes to the cost of the car rather than to the cost of the fuel as such a payment would then reduce the overall benefit charge.

What cost should be repaid to ensure that the private fuel is fully reimbursed to avoid this fuel benefit charge? HMRC helpfully publish guidance figures to help an employer ensure they collect enough reimbursement (called Advisory Fuel rates). The current guidance (from 1 June 2018 – these are reviewed quarterly) for petrol cars is:

Engine size	Petrol	LPG
1400cc or less	11p	7p
1401cc to 2000cc	14p	9p
Over 2000cc	22p	14p

The corresponding rates for diesel cars are:

Engine size	Diesel
1600cc or less	10p
1601cc to 2000cc	11p
Over 2000cc	13p

Lower rates of repayment may be acceptable to HMRC however, so long as evidence of actual costs is then provided and accepted by them. (Note – these rates are reviewed four times a year currently so you should check them on the HMRC website to confirm the current rates – search for 'Advisory fuel rates').

For any reimbursement to count in preventing the fuel benefit falling due it must also be paid in the tax year (i.e. by the 5 April at the end of the tax year) or a short time after this date or the payment may not be counted as a 2006 case has illustrated (see *Impact Foiling Ltd v HMRC*, 2006).

Fiscal Fact

Budget 2008 stated that the number of company car drivers getting free fuel for private use has dropped by approximately 600,000 since 1997 to around 300,000, in part due to these various measures being introduced. In 2014/15 there were approximately 190,000 recipients of fuel benefit in kind creating £250 million in tax liabilities and £100 million in national insurance contributions. The average car fuel benefit tax liability paid in that year was £1,370 and NIC liability of £570.

If the employee does not repay all the fuel costs related to private mileage, then an emissions-based charge has been used since 6 April 2003. To compute this charge, we use the same table on the previous page. Unlike car benefit itself (which multiplies the emissions level percentage by the car's new list price when it was new) the same relevant percentage is instead multiplied by a set monetary amount set for each tax year to go into the employee's tax computation. This amount is set at £23,400 for 2018/19 (£22,600 for 2017/18).

If an employee opts out of free fuel during the year, only the proportion (pro rata) of the annual charge will be assessable as a benefit. If the employee subsequently opts back in to receiving fuel paid for by the employer then they will have to pay the full annual charge – with no discount allowed for the opted-out period.

Activity

Sarah, a higher paid employee, had the use of a 1400cc, petrol-engined company car throughout the tax year. The car was first registered on 1 January, 2014, has an emissions rate of 148g/km of carbon dioxide and had a list price of £14,000 new (no accessories are attached to the car). Sarah contributed £50 per month towards the running costs of the car and £30 per month towards part of her private fuel. Sarah drove 18,000 miles in the year of which 70% is business mileage. Determine the benefit assessable to Sarah.

Feedback

The assessable benefit is therefore:

$$(14,000 × 30\%) – (£50 × 12) = £3,600$$

As Sarah only makes a partial contribution towards her private fuel a taxable benefit arises for this also. This will equate to £23,400 × 30% = £7,020. No reduction is given for her contribution towards her private fuel as it is not all paid back. Sarah's total benefit in kind cost related to her car is therefore £10,620 (£3,600 + £7,020). This should be added to her employment income for her tax computation.

It was very expensive for Sarah not to reimburse all her private fuel. If she had paid back the guidance price of 11p per private mile driven, she would have paid 11p × (30% × 18,000) = £594, or £49.50 per month. Not paying this extra £19.50 a month (£49.50–£30.00) therefore created a total of £6,426 (£7,020 – £594) as extra benefit which she could have avoided. She'd be better advised next year to pay back all her private fuel (unless she drives a lot more private miles).

Both of the charges for company cars given in the tables above are for full years. When the car is unavailable for part of the tax year then these rates fall pro rata to the time in the year the car was actually available to the taxpayer. Unavailable times obviously include before and after the taxpayer is allowed to use the car, but also if the car is not available to be used while being repaired for at least 30 consecutive days during the year this period can also be deducted from the benefit computation. (Note that no reduction is made if *you* are unable to drive the car, only if *the car* cannot be driven). [For an interesting case on this involving an antique dealer and a Ferrari, see the 2011 Tribunal case of *Michael Golding v HMRC* (TC01097)]

Activity

Jane, a higher paid employee, has an 1800cc, diesel-engined company car which was first registered in 2013 when it ha d a list price of £24,000 and produces emissions of 96g/km of carbon dioxide. Fifty per cent of Jane's mileage was for business purposes and she makes no contributions towards the cost of the car or her private fuel. Her car has no accessories attached. Calculate Jane's car related benefits assessable in the tax year if:

a) Jane has the use of the car for the whole year and drives a total of 4,800 miles during the year.

b) Jane has the use of the car only from 5 October 2018 and she drives 4,800 miles between 5 October 2018 and 5 April 2019.

c) She has the car for the whole year but has a satellite navigation system fitted as an accessory to the car (not standard) costing £250.

Feedback

(a) As for Sarah above, Jane's business miles and the age of her car is not relevant to the computation.
   The assessable car benefit is £24,000 × 24% = £5,760.
   Her fuel benefit for the year will be £23,400 × 24% =£5,616

(b) As she only had the car for six months her car benefit rate is halved to £2,880. Note that this calculation should ideally be done to the nearest day. Jane's fuel benefit will also be halved to £2,808.

(c)   The cost of the accessory must be added to the list price of the car in the computation as it is more than the £100 minimum that can be ignored, therefore the car benefit calculation will become a total of: £24,250 × 24% = £5,820 (the fuel charge is not affected).

Special rules for vans

5.32   For vans, as distinct from motor cars, special rules apply. If an employee is provided with a van in which they are allowed to do private motoring, he or she will be taxed on a flat rate charge of £3,350 for the year (£3,230 in 2017/18). As for other vehicles, this benefit cost is pro-rated if the van is only available to the employee for part of the year. An additional charge of £633 for the year (£610 for 2017/18) will apply if the employee is also provided with private fuel for the van (unless all of this fuel for private use is reimbursed).

Vans which produce 0g/km CO_2 emissions had a £0 van benefit rate for 2014/15 however, this increased to 20% of the value of the 'normal' van benefit rate in 2015/16 (i.e. was £630 in that year). It was held at the same 20% level for 2016/17 and 2017/18 but has risen further to 40% of the full van benefit rate (i.e. £1,340) for this year (2018/19). Unless the rules change again, there will be a further 20% increase for each of the next two years (to 60% in 2019/20 and to 80% in 2020/21) and then 10% rises will apply for the next two years until there is no difference between the zero emission and normal benefit rate (i.e. by 2022/23).

Van benefit charges now increases annually in line with inflation (RPI), since 6 April 2016.

These new rules have brought the benefit associated with private use of vans closer to that of other cars. It is suggested this was necessary to reduce tax avoidance that was occurring where employees are provided with vehicles that can be classed as vans just to reduce the normal tax benefit charge on cars.

The only way for employees who are drivers of company provided vans to avoid these rules is if they prove they do no (or very few) private miles in the van. However, these claims are carefully examined to prevent abuse.

Loans to employees

5.33   If an employee or director, or a member of their family, receives a loan which was obtained because of their employment and either no interest was paid on the loan for the year or the amount of interest paid on the loan in the year is less than interest at the *official rate* published by HMRC, then the employee will be assessed on the cash equivalent of the benefit of the loan. The cash equivalent is equal to the difference between the interest the employee has paid on the loan to the employer (if any) and the interest calculated at the official rate. However, a minimum level of loan applies before this charge is commenced. If the total amount of all loans the employee has received from the employer does not exceed £10,000 then no tax liability will arise (i.e. the benefit is therefore ignored for tax purposes). Once the loan or loans exceed the £10,000 threshold however, it is all liable for a taxable benefit calculation, not just the excess over this amount.

The amount of the loan for this benefit computation is normally taken to be the average of the balance at the beginning of the year and the balance at the end of the year, if the loan had been in existence throughout the year. Otherwise the balance on the dates on which the loan was taken out and/or repaid is used instead. Only complete tax months in which the loan existed are taken into account (a tax month runs from the 6th of the month to the 5th of the following month). Under this circumstance the taxpayer can also make an election for interest at the official rate on the outstanding balance to be calculated on a daily basis if they want to, which is obviously more accurate, and therefore could lower their final tax bill.

If an employee receives a loan that comes under the 'qualifying loan' rules for tax deductibility (e.g. typically to buy necessary equipment to carry out their job as an employee – see section 4.32 above) then no benefit will arise. Loans at full commercial rates to employees where the employer is in the business of providing loans, also give rise to no taxable benefit.

Activity

Harry has loans from his employer that have been in existence all year:
a) An interest-free loan of £50,000 which Harry used to finance the purchase of his main residence.
b) A loan of £1,500 to buy an annual season ticket for rail travel at an interest rate of 2% pa.
c) A personal loan of £2,000 at an interest rate of 3.5% which Harry used to refit the bathroom in his home.
d) A loan of £1,800 at an interest-free rate to buy equipment he needs for his job.

Take the official rate of interest to be 2.5%. Determine the benefit assessable on Harry for the tax year.

Feedback

Loan d) is qualifying and therefore does not form part of any benefit calculations. The other loans can be totalled to calculate the benefit arising.

		£
a)	50,000 × (2.5% – 0%)	1,250.00
b)	1,500 × (2.5% – 2%)	7.50
c)	no benefit as rate exceeds official rate	–
		1,257.50

Other benefits

5.34 It is not possible here to list and explain all the detailed rules relating to the full range of possible benefits in kind as so many exist; however, a number of other specific benefits in kind are worth mentioning briefly because of their relative importance for large numbers of employees.

Mobile phones

No benefit arises from provision and use of a mobile phone even if private calls are allowed and paid for by the employer. The 2006 Budget however, restricted this benefit to a single phone per employee, for their use only, to prevent possible exploitation of this benefit by the giving of multiple phones for use by an employee's family members, as well as the employee, on a tax-free basis. This restriction applies to all new phones issued to employees. Any money paid by an employer to an employee for the use of their own phone must be declared as taxable as normal (and will be taxed if reimbursements are greater than the cost therefore).

Computers

A second benefit worth specific comment is the loan of a computer to an employee for their home (i.e. part business, part private) use. Somewhat controversially and unexpectedly the rules for this benefit were changed in the 2006 Budget, and an exemption that existed then for the first £500 of this benefit was withdrawn.

Since 6 April 2006 the computer benefit is valued at the full 20% of the cost of provision, just like other loaned assets, to represent the private use element. This extra tax cost is only avoidable under these new rules if it can be proven that there is no private use of the computer of any kind.

For all other loaned asset benefits (other than cars) a rate of 20% of the cost when new applies each year as we saw earlier.

Scholarships

A final special benefit you may come across is the provision of scholarships. We saw in Chapter 4 that scholarships paid to employees for their own education are exempt from tax. The situation is different, however, when the scholarship is for an employee's family members. If a scholarship of any kind is made available to the employee's family the employee is taxed on the actual cost of the scholarship, except when no more than 25% of the award is available because of the fact the recipient is a family member of an employee (i.e. at least 75% of the amount needs to be available to any applicant irrespective of any family ties to the giver of the scholarship).

Pension Advice

With effect from April 2017, if you are an employee you can receive up to £500 worth of pensions advice arranged via your employer without a benefit in kind being deemed to have occurred (the cost of any advice above this level is however, taxable).

Fiscal Fact

Private medical and dental insurance is the largest benefit in kind by number of recipients at 2.35 million in 2014/15. This benefit produced £640 million in tax liability and £250 million national insurance contributions in that year.

Making Good

There has been a tightening of the rules on making good what would otherwise become taxable benefits in kind enacted as part of the Finance Act (no. 2) 2017. A firm date of the 6 July following the tax year end (i.e. by 6 July 2019 for the 2018/19 tax year) is now the cut-off date by which making good must have occurred for payments that would otherwise be considered to be benefits-in-kind.

You can see from this section that there are a number of benefits in kind that either have a low value, or are exempt from income tax. This gives rise to some tax planning opportunities for employers and employees. We will consider these, including salary sacrifice arrangements, in more detail in Chapter 11.

A summary of the benefits in kind treatment detailed in this section, together with some further examples, can be found as a handout in the student section of the website.

Termination payments

5.35 We saw in Chapter 4 that there are exemptions from income tax for certain types of payments received on termination of employment. When employment is terminated, the former employee may receive a number of types of payment for example, unpaid salary, damages, a payment in lieu of notice and compensation for loss of office. Some payments are fully taxable, some are fully exempt, and some are partly taxable, which can be confusing.

Fully taxable payments include unpaid salary, bonuses and payments made under a pre-existing contractual arrangement. Fully exempt payments include payments made where the employee has to give up work due to illness or injury, and statutory redundancy payments. Redundancy is where the employee has to leave employment because the job he or she was doing is no longer required.

Partly taxable payments arise due to a monetary limit on some termination payments, in particular those that are *ex gratia*, which means they are for gratuitous reasons and not a contractual entitlement. In this case only the first £30,000 is exempt. One complication that can arise is where the taxpayer receives a mix of payments e.g. statutory redundancy payment and also an ex gratia payment. In such cases, the £30,000 exemption is reduced by the amount of the statutory redundancy payment. From 6 April 2018, a reform to these rules came into force making taxable as earnings all contractual and non-contractual payments in lieu of working notice and requiring all employers to tax the equivalent of an employee's basic pay if notice was not worked. Employer's National Insurance Contributions would also become due on termination payments in excess of the £30,000 threshold under these proposals.

The following activity illustrates these rules:

Activity

Oliver was made redundant on 31 August 2018 and received the following payments:

Statutory redundancy pay	£1,600
Discretionary payment for loss of employment	£42,000
Payment in lieu of notice	£4,300
Bonus under employment contract	£5,000
Holiday pay owing	£1,200

How much (if any) is taxable?

Feedback

	£
Oliver's taxable redundancy payment is calculated as follows:	
Statutory redundancy pay – exempt	nil
Discretionary payment – partly taxable	42,000
Payment in lieu of notice – fully taxable	4,300
Bonus – fully taxable	5,000
Holiday pay owing	1,200
Total before partial exemption	52,500
Partial exemption (£30,000 – £1,600)	(28,400)
Taxable amount	24,100

Pensions

5.36 There are a number of different methods for dealing with income tax on pensions used throughout the world. What makes pensions different from other forms of income receipt is the fact that they are earned over a long period of time. Governments have to make decisions about whether to allow tax concessions:

- to taxpayers for contributions they make to their pension fund;
- for the pension fund as it invests the contributions and earns income over the years; and finally,
- for the pension income itself when the taxpayer eventually withdraws from the fund.

The rationale for giving tax relief for pensions is to encourage taxpayers to provide for their own income in retirement, so they are not entirely dependent on state benefits. The UK adopts an 'EET' method, meaning that contributions to the fund receive tax relief (i.e. payments into a pension fund are exempt from income tax (E)), the pension fund is exempted from income tax on its earnings (E), but the pension received is taxable once the taxpayer starts to draw it (T).

In the UK, until 6 April 2006, an individual could potentially derive a pension from at least three direct sources: the basic state pension schemes, an occupational pension scheme and a personal pension scheme. A fourth type of pension available to everyone, working or not, had also been available since 6 April, 2001, called a *stakeholder pension*. A significant change however, occurred for pension provision in the UK on 6 April, 2006. While the basic state pension entitlement continued, the other three methods of providing for your own pension were rationalised into what effectively became one scheme. The aim was to make pension provision easier understand, and therefore easier for more people to invest in.

The state pension schemes are funded from the Government's general funds, as discussed in Chapter 1. Entitlement to state pensions is determined in part by national insurance contributions made over your working life. Contributions to the state pension schemes via national insurance contributions have no specific income tax computation consequences, however, when state pensions are received on retiring, they are potentially taxable as part of a taxpayer's employment income. State pensions must therefore be added into the tax computations of anyone who receives them along with any other income when computing what, if any, income tax is payable (this is listed as 'pension income' and is treated like employment income in the tax computation). The current rate of payment for basic state pensions can be found in Appendix A.

After April 2006 the new pension structure relates to all other pension funds created directly by taxpayers during their working lives. We briefly review below the options now available to taxpayers for providing their own pension incomes. In all cases however, for your tax computations the treatment is the same. If a taxpayer is in receipt of a pension it must be added to their income tax computation as if it were an earned source of income. Non-cash benefits received as part of a pension are also taxable just like benefits received as part of employee incomes. The rules for taxing non-cash items are broadly the same as we reviewed in this chapter for benefits in kind.

Pension contributions are a tax efficient way of saving for retirement as the fact that pension contributions do not attract income tax makes them effectively tax deductible and what's more, deductible at the taxpayer's marginal tax rate. Therefore, higher (40%) or additional (45%) rate taxpayers get a better tax deduction per £1 paid into their pensions than do basic rate (20%) taxpayers. This tax deductibility is however, not allowed without limits, as we will see below.

From April 2017 a new benefit in kind exemption related to pensions has also been available. If you are an employee, up to £500 of advice can be received via your employer without creating a benefit in kind, irrespective of what level taxpayer you are. These cash sums have become important now pensions advisors (like all financial advisors) are now required to charge fees for their advice (rather than take commission on products sold).

For all taxpayers, from April 2017, a sum up to £500 can also be taken from your pension pot tax-free to pay for the cost (or part of the cost) of pensions advice. This is only available however, to people under the age of 55. This item, and the one above, can be used together by employees to create a £1,000 pot for obtaining advice.

A good source of further information about pensions is the Gov.uk website. For example, see:

https://www.gov.uk/browse/working/workplace-personal-pensions or
https://www.gov.uk/browse/working/state-pension

Current pension regime

5.37 Pension contributions have long been allowed as deductible expenditure from employment or trading income. This deduction has historically been allowed at the marginal rate of the taxpayer. This was introduced to encourage people to make personal pension provision, rather than relying solely on state provision, by making contributions effectively made out of untaxed income. Tax relief under the new pension regime is usually given to the taxpayer in one of two ways depending how the pension scheme operates.

Contributing to a pension

5.38 First, for an employee contributing to a pension directly through their salary (e.g. as they participate in their employer's occupational pension scheme) their deduction will be taken out before PAYE is computed to ensure that they receive the full tax deduction they are entitled to at the correct marginal rate. This is referred to as a 'net pay arrangement'. In this circumstance you will not need to make any further adjustment to their tax computation.

Second, members may receive 'relief at source' by making their pension contributions to a pension provider net of the basic rate of income tax. This is how self-employed taxpayers will typically make contributions. A pension scheme member, for example, who wanted £100 added to their scheme, would actually pay only £80. The scheme administrator then claims basic rate tax applicable to that net sum paid (in this case £20) from HMRC and credits the member with having paid £100. If the member is a higher or additional rate taxpayer, they can get the extra higher or additional rate relief (i.e. a further 20% or 25%) on their self-assessment return by extending the basic rate band limit by the gross amount of the contribution (i.e. using the same process we used for charitable donations, as shown in Chapter 4 section 4.45).

Activity

Bert earns £63,000 from his business in the tax year. He has no other taxable income. He makes a personal pension contribution in the tax year of £8,000 (net). What is his tax liability for this tax year?

Feedback

Bert's tax liability will be:

	£
Trading income	63,000
Personal allowance	(11,850)
Taxable income	51,150

The grossed-up pension contribution Bert has paid (£8,000 x 100/80) will extend his basic rate tax band to £44,500 (i.e. £34,500 + £10,000).

44,500 @ 20%	8,900.00
6,650 @ 40%	2,660.00
Tax liability	11,560.00

Fiscal Fact

The cost to the Treasury of income tax relief for contributions to registered pension schemes is estimated to be £24.05 billion for 2017/18. This is the largest non-structural relief provided in the UK underling how important the Government considers supporting pension provision in the UK. There are calls however, for a review of this sum as a significant percentage of this goes to the wealthier pension savers given the extra benefits they accrue under the current system either because they can afford to make larger contributions, or because if they are higher or additional rate taxpayers, the cost of these deductions fall due to higher tax relief levels they can claim. (Source: 'Estimated costs of principal tax reliefs' – HMRC website)

Fund and contribution caps

5.39 Under the current rules while there is no limit on the size of an individual's total pension funds there is a life-time maximum limit on the total size of the pension funds on which tax relief can have been claimed. This is set at £1.03 million for this tax year (rising from £1 million in 2017/18 – although this level was a reduction from the £1.25 million in 2014/15). If your total pension funds rise above this sum then a tax charge on the excess will need to be paid when the pension is taken. This is at your marginal rate for income tax whether you take the extra benefits as a lump sum or you take them as income (before April 2015 this was 55% if you took the benefits as a lump sum and 25% if you took it as income).

In addition to the cap on the overall size of the pension fund that can be accumulated, there is an annual maximum cap for the amount you (and your employers if they also make contributions on your behalf) can contribute to your pension funds each year and claim tax relief on the contributions. This is set at £40,000 for 2018/19 (unchanged for the last two years). This was much higher for 2010/11 at £255,000 but was dramatically cut by the Coalition Government that year and subsequently. If you wish to make contributions to your pension fund in excess of this sum this is allowed (there is no maximum that can be contributed) however, you will then be charged at your marginal income tax rate on your extra contributions so that they are no longer tax relieved (i.e. the excess effectively becomes like any other form of saving paid out of after tax income with no special tax treatment).

This £40,000 per annum cap is transferable to future years, if not fully used in any year, for up to three tax years. When a carry forward is claimed, all of the current year's sum must be used first. The oldest sums being carried forward should then be used before more recent ones. In this way, the maximum anyone would be able to contribute to their pension in a future period, and still get a tax deduction on the contribution, would be £160,000 – i.e. assuming no contributions had been made in the preceding three years since the cap became £40,000.

From April 2016 further cap restrictions have applied for those earning over £150,000. Their cap will be reduced by £1 for every £2 of adjusted income over this sum, to a minimum cap level of £10,000. Adjusted income here means income plus pension contributions.

Drawing your pension

5.40 Once a taxpayer decides to withdraw their pension they are allowed to take up to 25% of the accumulated fund as a tax free lump sum to do with as they wish. Until April 2015 the remainder had to be invested in a product called an *annuity* – that provides a regular (usually monthly) payment to the taxpayer in return for the lump sum they invested. This option is still available, but not compulsory now. The rate the annuity paid depends on:

- the amount of the initial lump sum invested,
- the predicted life expectancy of the applicant,
- the current stock market conditions.

This rate would normally be fixed for the remainder of the taxpayer's life so they have a fixed, known, level of income to rely on from then on.

From April 2015, more flexibility has been introduced to how these rules apply so that, for example, an annuity is now only one way to access these funds in future. You are also able now to draw from your capital held in your pension as you wish (for those in defined contribution pensions at least) and you pay tax only at your marginal rate of tax on the income (i.e. as you would if it was any other source of income).

If you have small pension pots, of up to £10,000 value each, these can be withdrawn fully as cash. Up to three such pots can be taken this way.

The minimum age at which a taxpayer can take their pension is 55, but they can delay this as long as they wish to enable their fund to continue to grow so as to maximise their tax free lump sum, annuity levels or the size of the pot from which they can withdraw capital flexibly. This flexibility is also important to allow the taxpayer to pick the market conditions that will give them the best long-term rate for their annuity, if they take one, rather than forcing them to take a lower rate just because the market conditions were weak at the time they reached a particular age.

Further, from April 2015, if a pension recipient dies before their 75th birthday, their nominated beneficiary can receive the funds remaining in their pension tax-free. If they die after becoming 75, the beneficiary will only pay tax on the remaining funds they receive at their own marginal rate of tax (or at 45% if funds are withdrawn as a lump sum – although this rate became their marginal rate of tax from April 2016). Before April 2015 there was a penalty rate of 55% that had to be paid by beneficiaries on funds they gained access to this way.

The Pension Credit

5.41 Additional pensions give recipients an additional source of income in retirement to supplement the basic state pension. As such they are an important part of an individual's financial planning, at least for those that can either afford to pay into them during their working life or have an employer who does it for them. However, a significant number of pensioners do not have these extra sources of income to rely on. A pension credit system is therefore in place to provide a minimum income for all pensioners.

Fiscal Fact

In August 2017 there were 1.8 million pensioner claimants (2.1 million including partners) receiving this credit, a fall of 1025,000 on the previous year continuing a trend since 2010 of fewer and fewer people claiming this credit. It is expected this will continue to fall perhaps by another 350,000 by 2022/23. [Source: Department of Work and Pensions Statistics]

The Pension credit commenced in October 2003 and operates with similar aims to the Child Tax Credit and Working Tax Credit we discussed in Chapter 4. Its aim is to ensure no pensioner lives on less than £163.00 a week (£159.35 in 2017/18) or £248.80 a week as a couple (£243.25 in 2017/18). Direct credit payments are made to qualifying pensioners to ensure this is the case.

Summary

In this chapter we have focused on the taxation of income from employment and pensions. Since the majority of the UK workforce are employees it is an important area of the UK tax system. The general rule is that, unless specifically exempted, every benefit received from an employment is taxable, with just a very few deductions allowable. There are some tax planning opportunities for employers and employees. These particularly include the provision of some benefits in kind and planning for retirement.

You have encountered a number of different forms of tax relief in this chapter and the previous one, and may well be confused about how they all work. The following table should help clarify this for you.

Type of payment	how paid	how relief is given
Charges on income		
Patent royalties	net	Deduct gross amount paid (step 2) Add tax to tax liability
Copyright royalties	gross	Deduct gross amount paid (step 2)
Interest	gross	Deduct gross amount paid (step 2)
Gift aid donations		
Gift to charity	as if net	Don't deduct payment. Extend basic rate band by grossed up amount (higher and additional rate taxpayers)
Pensions		
Relief at source	net	Don't deduct payment Extend basic rate band by grossed up amount (higher and additional rate tax payers)
Net pay arrangement	gross	Paid before PAYE is calculated so relief is automatic, i.e. doesn't affect the tax computation. If the salary figure you're given in a question is before this has been deducted, deduct from gross salary.

Project areas

The taxation of income from employment provides a number of interesting areas to research. One such topic would be to undertake a comparison of the taxation of employment throughout the EU. Another interesting area of research is the question of the impacts and costs of altering benefits in kind, for example, extending the existing tax relief for workplace nurseries to all kinds of child-care costs.

A topical project would be an investigation into the provision of private versus company cars or of private fuel by employers. It would be interesting to find out how the role and use of company cars is changing in the UK as a result of the new rules introduced for fuel and for car benefit, or how many employers pay for their employees' private fuel and whether their decisions will change as a result of the Chancellor's measures.

Given the recent introduction of various radical changes to the pension regime in recent years, and further major changes in 2011, you could also look at how these differences have changed the nature of pension provision.

Discussion questions

1. Is it right to tax heavy users of vehicles more under the emissions-based rules when they need to use their cars for work?

2. Is it right to impose the extra 'necessary' rule, not present for sole-traders, on employees for deductibility of expenses from their taxable income?

3. Is it appropriate that some benefits in kind should not be taxable? (e.g. mobile phones provided to employees).

4. What are the implications for individual taxpayers, employers, the Government and society as a whole of our current pension provision options? Is the reduced focus on state pensions appropriate for those who can and can't fund their own pensions? What are the implications of such frequent changes to the pension rules?

Quick quiz

1. Helena, who is not a director, receives a bonus from her employer of £5,000. She became entitled to payment on 31 March 2019 but agreed to delay receipt until 30 April 2019 because of cash flow problems being experienced by the employer. When will Helena's bonus be taxed?

2. Iain makes £125 worth of business calls on his (non-business dedicated) home telephone and pays line rental on this phone of £28 per quarter. How much of these costs could he deduct from his employment income if his employer doesn't reimburse him for these costs.

3. Julia receives a mileage allowance of 30p per mile and drives her car 3,000 business miles during the year. How much (if any) is chargeable as employment income?

4. Keith's employer supplies him with the use of a company house which cost £250,000 and has an annual value of £10,200. He makes no contribution towards the running costs, which cost his employer £2,500 for the year. How much (if any) is chargeable as employment income, assuming an official rate of 2.5%, and that the accommodation is not job related?

5. Lorna is provided with a diesel-engined company car with a list price of £27,000 and an emission rating of 216g/km. How much (if any) is chargeable as employment income?

6. Michael works for a Big 4 accounting firm. He joins the local golf club and uses the club to meet with clients. He pays for the subscription himself. Is Michael entitled to a tax deduction for this payment?

7. Nola works for a company that provides her, from 6 October 2018, with a DVD recorder that cost £1,500. What is its value as a benefit in kind?

8. Pauline is provided with a bicycle by her employer on 6 April 2018 for her private use including traveling to work. The bicycle cost the employer £975 when new and was transferred to Pauline free of charge on 6 October 2018, when it was valued at £500. What is Pauline's taxable benefit in 2018/19?

9. Quentin starts a new job during the tax year and his new employer pays for his removal expenses of £3,500. What is his taxable benefit?

10. Ravi's employer provides him with free car parking close to the building where he works. If he had to pay for the parking, it would cost Ravi £700 p.a. What is his taxable benefit?

11. Sumo has earnings from a business of £85,500 for the tax year and no other income. She pays personal pension contributions of £7,200 (net). What is her income tax liability?

12. Tiffany has employment income of £30,850 (gross). Her contribution to the occupational pension scheme is £5,000. His employer contributes £2,000. What is her income tax payable?

Questions

Question 1 (based on ACCA December 2007).

Serene Volley is employed as a sports journalist by Backhand plc, a newspaper publishing company. During the tax year 2018/19 she was paid a gross annual salary of £26,400. Income tax of £4,190 was deducted from this under PAYE.

Throughout the tax year 2018/19, Backhand plc provided Serene with a petrol-powered car that has a list price of £16,400. The official CO_2 emission rate for the car is 142g/km. The company did not provide Serene with any fuel for private journeys. Serene contributed 5% of her gross salary of £26,400 into Backhand plc's HMRC registered occupational pension scheme. In addition to her employment income, Serene received interest of £1,200 on the maturity of a savings certificate from the National Savings & Investments Bank during the tax year 2018/19. This was the actual cash amount received.

Required: Calculate the income tax payable by Serene for the tax year 2018/19.

Question 2 (based on ACCA June 2008).

Kim White is employed as a sales person by Sharp-Suit plc, a clothing manufacturing company. During the tax year 2018/19 she was paid a gross annual salary of £21,600.

On 1 June 2018, Sharp-Suit plc provided Kim with an interest free loan of £18,750 so that she could purchase a new car. During the period from 1 June 2018 to 5 April 2019, Kim used her private car for business and private purposes. She received no reimbursement from Sharp-Suit for any of the expenditure incurred. Kim's mileage during this period included the following travel:

Normal daily travel between home and permanent workplace	3,400
Between permanent workplace and Sharp-Suit plc's customers	9,200
Between home and a temporary workplace for one month	1,300

During the tax year 2018/19, Kim paid interest of £140 (gross) on a personal loan taken out on 1 January 2019 to purchase a laptop computer for use in her employment with Sharp-Suit plc. Kim received building society interest totalling £750 during the year, which was the actual cash amount received.

Required: Calculate Kim's income tax liability for the tax year 2018/19 (before PAYE). Assume an official interest rate of 2.5%. You should ignore any capital allowance that Kim might be entitled to.

Question 3 (based on ACCA June 2009).

Domingo and Erigo Gomez are brothers. The following information is available for the tax year 2018/19:

Domingo Gomez
1. Domingo is aged 78
2. During the tax year he received a state pension of £6,082 and a private pension of £3,480.
3. In addition to his pension income, Domingo received building society interest of £18,160 and interest of £600 on the maturity of a savings certificate from the National Savings and Investments Bank during the tax year. These were the actual cash amounts received.
4. During the tax year Domingo made donations of £300 (gross) to local charities. They were not made under the gift aid scheme.

Erigo Gomez

1. Erigo is aged 66.
2. He is employed as a business journalist by Economical plc, a magazine publishing company. During the tax year Erigo was paid a gross annual salary of £36,000.
3. During the tax year, Erigo used his private car for business purposes. He drove 18,000 miles in the performance of his duties for Economical plc, for which the company paid an allowance of 20p per mile.
4. During June 2018, Economical plc paid £11,400 towards the cost of Erigo's relocation when he was required to move his place of employment. Erigo's previous main residence was 140 miles from his new place of employment with the company. The £11,400 covered the cost of disposing of Erigo's old property and of acquiring a new property.
5. Erigo contributed 6% of his gross salary of £36,000 into Economical's HMRC registered occupational pension scheme.
6. During the tax year, Erigo donated £100 (gross) per month to charity under the payroll deduction scheme.

Tax returns

For the tax year 2018/19, Domingo wants to file a paper self-assessment tax return and have HMRC prepare a self-assessment on his behalf. Erigo wants to file an online return.

Required:

(a) Calculate the respective income tax liabilities for the tax year 2018/19 of Domingo and Erigo.
(b) Advise Domingo and Erigo of the latest date by which their respective self-assessment tax returns for the tax year 2018/19 will have to be submitted given their stated filing preferences.
(c) Advise Domingo and Erigo as to how long they must retain their records used in preparing their respective tax returns for the tax year 2018/19, and the potential consequences of not retaining the records for the required period.

Question 4 (based on ACCA December 2014).

Edward King is trying to calculate his tax liability for the tax year 2018/19 and the following information is available:

1. Edward was born on 29 October 1951 and is employed by Stately Ltd as a marketing director. During the tax year 2018/19 he was paid gross director's remuneration of £179,000.

2. On 1 December 2018, Stately Ltd provided Edward with an interest-free loan of £87,000, which he used to purchase a holiday cottage.

3. Stately Ltd has provided Edward with a home entertainment system for his personal use since 6 April 2015. The home entertainment system had been purchased by Stately Ltd on 6 April 2015 for £5,200. The company gave the home entertainment system to Edward on 6 April 2018 for no charge, although its market value at that time was £2,200.

4. During the tax year 2018/19, Edward contributed 4% of his gross director's remuneration of £179,000 into Stately Ltd's HMRC registered occupational pension scheme. The company contributed a further 6% on his behalf.

5. During the tax year 2018/19, Edward donated £200 (gross) per month to charity under the payroll deduction scheme.

6. During the tax year 2018/19 Edward used his private motor car for business purposes. He drove 12,000 miles in the performance of his duties for Stately Ltd, for which the company paid an allowance of 35 pence per mile.

7. On 1 January 2019, Edward paid a professional subscription of £240 to the Guild of Marketing, an HMRC approved professional body.

8. For the tax year 2018/19, Stately Ltd deducted a total of £62,600 in PAYE from Edward's earnings.

Required: Calculate Edward King's tax liability for the tax year 2018/19. He has no other income or expenses for the year.

Question 5 (based on ICAS TPS Tax Paper December 2010).

Jon was working as a dentist in a long established local practice but was recently offered an exciting new job at a dental research company. He left the dental practice on 5 April 2018 and started his new job the following day. Details of Jon's new salary and benefits are given below, together with details of his other income.

Salary

Jon started his new job on 6 April 2018. His annual salary is £110,000 (gross). In addition, the company will make contributions to its approved pension scheme of 6% per annum, while Jon will make employee contributions of 5% per annum. Jon has advised you that monthly PAYE of £3,000 was deducted from his salary.

Benefits

- The company has provided Jon with a diesel BMW 1 Series company car. It has CO_2 emissions of 55g/km and its list price is £21,000. Optional extras which Jon asked the company to add to the car totalled £800. Jon's local garage was offering the same car (with extras) at a cost of £20,500. The company have agreed to meet the cost of Jon's fuel. The car was made available from 6 April 2018.

- Jon has been provided with a laptop, which he uses for both business and private purposes. He estimates that his private use will be approximately 50%. The laptop cost £950 when he was given it on 1 June 2018.

- Jon was provided with an iPhone which he uses principally for business. The rental is £15 per month and it cost £150. He has had use of the iPhone since the first day of his employment.

- Jon and his wife travelled to Paris for a weekend in the middle of November where Jon attended an introductory company conference. Other than attending the end of conference dinner, Jon's wife was free to shop and sightsee. Travel and expenses met by the company amounted to £850 each.

Other receipts

Jon received the following amounts in 2018/19:	£
UK dividends	20,000
Bank interest	800
Interest on ISA account	1,500
Premium bond winnings (received in May 2018)	1,000

Required: Calculate the income tax payable by Jon for the tax year 2018/19.

(Note: answer available via lecturer's website)

Question 6 (based on ACCA December 2008).

Peter Chic is employed by Haute-Couture Ltd as a fashion designer. The following information is available for the tax year 2018/19:

1. During the tax year Peter was paid a gross annual salary of £45,600 by Haute-Couture Ltd. Income tax of £15,558 was deducted from this figure under PAYE.

2. In addition to his salary, Peter received two bonus payments from Haute-Couture Ltd during the tax year. The first bonus of £4,300 was paid on 30 April 2018 and was in respect of the year ended 31 December 2017. Peter became entitled to this bonus on 10 April 2018. The second of £3,600 was paid on 31 March 2019 and was in respect of the year ended 31 December 2018. Peter became entitled to this second bonus on 25 March 2019.

3. Throughout the tax year, Haute-Couture Ltd provided Peter with a diesel car which has a list price of £22,500. The car cost Haute-Couture £21,200, and it has an official CO_2 emissions rate of 232g/km. Peter made a capital contribution of £2,000 towards the cost of the car when it was first provided to him. Haute-Couture Ltd also provided Peter with fuel for private journeys.

4. Haute-Couture Ltd has provided Peter with living accommodation since 1 January 2009. The company had purchased the property in 2007 for £160,000, and it was valued at £185,000 on 1 January 2018. Improvements costing £13,000 were made to the property during June 2015. The annual value of the property is £9,100.

5. Throughout the tax year Haute-Couture Ltd provided Peter with two mobile telephones. The telephones had each cost £250 when purchased by the company in January 2015.

6. On 5 May 2018, Haute-Couture Ltd paid a health club membership fee of £510 for the benefit of Peter.

7. During June 2018, Peter spent five nights overseas on company business. Haute-Couture paid Peter a daily allowance of £10 to cover the cost of personal expenses such as telephone calls to his family.

Other information:

1. During the tax year Peter received building society interest of £2,200 and dividends of £800.

2. On 4 August 2018, Peter received a premium bond prize of £100.

3. During the tax year Peter made gift aid donations totalling £2,340 (net) to national charities.

Required: Calculate the income tax payable by Peter Chic for the tax year 2018/19. Assume the official rate of interest is 2.5%.

(*Note: answer available via lecturer's website*)

 Further test questions for this chapter to test your knowledge can be found in the student section of the website at:

http://www.taxstudent.com/uk

Further reading and examples

Combs, A., R. Tutin & Rowes, P. (2018), *Taxation: incorporating the 2018 Finance Act*, Fiscal Publications: Birmingham.
 – use this book for many other examples to further develop and test your knowledge of this chapter's contents. See http://www.fiscalpublications.com/rowes/2018

Full guidance on the taxation of expenses and benefits in kind can be found in Tax Guide 480(2013) – see http://www.hmrc.gov.uk/guidance/480.pdf

6 Taxing trading and property income

Introduction

6.1 In this chapter and the next we will study the taxation of unincorporated businesses, which are businesses that are not run as limited liability companies, focussing on taxation of sole traders. Unincorporated businesses are not treated as separate taxable entities for tax purposes. Rather, in the case of a sole trader, the trading income rules are used to determine the taxable income resulting from their business activities so that this can then be included in the taxpayer's tax computation alongside any other income categories they have to pay tax on for the tax year.

As property income is also calculated using similar rules to trading income, the final section of this chapter reviews this component of income.

At the end of this chapter you will be able to:
- state the badges of trade and use them to identify trading activities;
- identify income that is chargeable and expenses which are deductible under the trading income rules;
- convert accounting profits into trading profits for tax purposes; and
- compute property income and discuss the special property related tax schemes currently in operation.

Introduction to the trading income rules

6.2 In Chapter 4 we discussed how income taxed by direct assessment is assessed for tax purposes. Such income is taxed under one or other of the various tax categories. The basis of assessment that applies, and other rules to determine how much tax will be due on the income, depends on which category the income is assessed under. We saw in Chapter 5 how income from your job is taxed under the employment income rules. Income from a trade or business and income from a vocation or profession are taxed under the *trading income* rules. There are some small differences in the way that the tax due is calculated for trade and vocation/professional incomes (we'll meet one later as an illustration), but for our purposes we can treat them as being the same.

Although we focus on sole traders, many of the rules also apply to partnerships as the other form of unincorporated business structure.

We will not discuss the rules for partnership income tax in more detail in this book however you can find information and worked examples on our website.

Many of the trading and property income rules also apply to companies, with some modifications that we will discuss further in Chapter 9.

There are approximately 4.8 million people, or about 15% of the current working population, who are self-employed and therefore are taxed under the trading income rules (Source: ONS – Trends in self-employment in the UK, February 2018). They pay a total of approximately £30 billion in taxes each year (Source: HMRC Income tax receipts, Table 2.8). While some trading taxpayers run large businesses, many are running relatively small undertakings where they may be the only person working in the business or where there are only a handful of other employees.

Fiscal Fact

The Department for Business, Energy and Industrial Strategy reported in November 2017, there were an estimated 5.7 million private sector enterprises in the UK at the start of 2017. This is 2.2 million (or 64%) more than at the start of 2000 (although 89% of this growth is in the form of non-employing businesses – i.e. they have no employees listed working for these businesses). The total number of businesses increased by approximately 197,000 between the start of 2016 and the start of 2017. These businesses employed 26.7 million people and had an estimated combined turnover of £3.74 trillion. The same report said that almost 2/3rds of these businesses (3.4 million or 60%) were sole traders, 33% (1.9 million) were companies and 7% (414,000) were partnerships. Taken together, small and medium sized enterprises count for 99.9% of all businesses. (Source: Business Population Estimates for the UK and Regions 2017 - Statistical Release November 2017)

This large number of business can be split into three groups for the purposes of determining how they must account for tax on their profits:

1. All larger businesses, sole traders and partners are assessed on the profits which arise in the business' accounting period that ends during the tax year being assessed. Before April 2013 this was always computed in the same way for all businesses, whatever their size, using generally accepted

accounting principles where receipts and expenditure are matched to the period on an accruals basis, whether or not they had been received or paid. Adjustments are then made for any receipts or payments that relate to a different period. For many businesses this remains the way which they account for their tax liabilities.

2. From 6 April 2013 smaller businesses have been able to opt to use cash accounting rules (the so called 'cash basis') to compute their tax liability (and from April 2017 this has in fact become the default approach for many individuals operating a property business). This option is available to businesses with a *turnover* below the current VAT registration threshold (£85,000) (or £150,000 if a property business) who are not benefiting from limited liability (as a company or partnership). We will review these rules in more detail in section 6.6 and 6.46.

3. New rules commencing in 2017/18 actually allow the very smallest of businesses (those with a turnover of less than £1,000) to not have to file tax returns on this income and not to have to pay any tax on it at all. We introduced this new 'trading allowance' rule in section 4.37 that in effect means where an entity that would normally be subject to trading income tax has a turnover of less than £1,000, this can be completely covered by the new allowance and no tax becomes due. This excludes the very smallest of business from having to use either the cash-basis or the accruals-basis to compute their profits.

Most businesses continue to use an accruals based accounting system (i.e. group 1 above) to determine their tax liability. This is therefore the system we will focus on in this chapter but some details of the cash basis approach are also provided (see section 6.6 and 6.46).

Before any taxable profit under the trading income rules can be calculated (i.e. if the business is in any of the groups above) it is first necessary to demonstrate that trading is actually taking place. In this chapter we will review the principles referred to as the *badges of trade*, which are used to determine this. Once the existence of trading has been established, you will then need to undertake at least two steps in order to determine the trading income for a tax year. These are:

1. determine which of the trader's accounts will form the basis period for the tax year; and

2. adjust the accounting profits to derive the tax adjusted trading profits.

In order to fully determine the trading income, for tax purposes you may need to establish the tax implications of any investment in capital assets, so we will look at those rules in the next chapter.

Once you have computed the tax adjusted trading profits, you can add this amount to the tax computation to determine the total income (or it can be ignored in this computation if the business falls under group 3 above). The Thomas Lester example at the beginning of Chapter 4 showed you how to do this. Look back to this illustration if you need to be reminded which number we are now working towards determining.

Identification of trading activities

6.3   The first thing for us to do is to consider when an activity is 'trading' and so is subject to trading income rules. The definition of 'trade' is quite wide and is defined to include 'any venture in the nature of trade' (ITA s989). This brings some isolated (single, or 'one-off') transactions within the concept of 'trade'.

For anyone who is not an employee, it is very important to determine whether money received in conjunction with carrying out an activity is trading income or not, as this could significantly affect how much tax is due.

Before 1965, if a receipt was determined not to be trading income then it was likely to be a *capital gain* (meaning simply, selling something for more than its purchase price). At that time capital gains were not taxable and therefore obtaining receipts in this form was a tax free source of increased wealth. Since 1965 however, capital gains have been taxable in the UK. Until 1988 capital gains were taxed at the single rate of 30%. This rate was often lower than the taxpayer's marginal rate of tax and so even after 1965 there was an advantage to having a receipt of money classed as a capital gain.

Between 1988 and 2008, this distinction became less important because capital gains were taxed at the taxpayer's marginal rate of income tax and so the amount of the tax saving resulting from the classification of the receipt as being outside of trading income largely disappeared. This has now re-appeared following Budget 2008 which created a new single rate of tax for capital gains tax for individuals (currently at 10%, but at 18% until April 2016) – a rate which provides a lower marginal rate of tax than for income receipts for most taxpayers (we will discuss how to tax capital gains in more detail in Chapter 8). This distinction was reduced in the 2010 Budget with the introduction of a second capital gains tax rate (at 20% but at 28% until April 2016) for higher/ additional rate income tax payers, however, this still remains below their marginal rate of tax on income, so doesn't completely remove this continued benefit.

Because of these different potential tax rates, it is important to know whether trading is occurring, or some other type of activity (e.g. just a hobby or one-off activity), so that the correct method of taxing this activity is applied. For example, if you bought and sold a number of works of art or collectables (e.g. perhaps on Ebay or via newspaper ads), at what point would this go from being a hobby or occasional pastime (on which you may have to pay capital gains tax if you sell anything for more than you bought it for, but no income tax) to being a 'trade' you are engaged in (which is then subject to trading income tax rules)?

For most of us hobbies cost money rather than make money; the tax system will not give us tax relief on any losses (e.g. costs) related to hobbies, however, relief is often available for costs/'losses' incurred when trading. Correct classification is therefore important for a variety of reasons.

Unhelpfully, the UK tax legislation does not give us a neat definition of what constitutes trading. We must therefore look to case law or other sources of tax principles, for guidance in determining whether trading is taking place.

Often the decision whether trading is occurring or not is fairly clear cut e.g. if the taxpayer is running a shop and selling goods to the public, they will very likely be considered to be trading for tax purposes. But, where doubt exists, and in the extreme where there is perhaps only a one-off transaction occurring, a mechanism is needed to confirm if activities (one-off and other) can be taxed as trading income. In 1955 a Royal Commission (Cmd 9474) reviewed the existing case law in this area, particularly on one-off transactions, and drew together the principles applied by the courts when considering cases of whether trading was occurring or not. These principles (six in total) have become known as the 'badges of trade'.

None of the six badges offer a conclusive test of trading by themselves, although some are stronger indicators than others in practice. If trading is taking place it is likely that there will be evidence of this in more than one 'badge'. HMRC use these tests in deciding whether they agree with a claim made by a taxpayer to be trading, or not. If they disagree with the taxpayer's assessment, they may challenge this opinion and seek to tax them on that activity differently.

Badges of trade

6.4   The six badges of trade are as follows:

1   The subject matter of the transaction

6.5   If the property forming the subject matter of the transaction does not provide either direct income or enjoyment to the owner, it is likely that the transaction will be considered to be trading. It seems unlikely that commodities or manufactured articles which are normally the subject of trading will be treated as anything other than a trade. For example, in *Rutledge* v *IRC* (1929) while in Berlin on business the taxpayer bought one million rolls of toilet paper from a bankrupt German firm for £1,000. The toilet rolls were sent to the UK and the taxpayer endeavoured to sell them. Eventually he found a buyer who bought the whole quantity for £12,000, earning him a considerable profit. The transaction was held to be 'in the nature of a trade' largely because of the quantity of the goods involved but also because of the nature of the goods (one million toilet rolls are unlikely to be used by the taxpayer personally!). This case demonstrates that even a single transaction can sometimes be trading.

In contrast, in *IRC* v *Reinhold* (1953) the taxpayer had bought four houses within a two year period intending to sell them on. The Court of Session stated that 'heritable property is not an uncommon subject of investment' and so the taxpayer was not considered to be trading on this occasion.

In the case of *Marson* v *Morton* (1986) the taxpayer bought land intending to develop it, but in fact sold it on for a profit. The taxpayer was held not to be trading, confirming that land can be held for investment purposes even if it does not yield an income.

2 The frequency of similar transactions

6.6 Although a single transaction can be considered to be trading the repeated undertaking of transactions in the same subject matter is likely to be a stronger indicator that trading is being conducted.

In *Pickford* v *Quirke* (1927) the taxpayers formed a syndicate to buy and resell cotton mills. There were four such transactions over a period of time. The membership of the syndicate was not identical for each transaction. It was held that any one transaction would not have constituted trading but the four taken together did.

3 The circumstances responsible for the realisation

6.7 There is a presumption that trading is not occurring if the property is disposed of to raise money for an unexpected event.

In the case of *The Hudson's Bay Company* v *Stevens* (1909) the taxpayer company had sold off a large quantity of land over a number of years which it had acquired in return for the surrender of its charter. The company was held not to be trading, the court offering the following explanation: 'The company are doing no more than an ordinary landowner does who is minded to sell from time to time as purchasers offer, portions suitable for building of an estate which has devolved upon him from his ancestors.'

4 Supplementary work on or in connection with the property realised

6.8 Trading is more likely to be taking place if either work is done on the property to make it more marketable, or an organisation is set up to sell it. The courts have decided that if there is an organised effort to obtain profit there is a source of taxable income but in the absence of such effort the presumption will be that trading is not taking place.

In *Cape Brandy Syndicate* v *IRC* (1927) a group of accountants bought 3,000 casks of Cape Brandy, blended it with French Brandy, re-casked it and sold it in lots over a period of 18 months. They were held to be trading because they did not simply buy an article which they thought was cheap and then resold it; the syndicate bought the brandy intending to modify its character so that it could be sold in smaller quantities.

5 The motive for the transaction

6.9 There is some evidence of trading taking place if the objective of undertaking the transaction is to make a profit. However, even in the absence of a motive to make a profit it may still be concluded that trading is taking place. The subject matter of the transaction may be crucial.

In *Wisdom v Chamberlain* (1968) the taxpayer, a well-known comedian, bought silver bullion as a hedge against an anticipated devaluation of the pound. It was held that the taxpayer had undertaken an 'adventure in the nature of a trade' when he realised a profit three months later, because the transaction was entered into on a short-term basis with the sole intention of making a profit from the purchase and sale of a commodity.

6 The length of ownership

6.10 The presumption in this badge of trade is that the shorter the period of ownership the more likely it is that trading is taking place. This is a weaker badge than some of the others, however, because the short period of ownership can often be explained by the taxpayer if they need to, perhaps for example, by demonstrating a need for cash at the time of the sale. Hence there are many exceptions to this as a universal rule.

In addition to these six main badges of trade, other factors might be considered by HMRC when deciding whether trading is taking place. There could perhaps include:

- the source of finance for the transaction;
- the circumstances surrounding the acquisition of the asset; and
- whether the subject matter of transaction is in any way related to trades and other activities carried on by the taxpayer.

To summarise this section, and to illustrate the practical difficulties courts have in deciding over the trading question, attempt the following activity:

Activity

Stirling Hill is a vintage motor car enthusiast. On 1 January, 2016 he took out a loan of £40,000 at a fixed rate of interest of 10%, and spent £30,000 on having a workshop built. This was completed on 31 March 2017, when a further £8,000 was spent on tools and equipment. On 6 April 2017, Stirling bought a dilapidated vintage motor car for £3,000, and proceeded to restore it at a cost of £7,000 in spare parts. The restoration was completed on 30 June, 2017. Unfortunately, Stirling was made redundant on 15 September 2017, and was forced to sell the motor car for £25,000. Not being able to find further employment, Stirling proceeded to buy three more dilapidated vintage motor cars on 15 October 2017 for £4,000 each. The restoration of these was completed on 28 February 2018 at a cost of £7,000 per motor car, and two of them were immediately sold for a total of £50,000.

On 31 March 2018 Stirling obtained employment elsewhere in the country, so he immediately sold the workshop for £25,000, and repaid the loan of £40,000. Stirling personally retained the tools and equipment, which were worth £4,500, and the unsold vintage motor car which was valued at £25,000.

You are required to:

(a) Briefly discuss the criteria which would be used by the courts in deciding whether or not Stirling will be treated as carrying on a 'trade' for his vintage motor car activities; and

(b) Explain whether or not you would consider Stirling to be carrying on an adventure in the nature of a trade.

Feedback

To answer this part of the question you need to discuss the six badges of trade.

The acquisition and disposal of the first car, taken in isolation, is unlikely to be deemed to be trading because:

- Vintage cars are often owned and restored by individuals in order to derive enjoyment and/or as investments.
- The length of ownership after the restoration work is completed does not suggest trading is taking place.
- The circumstances surrounding the sale of the car suggests that the disposal was a forced sale rather than trading.

However, the loan taken out to build and equip the workshop and help to finance the acquisition of the car might be taken to be a sign that trading is taking place. The acquisition and disposal of the next three cars is likely to be treated as an adventure in the nature of a trade because:

- Stirling devoted the whole of his time to the activity.
- There were three acquisitions and disposals.
- Two of the cars were sold as soon as their restoration was completed.

If, as seems likely, Stirling Hill is deemed to be trading it is now necessary to determine whether the first transaction will be deemed to be trading as a result of the subsequent transactions. To decide this we need to refer to case law again. In the case mentioned above of *Pickford* v *Quirke* (1927) the taxpayer bought a mill and sold all the assets. This would normally be treated as a capital transaction but the taxpayer carried on to asset strip a total of four mills. The courts decided that the taxpayer was trading and that the three later transactions could be taken into account when deciding whether the first transaction was trading.

In the case of *Leach v Pogson* (1962) the taxpayer set up 30 driving schools which were then sold. Again, the courts decided that the 29 later transactions could be taken into account when deciding whether the first transaction was trading and hence the taxpayers were considered to be trading.

Finally, in the case of *Taylor v Good* (1974) the taxpayer bought a country estate, intending to live in the house. His wife refused to live in the house and so he instead obtained planning permission to build 90 houses on the land. He then sold the property to a property developer having owned the property for about four years. The courts decided that the transactions undertaken to enable the taxpayer to sell the property at a profit were not enough for the first transaction, the acquisition of the property, to be considered trading.

On balance it seems likely that Stirling Hill will be taken to be trading on all his transactions. Do you agree? You might like to think about what arguments Stirling Hill could offer against this decision if he challenged it in court.

Adjustment of profits

6.11 Now that you are able to identify trading activities you need to be able to calculate the taxable trading income that arises from any trading transactions.

Taxable trading income is made up of the difference between trading receipts and allowable expenses during a period of assessment. As we noted earlier, from 6 April 2017 this computation can be undertaken in one of three ways for businesses:

1. using generally accepted accounting principles (an *accrual basis*). HMRC refer to this as 'traditional' accounting;
2. using a *cash basis* (small businesses only);
3. applying the *trading allowance* so that any trading income is not taxable (the very smallest of businesses)

We review the first of these options, the accruals basis, in sections 6.12 to 6.39, and provide an example to illustrate how this is applied in practice in section 6.40.

We will review the cash basis option in more detail in section 6.41. The cash basis is used by relatively few, mainly new businesses. In section 6.42 we look more closely at the basis of assessment for trading activities.

The accruals basis

6.12   The normal approach to the adjustment of profits for tax purposes, starts with the net profit for accounting purposes i.e. using accruals based accounting. Under this approach, accounting profit includes all receipts that relate to the relevant period, whether actually received in the period itself or not. From this accrued income is then deducted all relevant expenses. These will include all those relating to the period you are computing the profit for, whether actually paid or not within the period itself.

The tax rules then require a number of adjustments to convert the accounting profit to a tax adjusted profit. To do this, you will need to:

- determine which accounting period will form the basis of assessment for trading income for the tax year; and
- identify taxable income and allowable expenditure for the basis period.

In the remainder of this section we will first briefly summarise the rules for recognising receipts and allowable expenditure for tax purposes. Then we will explore specific trading receipts that form part of the trading income in more detail. Finally we will consider what expenses are allowable in determining trading income.

We will now look more closely at the calculation of trading income to illustrate how these general rules are applied in practice.

Recognition of income - Trading receipts

6.13   A receipt is a trading receipt if it is a payment for services or goods supplied by the taxpayer. But how do we determine when a trading receipt has been received, and how much should be recorded in our tax computation? There are a number of rules and principles we must apply in practice to answer this question to ensure we don't either under or over report the amount (so we don't under- or over-pay tax). These include, for example:

1.   The receipt must be income and not capital;
2.   Voluntary payments received are not trading receipts; and
3.   Goods taken from the business for private purposes must be valued at market price and not cost.

We will now examine each of these principles in more detail:

1 Income versus capital receipts

6.14 As a general rule, to be taxable as trading income, a receipt must be income related and not related to the non-current assets of the business (also referred to as its 'capital'). Receipts related to capital assets (i.e. the proceeds from selling a capital asset) are instead generally taxed under the capital gains tax rules (see Chapter 8). The distinction has proved difficult to draw in practice and a number of tests have been developed over a long period of time to help get this right. The most straightforward is to determine if the receipt relates to an asset that is part of the businesses' non-current assets (therefore likely to be a capital receipt) or to the current assets of the business (therefore likely to be an income receipt). While this might on the surface seem a fairly straight forward rule, it isn't always easy to determine if an asset is inventory or a non-current (capital) asset as it can depend on the type of business being carried on. You will have looked at this distinction if you have studied accountancy and will have seen how difficult this can be to determine.

The courts have devised a broad test, called the 'trees and fruit' test, which can be applied to help resolve this issue in practice. Here the analogy is that the tree is the enduring part (considered to be the capital), producing the fruit, which is the recurring product (considered to be the income).

One characteristic of income receipts is that they are often recurring, compared to capital receipts that are often (but not always) one-off items. So how often a taxpayer receives a particular kind of payment may be a clue as to whether it is income or capital for tax purposes.

In order to decide whether a receipt is income or capital, we also need to think about what it is paid for and how it relates to the taxpayer's particular activities. Case law gives us a number of examples and general principles that can be used to help make this decision.

For example, what if an amount is received in return for a taxpayer restricting his or her activities in some way (e.g. agreeing not to trade in a particular area)? If the receipt is to compensate the taxpayer for not being able to use a business asset at all, sometimes referred to as 'sterilisation' of the asset, then it will probably be a capital receipt. However, if it is to substitute for a receipt that would have been a trading receipt, then it is more likely to be treated as income.

In *Higgs v Olivier* (1952), Sir Lawrence Olivier received £15,000 from the makers of the film Henry V, in which he starred, in return for an agreement not to act in another film for 18 months. This payment was separate from the fee he was paid for starring in the film. The Court of Appeal held that the payment was for a substantial restriction of his income earning activities, and so was not a trading receipt. If a restriction is not substantial, or only short term, it may be classified as an income receipt.

In *Glenboig Union Fireclay Co Ltd v IR Commrs* (1922) the company leased some fireclay fields and the seam ran underneath a railway track. The railway company paid a large sum of money to stop the company from working the fireclay seam, and the House of Lords held that this was a capital receipt. It was considered to be a payment for the sterilisation of an asset of the business.

In *Burmah Steamships Co Ltd v IRC* (1930), the company bought a ship that needed extensive repairs before it was seaworthy. The repairer took longer than agreed to finish the repairs and so paid compensation to the company, calculated by reference to the profits lost during the delay. This was held to be income because the compensation filled a 'hole' in the taxpayer's profit.

Some other areas where the distinction between capital and income arise are:

- Compensation for cancellation of commercial contracts or connections. Where the compensation relates to contracts which are relatively small compared to the overall size of the business activities, they will usually be income in nature and form part of the trading profits. Receipts which are compensation for contracts which are large compared to the size of the business, on the other hand, are generally considered to be capital.
- Appropriations of unclaimed deposits and advances.
- Receipts from the sale of information. This receipt is covered by statute, unlike the two above which have been decided by means of case law. Provided that the vendor continues to trade after the sale, the receipt will be treated as a trading receipt.
- A trade debt which has been deducted as a trading expense and is subsequently cancelled is treated as a trade receipt.

Sometimes a particular payment can be divided into both capital and income parts for tax purposes. This is what happened, for example, in the case of *London and Thames Haven Oil Wharves v Attwooll* (1967) where £100,000 compensation was paid after a tanker crashed into a jetty, causing serious damage. The sum was split into a capital sum, which was intended to be used to rebuild the jetty, and an income receipt, which was compensation to the jetty owners for loss of income due to the accident. The income part alone of this sum would qualify as a trading receipt.

2 Voluntary payments

6.15 Payments made on a voluntary basis for some personal quality of the taxpayer are not generally trading receipts. In *Murray v Goodhews* (1976), the brewing company, Watneys, made *ex gratia* (voluntary) lump sum payments to landlords of public houses when they terminated tied tenancies, partly as an acknowledgement of the good relationship they had with their tenant and partly to preserve their good name. These sums were held not to be trading receipts in the hands of the landlords since the amounts of the payments had no connection with the profits earned nor was it linked with future trading relations between Watneys and the taxpayer.

However, in *McGowan v Brown and Cousins* (1977), the taxpayer, an estate agent, received a lower than usual fee for acquiring property for a company in the expectation that he would be retained to deal with letting the property. The company owning the property later paid the taxpayer £2,500 as compensation when they retained another agent instead to deal with the lettings. The payment was held to be a trading receipt this time despite the lack of a legal obligation to pay it.

HMRC (BIM15035) provides an example of a payment that is outside of income tax: a greengrocer witnesses a car breakdown, helps the passengers to their destination and repairs their car. In return, he or she receives an unsought payment for the assistance. The payment is unsolicited and made in recognition of personal qualities and so is outside of income tax altogether.

3   Goods taken for private purposes

6.16   For tax computation purposes goods disposed of, other than in the ordinary course of business, must be accounted for at market value as a trading receipt. In *Sharkey v Wernher* (1956) the taxpayer who ran a stud farm as a business also raced horses as a hobby. She transferred five horses from her stud farm to her racing stables and recorded the cost of breeding the horses as a receipt of the stud farm. The Revenue argued that the market value of the horses should be entered in the accounts rather than cost, and the courts agreed. The rule derived from this case applies to all goods taken by owners for their own use, as well as goods they give to others for non-business purposes. Finance Act 2008 enshrined this rule in statute. Beware, as this is usually different to the way such adjustments are made in accounting (where cost is used not market value). We will illustrate this principle for you later with an example when we discuss common adjustments needed to convert accounting profits to tax profits.

This rule can also apply if goods are sold at less than their market value. However, provided that the disposal can be shown to have been made for genuine commercial reasons (e.g. as the result of a sale or special offer) the rule in *Sharkey v Wernher* does not apply. Additionally, the rule applies to traders only. It does not apply to professional persons (i.e. it does not apply in relation to intangible goods or services). In *Mason v Innes* (1967) the novelist Hammond Innes gave the manuscript of *The Doomed Oasis* to his father. The writer had deducted allowable travelling expenses, which had been incurred while researching the book, from his income. The Revenue wanted to assess the writer on the market value of the script. Lord Denning said:

> "Suppose an artist paints a picture of his mother and gives it to her. He does not receive a penny for it. Is he to pay tax on the value of it? It is unthinkable. Suppose he paints a picture, which he does not like when he has finished it and destroys it. Is he liable to pay tax on the value of it? Clearly not. These instances therefore show that that *Sharkey* v *Wernher* does not apply to professional men."

This latter example is one of the main differences between business and professional income categories. Other examples are beyond the scope of an introductory tax course.

Deductible expenses

6.17 Having looked at the income element in determining a trader's taxable income we should now consider the allowable expenses that can be deducted from this income. For expenditure to be an allowable deduction for tax purposes it must satisfy three criteria:

1. it must be incurred *wholly and exclusively* for the purposes of the trade;
2. it must be a *revenue* item, not a *capital* expense (unless specifically allowed for in the legislation); and
3. it must not be specifically disallowed by statute.

We will now examine each of these concepts in more detail before discussing how a simplified expenses scheme can be used by some businesses who wish to account for their allowable costs in a different way:

1 Wholly and exclusively

6.18 Only expenditure that is wholly and exclusively for the purposes of the trade or business will be deductible to determine taxable trading income. This concept is similar to the one we met in section 5.2 when discussing employment income, except the requirement there was for expenses to be wholly, exclusively and *necessarily* for the purposes of employment. For a self-employed taxpayer there is no need, however, to prove an expense they incur is necessary to perform their income earning activities. As long as the wholly and exclusively aspects are met then an expense can be allowable. This means more expenses may be allowable for self-employed taxpayers than for employees.

There are two situations where a business is likely to fall foul of the wholly and exclusively requirement. The first is when the payment is not directly related to the business activities, which is tested using what is called the *remoteness test*. The second is where the expenses have a more than one purpose, tested using the *duality test*.

The remoteness test

6.19 This test considers whether the expense is closely enough related to the day to day running of the business, or whether it really relates to an activity outside of the business. For example, consider whether subscriptions and donations are deductible or not. Subscriptions to trade associations will generally be deductible as it is usually easy to see the benefits that arise to the business from membership of a trade association, and it is closely related to the running of the business. Subscriptions and donations to political parties on the other hand are likely to be disallowed, as they are usually remote from the business activities of most businesses. It is therefore difficult to create a case to demonstrate how they can relate to business operations directly.

In one case, however, a donation to a political party was held to be allowable where this link to business operations was considered to have been adequately made (i.e. payment was not considered to be remote). This was the case of *Morgan v Tate and Lyle Ltd* (1954) where a donation to the Conservative Party was allowed as a business expense because it was made in order to resist the nationalisation of the sugar industry proposed by the Labour Party, which would have led to the cessation of the business.

Donations to charity will generally not be deductible as they are considered to be remote from the business activities. However, where the donations are only small and are to local charities, they are often allowable as a deduction in practice.

In applying the remoteness test you also need to consider in what capacity the proprietor has incurred the expense. In a 1906 case, *Strong & Co of Romsey Ltd v Woodifield*, a guest at a hotel was injured when a chimney fell, and the company paid an amount of damages to the guest as compensation. These were considered to be paid by the company in its capacity as an owner of property, and not in the context of the business operations and so were not allowed as a business deduction.

Similarly, a misappropriation, or theft, of profits by the owner or a director of the business will be considered to be outside of the business activities and not deductible (e.g. see *Curtis v J & G Oldfield* (1933)). On the other hand, if the theft is by a member of the staff, the loss will usually be an allowable deduction.

The duality test

6.20 If an expense has a dual purpose, for example, the sole trader gets some private, as well as business related, benefit from the expense, then the duality test will operate to deny deductibility of the expense. In *Caillebotte v Quinn* (1975) the taxpayer, a self-employed carpenter, claimed the difference between the cost of eating at home (at 10p a meal) and the cost of eating in a café (at 40p) for those days when he was working away from home. It was held that the expenditure was disallowable because he ate to live as well as to work and so the expenditure was 'tainted' by the private purpose.

There have been a number of other cases dealing with this rule, such as *Mackinlay v Arthur Young McClelland Moores & Co* (1990) where the House of Lords ruled that removal costs paid to two partners to move house were disallowable. It was accepted that the partnership benefited from the move because the partners were able to work at different offices, but there was a duality of purpose where the business and private benefits were too closely intertwined to separate them from each other. In another case, *Mallalieu v Drummond* (1983), a barrister tried to deduct the cost of the clothes she wore in court. The House of Lords said that in addition to a business purpose, there were other purposes, namely to provide 'warmth and decency' which meant that the expense had a dual purpose and was not deductible.

Sometimes when it is not possible to split an expense into a business and a personal element directly, it may be possible to split the payment up using an acceptable allocation formula and allow the business portion as a deductible expense. A common example of this situation that occurs for a large number of self-employed taxpayers are expenses relating to a car which is used for both business and pleasure. The proportion of business miles compared to total miles can usually be used to determine the proportion of expenses such as servicing, insurance and petrol which are allowable deductions.

In a case heard by the tax tribunal, *Interfish v HMRC* [2012] UKFTT 599], a successful seafood supplier based in Plymouth donated over £1m to the local rugby club. The taxpayer argued that the donation benefited the business, but the tribunal held that it wasn't wholly and exclusively for the purposes of the trade. It had the dual purpose of improving the rugby club's financial position as well as improving the taxpayer's business. If Interfish had been able to separate part of the payment as advertising, for example having the logo on players' shirts, it would probably have been able to deduct that component. This decision of the First Tier Tribunal was upheld by the Upper Tribunal in August 2013.

Other examples of this occur for taxpayers who undertake all or part of their business from their home. Part of the cost of running their house is deductible from their trading profits as long as they can justify that these shared costs are allocated to the business correctly or (from April 2013) the fixed rate deductions are used (see Chapter 5 for these details).

2 Revenue not capital expenditure

6.21 The second question we need to consider in determining if an expense is deductible is whether it is a revenue or capital expense. As we discussed above, there is a need to distinguish between revenue and capital receipts, as generally only revenue receipts are part of trading income for tax computations. Equally revenue expenses are normally deductible from trading profits whereas capital expenses have to be dealt with differently - using the capital allowances rules (we'll discuss these rules in Chapter 7). These principles will sound familiar to those of you who have studied accounting where what goes directly into the income statement, or what needs to go into the balance sheet, is considered on a very similar basis.

The distinction between *revenue* and *capital* expenditure for tax deductibility has developed over the years, largely from case law, which tries to be consistent in its treatment of revenue income and expenditure. The tests that are used to determine whether a receipt is capital or revenue, as we discussed above, are generally also used to test whether expenses are of a capital or revenue nature. These rules largely follow normal accounting principles, however, there is not always a clear cut distinction and some cases appear to be at odds with these tests. For example, in the case of *Lawson v Johnson Matthey plc* (1992) a payment of £50 million was made as part of a deal with the Bank of England in order to save the banking subsidiary from a threat of insolvency. Despite the size and one off nature of the payment it was allowed as revenue expenditure.

The question of how often a payment is made can play a part in deciding whether it is capital or revenue in nature. As we saw with receipts, capital payments are often one-off, single payments, whereas revenue payments are often recurring. One of the tests the courts have established is the *enduring benefit test*, where we ask 'does the expense bring into existence something that has enduring benefit for the trade?' If so, it is probably capital and therefore not deductible.

In *Tucker v Granada Motorway Services Ltd* (1979), the rent payable by the taxpayer company under a lease agreement was calculated based on the previous year's takings, which included an amount of tobacco duty. By paying a lump sum to the lessor, the company was able to have the formula changed to take out the tobacco duty and so in the future the rent paid under the lease would be lower. The House of Lords held that this was a capital payment, because it created an enduring benefit, i.e. future reduced rent payments.

To help explain these rules in more detail, and to show you how these rules work in practice, let us review some commonly encountered items for which the revenue/capital distinction is important:

Self education expenses

6.22 Expenditure on a training course for the proprietor of a business which is intended to provide new expertise, knowledge or skills brings into existence an intangible asset which has enduring benefit for the business and is therefore really of a capital nature. On the other hand, if the training course is to update expertise, knowledge or skills already possessed by the proprietor it will normally be regarded as revenue expenditure. The Government is currently consulting on the extension of tax relief for training by the self-employed. The consultation document (including a description of the current rules as well as proposals for change) is available here:

https://www.gov.uk/government/consultations/taxation-of-self-funded-work-related-training

Repairs and improvements

6.23 Amounts spent on repairs to an asset will generally be allowable for tax purposes but amounts spent on improvements will not be deductible. As a general rule, repair means restoring an asset to its original condition, whereas an improvement means making the asset bigger or better in some way, therefore changing its character. Given the frequency of these kinds of payments occurring in business, this distinction is very important to understand. Normal accounting principles are used as guidance when differentiating between repair and improvement expenditure and case law has been used to decide marginal cases.

Two types of expenditure cause particular difficulties. The first is expenditure which is incurred to renovate assets soon after they were acquired. When a taxpayer buys an asset, the purchase price is, of course, a capital expense. What if the asset needs to be repaired soon after purchase? There is an argument that if the asset was purchased for a low price because it needed to be repaired, then the cost of those repairs is also a capital expense, because it is effectively an additional purchase cost. In *Law Shipping Co Ltd v IRC* (1924) a ship, which was built in 1906, was bought in December 1919 for £97,000. The ship was ready to sail with freight that was booked for transport at the time of the purchase. The required periodic survey of the ship (for sea-worthiness etc.) was then considerably overdue and an exemption from the survey had to be obtained. The ship was granted a Lloyd's Certificate for a single voyage to enable it to be taken into dock to undergo its survey. The purchaser had to spend £51,558 on repairs.

It was agreed that the expense of keeping a ship, which is employed in trade, in proper repair is normally an expense 'necessary for the purpose of trade' (i.e. a revenue expense), even if that expense is deferred. In fact, had the previous owners undertaken the repairs, they would have been able to set the costs against their income for tax purposes. However, the accumulation of repairs required extended partly over a period during which the ship was used, not in the purchaser's trade, but the seller's. A ship which is dilapidated is worth less than a ship which has been well maintained and is in good condition. The condition of the ship at the time of the sale was reflected in the price paid. The value of the ship was presumably increased by the repairs undertaken and hence some of the cost of the repairs should be treated as capital expenditure since they increased the value of a capital asset.

It was held that most of the expenditure was incurred because of the poor state of repair of the vessel when it was bought and this amount was disallowed as a capital expense, but £12,000 of the total expenditure was allowed for post-acquisition repairs.

In a contrasting case of *Odeon Associated Theatres Ltd* v *Jones* (1972) a cinema had been bought which was in a fairly dilapidated condition after the Second World War. The cinema was used for a number of years by its new owners before it was refurbished. In this case all of the refurbishment expenditure was allowed despite the poor condition of the cinema when it was bought.

There are two essential differences between the two cases which led to the differing conclusions. First, when the cinema was bought, the purchase price was not reduced to reflect the condition of the property which was both usable and used immediately after purchase. In the *Law Shipping* case, however, the purchase price did reflect the condition of the ship which was not seaworthy immediately after purchase. Second, the Court of Appeal decided that the costs of refurbishment for the cinema were deductible expenses in accordance with accounting principles (i.e. would go directly to the income statement, not to the balance sheet) and therefore tax principles should not deviate from the normal accounting rules unless there was strong reason to – which they argued was not so in this case.

The second area which has depended on case law for clarification concerns the question of *repair or replacement*. That is, has an asset been repaired or effectively replaced following the expenditure? The cost of replacing part of an asset will generally be deductible as a revenue expense, but if it is the whole of the asset that has been replaced, it will generally be considered capital expenditure and therefore not be deductible.

To illustrate these situations, we can use the example of the case of *Samuel Jones & Co (Devondale) Ltd* v *CIR* (1951) where expenditure on a new chimney to replace the existing one was allowable because the chimney was held to be a subsidiary part of the factory. In a second case, *Brown v Burnley Football and Athletic Co Ltd* (1980), the football club replaced a wooden spectators' stand with a concrete structure which also provided additional accommodation. The expenditure was disallowed because the entire stand was replaced, which was held not to be part of a larger asset, but a distinct and separate part of the club.

Professional fees and charges

6.24 In some cases you will need to look behind the expenses to see what they relate to in order to classify them as revenue or capital. This is the case with professional fees and charges. Where they relate to capital assets or non-trading items, they will not be deductible. Use the following activity to see how these rules can be applied.

Activity

For each of the following legal and professional charges decide whether they are allowable deductions for the purposes of computing trading income:

1   Charges incurred when obtaining a long (more than 50 years) lease.

2   Charges for trade debt collection.

3   Charges incurred with respect to an action for breach of contract.

Feedback

The first charge would be disallowed because it relates to a non-revenue item. The second charge would be allowable and the third charge would be allowable provided that the contract itself has the quality of revenue and not capital.

However, while this rule works most of the time, it is not always possible to classify all legal and professional charges using this rule alone. Some further exploration of the actual purpose of the expenditure may be needed to determine if it can, or cannot, be deducted for tax purposes. For example, the normal fees for preparing accounts and agreeing tax liabilities are allowable while legal fees incurred during tax appeals are not deductible, regardless of the outcome of the appeal. However, accountancy expenses incurred due to a HMRC investigation will be allowable provided that taxable profits for earlier years are not increased and that an increase, if any, made to the taxable profits of the year under review does not lead to interest charges or penalties.

Costs of obtaining finance

6.25 In relation to loans, interest on qualifying loans for partners or employees is treated as a tax relief, and dealt with in the personal tax computation (as we saw in Chapter 4). However, for the self-employed, interest on other types of business loans such as overdrafts, credit cards and hire purchase agreements will be allowable as revenue expenses (i.e. fully deductible in the year it is accrued) so long as they meet the 'wholly and exclusively' rule. If there is any private use of the assets purchased with the loan then this part of the interest paid is not tax deductible. Note, however, that interest paid on overdue tax is not an allowable expense for those who are self-employed (for what should be obvious reasons!). [These are however, deductible for companies who can in fact claim a non-trading loan relationship expense for this as we will see in Chapter 9, section 9.7]

The incidental costs of obtaining finance for the business could be considered to be capital expenses on the basis that they are one-off expenses. A special rule, however, provides that if the interest paid on the loan is tax deductible, then the incidental costs of obtaining the loan will also be deductible. This includes fees, commission, advertising and printing but does not include any stamp duty costs.

Registration of Patents
6.26   A patent is an item of intellectual property that is an asset of the business. It would be reasonable therefore to classify the cost of registering a patent as a capital expense, however the legislation specifically allows for this cost to be deductible.

Staff secondments
6.27   A secondment is the temporary transfer of a worker to another position or employment. Where staff of the business are seconded to work for another organisation, but the business continues to pay their wages, it is arguable that the wages are no longer paid wholly and exclusively for business purposes. By special provision, where the secondment is to a charity or to an educational institution, the business can continue to claim the salary of the seconded employee as a tax deduction.

Lease premiums
6.28   If a taxpayer leases premises he or she may be required to pay a premium when the lease is granted as well as periodical rent. Because it is a one-off payment related to the acquisition of a right to use whatever is being leased, a lease premium is really capital in nature. However, a special provision allows for the premium to be claimed as a deduction. The lessee can claim the amount on which the landlord is assessable under property income for the premium paid; spread over the term of the lease agreement.

Activity

The lessee of business premises pays a premium of £36,000 on the grant of a 25 year lease. How much, if any, can be claimed as a deduction under the trading income rules?

Feedback

For the landlord, under the property income rules (see later in this chapter) the assessment will be the amount of the premium reduced by 2% for each year of the lease except the first. Therefore 48% (24 × 2%) of the premium is not taxable and the remaining 52% is taxable. The property income assessment is therefore 52% of £36,000 or £18,720.

The tenant can claim a deduction for that amount spread over the lifetime of the lease, i.e. £18,720 ÷ 25 or £748.80 each year.

3 Specifically disallowed items

6.29 The final of our three criteria for deductibility of expenses in trading income tax computations is whether the expenses are specifically disallowed by legislation. There are a number of items which would appear to be deductible for trading income purposes using the first two rules we outlined at the start of this section (namely incurred wholly and exclusively for the purpose of trade and not of a capital nature) but are specifically excluded from being deductible by legislation. The following are some of the more commonly encountered cases in this category:

Fines and penalties
6.30 Any payments made which are held to be contrary to public policy, such as fines or penalties, are disallowable. However, in practice, deductions for parking fines incurred by employees parking the employer's cars during the course of their employer's business are usually allowed, although such fines incurred by directors and proprietors are never allowed.

In the 2012 McLaren case (*McLaren Racing Ltd v Revenue and Customs UKFTT 601*), the Formula One racing team was fined £32m for breaching the FIA International Sporting Code. The first tier tax tribunal held that the penalty was deductible because McLaren were obliged to pay it under its contractual terms. This case may be appealed by HMRC because it undermines the principle that it is in the public interest not to allow a tax deduction where there has been a breach of non-statutory regulations. With effect from 1 April 2002, deductions also cannot be claimed for any payments, such as bribes, made overseas that would be a criminal payment if made in the UK.

Entertainment
6.31 Most expenditure on hospitality and entertainment is disallowed. This includes entertaining customers and clients whether they are UK based or overseas. The main exception is the entertainment of genuine employees of the business. This expense, as with most expenses relating to employees, is fully

deductible. You will recall from section 5.16, however, that where an employee is entitled to attend an annual Christmas party or similar, the value of which is more than £150 a person, a benefit in kind will arise to the employee. The full cost of the function will still be deductible to the employer however much they spend per employee.

Gifts

6.32 Gifts to charities are given special treatment in the personal income tax computation outside of the trading income calculation. Businesses may, however make gifts to other categories of people, including customers and employees. As a general rule, gifts to customers are disallowed unless they cost less than £50, contain a conspicuous advertisement for the business and are not food, drink or tobacco. Gifts to employees are allowable deductions for the business, but may be a taxable benefit in kind in the hands of the employee, as we saw in Chapter 5.

Expensive car leases or hire charges

6.33 The cost of hiring or leasing plant and equipment for business purposes is generally deductible. The on-going lease rental payments are of a revenue nature, not a capital expense which their outright purchase would be.

For lease agreements entered into before 6 April 2009, there was an exception to this general rule in the case of expensive motor vehicles. Where a car cost more than £12,000, the amount of car hire, or lease expense, was restricted using a formula. Since 2009 the restriction refers to the CO_2 emissions of the vehicle instead. For leased cars with CO_2 emissions of more than 130g/km (160g/km before April 2013) a flat 15% disallowance applies, i.e., only 85% of the lease payments are deductible.

Do note however, that since 17 April, 2002, where the car is a low-emission vehicle, this special rule does not apply and the full amount of the lease expense is deductible irrespective of the cost.

Redundancy payments

6.34 Where payments are made to staff who are made redundant, they will be deductible so long as it can be shown that they are wholly and exclusively for the purposes of the trade. If the payments are made by a business that is ceasing to trade, however, there is a restriction on the amount that can be claimed as a tax deduction. The limit is the statutory amount plus three times this statutory amount for each employee (i.e. a total of four times whatever that employee's statutory redundancy pay entitlement is).

Pre-trading expenses

6.35 Expenditure can only be a deductible expense from trading income if it is incurred on or after the date on which the business commences to trade. However, expenses incurred in the seven years prior to this date will be treated as a loss which arises on the date of commencement provided they relate directly to the new business. The reason for treating it this way relates to the way in which the basis period rules work for commencing businesses.

Appropriations of profit

6.36 Where a sole trader makes drawings from the business profits (this typically may include paying themselves an income from the business' assets), this is an appropriation and is not deductible. As such, any drawings must be included in the taxable profit calculation.

Provisions

6.37 Another item that is not deductible is a provision for accounting purposes. For tax purposes, to be deductible an expense must be reasonably certain to arise. Where for accounting purposes an adjustment is made to profit in the interests of prudence, for example a provision for doubtful debts, this will not be deductible. In the case of adjustments to debtors, for tax purposes, only debts written off or which are reasonably estimated to be bad will be deductible.

A further example of an unacceptable provision is depreciation for accounting purposes. Where depreciation is included in the accounts, it cannot be claimed as a tax deduction. As depreciation is related to apportioning the costs of capital assets over time and may be subject to abuse (at least in theory) to affect reported tax profits, the tax system has its own regime for calculating allowable costs related to the purchase of certain capital assets (called capital allowances) which we will examine more closely in the next chapter.

A question of timing

6.38 The timing of expenses deductions usually follows the accounting rules, i.e. expenses are deducted for tax purposes in the year in which they accrue (not when they are paid). There are two main exceptions to this general rule. One is for payments to employees. A special rule says that if a business deducts payments to employees on an accrued basis, but then the actual payment is not made until more than 9 months after the end of the accounting period, then the deduction is disallowed and deferred to the following year.

Another variation is for pension contributions made by a business for its employees. Where contributions are made to registered pension schemes, they are deductible in the period in which they are paid, which is different to the accounting treatment.

Simplified Expenses Scheme

6.39   In addition to changes to introduce the cash basis scheme in 2013/14, the Government also introduced a *simplified expenses scheme*. This scheme can be used by business that are sole-traders, by business partnerships or limited liability partnerships (as long as they have no companies as partners). It is not available to limited companies.

This scheme creates the possibility to use more flat rate expense deductions i.e. a fixed amount can be deducted irrespective of what was actually paid out. For example, if you are eligible to use the cash basis, any business mileage expenses can be computed on a flat rate basis that mirrors the rates we discussed for company car mileage rates in section 5.10 i.e. 45p/mile for the first 10,000 business miles driven annually and then 25p/mile for any further miles.

Some restrictions do apply to these rules for business mileage however. If the business is already in operation and claims capital allowances for the vehicle currently (see Chapter 7) then switching to the cash basis does not allow you to use the flat rate scheme for deductions for this vehicle. You will have to continue to use actual expenses incurred for this vehicle for the duration of the time you own it.

Businesses can also opt for certain other expenses to be deductible at a flat rate. For example:

- *Use of your home to work from* – the fixed rate deduction will be based on the number of hours your home is used for work purposes each month as follows:
  - 25-50 hours/month   £10
  - 51-100 hours/month   £18
  - 101+ hours/month   £26
- *Premises used for business and as a home* – for example, if you run a guest house it may be expected that you will live in part of the property and let out other parts. In this situation you will be allowed a fixed rate deduction based on the number of occupants you have each month;
  - 1 occupant   £350/month
  - 2 occupants   £500/month
  - 3 or more occupants   £650/month.

In either case, these are optional flat rate deductions if the taxpayer wishes to use them, regardless of whether the cash basis scheme is used. Alternatively they can opt to deduct the allowable part of any actual expenditure incurred – as usual.

It can reasonably be expected that other flat rate deductions will be introduced in future years if this scheme proves popular and workable.

Calculating tax adjusted trading profit

6.40 You can now identify taxable revenues and allowable deductions for trading income purposes using the accruals basis. To determine tax adjusted trading profit, rather than start a whole new calculation from scratch, we instead start with the net accounting profit. This is then adjusted to take into account those items where the tax treatment of items is different to the accounting treatment. Because the final figure we are calculating is the trading income, adjustments also need to be made to remove items that are dealt with under different categories for tax purposes, but form part of the accounting profit for the business, for example, savings or property income. Remember these have their own separate rules in a taxpayer's tax computation. In undertaking this computation for exam questions, or in practice, you may find it helpful to use this pro forma to undertake the adjustment of profits to the trading income (Note: figures are for illustration only):

Computation of the trading income assessment:

	£	£
Net profit per accounts		20,000
Add:		
Expenditure in the accounts which is not deductible for tax purposes	3,000	
Income which is taxable but not directly credited to the P & L account	1,000	4,000
		24,000
Less:		
Income in the accounts which is not taxable	2,000	
Expenditure not in the accounts which is deductible for tax purposes	3,000	(5,000)
Tax Adjusted Trading income		19,000

To see how this is useful in practice, examine the following activity.

Activity

Monica has been in business for a number of years. Her income statement for the year to 31 August, 2018 is as follows:

	Note	£	£
Sales			100,000
Less: Cost of sales			(40,000)
Gross profit			60,000
Add:			
Bank interest		500	
Profit from sale of plant		300	
Rental income		1,000	1,800
			61,800
Less:			
Rent and rates		3,000	
Insurance		1,000	
Heating, lighting and power		1,500	
Repairs and renewals	(a)	1,500	
Telephone	(b)	400	
Motor expenses	(c)	500	
Bad debts	(d)	200	
Wages and salaries	(e)	20,000	
Legal fees	(f)	300	
Sundry expenses		1,000	
Interest on a credit card		100	
Depreciation		3,000	(32,500)
Net Profit			29,300

Notes:
(a) This figure includes £1,000 spent on furnishing a new showroom and £200 redecorating the reception area.
(b) 30% of the telephone cost relate to private use.
(c) 20% of the motor expenses relate to private use.
(d) Bad debts is made up of £120 trade debt written off and £80 increase in the general provision for bad debts.
(e) This figure includes drawings of £8,000.
(f) The legal fees related to the purchase of plant and machinery.

Required: Determine the tax adjusted trading profit using the accrual basis for the year ended 31 August, 2018.

Feedback

	£	£
Net profit per the accounts		29,300
Add: Disallowed expenditure		
Drawings	8,000	
Capital expenditure	1,000	
Telephone 400 × 30%	120	
Motor expenses 500 × 20%	100	
General provision for bad debts	80	
Legal fees	300	
Depreciation	3,000	12,600
		41,900
Less: Non-trading income		
Rental income	1,000	
Bank interest	500	
Profit from sales of plant	300	(1,800)
Tax adjusted profit		40,100

Notes:

- Drawings are not allowable as they represent an appropriation of profit by the proprietor.
- The £1,000 spent on furnishing the new showroom is capital expenditure. This may qualify for capital allowances which we will discuss in the next chapter. Note that the cost of redecoration, which has to be done periodically, is of a revenue nature, so no adjustment is necessary for that expense.
- Private expenditure must be excluded under the wholly and exclusively rule (e.g. for telephone and car expenses).
- General provisions are not allowable for tax purposes.
- To decide whether legal fees are deductible, you must consider what they relate to. Here it is for purchase of plant and machinery, a capital transaction, and so the legal fees are also considered to be capital and disallowable.
- Accounting depreciation is not deductible for tax purposes (capital allowances related to these assets will potentially be claimable instead as we will see in the next chapter).
- Rental income is taxed as property income and so must be excluded from the trading income computation. It will appear in a separate part of Monica's overall tax computation.
- Bank interest is taxed as savings income and so must also be excluded here. Again, it is instead listed separately in Monica's overall tax computation.
- Profit on sale of plant is a capital receipt and must be excluded. There may be capital gains tax liability on this item, see Chapter 8 for details of how this could be calculated and taxed.

To draw together all the points made in this section outlining the normal rules for computing trading income, we will use another activity. You are advised to work through this long example carefully so that you can be sure you understand how the principles we have discussed are translated into a trading profit adjustment and how these are placed into a simple tax computation.

Activity

Roger Riviere is a self-employed wholesale clothing distributor who commenced trading on 1 July, 1998. His summarised accounts for the year ended 30 June, 2018 are:

			£	£
Sales	(1)			400,000
Opening inventory	(2)		40,000	
Purchases			224,000	
			264,000	
Closing inventory	(2)		(32,000)	232,000
Gross profit				168,000
Wages and national insurance	(3)		52,605	
Rent and business rates			31,140	
Repairs and renewals	(4)		3,490	
Miscellaneous expenses	(5)		665	
Taxation (Roger's income tax)			15,590	
Bad debts	(6)		820	
Legal expenses	(7)		1,060	
Depreciation			570	
Loss on sale of office furniture			60	
Transport costs			4,250	
Interest	(8)		990	
Motor car running expenses				
(Roger's car)	(9)		2,000	
Lighting and heating			1,250	
Sundry expenses (all allowable)			710	
Relocation expenditure	(10)		2,400	117,600
Net profit				50,400

Notes to accounts:

1. Sales include £500 reimbursed by Roger's family for clothing taken from stock. This reimbursement represented cost price.

2. Inventory: The basis of both opening and closing inventory valuations was 'lower of cost or market value' less a contingency reserve of 50%.

3. Wages: Included in wages are Roger's drawings of £50 per week, his national insurance contributions of £320 for the year and wages and national insurance contributions in respect of his wife totalling £11,750. His wife worked full-time in the business as a secretary.

4. Repairs and renewals: The charge includes £3,000 for fitting protective covers over the factory windows and doors to prevent burglary.

5. Miscellaneous expenses:

	£	£
Theft of money by employee	65	
Political donation to Green Party	100	
Gifts of 100 'Riviere' calendars	500	665

6. Bad debts:

	£	£
Trade debt written off		720
Loan to former employee written off		250
Provision for bad debts (2% of accounts receivables)	450	
Less: Opening provision	(600)	(150)
		820

7. Legal expenses:

	£
Defending action in respect of alleged faulty goods	330
Costs in connection with lease of new larger premises	250
Successful appeal against previous year's income tax assessment	200
Defending Roger in connection with speeding offence	190
Debt collection	90
	(1,060)

8. Interest:

	£	£
Bank overdraft interest (business account)	860	
Interest on overdue tax	130	990

9. Motor car running expenses. One-third of Roger's mileage is private. Included in the charge is £65 for a speeding fine incurred by Roger whilst delivering goods to a customer.

10. Relocation expenditure. The expenditure was incurred in transferring the business to new and larger premises.

The following information is also provided:

1. Capital allowances for the year to 30 June, 2018 are £480 (in Chapter 7 we will show you how to undertake the computation to produce these numbers).

2. Roger was born on 8 April, 1969 and, due to his rapid aging, decided to increase his pension pot by £13,500 by making a 'relief at source' pension contribution.

3. Roger has no other sources of income.

You are required:

a) To prepare a profit adjustment in respect of the accounting period to 30 June, 2018 showing the tax adjusted profit.

b) To calculate the Class 4 national insurance contributions payable for 2018/19 (using the data provided)

c) To prepare an estimate for Roger of the income tax payable for 2018/19 and to advise him when the tax will become due for payment.

Feedback

(a) Profit adjustment statement year ended 30 June, 2018

	£	£
Net profit per accounts		50,400
Add:		
(1) Sales: Goods for own use (see working 1 below)	334	
(3) Wages: Roger's drawings (appropriation)	2,600	
Roger's NIC (private)	320	
(4) Capital cost of fitting covers	3,000	
(5) Miscellaneous:		
Political donation (not wholly and exclusively)	100	
Taxation (private)	15,590	
(6) Loan to former employee (not business)	250	
(7) Legal expenses:		
Lease of new and larger premises (capital)	250	
Cost in connection tax appeal (private)	200	
Defending re: speeding offence (private)	190	
Depreciation	570	
Loss on sale of office furniture (capital)	60	
(8) Interest: on overdue tax (private)	130	
(9) Motor car running expenses:		
Fine (not deductible)	65	
1/3 of remaining expenses (private)	645	
(10) Re-location expenditure (capital)	2,400	26,704
Less:		
Capital allowances	480	
(Chapter 7 will discuss this item further)		
(2) Inventory adjustment for contingency (working 2)	8,000	
(6) Reduction in general bad debt provision	150	(8,630)
Tax adjusted trading profit		68,474

(b) Class 4 National insurance contributions

9% x (£46,350 – £8,424) + 2% x (68,474 – 46,350) = £3,855.82

(c) Computation of income tax liability 2018/19

	Non-savings £	Total £
Income:		
Trading income		
(adjusted profits)	68,474	68,474
Total Income	68,474	68,474
Less Personal Allowances	(11,850)	(11,850)
Total Taxable Income	56,624	56,624

Roger has made pension contributions of £13,500. This is the gross amount of the payment. As we saw in section 5.3, basic tax relief for the pension payment is obtained by Roger making the payment net of income tax at the basic rate. That is, he will pay only £10,800 (£13,500 × 80%). Higher rate relief is given by extending his basic rate band by the gross amount of the premium, £13,500. Roger's basic rate band is therefore increased to £48,000 (£34,500 + £13,500).

Tax Due:

		£
Non savings income	48,000 @ 20%	9,600.00
	8,624 @ 40%	3,449.60
Tax Liability		13,049.60

Workings

1. Goods taken for Roger's own use must be included at market value. They have been reimbursed at cost, so we need to increase Roger's profit by the tax profit associated with goods costing £500:

	£
Sales £500 × 399,500/239,500	834
Less cost of sales	(500)
Profit	334

The sales price of the goods for Roger's own use is arrived at by multiplying the cost of those goods (£500) by Roger's gross sales figure (£400,000) less the cost of those goods taken for Roger's own use (£500) divided by the restated cost of sales (£240,000 – see working 2 below) again without the reimbursed goods' cost (£500) i.e. £239,500.

2. The valuation of inventory for tax purposes is on the basis of 'lower of cost or market value'. Therefore the cost of goods sold by Roger for tax purposes is:

Opening inventory	80,000
Plus purchases	224,000
	304,000
Less closing inventory	(64,000)
Cost of goods sold	240,000

Roger has only deducted cost of goods sold of £232,000 in his profit and loss account – a further deduction of £8,000 is required.

The Cash Basis Scheme

6.41 Having examined the normal method for determining trading income in sections 6.12 to 6.39, we can now turn to the second of the methods listed at the start of section 6.11. This is now an alternative allowable way of determining the taxable trading income (the cash basis) for some businesses. Under this basis, trading income is simply determined using business cash received in the year (of whatever type and in whatever form payment is received, including payments in kind) and deducting business expenses that have actually been paid during the period (irrespective of the tax or accounting years to which they actually relate).

This new scheme for small business started in 2013/14. Before this time only barristers could use the cash basis for determining their trading income. The Government believes this is a simpler way to do tax accounting for the smallest businesses, decreasing their tax compliance costs, and better reflecting in their tax computations the way in which they run their businesses already (i.e. on a cash basis). It is therefore most likely to be used by new start-up businesses.

To be eligible to use the cash basis turnover must be less than £150,000 for 2018/19 (unchanged from 2017/18 but significantly increased from £83,000 in 2016/17). If you are an individual who is in receipt of Universal Credit, however, this threshold is £300,000 (was double the VAT threshold, i.e. £166,000, in 2016/17). For businesses below the threshold, the cash basis scheme is optional. You can use accrual accounting if you wish to.

Fiscal Fact

Approximately 1.1m sole traders made use the cash basis as their tax computation basis in 2014/15. Following the increased threshold to £150,000 the Government anticipates up to 135,000 extra businesses could be eligible to use the cash basis if they wished to. [Sources: Office for Tax Simplification Micro-business tax report, March 2016; Increase to the cash basis threshold for unincorporated business, HMRC Policy Paper, 8 March 2017.]

If your business receipts exceed the threshold, you will be required to start using the accruals basis rules from the following tax year onwards (unless your receipts fall back below the relevant limit in the following year). You can also opt to switch out of the cash based system at any point should you so wish. In either case there are transition rules that must then be applied (see the HMRC website for guidance on these if you need them as they are beyond the scope of this book).

The cash basis rules apply for all business an individual runs either as a sole-trader or in partnership. That is, if the taxpayer runs more than one business, then the cash receipts in the year for all the businesses are added together in checking if they all can use the cash basis. This will prevent taxpayers artificially splitting up their businesses to stay under the thresholds.

A cap exists for the deductibility of loan interest under this scheme. You can only claim up to £500 a year as a deduction for interest on borrowing to fund your business. If the interest expense is more than £500, it may be better not to use the cash basis scheme as you could lose some of your tax deductible interest.

Bad debts (actual or provisions for) are not deductible under the cash basis. Income from sales is recorded when received and so no adjustment for bad debts will be needed.

Budget 2017 outlined a new list of expenses that were specifically disallowed for cash basis use to reduce uncertainty in this area. This list however, was cut from the first Finance Act 2017 as a result of the General Election – it seems highly likely though this will be provided in due course.

Not all business ventures are eligible this scheme, even if their business receipts come below the threshold levels. Specifically excluded business types include the following examples:

- Companies and Limited liability partnerships (LLPs);
- Businesses that have claimed research and development allowances (see Chapter 7); and,
- Businesses that are involved in the mineral extraction trade.

The cash basis scheme does not affect the decisions about your tax year. This can still be determined as best suits business needs, as we will see in section 6.7.

Basis of assessment

6.42   Income tax is calculated for individuals for tax years (6 April to following 5 April). These are called 'Assessment Years'. For employed people it is easy to assign their income to these periods to calculate their income tax liability as most employees are paid on a weekly, or monthly, basis – so we can just add up their payslips for the twelve month period (or use their P60 issued annually by their employer if they have this). For self-employed people paying tax on trading income however, this is not quite so straightforward because their income is based on their accounts, as we have just seen in the previous section. Accounts are produced in periods usually, but not always, of twelve months in length. These accounting periods may start and finish at different point during the year to the tax year, as suits the business. To perform tax computations for self-employed people we therefore need rules for how to allocate their trading income to tax years.

In this section we will discuss how these rules operate in the UK at present. These rules were introduced in 1998/99 for all unincorporated businesses as part of the self-assessment regime currently in operation in the UK for individual taxpayers.

As described in section 4.5, the normal basis of assessment for unincorporated businesses is the *current year* basis. If a sole trader or partnership uses an annual accounting date that is not 5 April, the accounting period ended in the tax year will normally form the basis period for the tax year.

To ensure you understand these rules, try the following activity:

Activity

For each of the following annual accounting dates state the tax year for which they will form the basis period.

  a) 30 June, 2018
  b) 31 August, 2017
  c) 30 November, 2018
  d) 31 January, 2018
  e) 31 March, 2019
  f) 30 April, 2019.

Feedback

The tax years for which these accounts form the basis period are:

  (a) 2018/19
  (b) 2017/18
  (c) 2018/19
  (d) 2017/18
  (e) 2018/19
  (f) 2019/20

 There are some circumstances in which the normal basis of assessment cannot be applied. These usually fall in the opening and closing years of a business trading or when the business decides to change its accounting date. Further explanations and worked examples for these extra rules can be found on the website.

Loss relief

6.43   What happens then, if the allowable expenses of a trading business exceed the revenue for tax purposes? In such a case, there are a number of possible ways of relieving the tax loss. These differ depending on the basis used to compute the trading loss for the year. If the cash basis is used the loss can be carried forward to the following year to offset trading income for that year, or subsequent years. If the accruals basis is used, in addition to the option to carry losses forward, the loss can be also offset against other categories of income that the taxpayer has during the year (sideways relief). Alternatively, the loss can be carried back to previous years to be offset against the general income of that year. The accruals basis therefore gives extra options for loss relief over the cash basis. We will look more closely at these rules in section 7.24 onwards.

Property income

6.44   Having examined how tax adjusted trading profit is computed, the final income component we will examine is property income. Most income from land and property located in the UK is taxed under the property income rules. This includes rents, lease premiums (if the lease is for not more than 50 years), income from rights of way or sporting rights over land or income from letting of fixed caravans or permanently moored house boats. The exceptions to this rule are hotels and guest houses as these are treated as trading income (use the rules therefore contained in the earlier parts of this chapter).

Taxable income from UK property is pooled (i.e. added together) to create one net profit or loss from all property belonging to a taxpayer. This profit or loss is calculated in the same way as trading income is computed (i.e. as discussed previously) – on either the accruals basis or, if eligible, the cash basis. Receiving money from UK property is referred to as running a 'property business'.

Income from most property (apart from furnished holiday lettings) is treated as 'unearned' income in a taxpayer's income tax computation, not 'earned' income (i.e. not considered to be trading income). A key implication of this is that it cannot be used as a source of income to count towards deductible pension contributions, nor can this type of property usually gain from business asset rates for rollover relief when calculating capital gains tax on property sales. The rules for furnished holiday lettings are different – these can count for pension contributions and for business asset rates of rollover relief etc. We will examine these specific differences later in this section.

The basis of assessment for property income is the income for the tax year, most often computed using the accruals basis. However, for very small, simple businesses, for example where income is only received from one property, and the taxpayer is trading below the VAT threshold, the cash basis can be applied.

Normal rules

6.45 Under the normal property business rules, we include the total income from land and property in the UK, regardless of the source, less total allowable expenses – i.e. to follow the same principles as we outlined above for trading income. Examples of allowable expenses include:

- expenses incurred wholly and exclusively for the purpose of the business such as repairs, insurance, advertising, legal costs, etc.;
- capital allowances for plant and machinery which enable taxpayers to carry on their business (unless the property is a dwelling where no capital allowances are available – see Chapter 7 for more on this);
- capital allowances for landlords of residential property on loft and cavity wall insulation up to a value of £1,500; and
- rent paid by the property business to another landlord (e.g. when rental income results from sub-letting).

If the rental comes from a fully furnished residential dwelling (of any kind other than holiday lettings – see below), the cost of replacing furnishings, appliances and kitchenware is allowed as a deduction. The replacement must be like for like, or nearest modern equivalent and relief is also given for any costs incurred in disposing of the asset being replaced. The deduction is reduced by any amounts received on disposal of the old item.

Before April 2016, a 'wear and tear' rules allowed for usage of fixed assets to be claimed at 10% of the relevant receipts from furnished lettings as relief for the wear and tear of furniture and equipment provided as part of the letting. Relevant receipts were gross receipts less any sums for services that would normally be borne by the tenant (payment of the council tax by the landlord would be an example of this). This approach is no longer allowed however.

Unlike normal trading businesses (see Chapter 7), these are the only capital expenditure deductions allowed for property businesses.

This activity illustrates how property income can be assessed in practice:

Activity

Andrew has a furnished house which is let for £4,800 per annum payable monthly in advance. Andrew incurred the following expenditure in the tax year.

		£
June 2018	Replacement of doors and windows with double glazed units.	1,500
July 2018	Annual insurance premium runs from 1 August to 31 July (last year's premium was £600)	900
November 2018	Redecoration	500
June 2019	Repairs to boiler – the work was undertaken and completed in January 2017	200

Andrew's tenant left in May 2018 without paying the rent due for May. Andrew was unable to recover the debt but he let the house to new tenants from 1 July, 2018. Determine Andrew's property business profit for 2018/19.

Feedback

	£	£
Rent accrued (£400 × 11)		4,400
Less allowable expenses:		
Doors and windows replacement	1,500	
Insurance (4/12 × £600 + 8/12 × £900)	800	
Redecoration	500	
Repairs to boiler	200	
Bad debt – May 2017 rent	400	
	(3,400)	
Property business profit		1,000

Cash basis

6.46 Alternatively, when eligible (e.g. if total turnover from the property business was less than £150,000, the business is not run by a limited company or limited liability partnership but only be an individual - or where jointly owned, for that part only that is owned by an individual), since 6 April 2017 the property owner will usually be presumed to use the cash basis for computing their property income for the tax year unless they specifically make an election to be assessed under the accruals basis rules (before this point, and since the cash basis was introduced on 6 April 2013, the property business owner had a choice which basis they used). Where no election is made the same rules will then apply as were described above for trading income i.e. the property income total to be subject to taxation will be determined by using the income received from the property (or properties if more than one owned by the business) in the year from which actual expenses paid in the period (including costs that would be classified as capital outlays in the accruals basis rules) will be deducted. This implies that no capital allowances will apply.

Where a property business owner has more than one property in their portfolio they can opt to use different basis for different properties if they so wish (i.e. some could be assessed under the cash basis and some under the accruals basis).

The cap of £500 for allowable loan interest deductions that applies when using the cash basis for trading income computations does not apply when using the cash basis for property income computations. Instead, the rules applying for determining the allowable deductions for the costs of the financing of the property (or properties) are outlined in the next section.

Activity

If Andrew (as in the activity above) used the cash basis, what would his property business profit be for 2018/19?

Feedback

	£	£
Rent received (£400 × 10)		4,000
Less allowable expenses:		
Doors and windows replacement	1,500	
Insurance	900	
Redecoration	500	(2,900)
Property business profit		1,100

Notes:

1. Rent received is now just recognised for 10 months as the total amount received in the tax year (as no payments were received in May and June 2018). The tenth payment is received at the start of April 2019 which, whilst is primarily for rent for the period that falls into 2019/20 (i.e. the period after 6 April 2019), is actually received in the 2018/19 tax year and so must be counted as income for that year under the cash basis. In the accruals basis case above, the tenth payment would be treated as a pre-payment for April 2019 that would need to be partly allocated to 2018/19 and partly to 2019/20. As bad debts do not apply under the cash basis, the eleventh payment under the accrual system, (then deducted as an expense determined as bad) is not relevant under the cash basis.

2. Each expense that occurred in the year is included (i.e. doors and window replacements, redecoration and the actual insurance premium payment made – in full, not adjusted for accrual or pre-payment). The repairs to the boiler will not be included as, despite this work occurring during the year, it is not actually paid for until June 2019 and so will be a deduction in 2019/20, not this tax year.

In this case, Andrew is better off not electing to use the cash basis, but the position may be different in future years.

Finance costs

6.47 Before 6 April 2017 landlords of residential property could fully deduct the cost of financing any loans they took out related to a property they were letting (e.g. the cost of interest they paid in the year on a mortgage taken out to buy the property). Budget 2017 announced that the ability to fully deduct these costs will be restricted in stages between April 2017 and April 2020 to the point where only basic rate (20%) tax can be reclaimed on these particular costs as a tax reduction at the end of this period. This means instead of the full cost being deducted against the income as an allowable expense of doing business, once the tax due is computed, an adjustment will be made to provide basic rate tax relief only.

The tax reduction is 20% of the lower of:

- The finance costs not deducted from rental income in the tax year
- Property business profits after using any brought forward losses
- Adjusted total income, after losses and reliefs (but excluding savings and dividend income) that exceeds the personal allowance.

Between 2017/18 and 2020/21 there will be a transition arrangement where part of the financing costs is deductible and part is applied as a reduction. The relevant percentages are as follows:

Tax year	% of finance costs deductible	% of basic rate tax reduction
2017/18	75%	25%
2018/19	50%	50%
2019/20	25%	75%
2020/21	0%	100%

To illustrate using Andrew's case above – if Andrew had purchased the house with a mortgage on which he paid £700 in interest in the year to 6 April 2017 this would have all been an allowable expense in computing his tax due from the property letting for 2016/17 (i.e had he incurred all the costs listed above in the

2016/17 year, instead of 2017/18, then the £1,000 property business profit computed above under the accrual basis would go down to £300, or the £1,100 profit computed under the cash basis would become £400).

Since 2017/18 however, he can't claim the whole £700 as a deduction. In 2018/19, the second year of the transition period, only 50% of this (i.e. £350) can be claimed (in 2017/18 this would have been 75% ie £525). The remaining 50% of this interest (£350) would be applied as a tax reduction at the basic rate of tax (20%) at the end of his income tax computation i.e. his revised property business profit for 2018/19 will become (using the accrual computation as an example although the same process applies if he is using the cash basis), assuming he is a higher rate taxpayer:

	£
Property business profit (per computation above)	1,000
Finance Costs deduction:	
Mortgage interest (£700 x 50%)	(350)
Property business profit	650
Tax @ 40%	260.00
Finance costs reduction:	
(£700 x 50%) x 20%	(70.00)
Income tax due on the property business	190.00

The new rules, in Andrew's case, therefore mean he will be paying £70 (£190 – £120 (i.e. £1,000 – £700 @40%) in extra tax in the year compared to the previous rules.

Do note that the new finance costs reduction computation should be applied at the same stage in Andrew's personal income tax computation as other tax reducers, i.e. at Step 6 of the computation (see Chapter 4.2 for a reminder of the steps if necessary).

One further complication of these new rules is that if this computation creates a tax refund (e.g. as finance and other costs exceed income in the year) then the reduction allowed is capped and any further reduction that would have otherwise been allowed from these new finance costs rules is carried forward as extra allowable finance costs for use in the following year.

Examples of how the tax reduction may be limited if it creates a tax refund can be found on the gov.uk website if required at: https://www.gov.uk/guidance/changes-to-tax-relief-for-residential-landlords-how-its-worked-out-including-case-studies

Loss relief

6.48 Unlike trading losses, options to relieve property income losses are the same irrespective of basis used for the tax computation. Losses arising under property income rules can only be carried forward and set against the first available property income profits in the future. If a loss arises across all a taxpayer's property business, the assessment for that year will then be nil. If a loss arises for one part of the property business only it will be netted against any gains in other parts first however, as part of the pooling of property income.

Where a difference does occur between the cash and accruals basis computations however, is where the loss results from the use of capital allowances, as this can occur when using the accruals basis. These losses can be applied sideways (against other current non-property income). Where it is to be used as a relief against general income in this way, it is included in the tax computation at step 2. If the cash basis is used, carrying forward of losses will be the only option allowed.

An illustration of the property income loss rules can be found on the website. This demonstrates how they work in practice.

Furnished holiday lettings

6.49 A special tax position exists for furnished holiday lettings (including both houses and caravans). Income from this kind of property is assessed under property income rules, however, the regulations which apply to trading income are used to determine the taxable income as this income is normally treated as "earned income" unlike other property income (which you will recall we said at the start of this section is treated as unearned income). This means if you wish to, you can use the accruals basis system. If you don't opt for the cash basis, normal capital allowances can be claimed (i.e. instead of the renewals basis as for other dwellings), capital gains tax relief for the disposal of business assets (i.e. entrepreneurs' relief and rollover relief, which are explained in Chapter 8) is available and loss relief can be claimed under the regulations which apply to losses incurred by traders (see Chapter 7).

If the cash basis is used, then the usual rules will apply i.e. all trading receipts received in the year will form the basis of the income to be reported with only expenses paid in the year (of whatever kind) being deductible.

Because these profits are treated as earned income the taxpayer can also provide for retirement by making contributions to a pension fund that include this income in their computation (see the section in this Chapter 5 for more detail on pensions). However, no Class 4 national insurance contributions are due on this income source as Class 4 only applies to income assessed under trading income.

Note that the basis period rules for property income rather than trading income still apply to income from furnished holiday lettings despite this special treatment (i.e. you use the tax year).

To be eligible for this advantageous treatment the accommodation must be let commercially with the aim of making a profit. Also, these rules must apply:

1. *The availability condition:* the property must be available for letting to the public for at least 210 days in the tax year.
2. *The letting condition:* the property must have actually been let for at least 105 of those days.
3. *Pattern of occupation condition:* For at least 155 days (including the 105 days from rule 2) the property must not normally be occupied by the same tenant for more than 31 days.

In addition, if the taxpayer owns more than one property, each of which satisfies the 210 day rule, they will all be deemed to satisfy the 105 day rule providing their average number of days let is at least 105.

Also, from April 2011, if a property meets the 'actually let' threshold for any one year, the owner can elect for it to be treated as having also met this criteria for the following two years (called the 'period of grace') providing certain conditions are met. This may be useful if these criteria are periodically missed (e.g. while under refurbishment).

Activity

Leonard owned four furnished houses in a village in the Yorkshire Dales which are let as holiday homes. None of the houses are normally let to the same tenant for more than 31 consecutive days. The numbers of days for which each house was available for letting and actually let in this tax year were:

House	Days available	Days let
1	250	115
2	290	87
3	200	180
4	365	100

Determine Leonard's potential averaging claims.

Feedback

House 3 does not satisfy the 210 day availability rule and so cannot be included in an averaging claim even though it is let for more than 105 days, so meets the letting condition. If no averaging claim is made, only house 1 qualifies as furnished holiday accommodation.

Possible averaging claim	Average days let
House 1 and 2	101.0
House 1 and 4	107.5
House 2 and 4	92.5
House 1, 2 and 4	100.7

Averaging house 1 and 4 is beneficial because the average number of days let is more than 105. No other averaging claim would succeed.

The furnished holiday lettings rules only applied to UK property, until 6 April 2009 when they were extended to include property in the European Economic Area. It was proposed that the special rules for furnished holiday lettings would be abolished in 2010/11, however the Emergency Budget in June 2010 confirmed these rules would continue but were subject to revised plans from April 2011. These included requiring the splitting off of any EEA property in the portfolio from the UK property to form separate 'property businesses'. The significance of this change is that any losses incurred can only be offset by the same 'business' (i.e EEA property losses can't be offset against UK property income).

The 'rent a room' scheme

6.50 If an individual lets one or more furnished rooms in his or her main residence then rents received up to a limit of £7,500 in 2018/19 (previously £4,250 for many years but significantly increased in 2016/17) are exempt from tax under property income. If another individual is also receiving rent from letting accommodation in the same property (for example, as joint owner) the limit of £7,500 will be halved. If the total receipts are in excess of £7,500 (£3,750 if halved) then the taxpayer has a choice as to how they are taxed. Either the excess receipts over £7,500 (£3,750) is taxed in full (i.e. no deductions are allowed) or they can choose to be taxed on a normal trading computation principle (i.e. the gross rents received minus any allowable deductions, such as heating costs is taxed instead - although note that for capital expenditure deductions, such as for the furniture for the room, normal capital allowances are not available as this is in a dwelling house, instead the replacement basis rules would be applied for these expense. If the cash basis is used, only actual expenditure in the year will be deductible. The taxpayer has the choice of which of these two calculations should determine their taxable income in this case.

Any income arising from the 'rent-a-room' scheme is normally likely to be treated as part of property income in the taxpayers' tax computation. If a trade is being carried out however, (e.g. if meals are cleaning/laundry services are also provided in addition to just the charge for the use of a room itself) then this income can probably be added to trading income totals.

This allowance cannot be claimed in addition to the new £1,000 property income allowance (as introduced in 2017/18 and described in section 4.37). The property owner must decide which of this allowance or this relief to claim.

HMRC have announced a consultation on the 'rent a room' scheme will be undertaken in 2017/18 aiming to make sure the scheme is well-targeted to support longer term lettings. The results of this consultation was not available at the time of updating this text. Details can be found at https://www.gov.uk/government/consultations/rent-a-room-relief .

Fiscal Fact

The estimated cost to the UK Government of allowing the rent-a-room scheme for 2015/16 is £110 million. The cost is forecast to increase in 2017/18 to £140 million with the increase in the threshold from £4,250 to £7,500 (Source: 'Estimated costs of principal tax reliefs' – HMRC)

Premiums on leases

6.51 We saw in our discussion of trading expenses that when a lease is granted the lessee may have to pay a premium to the lessor. A premium is a lump sum payment at the commencement of the lease and is different to the regular lease or rental payments made throughout the course of the lease. In fact, some leases are structured so that the lessor receives very little rent for the duration of the lease but has to depend on the lease premium for income from the property. This situation is most typically found in commercial (e.g. office space) leases.

If the lease term is more than 50 years (termed a *long lease*) then the premium is taxable as a capital gain rather than an income. If the lease is for 50 years or less (a *short lease*) income tax is paid on the value of the premium less 2% of the premium for each complete year of the lease after the first. Written as a formula the assessable amount of the lease premium therefore equals:

$$P - (P \times (L - 1) \times 2\%)$$

where P is the premium on the lease and L is the length of the lease.

Activity

Amanda granted a 21-year lease on a property on 1 January, 2019 for an initial premium of £30,000 and an annual rent of £6,000 payable monthly in advance. Determine Amanda's property income for 2018/19 and 2019/20 using the accruals basis.

Feedback

In 2018/19 the assessment on the premium of the lease is £18,000 (£30,000 − (£30,000 × (21 − 1) × 2%)). The rent due in 2018/19 is £1,500 (£6,000 × 3/12). Hence the total property income for 2018/19 is £19,500 (£18,000 + £1,500). In 2019/20 the property income will be £6,000. The remaining £12,000 of the lease premium will fall to be taxed under the capital gains tax rules (see Chapter 8). It is an interesting example of how the law takes a capital receipt and turns part of it into an income equivalent receipt to be taxed under income tax, and leaves the balance to be dealt with as a capital gain under the capital gains tax rules.

We saw earlier that if the property is used for business purposes, the lessee on a short lease can claim a tax deduction against their trading profits of the annual equivalent of the amount of premium they paid and on which the landlord is liable to pay tax in each year of the lease. In the activity above, Amanda's tenant would therefore be able to claim a deduction of £18,000÷21 = £857 in each year of the life of the lease.

Note that the above rules on premiums only apply on the granting of the lease (i.e. from landlord to lessee) not if it is subsequently assigned (i.e. transferred from one lessee to another lessee).

In some cases, a premium may actually be paid by the landlord to the lessee (rather than the lessee to the landlord) perhaps as an inducement to the lessee to take on the lease. This occurs most commonly in commercial leasing. This type of premium is usually called a *reverse premium*. When a reverse premium is paid the landlord can usually either treat the payment made as an enhancement expenditure against their capital gains tax bill when they sell the property (see Chapter 8 for details of how this works in practice), or as an allowable business expense if they are a property developer or dealer. Of course, the lessee must declare the receipt of the premium as income on which they will have to pay tax (under trading income if the property rented is used for this business, or under property income if it is not for commercial use).

Summary

This chapter looks trading and property income. It outlines how to distinguish between a trading activity and an activity that is carried out as a non-trading activity, maybe as a hobby. It outlines how the 'Badges of Trade' are used in practice for this assessment given we have no legal definition for trading. As accounting profit for the business is the foundation for trading income computations, it then focuses on how to adjust the accounting figures to arrive at the tax computation using either the traditional 'accruals basis' or the new simpler income tax 'cash basis' scheme introduced in April 2013 for some small businesses. This involves manipulation of both receipts and expenses from the accounts. A detailed worked example was then provided to illustrate these principles in practice.

The question of what happens when a trading activity results in a loss was outlined but this will be considered in more detail in Chapter 7.

Property income is discussed illustrating the specific rules used for computing this component of income, particular focusing on how income from furnished holiday letting property can be taxed differently to income from other dwellings. The special rules for the 'rent-a-room' scheme and for lease premiums were also outlined.

Project areas

This chapter provides a rich source of material for projects including:

- the impact of taxation on reported profit.
- the differences between trading and non-trading activities in practice
- the classification of expenses into revenue and capital items
- the use of different recognition bases for reporting profits
- the advantages of income from furnished holiday lettings being considered to be trading income. Does it just give special tax breaks to rich people with second homes distorting local housing in some areas of the UK?

Quick quiz

(Assume all the following relate to activities that are trading and the accruals basis is used unless otherwise stated)

1. Matthew charges £800 to his profit and loss account for bad and doubtful debts. This figure consists of £300 trade debts written off, £150 staff loan written off, £100 increase in specific provision and £250 increase in general provision. What amount (if any) is to be added back in the course of adjusting profits for tax purpose?

2. How would Matthew's (from Q1) assessment change if he opted to use the cash basis for this tax year?

3. Nola leases a car for use in her business, which costs £25,000 when new, for £4,200 per annum.

4. Orlando spends £500 on 100 T-shirts, printed with his business logo, to give to his customers, and spends £200 per head on a Christmas party for his 5 staff. How much (if any) of this expenditure is deductible?

5. Pauline takes goods costing £90 from her business stock for her own personal use. She normally sells such items for £115. What adjustment is required to her net profit for tax purposes if she pays nothing for the goods and records the £90 as a cost of sale?

6. Quentin pays a lease premium of £10,000 for the 15 year lease of his business premises. How much of this (if any) can he deduct?

7. Rachel incurs legal fees for her business of £500 being £30 for debt collection, £270 for the acquisition of new business premises and £200 for registration of a patent. How much (if any) can she deduct?

8. As a personal landlord Gerald owns a second house which he lets to a tenant for a rent payable monthly in advance. The annual rent of £8,400 was increased to £8,600 on 6 October, 2017. How much is assessable as Gerald's property income?

9. Heather receives a lease premium of £48,000 in respect of a 40 year lease. How much (if any) is chargeable as property income?

Questions

Question 1 (based on CIMA May 1992 - updated).

The following events occurred and were reflected in the profit and loss account of Mr Jones' self-employed business for the year ended 31 March, 2019.

Debits

(a) Expenditure of £8,500 was incurred on the reconstruction of a roof on a second-hand warehouse which was recently purchased. This had been damaged in a fire some months before Jones acquired it.

(b) During the year a director was convicted of embezzlement and the amount of the loss, as established in court, was £18,000.

(c) Due to a contraction of the trade, a works manager was made redundant. His statutory redundancy entitlement was £12,000 and the total gratuitous lump sum paid to him (including the £12,000) was £38,000.

(d) For the whole of the year, one of the senior managers was seconded to work full-time for a national charity. Her annual salary, included in the salaries charged in the profit and loss account, was £24,000.

(e) Costs of £24,000 were incurred in constructing a crèche to be used for employees' children. Administration costs include £8,000 in respect of the running costs of the crèche incurred during the year.

Credits

(f) £24,000 was received from an insurance company in respect of damage caused to a processing plant as a result of a fork-lift truck colliding with it. The cost of repairing the plant was £18,000 and this was credited against the repairs account. The additional £6,000 was an agreed sum paid for loss of profits while the plant was unusable and this was credited to the profit and loss account.

(g) A gain of £30,000 arose on the sale of selected investments. No details of the original cost or disposal price are given at this stage.

(h) Mr Jones has included in his sales figure for the year, sales amounting to £50,000 to X Ltd, a company in which he has an interest. These sales have been heavily discounted and, if they had been made at the normal retail price, would have been sold for £80,000.

Required: Indicate, giving full reasons and quoting case law where appropriate, how each of the above items would be dealt with in arriving at the tax adjusted trading profit figure for the year if Mr Jones is using the accruals basis.

You must state in your answer whether each item would be added to or subtracted from the profit shown by the profit and loss account (which is not given) or left unadjusted.

Question 2 (based on ACCA June 2008).
Sam is self-employed running a retail clothing shop. His income statement for the year ended 5 April 2019 is as follows:

	£	£
Gross profit		140,300
Depreciation	7,600	
Motor expenses [1]	8,800	
Patent royalties [2]	700	
Professional fees [3]	1,860	
Other expenses [4]	71,340	
		(90,300)
		50,000

Notes:

1. During the year ended 5 April 2019 Sam drove a total of 25,000 miles, of which 5,000 miles were driven when he visited his suppliers in Europe. The balance of the mileage is 25% for private journeys and 75% for business journeys in the UK.

2. During the year ended 5 April 2019 Sam paid patent royalties of £700 (gross) in respect of specialised technology that he uses when altering clothes for customers.

3. The figure for professional fees consists of £1,050 for legal fees in connection with an action brought against a supplier for breach of contract and £810 for accountancy. Included in the figure for accountancy is £320 in respect of personal capital gains tax advice for the tax year 2017/18.

4. The figure for other expense of £71,340 includes £560 for gifts to customers of food hampers costing £35 each and £420 for gifts to customers of pens carrying an advertisement for the clothing shop costing £60 each.

5. Sam uses one of the eight rooms in his private residence as an office when he works at home. The total running costs of the house for the year ended 5 April 2019 were £5,120. This cost is not included in the income statement's expenses of £90,300.

6. Sam uses his private telephone to make business telephone calls. The total cost of the private telephone for the year ended 5 April 2019 was £1,600 and 25% of this related to business telephone calls. The cost of the private telephone is not included in the income statement expenses of £90,300.

7. During the year ended 5 April 2019 Sam took goods out of the clothing shop for his personal use without paying for them and no entry has been made in the accounts to record this. The goods cost £820 and had a selling price of £1,480.

8. Sam is entitled to claim capital allowances of £ 6,100.

Required: Compute Sam's tax adjusted profits for the year ended 5 April 2019.

Question 3 (based on ICAS TPS Tax Paper June 2010).

Ben Roberts was employed for many years as a design engineer until he was made redundant on 5 June 2017. After a period out of work, Ben started his own design consultancy, BR Associates, on 1 February 2018. Ben wishes to draw up accounts to 31 January 2019 and has kept a cash book record of his receipts and payments as follows:

	Cash payments	Cash receipts
	£	£
Sales income received from customers [1]		75,000
Materials [2]	29,429	
Rent paid [3]	11,000	
Wages for Ben Roberts	12,000	
Machinery purchased	4,122	
Entertaining [5]	2,103	
New computer purchased	1,855	
Heat and light	1,123	
Travel and subsistence [6]	1,426	
Repairs [7]	1,250	
Interest paid	964	
Clothing [8]	680	
Motor expenses [4]	636	
		(66,588)
Surplus		8,412

Notes:

1. Accounts receivable at 31 January 2019 amounted to £2,900; the sales value of work done but not invoiced at this point came to £1,300.
2. The only accrued expense at 31 January 2019 was interest of £74. All materials are used up in the period.
3. Ben signed a 15-year lease on 1 March 2018. He pays rent of £1,000 each month in advance.
4. Ben's car is used two-thirds for business purposes. Ben wishes to use actual costs for this tax computation and not make use of optional fixed rate expenses.
5. Entertaining comprises £986 for entertaining UK customers and £1,117 in respect of potential overseas customers.
6. All travel was to clients and no overnight stays were involved. Subsistence includes £246 lunch costs while travelling undertaking his business activity, of which £158 relates to the extra cost of buying lunch over and above what Ben spends normally.
7. This relates to repairs which were necessary before the machinery purchased in the period could be used.
8. This relates to the cost of two new suits used only for work.
9. Ben is entitled to tax capital allowances of £6,830 for the year.

Required: Compute Ben's tax adjusted profits;

    a)   on an accruals basis;

    b)   on a cash basis.

You may ignore the VAT implications of the business. All costs were incurred within the tax year, and were paid in the tax year, unless otherwise indicated.

Question 4

Vincent's profit and loss account for the year to 31 August, 2018 was as follows:

	£		£
General expenses(1)	114,000	Gross trading profit	295,000
Repairs and renewals(2)	20,000	Bad debts recovered	
Legal and accounting charges(3)	1,200	(previously written off)	400
Subscriptions and donations(4)	3,000	Commissions received(5)	800
Manager's remuneration	40,000	Bank interest	1,000
Salaries and wages to staff	38,000		
Depreciation	20,000		
Rent and rates	1,500		
Net profit	59,500		
	297,200		297,200

Notes

(1) General expenses include the following:

	£
Travelling expenses of staff	1,000
Entertaining suppliers	600

(2) Repairs and renewals include the following:

Redecorating existing premises	300
Renovations to new premises to remedy wear and tear of previous owner (the premises were usable before these renovations)	500

(3) Legal and accounting charges are made up as follows:

Debt collection service	200
Staff service agreements	50
Tax consultant's fees for special advice	730
Audit and accountancy	220
	1,200

(4) Subscriptions and donations include the following
Donation to a political party   700
Staff Canteen facilities – running costs   500

(5) The commissions received were not incidental to trade

(6) Capital allowances for tax purposes for the year   4,000

(7) No payment to Vincent is included in the Manager's remuneration or Salaries and Wages to staff

Required: Compute Vincent's tax adjusted profits and, assuming he has no other income or deductions, calculate the income tax and national insurance contributions payable.

(Note: answer available via lecturer's website)

Question 5 (based on ACCA Paper 7 December 2007)

Edmond Brick owns four properties which are let out. The following information relates to the tax year 2018/19:

Property one: This is a freehold house (purchased outright) that is let out furnished. The property was let throughout the tax year 2018/19 at a monthly rent of £575, payable in advance. During the tax year 2018/19, Edmond paid council tax of £1,200 and insurance of £340 in respect of this property. He brought no new capital items in this tax year.

Property two: This is a freehold house that is let out unfurnished. The property was purchased on 6 March 2018 and it was empty until 30 June 2018. It was then let from 1 July 2018 to 31 January 2019 at a monthly rent of £710 payable in advance. On 31 January 2019, the tenant left owing three months rent that Edmond was unable to recover. The property was not re-let before 5 April 2019. During the tax year Edmond paid insurance of £290 for this property and spent £670 on advertising for tenants. He also paid loan interest (i.e. financing costs) of £500 in respect of a mortgage that was taken out to purchase this property.

Property three: This is a leasehold office building that is let out unfurnished. Edmond pays an annual rent of £6,800 for this property, but did not pay a premium when he acquired it. On 6 April 2018 the property was let to a sub-tenant, with Edmond receiving a premium of £15,000 for the grant of a five year lease. He also received the annual rent of £4,600 which was payable in advance. During the tax year 2018/19, Edmond paid insurance of £360 in respect of this property.

Furnished room: During the tax year 2018/19, Edmond rented out one furnished room of his main residence. During the year he received rent of £5,040, and incurred allowable expenditure of £1,140 in respect of the room. Edmond always computes the taxable income for the furnished room on the most favourable basis.

Required: Calculate Edmond's property business profit in respect of the three properties and the furnished room for the tax year 2018/19;

a)   using the accruals basis;

b)   using the cash basis.

(Note: answer available via lecturer's website)

Question 6 (based on ACCA Paper June 2014)

Richard Tryer was born on 22 June 1971. He is employed by Prog plc as a computer programmer and is also self-employed as a website designer. Richard has tried to prepare his own income tax computation for the tax year 2018/19, but he has found it more difficult than expected. Although the sections which Richard has completed are correct, there are a significant number of omissions. The omissions are marked as outstanding (O/S). The partly completed income tax computation is as follows:

Richard Tryer – Income tax computation (2018/19)

	£	£
Trading profit 1 (note 1)		O/S
Employment income		
Salary	41,000	
Car benefit 2 (note 2)	O/S	
Fuel benefit 2 (note 2)	O/S	
Living accommodation 3 (note 3)	O/S	
		O/S
Property business profit (note 4)		O/S
Building society interest		1,260
Dividends		1,800
		O/S
Personal allowance		(11,850)
Taxable income		O/S

Note 1 – Trading profit

Richard commenced self-employment on 1 January 2018. He had a tax adjusted trading profit of £11,592 for the year ended 31 December 2018.

Note 2 – Car and fuel benefits

Throughout the tax year 2018/19, Prog plc provided Richard with a petrol-powered motor car which has a list price of £17,900. The motor car cost Prog plc £17,200, and it has a CO_2 emission rate of 144 g/km. During the tax year 2018/19, Richard made contributions of £1,200 to Prog plc for the use of the motor car.

During the period 1 July 2018 to 5 April 2019, Prog plc also provided Richard with fuel for private journeys. The total cost of fuel during the period 1 July 2018 to 5 April 2019 was £4,200, of which 45% was for private journeys. Richard did not make any contributions towards the cost of the fuel.

Note 3 – Living accommodation

Throughout the tax year 2018/19, Prog plc provided Richard with living accommodation. The property has been rented by Prog plc since 6 April 2018 at a cost of £1,100 per month. On 6 April 2018, the market value of the property was £122,000, and it has an annual value of £8,600.

On 6 April 2018, Prog plc purchased furniture for the property at a cost of £12,100. The company pays for the running costs relating to the property, and for the tax year 2018/19 these amounted to £3,700.

Note 4 – Property business profit

Richard owns a freehold shop which is let out unfurnished. The shop was purchased on 1 October 2018, and during October 2018 Richard spent £8,400 replacing the building's roof. The shop was not usable until this work was carried out, and this fact was represented by a reduced purchase price. During November 2018, Richard spent £800 on advertising the property for rent.

On 1 December 2018, the property was let to a tenant, with Richard receiving a premium of £12,000 for the grant of a 30-year lease. The monthly rent is £830 payable in advance, and during the period 1 December 2018 to 5 April 2019 Richard received five rental payments.

Due to a fire, £8,600 was spent on replacing the roof of the shop during February 2019. Only £8,200 of this was paid for by Richard's property insurance.

Richard paid insurance of £480 in respect of the property. This was paid on 1 October 2018 and is for the year ended 30 September 2019.

Required: Calculate the income tax payable by Richard Tryer for the tax year 2018/19.

(Note: answer available via lecturer's website)

Further test questions for this chapter to test your knowledge can be found in the student section of the website at:
http://www.taxstudent.com/uk

Further reading and examples

Combs, A., Tutin, R. & Rowes, P. (2018), *Taxation: incorporating the 2018 Finance Act*, Fiscal Publications: Birmingham.
    – use this book for many other examples to further develop and test your knowledge of this chapter's contents. See http://www.fiscalpublications.com/rowes/2018

7 Capital allowances and trading losses

Introduction

7.1 This chapter continues the subject discussed in Chapter 6 – the taxation of unincorporated businesses. Here we consider the tax treatment of capital (i.e. non-current) assets under the capital allowances rules. Although we focus in this chapter on examples related to unincorporated businesses, you need to be aware that in fact these rules also apply for employees and companies that are eligible for capital allowances. The rules on capital allowances in this chapter do not apply if a business chooses to use the cash basis as discussed in Chapter 6.

At the end of this chapter we also consider the special tax rules that apply when an unincorporated business makes a loss.

At the end of this chapter you will be able to:
- identify plant and machinery that qualify for capital allowances;
- undertake capital allowance computations for plant and machinery;
- state the capital allowance rules for patents; and
- state the special tax rules that deal with the offset of trading losses for unincorporated businesses.

Overview of capital allowances

7.2 You will remember from the previous chapter that (as a general rule) neither actual capital expenditure (i.e. related to non-current assets) nor depreciation are allowable deductions for income tax computations when using the accruals basis. Tax relief for capital expenditure is instead given by means of capital allowances. This ensures consistent treatment of capital assets for tax purposes, rather than allowing the multiple possible treatments that would occur if accounting depreciation policies were used in tax computations. It also allows for special tax treatment of particular assets, asset groups or types of company as Government policy may require. We will see how the current special treatments are applied later in this chapter.

The bulk of the current legislation relating to capital allowances is contained in the Capital Allowances Act 2001 (CAA 2001).

Capital allowances are available to businesses on certain, but not all, capital assets. Just because you depreciate the asset for the accounting profit computation does not automatically mean you will also qualify for a comparable capital allowance for tax purposes.

Capital allowances allowed as a deduction each year are a fixed percentage of the value of the capital asset, or *pool* (collection) of assets, in question. They are usually given on a *reducing balance* basis and are called *writing down allowances* (WDA). Capital allowances are available on the date the payment made when buying qualifying assets becomes unconditional.

For expenditure on capital assets to be eligible for capital allowances they must fall into one of these categories:
- plant and machinery;
- integral features;
- patents; and
- agricultural buildings and works.

The first two categories are the most common and so we will concentrate on these in this chapter. The rules for patents will be commented upon briefly at the end of this chapter. Prior to 2011/12 capital allowances were also available for industrial buildings (such as factories or workshops). This ceased to be available from April 2011. Now neither buildings nor land (which didn't qualify before either) qualify for any capital allowances, although some integral features of buildings may, as we will see later.

Plant, machinery and integral features

7.3   To calculate capital allowances for plant and machinery and integral features, we need to go through a number of steps to decide:
1. whether the capital asset qualifies for capital allowances in the first place;
2. if so, which pool the asset belongs to and the rate of capital allowance;
3. whether the Annual Investment Allowance or Enhanced Capital Allowances apply;
4. whether the asset requires some special treatment; and
5. whether any disposals need to be dealt with.

Only after considering each of these steps, will you be ready to do a full capital allowance computation for the year.

Capital allowances pro forma

7.4   This is what a capital allowance computation will look like for a straightforward case. It is important to make sure you deal with things in a logical order. If you know the way to lay out a capital allowances computation you will be able to calculate the capital allowances for a business with relative ease. Therefore, this is the way we have laid out the answers to activities in this section and we advise you to use it wherever you do a capital allowance calculation.

Capital allowances on the main pool for plant and machinery (numbers given are just for illustration).

	£	Main Pool £	Allowances £
Balance brought forward		130,000	
Additions qualifying for AIA:			
Plant	20,000		
AIA	(20,000)		20,000
Excess additions over AIA cap		0	
Disposals		(40,000)	
		90,000	
Writing down allowance (90,000 × 18%)		(16,200)	16,200
Written down value c/f		73,800	
Allowances for the accounting period			36,200

The 'allowances' column at the end is the one in which we record the amounts that will be allowed as a deduction in the computation of the tax adjusted trading profit for the business (or other qualifying activity).

Fiscal Fact

The estimated cost to the government of providing capital allowances under income tax and corporation tax is £21.5 billion for 2017/18. (Source: 'Estimated costs of principal tax reliefs' – HMRC)

Take careful note of the order in which adjustments are made to the value of the capital allowance pool in the above pro forma. This order is important to ensure you calculate the correct writing down allowances each year. We will now consider each of the steps in turn so that you can see how the capital allowance computation is constructed.

Step 1: Does the asset qualify?

7.5   The first step is to decide whether the capital asset purchased by a business qualifies for any capital allowances or not. Like previous legislation on capital allowances, the CAA 2001 does not define plant and machinery and so it is necessary to look to case law for guidance. There has been a considerable amount of case law on this subject. One of the most important is *Yarmouth v France* (1887) in which the status of a horse was questioned. Lindley LJ concluded:

> "There is no definition of plant in the Act but in its original sense, it includes whatever apparatus is used by a businessman for carrying on his business, not his stock-in-trade which he buys or makes for sale; but all goods and chattels, fixed or moveable, live or dead, which he keeps for permanent employment in his business."

The *Yarmouth v France* decision therefore excludes trading stock from the meaning of 'plant' and implies that business premises are also excluded.

A number of subsequent cases have refined this definition somewhat. In *Wimpy International Ltd v Warland* (1988) three types of asset were excluded from the definition of plant and machinery:

- assets which are not used for carrying on the business;
- assets with a useful life of less than two years; and
- assets which form part of the setting in which the business was carried on, as opposed to assets actively used in the business.

As this judgment is actually the cumulative result of a number of earlier cases, it would be useful for us to review some of the more interesting ones. Understanding these rules is important as not having a proportion of capital expenditure allowed as a tax deduction has significant cost implications for businesses.

The last requirement is referred to as the 'function v setting' test and has been the subject of a considerable number of cases, as it can be a difficult test to apply in practice. In *CIR v Barclay Curle & Co* (1969) the costs of building a dry dock, which is used for repair and maintenance work on ships, was held to be expenditure on plant and machinery because the dock played an active part in the operation of the company's trade as a ship builder. In *Cooke v Beach Station Caravans Ltd* (1974) the costs of excavating and installing a swimming pool were held to be expenditure on plant and machinery because the swimming pool performed a function, that of 'giving buoyancy and enjoyment to the swimmers' using the caravan park.

In *Benson v Yard Arm Club* (1978) a ship which was being used as a floating restaurant was held to be ineligible for capital allowances because it failed the functional test. It played a passive role as the setting for the restaurant business, rather than an active role. However, in another restaurant case, *CIR* v *Scottish and Newcastle Breweries Ltd* (1982) it was held that light fittings, decor and murals performed the function of creating an atmosphere and so were plant. In contrast, in *Wimpy International Ltd* v *Warland* (1988) a raised floor was held not to be plant as it was considered setting, despite the argument made that it was there to make the restaurant attractive to customers.

In another case, *Carr* v *Sayer* (1992), quarantine kennels were held not to be plant, despite being purpose built.

In the case of *Brown* v *Burnley Football and Athletic Co Ltd* (1980) expenditure on a new football stand was held not to be plant because it did not perform an active function in the business, just provided the setting. You will remember from the last chapter that *Burnley Football and Athletic Co Ltd* had also failed to claim the expenditure as a repair because the entire stand was replaced. Today, however, such expenditure would in fact be allowed under the special provisions currently in force, as below.

The following is automatically deemed to be plant and machinery by statute. Expenditure:

- on equipment in order to comply with fire regulations for a building occupied by the trader;
- on thermal insulation in an industrial building;
- in order to comply with statutory safety requirements for sports grounds;
- on computer software;
- on alterations to buildings connected to the installation of plant and machinery; and
- on personal security equipment.

In order to claim capital allowances, a person carrying on a trade must incur capital expenditure on machinery or plant wholly or partly for the purposes of the trade, and the machinery or plant must belong to him or her. The extent to which assets can be described as plant and machinery is highlighted in *Munby* v *Furlong* (1977) when a barrister successfully argued that his law library was plant because it was the apparatus used for carrying out his profession.

Integral features

7.6 One of the problem areas for deciding what qualifies as plant and machinery is items that are attached to buildings. In 2008/09 the government introduced a new category of items that qualify for capital allowances, called integral features. It consists of the following items which are integral to a building:

- An electrical system (including a lighting system);
- A cold water system;
- A space or water heating system, a powered system of ventilation, air cooling or air purification, and any floor or ceiling that is part of such a system;
- A lift, escalator or moving walkway; or
- External solar shading.

This measure was first announced in Budget 2007, and there was a considerable amount of consultation with business about its design and technical approach. Some items that were previously treated as part of a building and therefore didn't qualify as plant and machinery for capital allowance purposes now qualify under this category. The category does not just include newly acquired items; it also extends to replacements where the whole or the majority (more than 50%) is replaced within a 12 month period.

Once we have decided whether a new capital asset qualifies for capital allowances by being either plant and machinery or integral features, the next step is to decide how much the capital allowance will be.

Step 2: Pooling and rates

7.7   If businesses were required to calculate capital allowances for each and every asset separately, the compliance costs would be very high. In order to reduce these costs, and keep the system relatively simple, the Government allows taxpayers to 'pool' certain categories of assets and perform a single calculation based on the aggregate value of the pool. There are two pools, a 'main pool' and a 'special rate pool'. There are also some special rules for items that are not put into either of these pools and are treated separately for their capital allowances computation. We will consider these at the step 4 stage.

For both the main and special rate pools, capital allowances are calculated on a reducing balance basis. This means that the starting point in any year's computation is the balance brought forward from the previous year. Before calculating the annual writing down allowance, however, we first must add to the balance brought forward the value of any new items, and subtract the value of any disposals. This again is in the interest of simplicity, and means that new items qualify for writing down allowances for the full year, and items disposed of don't qualify for any writing down allowance in the year of disposal. Writing down allowance is not apportioned for the part of the period that the asset has been owned - it is either allowed for the whole period or not at all. This is an important difference from the way depreciation may be computed for accounting profit calculations where part year ownership may be taken into account.

Main pool

7.8 The main pool consists of all of a taxpayer's plant and machinery other than special rate pool assets (see below) or items that have to be treated separately (which we consider later). The current rate, applicable from 6 April 2012 (1 April 2012 for companies) is 18%. For expenditure incurred before 6 April 2008 (1 April 2008 for companies) the rate at which the writing down allowance was calculated on the main pool was 25%. Between these dates and 6 April 2012 (1 April 2012 for companies) the rate changed to 20%. Where a business has an accounting period that spans the introduction of this new rate, a hybrid rate may have to be calculated, based on the number of days in each period to determine the relevant maximum percentage that can be used.

Special rate pool

7.9 The 'special rate pool', was introduced in 2008 and attracts a lower rate of 8% writing down allowance (was 10% until April 2012), which means the cost of the asset is spread over a longer period of time. As with the main pool, a hybrid rate may be needed if the accounting period spans the changeover date.

Initially, there were three categories of asset that qualify for the special rate, long life assets, integral features, and thermal insulation. FA 2009 included a fourth: high CO_2 emission cars.

Long-life assets are those items of plant and machinery purchased since 26 November 1996 that have a useful life of 25 years or more when new.

Note, however, that the long-life asset rules only apply to businesses spending more than £100,000 per annum on such long-life assets. Also, some assets are never treated as long life assets including:

- machinery or plant in a building used wholly or mainly as (or for purposes ancillary to) a dwelling-house, retail shop, showroom, hotel or office
- cars (including hire cars) and taxis
- sea-going ships and railway assets bought before the end of 2010.

Many businesses will not spend more than £100,000 a year on long-life capital assets, and so these assets are instead dealt with as part of the main pool, and not put into the special rate pool.

Basis periods

7.10 The rates of writing down allowance, 18% for the main pool and 8% for the special rate pool, assume that we are dealing with a normal 12 month accounting period. What happens, however, if the taxpayer's business has an accounting period that is not 12 months in length? In this case the relevant rate needs to be reduced, or expanded, pro-rata to the length of the accounting period (e.g. an 18 month accounting period will result in 18% × 1.5 worth of allowances for the main pool, or 8% x 1.5 for the special rate pool).

Step 3: Annual Investment Allowance

7.11   In this step we need to consider whether the new capital asset qualifies for the annual investment allowance (AIA). This incentive, introduced in 2008, is designed to stimulate investment in new capital assets. The allowance is available to individuals carrying on a qualifying activity, which includes trades, professions, vocations, ordinary property business (and also includes being an employee) as well as companies.

The AIA allows businesses (of any size) to claim an allowance of 100% of the first £200,000 of expenditure incurred on plant and machinery and integral features.

Activity

Mulder, a small sole trader, prepares accounts to 31 December annually. His main pool of unrelieved expenditure on plant and machinery brought forward on 1 January 2018 was £20,000. During the year ended 31 December 2018, the following transactions took place:

			£	
31 August 2018	Bought	Plant	20,000	
31 October 2018	Sold	Plant	5,000	(originally cost £10,000)
31 December 2018	Bought	Plant	14,000	

Calculate the capital allowances for the year ended 31 December 2018.

Feedback

To perform this calculation there is a series of questions we need to ask:

1. Do the new additions belong in the main pool? Yes, they are neither long life assets nor special rate assets.

2. Do the new additions qualify for AIA? We can assume they do unless told otherwise.

3. For disposals, which is lower, the net disposal proceeds or the original cost? It is the lower of the two that we must use.

	£	Main Pool £	Allowances £
Written down value b/f		20,000	
Additions qualifying for AIA:			
Plant (£20,000 + £14,000)	34,000		
AIA (max)	(200,000)		34,000
Balance to main pool		0	
Sale/proceeds		(5,000)	
		15,000	
WDA 18%		(2,700)	2,700
Written down value c/f		12,300	
Total allowances for year			36,700

In this example, the new plant and machinery purchased in the chargeable period (I January 2018 to 31 December 2018) does not exceed £200,000 so it can be fully covered by the AIA deduction available throughout this period. Had this not been the case the excess over £200,000 is simply added to the main pool and increases the sum available for the 18% WDV for that period and subsequently (see activity below to illustrate this). If the item had been special rate expenditure such as an integral feature, then the excess over the AIA limit would have been transferred to the special rate pool instead (usually shown as an additional column alongside the Main Pool column so these assets can be separately tracked).

Activity

During the year ended 31 December 2018, Mulder (from activity above) instead undertook the following transactions:

			£	
31 August 2018	Bought	Plant	400,000	
31 October 2018	Sold	Plant	5,000	(originally cost £10,000)
31 December 2018	Bought	Plant	150,000	

Calculate the revised capital allowances for the year ended 31 December 2018.

Feedback

	£	Main Pool £	Allowances £
Written down value b/f		20,000	
Additions qualifying for AIA:			
Plant (£400,000 + £150,000)	550,000		
AIA (max)	(200,000)		200,000
Balance to main pool		350,000	
Sale/proceeds		(5,000)	
		365,000	
WDA 18%		(65,700)	65,700
Written down value c/f		299,300	
Total allowances for year			265,700

The AIA level is currently £200,000 from 1 January 2016, but previously was:

£500,000	between 1 April 2014 and 31 December 2015.
£250,000	between 1 January 2013 and 30 March 2014.
£25,000	between 6 April 2012 (1 April for companies) and 31 December 2012.
£100,000	between 6 April 2010 (1 April 2010 for companies) and 5 April 2012 (1 April for companies)
£50,000	between 6 April 2008 (1 April for companies) and 6 April 2010 (1 April for companies).

If a business has a chargeable period that spans the dates when the AIA rate changes, a transitional amount has to be calculated for the respective periods either side of the date the rate changes based on the number of months falling before and after the date of the change. This then becomes the maximum AIA that is allowed in that period, referred to as a 'cap'. The following activity shows how this transitional amount is computed.

Fiscal Fact

The estimated cost to the Government of AIA was £2.52 billion for 2017/18 (Source: HMRC – Estimated costs of principal tax reliefs.)

The AIA can only be given for the chargeable period in which the expenditure is incurred, so any unused allowance (i.e. if a business spends less than the AIA limit for the period) can't be carried forward and can't be transferred to another business. The allowance can't be claimed in the period when the qualifying activity ceases, and is not available for cars. Apart from these restrictions, businesses have a choice about how to apply the allowance to best effect, so as to maximise their capital allowance claim.

Step 4: Special treatment

7.12   Having looked at the rules that apply to main and special rate pool items, we now consider some categories of capital asset that require special treatment. First, the special case of cars, then items that qualify for enhanced capital allowances, which gives immediate write off (100% allowance) in the year of acquisition. We finally consider some categories of capital asset that need to be treated separately, i.e. not included in either the main or special rate pools.

Cars

7.13   The capital allowance system has always treated cars differently from other plant and equipment and the rules for cars were changed with effect from 6 April 2009 (1 April 2009 for companies). We won't consider the pre 2009 rules here.

Post April 2009 rules

For cars purchased after 6 April 2009 (1 April 2009 for companies), there are three possible treatments depending on the level of CO_2 emissions:

1.   Cars with emissions equal to or below 75g/km (95g/km for purchases before 6 April 2014 and110g/km for purchases before 6 April 2013) qualify for a 100% allowance in the year of purchase;
2.   Cars with medium range emissions, i.e. between 75 and 130 g/km (95 and 130g/km for purchases before 6 April 2014 and 110 and 160g/km for purchases before 6 April 2013), go into the main pool with writing down allowance of 18%; and
3.   Cars with high emissions of 130g/km or more (160g/km before 6 April 2013), go into the special rate pool and receive writing down allowance of 8%.

The CO_2 emissions ratings are used to determine what annual capital allowances rates will apply. These rules deliberately attempt to encourage use of more environmentally friendly company cars.

The following activity illustrates the use of the capital allowances rules for cars.

Activity

Luxury Travel, a business offering premium taxi services to customers to 'arrive in style' at airports, buys a car for one of its employees, Diane. The car costs a total of £30,000. A deposit of £5,000 was paid on 1 November 2016 and the balance of £25,000 when the car was delivered on 31 January 2017. The car's CO_2 emissions were 145g/km. No private usage of Diane's car occurs. Luxury Travel's accounting date is 31 December and had a special rate pool balance of £125,000 on 1 January 2016. Illustrate the maximum capital allowances that Luxury Travel could claim for the car for 2016/17, 2017/18, 2018/19 (assuming that no further acquisitions or disposals were made by Luxury Travel in these years).

Feedback

Based on the CO_2 emissions of more than 130g/km (as the applicable threshold when the car was purchased), the car would have been allocated to the special rate pool. It will therefore qualify for 8% capital allowances. The deposit payment will fall into the 2016/17 tax year (as falls before Luxury's 31 December 2016 accounting year end). The final payment will fall into the following tax year (i.e. 2017/18).

	Special Rate Pool £	Allowances £
WDV b/f at 1 Jan 2016	125,000	
y/e 31 December 2016		
Acquisition	5,000	
	130,000	
WDA (@8%)	(10,400)	10,400
WDV c/f	119,600	
y/e 31 December 2017		
Acquisition	25,000	
	144,600	
WDA (@8%)	(11,568)	11,568
WDV c/f	133,032	
y/e 31 December 2018		
WDA (@8%)	(10,642)	10,642
WDV c/f	122,390	

Enhanced (100%) capital allowances

7.14 Since the 2000 Budget the government has introduced a number of enhanced capital allowances for certain 'green' capital items where the rate is 100%. It applies in a computation before the AIA cap is considered and so 100% is given for these assets even if the AIA cap is exceeded. The 100% ECA is available to all businesses, small, medium and large and can apply to assets for leasing, letting or hire purchase from 17 April 2002 where services are sold with the leasing arrangement (although leased cars do not get this special treatment from April 2013). Examples of items qualifying for the 100% ECAs are:

Energy saving plant and machinery [1]
Low emission cars [2]
Water conservation equipment [3]
Refuelling equipment[4]
Zero-emission goods vehicles[5]
Energy efficient hand dryers[6]
Heat pump driven air curtains[6]
Heat pumps for water heating and grey water re-use technologies[6]
Installation of electric vehicle charging points

Notes:

(1) A list of qualifying items can be found at the Department of Energy and Climate Change website, https://www.gov.uk/guidance/energy-technology-list. Initially included were boilers, motors, refrigeration equipment, thermal screens, lighting and pipe insulation. Added in 2002 Budget were heat pumps, radiant and warm air heaters, and solar heaters.

(2) These are for new cars that are registered after 6 April, 2014 and are either fully electric or emit not more than 75 g/km of carbon dioxide (the applicable limits were: 95g/km from 6 April 2013 to 5 April 2014, 110 g/km from 6 April 2008 to 5 April 2013 and 120g/km for new cars purchased between the start of the scheme on 12 April 2002 and 5 April 2008).

(3) This includes flow meters, leakage detection equipment and efficient taps and toilets. From April 2008 there are additions to this category including waste water recovery and reuse systems.

(4) For natural gas, bio-gas and hydrogen refuelling equipment.

(5) This measure commenced 1 April 2010 for companies and 6 April for other businesses. It applies to vehicles that cannot, under any circumstances, produce CO_2 emissions when driven, are design primarily to convey goods or 'burdens' and on which expenditure occurs by these applicable dates.

(6) Budget 2011 announced that enhanced capital allowances will also apply to certain energy efficient hand dryers. Budgets 2012 and 2013 made further additions and refinements to these lists.

Fiscal Fact

There are currently nearly 17,000 products listed on the Energy Technology List (ETL). It is claimed by the Carbon Trust, who oversees this scheme for the Government, that annual CO_2 emissions savings brought about directly by this scheme is 6,176 million tonnes (equivalent to 1 million hot air balloons). (Source: Carbon Trust statistics)

Capital allowances are a deduction in the tax computation. This means that they are only really useful as an investment incentive if you are a taxpayer. But what if the business has a loss? With effect from 1 April 2008, this situation was partly addressed as companies in loss situations that are entitled to enhanced capital allowances are able to convert them to cash refunds of up to 19% of the expenditure up to a maximum of £250,000 (or the total of their annual PAYE and NIC liabilities – whichever is the greater) From 1 April 2018, the 19% rate has been replaced by a rate equivalent to $2/3^{rds}$ of the corporation tax chargeable on the profits of the qualifying activity, or the average of the rates if there is more than one rate for the chargeable period.

According to the Government when this was first introduced, this provides a cash flow benefit to loss making companies that invest in environmentally friendly products and technologies. Note that this special cash refund only applies to companies and not to sole traders, which some commentators feel is unfair and may lead to some businesses switching to being companies just for tax purposes.

ECAs are also now available to companies (not individual sole-traders) for plant and machinery purchases in various designated *enterprise zones*. Several such zones were created in England in 2011. New zones were added in Scotland and Wales in 2012. These ECAs are available currently until 31 March 2020.

The following activity illustrates the use of AIA and enhanced capital allowances (ECAs):

Activity

Philip, who runs a small printing business, buys a computer and software costing £2,500 on 1 May, 2018. He purchased a delivery van for £5,500 on 19 June, 2018 and a qualifying boiler on 25 June, 2018 for £3,600. His normal accounting year runs to 30 June and the brought forward written down value of his main pool at 1 July, 2017 was £15,000. No other purchases or sales of assets occurred in the year. Calculate the capital allowances available to Philip for the year ended 30 June, 2018.

Feedback

	£	Main Pool £	Allowances £
Additions qualifying for ECA:			
Boiler	3,600		
ECA (100%)	(3,600)	–	3,600
Additions qualifying for AIA:			
Plant (£2,500 + £5,500)	8,000		
AIA	(8,000)		8,000
Balance to main pool		nil	
Writing down allowance:			
Written down value b/f		15,000	
WDA 18%		(2,700)	2,700
Written down value c/f		12,300	
Allowances for tax year			14,300

Philip can claim all of his expenditure on the computer and delivery van as a deduction under the AIA rules. He can also receive 100% ECA on the boiler and so in this way he can get all the eligible tax allowances for this purchase immediately. Note that it is important to list ECAs separately to AIAs available assets as these are entitled to a 100% allowance rate even if the taxpayer uses up all their AIA in any given year.

Recap

7.15 At this point, we can now create an order of priority for the different allowances we have considered so far as follows:

1. ECA is top priority so your first question must be – does the new asset qualify for 100% ECA as a 'green' asset or as plant and machinery for use in a designated Enterprise Zone in the case of a company?
2. Then consider the AIA – do the other new assets qualify for AIA? If so, up to £200,000 becomes fully deductible in addition to any ECA items.
3. Finally, what is left, i.e. the assets that don't qualify for ECA or AIA; or AIA expenditure in excess of £200,000, will be placed in either the main pool or the special rate pool and receive a 18% or 8% writing down allowance respectively.

Separately pooled assets

7.16 To determine the correct capital allowances some plant and machinery need to be treated separately rather than being placed into either the main or special rate pools. In this section we will review these situations. These include assets with some private use, leased assets, and short life assets.

Private use of assets

7.17 As we saw in the earlier discussion of cars, if plant and machinery is only partly used for the purpose of trade (e.g. the owner also gets some private benefit from their ownership) the capital allowances and charges described above are multiplied by the fraction A÷B, where A is the proportion of the time during which the asset was used for the purpose of trade while B is the total period of ownership. Because of the need to apply this fraction for each asset with any element of private usage, a separate capital allowances computation must be carried out for each asset. This means you should create a separate column in your proforma for assets with any private usage. Only the business use part of the total capital allowances can be claimed.

Activity

Jane bought a car for use in her car hire business for £30,000 on 9ᵗ August 2016. The car has CO emissions of 220g/km. She uses the vehicle 25% for private purposes and has a 31 December year end. What are the maximum capital allowances she could claim for 2016/17, 2017/18 and 2018/19.

Feedback

As the car has CO_2 emissions of more than 130g/km it would normally need to be allocated to the special rate pool as before, however, as it also has private usage, it will instead need its own pool – with WDA being applied at the same rate as for the special rate pool to which it otherwise would belong.

	Diane's car (25% private) £	Allowances £
y/e 31 December 2016		
Acquisition cost	30,000	
WDA (@ 8%)	(2,400) x 75%	1,800
WDV c/f	27,600	
y/e 31 December 2017		
WDA (@ 8%)	(2,208) x 75%	1,656
WDV c/f	25,392	
y/e 31 December 2018		
WDA (@ 8%)	(2,031) x 75%	1,523
WDV c/f	23,361	

Note that, even though only 75% of the allowances computed are claimed each year (£1,800, £1,656 and £1,523 respectively), it is the full WDA that is deducted to work out the asset's WDV – not just the 75%.

This rule for separately pooling items with private usage applies to all asset types, not just cars (although for companies the rules differ, see Chapter 9).

Leased assets

7.18 Assets which are owned by the business and leased to other people are not pooled with the assets owned directly by the business. Instead, they are aggregated in a separate pool (i.e. they also get their own column in the computation but not separate columns for each leased asset). The same WDA rate will apply however.

Short-life assets

7.19 The taxpayer may elect for certain machinery and plant to be treated as a short-life asset and given its own pool (called de-pooling) in order for the balancing allowance to be computed when the asset is disposed of. This is a useful concession as it means the full allowances for the asset can be claimed sooner rather than the taxpayer only receiving 18% of it, on a reducing balance, each year as part of the main pool of plant and machinery for the remainder of the life of the business (Note, that this option is not available for special rate pool items).

The election to treat a purchased capital asset as a short life asset must be made not more than two years after the end of the chargeable period, or its basis period, in which the capital expenditure was incurred and once made is irrevocable. However, if the asset is not disposed of in a chargeable period ending on or before the eighth anniversary of the end of the chargeable period in which the cost of the asset was first recorded, then the tax written down value of the asset is transferred into the general pool at the beginning of the next chargeable period. (This limit was the fourth anniversary prior to April 2011.) From then on it will receive the normal treatment for other capital assets and the advantage of gaining a balancing allowance (if applicable) early is lost.

The legislation identifies a number of assets which cannot be treated as short-life assets, these are:

- ships;
- cars; and
- machinery or plant provided for leasing.

 An example can be found on the website to illustrate the operation of the short life asset rules.

Step 5: Disposals

7.20 When assets are disposed of, we may need to calculate a balancing adjustment. This will happen in the year in which a trade ceases, or when an item that has been kept out of the main or special rate pools is sold. The process is similar to the calculation of profit or loss on disposal for accounting purposes, and is to ensure the correct changes have been made to the records over the life of the asset.

Note that any disposals are dealt with before calculating the current year's writing down allowance. This means that no writing down allowance is allowed in the year of disposal.

When performing this balancing adjustment computation we compare the disposal proceeds (or original cost if lower) with the written down value. Thus the disposal value deducted from the pool total when an asset is disposed of is equal to the lower of the net proceeds of disposal, including any insurance money received, and the capital expenditure incurred on its original acquisition, that is, the lower of the original cost or its disposal value.

If the written down value exceeds the disposal value (or original cost if lower), then a balancing allowance equal to the whole of the excess can be claimed. This balancing allowance is effectively an additional capital allowance claim. If the disposal value exceeds the written down value, a balancing charge equal to the excess will be levied on the taxpayer. This can be thought of as a 'negative capital allowance' and is effectively added to the trading profit for that year.

In the case of pooled assets, a balancing charge will arise if the disposal value is more than the balance in the pool. A balancing allowance, however, will not be allowed until such time as the qualifying activity itself ends (for example when the trade ceases to operate). This is the reason for using the 'short life asset' option that we discussed earlier. If a taxpayer thinks that he or she will sell an asset within eight (previously four) years and make a loss (balancing allowance), by de-pooling the asset, the balancing allowance can be claimed in the year of disposal.

Activity

Catherine retired on 31 December, 2018 after trading for many years. The opening tax written down value of her capital allowances pool was £10,000 and of a short life asset (acquired in 2015 and used solely for the purposes of the business) was £4,500. The plant and machinery in the main pool had originally cost £12,000. Catherine sold the plant and machinery for £16,000 and the short life asset for £3,000 when she retired. Calculate the capital allowances and charges for 2018/19.

Feedback

Remember, short life assets have their own column, therefore, the capital allowances computation is:

	Main Pool £	Short life asset £	Allowances £
WDV b/f	10,000	4,500	
Disposal proceeds/cost	(12,000)	(3,000)	
	(2,000)	1,500	
Balancing allowance		(1,500)	1,500
Balancing charge	2,000		(2,000)
Net capital allowances			(500)

Although the plant in the main pool was sold for £16,000, it had originally only cost £12,000 so this is the figure we use as the disposal value to work out the balancing adjustment.

Small pools

7.21 As part of the process of simplifying the capital allowances regime, particularly for small businesses, and in response to suggestions from business, in 2008, the Government decided to allow for small pools to be written off. Small pools of unrelieved expenditure can be written off where the balance brought forward is less than or equal to £1,000. This applies to both the main pool and special rate pool, but not to single asset pools such as short life assets. It is not compulsory to write off all of any small pools, and the taxpayer can choose how much, if any, to be written off each year.

Waiving rights to capital allowances

7.22 All or part of the capital allowance entitlement for any given year can be waived by the taxpayer. This means a taxpayer can make a choice each year whether or not to claim any of their capital allowance deduction. Any amount waived simply has the effect of increasing the balance of qualifying expenditure which is eligible for capital allowances in future years.

Clearly it is usually in the interest of the business to claim tax relief as quickly as possible, but this may not always be the case, for example if the business makes a loss that year. Rather than adding to this loss, the business may decide instead to carry forward their capital allowances by not including the deductions they could claim in this year's computation. Instead, the value of the pool will remain the same and so their claim is effectively deferred to offset against profit in later years.

A business might also waive the capital allowance on these occasions:

- if taxable profits would be reduced to such an extent that it would not be possible for the taxpayer to use all of his or her personal allowances
- if the taxpayer believed that his or her marginal rate of tax would increase significantly in future years and so the deduction will be more valuable to them in the future.

Patents

7.23 If patent rights are purchased (i.e. rather than developed in-house) and used for trading purposes, a separate capital allowances pool is formed for all rights held on which writing down allowance of 25% per annum on a *reducing balance* basis is available for tax purposes, if the owner wishes to use them. These rules however, only apply to unincorporated business. For companies with expenditure on patent rights after 1 April, 2002, the write downs used in producing the accounts are now used (see the intangible assets description in section 9.17 for further details).

The rules for balancing allowances and charges are largely the same as for plant and machinery. If sale proceeds exceed the original cost the deduction from the pool is limited to the original cost, as for plant and machinery. One difference, however, is that the excess of proceeds over the original cost is taxed as miscellaneous income, and not as capital gains as plant and machinery are.

Trading losses

7.24 In this section we will briefly look at the special tax rules that apply for dealing with losses on trading activities. These differ if the cash basis is used to compute the trading loss as we will see later.

Calculating a tax loss is straight forward. If, after adjusting the profits for tax purposes (using either basis), the end result is a negative amount, i.e. the allowable expenditures exceed the taxable income, then you have a trading loss for tax purposes. Such a loss can be used to offset future tax bills, however, a loss can only be relieved once and the taxpayer may have to make a choice about how best to use the loss if using the accrual basis.

There are special rules for losses incurred in the early years of business, or at the end of the life of a business, but in this chapter, we will only consider the position of an established, on-going business. In this case, the loss can be relieved by:

- Deducting it from general income, for the current year, the year before, or both years, or
- Carrying it forward to be offset against subsequent trade profits.

Deduction from general income

7.25 Where a taxpayer carries on a trade in the tax year and makes a loss in that year he or she can claim a deduction for that loss against general income for that year as a tax relief (at step 2 of their income tax computation) instead of having to carry it forward against future profits. If there is still some loss left over after applying it against general income of the year, the remaining part can then be used to reclaim income tax paid in the previous tax year. This is done in practice by creating a deduction equivalent to the loss available to be carried back. This deduction can then be used to claim a repayment of tax previously paid or can be used to offset later year taxes (see below) – the taxpayer has the choice.

Alternatively, the taxpayer can choose to first use the loss in the previous tax year and then, if there is still some left over, use it in the current year. This means that the taxpayer has to think about how much tax saving can be made from each course of action.

There are some conditions that have to be met for this relief to apply. The main condition is that relief against general income is not available unless the trade is "commercial". This means that it is carried on during the year on a commercial basis and with a view to making a profit.

Losses have to be used to the full extent of the net income of the year to which they are applied. This can mean the loss of personal allowances for that year (as losses are deducted at step 2 of the tax computation – before personal allowances are dealt with at step 3).

Carry forward

7.26 As an alternative to deduction from general income, a trading loss can be carried forward to be relieved against subsequent trade profits. However, this carry forward does have an important restriction; the loss can only be offset against the profits of the same trade in later years, not against profits from a different trade.

Any loss that is not used up in the following tax year can then be carried forward to the next year and so on indefinitely until it is all eventually used up.

There are several drawbacks to this form of relief:

- Once a taxpayer has decided to use this form of relief, there is no flexibility, and the first available profits have to be used to relieve the loss. If the taxpayer has little income from other sources, this could mean a loss of personal allowances in these future periods that would ordinarily reduce the income tax liabilities anyway.

- There is also a delay in receiving the relief, until the year of assessment for the year in which profits are next made. As well as having potentially serious cash flow implications, the relief may be worth less because the tax rate applied to the relief is the one in force when the relief is received, not when it was incurred.

- In addition, the law is strict about what exactly constitutes the 'same trade'. In *Gordon and Blair Ltd v IRC* (1962), losses incurred from the trade of brewing could not be carried forward and relieved against profits earned from bottling. Whether the same trade is being carried on is a question of degree and so the facts of each case must be considered carefully. Hence there is an element of risk in choosing to receive relief in this way.

This is the default way HMRC will apply losses if the taxpayer does not tell them that they wish to do something different.

The Cash Basis

7.27 If the taxpayer is using the cash basis, it is not possible to use relief against general income, and the only way losses can be relieved is through the carry forward method.

Limit on Reliefs

7.28 There is a cap, or limit, on the amount of reliefs that taxpayers can claim. With effect from 6 April 2013 the limit is set at the greater of £50,000 or 25% of income. Income for this purpose is total income liable for income tax, adjusted for pension contributions and charitable donations.

 If your course requires you to also know the other special cases of loss relief, additional material and examples can be found in the student section of the website at:

http://www.taxstudent.com/uk

The rules for dealing with trading losses for companies are slightly different to these, which apply to sole traders. We will briefly examine the rules for corporation tax in section 9.22.

Summary

This chapter continues our examination of the tax rules for unincorporated businesses. It looks at the capital allowance rules for capital assets. We examined what kind of plant and machinery qualifies for capital allowances and how they are calculated. We also discussed the special cases of allowances for expenditure on patents. Finally, we briefly reviewed the basics of how trade losses can be handled for an ongoing business.

Project areas

This chapter provides some scope for projects including the:

- effectiveness of capital allowances as tools for accurately reflecting the real cost of using assets in businesses;

- question of whether increasing capital allowances leads to increased investment in plant and machinery (i.e do incentives like the regularly changing AIA, or enhanced 100% FYAs, work to encourage investment);

- implications of having different accounting and tax treatments for capital assets and even between tax treatments when using the cash basis or accruals basis;

- reasons why cars are singled out for special capital allowance treatment.

Quick quiz

1. Samuel bought a motor car for use in his business on 1 September, 2018. The car cost £15,000 and has CO_2 emissions of 145 g/km. He draws up his accounts to 31 December each year. What is the capital allowance rate he can claim this year if the car is used solely for business purposes?

2. Theresa bought a motor car for use in her business on 1 September, 2018. The car cost £15,000 and is not electric, but has CO_2 emissions of 70 g/km. How much capital allowance can she claim?

3. Umut has a year end of 31 December for his business, which he has operated for several years. On 12 September 2018 he spent £450,000 on a machine for use in his business. The machine does not qualify for enhanced capital allowances and qualifies for the main rate pool. What is the capital allowances that he will be entitled to for the 2018/19 year?

4. Vivian buys a state of the art computer for her small business on 30 June, 2018 at a cost of £2,500. What capital allowance can she claim for the year ended 30 September, 2018? Should she treat it as a short life asset?

5. Walter sold a car for £3,000 which had a tax written down value of £8,000 at the start of the year. He used the car 75% for business purposes and

had purchased it in October 2011. What adjustment is required to his capital allowance claim for the year?

6. Xanthe runs a clothing shop that she has operated for many years. At 1 April 2018, the written down value of her main pool was £15,000. In October 2018 plant and machinery that had originally cost £16,000 was sold for £14,200. What is the maximum amount of capital allowances that Xanthe can claim for the year ended 31 March 2019?

7. Yolande started a new business on 1 October 2018 and prepared her first set of accounts for the period ending 31 December 2018. On 5 November 2018 Yolande purchased a new machine for £100,000, what is the maximum capital allowance she can claim for the year ended 31 December 2018?

8. Zeus has been in business for many years and prepares his accounts to 31 March each year. In the year to 31 March 2018 Zeus made a taxable trading profit of £12,000 and in the year to 31 March 2019 he made a loss of £170,000. Zeus also has property business income of £250,000 in the year ended 31 March 2018, but no other income in the year ended 31 March 2019. What is the amount of loss that Zeus can set against his general income for the tax year ended 5 April 2018?

Questions

Question 1

Luke Skyrunner has a medium sized manufacturing business. The opening balance in his main pool of assets was £10,000. He has no special rate pool at the start of the year. All vehicles are used 100% for business purposes. During the year ended 30 June 2018, the following transactions occurred in relation to his fixed assets:

29 July, 2017	New van purchased for £4,000
25 October, 2017	New car (CO_2 emissions 65g/km) purchased for £6,000
15 February, 2018	Plant (bought on 1 August, 2001 for £8,000) was sold for £7,000
1 May, 2018	New plant purchased for £15,000
15 May, 2018	New car (CO_2 emissions 180g/km) purchased for £20,000
30 May, 2018	New lift installed in the warehouse for £8,000

Required: Calculate Luke's maximum entitlement to capital allowances for the year ended 30 June 2018.

Question 2 (based on ACCA December 2008)

Phil Fit, trading as 'Jogger' runs a business manufacturing running shoes. The following information is provided for the year ended 31 March 2019:

Depreciation of £12,340 has been deducted in arriving at the net accounting loss of £56,400. Phil Fit does not choose to use the cash basis.

On 1 April 2018, the tax written down values of plant and machinery was as follows (with no special rate pool):

Main pool	£21,600
Short life asset	£8,800

The following transactions took place during the year ended 31 March 2018:

20 July 2018	sold the short life asset	£11,700
31 July 2018	purchased Ford Focus car (CO$_2$ 155 g/km)	£11,800
14 March 2019	sold a lorry	£8,600

The short life assets sold on 20 July 2018 for £11,700 originally cost £18,400. The lorry sold on 14 March 2019 for £8,600 originally cost £16,600.

Required: Calculate Phil's tax adjusted trading profit/loss for 'Jogger' for the year ended 31 March 2019.

Question 3 (based on ICAS TPS Tax Paper December 2009)

Stitched Up is an unincorporated business involved in the manufacture and sale of ladies fashion that has a 30 June year end for accounting purposes. The tax written down values of the various pools of expenditure at 1 July 2018 were:

Main pool	£59,400
Special rate pool	£14,200
Mercedes car (acquired 1 October 2014)	£26,300

The Mercedes car is used by Stitched Up's owner, Joe Brown, and it is estimated that he uses it approximately 50% for business. It has CO$_2$ emissions of 165g/km.

The following fixed assets were acquired by Stitched Up during the year:

	Acquired	Cost
New air conditioning system for factory	October 2018	£28,000
Solar panels for heating system (see below)	December 2018	£27,000
New industrial sewing machines (five machines)	January 2019	£15,000

A grant of £6,000 towards the cost of the solar panels was received from the government as these were rated as energy efficient. The gross cost of the panels was £33,000.

The only fixed asset disposal by Stitched Up was the sale of five old sewing machines. They cost less than £6,000 each and were sold for £250 each.

Required: Calculate the capital allowances that Stitched Up is entitled to claim for 2018/19.

(*Note: answer available on lecturers' website*)

Question 4 (based on ACCA Paper June 2012).

Harry Heavy runs a music publishing business. His operating profit for the year ended 31 December 2018 is £433,100. Deprecation of £12,880 has been deducted in arriving at this figure.

On 1 January 2018, Harry acquired a leasehold office building, paying a premium of £90,000 for the grant of a ten year lease. The office building was used for business purposes by Harry throughout the year ended 31 December 2018. Amortisation of leasehold property of £9,000 has been deducted in arriving at the operating profit.

On 1 January 2018, the tax written down values of Harry's qualifying assets were as follows:

	£
Main pool (including motor car (1))	14,100
Motor car (2)	26,300
Special rate pool	21,700

The following purchases and disposals of qualifying assets took place during the year ended 31 December 2018:

		£
23 March 2018	Purchase of office equipment	900
19 July 2018	Sold motor car (1)	(14,600)
28 July 2018	Sold all special rate pool items	(12,300)

Motor car (1) is used by one of Harry's employees and originally cost £19,200.
Motor car (2) has CO_2 emissions of 185g/km. It is used by Harry and 50% of the mileage is for private journeys.

Required: Calculate Harry's tax adjusted trading profit for the year ended 31 December 2018.

(*Note: answer available on lecturers' website*)

Question 5 (based on ACCA Paper 2.3 December 2004).

Richard Desk has been a self-employed manufacturer of office furniture since 1993. His income for the previous three years is as follows:

	2016/17	2017/18	2018/19
Trading profit/(loss)	11,800	(26,300)	8,600
Property income	nil	3,000	2,800
Bank interest	600	400	500

Required: Calculate Richard's taxable income for each year on the basis that he relieves the trading loss against general income in the previous year.

(Note: answer available on lecturers' website)

Further test questions for this chapter to test your knowledge can be found in the student section of the website at:

http://www.taxstudent.com/uk

Further reading and examples

Combs, A., Tutin, R. & Rowes, P. (2018), *Taxation: incorporating the 2018 Finance Act*, Fiscal Publications: Birmingham.

– use this book for many other examples to further develop and test your knowledge of this chapter's contents. See
http://www.fiscalpublications.com/rowes/2018

8 Capital taxes

Introduction

8.1   Until capital gains tax was introduced in 1965, capital receipts (such as sums received from selling privately owned, or non-current business, assets) were largely free of tax. This meant that increases in wealth through growth in capital value, as opposed to receiving income, resulted in substantially less tax being paid. Some of the incentive to classify a receipt as capital rather than income was removed by the introduction and development of capital gains tax, although there are still differences between the operation of the income tax and capital gains tax systems, as you will see in this chapter.

During its life capital gains tax has undergone many changes as successive Chancellors have attempted to improve the tax or change its focus. Capital gains tax is charged on both individuals and companies, however, in recent years, this tax has become increasingly different for these two groups. For this reason, in this chapter we consider the basic principles and their application for individual taxpayers. We will examine how capital gains tax works for companies in Chapter 9, alongside corporation tax.

There are other forms of taxes on capital transactions in operation in the UK at present and in this chapter we will also briefly describe the operation of stamp duty, and inheritance tax.

After reading this chapter you will be able to:
- describe the introduction and development of capital gains tax;
- calculate the capital gains tax liability which arises as a result of a range of transactions;
- describe the capital gains tax reliefs available to taxpayers;
- briefly describe the application of stamp duty; and
- briefly describe the operation of inheritance tax.

Capital gains tax

8.2   We saw in Chapter 6 that one of the key concerns of the income tax system is to distinguish income receipts from capital receipts given that, as a general rule, capital receipts are not subject to income tax. A consequence of not taxing capital receipts, as happened in the UK before 1965, is that it creates a significant distortion in the tax system, i.e. an incentive for taxpayers to manipulate transactions so that they escape tax as capital receipts rather than attract tax as income, or revenue, receipts. Many tax systems therefore tax capital receipts to reduce these distortions, however, not always at the same rates, or using the same rules, as for income. Where these differences exist there will continue to be an incentive towards capital receipts over income receipts (where capital receipts attract lower tax and vice versa if income is taxed more lightly). Most tax systems try to recognise, and do something about, this tax induced distortion.

The first modern attempt to tax capital gains in the UK was a short term capital gains tax introduced in 1962. The tax was replaced in 1965 by James Callaghan, as Labour Chancellor, by a full capital gains tax which was intended to tax 'profits' which were not subject to income tax. You will remember from Chapter 2 that taxes are sometimes introduced into a tax system because they are needed to make it fairer. Capital gains tax is an example of this as it tries to ensure some tax is paid on capital receipts to bring them into line with income.

Today capital gains tax accounts for only 2–3% of the revenue raised by direct taxation but, as James Callaghan said at the time he introduced it, the tax was not primarily introduced to raise revenue for the Government but to 'provide a background of equity and fair play'. So, it has an importance beyond the sums it raises in tax revenue.

Fiscal Fact

In 2008/09 142,000 individual taxpayers paid capital gains tax of £7.8billion, however, for 2013/14 this sum dropped dramatically to £3.9billion from 211,000 taxpayers – a sign of the economic situation in the UK over that period. It had been down as low as £2.5bn for 2009/10 but the forecast for 2016/17 is an upward trend again to £8.7billion and in 2015/16 (latest available figures) 239,000 individual taxpayers paid this tax. [Source: HMRC Tax Receipts & Table 14.1]

Look again at some of the legal cases in Chapter 6 which help to determine whether trading has occurred. Some of these pre-1965 cases may not be brought today because if the receipt is not a trading receipt it will now be considered under capital gains tax although maybe with different consequences as you will see later.

When capital gains tax was introduced in the UK it was not intended to be retrospective so only gains which arose after 6 April, 1965 are liable to capital gains tax. There were two possible ways of achieving this aim. Firstly, the 'Budget day value' at 6 April, 1965 could be substituted for the original cost of assets acquired before that date in computing the gain. This would enable the tax to be levied only on gains which arose after 6 April, 1965. The second solution was to 'time-apportion' the gain. That is the total gain which arose throughout the period of ownership was calculated and then apportioned to the periods of ownership prior to and subsequent to 6 April, 1965. Only the gain which was attributable to the later period of ownership was subject to tax. You are unlikely to encounter assets owned before April 1965 in an introductory tax course.

In 1988 the tax was rebased so that gains before March 1982 would no longer be liable to capital gains taxation. This is achieved by using the market value at 31 March 1982 as the cost of the asset.

Values of assets and the effects of inflation

8.3   Assets may increase in value over time for a number of reasons. For example, shares may become more valuable as the company's profits are accumulated year on year and if it is thought to have good prospects of continuing to earn profits in the future. You may also be able to sell assets for more than you paid for them, for example, if you buy 'collectables' that appreciate in value. However, one other factor that causes an increase in assets' 'value' over time is inflation. That is, as the value of money decreases over time, so higher prices are sought for assets to enable the cash equivalent value to be maintained. While a gain can therefore be said to be made when selling an asset for more in absolute cash terms than it was bought for, you are only really better off if the cash value of that sale buys you more now than the original cash value of the cost.

The question of what to do with gains resulting from inflationary increases in prices is one that affects all countries that try to tax capital gains. While assets are being sold for higher prices over time, at least part of any gain simply reflects the general inflation in prices that occurred while the asset was owned – i.e. it isn't a 'real' gain. Inflation results in changes to the real value of capital assets and creates a key question of whether to tax the inflation component of any change in value. The problem became particularly acute in the 1970s and 1980s when inflation was relatively high.

When capital gains tax was first introduced no relief was given for the effects of inflation. Broadly speaking tax was paid on the difference between the allowable costs of acquiring the asset and the disposal proceeds. In 1985 the law was amended to give full relief for inflation. The retail price index (RPI) was chosen as the inflation measure to be used for capital gains tax computations. The changes in the RPI between the date the asset was acquired and disposed of produced an *indexation allowance* that was used to reduce the total gain and remove the effect of inflation on the asset's value, but (from 1993) could not create a loss.

After a period of consultation, the then Chancellor, Gordon Brown, announced a major reform of capital gains tax for individuals in his 1998 Budget. In the interests of simplicity, the system of indexation allowances was replaced (for individuals only) by a fixed reduction based on the length of ownership of the asset, called *taper relief*. The new rules meant that for individuals the taxable amount of any chargeable gain diminished the longer they owned the asset.

The rules were intended to encourage individuals to undertake long-term investment by holding assets for relatively long periods. Taper relief was also significantly more generous for business assets (i.e. assets used for business purposes) than non-business assets to encourage investment by entrepreneurs.

So, for individuals, no indexation allowance was given for periods of ownership after April 1998. Instead, taper relief applied, ranging from 5% for non-business assets held for 3 years to a rate of 75% for business assets held for at least 2 years.

A further change took place with effect from 6 April 2008. Taper relief was abolished for individuals and replaced instead with a flat rate of tax at 18% for everyone. In 2010, a new rate of 28% was introduced for higher and additional rate income taxpayers. From 6 April 2016 these rates dropped to 10% and 20% respectively. These rates are, however, lower than comparable income tax rates, perhaps providing some acknowledgement of the impact of inflation. The justification for this new flat rate system (ironically perhaps) was to further simplify the system that the taper relief was supposed to have simplified.

We will examine how these rules work for individual taxpayers, in practice, with examples as we go through this chapter.

The charge to capital gains tax

8.4 A liability to capital gains tax arises when a *chargeable person* makes a *chargeable disposal* of *chargeable assets*. You need to be able to define each of these terms and list exemptions to capital gains tax to understand its effect.

Chargeable person

8.5 A chargeable person may be:

- *An individual who is resident in the UK during the tax year in which the chargeable disposal occurs.* If the individual is resident *and* domiciled in the UK, disposals anywhere in the world may give rise to a capital gains tax liability.

- *A partner in a business.* A partnership does not have a separate legal identity. When a partnership makes a chargeable disposal of partnership assets the partners are individually liable to tax in proportion to their share of the capital gain.

The legislation contains a list of exempt organisations that are not liable to capital gains tax on asset disposals (but also therefore cannot claim any losses). These are:

- charities using gains for charitable purposes;
- approved superannuation (i.e. pension) funds;
- local authorities;
- registered friendly societies;
- approved scientific research associations; and
- authorised unit and investment trusts.

Although companies are also chargeable persons for capital gains tax purposes, they don't pay a separate capital gains tax as individuals do. Instead, corporation tax is charged on total profits including chargeable (capital) gains. We will discuss the taxation of companies more fully in Chapter 9.

Chargeable disposal

8.6   The term *chargeable disposal* includes the sale or gift of all or any part of an asset. It also includes the loss or destruction of an asset, the appropriation of assets as trading stock and the receipt of a capital sum in return for the surrender of rights to assets. An example of this last case is the sale of rights which attach to shares when a company makes a rights issue. The chargeable disposal is deemed to take place when the title to the asset passes to its new owner.

A number of disposals are *exempt disposals* and do not give rise to a capital gains tax liability. These are:

- transfers of assets on death – the assets are instead deemed to be acquired by their new owners at their value at the date of death;
- transfers of assets to provide security for a loan or mortgage; and
- gifts of assets to charities and national heritage bodies.

Where an asset is damaged, and the taxpayer receives a capital sum as compensation (e.g. from an insurance payout), a special rule may apply. So long as the compensation is used to restore the asset (or most of it) the taxpayer can elect to have the compensation reduce the allowable cost of the asset instead of creating a chargeable disposal. This election can also be made if the capital sum is small (less than 5% of the value of the asset). Making such an election has the effect of delaying the capital gains tax payment until the restored asset is eventually disposed of.

Chargeable assets

8.7   All assets are *chargeable assets* unless they are specifically exempted from capital gains tax by law, or other regulation. Here is a list of some of the more common exempt assets:

- motor vehicles (whatever their age);
- national savings certificates, premium bonds and SAYE deposits;
- foreign currency, provided it was for private use;
- decorations for valour (e.g. brave conduct medals) unless the chargeable person purchased them rather than being awarded them personally;
- damages (compensation) for personal or professional injury;
- life assurance policies when disposed of by the original owner;
- works of art or scientific collections given for national purposes are treated as being disposed of on a no gain/no loss basis;
- gilt-edged securities, for example Treasury loans, Treasury stocks, Exchequer loans and War loans;
- qualifying corporate bonds (debentures);
- the disposal of debts, other than debts on a security, by the original creditor;
- pension and annuity rights;
- betting and gambling winnings; and
- investments held in individual savings accounts (ISAs/NISAs).

In addition, in certain circumstances tangible moveable property, also called *chattels*, is exempt from capital gains tax, as is an individual's principle private residence. We will consider both of these categories later in sections 8.19 and 8.26, as they are not always fully exempt.

If a taxpayer disposes of exempt assets no chargeable gain, or allowable loss, arises.

The basic computation

8.8   In this section we will first study the computation of the chargeable gain, or allowable loss. We will then illustrate how the calculation is applied in practice using a number of transactions.

The pro forma for calculating the chargeable gain or allowable loss is (numbers are for illustration only):

	£
Gross proceeds on disposal (or market value)	20,000
Less incidental costs of disposal	(1,000)
Net proceeds	19,000
Less allowable costs	(4,000)
Chargeable gain/(loss)	15,000

As you will see later, this calculation is performed for each disposal of a non-exempt capital asset; the results are then aggregated and an annual exemption applied (for individuals) to the total so that a certain amount of the total gain each year is tax free. For 2018/19 the annual exempt amount (AEA) is £11,700 (up from £11,300 in 2017/18). The following activity provides an overview of the CGT computation. We will then explore each stage in further detail.

Activity

Ernie sold two chargeable assets on 1 July 2018, and had no other asset disposals during the tax year:

Asset 1: cost £5,000, sold for £15,000

Asset 2: cost £15,000, sold for £20,000.

What is the amount on which Ernie will pay capital gains tax?

Feedback

Capital gains tax is based on the aggregated net chargeable gains for the year, less the AEA. In Ernie's case, this will be:

Asset 1 (£15,000 – £5,000)	10,000
Asset 2 (£20,000 – £15,000)	5,000
Total	15,000
Less annual exempt amount	(11,700)
Amount subject to capital gains tax	3,300

We will now consider each of the elements of the capital gains tax computation in more detail.

Gross proceeds on disposal

8.9 In general, the proceeds received from an *arm's length* transaction are used when performing a capital gains tax computation. An arm's length transaction occurs when vendor and purchaser are not *connected* in any way that could affect the price agreed between them i.e. the price is one which two strangers might mutually agree. If the disposal is not 'a bargain at arm's length' the consideration used for the computation will be the market value of the asset at the point of the sale, regardless of the value of any consideration actually given.

Disposals to connected persons and gifts are always taken to be not at arm's length. The market value is also used if the consideration for the disposal cannot be directly valued for any reason.

Connected persons are generally:

- For an individual – his or her spouse, siblings, direct ancestors, lineal descendants (children) and their spouses. He or she is not, however, considered to be connected for tax purposes to lateral relatives such as uncles, aunts, nephews and nieces.
- Companies are connected to each other if they are under common control. A company is connected to a person if, either alone or with individuals connected to him or her, that person controls it.

Sometimes a taxpayer may try to reduce a capital gains tax liability by disposing of assets piecemeal (ie piece by piece) to connected persons. Where this kind of disposal is made, the disposal proceeds for each transaction is taken to be an equivalent proportion of the value of the total of the assets transferred. Transactions in parts of an asset are generally considered to be linked if they occur within six years of each other.

For example, a majority shareholder of a company may pass their shares on to the next generation in a series of small gifts. If it were not for the above anti-avoidance legislation this might give a lower market value than if the shares were transferred in one single transaction.

There are strict rules for calculating the market value of some assets. When calculating the market value no reduction is made if several assets are sold at the same time. So if a large number of shares are disposed of to a connected person, then no account is taken of any reduction in the share price due to the size of the disposal. The market value of quoted securities is taken to be the lower of:

- The 'quarter-up': the lower of the two prices quoted in the Daily Official List plus a quarter of the difference between the two prices, and
- The 'mid price': half way between the highest and lowest prices at which bargains were recorded on the date of disposal excluding bargains at special prices.

Incidental costs of disposal

8.10   The incidental costs of disposal include fees, commission or remuneration paid for the professional services of a surveyor, valuer, auctioneer, accountant, legal adviser or agent as well as the cost of transfer or conveyance such as stamp duty. It also includes advertising to find a buyer, but does not include any payment of interest or any cost that is allowed as part of a trading profit computation.

Allowable costs

8.11   Allowable costs include the following:

- The base cost of acquiring the asset – this will usually be the purchase price. However, there are a number of situations in which some other value will be used. For example, if the asset is inherited rather than bought, the market value at the date of death will be used as the allowable cost. There are other examples which we will consider later on.
- Any incidental costs of acquisition such as legal fees.
- Any capital expenditure incurred in enhancing the asset or establishing, preserving or defending title to, or a right over, the asset. For enhancement expenditure to be allowed the benefits of the expenditure must be reflected in the state or nature of the asset at the time of disposal. There are a number of specific exclusions from this category of allowable expenses. These are the costs of repairs, maintenance and insurance and any expenditure which is either an allowable deduction for income tax purposes or was met by public grants, such as home improvement loans.

Calculation of the capital gains tax liability

8.12   In this section we will review how the capital gains tax liability is calculated once the relevant chargeable gain has been determined. We first discuss the basis of assessment that should be applied, then how to determine the relevant rates of tax applicable and then briefly deal with losses and transfers of assets between husbands and wives where special rules apply.

Basis of assessment

8.13   For individuals, capital gains tax is charged on the chargeable gains accruing during the year of assessment after the deduction of:

- allowable losses occurring during the year, and
- any allowable losses accruing from a previous year of assessment which have not already been allowed as a deduction from chargeable gains.

A year of assessment for an individual's capital gains tax runs from 6 April to the following 5 April, i.e. just like the income tax year. Capital gains tax is charged on a current year basis (i.e. what arises in the year of assessment). Any tax due is payable on the later of the 31 January following the year of assessment and 30 days after the issue of a notice of assessment from HMRC. Hence, for disposals made in the fiscal year 2018/19 the tax will be payable on 31 January, 2020.

Rate of tax

8.14 An individual can realise capital gains up to the annual exempt amount (AEA) each year before any liability to this tax arises. The annual exemption amount therefore operates for capital gains tax in a similar way as personal allowances do for income tax i.e. as a tax free threshold.

Fiscal Fact

The Government has estimated that cost to the Exchequer of annual capital gains tax exemption (AEA) of £11,100 for individuals in 2016/17 will be £3.9billion. [Source: HMRC Statistics – Estimated costs of principal tax reliefs as at December 2016]

After 22 June 2010, the rate of tax to be applied to net chargeable gains in excess of the annual exemption amount depends on the income tax band(s) the gain falls into. It is considered to be, in effect, the very top part of income for purposes of determining the applicable rate to pay on the gains. (There was a period of time between 8 April 2008 and 22 June 2010 when the link between CGT rates and income tax levels was dropped, but this was re-instated in 2010).

To determine the relevant rate of capital gains tax to use on any gain you therefore need to know what the individual's taxable income for income tax is for the tax year. The applicable rate of capital gains tax is determined by using the income tax bands. If enough of the basic rate band (£34,500) remains after dealing with non-savings, savings and dividends for income tax to absorb all of the gain, it is taxed at 10%. If the taxpayer is already paying income tax at the higher rate (i.e. taxable income is between £34,500 and £150,000) or additional rate (taxable income exceeds £150,000) then the capital gain is charged at a rate of 20%. If the taxpayer only paid basic rate tax on their income, but adding the capital gain to the taxpayer's taxable income takes them into the higher rate income tax band, then the part of the gain falling within the remainder of their basic rate band is taxed at 10%, and the rest is taxed at 20%. Before April 2016, these rates were 18% and 28% respectively.

Fiscal Fact

The Government estimated that cost to the Exchequer of reducing the rates of capital gains tax to 10% and 20% would be £735million per year by 2020/21. [Source: HM Treasury TIIN on Capital Gains Tax rate changes 16 March 2016]

The new rates applicable from 6 April 2016 (10% and 20%) however, do not apply to all disposals of all assets. If the taxpayer realises a chargeable gain from the sale of residential property (other than their own home which remains exempt under the rules for principal private residence relief – see section 8.26) this will remain at the 2015/16 rates of 18%/28%. The same rules apply to an interest in any land that was associated with a residential property at any time, including where the property has not yet been built (i.e. so called 'off-plan'). In effect there is now an 8% surcharge on the sales of residential property if subject to capital gains tax. The reason given for this in the associated TIIN was that the Government wanted this to motivate investments in companies, not in property.

Activity

Bianca's capital gains, on non-residential properties, after reliefs, are £13,000. What is her capital gains tax liability in 2018/19 if her taxable income, after deducting allowances and reliefs, is:

    a) £17,000

    b) £36,000

    c) £27,000

Feedback

In each case we need to compute what income tax band Bianca would be within once she added the capital gains to her income to determine the relevant rate of capital gains tax to apply.

a) £17,000 taxable income + £13,000 capital gain = £30,000. As this will all fall within the basic rate band for income tax in this tax year, her capital gain can all be taxed at 10%. Her capital gains tax liability will therefore be £1,300 (£13,000 x 10%).

b) £36,000 taxable income means she is a higher rate income taxpayer. All of her capital gains will therefore be taxed at 20%. Her capital gains tax liability will therefore be £2,600 (£13,000 x 20%).

c) £27,000 taxable income + £13,000 capital gain = £40,000. Therefore, part of the gain will be taxed at 10% and part at 20%. Her capital gains tax liability will therefore be:

(£34,500 – £27,000) x 10%	£750.00
£13,000 – (£34,500 – £27,000) x 20%	£1,100.00
	£1,850.00

These rules therefore mean two individuals with the same capital gain, perhaps even from selling the same asset bought on the same date, will pay different rates of capital gains tax depending on their level of taxable income for income tax purposes.

If the gain made by Bianca had come from the sale of a house that was not her home, she would have instead had to apply tax rates of 18% and 28%. We will explore how these rules apply in more detail in Section 8.26.

Capital losses

8.16 If a taxpayer incurs a capital loss in a year, the loss is first set against any gains for that year. If the taxpayer has an overall net loss for the tax year, ie total losses for the year exceed the total gains, the net loss is carried forward to future fiscal years.

Losses carried forward must be set against the first available gains in future years. In that year any losses for that year are deducted first before any prior year losses brought forward are deducted. However, the brought forward losses can be used to enable the taxpayer to gain the full benefit of the annual exemption limit for that year. Any remaining amounts still not used are then carried forward to the subsequent year.

Allowable losses cannot be carried back except on the occasion of the taxpayer's death – they can only be carried forward.

We can illustrate these rules with the following example:

Activity

Ewan had the following capital gains and losses:

Year	Gain	Loss	Annual exemption for year
	£	£	£
2016/17	4,000	9,000	11,100
2017/18	7,500	3,000	11,300
2018/19	12,000	nil	11,700

Calculate Ewan's net chargeable gain for each year.

Feedback

2016/17	£
Gain	4,000
Loss	(9,000)
Net loss	(5,000)

Ewan's annual exemption is wasted for this year and the loss of £5,000 is carried forward to the next year.

2017/18	£
Gain	7,500
Loss	(3,000)
Net current year gain	4,500
Annual exemption	(11,300)
Net chargeable gain	nil

Ewan's annual exemption covers his net current year gain and he pays no capital gains tax in this year. The £5,000 loss carried forward from 2016/17 does not need to be used; rather it is carried forward again into 2018/19.

2018/19	£
Gain	12,000
Loss	nil
Net current year gain	12,000
Loss brought forward	(300)
Annual exemption	(11,700)
net chargeable gain	nil

In 2018/19, Ewan has a net chargeable gain of £12,000. The annual exemption is £11,700. This means that Ewan only has to use £300 of his loss brought forward to make the chargeable gain equal to the annual exemption. He is then left with £4,700 of the loss to be carried forward into 2019/20.

Note that where a loss arises on the disposal of a chargeable asset to a connected person (using market value as the deemed proceeds), that loss can only be offset against gains on disposals to the same person.

Special capital gains tax rules

8.16 Now that you are able to calculate the basic capital gains tax charge on a disposal there are some special situations which you need to be able to deal with. We will look first at how the rules for transfers between husbands and wives and civil partners operate, then how gains on part disposals are computed followed by special rules for chattels and wasting assets. We will conclude this section with a discussion of negligible value claims.

Spouses and civil partners

8.17 Capital gains tax gets a little more complicated when it comes to its treatment of spouses and civil partners. For most purposes spouses and civil partners are treated as separate people. They each have the full annual exemption limit and each pays tax on their capital gains at either 10% or 20% depending on their marginal rate of income tax. As they are treated separately it is not possible for losses to be transferred from one spouse, or civil partner, to the other.

However, if an asset is jointly owned any chargeable gain, or allowable loss, on disposal to a third party must be split between the husband and wife, or civil partners. This is normally done by apportioning the gain between them using the beneficial interest of each in the asset.

Disposals between a husband and wife, or civil partners, living together, however, are treated on a 'no gain or loss' basis. This is done by taking the net proceeds to be the amount that makes the chargeable gain nil, regardless of any consideration actually given.

These rules obviously often give good scope for tax planning. Assets can be transferred between spouses or civil partners before their final disposal to make the best use of annual exemption allowances or may enable gains to be taxed at 10% instead of 20% if transferred from an higher rated income tax partner to a basic or non-taxable partner. The legislation also offers opportunities to maximise the benefit to be obtained from capital losses. We will review tax planning in more detail in Chapter 11, however, to illustrate these ideas, work through the following example.

Activity

Richard and Judy are a married couple. In May 2001, Judy bought a chargeable asset for £10,000 (net of incidental costs of acquisition and on which no further capital expenditure was incurred and which is not residential property), which she gave to Richard in November 2012. Richard sold the asset for £20,000 in March 2019. Calculate the chargeable gain that arises when Richard sold the asset.

Feedback

The transfer from Judy to Richard in November 2012 will be on a no gain/no loss basis. This means Richard is treated as having acquired the asset at the same value as Judy did in May 2001 – i.e. £10,000.

Assuming Richard is a basic rate taxpayer with taxable income of £15,000, when Richard sold the asset:

	£
Proceeds	20,000
Less Deemed cost	(10,000)
Chargeable gain	10,000

Note: Richard has an annual allowance this year of £11,700. This may mean that this sale attracts no capital gains tax. If he has used some or all of his AEA for this year on other disposals the 10% rate would apply to any remaining gain as it, together with his taxable income, does not exceed the income tax basic rate band.

This transfer may have made particular sense if Judy had perhaps disposed of other assets using up her allowance this year and would therefore had to pay 10% CGT on this disposal if she hadn't transferred it to Richard first. Even if Richard has used up his allowance, the transfer would still make sense if Judy was a higher rate income taxpayer and would have otherwise paid CGT at 20%.

Part disposals

8.18   A taxpayer may dispose of all or part of an asset or she may dispose of a part share in an asset; for example, selling a one-third interest in a race horse. A part disposal may still be a chargeable disposal even if the rest of the asset is still owned by the seller. A question then arises – how do we work out how much of the cost of the asset belongs to the part that has been disposed of? Suppose an individual buys a large plot of land and then sells a small part of it. It is possible that the large plot is worth more per acre than the part sold. If the taxpayer is simply allowed to apportion allowable costs by reference to the areas sold, a lower chargeable gain will arise than if the cost was apportioned according to the market value of the part disposed of and the part retained. Perhaps understandably, the legislation requires that the allowable costs are allocated according to market values when part disposals are made.

To calculate the portion of the cost that is attributed to the part disposed of, multiply the allowable cost for the entire asset by:

$$\frac{A}{A+B}$$

where A is the value of the part disposed of and B is the market value of the remainder.

To some extent this legislation acts as an anti-avoidance measure. Sales of parts of assets will typically be worth less than the aggregate value of all of the parts of an asset sold together. As such, selling parts can produce a lower capital gains bill overall than selling the whole asset in one transaction.

Activity

Susan gave a third interest in a painting of her great-grandfather, which had been commissioned at a cost of £30,000 in April 1982, to her daughter for her 21st birthday in June 2018. The market value of the third disposed of was estimated to be £20,000. The market value of the remaining two-thirds of the painting was estimated to be £55,000. Calculate Susan's chargeable gain.

Feedback

The allowable cost using market value in June 2018 is:

$$\frac{£20,000}{£20,000 + £55,000} \times £30,000 = 8,000$$

	£
Proceeds (deemed to be market value)	20,000
Less allowable cost	(8,000)
Chargeable gain	12,000

There is a special rule which deals with the part disposal of small areas of land. Where there is a part disposal of land, it will not be treated as a disposal if the taxpayer elects, so long as two conditions apply:

- the total consideration for all disposals of land for the year is not more than £20,000; and
- the consideration for the transfer of this land is not more than one-fifth of the value of the total just before the transfer.

Here, the consideration for disposal is deducted from any allowable expenditure when computing the gain on disposal of the rest of the land.

This special rule can also be used where part of a holding of land is compulsorily acquired, for example by a local government authority, so long as the consideration is small in relation to the market value just before the transfer (in practice, less than 5%).

Chattels

8.19   Another area of special capital gains tax rules you should be aware of is for chattels. Chattels are tangible, movable, property. Assets such as cars, paintings and horses are chattels. Securities and land are not chattels. *Wasting chattels* are chattels with an estimated remaining useful life of 50 years or less. Hence a horse, as an example, is a wasting chattel but a painting will probably not be. Machines are always considered to be wasting chattels.

Wasting chattels are usually exempt from capital gains tax, which at first sounds like a generous concession as it could then perhaps exclude lots of assets.

However, there are two special exceptions we must consider to this general rule. First, you will remember that cars are entirely exempt from capital gains tax anyway. Second, assets which are used during the course of a trade, profession or vocation and are eligible for capital allowances are subject to capital gains tax even if they are wasting chattels.

An interesting case in 2014 (*HMRC v The Executors of Lord Howard of Hendershelfe (decd) [2014] EWCA Civ 278*) involved a famous work of art, a painting by Reynolds, that was on display in one of the UK's stately homes, Castle Howard, until it was sold in 2001 for £9.4m. HMRC considered the sale to be subject to capital gains tax however, the taxpayer successfully argued that because the painting was on display, it was plant and machinery and therefore a wasting asset. Capital allowances over the years it was on display made the painting valueless for capital gains tax purposes, as we will see below. The First Tier Tribunal found in favour of HMRC, the Upper Tribunal found for the taxpayer, and the Court of Appeal also found for the taxpayer. In Finance Act 2015, the government responded to this decision by introducing a rule that says that for the plant exemption to apply, the asset had to be used in the taxpayer's own business, not that of another party.

The capital gains tax computation for assets that are eligible for capital allowances depends on whether a loss arises or not. If a loss arises, the allowable cost is reduced by the lower of the loss and the capital allowances, including any balancing allowance or charge given for the asset. If a gain is made the rules set out next, relating to the relief available for chattels, apply as normal.

A relief is available for all chattels subject to capital gains tax which have a relatively low value. If the proceeds of sale are £6,000 or less, no capital gains tax liability will arise. This is true even if the asset was eligible for capital allowances. If the sale proceeds exceed £6,000 the chargeable gain is equal to the lower of:

- $5/3 \times$ (gross proceeds – £6,000); and
- the gain computed in the usual way.

It is not possible to give a benchmark of when it is no longer worth checking both calculations, and so for relatively low value chattels both calculations will have to be done to be sure which applies.

The following activities illustrate the chattel rules we have just explained.

Activity

Jack sold a valuable book in June 2018 for £6,600. He had bought the book for £100 in November 1984 in an antique shop. Calculate the chargeable gain.

Feedback

A book is a chattel, but as the proceeds are more than £6,000 it is not exempt, although the maximum gain calculation can be used to cap any gain.

	£
Proceeds	6,600
Less cost	(100)
Chargeable gain	6,500
5/3 × (£6,600 – £6,000)	£1,000

The chargeable gain is the lower of £6,500 and £1,000. Hence the chargeable gain will be £1,000.

If a chattel is sold for less than £6,000 any allowable loss is calculated as if the chattel had been sold for £6,000. This will have the effect of reducing or extinguishing the loss, but cannot create a gain.

Wasting assets other than chattels

8.20   Not all wasting assets are chattels. Examples include intangible assets such as registered designs and copyrights with less than 50 years to run. In such cases the allowable cost is the full original cost of the asset written down over its useful life on a straight line basis. Note that this rule does not apply to leases, which generally don't lose value evenly over their life. Special rules apply for leases to work out how much of their cost is deductible.

Activity

Stephen sold a registered design, a business asset with a 30 year life and a remaining life of 14 years, for £12,000 in March 2019, which had cost £10,000 in March 2003. Calculate the chargeable gain.

Feedback

The registered design is a wasting asset, and so the acquisition cost must be restricted to reflect the wasting of its value over time. Only the part of the acquisition cost that has not been written off at the time of the disposal will be allowed.

	£
Proceeds	12,000
Allowable cost	
10,000 × 14/30	(4,666)
Chargeable gain	7,334

Chattels for which capital allowances are available and which are used throughout their period of ownership in a trade, profession or vocation do not have their allowable cost written off.

Negligible value claims

8.21 If an asset becomes effectively worthless the taxpayer can make a negligible value claim, which means the asset is deemed to be sold at its then market value and immediately re-acquired at the same value. This enables the taxpayer to create a capital loss which can be relieved in the normal way. Of course, the allowable cost on any subsequent disposal becomes the market value at the date of the negligible value claim which could lead to a future capital gains tax bill if the value of the asset goes up again later.

We have now considered some of the more common special situations for capital gains tax which you may come across. However, there are two more important ones that you need to know something about. The first is the treatment of quoted securities and the second is the treatment of houses which either have some element of private use as well as being used for other purposes or are not considered the taxpayer's principle private residence throughout the whole period of ownership.

Shares and securities

8.22 Special rules are needed for calculating the capital gains on the sale of securities because a taxpayer may undertake many transactions in the same securities and in these cases a *matching problem* may arise. For example, suppose a taxpayer acquires a number of ordinary shares in a company on several different dates. When they make a disposal it will be necessary to calculate the allowable cost of the shares. As the shares are effectively identical, but will probably have been purchased at different prices, rules are needed to determine which shares are actually being sold. This is much the same problem as arises in the valuation of stock for accounting purposes and many of the same techniques offer possible solutions, for example, First-in, First-out (FIFO), Last-in, First-out (LIFO) and average cost. In addition, there are circumstances when it may be difficult to identify the appropriate allowable costs, for example when rights and bonus issues are made. Since 1985, weighted average cost has been the method used to address these problems.

To work out the cost of shares disposed of, they shares are matched against acquisitions of shares in the same company and of the same class, in the following order:

1. any shares acquired on the day of disposal;

2. any shares acquired in the 30 days after the disposal (on a FIFO basis); and finally

3. any shares in what is known as the 's104 pool', which means all shares acquired before the date of disposal.

Capital distributions

8.23 A capital distribution is a repayment of share capital and is treated as a part disposal for capital gains tax purposes. Provided it has a value of more than 5% of the value of the shares, then the normal part disposal rules we examined earlier in the chapter will apply.

However, if the capital distribution is 5% or less than the value of shares the distribution can be deducted from the allowable cost of the shares. This has the effect of deferring any gain until a future disposal occurs. HMRC are able to exercise their discretion when applying this rule if, for example, they suspect tax avoidance is being deliberately entered into, although the taxpayer may appeal if the deduction is disallowed.

Reorganisations

8.24 During a reorganisation new shares, and possibly debentures, are exchanged for the original shareholding. If the exchange is for only one class of securities, for example ordinary shares, there is no difficulty. The allowable cost of the original holding becomes the allowable cost of the new holding.

If, however, shares are exchanged for more than one class of securities, such as ordinary shares and debentures, it is necessary to apportion the allowable cost of the original securities to the new holdings. If any of the new securities are quoted the allowable cost is split in proportion to their market values on the first day on which they are quoted after the reorganisation.

Takeovers and mergers

8.25 The way in which share exchanges which occur during a takeover or merger are valued is exactly as you might expect from reading the sections on reorganisations and capital distributions.

New shares and securities received in exchange for existing holdings do not lead to a capital gains tax liability. Their allowable cost is derived from the allowable cost of the original holding as described in the section on reorganisations above. If new capital is introduced it becomes an allowable cost. If part of the consideration is in the form of cash a capital distribution is deemed to have taken place and the procedure described in the section on capital distributions is followed.

Private residences and capital gains tax

8.26   An individual's only, or main, residence (termed their *principal private residence* or 'PPR'), including grounds of up to 5,000 square metres, is exempted from capital gains tax provided that he or she has occupied the whole of the residence throughout the period of ownership.

This exemption has helped to contribute to an attitude of homeowners to any increase in the value of their property that differs from the way they think about other capital assets. Homeowners are in a unique position to become highly geared, historically with loans of up to 100% (or even more in some cases) of the value of their house. This means that even a small increase in the value of houses could generate a nice tax-free increase in the value of the owner's equity. This has led to a sense of economic well-being when the price of houses goes up among the more than 65% of households who own their own homes. Few people however, see increases in house prices in the same light as increases in other commodities. Imagine the impact of applying capital gains tax to principal private residences. Increases in value would no longer be seen as beneficial to the same extent because of the large amount of tax which may be payable each time an individual moves.

There is some pressure on the Government to introduce a tax on the gains made by homeowners but it is hard to imagine a government accepting the level of unpopularity which would surely be the result of enacting such a policy and therefore we can probably expect no major change in this area in the near future.

There are, however, some restrictions to this generous rule that you should be aware of. For example, a husband and wife can claim only one principal private residence between them. If you own more than one property, and live in them both at any time, you must elect (i.e. tell HMRC in writing) which of them is your principal private residence. The sale of the other will be subject to capital gains tax under the rules explained below. This implies you can only have a single principal private residence at any one time. You must tell HMRC which is your principal private residence within two years of residing in the second or subsequent property.

Where the taxpayer has not occupied the residence throughout their period of ownership a capital gains tax liability may arise. To calculate the proportion of the gain which is exempt from capital gains tax multiply the total gain, calculated in the normal way, by:

$$\frac{\text{Period of deemed occupation since 31 March, 1982}}{\text{Total period of ownership since 31 March, 1982}}$$

(Remember that capital gains which arose prior to 31 March, 1982 are no longer taxable.)

For many years, provided that the residence was the taxpayer's principal private residence at any time during their period of ownership, the last 36 months of ownership were deemed to be a period of occupation, even if the taxpayer nominates another property to be their principal private residence during this period. This measure is designed to help taxpayers who have moved house and are trying to sell their old house and may otherwise be caught by the capital gains tax rules. For contracts for the sale of the property exchanged on or after 6 April 2014, this period of deemed occupancy has been reduced to 18 months, except for people who are disabled or in long-term care. According to the TIIN for this measure, it was designed to "make the tax system fairer by reducing the incentive for those with more than one property to exploit the rules while still providing people with sufficient time to sell a previous residence after moving to a new one." Some commentators expressed concern about this change, noting that it is not always possible to sell a property within 18 months.

Fiscal Fact

The cost of tax revenues foregone to the Exchequer of exempting gains on PPRs is forecast to be a huge £27.8 billion for 2017/18 [Source: HMRC - Estimated costs of principal tax reliefs as at January 2018]

There are a number of other occasions when a period of absence can be treated as a period of deemed occupation provided that the property both before and after the period of absence (although not necessarily immediately before or immediately after) was occupied as the taxpayer's principal private residence. The periods of deemed occupation are not affected if the property is actually let to tenants during them or not.

The periods of deemed occupation are:
- any periods of absence totalling up to three years;
- any periods during which the taxpayer was required to live abroad in order to fulfil employment duties; and
- any periods totalling up to four years during which the taxpayer was required to work elsewhere in the UK in order to fulfil employment duties.

Strictly, therefore, each period of absence should be followed by a period of occupation. However, as an extra-statutory concession, if a taxpayer's employment requires him or her to work in the UK immediately followed by a period of working abroad or vice versa the periods will still be allowed as periods of deemed occupation.

To try and make these complicated rules somewhat clearer we will illustrate them with the following example.

Activity

John bought a house on 1 April, 1994 for £45,000. He lived in the house until 30 June, 1996 when he obtained work in another part of the country. The house was let until he returned on 1 April, 2000. On 1 May, 2005 he went to work abroad until 1 May, 2010 when he returned to the UK and moved into his friend's house. John's house was sold on 1 January, 2019 for £220,000. John incurred fees and costs of £5,000 relating to the sale.

Feedback

It is first necessary to calculate the proportions of exempt and chargeable months to the period of ownership since 1 April, 1994. The total period of ownership is 297 months (24 years 9 months from 1 April 1994 to 1 January 2019).

Period	Exempt months	Chargeable months
1/4/94–30/6/96 (occupied)	27	0
1/7/956–31/3/00		
(working away (in UK) <4 years)	45	0
1/4/00–30/4/05 (occupied)	61	0
1/5/05–30/6/17 (see below)	0	146
1/7/17–1/1/19 (last 18 months)	18	0
	151	146

The period from 1 May, 2005 to 31 June, 2017 is not exempt because the absence was not followed by a period of owner occupation. Had John re-occupied the house after this period instead of moving in with his friend, even if only for a short time, the period from 1 May, 2005 to when he moved out would also have been exempted under the working away rules, and the normal principal private residence exemption.

Now the chargeable gain can be calculated:

	£
Gross proceeds	220,000
Incidental costs of disposal	(5,000)
Net proceeds	215,000
Less allowable cost	(45,000)
Gain	170,000
Private residence exemption:	
151/297 × 170,000	(86,431)
Chargeable gain	83,569

Remember, this chargeable gain will be taxed at either 18% or 28% depending on John's income tax band as this is tax due on the sale of a residential property for the periods when it was not his main home - i.e. the 8% surcharge therefore applies.

Taxpayers living in job-related accommodation will be able to claim any residence which they own as a principal private residence provided that they intend to occupy it as their main residence in due course. (See 5.27 for a definition of job-related accommodation).

Lettings

8.27 If a lodger (someone who rents a room in a house) lives with a family, sharing living accommodation and eating with them, there is no liability to capital gains tax when disposing of the residence because of this. However, if part or all of a property is let for residential purposes, the principal private residence exemption may extend to gains which relate to the period of letting. This relief is available if:

- the owner is absent and lets the property during a period which is not considered a deemed period of occupation; and
- only part of the property is let.

The relief available is the lowest of:

- the gain accruing during the letting period;
- £40,000; and
- the total gain which is exempt under the principal private residence provisions. However, this relief cannot turn a gain into an allowable loss for capital gains tax purposes.

Business use

8.28   If part of the residence is used wholly for business purposes, then any gain which is attributable to that part is taxable. This is an important point to bear in mind when deciding whether to claim that part of a residence is used for business purposes, perhaps an office or a workshop. In the short term it may be possible to set some expenses against income for income tax purposes but it may give rise to a substantial liability for capital gains tax purposes in the future if that use is claimed to be exclusively for business purposes.

Reliefs from capital gains tax

8.29   At the start of this chapter we discussed how capital gains tax is largely intended to help create a fairer and more equitable system of tax and to reduce the incentives to artificially create a capital receipt rather than an income receipt to decrease the tax payable on the transaction. However, there are a number of situations when relief is available to mitigate the impact of capital gains tax.

In this section we will look at four types of relief. The first three, Business Asset relief, Incorporation Relief and Gift Relief, all provide for a deferral of the capital gains tax liability, that is they affect the timing of payment rather than the amount to be paid. The fourth relief, Entrepreneurs' relief, actually reduces the amount of capital gains tax payable.

We will now consider each of these reliefs in more detail, in turn.

Business Asset Rollover relief

8.30   Businesses often sell an asset intending to replace it with another. For example, a business may move to new premises and thus sell the existing land and buildings they own in order to purchase the new property. Rollover relief, which defers capital gains tax due, may be available if the proceeds from a sale of assets are invested in new assets. You may consider this to be entirely reasonable since, although a liability to capital gains tax has arisen because of the sale, the business is clearly no better off than they were just before they sold the property, and may need the money it has raised from the sale to buy the new asset. In reality the taxpayer has simply exchanged one asset for another.

Such a favourable tax treatment may also encourage a business to reinvest their money into other businesses assets rather than to take it out of the economy. This is arguably good for an entrepreneurial society.

If the consideration received for the disposal of a capital asset is used, by the taxpayer, to acquire other capital assets, then rollover relief may be available. This will allow the disposal of the old asset to occur as if it gave rise to neither a gain nor a loss but the allowable cost of the new asset is then reduced by the amount of the gain on the old. This way the new asset absorbs the gain from the old asset until such time as it is disposed of. Both the old and the new assets must be used solely for the purpose of trade and also must fall into one of the following classes (Note: it does not matter if they fall into different categories.):

Class 1: any land or building or part of a building used only for the purpose of trade and fixed plant or machinery which does not form part of a building (but fixed plant and machinery is subject to holdover relief rather than rollover – see below)

Class 2: ships, aircraft and hovercraft

Class 3: satellites, space stations and spacecraft

Class 4: goodwill

Class 5: milk quotas and potato quotas

Class 6: ewe and suckler cow premium quotas.

Class 7: fish quota

Class 8: Lloyds syndicate rights

[Note that for Class 1 above, it can sometimes be difficult to decide whether plant and machinery is 'fixed'. Moveable items cannot usually be treated as 'fixed' plant and machinery for this purpose, but there have been some interesting cases on this question. It is one of the many areas of tax law that is the subject of considerable dispute.]

In order to claim the relief, the new asset must be acquired between 12 months before and three years after the disposal of the old asset. It is not necessary for the old and new asset to be used in the same business, just that they belong to the same taxpayer.

If the total proceeds from the sale of the old asset are reinvested in the new asset, then full relief will be given. However, if some of the proceeds are not reinvested then a chargeable gain equal to the lower of the chargeable gain before rollover relief and the amount which has not been reinvested will be subject to capital gains tax immediately.

Activity

Mike bought a ship in March 2001 for £500,000 and sold it for £1,000,000 in September 2011. He bought a factory in November 2011 for £850,000. Both assets are or were used in his trade. Determine any chargeable gain that arises on the sale of the ship assuming that rollover relief is claimed and compute the chargeable gain arising when Mike sells the factory in June 2018 for £1.5 million.

Feedback

Disposal of ship	£
Proceeds	1,000,000
Less allowable cost	(500,000)
Chargeable gain	500,000
Less amount not reinvested	
£1,000,000 – £850,000	(150,000)
Gain eligible to be rolled over	350,000

The chargeable gain is £150,000 as this is the amount not re-invested and is lower than the gain calculated (£500,000). This gain will be liable for capital gains tax in the 2011/12 year.

Base cost of the factory:	£
Cost	850,000
Less rolled over gain	(350,000)
Base cost of the factory	500,000
Disposal of factory June 2018	£
Proceeds	1,500,000
Less allowable cost	(500,000)
Chargeable gain (2018/19)	1,000,000

Holdover relief

8.31 Rollover relief cannot be claimed if the replacement asset is depreciable. This is defined to mean either the asset is:

- Fixed plant and machinery; or
- If it is, or within the next 10 years will become, a wasting asset. Remember that a wasting asset has a life of 50 years or less and so this rule will apply to any replacement asset with a life of 60 years or less.

In these cases, rather than rollover relief, we use another form of relief called holdover relief.

Holdover relief is given by reducing the amount of the chargeable gain according to the amount reinvested as we did with rollover relief, but instead of using the gain to reduce the cost of the new asset until it is finally sold, the gain is instead 'held over' until it crystallises, at which time it becomes chargeable.

The held-over gain becomes a chargeable gain on the earlier of:

- the date on which the taxpayer disposes of the replacement asset;
- the date on which the replacement asset ceases to be used for the purposes of a trade carried on by the taxpayer; or
- ten years after the date of the acquisition of the replacement asset.

If, before the held-over gain crystallised, the replacement asset is itself replaced by an asset which is not a depreciating asset then some or all of the held-over gain can be transferred to the new asset.

Activity

May bought a workshop in February 2004 for £25,000 and ran a business making and selling soft furnishings. In July 2008 she sold the workshop for £40,000 and in August 2008 she bought fixed plant for £50,000 to use in the new premises she was renting. In January 2011 May bought a new workshop for £35,000 and in October 2018 she sold the fixed plant for £80,000. Determine May's chargeable gains on each of the transactions, assuming that holdover/rollover relief is claimed where appropriate.

Feedback

July 2008 disposal:	£
Proceeds	40,000
Less allowable costs	(25,000)
Chargeable gain	15,000

The entire proceeds of £40,000 can be considered to have been reinvested in plant within the time period allowed for relief to apply, and so the £15,000 gain can be held over and no chargeable gain arises from the first transaction.

January 2011 purchase:

When the new workshop (not a depreciating asset) was bought part of the held-over gain from the first workshop could be rolled over to the new workshop because this asset was still bought within 3 years of the original workshop disposal. Rolled-over gains can be held indefinitely as long as the new asset is owned and as such is a better place to have the gain attached to than the plant. May is probably better off moving as much of the held-over gain (£15,000) as she can onto the new workshop.

	£
Total gain held over	15,000
Less proceeds not reinvested	
40,000 – 35,000	(5,000)
Gain eligible to be rolled over	10,000

The base cost of the new workshop would be £25,000 (£35,000 – £10,000). The £5,000 not eligible to be rolled over can continue to be held over until the charge crystallises.

October 2018 disposal of plant:

	£
Proceeds	80,000
Less cost	(50,000)
Chargeable gain	30,000

The remaining held-over gain of £5,000 crystallises as a result of the disposal of the fixed plant and will be chargeable in 2018/19.

Incorporation relief

8.32   A form of rollover relief is also available where a business and all its assets (other than cash) are transferred to a company in exchange for shares in that new company. This relief is referred to as incorporation relief. It is automatically applied although incorporations can be done without application of this relief if the taxpayer so elects, for example to use up allowances that may otherwise be lost. The election must be no later than the second anniversary of the 31 January following the tax year in which the transfer occurs.

The relief works by deducting any chargeable gains from the disposal of business assets from the value of the shares received and the company is treated as receiving the assets at their market value. The relief only applies if the business is transferred to the company as a going concern.

Activity

Zigmund decides to incorporate the business he has operated for a number of years as a sole trader. He transfers the business to the company as a going concern, and there is a chargeable gain of £75,000 for the business assets transferred. The market value of the shares in the new company is £200,000. What is the effect of incorporation relief on this transaction?

Feedback

The gain on the business assets is rolled over by reducing the value of the shares, so that their cost becomes £125,000 (200,000 – 75,000). This means that when Zigmund later sells the shares, the gain will crystallise at that time.

If only part of the consideration given by the company for the business is in the form of shares, for example part of the price is paid in cash, then only a proportion of the chargeable gain can be rolled over in this way and deducted from the value of the shares, based on the market value of the shares compared to the total consideration for the transfer of the business.

Gift relief

8.33   If a taxpayer makes a chargeable disposal for less than the market value of the asset (e.g. as a gift) then, providing both the donor and the beneficiary make an election, and provided the asset qualifies (see below), some or all of the chargeable gain can be deferred and transferred to the beneficiary by means of gift relief. This enables assets to be passed from one generation to the next without a capital gains tax liability arising and hence the name gift relief.

Gift relief only applies to qualifying assets, which means:

- it is, or is an interest in, an asset used for the purposes of a trade, profession or vocation carried on by:
  - the transferor, or
  - his or her personal company, or
  - a member of a trading group of which the holding company is his or her personal company or
- it is shares or securities of a trading company, or of the holding company of a trading group, and either:
  - the shares are not listed on a recognised stock exchange, or
  - the trading or holding company is the transferor's personal company.

If this election is made the transferee is deemed to acquire the asset at its market value less the gain which would otherwise have arisen.

Activity

Joe runs an IT firm. In October 2013, his daughter Lorna joins the business. Joe decides to gift to her the goodwill in the business. This was acquired for £150,000 in April 2001 when Joe first acquired the business and its market value in October 2018 was £450,000. Both parties elect to treat the gift under the gift relief rules. What amount of the gain qualifies for gift relief, and what will be the base cost of the goodwill for Lorna after the relief is applied?

Feedback

First, the chargeable gain needs to be computed for Joe. This will be £300,000 (£450,000 – £150,000). This sum reduces the allowable cost of the asset in Lorna's hands to £150,000 (£450,000 – £300,000). If gift relief is claimed, Joe has no capital gains tax liability to deal with at the point of the transfer and the gain is instead effectively transferred to Lorna to pay tax on when she disposes of the goodwill in the future.

If the transferee provides some consideration then the transferor's deferred gain is instead equal to the gain less any excess of the consideration over the allowable costs. This deferred gain is termed the held-over gain.

Activity

Alan sold the goodwill of a small paper recycling business to his daughter Sarah on 30 May 2011. The goodwill had a market value of £300,000 but Alan sold it to Sarah for £100,000 and both claimed gift relief. Alan had bought the goodwill in May 2001 for £50,000. Sarah intends to sell the business in May 2018 and believes that she will be able to obtain a price of £400,000 by then. Determine Alan's chargeable gain and advise Sarah on the amount of any chargeable gain if she sells the business as planned.

Feedback

	£
Alan	
Deemed proceeds	300,000
Less allowable cost	(50,000)
	250,000
Less gain held over	
£250,000 – (£100,000 – £50,000)	(200,000)
Chargeable gain	50,000
Sarah – if sold in May 2018	
Proceeds	400,000
Less allowable cost (£300,000 – £200,000)	(100,000)
Chargeable gain	300,000

Alan's chargeable gain is £50,000, while Sarah's chargeable gain will be £300,000 if she sells the business as planned.

If the taxpayer makes a disposal by way of a gift to a charity or for national purposes, or for a consideration which would give rise to an allowable loss, then the disposal and acquisition is treated as being made for a consideration that results in neither a gain nor a loss on the disposal. The recipient of the asset is deemed to have acquired the asset at the same time and for the same consideration as the donor of the gift.

A gift is for national purposes if it is made to the National Gallery, British Museum or National Trust or to a university, among others.

It should be noted that no gift relief is available for any transfers of shares or securities to a company by individuals or trustees.

If an individual gifts shares in a company to another person, however, an apportionment calculation must be done as only gains related to chargeable business assets are eligible for gift relief. Any sum represented by non-eligible assets (for gift relief), like investments held by the company whose shares are being gifted, become chargeable instead on the transferor.

Entrepreneurs' relief

8.34 Entrepreneurs' relief was introduced with effect from 6 April 2008 to complement the capital gains tax reforms introduced in 2008 (i.e. the abolition of taper relief for individuals, replaced by a flat 18% tax rate). It was introduced following public concern that the changes to the rate of capital gains tax would be detrimental to people selling all or part of a business as a going concern, or on cessation of the business, particularly as many small business owners treat the increase in goodwill which they will realise on sale of their business as a form of retirement provision.

Where individuals involved in running a business dispose of all or part of that business and make a gain on the disposal, the first £10million of gains that qualify for the relief for any disposals after 1 April 2011 will be charged to capital gains tax at a simple, fixed rate of 10%, instead of some having to be taxed at the higher 20% CGT rate. Any excess gains over the £10million limit are taxed at normal capital gains tax rates (i.e. likely to be 20%).

This limit of £10 million has been changed since the relief was introduced; it was initially £1million until 5 April 2010, then £2million for disposals 6 April 2010 to 22 June 2010, and £5million for the rest of 2010/11.

The £10million limit is a lifetime limit, so a taxpayer may be able to make several claims until this total is reached.

The relief also applies to gains which arise on the disposal of shares in a trading company, providing that the individual making the disposal has been an officer or employee of the company and owns at least 5% of the ordinary share capital of the company.

In Finance Act 2015, a new restriction was introduced in relation to gains arising from the transfer of goodwill to a limited company that is related to the claimant. This anti-avoidance rule was relaxed a little in Finance Act 2016 to remove this restriction if less than 5% of the shares and voting rights in the acquiring company were held by the individual disposing of the asset.

Activity

Bethan is a higher rate taxpayer who sold a business that she had run for 10 years. The chargeable gains are agreed to be £15,750,000. Bethan has not made an entrepreneurs' relief claim previously and has no other chargeable gains or losses for the year. What will be her capital gains tax liability?

Feedback

	£
Total chargeable gain	15,750,000
less Entrepreneurs' relief	(10,000,000)
less annual exempt amount	(11,700)
Chargeable gain	5,738,300
Tax @ 20%	1,147,660
Tax @ 10% on 10,000,000	1,000,000
Total tax	2,147,660

Without the benefit of entrepreneurs' relief, Bethan would have had to pay up to £3,147,660 in capital gains tax.

Investors' relief

8.35 In Finance Act 2016 a new extension to this relief was introduced related to new shares issued to external investors (i.e. not employees or directors of the business) with new money (i.e. not recycling money already invested in the company) in unlisted trading companies or their holding companies. Where new shares are issued in such companies after 18 March 2016, held for at least three years from 6 April 2016, and held for three continuous years prior to the disposal, then the gain from the disposal of the shares qualify for 'investors' relief', which is an additional relief subject to a £10 million limit.

Stamp duty

8.36 Stamp duty was introduced into the UK in 1694, and is therefore one of the oldest taxes still in existence in this country. Its origins can be traced all the way back to Roman times however. Stamp duty is a tax on transactions, imposed when certain types of property changes hands. As such it can therefore be thought of as a capital tax in the same category of taxes as capital gains tax.

Like income tax, when stamp duty was first introduced it was only supposed to be temporary and was introduced to provide revenue for the King and Queen (William and Mary) to 'carry on the war against France'.

Stamp duty was charged on certain documents when first introduced. These included insurance policies, documents in court proceedings, grants of honour, grants of probate (wills) and letters of administration.

Stamp duty is now administered in the UK by HMRC via various Stamp Duty offices that can be found throughout the UK.

Payment of stamp duty used to be denoted by affixing a stamp to the transfer document or receipt which is the subject of the duty. With the introduction of Stamp Duty Land Tax (SDLT) in December 2003, provision is now made for electronic conveyancing, i.e. without documentation. Stamp duty is calculated at either a flat rate or *ad valorem* i.e. varying according to the value of the transaction to which it relates.

Property transactions

8.37   The most common form of stamp duty now is SDLT on transfers of property (land and buildings), both residential and non-residential/commercial, and on share transactions. It is always payable by the purchaser in a transaction to which it applies.

A major reform of stamp duty on land and buildings was announced in Budget 2002 in order to close a number of loopholes in the new tax rules and reduce some distortions recognised as existing in the old system. Under the previous stamp duty regime, transactions were sometimes structured so as to avoid or reduce payment of stamp duty and the government was concerned that this was interfering with commercial decision making. The new regime includes increased powers of enforcement for HMRC to reduce this problem.

From 1 December, 2003, SDLT applies to all land transactions. This includes the purchase of freehold land as well as the acquisition of an existing lease. The only exemptions to this are the sales of school owned land and of zero carbon homes (on the first £500,000 of purchase price only in the latter case) from 1 October 2007.

Fiscal Fact

The exemption for first time buyers is expected to cost the government £125m for 2017-18 (HMRC estimated cost of principle tax reliefs, January 2018).

The act of entering into a contract to purchase land is not enough to be considered a land transaction (i.e. what is called an 'exchange' in house purchase terms) rather it is generally 'completion' or the point at which possession occurs that is important. As the date of completion normally occurs immediately before possession is allowed, this will normally be the date of the transaction for SDLT.

The rates of tax on transfers of property vary from 0% to 15%. The table below shows you how the property related stamp duty rates apply in the UK. For residential properties, prior to December 2014, as soon as the value of the property transferred crossed a boundary, all of the transaction was taxed at the higher rate, not just the excess over the lower band. This system, sometimes referred to as a 'slab' system, was modified in December 2014 to a 'slice' system where the tax is paid on increasing portions of the value of the property. This move to a 'slice' system also now applies to non-residential property and land transactions from 17 March 2016.

Fiscal Fact

The change of the rules for SDLT on non-residential property and land to a 'slice' basis from a 'slab' basis in March 2016 was estimated to produce more than £1billion in tax revenue for the Government each year according to the Budget 2016 summary of impact assessments.

The rates of SDLT vary depending on whether the purchaser is a natural person (an individual) or a non-natural person such as a company or trust (for simplicity we will use the term 'company' in this section to cover all types of non-natural entities).

In a move that angered many landlords, Finance Act 2016 also introduced an 'additional property supplement' to SDLT on purchases of buy-to-let residential property (but not for non-residential property). A 3% surcharge applies for all such property purchases over the £40,000 minimum limit. Note that a 'multiple dwellings relief' is available so that the surcharge does not apply if more than six properties are purchased in the same transaction.

For natural persons, the rates are now as follows:

Value of property (£)	Stamp duty rate (%)	
Residential property	*not buy to let*	*buy to let*
up to 40,000	0	0
40,000 – 125,000*	0	3
125,001 – 250,000	2	5
250,001 – 925,000	5	8
925,001 –1.5m	10	13
over 1.5m	12	15

* £150,000 for not buy to let in disadvantaged areas.

Value of property (£)	Stamp duty rate (%)
Non-residential property	
up to 150,000	0
150,001 – 250,000	2
over 250,000	5

In the case of residential property in disadvantaged areas that is not purchased for buy-to-let, the threshold at which SDLT starts to apply is £150,000 instead of £125,000.

From 22 November 2017, special rules are in place for first time buyers so that there is no SDLT for properties valued at up to £300,000, then 5% up to £500,000. This only applies to properties purchased for the first-time buyers only (or main) residence, i.e. it does not apply to buy-to-let purchases.

Activity

(a) Rhona enters into a contract in January 2019 to buy a residential house for her to live in, not in a disadvantaged area, for £243,000. How much SDLT will she have to pay on completion?
(b) What if this sale falls through and instead Rhona buys a house for £252,000. How much SDLT will now be due on completion?
(c) What if the second property was instead bought as a buy-to-let rather than for her to live in?
(d) What would the difference be in a-c if Rhona was a first-time buyer?

Feedback

(a) The house is in the 2% band and so she will have to pay
(£243,000 – £125,000) × 2% = £2,360 in SDLT.

(b) The second house is in the 3% band she will have to pay:

(£250,000 – £125,000) x 2%	£2,500
(£252,000 – £250,000) x 3%	£60
Total	£2,560

(c) As this is a buy-to-let property the new additional rates apply to increase the SDLT for each band by 3% so she will have to pay:

(£250,000 – £125,000) x 5%	£6,250
(£252,000 – £250,000) x 8%	£160
Total	£6,410

(d) If Rhona is a first-time buyer there would be no SDLT if Rhona purchased House (a) or House (b) as they are below £300,000. There would be no first-time buyer SDLT reduction if Rhona purchased a buy-to-let property like House (c)

Special rules for companies

8.38 From 20 March 2014 SDLT is charged at 15% on residential dwellings costing more than £500,000 purchased by companies. Prior to this date, the threshold for this 15% rate was £2million. There are exclusions from this special rate for property rental businesses, property developers and traders, properties that are made available to the public, dwellings occupied by employees and farmhouses.

This higher level of SDLT for companies buying expensive UK-based property is a direct attempt by the Government to reduce the avoidance of this tax by those buying property through overseas companies that otherwise escaped the need to pay this tax.

Leases

8.39 When a new residential property has a substantial annual rent, SDLT is payable on both the lease premium (if any) and the net present value of the rent payable over the life of the lease.

The SDLT on the lease premium is the same as for SDLT on residential property purchases. The SDLT on rent for new residential leasehold properties is 0% up to £125,000 and 1% on the excess over £125,000.

Where the property is non-residential, for example shops, offices and agricultural land, the SDLT on the premium is the same as for a freehold purchase.

For new leases on non-residential property the SDLT on the net present value of the rent is 0% up to £150,000 and 1% on the excess up to rents with net present value of £5million. From 17 March 2016 a new higher SDLT rate of 2% is charged for those with net present values exceeding £5million.

As with all SDLT, these measures do not apply in Scotland where a different tax (LBTT) applies to similar transactions under its devolved tax powers (see 8.40) and only applies in Wales until 2018 when it also introduced its own SDLT style rules.

Activity

Lewis is granted a 15 year lease over a warehouse building which is not in a disadvantaged area. He pays a premium of £50,000 and the net present value of the rent is £190,000. How much SDLT will he have to pay?

Feedback

	£
On the premium £50,000 × 1%	500
On the rental 1% × (190,000 – 150,000)	400
Total	900

Scottish Land and Buildings Transactions Tax

8.40 Following the devolution of taxing powers to the Scottish Parliament, from 1 April 2015, instead of SDLT a new tax, the land and buildings transaction tax (LBTT) applies to property in Scotland. The new tax is similar to SDLT and applies to 'slices' of consideration as follows:

Value of property (£)	LBTT rate %	Additional Dwelling Supplement%
Residential property		
0 – 40,000	0	0
40,001 – 145,000*	0	3
145,001 – 250,000	2	5
250,001 – 325,000	5	8
325,000 – 750,000	10	13
over 750,000	12	15
Non-residential property		
0 – 150,000	0	
150,001 – 350,000	3	
over 350,000	4.5	

The new tax is administered by Revenue Scotland, a new government body set up to administer all Scottish devolved taxes.

Welsh Land Transactions Tax

8.41 From 1 April 2018 stamp duty land tax no longer applies in Wales. Like Scotland, the devolved government has introduced a new tax, the land transactions tax (LTT). The tax is administered by the Welsh Revenue Authority (WRA). The tax is payable when buildings or land is purchased or leased, and is broadly consistent with SDLT. The following rates apply to purchases of land and buildings:

Value of property (£)	LTT rate %
Residential property **	
0 – 180,000*	0*
180,001 – 250,000	3.5*
250,001 – 400,000	5*
400,000 – 750,000	7.5*
750,000 – 1,500,000	10*
Over 1,500,000	12*

* 3% supplement on additional residential dwellings.

Non-residential property

0 – 150,000	0
150,001 – 250,000	1
250,001 – 1,000,000	5
over 1,000,000	6

Additional Property/Dwelling Supplement

8.42   From 1 April 2016 additional rates apply to all SDLT and LBTT rates where the purchase is related to an 'additional' residential property. This is called the 'additional property supplement' for SDLT and Welsh LTT and the 'additional dwelling supplement' for Scottish LBTT but the same 3% supplement rate applies to all the standard rates for each SDLT and LBTT property value 'slice' (see tables above).

Who will pay these additional rates? Broadly this will apply to:

(a)   Companies and funds (i.e. 'non-natural' persons) when buying residential properties for values more than £40,000 will always pay the additional rates;

(b)   Individuals holding large property portfolios – when buying residential properties for values more than £40,000 will always pay the additional rates unless the new property is replacing their main residence, or does so within 36 months;

(c)   Other individuals – buying (or leasing) properties for more than £40,000 (and at least seven years if a lease) if at the end of the day on which the purchase/lease transaction occurs the person buying, their spouse or civil partners, or any minor child of the purchaser/lessor (under the age of 18) have ownership interests in more than one residential property.

Overseas properties, or properties held in other parts of the UK, are also included in this count of residential properties owned for determining if additional rate applies if those properties are valued more than £40,000.

The rule for individuals is relaxed, however, if the property being purchased or leased is to become their main residence. It does not matter how many other properties they own for this exemption to apply. Proving that a property is a main residence is based on matters of fact (where you are registered to vote, where your children go to school if you have children etc.), not on the basis of an election, unlike the capital gains tax rules for property transactions (e.g. for determining which is the main residence for principal private property relief – see Section 8.26). This will work by payment being made at the additional rate when the new property is acquired, but where evidence is subsequently presented to show that this new property has become the main residence, a rebate of the supplement amount paid will be made. The current residence must be sold within 36 months of the purchase of the new one for this rebate to be payable.

Purchases of furnished holiday lettings also fall within these new rules as will any buy-to-let properties. However, the Government believes 90% of residential property transactions will be unaffected by these new rules. However, other forms of property you can live in (for example, caravans, mobile homes, timeshares and house boats) are excluded from these rules entirely. Accommodation provided by an employer is also not included within these rules.

Further, where less than 50% of a property is inherited the recipient is eligible for a rebate of the supplement if sold within 36 months of their inheritance, where this is not the only residential property owned by the person inheriting. Where larger shares in a property are inherited, or where sales do not complete within 36 months irrespective of the shareholding, these will be caught by these new supplement rate rules and no rebate will be paid.

Annual Tax on Enveloped Dwellings

8.43 An annual tax was introduced from 1 April 2013, designed to provide a disincentive to holding expensive UK residential property through a company or other non-natural entity. Liability to ATED arises where a company has a 'single-dwelling interest' in a dwelling worth £2million as at 1 April 2012. This is a freestanding tax, and so is not superseded by the Scottish LBTT as SDLT is.

A 'dwelling' includes the garden or grounds that go with the dwelling buildings. Where a company holds an interest in more than one dwelling, the interest is apportioned for ATED purposes and each interest in a single dwelling is treated as a separate chargeable interest, there is no aggregation.

ATED is chargeable for any day when the value of the single dwelling interest exceeds the threshold, unless any of the reliefs apply.

The flat rate of tax is as follows:

Value of property (£)	ATED charge £
500,000 – £1m	3,500
Over £1m, not exceeding £2m	7,000
Over £2m, not exceeding £5m	23,350
Over £5m, not exceeding £10m	54,450
Over 10m, not exceeding £20m	109,050
Over £20m	218,200

Prior to 1 April 2016, only properties valued at more than £1million were liable for ATED. From 1 April 2016, a new lower rate has been added. Properties worth between £500,000 and £1million are now charged at £3,500.

For the ATED period beginning 1 April 2014 onwards, an ATED return and payment are due by 30 April, i.e. for the ATED period 1 April 2016 to 31 March 2017, both the return and payment are due by 30 April 2017.

If residential property which has been subject to ATED is disposed of, some or all the capital gains will be 'ATED related'. A special tax return is required for ATED related capital gains which is separate from the usual capital gains tax return. The general capital gains rule that liability only arises if a person is a UK tax resident, does not apply for ATED related gains. Capital gains tax is charged under these rules on ATED related gains attributed to periods after 5 April 2013 at 28% (i.e. they are not reduced by the 2016 changes to capital gains tax rates).

The ATED related CGT charge takes into account the new ATED bands that apply for 2015 and 2016. Properties within the £1million to £2million bracket will be rebased to 6 April 2015, and those within the £500,000 to £1million band will be rebased to 6 April 2016.

Share transactions

8.44   The other main area to which UK Stamp Duty is applied is transactions in shares. When shares are purchased using a stock transfer form, stamp duty is payable at 0.5%, rounded up to the nearest £5 above.

Transactions with a purchase price of less than £1,000 are exempt from stamp duty, with effect from April 2008.

When you buy shares through a stockbroker, it will usually be a paperless (electronic) transaction. In this situation, Stamp Duty Reserve Tax (SDRT) is paid at a flat rate of 0.5% of the amount paid for the shares.

From 28 April 2014, stamp duty is no longer chargeable on transactions in eligible securities on London Stock Exchange's AIM or High Growth Segment.

Administration

8.45   Payment of stamp duty on share transactions is made by taking, or sending, the documents to be stamped to a Stamp Duty office. These offices can be found in various UK cities. Documents that need stamping should be presented to one of these offices within 30 days of the transaction occurring. If you are late making this presentation for payment you have to pay charges and interest as a penalty. The maximum penalty is an amount equivalent to the duty, or £300, whichever is less. This becomes a minimum of £300 if your presentation for payment is more than a year late. Interest is charged on overdue payments at normal official rates in addition to this penalty.

For property transactions, a self assessment system is now in operation that requires the purchaser to send HMRC a return notifying them of the completion of a taxable transaction within 30 days of the effective date of the transaction. The tax due should accompany this notification. Failure to submit a return and/or pay the tax due results in similar interest and penalty charges or legal proceedings that are linked with the self assessment procedures for other taxes, such as income tax.

Inheritance tax

8.46 Inheritance tax in its current form was introduced in 1986. A tax on the transfer of property on death has, however, been part of the UK tax landscape in some form or another since the eighteenth century. Like capital gains tax and stamp duty it is a further example of a capital tax in operation in the UK at present as it related to capital transfers (i.e. to inheritances in this case).

An inheritance tax liability will arise when a chargeable person makes a transfer of value of chargeable property. Let's consider these terms further:

- *Chargeable person*. Inheritance tax only applies to individuals and not to companies. All individuals are potentially liable for inheritance tax, for UK domiciled persons on all chargeable property wherever it is located, and for non-UK domiciled persons on UK-situated property only. (See Chapter 12 for an explanation of the concept of domicile for tax purposes). There is an exemption for those who die while on active military service, which has been extended to Emergency service and humanitarian aid workers killed in the course of duty by Budget 2014.
- *Chargeable property*. All property is potentially chargeable to inheritance tax, although there are some exemptions or exclusions which we will consider briefly below - see the website chapter for full details.
- *Transfer of value*. The key trigger for inheritance tax to arise is a transfer of *value* between its current 'owner' and the person or entity to whom it is being given. This does not always just arise on an individual's death however. A transfer of value is essentially a gift of an asset by a chargeable person which results in a decrease in the value of that person's estate (total net worth). Usually the decrease in value we consider for inheritance tax purposes will be the open market value of the property at the time of its transfer. Some transfers, or dispositions, are not caught by the inheritance tax net however, including genuine commercial activities and those that are allowable expenses for income tax or corporation tax purposes. Also excluded are dispositions for the maintenance of the transferor's family.

Lifetime transfers

8.47   There are three types of transfer made during the lifetime of an individual:

- *Exempt transfers*: These include certain gifts, for example, between spouses or to charities, small gifts (you can give up to £250 as single gifts to as many people as you want in the year with no IHT implications) and those within the annual exemption, currently £3,000 per annum. You can also make gifts out of any 'excess income' (i.e. income you may receive in a year that is over and above reasonable costs incurred in living normally). No inheritance tax is payable on any of these gifts either during the transferor's lifetime or on death. Unused parts of the annual £3,000 exemption can be carried forward one year (only) so that the maximum annual exemption based gift can be as much as £6,000 if nothing was given in the previous year.
- *Potentially exempt transfers* (PETs): These are gifts to another individual or certain types of trust. No inheritance tax is payable during the lifetime of the transferor, however, some tax will be payable if he or she dies within seven years of the transfer.
- *Chargeable Lifetime Transfers* (CLTs): These are mainly gifts to discretionary trusts. Here lifetime inheritance tax is payable at a rate of 20%, and if the transferor dies within seven years of the transfer, another 20% becomes payable to bring the rate up to the full inheritance tax rate of 40%.

Payment of inheritance tax on lifetime transfers depends on when the transfer is made. For transfers made after 5 April and before 1 October in any year, payment is required by 30 April of the following year. Where the transfer is made after 30 September and before 6 April in any year, payment is required within six months of the end of the month in which the transfer is made.

Inheritance tax payable on death

8.48   When an individual dies, inheritance tax is calculated at the rate then applicable, currently 40%, subject to a nil rate band of £325,000 for the current tax year (unchanged from 2011/12 and frozen at this level until April 2021). The nil rate band is applied first against lifetime transfers, i.e. CLTs and PETs which were made in the preceding seven years. Any remaining nil rate band after lifetime transfers have been considered then reduces the value of the total estate left at the point of death. The remainder of the estate after all the nil-rate band has been used up is taxed at 40%.

A reduction in this rate to 36% can be applied if 10% or more of the estate is left to charity. This is a new rule applying from April 2012.

Inheritance tax payable on death transfers is due six months after the end of the month in which the death occurs.

From 9 October 2007, the inheritance tax rules have been relaxed somewhat for married couples and civil partners. They are now allowed to share their nil-rate bands so that any unused sums from these bands on the first partner's death can be added to the surviving partner's nil-rate band for when they die.

From 2017-18 when a residence forms part of the estate passed on death to direct descendants (i.e. to children, grand-children etc.) – a so called 'family home allowance'. This was initially set at £100,000 in 2017/18, but rises by £25,000 each year to 2020-21, reaching a maximum of £175,000 (and so is £125,000 in 2018/19). As this extra nil-rate threshold is potentially available to both partners in a couple if the family home is owned between them, and worth more than £350,000 (i.e. 2 × £175,000), this will raise the overall combined inheritance nil-rate threshold they could get on the second death to £1million (i.e. £325,000 + £175,000 for each of the two partners). Properties worth more than £2million when sold however, will be subjected to a claw-back of this extra family home allowance, at the rate of £1 for every £2 the home is sold for over the £2million limit, back to the standard £325,000 limit.

Fiscal Fact

Despite the fact the published rate of inheritance tax is 40%, HMRC estimates that only 6% of value bequeathed in the UK is taxable due to the use of tax planning and the effect of the threshold; 94% of all estate value therefore is not subject to IHT. The estimated number of taxpaying estates in 2017/18 is 23,000, paying in total £4.8billion in IHT in cash and other assets. [Source: HMRC Receipts & Number of taxpayers and registered traders]

Business and agricultural property relief

8.49 Special relief applies to agricultural (farmland) and business property so that they do not have to be sold in order to pay any inheritance tax due on transfer of an on-going business. Property which qualifies for business property relief includes unincorporated businesses and shares in unquoted companies, so long as they have been owned for at least two years prior to the transfer.

See the website for a supplementary chapter on Inheritance Tax that provides more detail on how this part of the UK tax system works.

Tax planning

8.50 Capital gains tax is a tax which is amenable to tax planning because the timing of events is often within the control of the taxpayer. Tax planning is also an important issue because it is possible to incur a significant capital gains tax liability if good advice is not taken.

Consider the disposal of a company on retirement – the taxpayer can sell either the shares of the company or the business's assets and wind the company up.

If the assets are sold, a capital gains tax liability will accrue to the company. When the company is then liquidated the taxpayer will incur a second capital gains tax liability on the gain received on the shares. If instead the shares are sold directly, then only the gain on the shares will be taxable.

However, for a number of reasons the purchaser may rather buy the assets than the shares. If the company is sold the purchaser also acquires the liabilities and obligations of the company whereas acquiring the assets is more straightforward.

These factors, often together with many more, will become part of the negotiations which are entered into before the business is sold.

In general, capital disposals should be made as early as possible in the fiscal year in order to delay the payment of tax as much as possible to allow inflation to reduce the impact of the tax charge. An individual or married couple should try to fully utilise their annual exemption limit(s) each year since, if it is not used in the year, it cannot be carried forward.

If at all possible losses should not be wasted by being set against current gains which would otherwise have benefited from the annual exemption limit.

It is important to obtain good tax advice before making a large disposal so that any exemptions and reliefs available can be claimed.

Summary

Capital taxes, including capital gains tax, stamp duty and inheritance tax, are generally levied for reasons of equity and to reduce tax avoidance.

Capital gains tax was introduced in 1965. In the early years there were many changes in the legislation which were needed to correct fundamental flaws in the original legislation. One of the most important subsequent developments was the introduction of the indexation allowance. Of course, this significantly reduced the amount of tax which was collected by the Government but it might be argued that it made the tax 'fairer'- which seems to be one of the most important motivating characteristics of capital gains tax. Now that the indexation allowance and taper relief have gone, the question of whether the tax is still fair must be raised again particularly as the amount collected from these taxes is now rising year on year.

Taxpayers, both individuals and companies, pay tax on their chargeable gains. However, there is considerable scope for tax planning as the taxpayer can often choose the date on which to make the disposal. There are a number of reliefs which are available to taxpayers including relief on a principal private residence, rollover relief, holdover relief, incorporation relief and gift relief. Remember also that gains on assets held in pension funds and individual savings accounts are not subject to income tax or capital gains tax. These reliefs, together with the annual exemption limit, enable most individuals to avoid any liability to capital gains tax.

Stamp duty is imposed on documents which evidence certain transfers of property. New rules for computation of SDLT on residential property transactions were introduced in December 2014 to move the system from a 'slab' basis to a 'slice' basis which many advocated was long overdue to reduce the impact of tax on transaction levels, Non-residential property was also changed to this system from March 2016. With effect from April 2015, the Land and Buildings Transactions Tax applies instead of SDLT to properties in Scotland, and from April 2018, the Land Transaction Tax applies in Wales. Finally inheritance tax, which only applies to individuals, taxes the value of estates on the death of individuals, and sometimes also transfers of property during a taxpayer's lifetime.

Project areas

Because of the introduction and subsequent abolition of the taper relief regime for individuals, there is great increased scope for dissertations on the subject of capital gains tax. A survey of holders of chargeable assets, especially chargeable business assets, to determine if it affects their decision to hold or sell might be interesting. A comparison of the taxation of capital gains in more than one country is likely to be interesting. The question of whether capital gains tax is a fair tax is worth asking.

In the area of stamp duty you might like to consider what the impact of this tax is on the housing and share markets. What has been the impact of recent changes to a 'slice' based system on property transaction markets for example? Will the new additional property rates have an impact on buy-to-let and second home ownership markets?

For IHT, how has the significant increase in personal wealth of homeowners over the last 20 years or so affected the role of IHT as part of the tax system? Is this taxation of PPRs by the back door?

Discussion topics

1. It is sometimes possible for individuals to arrange their affairs in order to have receipts taxed as income rather than a capital gain and vice versa. For example, directors planning to sell a family company could either pay themselves high salaries taxable under ITEPA 2003 or take relatively low salaries thus increasing the funds retained in the business, leading to a higher value for their shares when the company is sold. List the taxation consequences of making this decision and discuss the circumstances in which income may be preferable to capital gains.

2. What impact do stamp duties have on capital transactions, if any?

3. Is inheritance tax an unfair tax in that it taxes people on the results of their life-time's hard work when they die?

Quick quiz

1. Andrew bought a fixed asset (not exempt from capital gains tax) for use in his business in June 1989 for £1,700 and sold it in May 2018 for £5,000. Compute the chargeable gain.

2. In August 1999, Barbara bought a second-hand hearse at an auction for £4,000 which she then sold to the Atherstone Vintage Car Museum for £7,000 in April 2018. What are the capital gains tax consequences?

3. Charlie bought a valuable modern impressionist painting for £3,400 in May 1998. He sold it in February 2019 for £5,500. What are the capital gains tax consequences?

4. In August 2018 Davina sold part of her trading business and realised a gain of £450,000 before entrepreneurs' relief. She has not previously made any claims for entrepreneurs' relief and has no other capital gains or losses for the year. If she claims entrepreneurs' relief, how much capital gains tax will be payable?

5. Eddie was given a chargeable asset (not a chattel) in August 2000 with a market value of £7,000. In June 2018 he was successful in claiming that the asset had a negligible value of only £50. What allowable loss (if any) will Eddie be entitled to?

6. Felicity sold one quarter of a parcel of land in May 2018 for £200,000. She had originally bought the land in May 2002 for £500,000 and the remainder was valued at £860,000 immediately after the part disposal. Assuming Felicity is a higher rate taxpayer and has no other gains for the year, what is her capital gains tax liability?

7. Gregory sold an asset that qualifies for rollover relief in August 2018, making a chargeable gain. When must he acquire a replacement asset in order to qualify for the relief?

8. Helen incorporated her business in May 2018 and received 1,000 £1 ordinary shares in the company plus £20,000 in cash. At the time of incorporation, the business was valued at £100,000, and the agreed chargeable gain on the assets transferred was £50,000. On what amount will Helen be liable to capital gains tax as a result of the incorporation assuming she does not elect for incorporation relief not to apply?

9. Ian has a chargeable gain for the tax year 2018/19 of £24,800 and a capital loss of £12,200. He also has unused capital losses of £7,100 brought forward from the tax year 2017/18. What amount of capital loss can Ian carry forward to the tax year 2019/20?

10. Julia is in business as a sole trader and sold a freehold warehouse for £184,000 in May 2018 resulting in a chargeable gain of £38,600. She purchased a replacement freehold warehouse the same month for £143,000. Both warehouses are used for business purposes and Julia wants to claim rollover relief. What will be the base cost of the replacement warehouse for capital gains tax purposes?

Questions

Question 1   (based on ICAS TPS Tax Paper June 2010).

Ben disposed of the following assets in January 2019:

1. An antique table which cost £25,000 in April 2001 was sold at auction for £35,000 before commission of 10%.
2. A holiday cottage which was transferred to his brother for £35,000 when its market value was £45,000. It had cost £47,500 in May 2003 and the costs of conveyance (paid for by Ben) were £1,100.
3. One acre of a four-acre plot of land acquired in April 1988 for £24,000. This was sold for £13,000 at which point the remaining acreage was worth £15,000. Expenses of sale were £500.
4. Ben sold 100 shares in Ryft plc held within his ISA. These cost £1,800 and were sold for £2,000 before commission of £50.
5. Ben sold 1,200 shares in PK plc bought in January 1999 for £6,000. Ben realised £8,500 from this sale. The price dropped significantly in the days after Ben sold and he decided to reinvest the proceeds back into PK plc one week later. He managed to buy 1,600 shares with his proceeds of £8,500.

Required: Calculate Ben's capital gains tax liability for 2018/19, assuming he made no other disposals during the year and is a higher rate taxpayer.

Question 2   (based on ACCA December 2007).

David and Angela Brook are a married couple. They disposed of the following assets during the tax year 2018/19:

Jointly owned property:

(a) On 29 July 2018, David and Angela sold a classic Ferrari car for £34,400. The car had been purchased on 17 January 2004 for £27,200.

(b) On 30 September 2018, David and Angela sold a house for £381,900. The house had been purchased on 1 October 1996 for £86,000. David and Angela occupied the house as their main residence from the date of purchase until 31 March 2000. The house was then unoccupied between 1 April 2000 and 31 December 2003 due to Angela being required by her employer to work elsewhere in the UK. From 1 January 2004 until 31 December 2014, David and Angela again occupied the house as their main residence. The house was then unoccupied until it was sold on 30 September 2018.

David Brook

(a) On 18 April 2018, David sold an antique table for £5,600. The antique table had been purchased on 27 May 2009 for £3,200.

(b) On 5 May 2018, David transferred his entire shareholding of 20,000 £1 ordinary shares in Bend Ltd, an unquoted trading company, to Angela. On that date, the shares were valued at £64,000. David's shareholding had been purchased on 21 June 2009 for £48,000.

(c) On 14 February 2019, David made a gift of 15,000 ordinary shares in Galatico plc to his son. On that date, the shares were quoted on the stock exchange at £2.90 - £3.10. David had originally purchased 8,000 shares in Galatico plc on 15 June 2010 for £17,600, and he purchased a further 12,000 shares on 24 August 2010 for £21,600. David's total shareholding was less than 1% of Galatico' plc's issued share capital.

Angela Brook

(a) On 5 May 2018, Angela sold an antique cabinet for £7,200. The antique cabinet had been purchased on 14 June 2009 for £3,700.

(b) On 7 July 2018, Angela sold 15,000 of the 20,000 ordinary shares in Bend Ltd that had been transferred to her from David. The sale proceeds were £62,400.

Angela has taxable income of £40,000 for the tax year 2018/19. David does not have any taxable income.

Required: Compute David and Angela's respective capital gains tax liabilities for the tax year 2018/19, and state the due date for payment.

Question 3 (based on ACCA June 2008).

Wilson Biazma disposed of the following assets during the tax year 2018/19:

(a) On 21 April 2018 Wilson sold a freehold office building for £246,000. The office building had been purchased on 3 January 1990 for £104,000. Wilson has made a claim to rollover the gain on the office building against the replacement cost of a new freehold office building that was purchased on 14 January 2018 for £136,000. Both office buildings have always been used entirely for business purposes in a wholesale business run by Wilson as a sole trader.

(b) On 26 May 2018 Wilson incorporated a retail business that he had run as a sole trader since 1 June 2009. The market value of the business on 26 May 2018 was £200,000. All of the business assets were transferred to a new limited company, with the consideration consisting of 140,000 £1 ordinary shares valued at £140,000 and £60,000 in cash. The only chargeable asset of the business was goodwill and this was valued at £120,000 on 26 May 2018. The goodwill has a nil cost. Wilson took full advantage of the available incorporation relief.

(c) On 17 August 2018 Wilson made a gift of his entire shareholding of 10,000 £1 ordinary shares (a 100% holding) in Gandua Ltd, an unquoted trading company, to his daughter. The market value of the shares on that date was £220,000. The shares had been purchased on 8 January 2011 for £112,000. On 17 August 2018 the market value of Gandua Ltd's chargeable assets was £180,000, of which £150,000 was in respect of chargeable business assets. Wilson and his daughter have elected to hold over the gain on this gift of a business asset.

(d) On 3 October 2018 an antique vase owned by Wilson was destroyed in a fire. The antique vase had been purchased on 7 November 2010 for £49,000. Wilson received insurance proceeds of £68,000 on 20 December 2017 and on 22 December 2018 he paid £69,500 for a replacement antique vase. Wilson has made a claim to defer the gain arising from the receipt of the insurance proceeds.

(e) On 9 March 2019 Wilson sold 10 acres of land for £85,000. He had originally purchased twenty acres of land on 29 June 2003 for £120,000. The market value of the unsold ten acres of land as at 9 March 2019 was £65,000. The land has never been used for business purposes.

Required: Calculate Wilson's chargeable gains for the tax year 2018/19, clearly identifying the effects of the reliefs claimed in respect of disposals (a) to (d).

Question 4 (based on ACCA June 2004).

Alice Lim disposed of the following assets during 2018/19:

(a) On 24 June 2018, Alice sold a freehold office building for £152,000. The office building had been purchased on 2 March 2003 for £134,000. Prior to this on 15 April 2002 Alice had sold a freehold warehouse for £149,000. The warehouse had been purchased on 20 November 1999 for £93,000. Alice made a claim to roll over the gain arising on the disposal of the warehouse against the cost of the office building. Both the office building and the warehouse were used entirely for business purposes in a manufacturing business run by Alice as a sole trader.

(b) On 9 January 2019 Alice sold 50,000 £1 ordinary shares in Alilim Ltd, an unlisted trading company, for £275,000. Alilim Ltd had been formed on 17 October 2002 in order to incorporate a retail business that Alice had run as a sole trader since 18 May 1998. She is an employee of, and active in, Alilim Ltd. The market value of the retail business on 17 October 2002 was £300,000. All of the business assets were transferred to Alilim Ltd. The consideration consisted of 200,000 £1 ordinary shares valued at £200,000, and £100,000 in cash. The transfer of the business assets resulted in total chargeable gains of £120,000. This figure is before taking account of any rollover relief that was available on incorporation.

(c) On 27 February 2019 Alice sold 40,000 £1 ordinary shares (a 40% shareholding) in Family Ltd, an unlisted trading company for £230,000. Alice had acquired the shares on 21 March 2003 when she purchased them from her mother for £120,000. Alice's mother had originally purchased the shares on 19 December 1998 for £128,000. Alice and her mother elected to hold over the gain arising on 21 March 2003 as a gift of a business asset. The market value of the shares on that date was £168,000. Alice has never been employed by Family Ltd.

Required: Calculate Alice's capital gains tax liability for 2018/19, given that her taxable income for income tax purposes is £30,000.

(*Note: answer available on the lecturer's website*)

Question 5   (based on ACCA June 2014).

Mick Stone disposed of the following assets during the year ended 5 April 2019:

(a) On 19 May 2018, Mick sold a freehold warehouse for £522,000. The warehouse was purchased on 6 August 2006 for £258,000, and was extended at a cost of £63,000 in November 2009. In January 2012, the floor of the warehouse was damaged by flooding and had to be replaced at a cost of £63,000. The warehouse was sold because it was surplus to the business's requirements as a result of Mick purchasing a newly built warehouse during 2017. Both warehouses have always been used for business purposes in a wholesale business run by Mick as a sole trader.

(b) On 12 August 2018, Mick sold an acre of land for £81,700. He had originally purchased five acres of land on 19 May 2003 for £167,400. The market value of the unsold four acres of land as at 12 August 2018 was £268,000. The land had never been used for business purposes.

(c) On 24 September 2018, Mick sold 700,000 £1 ordinary shares in Rolling Ltd, an unquoted trading company, for £3,675,000. He had originally purchased 500,000 shares in Rolling Ltd on 2 June 2010 for £960,000. On 1 December 2015, Rolling Ltd made a 3 for 2 bonus issue. Mick has been a director of Rolling Ltd since 1 January 2010.

(d) On 19 January 2019, Mick made a gift of his entire holding of 24,000 £1 ordinary shares in Sugar plc, a quoted investment company, to his son Keith. On that date the shares were quoted on the Stock Exchange at £6.98 - £37.10, with recorded bargains of £6.85, £6.90, £7.00 and £7.05. The shares had been purchased on 8 May 2013 for £76,800. Mick's shareholding was less than 1% of Sugar plc's issued share capital, and he has never been an employee or director.

Required:

1.   Assuming no reliefs are available, calculate the chargeable gain arising from each of Mick Stone's asset disposals during the tax year 2018/19. You are not required to calculate the taxable gains or the amount of tax payable.

2.   State which capital gains tax reliefs might be available to Mick Stone in respect of each of his disposals during the year ended 5 April 2019, and what further information you would require in order to establish if the reliefs are actually available and to establish any restrictions as regards the amount of relief.

(*Note: answer available on the lecturer's website*)

Further test questions for this chapter to test your knowledge can be found in the student section of the website at:

http://www.taxstudent.com/uk

8.18 Further reading and examples

Chamberlain, E (2016) A review of agricultural property relief and business property relief, *British Tax Review* 2016, 5, 509 – 519. (Inheritance tax: policy reform options)

Combs, A., Tutin, R, & Rowes, P. (2018), *Taxation: incorporating the 2018 Finance Act*, Fiscal Publications: Birmingham.

– use this book for many other examples to further develop and test your knowledge of this chapter's contents. See http://www.fiscalpublications.com/rowes/2018/

9 | Corporation tax

Introduction

9.1 Corporation tax is charged on the profits of companies. Until 1965 companies were taxed under the income tax rules. In 1965 a reform of the tax system led to the introduction of corporation tax as a separate tax. As you will learn in this chapter, there are still many similarities between the ways in which companies' profits are taxed under corporation tax rules and the taxation of sole traders and partnership profits, which are subject to income tax rules. However, there are some important differences between corporation tax and income tax that you need to be aware of.

At the end of this chapter you will be able to:
- describe the imputation system of taxation;
- state the basis of assessment of tax for companies;
- determine the taxable total profits;
- calculate a company's corporation tax liability; and
- determine the date on which the corporation tax is due

Further details of other, more complicated, aspects of corporation tax can be found on the website, specifically tax implications of corporate losses and company groups.

The liability to corporation tax

9.2 For corporation tax purposes a company is defined as being either a body corporate or an unincorporated association. The definition of a company extends to organisations such as clubs and political associations which are therefore subject to corporation tax. The definition excludes partnerships, however, which are subject to income tax like sole traders.

UK resident companies are liable to corporation tax on their total world-wide profits arising in an accounting period regardless of whether the profits are remitted to the UK or not. However, dividends received by a UK resident company from other companies are generally not liable to further corporation tax in the hands of the recipient. The exact details of how to determine the residence of a company for tax purposes is further considered in Chapter 12.

The capital gains of a company are not subject to capital gains tax as a separate tax. Instead, its capital gains are subject to corporation tax along with other income and profits.

The imputation system of taxation

9.3   Before looking at the UK system of corporation tax more closely, we need to think about what companies are and the reasons why governments tax them. Companies are separate legal entities. Their operations are managed by directors, but they are owned by shareholders. Companies undertake activities to make profit, which can then either be retained for reinvestment within the company, hopefully producing capital gains as the shares are then worth more, or distributed as dividends to shareholders. Company profits can be thought of then as passing through two layers; they are earned by the company itself, but then they are passed on to shareholders, who ultimately may have a right to the profits earned, either as capital gains as the value of their shares rise, or in dividends. So the question arises – should we tax companies on their profits? Most governments do so, and so corporation tax is a cost to the company in earning its profits. However, there is also a second question – should we tax shareholders on their dividends and capital gains as well? Some governments do and some don't.

When corporation tax was first introduced in the UK in 1965 the *classical system* was used. Under the classical system the relationship between a company and its shareholders is ignored for tax computations. A company pays tax on its profits without reference to its dividend policy and its shareholders pay tax on their dividends received without any relief for the tax already paid by the company on those profits. This is a simple system but does lead to profits effectively being taxed twice, once in the hands of the company and then again in the hands of the shareholders.

Fiscal Fact

In 1973-74 it is estimated that 175,000 companies paid corporation tax, by 2013/14 the number had reached 1,145,000. [Source: HMRC Statistics – Numbers of taxpayers and registered traders]

In 1973 the problem of double taxation of distributed profits led the Government to switch to an *imputation system* under which shareholders were given a tax credit for some of the corporation tax which had been paid by the company. The tax credit was used to offset at least some of the shareholder's liability to income tax resulting from their dividend receipts from the company.

This was the system in operation in the UK until 6 April 2016. (If you need to, look again at the way in which dividends are included in a tax computation in Chapter 4). The primary advantage of the imputation system of company taxation over the classical system is that the impact of double taxation on distributed profits is reduced.

For many years the dividend tax credit was set at a rate of 10%. Taxpayers received a tax credit equal to 1/10th of any gross dividend from a UK company. Gross dividends received by basic rate taxpayers, that is the dividend actually received together with the related tax credit, were subject to income tax at a rate of 10%. This meant that non-taxpayers and basic rate taxpayers were able to use their tax credit to fully satisfy their dividend tax liability, meaning they had a zero effective tax rate. After the dividend credit higher rate tax payers paid an effective 25% tax rate on dividends and individuals paying tax in the additional rate tax band ended up with an effective tax rate of 30.56%.

Individual non-taxpayers were not able to reclaim the tax credit under the previous tax system and therefore suffered tax on dividend income from UK companies even though they would not pay tax on income of other types. This may seem a little unfair, but it was the way the UK tax system worked.

From 6 April 2016 this system changed in that dividend tax credits no longer form part of the system. Instead, as we saw in Chapter 4, shareholders are now given a tax-free 'dividend allowance' of £2,000 (£5,000 before 6 April 2018) for any dividends they receive and only dividends above that level are subject to tax – at the special rates of income tax for dividends of 7.5%, 32.5% or 38.1% (which rate applies being determined by which tax band the dividends fall into as a top slice of their income). The reduction of the dividend allowance in 2018 from £5,000 to £2,000 means that more people who rely on dividend income, such as retirees, will now have to fill in tax returns and pay tax than previously.

The previous system operated on a 'gross up and credit' basis, but this no longer applies, which makes the system simpler. In effect therefore double tax does still form a part of the UK tax system for corporate profits. Individuals get an allowance for dividends paid out to them, offsetting part of any tax liability they otherwise have, so partial imputation still occurs, but no imputation is provided for dividends over £2,000. The system for taxation of corporate profits in the UK therefore remains a partial imputation system.

As we discussed in Chapter 8, the rules for paying tax on capital gains made when selling shares has not changed; so when companies retain profits, the increase in share value that results may be chargeable to capital gains tax when shares are sold.

Calculation of the corporation tax payable

9.4   Companies are taxed on the full amount of the profits or gains or income arising in the accounting period for a company (whether or not received in or transmitted to the UK), after any deductions authorised by the Corporation Tax Acts. Despite coming from a common Act originally (before the Tax Law Rewrite project) there are a number of key differences between how the rules are applied to sole traders to calculate income tax on their profits and to companies to calculate corporation tax on their profits and capital gains In this section we will examine the key similarities and differences.

In order to calculate corporation tax payable you will need to undertake a number of steps. These are:

1.   Determine the accounting period(s) which are to be assessed.
2.   Adjust accounting profits for tax purposes and allocate income and allowable expenditure to the correct period.
3.   Calculate the taxable total profits.
4.   Ascertain the rate at which corporation tax will be charged.

In the first section of this chapter we will review each of these stages in order.

1. Determining the accounting period

9.5   Look for the similarities and differences between the basis of assessment for companies and unincorporated traders when reading this section. Many of the calculations are the same but there are some important differences.

Corporation tax is assessed and charged for any accounting period of a company on the full amount of the profits arising in the period, whether or not received in or transmitted to the UK, minus allowable deductions. An accounting period of a company starts, for corporation tax purposes, whenever:

- the company comes within the charge to corporation tax; usually on commencing to trade as a company; or
- immediately after the end of the previous accounting period, if the company is still within the charge to corporation tax.

An accounting period of a company ends, for the purposes of corporation tax, on the earliest of the following:

- 12 months after the beginning of the accounting period;
- an accounting date of the company or, if there is a period for which the company does not make up accounts, the end of that period;
- the company starting or ceasing to trade;
- the commencement of a winding up;
- the date on which the company ceases to be UK resident; or
- the date on which it ceases to be liable to corporation tax.

Be careful that you do not confuse accounting periods for tax purposes (called '*accounting periods*') with the company's reporting period for financial accounting purposes (called '*periods of account*'). Whilst these two are often the same (usually 12 months long and ending on the same day) this is not always the case. The key rule to remember is a company's accounting period for tax purposes cannot be more than 12 months long. If the period of account (for reporting purposes) is longer than 12 months (e.g. perhaps when a company moves its year-end date) then the period of account must be split up into more than one accounting period for the tax calculations. If the accounting period is less than 12 months then it becomes its own chargeable period. This is one of the important differences between sole traders and companies. Sole traders can have tax periods longer than 12 months as we discussed in Chapter 6.

Activity

Apply the above rules to determine the accounting periods for tax when a company changes its year end from 31 December to 31 March by having a 15-month period of accounts starting on 1 January, 2018.

Feedback

For this company, 1 January, 2018 is the start of an accounting period because it is immediately after the end of the previous accounting period (i.e. 31 December 2017). Since it must end at the latest 12 months after it starts, the first accounting period must run from 1 January, 2018 to 31 December, 2018. The second accounting period must commence as soon as the first one finishes and so it begins on 1 January, 2019. It ends at the end of the period of account i.e. 31 March, 2019. This company will therefore have two accounting periods covering the 15 month period of account; one for the first 12 months and the other for the final 3 months.

2. Allocating profits to accounting periods

9.6 Income and expenses of a company are normally simply allocated to the accounting period in which they accrue to form part of the tax computations however, the fact that companies can't have an accounting period of more than 12 months may cause problems for this simple allocation process. For example, in the activity above you saw that a 15-month period of account was split into two accounting periods for tax purposes, the first one 12 months long and the second one three months long. If this happens we must then split the income and expenses of the company between the two periods in the following ways:

- Trade profits and miscellaneous income before capital allowances is *apportioned* on a time basis. In our example 12/15ths would be included in the first accounting period while the remaining 3/15ths would be included in the second. This apportioning approximates reality but won't necessarily reflect exactly when any particular income is earned.
- Capital allowances, including balancing allowances and charges, are calculated for each accounting period by computing figures based on actual expenditure or disposals. Do not forget that writing down allowance percentages need to be reduced for short accounting periods as they are normally cited on a per annum basis e.g. 18% per annum for main pool plant and machinery. Also note that for companies, although a short period of account will result in an adjustment to the capital allowances available, there are never any reductions in capital allowances for private use of assets owned by the company, because a company is an artificial legal entity and can't have 'private' expenses. Instead any private use by employees or directors of the company may be charged on the user as a benefit in kind under employment income rules.
- Property business income is treated like trading income and time apportioned.
- Bank interest (and income from other non-trading loan relationships e.g. building society interest) are allocated on an accruals basis.
- Other income is usually allocated on an actual basis to the period to which it relates.
- Charges on income are allocated to the period in which they are paid.
- Chargeable gains are allocated to the period in which they are realised.

Activity

Cherry Ltd. makes up accounts for the 18 months to 31 March, 2019. The company's results for the period of account are:

	£
Trade profit before capital allowances	300,000
Bank interest (gross) accrued:	
31/3/18	1,200
30/9/18	1,000
31/3/19	1,100
Chargeable gains on disposal of assets:	
31/12/17	5,000
6/6/18	3,000
31/12/18	7,000
Qualifying charitable donations:	
31/12/17	15,000
31/12/18	20,000

Calculate the taxable total profits for each accounting period within the period of account.

Feedback

The period of account will be split into two accounting periods, the 12 months to 30 September, 2018 and the 6 months to 31 March, 2019. The chargeable profits are:

	12 months to 30/9/18	6 months to 31/3/19
Trade profits		
12/18 × 300,000	200,000	
6/18 × 300,000		100,000
Bank interest received	2,200	1,100
Chargeable gains	8,000	7,000
	210,200	108,100
Less charitable donations	(15,000)	(20,000)
	195,200	88,100

Now you need to be able to adjust the company's trading profits for tax purposes. As for income tax, the easiest way of calculating the trade profits is to follow the proforma given here. (Note – the numbers are used in the proforma to make it easier to follow – they do not relate to the previous example.)

Adjustment of trade profits for the accounting period ended 31 December 2018.

	£000	£000
Net profits per accounts		3,270
Add expenditure disallowed		530
		3,800
Less: Income not assessable	120	
Expenditure not included in the accounts which is an allowable deduction	180	
Capital allowances	500	
		(800)
Tax Adjusted trade profits		3,000

Most of the rules you are already familiar with for sole traders, from Chapters 6 and 7, also apply to companies. These include the rules relating to capital receipts and expenditure, as well as prohibitions on certain deductions such as entertainment expenses. In the next section we will consider one particular area where companies are treated differently to sole traders. There are several more that we will consider later in the chapter.

Loan relationships

9.7   Individuals account for income and expenses, and gains and losses on loans, such as government stock and company debentures, using a combination of the income tax rules (for interest accrued and payable) and the capital gains tax rules (for any capital gain or loss when the loan is disposed of). Different rules apply to companies for loan relationships i.e. any relationship that involves borrowing or lending money.

Where a company borrows or lends money for the purposes of its trading activities, it is referred to as a *trading loan relationship*. Examples of trading loan relationships are bank overdrafts, loans to buy business premises or plant and machinery, and debentures. (Note: You will not usually see a company *receive* income under a trading loan relationship unless they are in the business of making loans but it is still useful to know how this should be handled).

Income, expenses, gains and losses from *non-trading loan relationships,* i.e. those which are not related to the company's trading activities, are dealt with as a separate category, under the non-trading loan relationship rules for companies as we will see later.

Income and other amounts receivable in this category by companies usually relates to interest from bank and building society accounts and other interest receivable that is not to do with trading activity. This income is assessed on an *accrued basis.* Trading loan relationships are dealt with as part of the trade profit computation, as we discussed above.

Any amounts receivable or payable under non-trading loan relationships must be pooled. If the net figure is positive (debits are less than credits) then the total becomes the non-trading loan relationship income for the company and is included in the company's taxable profit figure for the year. If a net deficit exists then it can either be set against other income for the same accounting period, carried back against any surpluses on non-trading loan relationships in the last twelve months or carried forward to set against future non-trading profits (i.e. future taxable total profits less trade profit). This process applies not just to interest, but also to other gains and losses for loan relationships, for example when a loan is written off.

An important point to note is that for all loan relationships, trade and non-trade, profits and losses (referred to as credits and debits respectively) are treated as income for companies, i.e. the capital/revenue distinction, which we discussed in Chapter 6, does not apply. This is an important difference between sole traders and companies for tax purposes.

3. Taxable Total Profits

9.8   Now that the trade profit has been computed and allocated to the correct accounting period for the tax computation we can calculate the rest of the taxable total profits (previously referred to as profits chargeable to corporation tax or PCTCT) of the company. This computation is the equivalent for companies of calculating taxable income for sole traders i.e. it is the aggregation of income from various sources minus any charges.

We will use a proforma (with example numbers) to illustrate how to do this:

Taxable total profits for the accounting period ended 30 September, 2018

	£000
Trade profit	3,000
Non-trading loan relationship	1,500
Property income	500
Miscellaneous income	300
Chargeable gains	700
Total profits	6,000
Less qualifying charitable donation	(1,000)
Taxable total profits	5,000

It is important to note that dividends received by a UK company from other companies are excluded from the tax computation because they are not subject to further corporation tax in the hands of the receiving company.

We have already explored how to determine trade profit earlier in the chapter but you need to know a little more about some of the other items in the proforma before you are ready to calculate the taxable total profits for specific companies. We will consider the relevant points in the order in which they appear in the pro forma above.

Non-trading loan relationships

9.9   We saw earlier that non trading loan relationships are treated as a separate category for the corporation tax computation.

Property income

9.10   Income from land and buildings owned by companies is taxed regardless of whether the property is located in the UK or not. As for individuals, property income includes rents due, income from holiday lettings and furnished lettings, premiums on short leases, ground rents and payments for sporting rights.

Property income will be determined using all the same trade profit rules that you are familiar with. Because this is in line with normal accounting principles, no tax adjustment will generally be necessary. Capital allowances will also be deducted to determine the property income.

Interest payable by a company on a loan related to rental property, however is dealt with under the loan relationship rules, and so it is not an allowable property expense.

Charitable donations

9.11 The special treatment of charitable gifts for individual taxpayers i.e. the extension of the basic rate band (see section 4.45), does not apply to companies. Qualifying corporate gifts to charities (and community amateur sports clubs (CASCs) from April 2014) are deductible under 'charitable donations relief' provisions introduced in Corporation Tax Act 2010. They are paid gross by the company (so no grossing up is required) and no further tax is reclaimable by the charity from the Government. The amount is deductible for the company making the donation when computing its taxable total profits.

An exception is donations to local charities which are small in amount and are made wholly and exclusively for the purpose of the trade. These are allowable deductions from the trade profits. An example of such a donation might be a gift to an employees' welfare organisation. Of course, there is no possibility of a double deduction, it must be used as one or the other and treated correctly in the tax computation.

The amount that is added back in the adjustment of trading profits computation is equal to that which is included in the profit and loss account. This figure will usually be determined using the accruals basis rather than the cash paid basis. The amount allowed in the calculation of taxable trade profits however is the cash actually paid. Hence the two figures may not be the same.

Companies and income tax

9.12 Where a payment is made net of tax, for example a patent royalty to an individual, the company must account to HMRC for the tax they have withheld. This is a separate calculation to the corporation tax computation. The income tax withheld is netted against any income tax that is withheld from the company as recipient and the difference is paid/reclaimed. Companies are required to submit quarterly returns to HMRC to reconcile any income tax on items received and paid. This process used to include all patent royalty (at 20%) and interest payments (at 20%), but since 1 April 2001, these payments can be made between UK companies without deduction of tax. Income tax will only need to be deducted from patent royalties and interest where either the payer or recipient is not a UK company, for example a partnership.

The following activity illustrates the key points from above.

Activity

Bournemouth Ltd had the following results for the year ended 31 March, 2019

	£000	£000
Gross profit on trading		1,200
Investment income (a)	300	
Profit on sale of land (b)	200	500
		1,700
Less:		
Depreciation	100	
Directors' emoluments	250	
Qualifying charitable donation	30	
Audit and accountancy fees	45	
Legal costs (c)	20	
Salaries	100	
Premium on lease written off (d)	25	
Miscellaneous expenses	30	(600)
Net profit for year		1,100

Notes:

(a) Investment income:	£000
Dividends from UK companies (gross)	200
Loan interest from UK company (gross- non-trading loans)	100

(b) Profit on sale of land:

The profit on the sale of land relates to a plot of vacant land no longer required by the company. The chargeable gain is	150

(c) Legal costs:

Costs re debt collection	5
Costs re issue of shares	12
Costs re renegotiations of directors' service agreements	3

(d) Lease premium

The lease premium written off relates to a lease entered into at the beginning of the accounting period for a warehouse for a period of 17 years. The premium paid was	25

(e) Capital allowances have been calculated as	50

Required: calculate the tax adjusted trade profits.

Feedback

First you needed to calculate the trade profit:

Trade profit	£000	£000
Net profit per accounts		1,100
Add: Depreciation	100	
Charitable donation (deducted from TTP)	30	
Legal costs (not allowable as capital)	12	
Lease premium written off (W1)	25	167
		1,267
Less: Investment income (loan relationship)	100	
Investment income (dividends)	200	
Profit on sale of investments	200	
Capital allowances	50	
Lease premium (W1)	1	(551)
Adjusted trade profit		716

Working 1

The amount of the lease premium assessable on the landlord under the property income rules is:

£25,000 – [£25,000 × (17 – 1) × 2%] = £17,000.

The amount which is allowable for the lessee in the accounting period ended 31 March, 2017 is therefore £17,000 ÷ 17 = £1,000.

Now you can calculate the taxable total profits.

	£
Trade profit	716,000
Non-trading Loan relationship	100,000
Chargeable gains	150,000
	966,000
Less charitable donation	(30,000)
Taxable total profits	936,000

You will notice the treatment of the lease premium is the same as for individuals as we saw in Chapter 6.7.

4. The rate of corporation tax payable

9.13 Having learnt the basics of the first three stages of calculating corporation tax, we now need to work through the actual computation of the tax liability.

The rate of corporation tax is set for *financial years*, rather than the *tax years* of the income tax legislation. A financial year (FY) runs from 1 April to the following 31 March i.e. the financial year 2018 (or FY 2018) runs from 1 April, 2018 to 31

March, 2019. The rate of corporation tax for a financial year is set after the year has started, in the annual Finance Act. Hence the rate for the financial year 2018 is set in the Finance Act 2018.

Prior to 1 April 2015, there were two rates of corporation tax, 20% for companies with small profits (below £300,000), and 21% for larger companies (with profits over £1.5million – a formula was used to compute the correct tax rate when a company's profits fell between these levels). The calculation of corporation tax payable was quite complicated because of this rate structure. From 1 April 2015, however, the system has been considerably simplified and now there is only one flat rate of corporation tax, 19% (the same as for 2017/18), that applies to the taxable total profits. It has been announced that the corporation tax rate will fall to 17% by April 2020. There is no equivalent to the personal allowance or annual exempt amount, and corporation tax must be paid from the first £1 of taxable total profit.

At present this rate is set for the whole of the UK, and so companies throughout the whole country pay the same flat rate of tax now. However, legislation has been passed to potentially allow Northern Ireland to set a different rate of corporate tax to the rest of the country for many businesses in the future. This is to enable them to compete with the currently lower rate of corporation tax in Ireland. These new powers for the Northern Irish Assembly commenced in April 2017.

Fiscal Fact

In 2017/18 corporation tax is expected to raise £53.2 billion, 7.8% of total tax receipts and 2.6% of national income. This has fallen from the pre-recession high of 3.2% of national income and is forecast to fall to 2.3% by 2021/22. [IFS briefing note BN206]

Other special rules for companies

In this section we will look at some of the other special areas where companies are treated differently from individuals, in particular research and development expenditure, intangibles, creative industry relief and the patent box regime.

Research and development expenditure

9.14 Companies are entitled to tax relief for research and development (R&D) expenditure. There are two systems in operation, one for small and medium sized companies (SMEs) that has been in operation since April 2000 and one for large companies which was introduced in 2013.

What are now the SME R&D relief rules were first introduced in April 2000 for SMEsand then extended in April 2002 to large companies, so between 2002 and 2013 the same system applied to all sizes of companies (we look at the system for large companies below at 9.15). The credits are only available to companies and not to sole traders and partnerships so the rules are another example of how the UK tax system treats companies differently from other forms of business.

For both systems, there is now no lower limit to R&D spend in the year to qualify for the credits but prior to 1 April 2012 companies had to spend more than £10,000 on research and development in a 12 month period.

Resesarch and development is defined by reference to Department for Business, Innovation and Skills guidelines which, at its most basic, implies the project concerned must be aiming to extend overall knowledge or capability in a field of science or technology, for example, creating a new process or product. R&D will not however, be allowable for enhanced credit if it is just increasing that business' level of knowledge or expertise with knowledge already known elsewhere.

Valid expenses include non-capital expenditure which directly relates to R&D activity, such as staff costs and consumables. The allowable expenses were extended in the 2004 Budget to include expenditure on software development and any power, fuel or water expenditure directly related to the research and development activity.

The SME R&D relief system works by allowing SMEs to deduct 230% of valid expenditure in their tax computation i.e. a 100% normal deduction for the allowable R&D costs plus a further 130% deduction (this was 225% prior to 1 April 2015, 200% prior to 1 April 2012 and 175% before April 2011).

Activity

Ardvark Ltd has a turnover of £56,000 and allowable expenditure (other than R&D) of £16,000 for the year ended 31 March 2019. During the year, the company incurs £20,000 of qualifying R&D expenditure. What is the corporation tax liability for the year?

Feedback

	£
Turnover	56,000
Allowable expenditure	(16,000)
R&D expenditure	(20,000)
Enhanced R&D deduction	
130% x £20,000	(26,000)
TTP	0
Net corporation tax	0

What happens then, when a company is making a loss and therefore can't get the benefit of the enhanced tax deduction? In that case, since April 2014, it may be eligible for a special payment from the government of £14.50 (previously £11) for every £100 of actual R&D expenses. This only applies to SMEs, however, and if they claim a cash payment in this way, they then lose the special 230% deduction.

In addition to R&D tax credits related to non-capital expenditure items, there is a separate 100% capital allowance for R&D capital expenditure such as the purchase of new buildings or machinery.

Research and development expenditure credit
9.15 A different system called research and development expenditure credit (RDEC) was introduced for R&D expenditure incurred on or after 1 April 2013. SMEs have a choice as to whether to use the old 130% deduction rule (i.e. 100% expense deduction for the cost incurred plus a further 30% deduction) or the RDEC credit rules. From 1 April 2016, RDEC is compulsory for large companies.

With effect from 1 January 2018 the rate of RDEC has increased to 12%, it was previously 9.1% when first introduced in April 2013, increasing to 10% from April 2014 and again to 11% after April 2015.

RDEC is designed to increase the visibility of R&D credits and also provide a cash flow for large companies that do not have a corporation tax liability.

The credit is first offset against the company's corporation tax liability for the current year. Any remaining credit is then limited to the amount of PAYE and NIC liabilities related to the staffing costs for qualifying R&D expenditure. This restricted amount can be offset against other HMRC liabilities such as VAT, but only after being converted to a 'repayable amount', by treating it as being net of tax. Finally, if there is any excess remaining, it will be repayable to the company, so long as the company is a going concern. The following activity shows how the RDEC works.

Fiscal Fact

The cost to the Government of providing research and development credits is estimated to be £3,010 million for 2017/18. [Source: HMRC Estimated costs of principal tax reliefs]

Activity

Einstein Ltd has a turnover of £105m and allowable expenditure (other than R&D) of £1.5m for the year ended 31 March 2019. During the year, the company incurs £1m of qualifying R&D expenditure. Show how the RDEC affects Einstein Ltd's corporation tax liability.

Feedback

	(£'000s)
Turnover	105,000
R&D expenditure	(1,000)
RDEC @ 12%	120
Other expenditure	(1,500)
Profit	102,620
TTP	102,620
Tax @ 19%	19,497.80
RDEC	(120.00)
Net corporation tax	19,377.80

Creative Industries Reliefs

9.16 The UK Government has for some time been encouraging creative industries using the corporation tax system. There are a number of corporation tax reliefs under this heading, which all work by increasing the amount of allowable expenditure.

Qualifying companies are those directly involved in the production and development of certain films, high end television programmes, animation programmes or video games. To qualify for creative industries tax relief, the films etc must pass a 'cultural test', ie be a British production.

There are currently eight creative industries reliefs available as follows:

- Film tax relief
- Animation tax relief
- High-end television tax relief

- Video games tax relief
- Theatre tax relief
- Orchestra tax relief
- Museums and galleries exhibition tax relief.

You can find details of the reliefs or credits available to qualifying companies on the HMRC website at https://www.gov.uk/corporation-tax-creative-industry-tax-reliefs.

Intangibles

9.17 Intangibles includes intellectual property such as patents, trademarks and copyright, as well as goodwill. Goodwill that only appears in the consolidated accounts and not in the individual company's accounts does not come under these rules, however, because the UK corporation tax system does not recognise groups of companies as a general rule (although see later at 9.22 in relation to losses).

Companies can claim tax relief for any amortisation or impairment claimed in the accounts for intangible assets. Alternatively, they can use a fixed rate of 4% per annum if the accounting treatment is not considered appropriate to use (e.g. where the asset is not amortised in the accounts or is amortised over a very long period). The company must justify why this will be the case to HMRC. Capital allowances for patent rights or know-how are not available to companies if acquired on or after 1 April, 2002.

If a company sells an intangible asset which was created or acquired after 1 April, 2002, any loss will be deductible from the total trading income and any profit will be taxable. In this way, the new rules remove the capital/income divide for these types of assets in a similar way to the loan relationship rules. If a profit arises but the proceeds are reinvested in a new intangible asset, the difference between the original cost and the disposal proceeds can be rolled over into the cost of the new intangible. This rollover rule applies to all intangibles, not just those acquired after 1 April, 2002, and for companies it supersedes the rollover capital gains tax rules we saw in Chapter 8.31.

Patent box regime

9.18 A special regime for taxing income from patents was introduced with effect from 1 April 2013. Under this regime, companies can elect for profits from the development and exploitation of patents to be taxed at the rate of 10%. The rules only apply to companies that make profit from exploiting patented inventions. The income to which the special tax rate will apply includes income from:

- selling patented products;
- licensing out patent rights;
- selling patent rights.

The aim of the Patent Box regime is to provide companies with an incentive to keep existing patents in the UK and also develop new and innovative patented products. It was first foreshadowed in the Government's *Plan For Growth* document, released in March 2011.

The regime was phased in over a period of time and now provides for a deduction from taxable total profits that equates to a 10% tax rate for qualifying income. The deduction is calculated using the following formula:

RP x FY% x ((MR – IPR) ÷ MR)

Where: RP is the profits of a company's trade relevant to Patent Box;
FY% is the appropriate percentage for each financial year;
MR is the main rate of corporation tax; and
IPR is the reduced rate of 10%.

Activity

Innovate Ltd is a UK resident company with no associated companies. In the year ending 31 March 2019, Innovate has tax adjusted trading profits of £10,000 all of which qualified for the Patent Box. Calculate Innovate Ltd's UK corporation tax liability for the year.

Feedback

Profit	£10,000
Patent Box Deduction:	
(10,000 ((19 – 10) ÷ 19))	(4,737)
Taxable Total Profits	5,263
Tax payable £5,263 @ 19%	£999.97

This is a very simplified example because it is unlikely that all of a company's profit would qualify for the Patent Box and there are some rules for calculating the profits that can benefit from the Patent Box. This is done in three stages:

1. Identify profits attributable to income from exploiting patented inventions (relevant IP income).

2. Remove an amount called 'routine profit', which takes into account that a business would probably earn a profit even if it didn't have access to patented technology or IP.

3. Remove the profit associated with intangible assets, e.g. brands. This is because the Patent Box regime doesn't apply to other forms of IP.

The government issued a consultation document in December 2015 proposing changes to the patent box regime to comply with a new internatonal framework for intellectual property tax regimes as set out by the OECD (see Chapter 12). Finance Act 2016 contains modifications to the rules to ensure that from 1 July 2016, the profits qualifying for the reduced rate of corporation tax are determined by reference to the company's direct engagement in R&D.

Close Companies

9.19 Close companies are those that are closely held, i.e. the shares are held by only a small number of people, often related as in family companies. There are concerns that these companies could be used for tax avoidance, and so a special set of rules applies to them. For tax purposes a close company is one that is controlled by five or fewer shareholders or any number of shareholding directors, who are referred to as 'participators'. When deciding whether this control test is met, it is not only the direct interests of the shareholders that is taken into account but also their 'associates', which are direct relatives or business partners.

There are two consequences of being classified as a close company. The first is an additional tax charge that arises when a close company makes a loan to one of its participators, a penalty tax of 32.5% must be paid (prior to 6 April 2016 the rate was 25%). The purposes of this rule is to make sure some tax is paid when profits are extracted from the company without a tax charge arising for the shareholder (ie not as a dividend). For non-large companies, the penalty tax must be paid nine months and one day after the end of the accounting period. For large companies, quarterly payments must be made. If the loan is repaid before the due date for payment of corporation tax, then the penalty tax will not be imposed. If it is repaid in full or in part, or if the company writes the loan off, the company may reclaim the penalty tax from HMRC. This is because the loan writing off of a loan is treated as a dividend in the hands of the particiaptor.

The second consequence of being a close company is that benefits given to participators and their associates that are not taxable as earnings, are treated as distributions. This means the company cannot deduct the cost of the benefit and its value is treated as a dividend in the hands of the participator or associate.

Chargeable gains for companies

9.20 Companies are not liable to capital gains tax as a separate tax, but their chargeable gains and allowable losses are subject to corporation tax. This mean they will not pay tax on chargeable gains at the fixed rates of 10% and 20% like individuals do. They will instead pay tax on chargeable gains at the rate of corporation tax.

Many of the same rules apply to companies that we examined in Chapter 8 for individuals. There are a few exceptions you should be aware of, however. For example, unlike individuals, companies do not have an annual exemption allowance to set against their chargeable gains, and they are also compensated for changes due to inflation using an indexation allowance rather than reduced rates of tax.

The pro forma for calculating the chargeable gain or allowable loss is (numbers included only for illustration purposes):

	£
Gross proceeds on disposal (or market value)	12,000
Less incidental cost of disposal	(2,000)
Net proceeds	10,000
Less allowable costs	(2,500)
Unindexed gain/(loss)	7,500
Less indexation allowance	(1,000)
Indexed gain/(unindexed loss)	6,500

The indexation allowance is applied to all items of allowable costs (except incidental costs of disposal as these are taken to already be in current money value). The allowance is designed to compensate for the inflation part of the increases in the value of the asset so that companies only pay tax on the real gains they make – not those solely due to inflation. It does this by using the percentage increase in the retail price index from the month in which the asset was acquired until the month in which the disposal took place.

In 1988, legislation was introduced so that only gains (losses) arising from 31 March 1982 are chargeable (allowable). If the asset being sold was acquired before 31 March 1982, two calculations are required, one based on the original cost and the other on the value as at 31 March 1982, and the higher value is used to calculate the indexation allowance. Companies can elect to always use 31 March 1982 values. In 2017, a further change means that indexation was frozen at December 2017, as you will see below.

The indexation factor for companies is:

$$\frac{\text{RPI for month of disposal* – RPI for month of acquisition}}{\text{RPI for the month of acquisition}}$$

* Note that the indexation allowance for the disposal of assets on or after 1 January 2018 is calculated using the December 2017 RPI figure.

The retail price index figure for the appropriate months can be found in the RPI table in the rates and allowances section in Appendix A.

The indexation factor should be stated as a decimal correct to *three decimal places*. It is important you round to three decimal place or your answers will be wrong – it is not more accurate to use more decimal places in this case.

Be careful in use of indexation allowance as it cannot create or increase a loss for the chargeable gains computation. At best it will reduce the gain to zero.

The following activities will illustrate how to compute indexation allowances for chargeable gains computations for companies:

Activity

Calculate the relevant indexation allowance for an asset purchased in June 1989 and sold in April 2018.

Feedback

a)   Using the RPI tables in the Appendix A, the indexation allowance will be:

$$\frac{278.1 - 115.4}{115.4} = 1.410$$

(Don't forget to use the December 2017 indexation factor in place of the actual disposal date as this was after 1 January 2018 and to round the indexation factor to three decimal places)

The indexation allowance is equal to the indexation factor multiplied by the allowable cost. Each element of the allowable cost has a separate indexation calculation as the expense may have been incurred at different times. For example, if there is enhancement expenditure this also is indexed but from the date of the expenditure on the enhancement, not from the date of the original acquisition of the asset of course.

Activity

Cream Ltd sold land and buildings for £200,000 in April 2018. The property cost £50,000 when bought in December 1991. Cream Ltd spent £30,000 extending the building in June 1996. Calculate the chargeable gain on the property.

Feedback

	£	£
Proceeds		200,000
Less allowable costs		
Cost	50,000	
Enhancement expenditure	30,000	(80,000)
Unindexed gain		120,000
Indexation allowance		

$$\frac{278.1 - 135.7}{135.7}$$

$1.049 \times 50,000$	52,450	

$$\frac{278.1 - 153.0}{153.0}$$

$0.818 \times 30,000$	24,540	(76,990)
Indexed gain		43,010

Other aspects of taxation of chargeable gains for companies

9.21   The treatment of the disposal of chattels, part disposals and negligible value claims is the same for companies as it is for individuals, subject only to the differences set out above. The principal private residence relief, gift relief and entrepreneurs' relief, are not available to companies.

Business Asset (rollover relief and holdover) relief is available to companies, but not for intangible assets after 1 April, 2002 (e.g. goodwill and the various quotas we listed in Chapter 8.9). As we saw earlier, a different form of rollover relief, is available on realising intangible assets where the proceeds are reinvested in new intangibles. The company has the right to choose which set of rules to apply if the assets were owned on 1 April, 2002.

Companies can also benefit from a special rule referred to as the substantial shareholdings exemption that provides that a gain on a disposal of shares by a company will not normally be a chargeable gain so long as certain conditions are met. 'Substantial' here means at least 10% of the ordinary shares and entitlement to at least 10% of the assets on a winding up. The shares must have been held for at least 12 months in the two years prior to disposal. The exemption only applies to sales of shares in a trading company (or holding company of a trading group), sold by a trading company itself or a member of a trading group.

Companies also need special rules for determining the cost of quoted securities, in much the same way as we saw for individuals. The rules for companies are slightly different however, and you will need to see the website for an explanation and worked examples.

Relief for losses

9.22 As with individual taxpayers, companies are entitled to relief for trade and property business losses. The rules are slightly different for companies, however, and companies are also entitled to loss relief for non-trading loan relationship deficits (which don't arise for individuals of course, as we saw earlier).

The rules for loss relief for companies were changed with effect from 1 April 2017. We now have two periods with different treatment ie pre and post April 2017.

Prior to 1 April 2017 trade losses could be set against taxable total profit of the same accounting period, carried back to the previous twelve months or carried forward to future accounting periods and set against future trade profit (not total profits) from the same source. As well as the recent changes to the company loss carry forward rules (below), the main difference between companies and sole traders is that before a trade loss can be carried back to the previous twelve months, it must first be used as much as possible against the current year's taxable total profits, i.e. only the excess can then be carried back.

Pre April 2017 property losses could be offset against current taxable total profits, or carried forward to future years.

A pre April 2017 non-trading loan relationship deficit (loss) could be offset against the company's taxable total profits for the period, carried back to be offset against interest income loan relationship profits falling within the previous twelve months, or carried forward to be offset against non trade profits in future years.

In the case of capital losses, the pre April 2017 relief was more restricted. A capital loss could only be set against chargeable gains of the same accounting period. It could not be offset against total profits, so if there were not enough gains to absorb the loss in the current year, the loss was then carried forward, but could only be set against future chargeable gains.

With effect from 1 April 2017 a 50% restriction now applies for all companies with carried forward losses. Pre 1 April 2017 losses can still only be offset against the same income stream, e.g. trading losses against future profits of the same trade. Losses carried forward post 1 April 2017, however, can be used against total profits of the company in future accounting periods, which includes future investment income and capital gains, as well as trading income.

Where an accounting period straddles the 1 April 2017, periods before and after are treated as separate accounting periods and it may be necessary to apportion profits, losses or deductions on a time basis. In both cases, the amount of annual profits that can be relieved by brought forward losses (old and new type) is limited to 50% of the company's chargeable profits in excess of £5million. The £5million is referred to as a 'deductions' allowance and needs to be pro-rated for accounting periods which aren't 12 months long and has to be shared by companies in a group (9.23 below). This means that large companies with profits over £5m will still pay some corporation tax despite having brought forward losses to use up.

Activity

Zoot Suit Ltd had a trading loss of £8m in the year ended 31 March 2017, a trading loss of £10m in the year ended 31 March 2018 and trading profit of £12m plus a property business profit of £3m in the year ended 31 March 2019. How will the trading losses be relieved?

Feedback

In the year ended 31 March 2019, Zoot Suit Ltd will be able to claim maximum relief of £5m plus 50% x ((£12m+£3m) – 5m) = £5m ie £10m in total.

The 2016/17 loss is an 'old' loss and can only be offset against the 2018/19 trading profit, subject to the 50% restriction, i.e. only £4m can be offset leaving £4m to be carried forward to 2019/20.

The 2017/18 loss is a 'new" loss and can be offset against total profits up to the maximum of £10m less the £4m already used, i.e. £6m. The remaining £4m can be carried forward to 2019/20.

There are winners and losers with the April 2017 changes to the corporate loss regime. SMEs will be winners because they will benefit from greater flexibility for using carried forward losses without the 50% profit restriction. The government estimates this will be 99% of all businesses. Larger businesses however, will face cash flow and forecasting difficulties with significantly more complexity, in particular if they are operating as a group, as we will see in the next section.

Company groups

9.23 While very small companies may operate alone, it is not unusual to find groups of companies, consisting of a parent company and subsidiary companies. The UK tax system does not allow for consolidation of group profits as is done for accounting purposes. Instead, as we have seen, each separate company is responsible for its own tax liability even if part of a group. There are, however, some special rules that recognise group relationships and allow for certain reliefs between group members.

There are three forms of group relationship that you should be aware of:
- Loss groups (75% groups and consortia);
- Capital gains groups; and
- Related companies (51% groups)

In this section we will look at the first and second of these type of groups. The third type is relevant for payment of corporation tax and we look at this in section 9.26

Loss Groups

9.24 There are two types of groups that are relevant for the transfer of losses, 75% groups and consortia. Members of these types of group are able to move certain losses between them. This then gives another way of relieving losses, rather than only using it within the company that created the loss, it can be passed over to a 75% group or consortium member. The losses that can be transferred are trade losses and non trade loan deficits. The ownership rules are actually quite complicated, so for our purposes we will assume that this means owning a percentage of the share capital of another company.

A 75% group is one where one company owns 75% of another company or a third company owns 75% of both of them. The 75% requirement refers to effective interest, so that, for example, a 90% subsidiary of a 90% subsidiary will qualify because the effective interest is 90 x 90 = 81%.

Activity

The group structure of the Canine group is as follows:

The parent company, Canine plc, owns 80% of the shares in Alsation Ltd, 80% of the shares in Beagle Ltd and 70% of the shares in Corgi Ltd. In addition, Alsation Ltd owns 80% of the shares of Doberman Ltd.

Which companies are able to transfer losses as part of the 75% group?

Feedback

Canine plc owns 80% of each of Alsatian Ltd and Beagle Ltd and so these three companies form a 75% group and may exchange losses between themselves. Corgi Ltd is excluded because Canine plc's interest is less than 75%.

Doberman Ltd does not form part of this wider 75% group, as Canine plc's indirect interest in it is only 64% (80% x 80%). Doberman Ltd and Alsatian Ltd, however, can exchange losses as they form a 75% group of their own. It is possible for a company, in this case Alsatian Ltd, to be a member of two or more separate 75% groups.

We refer to the company that is transferring a loss as a 'surrendering' company, and the company who is receiving it as the 'claimant' company. Companies can only use this 'group relief' for trading losses, excess property business losses and excess charitable donations.

The rules for group relief were also changed from April 2017. Prior to April 2017, only current year losses could be relieved and there are two limitations on this form of relief. First, the most that can be transferred is the available profit of the claimant company. Second, the companies must have corresponding accounting periods, and if they don't an adjustment is required to work out how much can be transferred. The group relief is restricted to the proportion of the profit or loss that belongs to the period where their accounting periods overlap.

From April 2017, carry forward losses can also be surrenderd as group relief, but only after the surrendering company has used as much of its loss as possible itself, and are subject to the 50% restriction and the £5m allowance. The £5m allowance can be allocated between group companies through a nominated company in a way to best suit the group.

Above the £5m allowance, only 50% of profits can be covered by carry forward losses whether they come from pre or post April 2017. The claimant company can only claim carry forward losses surrendered from another group company if it has first used its own brought forward losses.

A consortium is a different form of group with more limited ability to transfer losses. A company is owned by a consortium if 75% or more of its shares are owned by companies (the consortium companies), none of which has a holding of less than 5%. A consortium owned company can surrender current year losses in proportion to the stakes of the members of the consortium to be set against profits of a corresponding accounting period. A consortium member may surrender a loss to set against its share of the consortium owned company's profits. The surrendered loss made by a consortium owned company can only be surrendered after being offset as much as possible against current year profits.

Capital gains groups

9.25 It is possible for assets to be transferred between capital gains group members on a no gain and no loss basis; that is at cost plus indexation allowance up until the date of the transfer. Assets can be transferred in any direction between group members. There is a slightly different form of group relationship for capital gains. The rules for determining membership of a capital gains group are less stringent so that at each level there must be a 75% holding so long as the top company has an effective interest of more than 50% in the group companies. Unlike with 75% groups, it is not possible for a company to be a member of more than one capital gains group.

Activity

A plc owns 75% of B Ltd, which owns 75% of C Ltd which in turn owns 75% of D Ltd. Which of them will form a capital gains group?

Feedback

The capital gains group will consist of A, B, C but not D as A's interest in D is only 42.19%. Note that for group relief purposes A & B will constitute a group, as will B & C and C & D.

There are two situations that will give rise to a subsequent chargeable gain. First, if the asset is disposed of outside of the capital gains group and secondly if the company holding the asset ceases to be eligible to be a member of the group because of a change of shareholding. In the second case, where a group member leaves the group within six years of an asset transfer, it is deemed to have sold the asset on the date of the intra group transfer for its market value on that date, and immediately re-acquired it at that value. The effect of this is that the chargeable gain to the date of the transfer crystallises at the time the company leaves the group. It is possible for this "degrouping charge" to be transferred to another company in the group, which may have the advantage of allowing capital losses within the group to be absorbed.

Capital losses cannot be transferred between group members. However, because it is possible to transfer assets between group members on a no gain and no loss basis before they are sold outside of the group, capital losses can be offset against capital gains. Helpfully, in practice the asset doesn't have to actually (i.e. legally) be transferred, rather the tax calculation is based on a hypothetical transfer.

Payment of corporation tax

9.26   In the UK, companies are required to use a system of *self-assessment* for their corporation tax computation. Self assessment for companies commenced for accounting periods ending after July 1999, whereas individuals have been self-assessed for their income since the 1996/97 tax year.

A company is required to perform its own tax computation and pay over the tax due according to this computation on the correct dates. If HMRC wishes to query the calculations, they now have up to one year from the date the return is due to be filed (or at least a year after the return is filed if filed late) to say so. If they do not query the computation within this time then the year is completed.

Companies are also required to maintain full records of all the information they use to produce their tax computation for 6 years beyond the end of the period of assessment. Companies failing to be able to produce records if asked to by HMRC in this period could be prosecuted.

The advantage of the self-assessment scheme to HMRC is that they can operate a 'process now – check later' approach for dealing with corporate tax returns. This enables them to spread their work load throughout the year in more flexible ways than was previously the case. A disadvantage of the scheme for the company is that they now need to employ more expert help in completing their returns, which increases their compliance costs.

Since 2009 large companies are required to nominate a 'senior accounting officer' who will be required to certify each year that the tax accounting arrangements for the company are appropriate. If he or she fails to comply with this new rule, a personal fine of up to £5,000 could be imposed..

Payment dates

9.27   Companies with taxable profits of up to £1.5million mostly pay their corporation tax liability 9 months and one day after their accounting period end. For example, a company with a 31 December year end will be required to pay corporation tax on the following 1 October. However, for large companies there is a requirement for quarterly instalments of their corporation tax liability to spread their payments throughout the tax year.

Companies that have taxable profits of more than £1.5m required to pay a percentage of the total tax liability in four equal payments. The actual quarterly dates on which payments should be made are calculated using the rule: the first payment is due on the 14th day of the 7th month of the accounting period, then in three further equal payments at quarterly intervals.

Activity

Calculate the corporate tax payment dates for a large company with a 12 month accounting period ending 31 December 2018.

Feedback

The due dates will be:

1st instalment	14 July 2018
2nd instalment	14 October 2018
3rd instalment	14 January 2019
Final instalment	14 April 2019

You should note that the final instalment is not due until 3 months and 14 days after the accounting period ends. This enables the company to ensure all their records have been completed for the accounting period so that a full determination of the tax due is possible.

The Summer Budget 2015 announced that corporations with profits in excess of £20million will have to pay their corporation tax earlier than at present. This new measure was finally implemented by the Corporation Tax (Instalment Payments) (Amendment) Regulation 2017, with affected companies required to pay in the 3rd, 6th, 9th and 12th months from 1 April 2019.

Where accounting periods exist of less than 12 months, then fewer than four payments will be made. The final instalment will always be due 3 months and 14 days after the end of the accounting period. Earlier instalments are only due if the due dates of the usual gaps (six months and 13 days then 3 monthly intervals) fall before the due date for the final instalment.

This means:

Accounting period length	Instalments due
less than 3 months	final
3-6 months	first + final
6-9 months	first, second + final
9-12 months	all four instalments

Activity

Calculate the instalment dates due for a company with an accounting period of 1 January 2018 to 31 July 2018.

Feedback

First instalment	14 July 2018 (14th day of 7th month)
Second instalment	14 October 2018 (3 months after 14 July)
Third instalment	not due (would be due 3 months after 14 October 2018 which would fall after final instalment)
Final instalment	14 November 2018 (3 months and 14 days after the end of the accounting period)

Where a company has an accounting period of less than 12 months the amounts of tax due at each instalment should be calculated using the formula:

$$\frac{3 \times CTL}{n}$$

where:

- CTL is the amount of the company's total tax liability for the accounting period due for payment by instalments
- n is the number of months in the accounting period.

Where a company has reasonable grounds for believing that its total tax liability at the end of the year will be less than the total amounts that will be paid based on amounts currently being paid in instalments, then the company can adjust subsequent payments to reflect the correct liability (or make a claim for a repayment if they have already paid too much).

In working out whether a company is 'small' or 'large' for the purposes of paying corporation tax, by reference to the taxable profits, we need to take into account any 51% group companies, which means companies where more than 50% of its ordinary shares is beneficially owned by another company. Company A is a related 51% group company of company B if:

1. A is a 51% subsidiary of B
2. B is a 51% subsidiary of A
3. A and B are 51% subsidiaries of the same company.

If a company has 51% group companies, the £1.5million threshold for deciding whether instalment payments are required is divided by the number of associated companies. For a company with 4 related 51% group companies, the threshold becomes £1.5m/5 or £300,000. If any of these companies has taxable profits in excess of £300,000, it will be required to pay by instalments.

Corporation tax reform

9.28 For some years now the Government has been consulting widely on possible reform to the corporation tax system in the UK. One of the issues being discussed is the possibility of making tax profits and accounting profits the same so that companies only have to create one set of computations for both financial reporting and for tax computation purposes.

In some countries tax profit and accounting profit are already much more closely aligned, but in the UK the computation of tax profits has always been separate, even though it uses the accounting profit as the starting point, as we have illustrated.

One of the unique features of the tax profit calculation is the need to separate different types of income into different categories. One reason for separating different income sources is to give special treatment to losses (i.e. where the income from that source is less than the associated expenses). Whether or not this should continue is also under debate.

Several new measures introduced in recent years have deliberately adopted accounting rules for tax purposes. For example, the rules which allow companies to deduct goodwill written off in the accounts for tax purposes, allow the accounting value to be used to work out the tax deductible amount. Some have suggested that now all listed companies use International Financial Reporting Standards, and perhaps other companies will eventually do likewise, not only will it be possible to use accounting profits for tax purposes, but also that company tax systems will be able to be harmonised between countries.

One argument against using accounting profits for tax purposes is that it won't allow the Government to use the tax system to provide special incentives. There are also public policy implications, for example, the Government in the UK has decided that fines and penalties should not be allowed as deductions for tax purposes even though they will appear in the accounts.

The Treasury released a discussion document in conjunction with the Pre Budget Report in November 2009, in which it is proposed to allow small companies to use accounting profits for tax purposes, or be taxed by reference to cash flows rather than profit. The Institute for Chartered Accountants in Scotland has spoken out against these proposals, suggesting they are not helpful to small business and simplification to the current system would be preferable to such radical changes – despite the possible compliance cost benefits this might bring for small businesses. In March 2012 HMRC announced changes based on recommendations from the Office of Tax Simplification that SMEs be allowed to calculate their income tax on a cash basis using simplified expenses rules. As we saw in Chapter 6, from April 2013, small, unincorporated businesses with receipts of up to the VAT registration threshold are able to use the cash basis.

Further reforms to the system of paying and filing self assessment tax returns for companies were also recently proposed in a major review of the way the HMRC operate their electronic services. This report, called the Carter Review and published at the same time as the 2006 Budget (and revised during 2007), suggested that, for example, companies should file their tax returns sooner than they are at present. On-line filing of corporation tax returns will be required for accounting periods ending after 31 March 2010. HMRC also mandated the use of XBRL for corporation tax return filing from April 2011.

In December 2010, the Government released a 'Corporation Tax Roadmap' that set out plans for reform of corporation tax over the following few years. Many of the proposed changes related to international operations and we will look at these in Chapter 12. The Government has consulted with businesses during each stage of introducing the proposed changes, only some of which have been enacted to date, but they gave priority to reducing the tax rate. We have seen the highest rate of corporation tax that then applied fall first from its then level at 28% first to 26% in April 2011, then to 24% in April 2012, to 23% in April 2013, to 21% in April 2014, to 20% in April 2015 and from April 2017 it is 19% (a further fall is promised to 17% by April 2020). This now brings all companies in line with the same (flat) tax rate now from this year.

In March 2016 a new 'Business Tax Roadmap' was released by HM Treasury. This makes suggestions for further changes to all business taxes, particularly those paid by corporations. Some of these changes have been outlined above, such as changed rules for the carrying forward of corporate losses. Several other changes will be explored in Chapter 12.

The Office for Tax Simplification has published a report in July 2017 which makes recommendations for simplifying corporation tax, particularly for small companies, including closer alignment between tax rules and accounting rules.

Basic tax planning of UK resident companies

9.29 Companies which are family owned and managed may have some flexibility when remunerating their owner/managers. Paying dividends or providing benefits in kind rather than high salaries may reduce the total national insurance contributions which must be paid. For example, when employees make contributions to a pension scheme the contributions are allowable deductions for tax purposes but not for national insurance contributions. However, if the contributions are made by the employer, then they are fully deductible for tax purposes and do not give rise to a liability to either employee or employer national insurance contributions. Hence it may be tax efficient for small companies to operate non-contributory pension schemes.

Further discussion of tax planning related to companies can be found in Chapter 11.

Summary

This chapter has provided you with the skills needed to calculate the corporation tax liability of companies which are resident in the UK.

To calculate a company's tax liability it is necessary to undertake a number of steps:

- identify each source of income for a company;
- determine the category of income which is used to calculate the taxable income for each source of income;
- using the current year basis (which applies to the income and expenditure of companies) to calculate the income that is assessable and determine any deductions from that income which are allowable for tax purposes; and
- determine details of any charges on income which are paid by the company.

This will enable you to calculate the corporation tax liability using the small companies limit, and the marginal relief equation if necessary to determine the main corporation tax liability.

The imputation system was also briefly explained in this chapter.

You have been able to compare and contrast the taxation of companies with the taxation of individuals. You might like to list the similarities and differences and decide if the differences between the two are sufficient for one business medium to be preferred to the other. However, it is important to remember that tax is just one aspect of the environment in which businesses operate. Other considerations are at least as important, for example the benefit of limited liability and the ability to raise extra finance. We will look at this more in Chapter 11.

Discussion topics

1. What are the key differences between the application of trading profit rules for sole traders and for companies? Must these differences exist?

2. Is it fair that dividends paid by companies attract special treatment compared to other forms of income via a lower rate of tax?

3. Why are tax years and financial years different?

4. Why are special rules needed for describing how loan relationships, research and development costs and intangibles costs should be allocated to accounting periods for tax computations?

5. Should large companies have to pay their corporate tax bills so much earlier than smaller companies?

6. What are the pros and cons of using profits calculated using International Financial Reporting Standards as a basis for corporation tax?

7. Is it fair that the smallest company now pays the same rate of corporation tax as the very largest?

8. Why do companies in the creative industries appear to get special tax treatment? Is this fair on companies in other sectors?

Quick quiz

1. Grotius Ltd prepares accounts for the sixteen months to 31 December 2018. What are its accounting periods for corporation tax purposes?

2. Helvetius Ltd receives dividends from a UK company of £132,000. How will they be treated for corporation tax purposes?

3. Isocrates Ltd acquired a patent during the year ended 30 June 2018 and charged amortisation in its accounts at the rate of 3%. How will it be treated for corporation tax purposes?

4. Justinian Ltd licences a partnership to use its patent and accrues patent royalties of £3,900 (net) for the year. How will this be treated for corporation tax purposes?

5. Lycophron Ltd has a corporation tax liability of £650,000 and has an accounting period of 5 months to 31 May 2018. When will its instalments of corporation tax be due?

6. Magician Ltd's accounts for the year ended 31 December 2018 show the following accrued income received and interest paid:

Bank interest receiveable	£7,000
Interest payable on loan to purchase a rental property	£5,650
Interest payable on overdue corporation tax	£1,200
Interest on loan to purchase plant used in the trade	£3,600

What is the amount taxable as a non-trading loan relationship?

7. New Money Ltd is a small company. It spends £11,000 on hiring temporary staff to carry out scientific research in connection with its business activities. What effect will this expenditure have on the company's corporation tax liability?

8. Origami Ltd has trading profit of £7m and investment income of £4m for the year ended 30 June 2018. The company has a loss brought forward from the year ended 30 June 2017 of £10m. What is the maximum amount of loss that can be set off in the year ended 30 June 2018?

9. Perigrine Ltd sold an asset for £14,600 in August 2018 that had been originally purchased in February 2003 for £5,000. What is the amount of the indexed gain on the sale of the asset?

10. Quay Ltd, a small close company, made a loan of £30,000 to a shareholder in July 2017. The company's accounting period ends on 31 July each year. The loan was not repaid and penalty tax of £9,750 was paid to HMRC. In July 2018, the shareholder repaid £15,000 of the loan. How much of the penalty tax can be recovered and when?

11. Ranch Ltd is a close company and provides a new car for one of its participators, Billy. Billy is neither a director nor employee of Ranch Ltd. As a benefit in kind for income tax, the value of the car would be £2,750. What are the tax consequences for Ranch Ltd and for Billy?

12. Time Ltd has the following shareholding:

Usual Ltd	40%
Verity Ltd	60%
Wallace Ltd	80%

Which companies are related for the purposes of determining the limit for paying by instalments? Which companies are in a loss relief group and which are in a capital gains group?

Questions

Question 1

Ultimate Upholsterers Ltd is a UK resident company which manufactures leather upholstered chairs. It has been trading for many years. The company's results for the year ended 31 March 2019 are summarised as follows.

	£
Trading profits*	375,000
Net dividend from UK company (received 29 May 2018)	18,000
Gross (non-trading) loan interest receivable	12,000
Gross (non-trading) debenture interest payable	10,000
Profit on sale of land	37,000
Writing down allowances on plant and machinery	49,000

* As adjusted for taxation, but before capital allowances and adjustment for the lease premium on the factory (see below).

The company operates from a factory that was first occupied by Ultimate Upholsterers Ltd on 1 October 2000, under the terms of a 25-year lease which was acquired for a premium of £50,000. The land had been purchased in December 1984 for £10,000 and sold in February 2019 for £47,410.

Required: Calculate the corporation tax payable for the year ended 31 March 2019.

Question 2

ABC Ltd (a company with one related associate company) has augmented profit of £1.2million and a corporate tax liability of £228,000 for FY18.

Required: Calculate the due dates for instalments of corporation tax ABC Ltd will have to pay and the amounts due on each of these dates if:

(a) The company has a 12 month accounting period to 31 October 2018;
(b) The company produces accounts for 8 months to 30 June 2018 instead (assume the amount of the tax liability is not affected for the purpose of this question).

Question 3

Pendulum Ltd is a medium sized UK company that owns a gymnasium and leisure facility in Stafford. The company has been trading for several years. During the year ended 31 March 2019, the company's accounts revealed the following:

	£		£
Depreciation	43,150	Trading profit	262,772
Directors' fees (1)	37,840	Building society interest accrued	759
Patent royalty payable (2)	3,500	Debenture interest accrued (gross)	1,200
Qualifying charitable donation	5,000		
Entertaining customers	730		
Salary and wages	16,500		
Non trading loan interest payable (3)	700		
Rent of business premises	3,000		
Audit fee	1,320		
Trade expenses (4)	25,328		
Net profit before taxation	127,663		
	264,731		264,731

(1) Directors' fees were all paid within 9 months of the year end.
(2) The patent royalty is payable to a UK company.
(3) £100 of the £700 non-trading loan interest payable was accrued as at 31 March 2019.
(4) The trade expenses include the following items:

	£
Legal expenses in respect of the following:	
The non trading loan	500
Staff service agreements	90
Gifts to customers:	
6 bottles of malt whisky	280
1,000 diaries bearing the company's name	1,250
Redecoration of café area	3,200

(5) The written down value of plant and machinery on 1 April 2018 was £263,504. On 1 August 2018 the company sold some plant for £9,400 which had originally cost £11,000. On 31 January 2019 plant costing £10,500 was acquired. On the same day, a low emission car costing £13,000 was purchased for the use of the marketing director of the company, who used the vehicle 50% for private purposes.

Required: Compute Pendulum Ltd's trade profits, taxable total profits, and corporation tax payable for the accounting period 31 March 2019. State when the tax will be payable.

Question 4

(a) Burgundy Ltd bought an office block to use in its business in August 1992. In April 2018 the company sold the building for £300,000, resulting in an indexed chargeable gain of £125,400, and at the same time bought another office block to use in its business.

Assuming that Burgundy claims rollover relief calculate the chargeable gain arising on the disposal of the office block if the replacement block costs:
   (a)   £380,000
   (b)   £280,000
   (c)   £120,000.

(b) Navy Ltd sold a warehouse used exclusively for business purposes for £200,000 in November 2010 realising an indexed chargeable gain of £50,000. The company bought fixed plant for £240,000 in November 2010. The company elects to hold-over the gain on the warehouse against the fixed plant.

How will the held-over gain be treated (assuming current tax rules apply) if:
   (a)   Navy Ltd sells the fixed plant in January 2019
   (b)   Navy Ltd sells the fixed plant in April 2021
   (c)   Navy Ltd bought another warehouse for business use in December 2011 and elected to transfer the held-over gain on the fixed plant to the new warehouse which cost £220,000
   (d)   The new warehouse in part (c) cost £185,000.

(Note: answer available via lecturer's website)

Question 5 (ACCA June 2015)

Restro Ltd's summarised statement of profit or loss for the year ended 31 March 2019 is as follows:

	Notes	£	£
Gross profit			127,100
Operating expenses:			
Depreciation		27,240	
Gifts and donations	1	2,300	
Impairment loss	2	1,600	
Leasing costs	3	4,400	
Other expenses	4	205,160	
			(240,700)
Finance costs:			
Interest payable	5		(6,400)
Loss before taxation			(120,000)

Notes:

1. Gifts and donations are as follows:

	£
Gifts to employees (food hampers costing £60 each)	720
Gifts to customers	
(calendars costing £8 each and displaying Retro's name)	480
Political donations	420
Qualifying charitable donations	680
	2,300

2. On 31 March 2019, Retro Ltd wrote off an impairment loss of £1,600 relating to a trade debt. This was in respect of an invoice which had been due for payment on 10 November 2018.

3. The leasing costs of £4,400 are in respect of a motor car lease which commenced on 1 April 2018. The leased motor car has CO_2 emissions of 145 grams per kilometre.

4. The figure of £205,160 for other expenses includes a fine of £5,100 for a breach of health and safety regulations, and legal fees of £4,860 in connection with the defence of Retro Ltd's internet domain name. the remaining expenses are all fully allowable.

5. The interest payable is in resepct of the company's 5% loan notes which were repaid on 31 July 2018. Interest of £9,600 was paid on 31 July 2018, and an accrual of £3,200 had been provided for at 1 April 2018. The loan notes were issued to finance the company's trading activities.

Additional information:

On 1 April 2018, the tax written down value of the plant and machinery main pool was £39,300. The following vehicles were purchased during the year ended 31 March 2019:

	Date of purchase	Cost	CO_2 emissions
Motor car (1)	8 June 2018	14,700	124 g/km
Delivery van	3 August 2018	28,300	162 g/km
Motor car (2)	19 October 2018	12,400	86 g/km

Retro Ltd commenced trading on 1 Sepember 2016. The company's results for its two previous periods of trading are as follows:

	y/e 31/8/17	p/e 31/3/18
Tax adjusted trading profit	56,600	47,900
Bank interest receivable	1,300	0
Qualifying charitable donations paid	(540)	(330)

Retro Ltd is expected to return to profitability in theyear ended 31 March 2020 and continue to be profitable in subsequent years.

Required:
1. Calculate Retro Ltd's adjusted trading loss for the year ended 31 March 2019;
2. Assuming Retro Ltd claims relief for its trading loss as early as possible, calculate the company's taxable total profits for the year ended 31 August 2017 and the seven month period ended 31 March 2018.
3. Identify the amount of unrelieved trading loss which Retro will have at 31 March 2019, and state how this can be relieved.

(Note: *answer available on lecturer's website*)

Question 6   (ACCA June 2009)

Gastron Ltd, a UK resident company, is a luxury food manufacturer. The company's summarised income statement for the year ended 31 March 2019 is as follows:

	Notes	£	£
Gross profit			876,500
Operating expenses:			
Depreciation		85,660	
Amortisation of leasehold property	1	6,000	
Gifts and donations	2	2,700	
Professional fees	3	18,800	
Other expenses	4	230,240	(343,400)

Operating profit			533,100
Income from investments:			
Income from property	5	20,600	
Bank interest	6	12,400	
Dividends	7	54,000	87,000
Profit from sale of fixed assets:			
Disposal of shares	8		80,700
			700,800
Interest payable	9		(60,800)
Profit before taxation			640,000

Notes:

1. Leasehold property: on 1 April 2018, Gastron acquired a leasehold office building, paying a premium of £60,000 for the grant of a new ten-year lease. The office building was used for business purposes by Gastron Ltd throughout the year ended 31 March 2019.

2. Gifts and donations were as follows:
   Gifts to customers (pens displaying Gastron's name, £60 each) 1,200
   Gifts to customers (bottles of alcohol costing £25 each)   1,100
   Donation to local charity (Gastron Ltd received free advertising
   in the charity's magazine)   400
                                                                    2,700

3. Professional fees are as follows:
   Legal fees in connection with the renewal of a 45 year property lease in
   respect of a warehouse   3,600
   Legal fees for the issue of debentures (see note 9)   15,200

4. Other expenses: the figure for other expenses includes £1,300 for entertaining suppliers and £900 for entertaining employees.

5. Income from property: Gastron Ltd lets out the whole of an unfurnished freehold office building that is surplus to requirements. The building was let from 1 April 2018 to 31 December 2018 at a monthly rent of £1,800, payable in advance. On 31 December 2018, the tenant left owing two month's rent which Gastron Ltd was unable to recover. During January 2019, the company spent £3,700 redecorating the property. The building was re-let from 1 February 2019 at a monthly rent of £1,950, on which date the tenant paid six month's rent in advance.

6. Bank interest received: the bank interest was received on 31 March 2019. The bank deposits are held for non-trading purposes.

7. Dividends received: during the year ended 31 March 2019 Gastron Ltd received dividends of £36,000 from Tasteless plc, an unconnected UK

company and dividends of £18,000 from Culinary Ltd, a 100% UK subsidiary. Both figures are the actual cash amounts received.

8. Profit on disposal of shares: The profit on disposal of shares is in respect of a 1% shareholding that was sold on 14 October 2018. The disposal resulted in a chargeable gain of £74,800. This figure is after taking account of indexation.

9. Interest payable: this is in respect of the company's 5% debenture loan stock that was issued on 1 April 2018. The proceeds of the issue were used to finance the company's trading activities. Interest of £30,400 was paid on 30 September 2018 and again on 31 March 2019.

10. Plant and machinery: on 1 April 2018, the tax written down values of plant and machinery were as follows:

Main pool	16,700
Special rate pool	18,400

These transactions took place during the year ended 31 March 2019:

		£
19 May 2018	purchased equipment	12,792
12 July 2018	purchased car (1)	9,800
11 August 2018	purchased car (2)	16,200
5 October 2018	purchased lorry	17,200
5 March 2019	sold equipment	(3,300)

Motor car (1), purchased on 12 July 2018 for £9,800, has a CO_2 emission rating of 155g/km. Motor car (2), purchased on 11 August 2018 for £16,200 is a low emission car (CO_2 emission rate of less than 75g/km). The equipment sold on 5 March 2019 for £3,300 was originally purchased in 2004 for £8,900.

Required: Calculate Gastron Ltd's corporation tax payable for the year ended 31 March 2019 and state the due date for payment.

(*Note: answer available on lecturer's website*)

Question 7   (ACCA December 2007)

Sofa Ltd has three subsidiary companies as follows:

Settee Ltd
   Sofa Ltd owns 100% of the ordinary share capital of Settee Ltd. For the year ended 30 June 2018, Settee Ltd had taxable total profits of £240,000, and for the year ended 30 June 2019 will have taxable total profits of £90,000.

Couch Ltd
   Sofa Ltd owns 60% of the ordinary share capital of Couch Ltd. For the year ended 31 March 2019 Couch Ltd had taxable total profits of £64,000.

Futon Ltd

Sofa Ltd owns 80% of the ordinary share capital of Futon Ltd. Futon Ltd commenced trading on 1 January 2019, and for the three month period ended 31 March 2019 had taxable total profits of £60,000.

Required:

Advise Sofa Ltd as to the maximum amount of group relief that can potentially be claimed by each of its three subsidiary companies in respect of its tax adjusted trading loss for the year ended 31 March 2019 of £200,000.

(Note: *answer available on lecturer's website*)

 Further test questions for this chapter to test your knowledge can be found in the student section of the website at: **http://www.taxstudent.com/uk**

Further reading and examples

Combs, A., Tutin, R. & Rowes, P. (2018), *Taxation: incorporating the 2018 Finance Act*, Fiscal Publications: Birmingham.
- use this book for many other examples to further develop and test your knowledge of this chapter's contents. See
http://www.fiscalpublications.com/rowes/2018/

James, S. & Nobes, C. (2018) *Economics of Taxation: 18th edition*, Fiscal Publications: Birmingham.
– useful additional perspective on the role and design of corporation taxation in the UK.

Evans, C., Hasseldine, J., Lymer, A., Ricketts, R. & Sandford, C. (2017) *Comparative Taxation: Why tax systems differ*, Fiscal Publications: Birmingham.
– further details on the principles of how and why corporates are taxed and comparisons of how this is achieved in different countries.

For more information about how different systems of corporation tax work to reduce the double taxation of dividends, see Oats, L (2002) "Taxing Companies and Their Shareholders" in *The International Tax System*, Lymer & Hasseldine eds, Springer.

10 | Value Added Tax

Introduction

10.1 VAT (Value Added Tax) has become an increasingly important source of income for the government since it was introduced in 1973. It is the third highest tax revenue source for the UK Government after income tax and national insurance contributions.

At the end of this chapter you will be able to:

- state the broad principles of the UK's VAT system;
- state the criteria for compulsory registration and deregistration for VAT and explain the advantages and disadvantages of registration;
- identify taxable supplies and calculate a trader's VAT payable/repayable;
- list which goods are standard rated, zero rated and exempt from VAT and explain the differences in their treatment;
- describe the main characteristics of the administration of VAT including various special schemes that currently exist in the UK;
- state the VAT consequences of importing and exporting goods and services; and
- describe the system for administering VAT which operates within the EU.

Background

10.2 VAT was introduced in April 1973 partly as a consequence of the UK joining the European Union. It replaced purchase tax and introduced three classifications into which all goods and services are allocated – zero rated, exempt and standard rated. Sales and purchases of goods and services (from UK or overseas traders) are taxed according to their classification into one of these categories.

When VAT was first introduced it was a relatively simple tax, however it has increased in complexity and can now be a difficult tax to apply in practice. It has become a specialist area of tax compliance and planning.

The legal basis for VAT is contained in the Value Added Tax Act (VATA 1994) and subsequent Finance Acts. VAT was, until 2005, administered by HM Customs and Excise. However, like other taxes, VAT is now managed by HMRC.

Principles of VAT

10.3 VAT is an *indirect tax* and is the UK's primary *consumption* or *expenditure tax*. VAT is borne by the final consumer, although it is charged whenever a *taxable person* makes a *taxable supply* of goods or services in the course of business at each stage in a supply chain for any taxable supply. It is a tax on turnover, not on income or profit like the majority of other taxes we have seen in this book.

Before giving more detail of how VAT operates in practice, let's review what we mean by the terms taxable persons and taxable supplies.

A taxable person

10.4 A person is a taxable person for the purposes of VAT while he or she is registered under the Value Added Tax Act 1994. As we see below, a trader is required by law to register for VAT once their annual turnover of a taxable supply reaches a registration threshold that is set each year in the budget. For this tax year it is set at £85,000, unchanged from the previous year. However, any trader making a taxable supply can register for VAT even if their turnover for the year is less than the threshold that year.

A taxable person can be an individual or partnership, company, club, association or charity.

A taxable supply

10.5 A taxable supply includes all forms of business supply made in return for consideration (i.e. for money or payment in kind) unless it is explicitly exempted from VAT by law or regulation. For example, in addition to the normal sales activities a business may engage in, the following transfers are all taxable supplies:

- Any transfer of a whole asset is a supply of goods. The transfer of any share of an asset is a supply of services.
- The supply of any form of power, heat, refrigeration or ventilation.
- The grant, assignment or surrender of a major interest in land.
- The transfer of fixed assets or current assets, including transfers to the registered trader whether or not for a consideration.
- Business gifts are taxable supplies unless the transfer is either a gift of goods made in the course or furtherance of the business (which cost the donor not more than £50) or a gift to an actual or potential customer of the business of an industrial sample which is not ordinarily available for sale to the public.
- Goods which were owned by the business and are put to any private use or are used, or made available to any person, including the registered trader, to use for a private purpose are taxable at cost.

- Goods lent to someone outside the business or hired to someone are a taxable supply of services.

A taxable supply is considered to have occurred once the ownership of the asset being supplied transfers from one person to another. This means the actual physical transfer of the asset, if it is a good, may happen after the supply has actually been made and supplies of services will have occurred for VAT purposes once the service has been carried out.

The value of a taxable supply

10.6 If the supply is for a consideration in money, then VAT should be added to the price charged for the good or service. If the supply is for a consideration which is not wholly in money (e.g. involving payment in kind) then, the money value of the consideration is taken to be the VAT inclusive price.

The market value of a supply of goods or services is taken to be the amount which would be payable by a person in an *arms' length* transaction. This means that if a business makes a taxable supply to a *connected person* the VAT will be due on the price that would have been charged on the supply had this transaction been with an unconnected recipient. This rule ensures the correct amount of VAT is charged on all supplies.

From 4 January 2011, there was an increase in the VAT rate to 20%. This amount is added to the value of the sale of a good or service to determine the total amount to be collected from the customer. The VAT proportion of the total consideration is $20 \div (100 + 20) = 1/6$. This proportion is called the *VAT fraction* and can be used to find how much VAT will have been paid on any standard rated supply if you are only given the VAT inclusive amount of the supply.

The standard rate of VAT from 1 January 2010 until 3 January 2011 was 17.5%, and so the VAT fraction was $17.5 \div (100 + 17.5)$ or $7/47$.

For the period from 1 December 2008 until 31 December 2009, a different standard rate applied (15%) introduced to try and stimulate spending and reduce the severity of the recession. This means that the VAT fraction for this period was $3/23$.

Input and output tax

10.7 The VAT system operates by registered traders collecting VAT on behalf of the Government from customers they supply to – VAT is therefore an example of an indirect tax. Registered traders can also, however, reclaim VAT they suffer on their purchases. These two parts of the VAT system from the trader's perspective are referred to as *input tax* and *output tax*.

Input tax is the VAT a taxable person has to pay:

- on the supply to him or her of any goods or services;
- on the acquisition by him or her of any goods from another EU member state; or
- paid or payable by him or her on the importation of any goods from a place outside the EU provided that the goods or services are, or will be, used for the purposes of a business carried on by the taxable person.

A taxable person's output tax is the VAT charged on taxable supplies made. The difference between input and output tax is the amount they pay over to the Government on a regular basis. We will see how this works in practice on the next page.

The tax point

10.8   VAT is accounted for on a periodic basis, usually quarterly, and so we need to know the date on which transactions occur in order to determine which time period it belongs to. The deemed date of supply of taxable goods or services is termed the *tax point*. The basic tax point is the date on which a supply of goods or services is treated as taking place.

A supply of goods will be treated as taking place when:

- the supplier sends the goods to the customer;
- the customer collects the goods from the supplier; or
- the goods are made available for the customer to use. This might occur, for example, when the supplier assembles something at the premises of the customer.

A supply of services is any taxable supply which is not a supply of goods. As no physical transfers may take place when services are supplied, the supply of services will be treated as taking place at the time when the services are carried out and all the work is finished.

A trader can choose to use these basic tax points, however, if a tax invoice is issued within 14 days of the date on which the supply is considered to have taken place according to the basic rules, the supply can be treated as taking place at the time the invoice is issued instead. This makes the practical process of accounting for VAT more straight forward as it is then linked with the accounting part of the transaction not the physical movement of goods or supply of the service. HMRC can, at the taxpayer's request, substitute a period longer than the 14 days. For example, many companies generate all invoices at the end of the month and so some invoices may be generated more than 14 days after the basic tax point. If this is the case then it is likely that this end of month date will be treated as the date of supply.

The impact of VAT on registered traders and final consumers

10.9 The easiest way to illustrate the operation of VAT we have outlined so far in this chapter, and its actual impact on registered traders and their consumers, is to use an example. The following activity illustrates the cascade effect of VAT where traders account for VAT on their value added at each stage in a production process.

Activity

Susan runs a small farm as a business on which she keeps rare breed sheep. She sells fleeces for £200 to a local manufacturer, Country Crafts Ltd, which employs spinners and knitters to produce garments which are sold for a total of £600 to a shop, Country Clothes Ltd, which sells the clothes to members of the public for £1,000. All three businesses are registered for VAT purposes.

None of the above amounts include VAT, which you can assume is levied at the standard rate of 20% on each of the transactions. Calculate the impact of VAT on the transactions described above.

Feedback

Taxable person	Cost (£)	Input tax (£)	Net sales price (£)	Output tax (£)	VAT payable to HMRC (£)
Susan	0	0	200	40	40
Country Crafts	200	40	600	120	80
Country Clothes	600	120	1,000	200	80
					200

Note that the VAT suffered by the final consumer is £200 which is exactly the amount payable to HMRC over the three transactions (£40 + £80 + £80).

Each person has to pay input tax on taxable supplies received and charges output tax on taxable supplies made.

The difference between the output tax charged and input tax paid must be paid to HMRC. This simple example does not illustrate it, but if there is an excess of input tax over output tax the excess can be reclaimed from HMRC.

You can perhaps notice therefore that as registered businesses collect VAT from their customers, but can deduct (reclaim) VAT they pay on their inputs, these businesses are not affected by the direct cost of VAT. The only impacts they suffer are the cost they must bear to administer the tax and any impact on cash flow between when they pay input tax and receive output tax.

Registration and deregistration

10.10 A registered trader is a sole trader, partnership or company who is registered for VAT. Failure to register carries severe penalties as well as a liability to pay the VAT which should have been accounted for.

Initial registration

10.11 A person who makes taxable supplies, but is not already registered for VAT, becomes liable to be registered:

- at the end of any month, if the value of taxable supplies for the preceding 12 months has exceeded £85,000 in 2018/19 (unchanged from 2017/18), or
- at any time, if there are reasonable grounds for believing that the value of taxable supplies in the period of the next 30 days will exceed £85,000.

In determining the value of a trader's supplies for this purpose supplies of goods or services that are capital assets of the business are ignored.

The second of these tests is referred to as the future prospects rule and is designed to capture large, one off transactions that are standard rated. Traders can avoid registration under this rule, however, if HMRC can be persuaded that the business has only exceeded the limit because of unusual circumstances and its turnover will fall below the deregistration threshold once they have passed. In a recent case, *Mark Mills-Henning v Revenue & Customs Commissioners* [2012] UKFTT 444, the trader had a sudden short period of increased sales that took the business over the threshold, but because the turnover then fell so that it was below the threshold, his accountant didn't seek exemption from registration. The Tribunal found that Mr Mills-Henning should have been registered from the date the business exceeded the registration threshold. The decision whether to allow exemption from registration must be made by HMRC, and not by the trader.

The trader will be registered from the end of the month following the 12-month period in which they exceeded the limit. If HMRC and the trader agree to an earlier date, this will be used instead.

If a trader's taxable supplies will not exceed £85,000, then they are not required to register for but they may choose to do so, as we will see later.

Where a business is split so as to keep each part below the registration threshold, HMRC can treat it as a single business in determining if registration is required.

As soon as it becomes known that a trader is required to register they should keep VAT records and begin to charge VAT on any taxable outputs they supply (although they cannot issue VAT invoices until a VAT registration number is received). During this period the trader should notify customers that the price charged is VAT inclusive and a full tax invoice should be sent within 30 days of receiving the registration number.

Traders who should register, but fail to do so, will still be liable for VAT on taxable supplies made from the date on which they should have registered. If it is not possible to collect the VAT due from customers retrospectively, then they will be liable themselves for the tax they should have collected. This could prove very expensive of course as it could equate to up to 20% of the value of all the supplies made since they should have registered.

Fiscal Fact

The cost to the government of allowing small traders not to register for VAT where their turnover doesn't exceed the registration threshold is estimated to be £2.1 billion for 2017/18. [Source: HMRC Estimated costs of principal tax reliefs – updated January 2018]

Voluntary registration

10.12 It is possible to register for VAT even if the business' turnover is below the registration limit. There are a number of benefits of voluntary registration:

- input tax suffered can now be reclaimed; and
- the trader may appear to be a larger business than they actually are which may increase their status with customers.

The key disadvantages of voluntary registration are:

- customers who are not VAT registered cannot reclaim the output tax now charged on the supply and so the trader may lose their competitive edge with non-registered customers; and
- the administrative burden of registration (e.g. completing quarterly VAT returns and handling queries from HMRC) should not be overlooked.

The tax status of a trader's customers is an important factor when deciding whether voluntary registration is likely to be beneficial. Let's consider this in a little more detail with an example.

Activity

Elaine makes patchwork quilts. She can make a maximum of 40 quilts in a year which she can sell on the open market for £500 each (before VAT). She does not think that customers would be willing to pay any more. Alternatively, she has been made an offer to sell her total production for the year to an exclusive retail outlet, again for £500 a quilt excluding VAT. The materials to make a quilt cost £100 before VAT.

Under what circumstances should Elaine apply for voluntary registration for VAT?

Feedback

Sales to public	If registered £	If not registered £
Value of supply		
40 × (£500 × 120%)	24,000	
40 × £500		20,000
Less output VAT		
40 × (£500 × 20%)	(4,000)	
Net sales	20,000	20,000
Less costs 40 × £120	(4,800)	(4,800)
Reclaimed VAT	800	nil
Profit	16,000	15,200

The difference in the two positions is therefore a result of the extra cost to Elaine of her input tax – if she is a registered trader, this is not a cost she will have to bear. However, if she registers she will need to start charging her customers £600 (£500 + 20%) for her quilts, rather than £500 if she does not register. She must be certain that her sales will not be offset by this extra price as she only needs to lose 2 sales of her 40 to then have a lower overall profit.

If Elaine took the option of selling to the retailer instead, the numbers would be the same (i.e. a profit of £16,000 if she registered and £15,200 if she did not) but now as long as the retail outlet was also a registered trader, then the extra cost associated with the output VAT charge would not directly affect this transaction. It would just become part of the retail outlet's input VAT which they can then reclaim. It would be up to the retailer how much of this extra cost to pass on to their own customers.

Deregistration

10.13 Deregistration may also be compulsory or voluntary. Compulsory deregistration will occur if the trader ceases to make taxable supplies.

A trader may ask to be voluntarily deregistered if they can satisfy HMRC their taxable supplies, net of VAT, for the following 12 months will not exceed £83,000, the deregistration limit for this year (unchanged from 2017/18). Traders can not claim to be voluntarily deregistered if they intend to cease to trade (it will be compulsory when they do cease to trade) or if there will be a suspension of taxable supplies for a continuous period of 30 days or more in the next 12 months (their registration cannot be suspended therefore by trading inactivity alone).

The date of a voluntary deregistration is the later of the date on which the request is made or an agreed date between the trader and HMRC.

Fiscal Fact

The number of registered VAT traders was 2.199 million in 2017/18. This was compared with 1.961 million in 2008/9 and 978,000 in 1972/3, the year VAT was introduced. [Source: HMRC Statistics - Number of taxpayers and registered traders]

Taxable supplies and exempt supplies

10.14 The example above (Elaine) illustrated the use of the standard rate (20% currently) for calculating the VAT due. There are actually three possible rates of VAT. The standard rate of 20%, a reduced rate (5%) and zero (i.e. 0%). It might appear strange to have a rate of 0% for some items, but it is an important part of the VAT system as we will see later. The general rule is that any supply that is not exempt, reduced rated or zero rated will be taxable at the standard rate. In this section we consider what types of supply fall in these categories and how this classification affects the VAT system.

Exempt supplies

10.15 The exemptions to VAT are contained in Schedule 9 of the VATA 1994. The Schedule contains a number of groups, which are listed here, together with some important examples of exempt goods and services.

Group 1	Land, including:

- granting of any interest in or right over land
- holiday accommodation
- mooring fees including anchoring and berthing.

Group 2	Insurance.
Group 3	Postal services provided by the post office.
Group 4	Betting, gaming and lotteries.
Group 5	Financial services. Including:

- provision of credit
- issue, transfer or receipt of, or any dealing with, any security or secondary security.

Group 6	Education, including:

- provision of education or research by a school, eligible institution or university or independent private tutor
- supply of any goods or services incidental to the provision of any education, training or re-training.

Group 7　Health and welfare, including:
- supply of services by registered medical practitioners, ophthalmic opticians and dentists
- provision of spiritual welfare by a religious institution as part of a course of instruction or a retreat.

Group 8　Burial and cremation.

Group 9　Supplies to trade unions and professional bodies if in consideration for membership.

Group 10　Entry fees for sports competitions (if non profit making).

Group 11　Works of art when disposed of to public bodies.

Group 12　Fund-raising events by charities and other qualifying bodies (this was extended in the 2000 Budget to include participative events and events on the internet).

Group 13　Provision of cultural services (e.g. admission charges for museums, zoos, galleries, exhibitions, etc).

Group 14　Supplies of goods with unrecoverable input tax.

Group 15　Gold purchased as an investment.

A business of making any of these exempt supplies cannot charge VAT on the supply to a customer. If the trader only makes exempt supplies, they cannot register for VAT and therefore cannot reclaim any input tax they pay. Effectively, they become the final consumer in any supply chain and therefore must bear the full VAT costs as part of the costs of their business.

Fiscal Fact

For 2017/18, exempting education from VAT is estimated to cost the Government £3.9 billion, rent on domestic dwellings £5.8 billion, health services exemption £3.7 billion, postal services £300 million; finance and insurance £10.9 billion and betting/gaming/lottery dues £1.5 billion. [Source: HMRC Estimated costs of principal tax reliefs 2018]

Zero rated supplies

10.16 Zero rated goods and services are defined in Schedule 8 of the VATA 1983. The Schedule has a number of groups, listed below, together with some important examples of zero rated goods and services.

Group 1　Food, including:
- food of a kind used for human consumption
- animal feeding stuffs.

Exceptions include (these are standard rated instead):
- supply in the course of catering, including all food which is consumed on the premises and all hot food

- ice cream, confectionery and chocolate biscuits
- spirits, beer and wine
- pet food.

Group 2   Sewerage services and water for non-industrial use

Group 3   Books, including:
- books, booklets, brochures, pamphlets and leaflets (but not stationery).
- newspapers, journals and periodicals.

Group 4   Talking books for the blind and handicapped and wireless sets for the blind when supplied to a charity.

Group 5   Construction or conversion of buildings, for residential or charitable purposes.

Group 6   Sale by builders of restored 'protected buildings' (i.e. listed) if used for residential or charitable purposes.

Group 7   International services.

Group 8   Transport (apart from those with less than 10 seats which are standard rated, such as a taxi or hire car).

Group 9   Caravans and houseboats.

Group 10   Gold supplied between capital banks (through a new scheme of investment gold was introduced at the start of 2000).

Group 11   Bank notes.

Group 12   Drugs, medicines, as prescribed by a medical practitioner and aids for the handicapped.

Group 13   Certain exports, etc. (see further explanation on export handling later)

Group 14   Tax-free shops.

Group 15   Sales by charities of donated goods and some supplies to charities e.g. some advertising (not for paid staff), etc.

Group 16   Children's clothing and footwear and some protective clothing e.g. crash helmets and bike helmets (children's and adults – latter being added in the Finance Act 2001).

The VAT system is complex and full of anomalies, for example, individual knitting patterns are taxable supplies but booklets containing more than one pattern are zero rated. The classification or exclusion of supplies into or from groups gives rise to lots of disputes and litigation between taxpayers and HMRC.

Fiscal Fact

Currently the UK and Ireland are the only EU countries to zero rate food, water, books or children's clothes. It is estimated the cost of zero rating these items will be £23.75 billion in foregone tax revenues for 2017/18. [Source: HMRC Estimated costs of principal tax reliefs 2018]

A zero rated supply is a taxable supply; the VAT is calculated at 0% – but it is in effect charged, and therefore not the same as being exempt. Businesses making zero rated supplies can still register and reclaim input tax as a taxable person. As such, businesses will often prefer to be classed as making a zero rated supply rather than exempt supplies. Traders making only zero rated supplies can request exemption from registration. Traders with this exemption are responsible for notifying HMRC if there is any change in the nature of their supplies.

The standard rating of hot food became very controversial following the announcement at Budget 2012 of a simplification of the rule for deciding whether the food is 'hot' or not. The change would bring food such as pasties into the standard rated net, when previously they had been treated by some retailers as zero rated. This has been referred to as the 'pasty tax' and caused strident protests. The change was due to take effect in October 2012, but the Government subsequently backed down in the face of public opposition and pasties will now not attract standard rate VAT under certain conditions. This is an example of the approach of the coalition government, which has on several occasions announced tax changes and then not carried them through. It is also an example of the complexities in VAT that arise from the attempt to achieve equity by zero rating basic foodstuffs.

Reduced rated supplies

10.17 A handful of items that would normally fall into the standard rated category are, by special exception instead, taxed at a reduced rate of 5%. These are termed reduced rate supplies. This category includes:

- Domestic fuel or power (or for charity use);
- Installation of energy-saving materials in the home or a charity property (e.g. loft insulation);
- Government grant-funded installation, maintenance and repair of central heating systems or water heating system in homes;
- Ground source heat pumps (new from 1 June, 2004);
- Qualifying security goods installed in the homes of qualifying pensioners (when installed as part of a Government grant funded scheme);
- Renovations and alterations of homes that have been left unoccupied for at least two years;
- Women's sanitary products;
- Children's car seats, seat bases and booster seats/cushions;
- Certain conversions, alterations or renovations of non-residential property into residential property;

- Contraceptives (from 1 July 2006 – although note that prescription contraceptives are a zero rated supply);
- Nicotine patches and gum (and related 'over the counter', non-prescription, smoking cessation products). Initially this is for one year only (1 July, 2007 to 30 June, 2008) but was extended in Budget 08; and
- Housing alterations to provide mobility aids for the elderly, for example, grab rails and stair lifts (from 1 July, 2007).

Fiscal Fact

The cost to the Treasury of reduced rated supplies of domestic fuel and power is estimated to be £4.65 billion for 2016/17. [Source: HMRC Estimated costs of principal tax reliefs 2018]

The VAT fraction (for determining VAT exclusive costs from a VAT inclusive price) on reduced rated items is $1/21$ (i.e. $5 \div (100 + 5)$).

Accounting for VAT

You next need to understand the principles of accounting for VAT in a business and you need to know the basic legislation and practices which deal with the accounting for VAT.

VAT returns

10.18 Registered traders will pay and collect VAT over a *tax period*. They must submit a *VAT return*, together with any VAT payable, within one month of the end of a tax period.

A tax period is the length of time covered by their VAT return. It is normally three months long and ends on the last day of a month. HMRC have classified trades and businesses into various groups and allocate a tax period to a registering business, by reference to the type of trade that is being carried on, when the business first registers for VAT. This enables HMRC to spread their work evenly throughout the year so they receive roughly equal numbers of VAT returns each month. However, variations on this general rule are allowed. For example, a trader who operates four-week periods can apply to use this basis for VAT periods rather than using month ends. Some businesses also prefer to have one of the tax periods ending on the same date as the accounting year end to aid their accounting process and this is likely to be acceptable to HMRC.

It is even possible to shorten the length of the tax periods to one month. This would be attractive to traders who regularly receive a repayment of VAT (i.e. their input tax regularly exceeds their output tax for reasons we will explore later), and so could decrease the impact of VAT on their cash flow. However, this option carries the penalty of having to complete twelve VAT returns a year and so may not be a favourable option for many smaller businesses.

At the other extreme, small businesses can elect to complete only one tax return a year, although they must still pay VAT throughout the year (see below).

A transaction must be accounted for in the tax period in which the tax point occurs. The transaction is subject to the relevant rate of VAT which prevails on the date of the tax point.

A VAT return, called a VAT 100, is completed at the end of each tax period and sent to HMRC (in paper form or also now via electronic submissions if the registered person wants to do it this way – although from April 2008 returns have had to be electronically filed for businesses with turnover exceeding £5.6million. From 1 April 2010, newly registered businesses and those with turnover greater than or equal to £100,000 have to file their VAT returns on-line. The VAT return includes the following information:

- output tax collected in the period
- input tax paid in the period
- net amount payable or repayable
- value of supplies to other EU countries
- value of acquisitions from other EU countries
- input VAT due on acquisitions from other EU countries.

If an excess of input over output tax exists for the period this is repayable to the business. If the output tax exceeds the input tax (as would be normal for most businesses that are profitable over time) this difference will be paid over to HMRC from the sums collected by the registered person during the period.

Fiscal Fact

From 4 January 2011 the Government raised the VAT rate to 20% from its previous level of 17.5%. At that time they estimated that this would create additional tax revenue of £2.8 billion in 2010/11 and between £12-13 billion in each of the next 4 years.

Tax invoices

10.19 Once a person is registered for VAT they must provide a tax invoice to other registered people whenever they make a taxable supply to them. The trader must also retain a copy of the tax invoice (in paper or electronic form) to illustrate what output tax has been charged on the supplies they have made.

A tax invoice must include at least:

- supplier's name, address and registration number
- tax point
- invoice number
- name and address of the customer
- description of the goods or services including, for each type of goods or services supplied:
  - quantity purchased
  - unit price where supply can be measured in units
  - rate of tax
  - tax exclusive amount
  - type of supply, for example sale or hire
  - rate of any cash discount available and separate totals of the cash discounts which applies to zero rated and exempt supplies.

Retailers may issue less detailed invoices when the VAT inclusive total value of the supply is less than £250. They need only disclose:

- supplier's name, address and registration number
- date of the supply
- a description of the goods or services supplied
- rate of tax
- the total amount chargeable including VAT.

From January 2004 a European Commission directive (2001/115/EC) on invoicing came into force in the UK. These rules make the general items of information mandatory as listed above but also add additional items if necessary. They allow invoicing of small businesses and for small valued items to be simplified further than in the past and allow for electronic transfers of VAT invoices in some circumstances. They also introduced rules for outsourcing the burden associated with accounting for VAT – even allowing customers to self bill (i.e. generate invoices for themselves) under some circumstances.

From 1 January 2013, the EU rules for electronic invoicing were further simplified so that member states can no longer impose conditions on the use of electronic invoices provided that the customer agrees to the use of electronic invoicing. This means that paper and electronic invoices are now treated the same for VAT purposes.

Cash operated machines, for example in car parks, do not need to provide a tax invoice if the total value of the invoice is less than £25. Purchasers can still reclaim the input tax on these costs even though they do not have a tax invoice, as a practical concession from HMRC.

Mixed supplies

10.20 Sometimes goods and services are sold as a unit but are, in fact, made up of a mixture of standard rated, reduced rated, zero rated or exempt supplies. For example, if a book and cassette tape is sold together, perhaps as a foreign language course, the book is zero rated and the tape is standard rated. This is called making a mixed supply.

In this case the supplier must apportion the value of the supply between the different components using an equitable basis. VAT is then levied on each part at the appropriate rate. The legislation does not offer one method to be used to apportion the value, but acceptable methods are likely to include apportionment using the cost to the supplier of the components and apportionment using the open market value of each component.

Sometimes it may not be possible to apportion the value in this way. It is then necessary to consider the sale as a composite supply and one rate will be applied to the whole of the supply.

Cash discounts

10.21 Prior to 1 April 2015, with the exception of imports from non-EU member states, if a cash discount was offered for early settlement of an invoice (prompt payment discount), then VAT was levied on the value of the supply net of the cash discount. This rule applied whether the discount was actually taken up, or not. With effect from 1 April 2015, this concession has been removed and VAT is now payable on the full consideration paid.

Input tax: more detail

10.22 So far we have simply suggested that registered traders can reclaim input tax they pay against output tax they charge provided that they have a VAT invoices to prove these amounts. In principle this is correct, but there are a number of special situations that you need to know about where these basic principles of VAT are varied.

We will start by considering capital expenditure, then VAT and cars, and finally list the occasions on which input tax cannot be reclaimed or restrictions on reclaiming may be imposed.

Capital expenditure

10.23 Capital expenditure is not usually differentiated from revenue expenditure for VAT purposes. All input tax is therefore fully recoverable as it is incurred.

When a capital asset is disposed of, then VAT is charged on the disposal price just as for any other taxable supply.

VAT and cars

10.24 The exception to the VAT on capital expenditure rules is the treatment of cars. Generally, input tax on cars cannot be reclaimed. Equally, registered traders do not account for output tax when the car is subsequently sold, unless it is sold at a profit, when output tax must be levied on the profit element. However, there are a number of exceptions to these rules. VAT can be reclaimed on cars:

- acquired new and intended to be sold (i.e. if you are a car dealer);
- intended to be leased to or used in a taxi business, a self-drive hire business or a driving school.

Where input VAT on a car is recoverable, output VAT must be accounted for in the usual way when the car is eventually disposed of.

Accessories bought at the same time as the car suffer the same treatment as the car itself, but if they are acquired and fitted after the car was acquired, the input VAT can be reclaimed, provided that the expenditure is for business use.

Travelling and car maintenance costs

10.25 While VAT on the acquisition of a new car is generally not recoverable, what happens to the VAT on petrol and maintenance costs?

By concession, provided that a car is owned by a business and used for some business purposes, the VAT on the full cost of any repair and maintenance costs is reclaimable, even if the car is also partly used for private purposes.

VAT on fuel used for business purposes is reclaimable even if the fuel is paid for by an employee who is then reimbursed, either through a mileage allowance or by repayment of the cost of the fuel.

If a business provides its employees with petrol for private use, and the employee does not fully reimburse the company for the cost of the fuel, the business is considered to have made a taxable supply of that fuel to the employee. VAT car fuel scale charge tables can be accessed from HMRC website to show how this output tax should be charged. However, if the business chooses not to try to reclaim the input tax on the fuel they do not have to account for this special output tax.

If an employee reimburses an employer for the cost of either the use of the car or any private fuel used, then the payment is treated as if it were VAT inclusive provided that the payment is equal to or exceeds the cost of the fuel.

Bad debts

10.26 What happens when a supply is made to a customer, VAT is charged, but the customer doesn't pay, i.e. the debt goes bad? In this situation, the trader can obtain a refund of the amount of tax chargeable on that debt. Where the trader has supplied goods or services and has accounted for and paid tax on the supply, if either the whole or any part of the debt has subsequently been written off in the accounts as an impairment loss, and a period of six months from the date on which payment was due has elapsed, the trader is entitled to a refund of the output tax previously paid.

On the opposite side, registered traders must repay any input VAT which they have reclaimed on supplies for which they have not actually paid and on which bad debt relief is then claimed by the supplier, as we have just discussed. This ensures repayments made to suppliers for their bad debts are collected from the buyers whose debt was not paid and so the Government does not end up 'out of pocket'.

Those who use the annual accounting scheme for VAT (explained later in this chapter), and hence only complete one VAT return a year, will be able to account for output tax and claim bad debt relief on the same return.

VAT recovery on registration

10.27 When a business first registers for VAT, it may have already paid input tax prior to registration. The question then arises, what can be recovered once registered? The VAT regulations allow for recovery of VAT on assets used in the business for resale that were bought in the previous four years and on services received in the six months before registration. The newly registered business can recover this input tax in its first VAT return, or any time within the first four years of registration.

Input tax specifically disallowed

10.28 In addition to non-recoverable input tax on the acquisition of cars discussed above registered traders also cannot reclaim input tax on expenditure on:

- Business entertaining, unless the expense is allowable for income tax or corporation tax purposes e.g. entertaining overseas customers (see Chapter 6.4 for more on this).
- Living accommodation being paid for by the business on behalf of its directors.
- Non-business items which have been recorded in the business accounts.

If the taxable supply is partly for business use and partly for private use, the registered trader may either reclaim all of the input tax, and then account for output tax on the value of the supply taken for private use, or reclaim only the business element of the input tax. If the taxable supply is a service, then only the second method can be used.

Note that non-reclaimable input tax is deductible as an expense for income tax, corporation tax and capital gains tax purposes, just like other expenses, if the related expenditure is deductible for trading income or capital gains tax purposes.

Self-supply

10.29 A self-supply occurs when a trader produces a marketable output and then instead of selling it, uses it during the course of their business instead. For example, a business may own a printing operation which produces stationery which is used by the business.

If a trader makes a supply to themselves, output tax must be charged as if it were a supply to a third party. Input tax charged on the supply is only reclaimable up to the level of output tax they charged themselves on the supply. (i.e. input tax reclaimed cannot exceed output tax on the supply).

Partial exemption

10.30 Input tax is only recoverable if it has been paid on acquiring goods and services which are directly attributable to taxable supplies made by the trader. Remember that taxable supplies covers standard rated, reduced rated and zero rated supplies.

If a trader's outputs consist of both taxable and exempt supplies, then the rule is that only input tax which relates to taxable outputs is recoverable. The trader cannot reclaim input tax on the goods or services they purchased that went into making their exempt output supplies. This type of trader is referred to as 'partially exempt' to recognise this fact.

This necessary matching of inputs and taxable outputs is achieved by firstly determining how much input tax can be related directly to taxable outputs and exempt outputs. The input tax which relates directly to taxable outputs is fully reclaimable and that which relates to exempt supplies is not deductible. The remaining input tax is apportioned between taxable supplies and exempt supplies by using the percentage:

$$\frac{\text{Taxable turnover excluding VAT}}{\text{Total turnover excluding VAT}} \times 100$$

This is then rounded up to the next whole percentage point. The following items are omitted from this calculation:

- goods acquired and sold without any work being done to them.
- self-supplies.
- capital goods acquired for use within the business.

HMRC may be willing to allow an alternative basis to be used to allocate input tax between taxable and exempt supplies but this will not happen automatically and the trader will need to seek approval directly for the use of any alternative method.

As a concession to this allocation rule, if the amount of input tax which is deemed to relate to exempt supplies is less than an average of £625 a month (£7,500 pa) the above apportionment is ignored and all of the input tax is reclaimable anyway. This concession helps to reduce some of the compliance costs that would arise for managing a very small amount of exempt input tax.

The treatment of partial exemption is a complex area of the VAT rules and many cases exist in this area.

Since 1 April 2009, it is possible for a registered trader to use last year's annual percentage rather than perform separate calculations for each quarter. A potential problem with using last year's annual percentage is that actual proportions of total to taxable supplies might vary during the year, but it has the advantage of smoothing out seasonal fluctuations and may help the cash flow of the business. An annual adjustment is required in the final VAT return for the year.

Special schemes

10.31 You need to be aware of some of the special VAT schemes which are available to registered traders that affect how VAT is accounted for between the trader and HMRC. There are many VAT schemes in operation (and new ones are introduced from time to time). We illustrate only the most commonly used ones here. The payments on account scheme (see later) is compulsory for large organisations but other schemes are offered to taxpayers on a voluntary basis. The schemes don't normally alter the amount of VAT which must be paid (the exception being the new flat rate scheme which is deliberately designed to do this); they merely affect either the date of payments to HMRC or the administration of VAT.

In practice the take-up of these voluntary schemes is very low despite the apparent attractiveness of some of them. This may be partly due to the stringent conditions for joining the schemes, some of which have been relaxed in recent budgets to encourage wider take-up as we will see.

The payments on account scheme

10.32 Companies which have to pay £2 million a year or more to HMRC complete their VAT returns in the normal way once each quarter but are required to make two payments on account in each quarter in addition to the usual end of quarter payment. The first payment is made a month before the end of the quarter and the second payment is made at the end of the tax period. The final payment, which is sufficient to cover the remaining VAT liability for the tax period, is made at the usual time, i.e. one month after the end of the tax period. This means, in practice, that the trader will make a payment to HMRC at the end of each month of the year.

HMRC will use the previous twelve months' information in order to determine the monthly payments of the scheme members usually on the basis of 1/24th of the trader's total VAT liability for the previous year. Traders can opt to pay their actual VAT liability instead, however, if they so wish. This may be cheaper for them to do if their activity is less than in the previous year.

The cash accounting scheme

10.33 The cash accounting scheme allows members to bend the normal tax point rules we examined earlier in the chapter. Instead members of this scheme can use the following tax points:

- for output tax; the day on which payment or other consideration is received, or the date of any cheque, if later.
- for input tax; the date on which payment is made or other consideration is given, or the date of any cheque, if later.

This means members of the scheme only pay VAT on actual cash transactions. This can provide a considerable cash flow advantage to many businesses as it also avoids them having to deduct output tax on a VAT return when they have not yet received the payment from their customer.

Taxable persons are eligible for admission to the scheme if:

- the value of their taxable supplies for the next year after application is not likely to exceed £1,350,000;
- they have made all the returns which they are required to make and all their VAT payments are up to date
- they have not, in the last twelve months up to date of application, been convicted of any VAT offence.

The scheme does not apply to hire purchase agreements, conditional sale agreements or credit sale agreements.

Members of the scheme may remain in the scheme unless at the end of any quarter or relevant accounting period the value of taxable supplies made in the 12 months up to that point has exceeded £1,600,000 and in the year then beginning is expected to exceed £1,600,000. If this is the case, they must notify HMRC and stop operating the scheme on the anniversary of joining it.

Current members can withdraw themselves from the scheme if:

- they want to at any point; or
- they are unable to comply with the requirements of the scheme for any reason (e.g. their accounting systems do not comply).

HMRC can terminate membership of the scheme in certain circumstances.

A person whose membership has been terminated must account for, and pay in the current period, all the tax they owe to return to the normal VAT rules.

Fiscal Fact

Budget 2007 estimated that the increase in the cash accounting threshold to £1.35 million (from £600,000 as it was before April 2007) would allow an extra 56,000 businesses to benefit from the scheme.

The annual accounting scheme

10.34 Under this scheme, members:

- pay 90% of tax liability as estimated by HMRC for that current accounting year. This payment is normally made by direct debit from their bank account in nine equal monthly instalments commencing on the last day of the fourth month of their current accounting year. An option to pay in three larger instalments in the year was also introduced with effect from 25 April, 2002. Payments are then equal to 25% of the previous year's VAT liability.
- supply a return for the year by the last day of the second month following the end of that accounting year, together with any outstanding payment due to HMRC for their liability for tax declared on the return.

Taxable persons are eligible to apply for membership of the scheme if:

- the value of taxable supplies in the year from the date of application to join will not exceed £1,350,000;
- they have made all the VAT returns which they are required to make;
- total credits for input tax did not exceed total output tax in the year prior to application for authorisation; and
- they have not had membership terminated in the three years preceding the date of application for authorisation.

Members can remain in the scheme once they have been allowed to join unless:

- at the end of any current accounting year the value of the taxable supplies made by them in that year has exceeded £1,600,000, in which case their authorisation will be terminated immediately;
- at any time the value of taxable supplies made so far in the current accounting year will exceed £1,600,000 in which case they have 30 days in which to notify HMRC who may then terminate their membership

They are expelled from the scheme for non-compliance with its rules. As with the cash accounting scheme, HMRC can terminate membership in certain circumstances.

Activity

Why may a business choose to use the annual accounting scheme?

Feedback

The annual accounting scheme is useful in managing business cash flows as payments are predictable throughout the year and only one VAT return needs to be completed, helping to reduce compliance costs. However, it does require monitoring of the various membership limits to ensure the turnover maximum is not exceeded as well as some planning to ensure monies are available for payments when they fall due, irrespective of the cash flow position of the business. If you are down-scaling your business, or just having a less profitable year, larger payments may need to be paid than would otherwise be the case as payments due will be based on the previous year's figures. This is of course reversed if you have a better year again the following year.

Retail schemes

10.35 There are a number of special schemes which are used by retailers. The normal VAT legislation requires registered traders to maintain detailed records of every transaction. Retailers who make a mixture of standard rated, zero rated and exempt supplies face particular problems with accounting correctly for VAT. Retailers are allowed therefore to keep less detailed records by using one of the schemes and calculate output tax in a way which better suits their circumstances. Some of the schemes require totals for different sorts of supply rather than details of individual transactions while others allow the VAT liability to be estimated using purchases and mark-up percentages. The retail schemes are only available to retailers who cannot reasonably be expected to account for VAT in the normal way.

Retail schemes are not just for small traders. Individually agreed schemes for businesses with taxable retail turnover in excess of £100 million per annum have recently been introduced. From 1 April 2009, retailers with a turnover of more than £130million are required to enter into bespoke schemes and are no longer able to use the published schemes.

The second-hand goods scheme

10.36 The second-hand goods scheme is available to traders who buy second-hand goods from individuals who are not registered traders. HMRC can allow a reduction on the taxable supply amounts of such second-hand goods as such traders will typically have to charge output tax but not have any input tax to offset against it. The maximum reduction available is equal to the amount of tax which would have been due had the purchase of the goods been a normal taxable supply. This means that VAT is due only on the trader's profit margin rather than on the total sales price of the goods. Hence the trader has to only account for output tax of $1/6^{th}$ of the difference between their purchase price and their selling price.

Under this scheme the member selling the second-hand goods does not have to create a tax invoice when they make a sale. A registered trader who buys goods from a trader who is using the second-hand goods scheme will not therefore be able to reclaim the input tax because he or she will not have received a tax invoice.

This scheme can apply to sales of all second-hand goods, works of art, antiques and collectors' items. The scheme cannot, however, be applied to precious metals and gemstones.

Flat rate scheme

10.37 The flat rate scheme has been available since 25 April, 2002, and is for businesses with VAT-exclusive taxable turnover of up to £150,000 per annum.

The scheme allows businesses to account for VAT using a flat rate percentage applied to their tax-inclusive turnover (including exempt or zero rated supplies). The rate that applies depends on the nature of the business as different flat rates will apply to different businesses. To illustrate the range in these rates; the lowest flat rates can be enjoyed by suppliers of food and of children's clothing (flat rate of 4% applies) whereas the highest rate applies to suppliers such as builders who charge for labour only, accountants, architects and IT consultants (flat rate of 14.5% applies).

While many of the rates remain unchanged since the start of the scheme, several have been changed, for example, the rate applicable to accountancy or bookkeeping was 11.5% in 2009, then 13% in 2010 and 2011 and is 14.5% from 4 January 2011. In addition, newly registered businesses are now entitled to an extra 1% discount in their first year of operation.

The government is concerned that the flat rate scheme is being abused by so called 'limited cost traders', for example those who purchase no goods and so suffer limited input tax. From 1 April 2017, traders that meet the definition of limited cost traders will be liable for a new 16.5% rate under the flat rate scheme.

The full range of rates for both levels of VAT can be found on the HMRC website.

Businesses using this scheme still issue VAT invoices to and collect VAT from their customers but don't have to track input or output VAT specifically to calculate their VAT charge or repayment. The only exception to this is for capital purchases in excess of £2,000 (VAT inclusive). For such purchases traders who normally use the flat rate systems can recover the input tax on these purchases directly in the normal way (i.e. as for non-flat rate users). Of course, if these assets are subsequently sold, full VAT must be charged on the sale price and accounted for as output tax in the usual way.

The use of the flat rate scheme could save businesses significant compliance effort by reducing much of the separate accounting that is otherwise needed for recording the input and output VAT appropriately. This scheme needs careful monitoring, however, as it may not produce a lower tax bill for all business depending on the specific make-up of supplies and other inputs they buy.

In a recent case a mechanical engineer registered for the Flat Rate Scheme and, on advice from his accountant, adopted a flat rate of 12% which applies to activities not listed elsewhere. HMRC argued that he should have been registered under the category 'architect, civil and structural engineer or surveyor' with a rate of 14.5%. The taxpayer challenged this, and won in the first tier tribunal. This further demonstrates the need to take care when entering into this scheme, to make sure the appropriate flat rate is used, and also that HMRC are prepared to argue about the categorisation.

Imports and exports

10.38 Since the creation of a Europe without trade barriers (the 'Single Market') on 1 January, 1993 it has become necessary to differentiate between transactions with traders resident in other countries in the European Union and those resident in countries outside the European Union when a trader completes a

VAT return. The way we account for VAT on transaction with these two groups of purchasers and suppliers is different. We will outline differences in this section.

Imports

10.39 Imports into the UK may come from other EU member states or from countries which are not members of the EU. The VAT treatment of imports depends on the source country of the goods.

We will discuss the detail of the arrangements which are currently in force within the EU member states later in this section. First, we will consider imports from countries from outside the EU.

Goods

10.40 Tax on the importation of goods from places outside the member states will be charged and payable as if it were a customs duty. VAT due and any associated customs duty on imports is often in fact paid at the same time by traders. The rate of the duty is the same as the rate which would apply if the same goods were supplied in the home market by a registered trader. The registered trader is then able to reclaim the duty paid on the goods as input tax in the normal way.

A registered trader can apply for approval to make deferred payments until a fixed payment day once a month. Payment day is the 15th day of the next month following the one in which the amount of duty deferred fell due to be paid. Each period under this scheme commences on the 16th day of a month and ends on the 15th day of the next month. On each payment day an approved person has to pay to the Commissioners the total amount of customs duty deferred.

The Budget 2016 introduced further anti-avoidance rules for overseas traders who use online marketplaces to sell goods into the UK. Where they fail to comply with UK VAT rules they will be required to appoint a UK tax representative to deal with their VAT obligations and HMRC will notify their online marketplace of their non-compliance. If they continue to be non-compliant, HMRC will then require the VAT due to be paid by the online marketplace. This, they hope, will encourage the online marketplaces to police the tax compliance behaviour of those they allow to trade via their services more effectively. They are very unlikely to wish to pay over VAT due for their traders that they have not collected!

Services

10.41 If services are supplied to a registered trader who is UK resident by a person resident overseas, either within the EU or from outside the EU, the *reverse charge system* is used.

Relevant services include:

- transfers and assignments of copyright, patents, licences, trademarks and similar rights;
- advertising services;
- services of consultants, engineers, consultancy bureaux, lawyers, accountants and other similar services; data processing and provision of information;
- banking, financial and insurance services including re-insurance; any other service supplied to a registered trader provided that it is not exempt.

The reverse charge system requires the recipient trader to treat the supply received as if they were also the supplier. This means they account for a notional output tax, which then becomes the actual input tax on the supply.

Overseas (non-EU) companies can register for VAT in the UK if they wish to. If they do so they then follow the usual rules for charging VAT on their supplies we have examined in this chapter. Under this circumstance no reverse charging is then necessary by the recipient of the supply, even though the supplier comes from outside the EU.

Non-EU based suppliers of broadcast electronic services (e.g. via the Internet) to UK based non-registered recipients have also been required to charge VAT from July 2003 at the rate applicable for that sale in the customers' country. This, in effect, requires some non-EU based suppliers to become registered traders in at least one EU member country and to comply with their VAT regulations in making suppliers of services in the rest of the EU. That member state country will reimburse any taxes due to countries to whom that supplier has made supplies.

Imports of works of art, antiques and collectors' pieces from outside the EU are subject to VAT at a reduced rate of 2.5%.

Exports

10.42 A supply of goods is zero rated if HMRC are satisfied that the person supplying the goods has:

- exported them to a place outside the EU member states (evidence must be produced); or
- shipped them for use as stores on a voyage or flight to an eventual destination outside the UK, or as merchandise for sale by retail to persons carried on such a voyage or flight in a ship or aircraft.

VAT within the EU

10.43 The principles of the EU requires that, in effect, no borders should exist when goods and services are sold or purchased between suppliers and customers in more than one member state. This means that VAT should be applied as if both parties were in fact in the same state. In reality this situation has not yet come about fully. Meanwhile, the current position can be outlined as follows:

If a registered person in one member state supplies goods or services to a registered person in another member state they should make the supply at a zero-rate in the country of origin (i.e. no output tax is accounted for, but input tax associated with the supply can be reclaimed). The customer will then account for output VAT on the purchase in their accounts at whatever VAT rate is applicable in their home country. The VAT suffered can also then be treated as their input tax in their country and accounted for as normal. This is the same reverse charging process as we described above for services purchased from non-EU suppliers by EU registered persons. This has a net effect of zero so that the trader is in the same position as if they have acquired the goods from a trader in their own country. For this system to be applied evidence of the transfer or supply of the goods or services must be available and both traders must be able to provide details of the registration numbers of the other.

If the supply from a registered trader is to a non-registered customer (or one who has not proved their registered status by providing their registration number) then the supply should be made including VAT at the origin country's rate, as if it had been supplied within the supplier's own country. However, watch out for 'direct selling thresholds' that apply as once the volume of sales exceeds a certain limit (which differs from country to country). The supplier will need to register in that country and then be required to charge the local rate of VAT instead, and reimburse that to the local government.

As mentioned above, Budget 2016 tightened rules for collecting VAT due related to non-compliant traders from outside the UK. Tax in future may be collected from online marketplaces if traders fail to comply with their VAT collecting obligations.

Digital services within the EU

10.44 From 1 January 2015 new EU rules came into force for the supply of digital services from business to consumers so that the place of taxation will be determined by the location of the consumer, instead of the supplier as is the case with other supplies. The supplier must account for VAT on the supply at the rate applicable in the consumer's member state, which will remove the competitive advantage of some states with lower VAT rates. Suppliers can either register for VAT in each member state, or can elect to register under an EU wide scheme known as the Mini One Stop Shop (MOSS).

There is no minimum threshold for registration in this new scheme and special support is provided for micro businesses that are below the current UK VAT registration threshold but have to comply with these new rules. This will place an additional compliance burden on all businesses, impacting most heavily on small businesses.

Summary

In this chapter you have read about the operation of VAT, one of the most important taxes in the UK.

VAT has to be paid whenever a taxable person makes a taxable supply of goods or services in the course of business. Unless a supply of goods or services is specifically exempt in the legislation it is a taxable supply. With the exception of domestic fuel and a handful of other supplies, which are taxable at 5%, taxable supplies are either standard rated or zero rated. The standard rate of VAT for the UK was 17.5% for a number of years, but reduced to 15% for the period 1/12/08 to 31/12/09 and then increased to its current rate of 20% from 4/1/11.

A trader must register if turnover exceeds certain limits, for this tax year the limit is £83,000 a year. A trader whose turnover is lower than the registration limit may choose to register voluntarily.

A registered trader is able to reclaim allowable input tax but must account for output tax on taxable supplies.

VAT is normally paid quarterly to HMRC on the basis of invoices received and issued in the quarter. However, there are a considerable number of special schemes, some of which are compulsory for some businesses, which require VAT to be accounted for on a different basis.

There is debate about the acceptability of further increases in the amount of revenue which is raised using indirect taxation. This debate was considered in the first three chapters·

Project areas

Not all countries around the world use a VAT style tax on expenditure. Review how other countries tax expenditure and discuss the relevant merits/disadvantages of each approach.

The harmonisation of VAT within the EU provides considerable scope for dissertation titles. There are also opportunities for comparative studies, for example the special schemes on offer to small businesses in EU member states.

Since 1979 there has been a significant shift in taxation in the UK from direct taxation to indirect taxation. A number of titles may apply in this area, for example, is it possible for there to be further shifts from direct taxes to indirect taxes? Alternatively, would a shift back towards direct taxation be possible or desirable?

Since 1 July, 2003 a VAT regime has been imposed on non-EU companies selling electronic services (e.g. via the web) to European customers. This resulted in VAT having to be charged to consumers of these services where previously they were VAT free. This was welcomed by EU companies, who always had to charge this, but not of course by non-EU based companies. What are the implications of this for the growing market of electronic business related services in the UK?

Another EU development is the introduction of new rules from 1 January 2015 for supply of digital services which requires all businesses to account for VAT at the rate applicable in the consumer's member state. What impact will this have on compliance costs for micro businesses in the UK?

Reduced and zero rating particular items costs the UK Government lots of lost revenue. Should they instead impose a fixed rate on all purchases to collect as much tax as possible – and to improve fiscal neutrality? What would be the implications of so doing?

Quick quiz

1. Kieran makes taxable supplies of £87,000 p.a. Is he required to register for VAT?

2. Louise offers her customers a 5% discount for prompt payment. She sells a standard rated item for £500 in December 2018 to a customer who does not take up the discount. How much VAT should she charge?

3. Maurice owns a business which makes wholly zero rated supplies totalling £50,000 p.a. Should he register for VAT?

4. Nigella is registered for VAT and is partially exempt. During the year she incurred the following input tax:
    – attributable to taxable supplies   £50,000
    – attributable to exempt supplies   £5,000
    – unattributable   £4,000
    The total value of supplies excluding VAT for the year was £500,000 of which £100,000 was exempt. How much of Nigella's input tax is recoverable?

5. Omnibus Ltd is a company that makes office furniture. It received an order on 30 July, delivered the goods to the customer on 20 August and issued an invoice on 30 August. Payment was received on 13 September. What is the tax point for VAT purposes?

6. Portia uses the cash accounting scheme and in the quarter ended 31 September 2018 invoices sales of £6,000 plus VAT; purchases raw materials for cash of £4,000 plus VAT and receives cash from debtors of £5,525. How much VAT is due?

7. Quentin is a VAT registered trader who prepares quarterly returns for quarters ended 31 March, 30 June, 30 September and 31 December, and does not use the cash accounting scheme. He made a supply of goods on 22 September 2018 with a due date for payment of 10 October 2018. The customer did not pay, and Quentin has written the debt off in his accounts. Which quarterly return is the earliest in which relief can be claimed for the impaired debt?

8. Roxanne is a VAT registered trader. On 14 November 2018, she purchased a motor car for £14,000 (VAT inclusive) to use for both business (70%) and private (30%) purposes. The car was damaged in an accident on 5 November 2018 and repairs cost £2,000 (inclusive of VAT). What is the input tax that Roxanne can recover for the quarter ended 31 December 2018?

9. Suzanne has been running a small business for three years and has applied for VAT registration from 1 October 2018. Prior to that date, she had incurred the following expenses:

	£
Legal fees (invoice dated 13 January 2018)	500
Accountancy fees (invoice dated 4 September 2018)	300
Inventory of spare parts on hand on 30 September 2018	250

What amount of pre-registration input VAT can Suzanne recover for these items?

10. Victor commenced trading as a garden centre business on 1 May 2002, and became registered for VAT on the same day. Supplies made (exclusive of VAT) for the 31 October 2018 quarter are:

	£
Standard rated supplies	88,400
Exempt supplies	11,600
Total supplies	100,000

Input tax for the quarter is £24,000, of which £18,000 directly relates to taxable supplies and £1,500 to exempt supplies. How much is Victor's deductible input tax for the quarter ended 31 October 2018?

Questions

Question 1 (based on past CIMA exam question May 1988).

A trader started in business, selling mainly foodstuffs which are zero rated for VAT purposes, on 1 January 2018 and the following information was extracted from his records for the year ended 31 December 2018.
The purchases (but not the sales) are inclusive of VAT.

	£
Fixed assets purchased (all standard rated)	9,000
Other standard rated purchases and expenses	4,000
Sales of zero rated foodstuffs	78,000
Sales of standard rated items	9,000

He approaches you shortly after the end of the year and informs you that he does not intend to register for VAT since 'the sales liable to VAT were well below the threshold'.

Required: Advise him on the position regarding VAT registration, and show the final value added tax position which would have applied for the above year if the trader had registered voluntarily at the start of the year.

Question 2 (based on ACCA June 2015)

Zim has been registered for VAT since 1 April 2010. The following information is available for the year ended 31 March 2019 (all are VAT inclusive where applicable):

(1) Sales invoices totalling £126,000 were issued, of which £115,200 were in respect of standard rated sales. Zim's customers are all members of the general public.

(2) On 31 March 2019, Zim wrote off two impairment losses which were in respect of standard rated sales. The first impairment loss was for £780, and was in respect of a sales invoice which had been due for payment on 15 August 2018. The second impairment loss was for £660, and was in respect of a sales invoice which had been due for payment on 15 September 2018.

(3) Purchase invoices totalling £49,200 were received, of which £43,200 were in respect of standard rated purchases and £6,000 were in respect of zero rated purchases.

(4) Rent of £1,200 is paid each month. During the year ended 31 March 2019, Zim made 13 rental payments because the invoice dated 1 April 2019 was paid early on 31 March 2019. This invoice was in respect of the rent for April 2019.

(5) During the year ended 31 March 2019, Zim spent £2,600 on mobile telephone calls, of which 40% related to private calls.

(6) During the year ended 31 March 2019, Zim spent £1,560 on entertaining customers, of which £240 was in respect of overseas customers.

The expenses referred to in notes (4), (5) and (6) are all standard rated. Zim does not use either the cash accounting or flat rate schemes. He has forecast that for the year ended 31 March 2020, his total sales will be the same as for the year ended 31 March 2019.

Required: Calculate the amount of VAT payable by Zim for the year ended 31 March 2019.

Question 3   (based on ACCA June 2014)

Anne Attire runs a retail clothing shop. She is registered for VAT and is in the process of completing her VAT return for the quarter ended 30 November 2018. The following information is available (all figures are exclusive of VAT):

(1) Cash sales amounted to £42,000, of which £28,000 was in respect of standard rated sales and £14,000 was in respect of zero rated sales.

(2) Sales invoices totalling £12,000 were issued in respect of credit sales. These sales were all standard rated. Ann offers all of her credit sales customers a 5% discount for payment within one month of the date of the sales invoice, and 90% of customers pay within this period. The sales figure of £12,000 is stated before any deduction for the 5% discount.

(3) Purchase and expense invoices totalling £19,200 were received from VAT registered suppliers. This figure is made up as follows:

	£
Standard rated purchases and expenses	11,200
Zero rated purchases	6,000
Exempt expenses	2,000
	19,200

(4) On 30 November 2018, Ann wrote off two impairment losses (bad debts). The first was in respect of a sales invoice due for payment on 15 July 2018. The second impairment loss was for £800, and was in respect of a sales invoice due for payment on 10 April 2018.

Anne does not use the cash accounting scheme.

Anne will soon be 60 years old and is therefore considering retirement. On the cessation of trading, Anne can either sell the fixed assets of the business on a piecemeal basis to individual VAT registered purchasers, or she can sell the entire business as a going concern to a single VAT registered purchaser.

Required:

(a) Calculate the amount of VAT payable by Anne Attire for the quarter ended 30 November 2018, and state the date by which the VAT return for this period was due for submission.

(b) State the conditions that Anne Attire must satisfy before she will be permitted to use the cash accounting scheme, and advise her of the implications of using the scheme.

(c) Advise Anne Attire as to what will happen to her VAT registration, and whether output VAT will be due in respect of the fixed assets, if she ceases trading and then (i) sells her fixed assets on a piecemeal basis to individual VAT registered purchasers, or (ii) sells her entire business as a going concern to a single VAT registered purchaser.

Question 4   (based on ACCA June 2004).

Sandy Brick has been a self-employed builder since 2000. He registered for VAT on 1 January 2019 and is in the process of completing his VAT return for the quarter ended 31 March 2019. The following information is relevant to the completion of this VAT return:

(1) Sales invoices totalling £44,000 (excluding VAT) were issued to VAT registered customers in respect of standard rated sales. Sandy offers his VAT registered customers a 5% discount for prompt payment and 50% of customers took the discount.

(2) Sales invoices totalling £16,920 were issued to customers that were not registered for VAT. Of this figure, £5,170 was in respect of zero rated sales with the balance being in respect of standard rated sales. In this case, standard rated sales are inclusive of VAT.

(3) On 10 January 2019, Sandy received a payment on account of £5,000 in respect of a contract that was completed on 28 April 2019. The total value of the contract is £10,000. Both of these figures are inclusive of VAT at the standard rate.

(4) Standard rated materials amounted to £11,200 of which £800 were used in work on Sandy's private residence (VAT inclusive).

(5) Since 1 December 2011, Sandy has paid £120 per month for the lease of office equipment. This expense is standard rated (VAT inclusive).

(6) During the quarter ended 31 March 2019, £400 (VAT inclusive) was spent on mobile telephone calls, of which 30% relates to private calls. This expense is standard rated.

(7) On 20 February 2019, £920 (VAT inclusive) was spent on repairs to a motor car. The motor car is used by Sandy in his business, although 20% of the mileage is for private journeys. This expense is standard rated.

(8) On 15 March 2019, equipment was purchased for £6,000 (VAT inclusive). The purchase was partly financed by a bank loan of £5,000. This purchase is standard rated.

Unless otherwise stated, all of the above figures are exclusive of VAT.

Required:

Calculate the amount of VAT payable by Sandy for the quarter ended 31 March 2019.

(Note: answer available via lecturer's website)

Question 5   (based on ACCA December 2007).

Vanessa Serve is self-employed as a tennis coach. She is registered for VAT and is the process of completing her VAT return for the quarter ended 31 March 2019. The following information is available:

(1) Sales invoices totalling £18,000 (VAT inclusive) were issued in respect of standard rated sales. All of Vanessa's customers are members of the general public.

(2) During the quarter ended 31 March 2019 Vanessa spent £600 (VAT inclusive) on mobile telephone calls of which 40% related to private calls.

(3) On 3 January 2019, Vanessa purchased a car for £12,000. On 18 March 2019, £987 was spent on repairs to the car. The cars used by Vanessa for business, although approximately 10% of the mileage is for private journeys. Both figures are inclusive of VAT at the standard rate.

(4) On 29 March 2019, tennis coaching equipment was purchased for £1,465 (VAT exclusive). Vanessa paid for the equipment on that date, but did not take delivery of the equipment or receive an invoice until 3 April 2019. This purchase was standard rated.

(5) In addition to the above, Vanessa also had other standard rated expenses amounting to £2,200 (VAT inclusive) in the quarter ended 31 March 2019. This figure includes £400 for entertaining customers.

Required:

(i) Calculate the amount of VAT payable by Vanessa for the quarter ended 31 March 2019.

(ii) Advise Vanessa of the conditions she must satisfy before being permitted to use the VAT flat rate scheme, and the advantages of joining the scheme. The relevant flat rate percentage for Vanessa's trade as notified by HMRC is 6%. Your answer should be supported by appropriate calculations of the amount of tax saving if Vanessa had used the flat rate scheme to calculate the amount of VAT payable for the quarter ended 31 March 2019.

(Note: answer available via lecturer's website)

Further test questions for this chapter to test your knowledge can be found in the student section of the website at:

http://www.taxstudent.com/uk

Further reading

For more details on the UK's VAT system use the HMRC website at www.gov.uk/government/organisations/hm-revenue-customs. You can also refer to the detailed professional guides such as Tolley's VAT Guide.

For a discussion of VAT systems generally see S. Cnossen, 'Issues in Adapting and Designing a Value Added Tax' in C. Sandford ed. (1993) *Key Issues in Tax Reform*, Fiscal Publications, Birmingham 1993.

For an advanced examination of VAT on supplies of services, see I. Roxan, (2000), 'The Nature of VAT supplies in the Twenty First Century' *British Tax Review* 2000 (6): 603-623.

On the way in which VAT interacts with other taxes, see R.S. Nock, (1998), 'Value Added Tax and other Taxes: The Interaction' *British Tax Review*, 1998 (6):547-551.

For a fuller discussion of how VAT compares with other approaches to general and specific sales taxes, and various approaches used around the world to operating a VAT system (they aren't all identical), see Evans, C., Hasseldine, J., Lymer, A., Ricketts, R. & Sandford, C. (2017) *Comparative Taxation: Why tax systems differ*, Fiscal Publications: Birmingham.

Combs, A., Tutin, R. & Rowes, P. (2018), *Taxation: incorporating the 2018 Finance Act*, Fiscal Publications: Birmingham.
– use this book for many other examples to further develop and test your knowledge of this chapter's contents. See
http://www.fiscalpublications.com/rowes/2018/

11 Tax planning

Introduction

11.1 In Chapter 3 we discussed the concept of tax avoidance and the difference between avoidance and evasion. In this chapter we will first consider tax planning, which involves strategic use of available tax concessions in order to minimise your tax liability, before looking more closely at avoidance and then evasion. The distinction between tax planning and tax avoidance is by no means straightforward, and you might like to think of it as a continuum:

Tax planning   *Acceptable Tax avoidance*   *Unacceptable Tax avoidance*

We saw in Chapter 3 that tax planning, which involves availing yourself of legitimate tax concessions, is quite legal and acceptable. Tax evasion involves at least an element of fraud or non-disclosure including, for example, failing to declare income which is taxable. This is illegal activity.

It is the grey area of tax avoidance which is particularly problematic, as exactly where the boundary exists between 'acceptable' tax avoidance and 'unacceptable' tax avoidance is difficult to determine. Tax evasion is clearly different to other forms of non-compliance in that it occurs after a tax liability has already crystallised. Tax planning and avoidance, on the other hand take place before a tax liability crystallises. Importantly, the diagram above doesn't take into account the temporal aspect – i.e. that over time, things change and what might be acceptable or not acceptable will fluctuate over time. It is still useful, however, as a way of starting to think about this complex issue. We will come back to this question of the boundary between acceptable and unacceptable tax avoidance later in the chapter, using the illustration of personal service companies to demonstrate the problems associated with this grey area, but we will start by considering tax planning, in the white zone.

At the end of this chapter you will be able to:

- identify some ways in which transactions can be structured so as to minimise income or corporation tax liabilities;
- discuss the advantages and disadvantages of being an employee as compared to being self-employed;
- compare the tax and national insurance differences of operating a business as a sole trader or a company;
- understand how tax avoidance is dealt with at present in the UK; and
- discuss the concept of tax evasion.

Basic tax planning issues

11.2 A number of earlier chapters covered specific issues of tax planning and you may want to review these at this time. Chapter 4 looked at some basic income tax planning points for couples including shifting income from a high rate taxpayer to his or her basic rate paying spouse. In Chapter 8 we considered some basic capital gains tax planning issues which relate to controlling the timing of disposals and making sure that any available reliefs and exemptions are used. Chapter 9 looked at basic tax planning for UK resident companies, including avoiding having profits taxed in the marginal rate band. In Chapter 10 we considered VAT planning including the use of voluntary registration.

We can now consider some other basic planning issues before considering broader structural issues.

Remuneration packages

11.3 A number of tax planning options are available to employees which will have the effect of reducing their income tax and NIC liabilities. Benefits in kind can be tax effective, even if they do not reduce the amount of income tax payable compared to a salary or bonus. Remember that employee (primary class 1) NICs are not payable on most benefits in kind (only class 1A – paid by the employer only), making them a relatively cheaper way to receive extra remuneration – at least as far as the recipient is concerned.

In addition, pension plans allow for tax savings, you may like to review Chapter 5 for more details of these.

Salary sacrifice

11.4 Salary sacrifice is a technique that can be used to reduce tax liabilities for both employers (secondary Class 1 NICs) and employees (both income tax and NICs). A salary sacrifice is where the employee gives up the right to receive some of his or her cash salary in return for an agreement from the employer to provide some kind of benefit in kind. To be effective for tax purposes, any arrangement to substitute benefits in kind for cash salary must be a genuine contractual arrangement. There are some potential pitfalls for employees, however, and the 'package' needs to be worked out carefully. For example, reducing the amount of cash payment entitlement under an employment contract may affect pension scheme contributions or entitlement to working tax credit, child tax credit or state pension and other government benefits.

Typically, a salary sacrifice will involve a benefit that is not taxable such as pension contributions, childcare vouchers or mobile phones. The arrangement must be such that it is not possible for the employee to go back to the original salary whenever he or she wishes. This was established in a 1969 tax case *Heaton v Bell* where it was decided that because the taxpayer, who had the use of a car, could give up the benefit at any time, then it had a 'money's worth' that was taxable.

As we saw in Chapter 5, the Government has tightened up the rules on salary sacrifice and from 6 April 2017 this can only be used for employer pensions and pensions advice, childcare, cycle to work and ultra-low emission cars. For those who have salary sacrifice arrangements in place, the new rules apply from 6 April 2018 although for cars, accommodation and school fees current arrangements can continue until 6 April 2021.

Capital allowances

11.5 Capital allowances provide scope for some tax planning for both incorporated and unincorporated businesses. You will recall from Chapter 7 that it is not compulsory to claim capital allowances in any given year. The choice of whether, or how much, to claim is the taxpayer's. Taking less than the maximum allowances available will have the effect of increasing the profit for that year, but also increasing the capital allowance claim that can be made the next year. This may be beneficial where a business has losses to be absorbed in the current period.

Timing is also important when considering capital allowances. Remember that enhanced capital allowances and writing down allowances are not pro-rated if an asset is purchased part way through the period. This means that even if you purchase an asset on the last day of the capital allowance period you still get a full period's allowance for that asset. Also, remember to classify the capital allowances you want to claim carefully to ensure the allocation you decide on gives you the option to claim the maximum allowances.

An example of this occurs where assets qualify for treatment as short life assets. Businesses should consider de-pooling such assets so as to crystallise a balancing allowance if it is sold at a loss within eight years.

See if you can identify any other planning opportunities that arise in other chapters of the book. Remember these can include making sure that you meet the criteria for special tax treatment such as the special deduction for research and development expenditure that we considered in Chapter 9. In the remainder of this chapter, we will be looking at some structural issues, specifically the tax differences that arise between being an employee, self-employed and incorporated.

Employee or self-employed

11.6 There are a number of tax planning considerations that apply to the classification of employment status. To illustrate these we will use the following activity to provide a context for discussion.

Activity

Andrea is a management consultant who seeks your advice about the tax implications of being an employee compared to being self-employed. Discuss the issues that you would raise in the course of providing Andrea with advice.

Feedback

There are significant differences in how an individual is assessed for income tax as an employee or as a self-employed taxpayer. Self-employed persons generally enjoy tax advantages including:

- Payment of income tax later, through the payment on account system, than employees who are locked into payment through the PAYE system on a weekly or monthly basis;
- A wider range of deductible expenses. You will recall that to be deductible under earnings from employment rules, expenses generally must be *wholly, exclusively and necessarily* incurred in the performance of the duties of the employment. Under the trading income rules, expenses need only be *wholly and exclusively* for the purposes of the trade or profession, the *necessarily* requirement does not apply. In practice this means that some items of expenditure may be deductible to someone who is self-employed, but not to someone doing the same work but as an employee.
- Lower national insurance contributions under classes 2 (for now) and 4, although this must be weighed against reduced social security benefit entitlements that may then result.

Activity

Andrea (from the previous activity) expects to earn approximately £70,000 for a consultancy project she is to undertake. She will spend £2,000 on furniture for her home office, £1,000 on a computer, and it will cost her £500 travelling from her home to her client. She has asked you to provide some estimates of the different income tax and national insurance contribution liabilities arising if she is an employee or self employed.

Feedback

If Andrea is an employee of the client business, she will be taxed under employment income rules. While she may do some of her work at home, that in itself is not sufficient to make more than a very small amount of her household expenses deductible. The cost of travel between home and work is also not deductible for an employee. Andrea will be taxed as an employee on the full £70,000 salary as follows (assuming she has no other income and is entitled to just the basic personal allowance):

		£
Taxable income	(£70,000 – £11,850)	58,150
Non savings income	34,500 @ 20%	6,900.00
	23,650 @ 40%	9,460.00
Tax liability		16,360.00

As an employee, Andrea will also be liable for class 1 national insurance contributions; primary contributions will need to be paid by Andrea herself, and secondary contributions will be paid by her employer. These contributions are normally calculated on a periodical basis (see Chapter 4), however for simplicity we will calculate it on an annual basis using the annual thresholds that apply to some employees such as company directors:

Primary Class 1		
£37,926 (46,350 – £8,424) @ 12%	4,551.12	
£23,650 (£70,000 – £46,350) @ 2%)	473.00	£5,024.12
Secondary Class 1		
£61,576 (£70,000 – £8,424) @ 13.8%		£8,497.48

Although secondary class 1 contributions are the legal responsibility of the employer, they can be considered part of the employee's effective tax liability. We will talk more about this idea when we discuss the question of tax incidence in Chapter 14.

Therefore, earning the £70,000 as an employee will cost Andrea £21,384.12(£16,360.00+ £5,024.12) in income tax and NICs, and her employer £8,497.48 in NICs.

If instead of becoming an employee Andrea becomes self-employed, she will be taxed under the trading income rules. If she can establish that her home is a place of business, there is a case for capital allowances to be claimed for her office furniture and computer. In addition, the cost of travel to the client's premises will probably also then be deductible.

Her tax adjusted trading profits will therefore be:

	£	£
Gross fees		70,000
Expenses:		
Capital allowances:		
AIA: computer	1,000	
furniture	2,000	
Travel expenses	500	(3,500)
Net profit from business		66,500
Less personal allowance		(11,850)
Taxable income		54,650
Income tax due:		
Non savings income		
34,500 @ 20%		6,900.00
20,150 @ 40%		8,060.00
Tax liability		14,960.00
National Insurance Contributions:		
Class 2		
£2.95 per week x 52 weeks		153.40
Class 4		
£37,926 (£46,350 – £8,424) @ 9%	3,413.34	
£20,150 (£66,500 – £46,350) @ 2%	403.00	3,816.34
Total		3,969.74

Therefore Andrea's total income tax and NIC liability is £18,929.74 (£10,951.86 lower than the total she and her employer would pay if she were an employee).

Of course, this is an over-simplified example, and in reality other considerations will come into play. For example, Andrea's remuneration as an employee does not need to be salary only. A range of benefits in kind may be available which could help to reduce her total tax liability. Andrea may well decide to start a pension scheme of one or other type which will give her tax relief. It must also be remembered that the question of whether someone is an employee or self-employed is not a simple one (see Chapter 5) and care must be taken to ensure that the rules relating to personal service income are not invoked. These are referred to as the IR35 rules and will be discussed later in this chapter. As we will see later, Andrea may well have a problem with these rules if she operates as proposed above.

In March 2015, the Office of Tax Simplification published an Employment Status review because of the difficulties the tax system faces in determining the dividing line between employment and self-employment. While not able to find a solution to the problem, the OTS have recommended that better guidance be provided together with rules for an evidenced 'audit trail' to protect against HMRC going back over previous years to challenge employment status. More recently, a consultation has been launched by HM Treasury and HMRC into tax avoidance in the private sector with responses due in August 2018.

Sole trader or company?

11.7 A taxpayer wanting to carry on business on his or her own account, has to make a decision about how to operate that business, as a sole trader or as a company. It is also possible to operate a business as a partnership, but for the purposes of this chapter we will only be considering the first two options.

Activity

Andrea (from previous examples in this chapter) has decided that she would rather have the independence of being self-employed, and wants to set up her own management consultancy business. She now seeks your advice on the tax implications of operating her business as a sole trader or as a company.

Feedback

As a sole trader, Andrea will be liable for income tax on her business profits under trading income rules as well as class 2 and class 4 national insurance contributions, as we saw in the previous activity.

If Andrea incorporates a company, with herself as sole director/shareholder, the company will be liable for corporation tax on the profits, which can then be distributed to Andrea in a number of ways. As a director/shareholder, Andrea can decide how much of the profits should be distributed to her as employment earnings, to be taxed under employment income rules, or as dividends to be taxed under dividend rules. Remember, the profits do not have to be distributed at all, they can be retained in the company which gives Andrea control over whether and when the higher rate of tax will apply.

The dates on which payments to HMRC are due differ between self-employed taxpayers and companies. As we noted earlier (in Chapter 6), for self-employed taxpayers income tax and class 4 national insurance contributions are payable by payments on account. Class 2 national insurance contributions are paid monthly by direct debit. Corporation tax, for companies paying less than the full rate of corporation tax, is payable nine months and one day after the end of the accounting period. Income tax and class 1 NICs must be deducted from any director's remuneration and remitted to HMRC on a monthly basis. Tax on dividends in the hands of shareholders will be taxed under self-assessment.

 For a company, the choice of accounting date is not important for tax purposes, however for a sole trader, the current year basis rules may operate in the early years to create overlap profits. If you need to know about the current year basis period rules for unincorporated businesses, you may want to visit the website to refresh your memory of how these rules work in the early years of a new business.

There are also capital gains tax differences between sole traders and companies which you will recall from Chapters 8 and 9. For a sole trader, a flat rate of tax of 10% or 20% applies and an annual exemption is available, currently of £11,700. Some specific capital gains tax reliefs and exemptions are only available to individual taxpayers, for example, the principle residence exemption, gift relief, and entrepreneurs' relief. For companies, allowable costs are indexed to remove the inflation element and chargeable gains form part of the company's taxable total profits (TTP).

It should be noted that capital gains retained within the company will increase the value of the company's shares. If the shareholder sells the shares, he or she may be subject to further capital gains tax, which means that there is effectively double taxation of the gain.

Activity

Given that Andrea is expecting to earn £70,000, and incur expenses as noted in previous activities, how much corporation tax will be payable if she decides to incorporate her business? How will this change if the company pays her:

(a) £30,000 as a salary or

(b) £30,000 as a dividend?

Feedback

With TTP of £66,500 (the same net profit will apply whether she is trading as self-employed or incorporated in this case) the corporation tax due would be:

	£
Corporation tax on £66,500 @ 19%	12,635.00

Compare this with the income tax and NICs payable as a sole trader on the same amount of profit in the earlier activity.

(a) If £30,000 is paid as a salary, this, together with the secondary Class 1 NICs, will be deductible for the company as follows:

		£
Net profit before salary and NIC		66,500
Less:		
Salary to Andrea	30,000	
Secondary class 1 NICs		
(£30,000 – £8,424) x 13.8%	2,977	(32,977)
Taxable profit		33,523

The corporation tax then becomes:

$$£33,523 \times 19\% = £6,369.37$$

There will also be income tax and primary class 1 national insurance to pay by Andrea on the salary of £30,000 as follows:

	£
Taxable income (£30,000 – £11,850)	18,150
Non savings income	
£18,150 @ 20%	3,630.00
Income Tax liability	3,630.00
Primary Class 1:	
£21,576 (£30,000 – £8,424) @ 12%	2,589.12
Secondary Class 1:	
£21,576 (£30,000 – £8,424) @ 13.8%	2,977.48

Total tax and NICs payable by Andrea is therefore £6,219.12 (£3,630.00 + £2,589.12), with £9,346.85 (£6,369.37 + £2,977.48) payable by the company.

(b) If £30,000 is payable to Andrea as a dividend, and not a salary, the picture is a little different. The dividend will not be deductible for the company, and so the corporation tax will still be the same as we calculated earlier, i.e. £12,635.00.

In Andrea's hands, the dividend will then be taxed using the dividend income rules. Assuming she has no other income, her income tax liability will be £16,150 (£30,000 – £11,850 – £2,000 (the dividend tax free allowance)) x the basic rate of tax on dividends (7.5%) i.e. £1,012.50.

Dividends are not subject to NICs, and so the result is the only tax Andrea would have to pay on the dividend payment is the £1,211.25.

Therefore, in this particular case, it will be slightly more tax efficient for Andrea to have her income paid as a dividend not as a salary as the total tax cost to Andrea and her company combined is lower this way i.e. £13,846.25 (£12,635.00 + £1,211.25) compared to £15,565.97 (£6,219.12+ £9,346.85). This may reverse however, as the sums extracted by way of dividend versus salary increases given the rate of tax on dividends rises to 32.5% and then 38.1% as the sums paid out go into the higher rate tax band and then the additional rate band. It will not always therefore be more tax efficient to use dividends rather than salary.

It can be seen that the advantages of operating a business through a company depend, to some extent, on the amount of profit extracted from the company and the form that the extraction takes. Dividends are only taxed in the hands of basic and starting rate taxpayers at 7.5%, but are not deductible for the company and the corporation tax rate will be 19% on these dividends. Salary is deductible for the company, but taxable on the director under employment income rules.

It must also be remembered that the decision whether or not to incorporate a business, like all commercial decisions, should not be made with only tax in mind. Many other non-tax issues need to be considered. These include quite considerable extra legal reporting requirements that exist for companies that are not present for unincorporated businesses. This extra administrative burden needs to be considered when making the decision whether or not to incorporate as its cost could easily outweigh the tax advantages.

Constraints on the use of companies

11.8 Earlier in this chapter we mentioned some rules that may influence the decision whether to use a company as a vehicle through which to provide personal services to clients. Personal services in this context will include any work a taxpayer may perform for a specific client in return for payment of some kind. As we have seen in this chapter so far, being able to work as an employee, self-employed person or through a company you own can make a significant difference to the amounts of tax you have to pay. We have discussed in previous chapters how the timing of when tax must be paid is also different between these three ways of structuring your business activity. HMRC is concerned that these tax planning strategies are not used to avoid tax.

The use of personal service companies in the UK to avoid employment related tax obligations is by no means a new issue. Indeed, the 1981 Finance Bill contained provisions described by the Revenue then as being introduced to ensure that agency workers were taxed as employees even if they operated through a company. In April 1982, however, the then Financial Secretary announced that the Government had decided not to proceed with the legislation.

The IR35 rules

11.9 IR35, dated 9 March, 1999, was an Inland Revenue press release. In it the then Chancellor, Gordon Brown's 1999 Budget announcement of changes to counter avoidance 'in the area of personal service provision' was amplified. Clearly the Government sees this as an area of unacceptable tax avoidance, in the grey zone of the continuum we discussed at the start of the chapter.

The stated aim of the changes was "to ensure that people working in what is, in effect, disguised employment will, in practice, pay the same tax and national insurance as someone employed directly". This is an attempt by the Government to increase equity in the tax system so that all "employees" are taxed the same whether or not they consider themselves to be an employee.

Following a period of consultation after the initial press release, where many expressed concern about the proposed rules, a new set of rules was introduced with effect from the 2001/02 fiscal year.

The rules look at whether a worker, who wants to be taxed as a self-employed person, would have been considered to be an employee of a client, using the usual tests of an employment relationship for tax purposes (which we looked at in Chapter 5). This will be clear in many cases by looking at the terms and conditions of the particular engagement. So, if a taxpayer "pretends" to be in self-employment to benefit from the kinds of tax advantages we discussed earlier in this chapter, and particularly if they offer their services through an intermediary (usually a company) to disguise the fact that they are really an employee under the usual rules to test for this, IR35 will be applied.

The IR35 rules operate so that the fee received by the intermediary for duties a taxpayer performs and to which the rules apply (net of specified deductions) is treated as having been paid to the taxpayer in the form of salary and wages subject to PAYE and NICs. Before 10 April, 2003 these rules only applied to business relationships, but since that date all services are now potentially subject to these rules. Corporate intermediaries account for PAYE deductions and NICs as usual for any salary paid to the worker throughout the year and reconciliation is then required at the year end. Any shortfall between the actual salary paid and the amount to which the rules apply is then deemed to be paid to the worker on the last day of the year. The personal services company then has to remit PAYE and NICs to HMRC to cover this deemed payment.

Because the aim of the IR35 rules is to make sure that taxpayers do not avoid tax by disguising an employment relationship, the intermediary can deduct expenses otherwise deductible under employment income rules as well as employer pension contributions, when working out the amount of the year end deemed payment to the worker. In addition, because the Government recognises that running a company involves extra administration costs, the company can deduct a further flat five per cent of the gross payment in working out the deemed payment. If the interposed personal services entity fails to deduct and account for PAYE and NICs, the normal penalties for employer default apply.

HMRC has made available on its website detailed information on IR35 including a page entitled "IR35: Find out if it applies". This page provides a guide to determine whether the IR35 rules may be applicable to your circumstances and, if so, what to do. More detailed information which specifically deals with how to compute the deemed payment and pay any resulting income tax and NICs can also be found on HMRC's website under the IR35 section (https://www.gov.uk/topic/business-tax/ir35).

This means that taxpayers like Andrea need to be careful about the nature of the contracts their companies enter into with clients. If they are really contracts *of* service, rather than contracts *for* services, IR35 may come into play so that extra tax and NICs are payable.

The introduction of the IR35 rules has led to some further developments in recent years. One response was for groups of taxpayers to get together, with the help of professional advisers, and form 'composite' companies, to provide their services to clients. It was possible to argue that the IR35 rules did not apply to these arrangements because the intermediaries were now acting for a number of different taxpayers, not just the one as is the case with a personal service company. Out of concern that this new form of arrangement was also unacceptable tax avoidance, the Government introduced, following consultation, some more rules in 2008, described as the Managed Service Company rules. These rules now sit beside the IR35 rules and aim to remove the tax advantage of providing personal services through a company rather than directly as an employee.

From 6 April 2017, changes come into effect in relation to public sector (government) workers using personal service companies. Under these new rules, the public sector engager is treated as an employer and the amount paid to the worker's intermediary is deemed to be a payment of employment income. The prospect of this being extended to the private sector has become more real with the latest consultation mentioned above at 11.6.

Settlements and income splitting

11.10 Another potential problem area from a tax planning perspective is the settlement legislation. This was first introduced in the 1920s as a tax avoidance rule, but for many years had not been invoked by HMRC. In the early 2000s, however, the rule was used to challenge husband and wife companies. The rules require that if income from property arises under a 'settlement', and the settlor has an interest in the property, then the income is taxed as income of the settlor. In a key case, *Arctic Systems* (2007), Mr and Mrs Jones each owned one share in a company which earned fees by providing Mr Jones' services to clients. After drawing a small salary, the remaining profits were distributed as dividends to Mr and Mrs Jones. HMRC argued that this was an arrangement which came under the settlement rules and attempted to tax Mr Jones on the dividends distributed to Mrs Jones. On 27 April 2005, the High Court found in favour of HMRC. The Court of Appeal overturned the High Court decision in December 2005, but in July 2007, the House of Lords finally found in favour of the taxpayers.

Following the lack of success in the *Arctic Systems* case, Her Majesty's Treasury issued a consultation document suggesting alternative ways of dealing with the general problem of 'income shifting', that is using arrangements, including setting up family companies and partnerships, to split the income of one person between a number of taxpayers in order to reduce the overall tax liability. After consultation and discussion, it now seems that no action is to be taken at this stage to develop new ways of dealing with this issue; indeed the Chancellor announced in the 2008 pre Budget Report that HMRC will delay indefinitely bringing in the proposed new income shifting law.

IR35, the settlements legislation and proposed income splitting rules all deal with the tension in the tax system between acceptable tax planning and unacceptable tax avoidance. In the next section we will consider some of the court decisions dealing with the question of whether an activity constitutes unacceptable tax avoidance. One of the main tasks of the Office of Tax Simplification (OTS) is to consider options for dealing with these tensions and finding a better way of taxing micro businesses and personal service income. The OTS interim report of March 2011, entitled *Small Business Tax Review*, provides a menu of options to deal with the issue. The OTS recommended major structural change to integrate income tax and NICs, which would take away the need for IR35 or any similar rules, because the incentive to incorporate would largely be removed. This would be a major change that would take some time to put in place and so the OTS recommended some interim changes:

- Suspend IR35 with the intention of permanently abolishing it following investigation of taxpayer behaviour and costs;

- Keep IR35 but improve the administration of the rules by HMRC; or
- Introduce a new 'business test' to reduce the number of people caught by the current IR35 rules.

The Government announced in Budget 2011 that it will not be following the recommendation to merge income tax and NICs, and it remains to be seen what action will be taken in relation to IR35.

The question of payments through personal service companies once again hit the media in March 2012 when it was revealed that a number of people working for the BBC were being paid into their personal companies, which sparked an investigation into all government employees, but to date no further action has been taken to curb this practice. In November 2013, the House of Lords appointed an ad hoc Committee to consider the consequences of the use of personal service companies. A call for evidence was issued and by January, the committee had heard oral evidence from 28 witnesses and received 44 written representations. The Committee cast some doubt on HMRC estimates of the revenue at risk through the use of personal service companies of £550million. The Committee recommended that if IR35 is to be retained, it needs to be better managed by HMRC, including making sure that lower paid taxpayers are aware of the legal ramifications of operating through a personal service companies, and of the benefits they lose as a result of not being employees.

Meanwhile, in the Autumn Statement 2013, the Government set out a number of measures aimed at clarifying the distinction between employment and self employment. Further, in Budget 2016 it was announced that from April 2017 the rules for engaging 'off payroll' workers through their own companies in the public sector will be tightened to make the public sector body more responsible for determining the correct status of these workers. They also promised (yet further) consultation on how these rules can be made clearer and online tests could be improved.

Tax avoidance

11.11 Over the past 75 years there has been a shift in the attitudes of the courts in relation to the question of what constitutes tax avoidance. Earlier in the twentieth century the courts adopted a strict interpretation of taxation laws: they looked at what the words of the legislation said and only considered the legal nature of any avoidance scheme, not any underlying issues. This has now evolved into a wider review beyond just the legal form of transactions and arrangements.

In this section we will look at some of the more significant cases involving tax avoidance and trace the development of the courts' attitudes. Note, however, that we present here only a very simplified discussion of the case law to illustrate the developments over time.

Tax avoidance case law

IRC v Duke of Westminster (1936)

11.12 The early, strict, interpretation is illustrated by the case of *IRC v Duke of Westminster* (1936). In this case an arrangement was entered into so that domestic servants were not paid wages but instead received an income under a deed of covenant. A deed of covenant produced a tax deduction for the person executing the deed and was valid only if no valuable consideration was provided by the recipient in return. However, the Duke of Westminster and his servants had an understanding, that so long as the deed of covenant operated the servants would not claim the wages due to them. The scheme enabled the Duke to claim tax relief for the amounts paid to his servants whereas payment of wages to servants would not have been an allowable deduction Today such a scheme could not be used because payments made under deeds of covenant are no longer tax effective when paid to individuals. However, at the time, the House of Lords found for the Duke, declaring that they would only consider the legal nature of the transaction, that is, they were more concerned with the form of the transaction than its substance. Until the mid-1980s this case remained an important precedent and the Inland Revenue were rarely successful in challenging tax avoidance schemes in the courts.

WT Ramsay Ltd. V IRC (1981)

11.13 In *WT Ramsay Ltd v IRC* (1981) the House of Lords took a completely different view of an avoidance scheme. The case involved an artificial scheme which was used to create a large capital loss. The company had realised a capital gain and intended to set the artificially generated loss against the capital gain to avoid paying tax on the gain. The scheme was artificial because it was made up of a series of preordained steps which were to be carried out in rapid succession. The scheme required that all steps be completed once the first one had been made. At the end of the series of steps the taxpayers would be in the same position as they had been at the beginning and any loss created would not be a real financial loss – just a paper loss. In fact the only real losses which had been suffered were the professional fees which were paid for the scheme's operation. The House of Lords decided that although each step in the scheme was a separate legal transaction, it was possible to view the scheme not as a series of separate legal transactions, but as a whole, by comparing the position of the taxpayer in real terms at the start and finish of the scheme. When this was done no real loss was incurred and the scheme was self- cancelling.

Lord Wilberforce explained the decision as follows:

'While obliging the court to accept documents or transactions, found to be genuine, as such, it does not compel the court to look at a document or a transaction in blinkers, isolated from any context to which it properly belongs. If it can be seen that a document or transaction was intended to have effect as part of a nexus or series of transactions, or as an ingredient of a wider transaction intended as a whole, there is nothing in the doctrine to prevent it being so regarded; to do so is not to prefer form to substance, or substance to form. It is the task of the court to ascertain the legal nature of any transaction to which it is sought to attach a tax, or a tax consequence, and if that emerges from a series, or combination of transactions, intended to operate as such, it is that series or combination which may be regarded.'

Furniss v Dawson (1984)

11.14 The *Ramsay principle* established in the previous case was extended in *Furniss v Dawson* (1984). This time the objective was to defer capital gains tax by using an intermediary company based in the Isle of Man. The scheme was not circular or self-cancelling. However, the House of Lords decided that the scheme should still be set aside for tax purposes because once again the scheme required a series of artificial steps to be carried out in quick succession just to save tax rather than with a real business purpose in mind.

Craven v White (1989)

11.15 Later the case of *Craven v White* (1989) was used by the House of Lords to limit the application of the *Ramsay* principle somewhat. Once again an intermediary company in the Isle of Man was used to defer a capital gains tax liability. The key difference between *Craven v White* and *Furniss v Dawson* was that when the shares were transferred to the Isle of Man based company, their final disposal had not been agreed. Hence no preordained series of steps existed at the time that the first transaction was undertaken. Consequently the House of Lords refused to view the series of transactions as a whole and the scheme was successful this time in reducing the tax liability. This case has great significance for anti-avoidance schemes generally. It makes planning well in advance critical. If transactions are undertaken before the final step is known with certainty, there is a greater likelihood of the scheme being successful if challenged by HMRC as tax avoidance activity – although of course, not being certain of the full outcome makes such schemes inherently more risky.

IRC v McGuckian (1997)

11.16 IRC *v McGuckian* (1997) dealt with an issue in which there was a transfer of company shares to a non-resident trustee of a settlement, followed by the rights to a dividend being assigned to a resident company for consideration. The UK resident company then paid an amount of dividend less commission to the trustee. The question was whether this constituted a tax avoidance scheme, and the House of Lords were of the view that it did. The case raised some important issues, not so much because *Furniss v Dawson* was again applied, but from comments made by their Lordships in the course of the decision. They appeared to adopt a more purposive approach to interpretation which means the courts will look at what legislation is designed to achieve, rather than just what it says.

McNiven v Westmoreland Investments Ltd (2001)

11.17 In *McNiven v Westmoreland Investments Ltd* (2001) the House of Lords had to consider whether steps inserted into a transaction had any commercial purpose or were present simply to affect the tax outcome. The case involved a company with accrued unpaid interest. To be deductible for corporation tax at the time, the interest had to be paid. The lender, which was the parent company, made a loan to Westmoreland that was then repaid in discharge of the outstanding interest. It was a preordained, circular, arrangement, designed purely so as to secure a tax deduction. The House of Lords found, however, that the company had incurred a real economic outlay and that this was tax mitigation to take advantage of a statutory tax relief. It was therefore legitimate tax avoidance.

Barclays Mercantile Business Finance Ltd. v Mawson (2005)

11.18 In 2005, the House of Lords delivered its decision in *Barclays Mercantile Business Finance Ltd v Mawson* [2005] STC 1. In this case, the Barclays group purchased a gas pipeline from the Irish Gas Board for £91 million and leased it back to them. By a series of transactions, the £91 million found its way back into the group as a deposit. The bank claimed capital allowances on the pipeline, however the Revenue was of the view that the money was spent on "financial engineering" rather than plant and machinery qualifying for capital allowances. The House of Lords affirmed the decision of the Court of Appeal that whether or not an expense is incurred is a legal question and so the arrangement did not constitute unacceptable tax avoidance.

Astall v Revenue and Customs Commissioners (2008)

11.19 More recently, in 2008, the High Court delivered its decision in the Astall case [2008] EWHC 1471 (Ch), in which the taxpayer sought to deduct a loss arising from the transfer of discounted securities. The Special Commissioners had earlier found in favour of HMRC that the loss was not deductible, taking a purposive approach to interpreting the relevant legislation. Their decision was upheld by the High Court.

Tower MCashback (2011)

11.20 In this complicated case, a software company, MCashback, owned software that it licensed to third parties. The company wanted to raise funds, and so with the help of a finance company, Tower, agreed to sell an exclusive royalty free license to a limited liability partnership, the partners of which were high net worth individuals. The investing partners provided some of the funds, and borrowed the rest from a special purpose vehicle set up by Tower Finance. The Supreme Court found that not all of the funds spent on the license were eligible for capital allowances, because some of it (the part provided by Tower) was not incurred on the acquisition of software rights. The case is different to Barclays Mercantile Business Finance Ltd (above) mainly because in that case the asset was bought and the funds borrowed on normal commercial terms, which was not the case here.

The question of where the boundary is between acceptable and unacceptable tax avoidance will continue to be debated, and subject to further subtle shifts, as a result of a number of forces. These will include the constitution of the courts and prevailing attitudes in HMRC, government and of society at large.

Tower Radio Ltd v HMRC (2015)

11.21 In this case (TC02784) a company entered into a scheme devised by an accountancy firm that was designed to pay the managing director a substantial bonus without having to pay PAYE or NIC. The scheme involved awarding shares in a subsidiary company that was subsequently liquidated and the assets distributed to the managing director. The First Tier Tribunal (FTT) upheld the view of HMRC that the Ramsay principle (see above) applied and the interposition of the subsidiary company could be ignored. The Upper Tribunal, (UKUT 0060) however, subsequently upheld the taxpayer's appeal against the FTT decision in 2015. The judges found that the employees were given shares, not money, and said 'However unattractive the result may be, it seems to us that the appeals before us must be allowed". Therefore, no income tax or NIC liability arose, and the purposive approach could not be used to overcome a deficiency in the legislation.

UBS AG v HMRC (2016)

11.22 The UBS case, together with the Deutsche Bank case heard at the same time, also involved employees being given shares instead of cash, in this case bankers' bonuses. The Supreme Court handed down its decision in April 2016 finding in favour of HMRC and overturning the previous Court of Appeal decision, and applied a purposive Ramsay approach, albeit a narrower version. The case involved a large sum: UBS paid £91,880,000 to acquire the shares that were then given to the employees, and the arrangement to sidestep income tax and NICs was quite complex involving several steps. Some commentators have suggested that this decision means that what was once a popular way of avoiding tax cannot be guaranteed to work in the future.

Tackling tax avoidance in the UK

11.23 The question of whether a transaction or arrangement is tax avoidance, and how to distinguish avoidance and planning, is a difficult one. Graham Aaronson, QC, in evidence to the House of Lords Economic Affairs committee in January 2013 said:

'Avoidance' is a rather unfortunate word... because avoidance can be regarded as a particularly nasty thing to do or, if it is an accident, it is a very sensible thing to do – you avoid an accident. So I would rather use words that are less emotive when describing the intellectual process in determining whether you should be paying a smaller amount of tax than you would otherwise pay. You can call that tax planning because it is planning. Where it is good planning or bad planning, whether it is abusive or innocent planning, it is planning. Tax avoidance is a very dangerous expression to use if you want to have a serious debate because one person's avoidance is another person's perfectly reasonable planning.

HMRC define tax avoidance as "exploiting the tax rules to gain an advantage that Parliament never intended. It often involves contrived, artificial transactions that serve little or no commercial purpose other than to produce a tax advantages. It involves operating within the letter, but not the spirit of the law."

The UK currently has a multifaceted approach to tackling tax avoidance that has been developing over a number of years. In the previous section we saw how the judiciary play a role in changing their approach to interpretation and are now looking to the purpose of the legislation and not just its strict wording. Another facet is to deal with specific transactions by specific legislation introduced to curtail new schemes. These are increasingly being referred to as Targeted Anti Avoidance Rules (TAARs). The difficulty that arises with this approach is that there is an ongoing incentive for the creation of new schemes not covered by existing legislation. It is also often the case that specific measures leave room for further tax planning opportunities. Finally, in Chapter 2 we saw that tax advisers who are members of professional bodies are bound by a professional code of conduct. In 2016 this was revised to give some clarity around tax planning. The new standard states:

> 'Members must not create, encourage or promote tax planning arrangements or structures that (i) set out to achieve results that are contrary to the clear intention of parliament in enacting relevant legislation and/or (ii) are highly artificial or highly contrived and seek to exploit shortcomings within the relevant legislation.'

Disclosure of tax avoidance schemes (DOTAs)

11.24 The Finance Act 2004 introduced radical new rules as part of HMRC's attempt to modernise its approach to managing the risk from fraud, evasion, avoidance and error. The new rules require those who sell tax avoidance schemes, and those who use them, to disclose them to HMRC if they fit certain 'hallmarks' that may indicate they would come under these rules.

According to the regulatory impact assessment issued by the Treasury, "they will help to maintain the integrity of the tax system and ensure that everyone pays their fair share of tax and so contributes to the UK's needs". The rules were initially confined to tax avoidance products that were either financial or employment related. In Finance Act 2006, this was extended to a broader range of tax avoidance schemes with wider tests as to when disclosure is required.

The rules have caused quite a lot of controversy and there remains some doubt about what their impact will be in the long term. There is some anecdotal evidence, however, that the disclosure rules have put a brake on the mass marketing of generic tax avoidance schemes. Many of the TAARs referred to in the previous section have been introduced as a result of disclosure of tax avoidance schemes, and their introduction is adding significantly to the length and complexity of the tax legislation in the UK.

Several new hallmarks of tax avoidance arrangements requiring disclosure have been added in 2014, including an employment income hallmark and a new confidentiality hallmark.

In 2014 new rules were introduced to make sure that taxpayers who are party to tax avoidance arrangements that are subject to the DOTAS rules must pay the tax in dispute up front, or risk penalties if the courts find the scheme to be ineffective. Accelerated payment notices are issued to taxpayers known to have taken part in avoidance schemes.

Specific schemes identified by HMRC for examination are also now detailed in a series of 'Spotlights' published on their website – see:

https://www.gov.uk/government/collections/tax-avoidance-schemes-currently-in-the-spotlight

Accelerated payments

11.25 In 2014, the Government introduced rules that may require taxpayers who have used a disclosable (see above) tax avoidance scheme to make a payment of the amount that relates to their use of the scheme, even though the final amount has yet to be determined. HMRC can issue an 'accelerated payment notice' (APN) if a tax enquiry or tax appeal is in progress involving an arrangement which has been given a DOTAS number. It operates like a payment on account.

A general anti avoidance/abuse rule

11.26 In the UK there was for many years no general anti-avoidance rule (GAAR), as there is in some other countries, such as Canada and Australia. There is an argument that not having a general anti-avoidance rule causes uncertainty in the operation of the tax system. The Revenue proposed a draft GAAR in 1998, however it was rejected on the basis that it was too detailed, and so its application was uncertain. One commentator, Freedman (2003) suggested that we need a GANTIP – a general anti avoidance principle, rather than a rule. She suggests that a legislative, principles based framework would give guidance to both taxpayers and HMRC. With the change in government in 2010, the question of whether the UK should have a GAAR came to the fore once again.

In December 2010, the Exchequer Secretary commissioned Graham Aaronson QC to lead a study into the introduction of a GAAR in the UK. His report was published in November 2011. Aaronson concluded that a narrowly focussed GAAR would be appropriate to deter abusive tax avoidance schemes and reduce legal uncertainty. He was also of the view that it will help to build trust between taxpayers and HMRC, and in the longer term allow for simplification of the tax system.

Following extensive consultation, including a GAAR panel that involved lawyers, accountants, business representatives and even tax campaigners, the new rules were drafted and written into the Finance Bill 2013. It is a General Anti

Abuse (rather than avoidance) Rule and is designed to apply where HMRC judge that taxpayers enter into an arrangement that has obtaining a tax advantage as one of its main purposes. An independent panel has been established to examine arrangements to see if they fall within the GAAR.

It will take time for the scope of the new GAAR to be established, and there will be some uncertainty in the meantime about the kinds of arrangements that it will prevent. The introduction of the GAAR has not led to the removal of the various TAARs that are already in place, but will be yet another piece of equipment available to HMRC in its quest to tackle tax avoidance.

In January 2014, HMRC published two documents. The first relates to a consultation in 2013 called, 'Raising the Stakes on Tax Avoidance'. The second is entitled 'Tackling Marketed Tax Avoidance'. New measures proposed in these consultations include identifying and monitoring closely 'high risk promotors' of tax avoidance schemes, and even naming them publicly, and also requiring taxpayers to settle their tax returns in advance of their particular resolution when a similar issue is resolved in the courts for another taxpayer. In January 2015, HMRC launched another consultation – 'Strengthening the sanctions for tax avoidance which includes the possibility of a GAAR penalty'.

Tax evasion

11.27 As we noted earlier, tax evasion is illegal activity, and in recent years it has become an important area of academic research, particularly in the field of economics. Researchers around the world are trying to work out what factors affect people's decisions to evade payment of taxes, including attitudes and norms, both personal and social. This research has led tax authorities to develop new strategies for dealing with taxpayers who evade taxes. For a list of references, see the end of this Chapter.

One recent example of tax evasion on a very large scale is referred to as 'missing trader' fraud where huge amounts of VAT have effectively been stolen. A version of this fraud, referred to as 'carousel' fraud, involves evasion of VAT in trade within the European Union taking advantage of the zero rating of cross border transactions within the EU. Importers of goods are able to receive them without paying VAT, but charge VAT on their resale without remitting it to the revenue authority.

Fiscal Fact

In a press release dated 5 July 2010, HMRC announced that two members of a 21-strong criminal tax fraud gang have been ordered to pay £92.3m in the biggest ever confiscation order secured by HMRC. The gang stole £37.5m in VAT tax fraud involving import and export of computer processing units through a chain of companies using sham invoices. They used the cash to invest in luxury properties.

Summary

We opened this chapter with a brief look at the difference between tax planning, tax avoidance and tax evasion. We then considered a limited number of different basic tax planning strategies for both employees and businesses. From a structural viewpoint, we considered the differences in the tax system for employees, self-employed taxpayers and incorporated taxpayers. We found that there are some clear differences, with employees generally paying more tax than self-employed taxpayers and unincorporated businesses paying more than incorporated businesses on the same amount of profits. We noted, however, that the decision of how to structure an income earning activity is not just a tax issue, there are other commercial considerations involved.

We also considered how the attitudes of the courts towards tax avoidance have changed over time and looked at some current developments in this area.

Project areas

The issue of tax planning provides lots of opportunities for projects as it is a subject that can be approached from a number of different directions. The boundary between tax planning and unacceptable tax avoidance for example raises questions about the different attitudes of the revenue authorities, taxpayers and their professional advisers and can also raise some interesting moral and ethical questions.

The incorporation of tax considerations into strategic management decision making is another area of potential project topics as is considering the tax policy questions of providing opportunities for tax planning in the first instance.

Discussion questions

1. The treatment of corporations separately from their shareholders for tax purposes can lead to tax avoidance, particularly where there is a significant difference between the rate of tax applicable to corporations and that applying to high income individuals. What measures can the Government put in place to prevent high income taxpayers from sheltering profits behind the corporate form?

2. How can a government fairly determine the difference between employment and self-employment to ensure legitimate tax planning is allowed to continue but abuses of the system are minimised?

3. Discuss how tax planning can occur for other taxes, such as inheritance tax, stamp duty or VAT. Does the interaction of these taxes and income tax provide any opportunities for tax planning?

4. Do you think the decision in *WT Ramsay v IRC* was the right one?

5. How effective do you think the new General Anti Abuse Rule will be?

6. Is the current approach of HMRC – requiring tax avoidance schemes to be registered – an effective way to limit tax loss to the Government or an 'over-the-top' solution that prevents acceptable tax planning which would otherwise be allowed by the law?

Questions

Question 1

Zainab is employed by a company that does not currently contribute to her pension scheme, and she pays £80 per month to a pension scheme from her net (after tax) pay. What would be the effect of entering into a salary sacrifice arrangement so that the company pays pension contributions on her behalf?

Question 2   (based on ACCA June 2009)

Andrew Zoom is a cameraman who started working for Slick-Productions Ltd on 6 April 2014. The following information is available in respect of the year ended 5 April 2019:

1. Andrew received gross income of £50,000 from Slick Productions Ltd. He works a set number of hours each week and is paid hourly for the work that he does. When Andrew works more than the set number of hours, he is paid overtime.

2. Andrew is under an obligation to accept the work offered to him by Slick-Productions Ltd, and the work is carried out under the control of the company's production manager. He is obliged to do the work personally, and this is all performed at Slick-Productions Ltd's premises.

3. All of the equipment that Andrew uses is provided by Slick-Productions Ltd.

Andrew has several friends who are cameramen, and they are all treated as self-employed. He therefore considers that he should be treated as self-employed as well in relation to his work for Slick-Productions Ltd.

Required:

(a) List those factors that indicate that Andrew Zoom should be treated as an employee in relation to his work for Slick-Productions Ltd rather than self-employed.

(b) Calculate Andrew Zoom's income tax liability and national insurance contributions for the tax year 2018/19 if he is treated:

(i) as an employee in respect of his work for Slick-Productions Ltd (note, you are not required to calculate employer's national insurance contributions);

(ii) as self-employed in respect of his work for Slick Productions Ltd.

Question 3   (based on ICAS TPS Tax Paper 2002)

You are a tax partner for Chic Ltd ('Chic'), a designer clothing manufacturing company jointly owned by Mr and Mrs Style. Mr Style is the managing director. Chic has no associated companies. The management and work force total 45 people. The company has a year end of 30 September and owns the existing premises which cost £100,000 in 1992.

The projected management accounts for the year to 31 March 2019 show turnover of £1,800,000 and allowable trading expenses of £1,400,000. Capital allowances on existing assets for the accounting period will amount to £90,000. The company will also receive the following income:

1. Dividends from UK companies of £9,000 net;
2. Annual royalties of £15,600; and
3. Loan interest of £4,000.

You have had a meeting with Mr Style regarding year-end planning for capital expenditure. The Styles are thinking of selling the existing factory premises to a developer for £400,000. With the proceeds, the Styles are planning to:

(a) purchase new fixed plant and machinery at a cost of £250,000 to allow the company's production to expand;

(b) upgrade the computer system at a cost of £70,000 to improve the efficiency in production, stock control and accounting functions, and to launch the company on to the internet; and

(c) build a 'granny annex' to the Styles family mansion by borrowing £50,000 from the company. The loan will be repaid when Mrs Style's mother sells her own flat after moving into the annex.

Mr Style is concerned about the timing and tax implications of these transactions and the effect of any tax liabilities on the company's cash flow.

Required:

1. Calculate the corporation tax that would be payable by Chic for the year ending 31 March 2019 assuming that none of the proposed capital expenditure took place. State when the corporation tax is due.

2. Prepare notes for a meeting with Mr and Mrs Style:
   (a) detailing the tax implications for the company of the proposed sale of the factory and of each of the three capital transactions which will follow; and
   (b) revising the corporation tax that will become payable for the year ending 31 March 2019 after the capital expenditure.

Indexation factors:	April 1992	138.8
	December 2017	278.1

(*Note: answer available via lecturer's website*)

Question 4 (based on ACCA June 2014)

You work as a Tax Senior and your manager has received a letter from Ziti. Ziti owns and runs an unincorporated business which was given to him by his father, Ravi. Extracts from the letter and from an email from your manager are set out below.

Extract from the letter from Ziti:
"I have decided that, due to my father's illness, I want to be able to look after him on a full time basis. Accordingly, I am going to sell my business and use the proceeds to buy a house nearer to where he lives. My father started the business in 1999 when he purchased the building referred to in the business assets below. He gave the business (consisting of the goodwill, the building and the equipment) to me on 1 July 2014 and we

submitted a joint claim for gift relief, such that no capital gains tax was payable. I have no sources of income other than this business.

I have identified two possible methods of disposal:
(i) My preferred approach would be to close the business down. I would do this by selling the building and equipment on 31 January 2019, at which point I would cease trading.
(ii) My father would prefer to see the business carry on after I sell it. For this to occur, I would have to continue trading until 30 April 2019 and then sell the business to someone who would continue to operate it.

In each case I would prepare accounts for the year ending 30 April 2017 and then to the date of cessation or disposal. I attach an appendix setting out the information you requested in relation to the business.

Appendix: Business assets (all figures exclude VAT)

	Goodwill £	Building £	Equipment £
Original cost of assets	nil	60,000	18,000
Market value as at 1 July 2014	40,000	300,000	9,000
Expected value 31/1/19 and 30/4/19	40,000	330,000	10,000

Financial position of the business
The tax adjusted trading profits for the year ended 30 April 2017 were £55,000. From 1 May 2017, it can be assumed that the business generates trading profits of £5,000 per month. The only tax adjustment required to this figure is in respect of capital allowances.

The tax written down value of the main pool as at 30 April 2017 was nil. I purchased business equipment for £6,000 on 1 August 2017. There have been no disposals of equipment since 30 April 2017.

Extract from an email from your manager:
- Ziti was born in 1967 and both he and his father are resident and domiciled in the UK.
- All of the equipment is movable and no item has a cost or market value of more than £6,000.

The business is registered for VAT and no election has been made in respect of the building in relation to VAT.

Required:
a) Calculate Ziti's taxable trading profits from 1 May 2017 onwards, the income tax thereon and any capital gains tax payable, assuming the income tax and capital gains tax rates and allowances remain as the 2018/19 rates in the future.

b) Compare the financial implications of the alternative methods for disposing of the business (you may ignore national insurance contributions).

c) Explain whether or not VAT would need to be charged on either or both of the alternative disposals

(*Note: answer available via lecturer's website*)

Further test questions for this chapter to test your knowledge can be found in the student section of the website at:

http://www.taxstudent.com/uk

Further reading and examples

Aaronson, G. (2011), GAAR Study available at:

http://www.hm-treasury.gov.uk/d/gaar_final_report_111111.pdf

Bowler, T. (2009), *Countering Tax Avoidance in the UK: Which Way Forward?* Institute for Fiscal Studies, Tax Law Review Committee Discussion Paper No. 7

Braithwaite, V. (2009), *Defiance in Taxation and Governance*, Edward Elgar Publishing.

Combs, A., Tutin, R, & Rowes, P. (2018), *Taxation: incorporating the 2018 Finance Act*, Fiscal Publications: Birmingham.

– use this book for many other examples to further develop and test your knowledge of this chapter's contents. See http://www.fiscalpublications.com/rowes/2018/

Evans, C., Hasseldine, J., Lymer, A., Ricketts, R. & Sandford, C. (2017), Tax compliance in *Comparative Taxation: Why tax systems differ*, Fiscal Publications: Birmingham.

Freedman, J. (2003), Tax and Corporate Responsibility, *The Tax Journal* Issue 695. 2; 2 June 2003.

HMRC (2013), *Tackling Tax Avoidance*, available at http://www.gov.uk/government/publications/tackling-tax-avoidance

Kirchler, E. (2007), *The Economic Psychology of Tax Behaviour*, Cambridge University Press.

Seely, A. (2017), *Personal Service Companies: recent debate*, House of Commons Briefing Paper No 05976.

12 International tax

Introduction

12.1 The UK tax paid by an individual or company is influenced by the residence or domicile of the taxpayer.

As a general rule, an individual who is closely connected with the UK will pay tax in the UK on his or her income no matter where in the world it comes from. If an individual only has a vague connection with the UK, however, he or she will be taxed in the UK only on income arising in the UK. A similar principle applies to companies, although the system is becoming increasingly territorial for companies as you will see later.

With increased globalisation, more and more UK-based individuals and companies are conducting business or earning income outside of the UK. It is important to know how the returns from these activities will be taxed. Overseas investments also allow scope for tax planning, particularly as there are a number of countries with much lower tax rates than the UK.

International tax is an extremely complex area and in this chapter we will only cover some of these issues at a level that will give you an overview of the key issues involved. We will also have a brief look at how some of the special tax rules work that are related to international activity.

At the end of this chapter you will be able to:

- explain the terms residence and domicile;
- outline the general rules concerning whether an individual or company is liable to UK income and corporation tax;
- explain how payment of tax overseas can affect a UK tax liability and the measures available to prevent double taxation; and
- identify some international tax avoidance practices and the legislation which seeks to prevent them.

Residence of individuals

12.2 Residence rules are important as they determine a taxpayer's likely exposure to UK tax legislation; for both individuals and companies there are different liabilities arising depending on whether a taxpayer is considered to be tax resident or not.

Your residency status will determine how much of your income will be taxed in the UK and also when it will be taxed. Some income is taxed on an *arising basis*, that is the amount that is earned during the tax year, even if it is not brought over to the UK. Other income is taxed on a *remittance basis*, that is so long as it remains overseas it will not be taxed in the UK, but will attract tax as soon as it is remitted, or brought in to the UK.

The old rules

12.3 Prior to 6 April 2013, there were three connecting factors used to determine UK tax liability for individuals; *domicile*, *residence* and *ordinary residence*.

A person's domicile is generally either where he or she is born, or the place where the person intends to settle permanently. An individual has a domicile of origin from the moment of birth. Once the individual is aged 16 or over they may choose their domicile. To do this the individual must maintain a physical presence in the country concerned and must have evidence that he or she has an intention to remain there indefinitely. You can only have one domicile at any one time, although it may be possible to be tax resident of more than one country.

The terms *residence* and *ordinary residence* were not defined in the UK's legislation but could be determined from various court rulings via the case law system. The core principles were that an individual was deemed to be resident in the UK if he or she:

- Spent more than *183 days* in the UK in the tax year.
- Having been a resident, left the UK for permanent residence abroad but returned to the UK for periods which equalled an average (*over a period of four consecutive tax years*) of *91 days or more* in the tax year.

HMRC published a guidance booklet to help with this topic entitled *Residents Domicile and the Remittance Basis* (HMRC6). In general, a person could be a UK resident for only part of a tax year. He or she was either resident or not resident for the entire year of assessment. The only exception occurs when an individual either left the UK for permanent residence abroad or came to the UK in order to take up permanent residence. Under these circumstances, the tax year was split and the UK tax liability will only apply to the part of the year for which they were a UK resident. Once considered a resident, this status was not usually lost for temporary absences from the UK. A taxpayer remained a UK resident unless they are absent from the country for a whole tax year.

A taxpayer was *ordinarily resident* if the UK was normally their country of residence (where you were habitually resident). Under these rule a taxpayer may therefore have been resident but not ordinarily resident, or ordinarily resident but not resident (although this is rare), or both resident and ordinarily resident in any tax year. A British citizen who has been ordinarily resident in the UK but who leaves to live abroad was deemed to be resident during his or her absence unless they could prove otherwise.

The current rules

12.4 A statutory residence test was introduced in FA13, to resolve the uncertainty that arose under the old, case law based, rules. The idea behind the new rules is to provide clear, objective tests that will give certainty in most cases.

The current rules have three components:

1. An *automatic overseas* test. This test means that an individual meeting the following conditions will be a non-resident for UK tax purposes. The conditions are that they were:
    *   not resident in the UK for the previous 3 tax years and they are present in the UK for fewer than 45 days in the current tax year; or
    *   resident in the UK in one or more of the previous 3 tax years, and present for fewer than 16 days in the current tax year; or
    *   leave the UK to carry out full-time work overseas, provided they are present in the UK for fewer than 91 days in the tax year and fewer than 31 days are spent working in the UK in the tax year.

2. An *automatic UK* test. This test provides that an individual will be a UK tax resident if they:
    *   Are present in the UK for at least 183 days in a tax year; or
    *   Have a home in the UK for more than 90 days, spend at least 30 separate days in that home, there are 91 consecutive days during which they don't have an overseas home or if they do, they spend fewer than 30 separate days in each of them; or
    *   Work full time in the UK for a period of 365 days with no significant breaks.

3. A *sufficient UK ties* test. This test looks at the ties the individual has to the UK and specifies the number of days they can spend in the UK without becoming tax resident. The ties are:
    *   UK resident family:
    *   Accessible accommodation in the UK;
    *   Substantive work in the UK;
    *   UK presence in the previous tax years (more than 90 days in the UK in either of the previous 2 tax years;)
    *   More time in the UK than in any other single country.

If your course requires you to understand these rules in more detail, HMRC has published guidance, including detailed worked examples at: www.gov.uk/government/publications/rdr3-statutory-residence-test-srt

Non-domiciles

12.5 With effect from 6 April 2008, an annual charge (called the Remittance Basis Charge or RBC) of £30,000 applies to non-UK domiciled adults resident in the UK for the year and also at least seven of the previous 9 years (the charge does not apply to children). Budget 2011 announced a higher rate charge from April 2012 of £50,000 where such a person has been resident at least twelve in the last fourteen years. This rate rose to £60,000 from 6 April 2015. The £30,000 charge continues to apply where a person has been resident for at least seven of the last 9 years.

With effect from 6 April 2015 a third level of RBC of £90,000 applies to those who have been resident for 17 out of the previous 20 years.

In all cases a period of 6 years of non-residence is required to reset each clock.

The RBC applies when a non-domicile claims the right to be taxed on their foreign income and gains on a remittance basis, that is, not as they are earned, but when the income or gains are brought into the UK (which they may never be, of course). This charge is in addition to whatever UK tax is also due but the charge will not apply if the unremitted foreign income is £2,000 or less in any tax year.

Non-domiciled adult residents in the UK in the tax year who continue to claim the remittance basis do not have the right (from 6 April 2008 also) to UK income tax personal allowances against their remitted income (including the personal allowance itself, blind person allowance and tax reductions for married couples or civil partners). They also cannot use the capital gains tax annual exemption against capital gains remitted to the UK. However, a £2,000 de minimus rule also applies so that if unremitted income does not exceed this sum, non-domiciles will be allowed to keep their allowances to offset their remitted income for both income and capital gains taxes.

Fiscal Fact

Approximately 5,400 individuals paid the Remittance Basis Charge in its year of introduction (2008/09). HMRC estimate this will be around 5,000 taxpayers for the 2015/16 tax year.

[Source: HMRC – The reform of the taxation of non-domiciled individuals consultation, June 2011 and Increase to Remittance Charge basis - Explanatory Note Finance Bill 2015]

Finance Act 2008 also included rules to stop non domiciles bringing certain income and gains into the UK free of tax as was previously possible in some cases. However, since April 2012, non-domiciled individuals have been able to bring foreign income and capital gains into the UK without the need to pay the remittance charge where this money is used for commercial investment

The continuation of the relief for non-domiciles became controversial during the 2015 election campaign and the Conservative Government surprisingly announced in the Summer Budget 2015 that permanent non-domicile (non-dom) status would cease from April 2017. After this date, anyone who has been resident in the UK for more than 15 of the last 20 years is deemed domiciled in the UK and subject to normal rules for taxation of their income and wealth. Further, (also from April 2017), anyone born in the UK, to UK domiciled parents, would no longer be able to leave the country and later return as a non-dom.

Employment income

12.6 As we saw in Chapter 5, earnings from employment or pensions are assessed on an arising (taxed in the year it is received) basis. This applies to any employment earnings for any year of assessment in which the person holding the office or employment is resident in the UK.

These rules also detail how to tax income, also on the arising basis, for UK-based duties performed by a person who is not a resident. In this circumstance, the taxpayer is charged tax only on income generated in the UK.

A person who is resident but not domiciled in the UK, may pay UK income tax on a remittance basis. This means they only have to pay income tax if they bring their income into the UK, subject to payment of the £30,000, £60,000 or £90,000 fee if necessary.

Capital taxes

12.7 Capital gains tax is charged on individuals if they are resident in the UK. If they are also domiciled in the UK, this charge is on gains made anywhere in the world and tax due is reported and collected via the usual processes, as we saw in Chapter 8. If individuals are not domiciled in the UK then only gains arising in the UK, or remitted here, are taxed in the UK. Use of the remittance basis is subject to payment of the £30,000, £60,000 or £90,000 charge.

Resident status does not affect inheritance tax. If you are domiciled in the UK, when you die you pay UK inheritance tax on your worldwide property. If you are not domiciled here you only pay inheritance tax on your UK property. Finance Act (No. 2) 2017 extends inheritance tax to UK residential property held by a non-dom through an overseas structure such as a company.

From 6 April 2015, non-residents who dispose of residential property will be potentially liable to capital gains tax. Such taxpayers will be entitled to claim principal private residence relief, but subject to some new conditions: the property must be located in the same country as where the taxpayer is resident for tax purposes and the taxpayer spends at least 90 midnights in the property in the tax year.

Further, it was proposed that from April 2017, all non-doms who are deemed to be UK domiciled under the changes to the remittance basis charge rules outlined above would have assets rebased to April 2017 values. This measure was also removed from the Finance Bill 2017, however, as a result of the snap General Election in June 2017.

Rates of tax

12.8 For UK residents any foreign income earned is simply added to the other, UK-sourced, income as part of the tax computation. It is then taxed at the same rates as if it had arisen in the UK. If tax has been paid overseas on this income already however, a reduction may be available in the UK tax computation to compensate for the tax already deducted by another Government. We will look at when this might apply later in this chapter.

Individuals who are only charged tax on amounts they remit in the UK, pay tax on all foreign sourced income (including foreign savings and dividend income) at UK rates for non-savings income (i.e., 20% 40% or 45% based on the usual bands).

Residence of companies

12.9 Companies do not have a domicile, only a residence status for tax purposes. UK resident companies used to be liable to corporation tax on their total worldwide profits arising in an accounting period regardless of whether those profits are remitted to the UK – the same rule as applies to resident individuals. More recently, however, there has been a shift away from a 'worldwide' system to a 'territorial' system, so that in many cases foreign profits are exempt from UK tax.

A company is deemed to be a UK resident if it is either incorporated in the UK or, if it is not incorporated here, its central management and control is exercised in the UK. This is generally where the key operational decisions are made, often the place where directors' board meetings are held.

In addition to having subsidiary companies, i.e. where a parent company owns shares in another company which may be located in another country, many companies operate in other countries through a *permanent establishment (PE)*. A PE is a fixed place of business; the most common form of which is a branch.

Non-resident companies are liable to UK corporation tax if they trade in the UK through a UK based PE which usually involves staff, and often premises of some kind, based in the UK but owned by the non-resident company. The trading profits arising, directly or indirectly, from the UK-based PE are liable to UK tax, whether or not they are fully earned in the UK. The question of whether a foreign company has a PE in the UK is very complex and depends on the facts of the particular case. The recent controversies over large multinationals such as Google and Amazon have bought to the public attention how complex this area of tax law can be.

Income from property or rights either used by, or held by, the UK PE of a foreign company is chargeable to corporation tax as are any chargeable gains on the disposal of assets situated in the UK.

Double taxation relief

12.10 It is possible, because of the way tax systems in different countries interact, that a UK resident can pay tax in two countries on the same income source; in their country of residence and the country in which the income or profit arises (referred to as the source country). A UK resident (individual or company) is taxed on worldwide income and so may have to pay tax, for example, on foreign business profits in both the UK and the source country where the business is being carried on. This situation is called *double taxation*. Fortunately, the problem of double taxation is well recognised by tax authorities around the world and, in most cases, the full effects of double tax can be avoided.

There are two main methods for reducing double taxation on overseas income. One is a credit system, where the home government taxes the overseas income but then allows a credit, or reduction in tax payable, for at least some of the tax paid overseas (a worldwide system). The second is the exemption system where the home government chooses not to tax foreign income at all, i.e. it is treated as exempt from home country taxation (a territorial system).

In the UK, as in many other countries, double tax is reduced by a system of double tax reliefs. These reliefs are outlined in a series of agreements between countries on how they will each handle this problem. These agreements are called *double tax treaties*. The UK has a large number of double tax treaties with other countries that contain provisions explaining exactly how double tax is to be relieved and how taxable activities between their countries are to be reported. As a general rule, until recently, the UK tax was calculated on gross worldwide income and then double tax relief was deducted from that liability.

What if the country you pay tax to does not have a treaty with the UK? This does not mean that you will have to suffer double taxation. The UK tax rules also contain provisions which allow for unilateral (one sided) relief for at least some of this double tax for such cases. These provisions require that the foreign income is first included in the taxable income of an individual (or TTP of a company in some cases), grossed up for any foreign tax suffered.

The double tax relief under these relief provisions is usually the lower of the foreign tax suffered on the overseas income or profits, and the UK tax liability on that overseas income. More relief can be available where a double tax treaty exists, but this basic rule is true in most circumstances.

As part of the modernisation of corporation tax, a PE profits exemption was introduced in 2011. UK companies can now make an election to exempt foreign PE profits and losses from UK taxation. The election is permanent, so companies will have to be careful about making this election. If the location of the foreign PE has a lower rate of tax than the UK, and the PE makes profits, there will be a tax saving. However, if the PE is making a loss, then the election will mean that the loss cannot be offset against UK profits. If the foreign PE is in a location with a higher tax rate than the UK, then making the election to treat it as exempt will have no effect on the UK tax burden.

Activity

Aristotle Ltd is a UK resident company with no associated companies. During the year ended 31 March 2019, Aristotle had the following income:

	£
Tax adjusted trading profits from UK business	2,500,000
Tax adjusted trading profits from overseas branch office (PE) (net of 35% foreign tax)	208,000

Calculate Aristotle Ltd's UK corporation tax liability for the year, assuming the company does not opt to use the PE profits exemption.

Feedback

First, in calculating Aristotle's total taxable profits, it is necessary to gross up the foreign profits by the amount of foreign tax paid to determine the total overseas income.

	Total £	UK Income £	Overseas Income £
Tax adjusted UK profit	2,500,000	2,500,000	
Foreign profit			
(£208,000 × 100/65)	320,000		320,000
TTP	2,820,000	2,500,000	320,000
Corporation tax @ 19%	535,800	475,000	60,800
Less double tax relief:			
Foreign tax paid:			
£320,000 @ 35%	112,000		
UK tax on foreign income			
£320,000 @ 19%	60,800		
Relief is the lower of the two	(60,800)		(60,800)
Corporation tax payable	475,000	500,000	nil

Note: In this case £51,200 (£112,000 – £60,800) of foreign taxes payable cannot be offset against Aristotle's UK tax bill. FA2000 introduced a provision which allows eligible unrelieved foreign tax to be either:

- Carried back to accounting periods beginning not more than 3 years before the period in which the unrelieved tax arises; or
- Carried forward indefinitely.

In both cases the unrelieved foreign tax is treated as if it was paid in respect of the same source of income and may be relieved against corporation tax payable on that source of income, in the earlier or later accounting period.

Dividend income from foreign companies

12.11 With effect from 1 July 2009 the UK switched from a credit system of double tax relief to an exemption system, for companies that receive dividends from foreign companies in which they own more than 10% of the shares.

Where the exemption does not apply, the UK shareholder will be entitled to double tax relief. When a foreign company pays dividends to a UK resident shareholder, the country where the foreign company is located (the source country) is likely to levy what is called *withholding tax*, which is a tax at a fixed rate on dividends leaving that country to go to foreign shareholders. UK resident companies receiving dividends from foreign companies will usually be entitled to double tax relief for withholding tax paid.

Branch or subsidiary?

12.12 When a company is considering expanding overseas, a decision must be made about how best to establish its foreign activities. The most common options are to either set up the foreign business as a branch, or PE, of the existing business, or to incorporate a separate subsidiary company in the foreign country. This is a complex decision and, of course, does not only involve tax considerations. However from a tax point of view, we can note the following that must be considered at the minimum:

- A branch office of a UK business is not treated as a separate taxpaying entity. The profits of a branch will need to be included in the UK head office's trading income and so will be liable for UK corporation tax in the year in which they are earned in the same way as the profits of a UK based business are, unless the company elects for the branch profits exemption to apply.

- A subsidiary company is a separate legal entity and for tax purposes there is no consolidation of profits required as there is for accounting reporting to stakeholders. Dividends from overseas subsidiaries are exempt from UK corporation tax.

International tax avoidance

12.13 Double taxation of profits by two or more countries is an added cost of doing business overseas. Minimising worldwide taxes paid and, where possible, eliminating double taxation has led to the development of a large international tax planning community. This is of some concern to governments who want to protect their taxing rights and so the grey area between tax planning and unacceptable tax avoidance, which we discussed in Chapter 11, also arises in the international context. Some tax avoidance practices of multinational enterprises entail the use of tax havens, which are countries where little or no tax is imposed on the profits of organisations resident or doing business there.

In the UK, there are some specific anti-avoidance provisions which aim to protect the Government's tax revenue from what they consider to be unacceptable international tax avoidance. Here we will consider three common avoidance practices and see how the UK provisions operate to prevent their inappropriate use to artificially reduce taxes due to the UK Government. Specifically they are the transfer pricing rules, thin capitalisation rules and the rules dealing with controlled foreign companies.

Transfer pricing

12.14 Transfer pricing refers to the process of determining the price to be charged for goods or services flowing between related or associated enterprises. Where goods or services are bought or sold between unrelated enterprises, the parties will agree what is known as an *arm's length price*, which is the market price for the item being traded where both parties seek to get the best price they can from their perspective. Where the two enterprises are related to one another, through common shareholding or some other arrangement, it is possible to agree to set a price for trades between them which is not the same as an arm's length bargain. The way in which transactions are structured may then allow for some tax planning, particularly where the parties are in different countries and there is a difference in the tax rates in force in those two countries.

To illustrate how transfer pricing could be used to affect global tax liabilities, take the case where a company resident in the UK sells goods to a subsidiary company resident in France, which then sells the product to French customers. The product cost £1,000 to manufacture, £100 to ship to France and retails for £2,100 in France.

Depending on how the parties wish to price the transaction, the profit can appear to be made in either the UK or France or partly in both. For example, the UK company can sell the product to the French associate for £2,000 leaving a £900 profit in UK and a £100 profit in France. Alternatively, it can sell the product for £1,100 leaving £100 profit in UK and £900 profit in France.

The companies could also introduce a third party through which to trade to place the profits somewhere else again. For example, the company could create a wholly owned subsidiary, perhaps in a tax haven where there are no taxes on business profits. If this new company then charge say £900 to arrange the transport of the goods, £800 of the profit is shifted from either UK or France to the tax haven.

Given the flexibility transfer pricing across tax borders offers to companies, HMRC has been given the power under UK law to substitute an arm's length price for any prices they consider to be artificial, in situations where:

- Sales are made by a UK company to an overseas company at what they consider to be an undervalue; or
- Purchases are made by a UK company from an overseas company at an overvalue.

The legislation gives HMRC wide powers to enter premises and examine documents to obtain information relating to transfer prices.

The legislation applies not only to trading activities but also to:

- Sales or purchase of fixed assets
- Letting or hiring of property

- Loan interest
- Patent royalties
- Management charges

It should be noted that these rules did not used to apply to transactions between associated companies who are both UK residents for tax purposes. As HMRC is the relevant tax authority in both cases then they were less concerned about the use of transfer prices to artificially adjust inter-group profits in this way as the total tax paid across the groups was the same and was all paid to the same tax authority, however it is sliced up between the associates. With effect from 1 April, 2004, however, transactions between related companies will have to be at arm's length prices even when they are both residents of the UK. There are, however, some exceptions to these rules for small and medium companies.

There are comprehensive guidelines, published by the OECD, that advise how an arm's length price should be calculated, and the UK transfer pricing rules draw on these guidelines. There are several methods available and companies have a certain amount of choice about what method to use. This can lead to disputes with HMRC, and the tax authorities overseas if the transactions are with foreign companies or branches. Transfer pricing is therefore an area of considerable uncertainty and gives plenty of scope for disagreement.

It is possible for companies to enter into advance pricing agreements (APAs) with HMRC under which an agreed method can be used without being challenged for a certain period of time. Often these agreements are entered into bilaterally, that is not just with HMRC but also with another tax authority e.g. the US Internal Revenue Service, so that both countries commit to accepting the companies method for working out its transfer prices. This reduces the uncertainty for both the taxpayer and the tax authorities concerned.

In March 2011, the pharmaceutical company AstraZeneca plc received agreement from the US and UK tax authorities for an APA covering a 13 year period from 2002 to 2014. This agreement means that the company can resolve transfer pricing disputes with the US tax authorities which have been outstanding for many years, for payment of $US1.1 billion. The company had an accrual in its accounts of $US2.3billion, so this agreement means a significant reduction in the company's effective tax rate. This particular example demonstrates both the large amounts of money involved in international transfer pricing disputes, and also the way in which tax has an impact on financial reporting for companies.

Thin capitalisation

12.15 Thin capitalisation refers to a company's gearing; a thinly capitalised company is one which has a high proportion of debt financing compared to equity. The fact that dividends paid to holders of equity are not tax deductible, whereas interest payments to creditors are, means that there is a tax induced incentive for companies to finance operations through debt. The UK government, along with others, is concerned that companies may artificially inflate the amount of debt, and therefore interest payable, in order to get an extra tax advantage, which is viewed as a form of tax avoidance.

To counteract this, the UK government introduced a 'worldwide debt cap' that operates to restrict the deductibility of interest payments by a group of companies. The debt cap applies to periods of account beginning on or after 1 January 2010. Amendments to the rules were announced in the 22 June 2010 Emergency Budget following consultation with businesses and advisers about their practical application. The rules are complex and beyond this scope of this introductory chapter so we provide no further information here, but if you are interested, the HMRC website has useful details on these rules with further discussion in the June 2010 Budget document.

A further consultation on changes to the rules for how much interest can be deductible against taxable profits was launched by the UK Government in May 2016. Budget 16 announced that further changes to these rules will occur from April 2017 as a result of this consultation, however, these latest changes are on hold as a result of the General Election

Controlled foreign companies

12.16 We saw earlier that differences in the tax situation result from the choice of earning foreign profits through a branch office as compared to a separately incorporated subsidiary. Having a subsidiary company, where the UK parent company has a controlling interest, presents opportunities for at least the deferral of some tax, and maybe some tax savings. Remember that the profits of a subsidiary will not attract UK corporation tax until such time as they are remitted to the UK, although since 2009 dividend payments from subsidiaries are usually exempt as we saw above. If that overseas subsidiary is also located in a country where the tax rate is low, considerable overall tax savings can be made, so long as the profits are left in the hands of the overseas subsidiary.

When taken to extremes, this is viewed by the UK Government as being unacceptable tax avoidance, and so provisions are contained in the UK legislation to make deferring tax by leaving profits in the hands of some foreign companies less attractive. These rules specifically refer to what are called *Controlled Foreign Companies* (or CFCs). If the controlled foreign company rules are applied, then HMRC has the power to apportion the profits of the CFC between its corporate shareholders and charge those profits to corporation tax in the UK even though they have not yet been actually remitted to the UK as either dividends or in another form. The UK's CFC rules were overhauled and the current rules apply from 1 January 2013. They are quite complex, and here we will only provide an overview of how they work. The rules are designed to identify and bring to tax artificially diverted profits.

Under the current rules, a CFC is a company which is:

- resident overseas but is controlled by UK residents, and
- subject to taxation in its country of residence where the tax rate applicable is less than 75% of the corresponding UK tax rate.

In deciding whether or not an overseas company is controlled by UK residents, the rules look at legal, economic and accounting assessments. For example, shareholdings, voting power, other rights which give control and whether consolidated accounts are required under accounting rules. The foreign company does not need to be controlled by just one UK resident, a combination of UK residents can cause the foreign company to be classified as a CFC.

You will find a worked example of these control rules on the website.

There are several entity level exemptions. If any of these apply, then all the profits of the CFC will be exempted from a CFC charge. These include:

- Exempt period– for the first 12 months of coming under UK control;
- Excluded territories exemption – where the CFC is resident in a specified territory with a headline corporation tax rate of not less than 75% of the UK main rate;
- Low profits exemption – where the CFC's profits are not more than £50,000, or not more than £500,000 of which nor more than £50,000 is non-trading profits;
- Low profit margin exemption – where the CFC's profits are no more than 10% of its operating expenditure;

If the entity level exemptions do not apply, then a series of 'gateway' provisions operate to define the profits which are considered to have been artificially diverted from the UK and to which the CFC charge will apply. Where the profits do not fall within the gateway provisions, they are excluded.

The CFC provisions are very complicated and here we have provided only a very brief overview of their operation.

Under self assessment, UK companies are required to calculate their own liability to tax on the profits of CFC's. This is an onerous requirement, especially given the need to compute the CFC's profits as if they had been liable to UK corporation tax. Given, however, that the provisions only apply to UK companies with at least a 25% interest in the CFC, and then only if one of the exemption provisions does not apply, the rules do not have wide application.

The OECD BEPS project

12.17 Important work has been undertaken since 2013 by the OECD in relation to various aspects of the potential for international tax avoidance. This is primarily being undertaken under a project entitled 'Base Erosion and Profit Shifting' (BEPS). A number of working groups were set up to look into different problematic aspects of international taxation including the digital economy and the increased use of intangible assets. These groups reported on their considerations at the end of 2015 and 15 different Action Plans were proposed to implement their recommendations. Countries around the world are gradually introducing measures recommended by the BEPS project and in the longer term it is hoped that there will be greater consistency in the global rules.

The UK Government has started a process of implementing these Action Plans into UK legislation with Budget 16 announcing several resulting changes and the launching of further consultations for changes to occur from April 2017. Most of these changes are beyond the scope of this book. Further details can be found the *Business Tax Roadmap*, launched as part of the Budget 2016 papers – see http://tinyurl.com/jdm43wm .

For current information about the progress and recommendations of these working groups, you should refer to the OECD website: http://www.oecd.org/ctp/beps-frequentlyaskedquestions.htm.

In the UK, a new tax was introduced in 2015 that pre-empted some of the work of the OECD, the diverted profits tax, discussed below.

Diverted Profits Tax

12.18 Finance Act 2015 introduced a new tax, the diverted profits tax (DPT), which some call the 'Google' tax, because it is directed at the type of arrangements that Google entered into that left it paying little or no tax in the UK. The tax is at the rate of 25% on diverted profits that relate to UK activity.

The DPT is a highly complex tax and, according to HMRC, is designed to catch contrived arrangements used by large corporate groups to erode the UK tax base. There are some concerns among practitioners, however, that the scope of the tax is wider than HMRC suggested.

The tax is a radical departure from the usual principle that the UK will not attempt to tax the profits of foreign companies doing business in the UK unless they have a PE here. It was introduced largely in response to public concerns that technology multinationals like Google were avoiding UK tax through artificial arrangements.

Fiscal Fact

The new diverted profits tax is expected to bring in additional revenue to the UK government of £355m by 2019/20. [Source: HMRC Diverted Profits Tax TIIN]

Information access and exchange

12.19 A further anti-avoidance tool HMRC regularly uses is information access rights and information exchange agreements. HMRC has the power to obtain information from taxpayers to determine the extent to which they are telling the truth about their taxable activity overseas. The information can be supplemented by information from those with whom the UK has a tax treaty or tax information exchange agreement. Although such agreements do not exist with all countries, these agreements do cover a large number of the major trading countries where individuals or companies are likely to invest their wealth.

The question of information exchange is particularly sensitive in the case of dealings with countries that are tax havens, and the UK government, along with others, are concerned about the possibility of tax evasion through the use of offshore tax havens. In response to the G20 group's calls for more tax transparency throughout the world, to combat tax evasion, the OECD has been obtaining reports from countries about their exchange of tax information, including bank information. It released a report in March 2011 entitled *The Global Forum on Transparency and Exchange of Information for Tax Purposes,* which provides an in-depth analysis of 18 countries and is continuing to work to ensure that all jurisdictions adopt international standards on transparency and the exchange of information.

The release of the Panama and Paradise papers, which revealed information about monies placed in tax havens, has led to increased public pressure to tackle tax evasion through tax havens. In April 2015 new regulations came into force in the UK to implement automatic information exchange with certain jurisdictions.

Summary

In this chapter you have read an introduction to how the UK taxation system works in an international setting. The application of the UK income and corporation tax rules depends on whether the taxpayer concerned is a resident of the UK for tax purposes. In some cases, taxpayers may be subject to tax in more than one country on the same income or profits. When this happens, the UK tax laws provide for a credit to be allowed for the foreign tax paid in order to mitigate, if not eliminate the double taxation.

For companies setting up an overseas business, there may be different tax consequences depending on whether it is established as a branch operation or a subsidiary company.

The existence of countries with considerably lower tax rates than the UK allows scope for tax planning, and HMRC is concerned about the boundary between tax planning and unacceptable tax avoidance this opportunity offers. In this chapter we have considered three examples of special rules that allow HMRC to combat international tax avoidance, the transfer pricing rules, the worldwide debt cap and the controlled foreign company rules.

The international tax rules for companies are in the process of being changed following extensive consultation over a period of more than three years. The most significant change has been the shift to an exemption system, away from a credit system, that is consistent with developments in other parts of the world.

Project areas

This area of tax study is complex, but provides plenty of opportunity for projects. You may wish to explore some of the issues we have touched on in more depth, for example, the decision whether to adopt a branch or subsidiary structure for a new foreign operation.

The UK offers both a tax credit for foreign taxes paid (under treaty agreements or unilaterally) and exempts some forms of returns from UK taxation as we have discussed. However, other countries offer double tax relief in other ways. You might like to explore how these other methods work and compare the use of these different methods to the use of credits.

The UK Government is not the only one to tackle issues like transfer pricing, thin capitalisation and controlled foreign corporations, you could compare the approaches taken by governments in other jurisdictions to the question of international tax avoidance.

You might also like to review the work of the OECD in the area of co-ordinating international activity in this area, in particular the BEPS project which is gaining in profile and is likely to lead to significant changes in the tax rules for companies in the future in the UK and elsewhere.

Questions

Question 1

Petra is a resident in the UK, but is non-domiciled and has claimed to be taxed on a remittance basis. In the year ended 5 April 2019, she had income from the following sources:

i.   Bank interest paid on an account held in Jersey and not remitted to the UK

ii.   Salary paid by a UK employer for work performed in the UK, but paid directly into an Australian bank account.

Required: Explain how Petra's income will be taxed in the UK

Question 2

Andromeda Ltd is a company that is incorporated in France. Three of the four directors of the company are based in the UK and they hold their board meetings in London.

Required: Explain how Andromeda Ltd will be treated for UK corporation tax purposes.

Question 3

Zanzibar Ltd is a UK company that has a wholly owned overseas subsidiary, company called Zeus, located in a country with a lower corporation tax rate than in the UK. Zanzibar exports goods to Zeus at a price for tax purposes that is less than market price.

Required: Explain the consequences of the under-pricing of goods exported from Zanzibar to Zeus.

Question 4

Gerald is resident and domiciled in the UK and is employed by Pied Piper Ltd earning a salary of £42,000 for the year ended 6 April 2019. Gerald owns an overseas property which he rents to tenants earning gross rental income of £7,000 from which tax is paid overseas of £3,150.00. What will be Gerald's UK tax liability if the maximum double tax relief is claimed?

Question 5

Abacus Ltd is a UK resident that has two branches overseas. The results for the year ended 31 March 2019 are as follows:

	Abacus £	Branch 1 £	Branch 2 £
Trading profits	1,500,000	58,000	376,000
Overseas tax paid	n/a	5,800	112,800

Required:

(a) Calculate both the global and UK corporation tax payable by Abacus Ltd if Abacus does not elect for the PE profits exemption to apply.

(b) What difference would taking the PE profits exemption make to the global and UK tax liabilities?

(Note: answer available via lecturer's website)

Further reading and examples

Evans, C., Hasseldine, J., Lymer, A., Ricketts, R. & Sandford, C. (2017), *Comparative taxation: Why tax sytems differ*, Fiscal Publications: Birmingham;

James, S. & Nobes, C. (2018), *The Economics of Taxation (18th edition)*, Fiscal Publications: Birmingham;

Lymer, A. & Hasseldine, J. (2002), *The International Tax System*, Springer: Boston;

Oats, L, Miller, A. & Mulligan, E. (2017), *Principles of International Taxation (6th edition)*, Bloomsbury Professional: Haywards Heath, UK.

– all four books provide further explanation of international taxation issues.

Further information on the Automatic Exchange of Tax Information can be found on the OECD website at:
www.oecd.org/tax/transparency/automaticexchangeofinformation.htm

13 Environmental tax

Introduction

13.1 Environmental taxes are an important part of modern governments' strategy for dealing with the problem of climate change. As Fullerton et al (2010) observed in their research for the Mirrlees Review, we are currently seeing calls for much closer connections between the Government's environmental policy and tax policy.

At the end of this chapter you will be able to:

- explain the rationale for using environmental taxes and the different forms these take; and
- describe the types of environmental taxes and tax incentives used in the UK.

Rationale for environmental taxes

13.2 There are a number of possible ways of making businesses pay for their environmental impacts, including voluntary agreements, tradable permits and regulation. There is an argument, however, that the tax system is a more effective way of encouraging firms to reduce their impact.

A 2010 OECD publication *Taxation, Innovation and the Environment* made the following observations:

- OECD governments are increasingly using environmentally related taxes because they are typically one of the most effective policy tools available.
- The key is finding environmental policy tools which ensure that environmental improvement starts now, but which also stimulates innovation and development of cleaner technologies for the future.
- Taxes on polluters provide clear incentives to polluters to reduce emissions and seek out cleaner alternatives.
- Putting a price on pollution creates opportunities for a wide range of types of innovation. This gives taxation an advantage over more prescriptive environmental policy instruments which tend to focus on innovations that reduce emission of pollution but not the creation of it in the first place. Even for firms that do not have the resources to undertake R&D,

the presence of environmental taxes can make them use technologies developed by others.

- The higher the rate of tax, the more significant the incentives for innovation. Taxes levied at the source of pollution (e.g. CO_2 emissions) provide a greater range of possibilities for innovation. However, environmental tax policy needs to be stable and certain, and international aspects are also important. Policies that are too stringent may cause emission intensive activities to be relocated to other countries.

The main types of environmental taxes are those that impose a levy or charge on polluting activities, punishing polluters directly. However, the tax system can also be used in other ways, by providing incentives, or tax expenditures, that reward green behaviour with reduced tax liabilities. We will look at both ways of using the tax system for environmental purposes later in the context of the UK tax system but first we will have a brief look at another form of pollution control: emissions trading schemes.

Emissions Trading Schemes

13.3   Emissions trading schemes (ETS) are based on the idea that businesses are allocated permits that allow them to produce a certain level of emissions. The rationale is that they then have the incentive to reduce their level of emissions below their allocation and if they can do this, the excess permits can be sold to other businesses who perhaps cannot or will not reduce their own emission levels Businesses that reduce their emissions levels are referred to as 'abaters' and those that are efficient abaters will make money out of the ETS system, while those that are not efficient abaters will have to buy more permits and therefore are paying more for their polluting activities.

ETS schemes take different forms, for example some give permits free of charge to participants, and others work by an auction process so that participators bid for permits which generates revenue for the government from the auction process.

The UK introduced an ETS in 2002 as a 'cap and trade' system using an auction process. The initial auction set a cap on, or limit to, the level of emissions that could be produced each year, and this determined the number of permits made available, which businesses could then trade with other businesses. The scheme has now closed, but continues for businesses who have entered into climate change agreements, which are promised to reduce emissions levels in return for a reduction in their climate change levy (a form of pollution tax that we will examine later in the chapter).

There is also a European Union ETS which covers member states and therefore affects UK businesses. This scheme is different to the old UK scheme in two main features. Firstly, it is not voluntary as the UK system was, although it specifies which particular industries are covered. Secondly, it only covers CO_2 emission and not other forms of greenhouse gases. The UK system covered a wider range of polluting activities.

Economists believe that ETSs are a good way to encourage overall reductions in the level of greenhouse gas emissions, but there is also a case for having environmental taxes as noted above. In the next section we will look at some of the environmental taxes (so called 'green' taxes) that currently operate in the UK.

Green taxes in the UK

13.4 There are a variety of taxes the UK Government uses to deliver its environmental policy. These collectively are known as 'green taxes'. In this section we will review the most important of these taxes; transport related taxes, the climate change levy, landfill tax and aggregates tax. Some of these taxes re imposed on businesses, some on individuals, and some on both.

Transport taxes

13.5 For non-business taxpayers in particular, a key mechanism that the Government uses to encourage 'greener' behaviour is transport policy. Road traffic is a major source of nearly all air pollutants in the UK. The four most important tax measures currently affecting road transport are:

- Fuel duty rates
- Discounted duty rates for alternative fuels e.g. electricity and LPG;
- Vehicle excise duties which vary according to CO_2 emissions; and
- Taxation of company cars using CO_2 emissions to determine an additional charge on drivers of such cars to add to their income tax liability.

Fuel duties have a long history in the UK, in fact they have been around for over a hundred years. It is a form of excise duty that currently brings in most of the total revenue from green taxes. Because fuel duty is directly related to distance travelled, the more miles driven the more petrol or diesel consumed and so the more tax is paid. It is thought this will provide an incentive for people to reduce their journeys or switch to public transport instead.

Fiscal Fact

In 2004, HMRC assessed the impact of the change to CO_2 emissions for cars (introduced in 2002) and found that in the first year of the new system, average CO_2 emissions for new company cars fell from 196g/km in 1999 to 182g/km in 2002. This suggests their tax policy of making emissions levels affect tax bills is having an influence as hoped for by changing behaviour of company car buying taxpayers.

Discounted rates for less polluting forms of fuel are important to encourage people to switch to these and so reduce the overall level of pollution without affecting how much driving we do. We have seen, however, that the introduction of, for example, electric cars is a slow and difficult process. This is not least because of the lack of the infrastructure needed to make their widespread use viable, such as places where we can charge the vehicles up.

Vehicle Excise Duty (VED) is an annual 'tax' that is levied on road vehicles. This form of tax also has a long history in the UK and importantly, since 2001 has been based on the emissions ratings of the vehicles. This is to encourage drivers to use more fuel efficient, lower polluting vehicles, although this policy direction was reversed somewhat in April 2014 when VED for HGVs was reduced and cars manufactured before 1 January 1974 (starting a 40 year rolling exemption start date, so this becomes 1 January 1975 next year) became exempt – both are likely to be relatively high polluters.

In relation to company cars, Chapter 6 illustrated that the benefit in kind is calculated by reference to the CO_2 emissions of the vehicle. This is also to encourage employers to provide fuel efficient cars to their employees.

Many countries, including the UK, are now increasingly charging for road usage through bridge, tunnel and road tolls, and through congestion charging (city based charging as now in operation in London). While some of these charges cover the cost of provision of such infrastructure, charges made at levels over and above this cost are a useful rationing tool reducing usage. As the price is raised so at least this extra bit is, in effect, arguably a 'green tax'.

UK green transport policy doesn't only cover motor vehicles, but also airline travel. Air passenger duty was first introduced in 1993 and was initially levied on airlines based on passenger numbers but is now based on a per passenger rate. Increases in air passenger duty rates (brought in during 2007), and more recently the change to distance related tariffs (2008 Pre-Budget Report) which took effect from 1 November 2009, were also, at least in part, aimed at affecting the cost of air travel attempting to decrease the number of flights people take. As air transport is a significant polluter, any increases in prices of tickets will have a direct effect on pollution created, it is hoped.

Air passenger duty rates from 1 April 2018 are:

Band (distance from London in miles)	Reduced rate £	Standard rate £	Higher rate £
A (0-2,000 miles)	13	26	78
B (>2,000 miles)	78	156	468

The reduced rates apply for travel in the lowest class on the aircraft. The standard rates for travel in any other class. The higher rate applies to planes of 2 tonnes or more equipped to carry 19 or more passengers.

Climate change levy

13.6   The climate change levy was introduced on 1 April 2001 and is a tax on the use of energy in industry, commerce and the public sector. It doesn't apply to fuels used by the domestic or transport sectors and there are varying rates of levy depending on the type of energy used. It is possible to enter into a "climate change agreement" (CCA), where a discount on the levy is available to a business in return for agreeing challenging targets for improving energy efficiency or reducing carbon emissions. The discount is 90% for electricity and 65% for gas, LPG, coal and other solid fuel. At present there are 53 sectors across 9,000 sites participating in the climate change agreement scheme, which the Government has announced will continue until 2023.

There are two rates of climate change levy. The main rates tax the supply of certain energy products for business consumers. These rates are intended to change the behaviour of businesses and encourage them to turn to renewable energy sources. The second rate of climate change levy is referred to as the Carbon Price Support (CPS) rate which applies from 1 April 2013 to certain energy products and is intended to maintain a clear price for carbon emissions.

Rates of climate change levy can be found in Appendix A:

Fiscal Fact

The numbers of traders registered to pay these environmental taxes in 2017/18 were not large at: landfill tax 153 (down from more than 1,000 in the 1990's when it was introduced), climate change levy 428 (up from 360 in 2012/13 and continuing to rise slowly year on year) and aggregates levy 723 (up from its lowest point - since its introduction in 2002/3 - at 692 in 2013/14). Combined, however, these three taxes are estimated to have raised nearly £2.99 billion in 2017/18 (up from £1.99 billion in 2012/13). [Source: HMRC receipts and number of taxpayers and registered traders]

As further encouragement to businesses, there are 100% capital allowances available for investment in certain energy efficient equipment, as we saw in Chapter 7.

In Budget 2016 the government announced that, following consultation, the business energy efficiency landscape will be simplified including rebalancing the CCL for different fuel types. The main rates of CCL will be increased from April 2019 to cover the cost of the abolition of the Carbon Reduction Commitment.

Carbon Price Floor

13.7 The carbon price floor (CPF) is designed to make carbon based energy sources more expensive and to encourage energy suppliers to look for alternatives such as wind and wave power. The idea is to have a minimum price for carbon, which will artificially increase prices for carbon based energy. The legislation introducing the carbon floor price of £16 per tonne of CO_2 came into effect from 1 April 2013. It is planned to increase gradually every year until it reaches £30 per tonne by 2020 and £70 per tonne in 2030.

The tax applies to fossil fuels used in the generation of electricity, and works through alterations to the CCL rules, setting up new carbon price support rates of CCL. Carbon support rate commodities include gas of a type supplied by a utility, liquefied petroleum gas and coal and other solid fuels. From 1 April 2015, fossil fuels used in combined heat and power stations to generate electricity that is self supplied or supplied locally are exempt from carbon price support rates.

The Government has stated that "putting a price on carbon emissions is at the heart of the Government's strategy for enabling the UK to reduce emissions over the long term. The carbon price floor firmly establishes the 'polluter pays principle'".

Landfill tax

13.8 The landfill tax was introduced in 1996 and affects a wide range of businesses from landfill site operators to waste carriers, local authorities and every commercial producer of waste that is disposed of at a landfill site. Landfill is currently the main method of waste disposal in the UK and the tax is designed to discourage businesses from using landfill by making it relatively more expensive than alternatives and so instead will encourage them to find alternative ways of disposing of waste.

The rate of tax depends on the type and volume of wasted disposed of, and there are exemptions for certain types of 'waste' disposal, including pet cemeteries. The tax operates in a similar way to VAT (see Chapter 10 for a discussion of VAT). It is currently charged at £88.95/tonne (£86.10/tonne

2017/18) of waste landfilled. A lower rate of £2.80 per tonne applies to inactive waste (£2.70/tonne 2017/18). Provision is made for 'tax free areas' where a landfill operator also recycles, composts or incinerates waste. In this way, the tax ultimately falls on waste that is landfilled. This tax, and particularly its above inflation annual increases, explicitly aims to increase the cost of landfilling waste with the hope that businesses will look for more environmentally friendly ways to dispose of waste.

Aggregates levy

13.9 The aggregates levy applies to all aggregates extractors/producers in the UK and is currently £2.00/tonne (unchanged for the last few years). Aggregates are sand, gravel and rock, although not all aggregates are chargeable to this tax, there are some exemptions, for example, silica sand which is used in glass manufacture. The levy was introduced because of the high environmental costs associated with quarrying including noise, dust and damage to biodiversity. The Government hopes that by increasing the price of aggregates, it will encourage recycling although there is some dispute about how effective the levy is in this regard. The British Aggregates Association is opposed to the levy and has been lobbying Treasury to replace it with a 10p per tonne levy across the board.

Any business that exploits aggregates in the UK for profit has to register with HMRC and pay the levy, which came into effect on 1 April 2002. Exporters of aggregates are exempt from the levy. The system works a bit like VAT in terms of the registration process, although there is no registration threshold and no provision to reclaim input tax.

Summary

In this chapter you have provided an overview of the rationale for environmental taxes and the different forms it can take. We have also looked at several UK environmental taxes. Transport taxes, and particularly fuel duty, are the biggest green tax revenue raisers for the UK Government. They are controversial, however, because their incidence is uncertain, although it is clear that they affect different types of taxpayer differently, for example, those living in rural areas compared to those in urban areas. Other forms of green tax in the UK include climate change levy, landfill tax and aggregates levy. The whole area of environmental taxation is certainly important to society and can be expected to become even more important in the future if the current Government policy direction is maintained, as seems highly likely.

Project areas and discussion questions

Some interesting questions arise in relation to environmental taxes, for example in the case of transport taxes, is there a way we can match the damage to society (not just the environment) through the use of transport such as cars, with an appropriate tax that covers the cost of such damage? Further, determining appropriate levels of such activity to maintain desirable business and personal activity is an important political and social question. What is the right level of tax to reduce usage to sustainable, acceptable, impact levels but not to levels that might adversely harm society by reducing activities too much? What should the right balance be?

Other questions include whether an ETS is a better mechanism for controlling pollution than taxes on polluting activities? This is not just an issue of concern to the UK, of course, and it would be interesting to examine policies and practices that are being adopted in other countries to compare with the UK.

Further reading

ACCA (2009), Position Paper: *Green Taxation in a Recession* - http://www.accaglobal.com/content/dam/acca/global/PDF-technical/tax-publications/tech-tp-gtiar.pdf

Evans, C., Hasseldine, J., Lymer, A., Ricketts, R. & Sandford, C. (2017) Environmental Taxes in *Comparative Taxation: Why tax systems differ*, Fiscal Publications: Birmingham.

Fullerton, D., Leicester, A. & Smith, S. (2010) Environmental Taxation in *Mirrlees Review: Dimensions of Tax Design* available at: https://www.ifs.org.uk/publications/mirrleesreview/

Heine, D., Norregaard, J. & Parry, I. (2012), *Environmental Tax Reform: Principles from Theory and Practice to Date*, International Monetary Fund, New York.

HMRC Green Tax web pages can be found at: https://www.gov.uk/green-taxes-and-reliefs

House of Commons (2009), *The Future for Green Taxes*, Research Paper 09/86.

KPMG Green Tax Index – https://home.kpmg.com/xx/en/home/insights/2015/03/green-tax-index-an-exploration-of-green-tax-incentives-and-penalties.html

Leicester, A. (2006), *The UK Tax System and the Environment*, Institute for Fiscal Studies, London.

Milne, J. (ed) (2012), *Handbook of Research on Environmental Taxation*, Edward Elgar Publishing, Cheltenham, UK.

OECD (2010) *Taxation, Innovation and the Environment* - http://www.oecd-ilibrary.org/environment/taxation-innovation-and-the-environment_9789264087637-en.

14 Impacts of the UK tax system

Introduction

14.1 In Chapters 1 and 3 we saw how tax can affect the economic and commercial decisions made by taxpayers. When a tax on windows was introduced in 1696 homeowners blocked them up to reduce their tax bills, even though this led to health problems. Today the Government uses this same eagerness of taxpayers to avoid tax to influence their behaviour. In Chapter 13 we discussed how this fact is used to deliver the Government's environmental agenda but it is also used more generally than just in environmental policies. For example, fairly generous tax reliefs are available for those who are willing to put aside income into a private pension scheme. This tax reliefs makes the cost of providing a private pension relatively cheaper than it would be otherwise. Therefore, the Government hopes this will change taxpayers' behaviour and encourage take up of greater private pension provision than might otherwise have occurred without the tax break. This will then, in turn, reduce the reliance on the state benefits system for those taxpayers in the future.

When making a relief available, such as the one for pensions above, the Chancellor will have undertaken some sort of cost/benefit analysis. For example, if the only people who took advantage of the scheme were those who were already subscribers to a private pension scheme the Chancellor would have lost some tax revenue he would otherwise have collected without encouraging anyone else to help to reduce the costs of the benefits system by investing in their own pension provision. Although using taxes to affect people's behaviour is common, determining exactly how a tax change will affect behaviour is very difficult to predict reliably and governments can sometimes get it wrong.

In this chapter we will expand on some of the concepts we looked at in Chapter 3 to help us understand the effects of taxation on the economy generally (i.e. macro effects). We will then look at a number of other ways in which the tax system in the UK affects the decisions made by individual taxpayers (i.e. micro effects). We will introduce some new economic concepts that help us understand the effect of taxation on society.

At the end of this chapter you will be able to discuss the:

- concepts of tax incidence and excess burden;
- distorting effects of UK taxation on the decisions made by individuals, businesses and companies;
- the concept of tax expenditures;
- impact of tax on personal and business investment decisions;
- use of taxation to affect decision making, and
- problems of achieving fiscal neutrality.

The incidence of taxation

14.2   In Chapter 3, we looked at the burden of taxation in terms of the tax rate structure. Now that you know more about the UK tax system in current operation, we can extend that analysis by looking more closely at a wider range of issues relating to the incidence of taxation. The tax system affects many people – both directly and indirectly. The *formal incidence* of a tax falls on those who must actually pay the tax while the *effective incidence* of tax falls on everyone whose wealth or income is reduced, or purchase opportunities changed, in any way by the tax. This will often include people other than those who directly pay the tax.

While it is often easier to identify where most of the *formal* incidence of tax will fall, it is, in practice, often impossible to identify the full effective incidence of tax. However, to plan for the effects of tax changes this wider incidence should ideally be taken into account.

To illustrate this problem consider the example of a newspaper purchase. Currently VAT is not levied on the sale of newspapers. If, however, the Chancellor decided he wanted to reform VAT and introduce such a tax, he would want to assess the incidence of this tax change. The formal incidence of the new VAT cost would fall on the people who buy newspapers. That impact would be relatively easy to track and measure. The effective incidence is, however, likely to fall not only on the buyers but also on the newspaper sellers and their distributors. This is because, other things being equal, it is likely that the increase in price of a newspaper the tax will bring will result in a fall in the volume of sales of newspapers leading to reduced profits for the newspaper owners, their distributors and the retailers. In addition, in order to reduce the impact of the tax on the volume of sales, the newspaper proprietors, their distributors and retailers may decide not pass on the full amount of the VAT to their readers but may choose to reduce their profit margins instead. These 'ripple' effects may then spread further still, for example, creating reduced profitability for newspaper proprietors that may mean lower wage increases can be funded for their workers or lower dividends paid to their investors so these groups could also be affected – and so on as the ripples of tax incidence spread.

For the Chancellor to fully understand the likely impact of this tax change he would therefore need to review both the formal and, as far as possible, the likely effective incidence of the tax changes or he may introduce undesirable changes into the economy. This same principle applies to any tax change not just for VAT.

Tax wedges

14.3   The effect of the incidence of taxation can be assessed by looking at what is called the *tax wedge*. This is the difference between what the purchasers pay for a good or service and what suppliers get of this payment (i.e. after tax). As demand and supply levels are changed as prices of goods or services change, e.g. by imposing a tax or changing tax rates, a tax wedge is created by the interaction of the new demand and supply levels caused by the tax inclusive/exclusive price.

In the case of indirect taxes, such as VAT, the tax wedge is the difference between the marginal cost of producing and selling a good and the marginal benefit from consumption. In the UK then the tax wedge is equal to the VAT (and any customs duty levied if applicable on a sale). An item which is sold for £100 before VAT has a marginal benefit from consumption of £120 (£100 plus VAT at the usual standard UK rate of 20%), because this is what the purchaser is prepared to pay for it, and a marginal cost of producing and selling the good of £100 since this is the price at which the seller is prepared to produce and sell the good. Hence the tax wedge is £20, the amount of VAT which is due from the consumer.

In the case of a direct tax, such as income tax, the tax wedge can be said to be the difference between the marginal value of leisure sacrificed by a worker and the marginal value to society of another hour of work.

In the case of taxes on unearned income the tax wedge is the difference between the gross and net after-tax rates of return.

Activity

Determine the variables that make up the tax wedge when a trader employs a new worker.

Feedback

The tax wedge will be equal to the difference between the total cost of the worker to the employer and the after-tax salary of the employee.

This difference will be made up of four elements: the income tax which is levied on the employee's salary, the employee's national insurance contributions, the employer's national insurance contribution and finally the value of any business tax relief which will be available to the employer related to the cost of employing the extra member of staff.

The distorting effects of taxation are not just dependent on the formal incidence of tax; rather it is dependent on the size of the tax wedge. For example, in understanding the full distortion effects of employing a new worker, it is not as important to draw a distinction between employer and employee national insurance but the total amount of national insurance which must be paid. The total payment will determine the distortion effect.

The larger the tax wedge the greater the potential for distortions. We will be exploring these in more detail in the next section.

The ultimate payer of tax

14.4 The concept of the incidence of taxation is concerned with the question of who ultimately pays the tax.

In theory the burden of indirect taxes, like VAT, falls on the final consumer. Yet there is evidence that sometimes traders absorb some of the burden of VAT, rather than passing it on in full to their customers, either by not charging as much as they should with the tax included or by offering special sales deals. For example, many traders offered to fit double glazing free of VAT for some time after VAT was extended to double glazing. They, of course, aren't actually selling it free of VAT – but are paying it on their customers' behalf as a sales discount, thus absorbing the burden of taxation themselves in the form of lower profit margins.

In many cases, at least some of the burden of an indirect tax will fall on the supplier – not just the intended consumer – as whenever a price is adjusted (e.g. by applying or changing a tax like VAT) both the levels of demand and supply are likely to be affected. For example, normally as prices increase because of a tax change, demand will correspondingly fall, therefore suppliers have to either lower their price to attract back lost demand, or accept lower sales levels at the price they previously charged; Either way, their profits are likely to be affected even though the tax is supposed to fall only on the consumer.

Distortions and the excess burden of taxation

14.5 The burden of taxation is the amount by which a taxpayer's economic wellbeing is reduced because of taxation. However, direct burdens (i.e. actual costs of tax directly affecting investments or wealth) are only part of the impact we must consider from the presence of taxation. Further, secondary, impacts can occur when taxes are charged. For example, as we noted earlier, consumers may change their purchasing patterns if VAT changes, resulting in a secondary impact on consumption. When organising or planning for tax system changes policy makers must not only take into account the direct impacts or distortions they expect to create – but also look for the wider (excess) burdens that may be created elsewhere that may need to be mitigated if the knock on, or ripple, effects of a tax change is to be controlled. Managing these wider changes is a key headache for all tax policy makers as you can never be sure exactly how people will react to changes in the tax system. However, two economic principles of possible behaviour can help us better understand what may happen as a result of a tax change. The first is the substitution effect, the second the income effect. In this section we will review each of these and illustrate how they are useful to tax system designers in understanding the distortions to 'normal' behaviours they may create because of the presence of, or changes to, tax.

The substitution distortion

14.6 Tax induced substitution distortion arises when individuals consume more of one item rather than another because of the effect of taxation i.e. tax affects their relative levels of consumption or use of something.

This substitution distortion is also called the *excess burden of taxation*. The burden of tax caused by a government transferring spending power from the taxpayer to the state when they collect tax from them is not, in itself, inefficient but if it is done in a way that affects the economic choices of the taxpayer, the cost to the taxpayer is the excess burden of taxation.

There are many examples of taxes that cause a distortion in the economic decisions made by a country's citizens. For a number of historical examples, look again at Chapter 1. You could also include perhaps brewing your own alcohol to avoid excise duties on purchased drinks, so called 'booze cruises' to France to buy drinks at a lower VAT rate, or even emigrating for tax reasons, and so on.

We will see later in this chapter that taxes can also distort the capital investment decisions of businesses. Investment projects which have a positive net present value before tax can have a negative net present value after tax. If this happens a company may choose to use its money in some other way than would have been the case without the effect of taxation. Suppose that the company decides to distribute the funds they would have used for the investment to its shareholders. The shareholders then suffer a loss equal to the before-tax net present value of the project. The community more generally could also be said to have lost the benefit of the expenditure planned by the company that will now not happen because of the distortion tax has created. This may have been for the consumption of goods or services from other businesses, causing other businesses to lose potential orders, with the knock-on impact to their profitability also. The total number of jobs may also fall (or at least not rise, as may have resulted from the new investment). Finally the Government has lost tax because the project was not undertaken. The 'ripple effect' of substitution distortions can be significant.

The income distortion

14.7 A second tax related distortion to consider is the *income distortion*. This is when there is a transfer of wealth from the taxpayer to the Government caused by taxation. The income distortion describes the reduction in the amount that the taxpayer can consume out of the money they earn resulting from having to pay taxes on their income. Of course, all taxation creates at least some income distortion when viewed in isolation from the rest of the tax, benefits and public expenditure systems as the imposition of a new, or extra, tax will usually move wealth from the taxpayer to the Government. Taxpayers may respond in different ways to this distortion – but it will often encourage them to put in more effort, work harder, seek better investments and so on to cover the loss to their returns the cost of tax creates. However, if they believe taxation is becoming excessive they may either to give up the effort entirely (e.g. stop work and retire) or switch to another activity or investment type where lower taxes are found (e.g. substitution distortions drive a change of behaviour as outlined in the previous section).

Later in this chapter we will look at these possible responses in more detail to assess their possible impact on work versus leisure decisions, personal and business investment choices (where the presence of a tax affects returns earned, and therefore the investments that may be made) in more detail. Understanding the likely responses at a micro level to tax changes through these two distortions is a critical part of effective tax policy making by a government.

A lump-sum tax

14.8 The degree of income distortion resulting from a tax will be dependent on the average rate of tax applicable to the taxpayer. The greater the average rate of tax, the greater the income distortion. However, the degree of the substitution distortion will be dependent on the marginal rate of tax (the amount of tax paid on the next pound of the tax base being examined). In the context of taxes on income, it is argued by some economists that a *lump-sum tax*, where an individual pays a given amount of income tax regardless of the amount of work which he or she undertakes, would eliminate the substitution distortion when individuals decide whether to work harder or enjoy more leisure time. This is because if a lump-sum tax were to be introduced then a taxpayer's marginal rate of tax would be zero (once the lump sum is paid there is no further tax to pay).

A lump-sum tax would be likely to affect the behaviour of individuals less compared with variable taxes that change with changes in the tax base. The benefit of working for an extra hour will increase because there is no corresponding increase in taxation and so more work is likely to be undertaken by rational taxpayers. This does not mean that the lump-sum tax is not distortionary; any tax will introduce a cost which will change the taxpayer's behaviour, however, lump sum taxes will not have further distortionary effects after their fixed payments have been met as further activity then is tax free.

To achieve this reduction in the distortionary effect by a lump-sum tax the amount of a lump-sum tax paid by an individual must be independent of characteristics which the individual can influence. For example, a tax which increases with the educational and vocational qualifications of the individual is not a lump-sum tax because it may have a distortionary effect on the decisions made by individuals about their education and training. The same principle would apply if the lump sum were differentiated on other characteristics such as wealth, geography, etc.

While the lump-sum tax approach has some advantageous impacts, its use would not be without knock-on effects. For example, if only members of the workforce paid the lump-sum tax, there may be a distortionary effect as low paid individuals may be deterred from joining or remaining in the workforce.

The excess burden of taxation, and the distortions to economic decisions that result from the incidence of taxation, are therefore important considerations for the Government in making choices on the best way to develop the tax system.

Fiscal neutrality

14.9 We introduced the idea of fiscal neutrality briefly in Chapter 3 under the heading of economic efficiency. We can now explore this idea further as it is important in helping us understand and assess tax impacts.

You will recall that a tax system, or a sub-set of the tax system, can be said to be *fiscally neutral* if it does not cause a taxpayer to discriminate between economic choices. In practice this implies that the introduction of changes to the tax system does not change the economic choices made by taxpayers. Hence a fiscally neutral system seeks to raise revenue in ways which avoid distortionary effects.

A tax has a distortionary effect if it changes the relative cost of goods and services. If tax changes are made in one part of the tax system, and not in another, the changes could result in a distortion to the relative costs of goods or services. If such goods or services are substitutes of one another, this can create a distortion (termed therefore a substitution distortion) in their consumption patterns.

Consider, for example, how VAT is levied when you purchase a product. VAT of 20% is added to the purchase price of chocolate biscuits, like Hobnobs, because they are classed as a luxury good, but not to Jaffa Cakes which are deemed to be cakes and therefore as an item of food are a zero rated supply (as was discussed in Chapter 10). The laws of supply and demand tell us that the increase in the price of Hobnobs due to the tax, will lead to a decline in the number of packets of Hobnobs sold as purchasers will choose to buy other products instead (or maybe just go on a diet!). Some individuals may purchase Jaffa Cakes rather than Hobnobs because of the price differential the increase in Hobnobs' price has created (i.e. Jaffa cakes are now relatively cheaper than Hobnobs as their price does not need to include VAT). This switch from one product to another, because of taxation, is an example of the *distortionary substitution effect* as we discussed earlier in the Chapter. (Of course, some people just prefer Hobnobs and will continue to buy them – but there are always exceptions to the rule!). Other such anomalies in the tax treatment of similar products or activities can be found throughout the UK tax system, as we have seen in earlier chapters.

VAT would be a fiscally neutral tax if all goods and services were taxed at the same rate. If this was so, the marginal rate of substitution of one product for another will be the same including and excluding VAT. As this is not the case in the UK, then VAT cannot be said to be entirely fiscally neutral. However, as the majority of products are taxed at one general rate (20%) VAT can be said to be fairly neutral in practice. Fiscal neutrality only becomes an issue for VAT therefore when the Government changes the VAT tax base (which products are taxed at different rates) which it does periodically.

If a tax system is not fiscally neutral it is possible that the economic cost to the consumers and producers because of the impact of the tax may be greater than the revenue raised by the tax. The difference between the economic loss and the revenue raised is termed the economic, or excess, burden of taxation as we discussed earlier in this Chapter.

Since VAT is charged only when goods or services are purchased, VAT in effect makes saving relatively more attractive than spending money. This is another example of the inefficiencies introduced into our economy by our tax system and explains why expenditure taxes are considered by some people to be recessionary – because they encourage saving at the expense of consumption, thereby artificially reducing expenditure in the economy. This was illustrated in 2008/09 with the temporary reduction in the general rate of VAT (17.5% to 15%). The claimed reason for this reduction was to help stimulate spending as part of the Governments' anti-recessionary policies.

Is this a useful economic concept in tax therefore if tax systems aren't likely to achieve fiscal neutrality in practice? In fact, yes, it is useful if we want to assess the impact of relatively small changes to tax systems rather than as a goal in its own right for larger scale tax reform. Also, as we have been discussing throughout this chapter, the fact that the presence of tax may affect economic decisions is an important feature of the tax system which can then be used to achieve political, social and economic goals that may otherwise be difficult to make possible.

Decisions about work and leisure activities

14.10 While it is not always the case, in most jobs there is generally a relationship between how hard you work and how well you are paid (premiership footballers aside!). Many individuals therefore have the opportunity to earn more money by working harder. Some people may be able to work overtime, others may choose to do jobs which have longer basic working hours in order to earn more money and still others may work many unpaid extra hours in the hope of gaining promotion and higher pay in the longer term. Of course, many people also make decisions which reduce their income, for instance taking early retirement, working part time or taking unpaid holidays.

In this section we will consider the tax factors which influence an individual when making a decision about how hard to work and then briefly consider the effect of their decisions on wealth creation and the revenues collected by governments.

Marginal rates of taxation

14.11 When considering the role that tax plays in the decision to work harder or not it is the *marginal tax rate* (MTR) which is important, rather than the *average tax rate* (ATR). We briefly introduced these in Chapter 3; the marginal rate of tax is the rate of tax which is due if the taxpayer earns £1 more than their current income. The average rate of tax is the total amount of tax paid as a proportion of their total income.

MTR (on income) = amount of tax paid on next £1 of income

ATR (on income) = $\dfrac{\text{total tax due on income}}{\text{total income}}$

The role of marginal rates of tax in work/leisure decisions was one of the reasons given by the Government to explain their overall policy of the last thirty or so years of systematically reducing the top rate of income tax (Budget 2010 reversing this trend with the introduction of a new 50% top rate of income tax for very high earners). Their argument had been that lower marginal rates of tax can encourage individuals to work harder and that is a good thing for the economy generally as it generates more tax revenues, creates wealth and helps produce economic growth for the country.

Firstly, if marginal tax rates are so important to people's work/leisure decisions, what are the marginal rates of tax which are in force in the UK at the current time? The *effective tax rate* (ETR) on earned income can be considered to be the combined rate of income tax and national insurance contributions, since they are both compulsory. National insurance contributions are a contribution 'insurance' paid to earn the rights to certain benefits – however, as they are a compulsory levy on an employee's income, and contributions made only partly determine what benefits might be received in return, they are effectively a tax in all but name, hence the current debate about merging income tax and NICs.

Prior to April 2003, an upper limit on incomes subject to national insurance contributions applied so that incomes above a certain level did not attract the charge. From April 1, 2003, however, the Labour Government introduced a 1% levy to apply to all incomes without a ceiling. This may not seem to be a large amount, but nevertheless marks the breaking of a barrier that has existed for a number of years and indeed led to a further increase (to 2%) with effect from 6 April 2011.

To work or play?

14.12 As already suggested, many taxpayers are able to decide whether or not to increase their income by increasing their work effort. Let us take a simple example, an employee is offered the opportunity to work for an extra hour one evening. When making the decision whether or not to accept this overtime, an individual is likely to weigh the benefit of any extra money they might earn against the costs of working an extra hour.

Some individuals will be offered pay at a higher hourly rate to encourage them to work overtime. This may help persuade an employee to work the extra time offered as it increases the gap between their marginal benefit and cost of working or not working overtime (their marginal cost). Of course, employers usually offer their employees the opportunity to work overtime because they believe that the marginal cost to them, even at a higher rate of pay offered to the employees, is less than the marginal benefit to be gained from the work which the employee will do (i.e. they'll still make a profit).

In addition to the extra money being earned, an employee should also consider the tax consequences of the decision. An employee who undertakes overtime will, of course, pay tax at his or her marginal rate on their overtime income.

Activity

What are the costs and benefits to an individual of deciding to work overtime?

Feedback

On the benefit side, of course there is their overtime pay. There may also be some cost savings associated with working these longer hours; for example, the employee might have socialised with friends otherwise and they will therefore save the cost of the drinks etc. they would have bought.

There may also be some benefits from working overtime which are difficult to express in monetary terms. For example, if some kind of emergency has created the need for overtime, there may be an enjoyable sense of camaraderie among the individuals who undertake extra work to help fix the problem.

What about the direct costs of working overtime? These may be zero, but some employees may incur significant costs if they work for an extra hour including any of the following:

- extra child care costs
- transport costs
- additional eating out, and so on.

In addition, there may be many other costs which cannot easily be assigned a monetary value, for example, missing spending time with their family.

Now that we have identified some of the costs and benefits of making the decision to work overtime we can consider the marginal utility (i.e. value to the employee) of an extra £1 to a taxpayer. This may seem an odd thing to suggest at first; surely £1 is £1? However, value, as a comparison of relative costs versus benefits, can in fact change over time. For example, individuals may be willing to work more overtime in the month before they go on holiday than at other times as their need for this money (called by economists their *expected utility*) may be greater at that time than other times in the year. This is just one example of a complex set of circumstances which combine to determine whether an individual employee would rather work more hours at one time than another or one employee might choose to work overtime and another might decline the offer.

We identified one reason for the employer to offer extra work: the marginal benefit to them (e.g. profit earned from extra work produced) is greater than the marginal cost to them (i.e. over-time wages). For the employee therefore the decision is effectively the same one. That is, the collective marginal benefit is greater than the collective marginal cost. In practice, of course, identifying the marginal benefits and the marginal costs is likely to be difficult sometimes but, as employees, most people can make this rational decision even if we cannot fully justify why in monetary terms.

Activity

What effect does a change in the rate of taxation have on the decision to work overtime?

Feedback

Once again, we only need to consider marginal rates of taxation faced by a particular employee rather than the total tax paid or the average rates of tax. Suppose an employee habitually works overtime. If their marginal rate of tax is increased they may choose to work more hours to maintain their net (after tax) income. Alternatively, they may decline to work overtime because their net income per hour is such that the marginal costs exceed the marginal benefits.

We can illustrate these two possible situations with two examples. The first is an individual with a large mortgage who has to earn a given amount in overtime each month to sustain his/her lifestyle. The second is an individual with children who has to pay a child-minder an hourly rate to look after the children. The first taxpayer may choose to increase his hours of overtime to maintain his level of income because his marginal rate of tax has increased. The second may conclude that the net benefit of working overtime, that is the extra gross income less the tax and the costs of childcare, is too low to be worthwhile.

Similarly, a rise in the marginal rate of tax may provide an incentive to some taxpayers to work extra hours so as to maintain their previous net income while others may lower the number of hours they work as the marginal benefits gained perhaps then no longer exceed the marginal costs.

However, if we return to our original hypothesis, that the extra work would be undertaken so long as the marginal costs are less than the marginal benefits, then the lower the marginal rate of tax is, the higher the marginal benefits will become relative to the marginal costs associated with the extra work, and it is reasonable to expect that most individuals will undertake the extra work.

So far we have only considered individuals who are already working and are deciding whether or not to accept overtime. We could also consider the situation of those who do not currently work but may be able to obtain work if they chose to. This category may include, for example, single-parent families, who may have to rely on the state benefit system instead of any earned income they would otherwise be able to receive because marginal tax rates trap them into this position. If benefit dependent people start to work often their benefits are reduced once they earn over a relatively low limit of income. Once they start to work, therefore, their effective marginal rate of tax can be extremely high. Not only do they pay tax and national insurance contributions now on their new income, but they lose state benefits and may incur other direct costs such as extra travelling and child care costs they otherwise would not have to bear. This can mean the overall effective cost impact to them is prohibitive – much more than others on similar incomes may be bearing. This may make it difficult in practice for some people, particularly those reliant on benefits, to get into work when they want to.

Previous Chancellors went some way towards addressing these problems when providing parents with some relief for the cost of child care and substantial additional help for low income families in the March 1998 budget. This was helped further by the introduction in 2001/02 of the Children's Tax Credit Scheme and was further developed by the provision of the Child Tax Credit from April 2003, as we saw in Chapter 4.

There is evidence to suggest that different types of taxpayer respond differently to changes in the rate of tax and benefits. For example, mothers of school age children and those in later working life are particularly responsive to tax incentives, according to economic analyses. There are many other important issues in judging the decision to work or play which are beyond the scope of this text, but we can generally conclude that the lower the marginal rate of tax the more likely it is that individuals will choose to work harder.

Do-it-yourself or subcontract?

14.13 So far we have considered the marginal costs and benefits of work versus leisure decisions without looking at the impact on this decision caused by the varying alternatives to working over-time. This section looks at some of these alternatives and how they may affect this decision.

Activity

Suppose that Joe can choose to work overtime regularly on Saturday mornings. If the overtime is worked Joe will employ a self employed person to maintain his garden. Assume that Joe does not enjoy gardening any more than he enjoys work and that he works less efficiently in the garden than in his normal job. We will also assume that the gardener, who has special skills and equipment, works more efficiently in the garden than Joe. List the tax implications of the work or not work overtime options for both Joe and the gardener. (You may assume that all the transactions are recorded and tax is not evaded.)

Feedback

If Joe chooses to reject the opportunity of overtime and maintains his own garden, there are, at least, the following tax related consequences:

- his direct income taxation is unchanged
- his employer does not benefit from his extra work and so his profits are not increased and the corporation tax payable is unchanged
- Joe is likely to be working less efficiently than an experienced gardener and the economic value of the work he produces to society is likely to be less valuable than the economic value of the work which he would have undertaken during the period of overtime he has declined.

If Joe chooses to work the overtime and employ a gardener there are the following tax consequences:

- his direct income taxation increases as his earnings increase
- his employer's profits (should) increase and so the corporation tax payable increases
- the gardener receives an income
- the amount of direct income tax paid by the gardener increases
- the gardener may also charge VAT on his supply of labour.
- all three people have increased their net income which potentially enables them to spend more money and thus potentially pay more tax in the future, perhaps in the form of VAT on their expenditures.

As you can see, from a government's point of view, there is an increase in tax revenues and an increase in the income generating activity of the economy if Joe chooses to work overtime and employ a gardener compared to gardening himself.

Now what about the monetary factors which would increase an employee's desire to undertake additional hours at work and employ others to work for him?

The gardener will probably decide how much to charge for his services by deciding how much money he wants for himself and then adding on the cost of any tax, direct and indirect, which he must pay.

Other things being equal, the greater the difference between the after-tax income which the employee can earn and the gross cost of employing the gardener the more likely it is that the employee will undertake the overtime.

The after-tax income of the employee will also be increased if his marginal rate of tax is reduced. Similarly, the gross cost of employing the gardener will be reduced if either his marginal rate of tax is reduced or the rate of VAT he must charge is reduced.

Activity

In reality, a whole series of non-monetary factors will also affect this decision. You may wish to make a second list, like the one above, of these other factors to have a more complete picture of how decisions are really made in practice.

Feedback

Your list may have included items such as enjoyment of work/gardening, opportunity cost of spending time away from friends/family, pressure to work overtime as normal work practice, desire for promotion and so on. Each of these factors may influence the decision (i.e. affect the marginal benefit part of the calculation).

In conclusion then:

- the lower the rate of corporation tax the more likely the employer is to increase his level of economic activity and therefore offer overtime to the employee
- the lower the rate of income tax the more likely it is that the employee will undertake extra work and employ others to do the jobs he does not now do for himself
- the lower the level of VAT the more likely it is that an individual will purchase services from registered traders.

Tax expenditures

14.14 In Chapter 3 we considered how governments use deliberate variations in the tax base to influence taxpayers' behaviour. We noted that doing this violates the principle of economic efficiency, or neutrality, but nonetheless, governments continue to introduce special rules to encourage particular activities or to benefit particular categories of taxpayer.

These variations in the tax base are often referred to as 'tax expenditures', and some of the special rules we've previously discussed can be classified as tax expenditures, such as not imposing VAT on newspapers and Jaffa cakes.

In April 2014, the National Audit Office (NAO) in the UK produced a report on Tax Reliefs as a precursor to more intensive scrutiny of several tax reliefs in operation of the UK. The term tax relief is used to describe provisions that are an essential part of defining the scope and structure of a tax by providing rules which establish where the tax burden is and is not intended to fall. The term 'tax expenditures' is used to describe those reliefs that are "designed to deliver specific policy by providing behavioural incentives to achieve economic and social objectives". As at March 2013, it was estimated there were 1,128 tax reliefs for individuals and businesses in the UK. There are currently in excess of 1,500.

Tax reliefs can be delivered through a variety of different methods:

- Exemption – where an amount is excluded from the tax base;
- Deduction – an amount that is deducted when calculating the tax base;
- Credit – a direct reduction in the calculated tax liability;
- Rate relief – where the normal rate of tax is reduced;
- Deferral – where a tax liability is temporarily delayed, to be paid at a later time.

Think back to the previous chapters where we considered the UK tax base for the various taxes. You will have seen a variety of tax expenditures among these rules, providing for reductions in tax using one or other of the above methods.

Activity

If the Government wants to encourage certain activities or taxpayers, why not just hand out money rather than use tax expenditures?

Feedback

This is an interesting question, for example, if a government wants to encourage say research and development expenditure (R&D), it could do this by giving companies that are doing research and development work a grant of money to support their activity – and this does happen. Yet many governments, including the UK, also use the tax system to encourage R&D.

One difficulty with using government grants rather than tax expenditures to encourage activity is that it requires some form of application process. Companies wanting to get help with their R&D would have to apply for funding, wait for their application to be considered and then eventually receive the government grant if they are successful. There will usually be some sort of accountability attached to a government grant, the company will have to explain how the money has been used so that the government can be sure that it has been used for the purposes for which it was given. The government too will be accountable to the public through the budget process for grants that it gives for this kind of activity.

By using a tax expenditure instead, for example, allowing a reduced tax liability to arise when a company spends money on R&D, there is no need for an application process, and for the government the reduced tax will not be as visible in the government accounts. Arguably this last point means that the government is not as politically accountable for tax expenditures as for direct grants.

One danger with tax expenditures is that the government loses control over which taxpayers are benefitting. The law is put in place allowing for a reduction in tax liability if certain requirements are met, and anyone who meets those requirements will get the tax reduction. This means that there is potential for a tax expenditure to be used by taxpayers who weren't supposed to benefit from it, and in some cases there is evidence that tax expenditures are used for tax avoidance purposes.

In the next few sections we will look at a selection of UK tax expenditures that are designed to specifically influence taxpayer behaviour in the areas of personal investments, business decisions generally and for companies in particular.

The personal investment decision

14.15 Having reviewed 'work versus leisure' decisions in the previous section, this section provides a discussion of personal investment decisions as another subject where the tax system can have significant impacts.

The financial services sector has proven to be very creative and there is a huge choice of investment types for individuals who wish to save money they receive rather than spending it. In this section we will consider the way the tax system impacts on individual's savings choices. In particular, we will consider ISAs, pensions and investments in housing.

Individual Savings Accounts (ISAs)

14.16 ISAs are a type of investment first made available to investors in April, 1999, then refreshed in 2014 as new ISAs. The Chancellor's stated objective for ISAs when they were introduced was to maintain the total tax relief given for two prior schemes that offered similar tax efficient savings opportunities (TESSAs and PEPs) but use it to encourage people who were not currently savers to start saving. In 1999 only half of the population had savings in excess of £200, so there was clearly scope for increasing the number of savers. These savings accounts became available from a much wider range of suppliers (even from supermarkets) as well as the usual financial institutions such as banks and building societies.

The accounts initially had a guaranteed life of ten years but this was extended and became permanent in the 2007 Budget as they had proven effective in increasing savings in at least some parts of the population (sadly not all – the latest data suggests 40% of the UK population do not have £500 in savings). There is no lifetime limit on how much can be saved in the scheme in total, however, the maximum which can be saved in a particular fiscal year is set each year. From 6 April 2017 the overall limit for 2017/18 is £20,000 for ISAs.

An ISA can be made up of cash and stocks and shares. The account can either be of one single investment in equities or split between cash and shares. Previously there was a restriction on the amount that could be held as a cash ISA, but under the new rules applying from July 2014 the restriction has been removed.

Fiscal Fact

The cost to the government of providing an exemption for ISAs is estimated to be £2.9 billion for 2017/18.

The key tax aspect of these accounts is that, unlike most other forms of savings, qualifying schemes are completely free of income tax and capital gains tax on their investments.

ISAs are therefore a good example of how tax expenditures are used to affect the decisions people make about their financial position. Their tax free status is used to influence the level, and type, of savings people undertake.

Personal pensions

14.17 We saw in Chapter 5 that saving through a personal pension plan, particularly if it is a scheme to which a taxpayer's employer contributes, has historically been tax efficient. Contributions to a HMRC approved pension fund are eligible for tax relief (i.e. a reduction in the payer's tax bill) at the taxpayer's marginal rate of tax (at least up to a reasonably high limit historically). Employer contributions, if they make any for their employees, are also eligible for tax relief through their tax calculation. Investment returns in a pension fund are also free of income tax and capital gains tax. However, apart from a tax-free lump sum that is usually paid when the pension is eventually taken by the taxpayer, other income from a pension once you start to draw on it is taxed as earned income (i.e. is treated as part of your non-savings income in your personal tax computations). All inputs into approved pension funds therefore get tax relief and you only pay tax on the income the fund generates once you start getting back these funds as your pension.

The significant tax benefits attached to private pensions is a key way the Government encourages people to save for their own retirement. The benefit for society of them doing this will be the decrease in their reliance on the state for income when they stop working. The UK Government has been reviewing tax relief on pensions however, to ensure it continues to act as an adequate incentive to save for retirement while at the same time doing so cost effectively in terms of tax revenues foregone from these reliefs.

Chapter 5 outlined a number of changes the first stage of this review brought about in 2014, including a significant reduction to the sums that can be contributed to a personal pension each year that qualify to get a tax deduction (to £50,000 from previous level of £255,000). From 6 April 2015, the allowance was further reduced to £40,000. Pension holders are also now able to extract capital from their pension accounts as they wish – subject to tax at their marginal rates once they withdraw more than 25% of the pension pot (i.e. the previously allowed tax-free sum).

Home ownership

14.18 Finally, we can consider the tax incentives that are, or have been, available for home owners.

Prior to April 2000, the interest paid on the first £30,000 borrowed to buy the taxpayer's main residence attracted tax relief as part of a scheme called MIRAS (Mortgage Interest Relief at Source). In 1998/99 and 1999/2000 this was at a rate of 10%. This scheme provided a significant tax advantage to owning the house you lived in rather than renting it as tax deductions did not apply to rental costs. During the 1980s homeowners could obtain this relief at their marginal rate of tax. This tax relief is no longer available so this particular tax incentive to own property rather than renting no longer exists (although the culture of owning your own home that this tax break helped create is now well established in the UK).

The real tax advantage of buying your own home now, however, is that capital growth does not give rise to a capital gains tax liability, unlike most other assets you may own. Imagine the attitude of home owners to increases in house prices if 18% (or worse, 28% as a higher or additional rate taxpayer) of any increase in their house values had to be paid in tax – clearly not likely to be a vote winner, which is perhaps why this key personal asset remains largely untaxed compared to other personal assets.

Activity

Could taxation be used to reduce the volatility we experience in housing markets? How should this be done? What knock-on impacts might taxing homeowners have?

Because of the privileged tax position of housing, people have often been persuaded to commit more of their wealth to their main residence than might otherwise be the case. Remember the case of Hobnobs and Jaffa Cakes in the section on fiscal neutrality? The distorting effects of taxing Hobnobs and not Jaffa Cakes made buying Jaffa Cakes relatively more attractive. Likewise, the tax advantages of owning a house over other forms of investment create a propensity to hold wealth in property rather than in other forms. As we have seen in recent years, holding wealth in property isn't always guaranteed to be a safe investment however, (house prices can go down as well as up) so tax-induced bias to hold assets this way may have added to the current housing pricing problems even if this tax policy was useful in other ways (another example of the difficulty of controlling tax incidence).

Tax and the business investment decision

14.19 Having reviewed some tax induced impacts on personal investment decisions, what about businesses and the investment decisions they make? Does the tax system also impact on these?

Businesses grow by incurring expenditure now in order to increase revenue in the future. There are often a number of ways in which this investment can be undertaken and the business must decide what is the optimal allocation of its resources to these opportunities to achieve its goals – including improving its long term profitability. For example, a business might invest in property plant and equipment or could instead incur training costs to prepare its workforce for new technologies. One of the features that marks a successful business from an unsuccessful one is the ability to determine which of these expenditures will lead to the best, or most sustainable, future profit.

When businesses undertake investment appraisal analysis they are encouraged to evaluate the cash flows associated with the project options. Cash flows are however, influenced by tax, and, as we will see, the tax treatment of the cash flows depends on their nature.

In this section we discuss the distortions that the tax system creates when a company is evaluating investment options with a life of several years.

Investment in long-term projects and fiscal neutrality

14.20 There are a number of techniques used by companies to evaluate a potential capital project. We will just consider discounted cash flow (DCF) techniques using the net present value (NPV) method as just one example of a widely used technique, as the impact of the tax system is similar on all evaluation techniques. There are a large number of books which explain this method very well, however, the basic principle is that all future cash flows resulting from the investment are stated at their value today, i.e. their present value, by discounting them using the company's cost of capital (i.e. what it would cost them to fund this investment). If the sum of all these present values of predicted future cash flows is positive, the investment is considered to be financially worthwhile. A simple example will help to explain the technique.

Activity

A Ltd. is considering investing £10,000 in a project which will generate a cash flow of £6,000 for two years starting one year after the initial investment. The company's after-tax cost of capital is 12%. (A company's cost of capital might be the company's cost of debt. The after-tax rate is used because interest payments are tax deductible and that should be included in the evaluation calculation).

Feedback

You need to undertake the following calculation in order to calculate the net present value:

Year	Cash flow £	Discount factor 12%	Present value £
0	(10,000)		(10,000)
1	6,000	0.8929	5,357
2	6,000	0.7972	4,783
		Net present value	140

Because the net present value of this scheme is positive, other things being equal, the theory tells us that the investment should be undertaken. Projects which generate a negative net present value should normally be rejected unless there are other, secondary, reasons to do them.

Notes on above example:
- payments of cash are cash outflows and are shown as negative numbers
- the discount factor for each year is calculated by using the formula:

$$\frac{1}{(1+r)^t}$$

- where r is the discount factor expressed as a decimal, i.e. 12% is written as 0.12, and t is the number of the year in which the cash flow arose

- the first cash flow, usually a cash outflow, is deemed to take place immediately and hence is recorded as occurring in year 0 and is already stated at its present value
- cash flows are deemed to arise at the end of the year in which they are recorded and so need to be discounted in full for that year.

From this example we can generate a simple test for fiscal neutrality. A business tax is fiscally neutral if the decision about whether to undertake the investment is the same using the before-tax and after-tax cash flows.

The only way for a tax system to be fiscally neutral for business investment is if tax is charged on positive cash flows at the same time as the cash flow arises, and tax relief should be available for cash outflows at the time the cash payment is made. If this situation exists, the rate of tax is 'T' and if the before-tax net present value is £B then the after-tax cash flows will be £$B(1 - T)$. Provided the rate of tax is less than 100% and if B is positive, then $B(1 - T)$ will also be positive. Equally if B is negative then $B(1 - T)$ will be negative. This means that so long as projects which give a positive net present value are accepted regardless of the numerical value of the net present value, the before-tax decision will be the same as the after-tax decision and the system is fiscally neutral.

The impact of the UK corporation tax system on investment appraisal

14.21 In practice, the UK corporation tax system does not tax cash flows, but neither does it simply tax accounting profits (those you will see in a company's annual reports and accounts). In Chapters 6, 7 and 9 we saw that the system is instead something of a hybrid with some accounting adjustments, such as depreciation, being ignored for tax purposes and other expenses taxed on the accruals basis. In addition, there is a nine-month gap for all but large companies between the end of the accounting period and the payment of tax on that period's profits.

Expenditure on a new project may include any, or all, of the following items:
- land and buildings
- plant and machinery
- working capital
- advertising
- staff training.

You can probably think of more examples but let us consider the tax treatment of each of these types of expenditure.

In some cases, tax relief is available for expenditures related to business activities. In assessing the impacts of the corporation tax system on investment appraisal, we need to take any reliefs into account. There is no tax relief for expenditure on land and buildings following the phasing out of industrial buildings allowances in 2011.

We saw in Chapter 7 that expenditure on plant and machinery is likely to qualify for a writing down allowance of at least 8% of the reducing balance each year.

Expenditure on working capital, that is unsold stock and money invested in debtors which has yet to be realised, is not eligible for any tax relief (although a stock relief of this kind used to be given in the UK on changes in stock holdings over a year, but was scrapped in the 1980s because of its significant impact on business activity).

The costs of advertising and staff training are likely to be considered expenditure 'wholly and exclusively' for the purpose of trade and so are fully deductible for tax purposes. Which expenses can or cannot be deducted from our profits in practice will, of course, affect how much tax we then have to pay.

There is a wide variety of tax treatments of expenditure incurred to set up and operate a new project. This makes assessing the full impact of tax on a business investment decision very difficult in practice. In the light of the different tax treatments of different items of expenditure it seems unlikely that any move towards fiscal neutrality is feasible. However, the lower the rate of business tax the smaller the distortions caused by the tax system, but the tax system clearly has important impacts on business investment decisions.

In the next section we discuss a number of special incentive provisions in the UK's tax system and some research reports that have analysed their effectiveness. These research reports are all available on the HMRC website.

Enhanced capital allowances

14.22 We saw in Chapter 7 that there is a special set of rules within the capital allowances regime that is designed to encourage investment in certain types of capital assets – the enhanced (100%) capital allowances for energy saving equipment. In May 2008, HMRC published a research report of a study that was undertaken in 2005 into the effects of this incentive, which was originally introduced in 2001. The study found some changes in the equipment purchasing patterns between those businesses who were aware of the allowances, and those who were not, but it looks like other factors are involved in this decision making process too. In terms of the CO_2 savings resulting from the purchase of the technologies considered in the survey, the savings are estimated to be 2,800 kT of CO_2 over the life of the equipment.

Intangibles

14.23 In Chapter 9 we explored the special set of rules for corporation tax that deals with intangible assets that was introduced in 2002. In 2010, HMRC commissioned a report into the intangibles regime, specifically to explore the decision making processes in companies regarding intangible assets. Interestingly, the UK intangibles regime was viewed by the tax directors interviewed as being neither favourable nor unfavourable. The taxation of intangible assets was seen as being part of doing business, rather than a direct influence on decision making processes. For most of the companies interviewed, the creation or purchase of intangible assets was first of all a question of corporate strategy. Only once a decision has been made on a commercial basis, were tax effects then taken into account.

One interesting factor that this research project identified was that the introduction of the intangibles regime seems to have affected buyers and sellers of intangibles differently. For example, an intangible asset, such as a brand, in the hands of a company can be sold either as an asset, or by selling the shares of the company itself. Sellers generally want to sell the shares, because as we saw in Chapter 8, there is a capital gains tax exemption for the sale of substantial shareholdings. Buyers on the other hands want to buy the assets rather than shares, because then the intangibles rules allow them to write off the cost of purchase, which can't be done for shares.

Research and development

14.24 Like many other countries, the UK provides tax incentives to encourage businesses to invest in research and development (R&D). We discussed R&D credits in Chapter 9.

HMRC, together with the Department for Business Innovation and Skills, commissioned a research study into the R&D tax credit system and the impact on the behaviour of companies. The study involved a series of interviews with managing directors, finance directors and directors responsible for R&D in 69 companies varying from micro businesses to multinational corporations, and was undertaken between October 2009 and March 2010. The study found that applying for R&D credits is often not connected to the R&D functions within the organisation, and that many companies see the R&D tax credit as a 'bonus', that is, it had little effect on the actual decision to conduct individual R&D projects. There is a general view that the R&D tax credit system does increase the overall amount of R&D in the UK and is especially important for small companies.

EIS and VCT Schemes

14.25 In 2007, HMRC commissioned a study into the impact of the Enterprise Investment Scheme (EIS) and Venture Capital Trusts scheme (VCT) on recipient companies to evaluate whether the incentives are worthwhile. These incentives are designed to encourage profitable risk-taking by private investors by investing in entrepreneurial activity in the small and medium sized business sector. The EIS was introduced in 1994 and gives tax relief to private individuals who invest in qualifying shares in small unquoted trading companies. VCTs are also designed to increase the supply of finance to small business, but indirectly. VCTs were introduced in 1995 and are a form of collective investment vehicle that allows private investors to invest in a diversified range of activities through a professional investment manager.

The study employed econometric techniques using HMRC data about companies. It found that investments under EIS and VCT were associated with growth in fixed assets and employment and expansion in sales, although on average the schemes seem to have little impact on real gross profits.

Another study was recently conducted into the use and impact of EIS and VCT (HMRC Research Report 355, published February 2016). A survey revealed that nearly 80% of respondents report that income tax relief is an important driver of their investment decision. Follow up qualitative interviews showed that the expansion of both EIS and VCT schemes in 2012 were viewed positively.

Community Investment Tax Relief

14.26 In Chapter 4 we saw that, since 2002, the Government has been attempting to stimulate the flow of private finance to deprived communities in the UK through the use of Community Investment Tax Relief (CITR). The system requires Community Development Financial Institutions (CDFIs) to be registered and become accredited, receive investments in the form of loans, equity investments or deposits, then lend on the funds to qualifying enterprises.

According to Responsible Finance (previously called the Community Development Finance Association or CDFA), members reported raising £8.7million in 2012 using CITR, and £86million since 2003. On average this is £10million raised per year, much lower than the £200million that was predicted when the scheme was first introduced.

If you are interested in learning more about community finance, see the Responsible Finance website at http://responsiblefinance.org.uk/

Real Estate Investment Trusts

14.27 The Real Estate Investment Trust (REITs) regime was introduced in 2007 and allows for quoted property investment companies to elect to not pay corporation tax, but rather be taxed only at the shareholder level. To join the system, companies must pay a charge of 2% of the market value of its property. To benefit from the system, at least 90% of the annual tax exempted rental income must be paid to shareholders. The original policy purpose of REITs was to stimulate investment in property. For a study that looks at market responses to REITs, see Holland (2014).

It seems the case that, while tax incentives are important in overall business planning, many are not driving business decisions in their own right. Whether this is as it should be (i.e. existing taxes are relatively efficient taxes in that sense) or whether this means they are having only limited impacts and as such are simply unnecessary complications to our tax system, is an interesting question for discussion. However, it is clear that understanding tax effects more generally has an important role to play in business decision making.

Summary

In this chapter we began by attempting to identify the individual who suffers a loss in his or her wealth because of the requirement to pay tax. We found that the actual incidence of tax was often difficult to determine and that it was often different from the formal incidence. We then spent some time discussing some of the limitations of the existing tax system before considering some of the distortions which exist. We have considered the distortions caused by both income and expenditure taxes for both individuals and companies. We have seen that lower marginal rates of tax are less likely to lead to distortions than higher marginal rates of tax. In order to achieve low marginal rates of tax it will be necessary to levy the tax on a wide range of income or expenditure as possible. For example, if VAT was extended to include food, children's clothing, books and newspapers it would be possible to reduce the rate of VAT and still generate the same amount of revenue for the Government.

We concluded the chapter by then examining the role and impact of tax expenditures. We did this by looking at a number of micro level impacts of taxation on individuals' work versus leisure choice, on their personal investment decisions and on business investment appraisals.

On the question of managing the impacts of taxation generally, we can conclude that a broad tax base and low marginal rates of tax leads to fewer distortions than a narrow tax base with high marginal rates of tax.

Project areas and discussion questions

There are many interesting projects contained within the material of this chapter. A topical area is that of the disincentive to work shared by many single parents who simply cannot afford to work. An evaluation of the Working Tax Credit systems or the Child Tax Credit systems, combined with the benefits system, would be an interesting project in this area.

An investigation into the impact of ISAs on savings patterns would make a good topic for a dissertation. For example, has their use increased or decreased savings in total? (i.e. have they cost the Government foregone tax revenue they would previously have received on taxed savings products?).

An examination of the impact of marginal tax rates on employee decisions to work or not to work may be an interesting area for a project. What impacts might the introduction of capital gains (or other) tax on profits of sales of houses have on house prices, peoples' desire to see house prices keep rising, and related housing costs?

An interesting project could be undertaken to review how flat taxes are working in countries that are using them and considering its potential use in the UK.

Further reading

Brown, C. and Sandford, C. (1993), Tax Reform and Incentives: A Case Study from the United Kingdom, in *More Key Issues in Tax Reform*, Sandford, C. (ed), Fiscal Publications, Birmingham, UK.

Evans, C., Hasseldine, J., Lymer, A., Ricketts, R. and Sandford, C. (2017), *Comparative Taxation: Why Tax Systems Differ*, Fiscal Publications, Birmingham, UK.

Holland, K (2014) *Market Valuation of UK Real Estate Investment Trust (REIT) legislation*, ICAEW Charitable Trusts.

James, S. and Nobes, C. (2017), *The Economics of Taxation (17th edition)*, Fiscal Publications, Birmingham, UK – a very useful guide to tax incidence, tax distortions and the subject matter of this chapter.

NAO (2014), *Tax Reliefs* available at:
http://www.nao.org.uk/wp-content/uploads/2014/03/Tax-reliefs.pdf

Potter, S & Parkhurst, G. (2005), Transport Policy and Tax Reform *Public Policy and Management* June, pp 171 – 178.

Scholes, M., Wolfson, M., Erickson, M., Maydew, E. and Shevlin, T. (2001), *Taxes and Business Strategy: A Planning Approach (2nd Edition)*, Prentice Hall: Englewood Cliffs, New Jersey.

Smith, S. (1993), 'Green Taxes' – The Scope for Environmentally Friendly Taxes in *More Key Issues in Tax Reform*, Sandford, C. (ed), Fiscal Publications: Birmingham, UK.

HMRC research reports, including the ones discussed in this chapter, can be found at http://www.hmrc.gov.uk/research/reports.htm

A Appendix A: 2018/19 Tables of tax rates and allowances

The current rates and allowances for income tax, corporation tax, capital gains tax, inheritance tax and other taxes are set out below.

Income tax rates***

	Non-savings	Savings	Dividends
£0 – £2,000	–*	0%*	0%**
£0 (or £2,000) – £34,500	20%	20%	7.5%**
£34,501 – £150,000	40%	40%	32.5%
Over £150,000	45%	45%	38.1%

* 0% rate on savings only available up to £5,000 of savings income if non-savings income does not exceed this sum. In addition, a £1,000 personal savings allowance is available to basic rate taxpayers (£500 for higher rate taxpayers and nil for additional rate taxpayers).
**Dividend allowance of £2,000 (£5,000 2017/18)
*** Scottish IT rates: £1-£2,000=19%, £2,001-£12,150=20%, £12,151-£31,580=21%, £31,581-£150,000=41%, over £150,000=46%

Personal income tax allowances

	2018/19 £	2017/18 £	Increase £
Income tax allowances:			
Personal allowance	11,850	11,500	350
Income limit: personal allowance	100,000	100,000	0
Transferrable tax allowance (married couples)	1,190	1,150	40
Income limit: transferable tax allowance	28,900	28,000	900
Dividend allowance	2,000	5,000	–3,000
Personal savings allowance:			
Basic rate taxpayers	1,000	1,000	0
Higher rate taxpayers	500	500	0
Blind person's allowance	2,390	2,320	70

Car and fuel benefits in kind

Car benefit charge: round down to find the correct percentage:

CO_2	Taxable %		CO_2	Taxable %		CO_2	Taxable %	
g/km	Petrol	Diesel	g/km	Petrol	Diesel	g/km	Petrol	Diesel
0(EV)	13	17	115	24	28	150	31	35
51	16	20	120	25	29	155	32	36
76	19	23	125	26	30	160	33	37
95	20	24	130	27	31	165	34	37
100	21	25	135	28	32	170	35	37
105	22	26	140	29	33	175	36	37
110	23	27	145	30	34	180+	37	37

Car fuel benefit charge	£23,400
Van benefit charge	£3,350
Van fuel benefit charge	£633

Approved mileage rates

	Business Miles	Allowance rate per mile
Cars and vans	0 – 10,000	45p
	10,000+	25p
Motor cycles		24p
Bicycles		20p

Excess payments over these rates are taxable. Shortfalls can be claimed as tax relief by the employee.

Income tax reliefs and incentives: annual limits

	2018/19 £	2017/18 £
Individual Savings Account (ISA)	20,000	20,000
Junior ISA	4,260	4,128
Help to buy ISA – maximum saving	12,000	12,000
Child Trust Fund	4,268	4,128
Enterprise investment scheme (EIS)	2,000,000	1,000,000
Seed Enterprise investment scheme (SEIS)	100,000	100,000
Venture capital trust (VCT)	200,000	200,000
Social investment tax relief (SITR)	1,000,000	1,000,000
Employee shareholder status	2,000	2,000
Pension scheme allowances:		
Annual allowance	40,000	40,000
Lifetime allowance	1,030,000	1,000,000

National Insurance Contributions

Item	2018/19	2017/18
Class 1:		
Lower Earnings Limit – LEL (per week)	£116	£113
Primary (employees) Threshold (per week)	£162	£157
Secondary (employers) Threshold (per week)	£162	£157
Upper Earnings Limit – UEL		
(per week – employees only)	£892	£866
Upper Secondary Threshold		
(per week – <21yr old)	£892	£866
(per week – <25yr old apprentices)	£892	£866
Employment allowance (per employer)	£3,000	£3,000
Employee's contributions	12%	12%
(£162pw to £892pw +2% over £892pw)		
Employer's Contribution Rates	13.8%	13.8%
(all earnings over £157pw)		
Class 1A and 1B	13.8%	13.8%
Class 2: Self employed Contribution (per week)	£2.95	£2.85
Small Profits Threshold (per annum)	£6,205	£6,025
Class 3: Contribution (per week) (voluntary)	£14.65	£14.25
Class 4: Contributions – Upper Profits Limit	£46,350	£45,000
Contributions – Lower Profits Limit	£8,424	£8,164
Contribution Rate	9.0%	9.0%
(£8,424pa – £46,350pa then 2% over £46,350pa)		

Apprenticeship Levy

	2018/19	2017/18
Apprenticeship Levy Allowance (per employer)	£15,000	£15,000
Apprenticeship Levy rate (gross employee earnings)	0.5%	0.5%

Capital taxes: Individuals

	2018/19 £	2017/18 £	Increase £/%
Capital gains tax annual exempt amount			
Individuals, etc.	11,700	11,300	400
Capital gains tax standard basic rate	10%*	10%*	0
Capital gains tax standard higher rate	20%*	20%*	0
Entrepreneurs' Relief limit	10 million	10 million	0
Entrepreneurs' Relief rate	10%	10%	0
Investors' Relief limit	10 million	10 million	0
Investors' Relief rate	10%	10%	0
Inheritance tax threshold (each if couple/partner)	325,000	325,000	0
Residence nil rate band limit	125,000	100,000	25,000
Inheritance tax rate	40%	40%	0
Lower rate (10%+ of estate left to charity)	36%	36%	0

* An 8% surcharge applies in respect of residential properties and carried interest.

Corporation tax, allowances and reliefs

	2018/19	2017/18
Corporation Tax rate	19%	19%
Plant and machinery: Main rate	18%	18%
Special rate	8%	8%
Annual investment allowance	£200,000	£200,000
First year allowances	100%	100%
R&D tax credits SME scheme	230%	230%
R&D SME repayable credit	14.5%	14.5%
R&D Expenditure credit	12%	11%
Patent box	10%	10%
Film, High end TV and videogame tax relief	25%	25%
Bank levy: 1.1.18 – 31.12.18 – equity and LT liabs	0.08%	
ST liabs	0.16%	
Bank Surcharge	8%	8%

Corporation tax on chargeable gains: indexation allowance

Retail prices index (January 1987 = 100.0)

	Jan	Feb	Mar	Apr	May	Jun	Jul	Aug	Sep	Oct	Nov	Dec
1982	–	–	79.44	81.04	81.62	81.85	81.90	81.90	81.85	82.26	82.66	82.51
1983	82.61	82.97	83.12	84.28	84.64	84.84	85.30	85.68	86.06	86.36	86.67	86.89
1984	86.84	87.20	87.48	88.64	88.97	89.20	89.10	89.94	90.11	90.67	90.95	90.87
1985	91.20	91.94	92.80	94.78	95.21	95.41	95.23	95.49	95.44	95.59	95.92	96.05
1986	96.25	96.60	96.73	97.67	97.85	97.79	97.52	97.82	98.30	98.45	99.29	99.62
1987	100.0	100.4	100.6	101.8	101.9	101.9	101.8	102.1	102.4	102.9	103.4	103.3
1988	103.3	103.7	104.1	105.8	106.2	106.6	106.7	107.9	108.4	109.5	110.0	110.3
1989	111.0	111.8	112.3	114.3	115.0	115.4	115.5	115.8	116.6	117.5	118.5	118.8
1990	119.5	120.2	121.4	125.1	126.2	126.7	126.8	128.1	129.3	130.3	130.0	129.9
1991	130.2	130.9	131.4	133.1	133.5	134.1	133.8	134.1	134.6	135.1	135.6	135.7
1992	135.6	136.3	136.7	138.8	139.3	139.3	138.8	138.9	139.4	139.9	139.7	139.2
1993	137.9	138.8	139.3	140.6	141.1	141.0	140.7	141.3	141.9	141.8	141.6	141.9
1994	141.3	142.1	142.5	144.2	144.7	144.7	144.0	144.7	145.0	145.2	145.3	146.0
1995	146.0	146.9	147.5	149.0	149.6	149.8	149.1	149.9	150.6	149.8	149.8	150.7
1996	150.2	150.9	151.5	152.6	152.9	153.0	152.4	153.1	153.8	153.8	153.9	154.4
1997	154.4	155.0	155.4	156.3	156.9	157.5	157.5	158.5	159.3	159.5	159.6	160.0
1998	159.5	160.3	160.8	**162.6**	163.5	163.4	163.0	163.7	164.4	164.5	164.4	164.4
1999	163.4	163.7	164.1	165.2	165.5	165.6	165.1	165.5	166.2	166.5	166.7	167.3
2000	166.6	167.5	168.4	170.1	170.7	171.1	170.5	170.5	171.7	171.6	172.1	172.2
2001	171.1	172.0	172.2	173.1	174.2	174.4	173.3	174.0	174.6	174.3	173.6	173.4
2002	173.3	173.8	174.5	175.7	176.2	176.2	175.9	176.4	177.6	177.9	178.2	178.5
2003	178.4	179.3	179.9	181.2	181.5	181.3	181.3	181.6	182.5	182.6	182.7	183.5
2004	183.1	183.8	184.6	185.7	186.5	186.8	186.8	187.4	188.1	188.6	189.0	189.9
2005	188.9	189.6	190.5	191.6	192.0	192.2	192.2	192.6	193.1	193.3	193.6	194.1
2006	193.4	194.2	195.0	196.5	197.7	198.5	198.5	199.2	200.1	200.4	201.1	202.7
2007	201.6	203.1	204.4	205.4	206.2	207.3	206.1	207.3	208.0	208.9	209.7	210.9
2008	209.8	211.4	212.1	214.0	215.1	216.8	216.5	217.2	218.4	217.7	216.0	212.9
2009	210.1	211.4	211.3	211.5	212.8	213.4	213.4	214.4	215.3	216.0	216.6	218.0
2010	217.9	219.2	220.7	222.8	223.6	224.1	223.6	224.5	225.3	225.8	226.8	228.4
2011	229.0	231.3	232.5	234.4	235.2	235.2	234.7	236.1	237.9	238.0	238.5	239.4
2012	238.0	239.9	240.8	242.5	242.4	241.8	242.1	243.0	244.2	245.6	245.6	246.8
2013	245.8	247.6	248.7	249.5	250.0	249.7	249.7	251.0	251.9	251.9	252.1	253.4
2014	252.6	254.2	254.8	255.7	255.9	256.3	256.0	257.0	257.6	257.7	257.1	257.5
2015	255.4	256.7	257.1	258.0	258.5	258.9	258.6	259.8	259.6	259.5	259.8	260.6
2016	258.8	260.0	261.1	261.4	262.1	263.1	263.4	264.4	264.9	264.8	265.5	267.1
2017	265.5	268.4	269.3	270.6	271.7	272.3	272.9	274.7	275.1	275.3	275.8	278.1

Note – no further indexation allowance will apply for disposals after 1 Jan 2018 – the Dec 2017 rate should be used for all subsequent sales.

VAT

	after 1 April 2018	after 1 April 2017
Standard Rate	20%	20%
Reduced Rate	5%	5%
Annual Registration Limit	£85,000	£85,000
De-registration Limit	£83,000	£83,000
VAT Fraction – standard rate	1/6	1/6
Maximum turnover to join:		
Cash Accounting Scheme	£1,350,000	£1,350,000
Annual Accounting Scheme	£1,350,000	£1,350,000
Flat Rate Scheme (ex VAT)	£150,000	£150,000

Stamp Duty Land Tax

Value of property (£)	Stamp duty rate (%)
*Residential property***	*not buy to let*
0 – 125,000	0*
125,001 – 250,000	2*
250,001 – 925,000	5*
925,001 –1.5m	10*
remainder (over £1.5m)	12*

* 3% supplement on additional dwelling purchased over £40,000.
** From 22.11.17 full SDLT relief for 1st property purchased up to £300,000 and then 5% up to £500,000.

Value of property (£)	Stamp duty rate (%)
Non-residential property	
up to 150,000	0
150,001 – 250,000	2
over 250,000	5

Annual Tax on Enveloped Dwellings

Value of property (£)	ATED charge (£)
500,000 – 1,000,000	3,600
1,000,001 – 2,000,000	7,250
2,000,001 – 5,000,000	24,250
5,000,001 – 10,000,000	56,550
10,000,001 – 20,000,000	113,400
20,000,000	226,950

Scottish Land and Buildings Transactions Tax

Value of property (£)	LBTT rate %
*Residential property***	
0 - 145,000*	0*
145,001 - 250,000	2*
250,001 - 325,000	5*
325,000 - 750,000	10*
Over 750,000	12*

* 3% supplement on additional dwelling purchased over £40,000.
** LBTT relief for 1st time purchasers up to £175,000.

Non-residential property	
0 - 150,000	0
150,001 - 350,000	3
over 350,000	4.5

Welsh Land Transaction Tax

Value of property (£)	LTT rate %
*Residential property***	
0 - 180,000*	0*
180,001 - 250,000	3.5*
250,001 - 400,000	5*
400,000 - 750,000	7.5*
750,000 - 1,500,000	10
Over 1,500,000	12*

* 3% supplement on additional dwelling purchased over £40,000.
** LBTT relief for 1st time purchasers up to £175,000.

Non-residential property	
0 - 150,000	0
150,001 - 250,000	1
250,001 - 1,000,000	5
over 1,000,000	6

Environmental taxes

	2018/19 (2017/18)
Landfill tax:	
Standard rate (per tonne)	£88.95 (£86.10)
Lower rate (inactive waste per tonne)	£2.80 (£2.70)
Aggregates levy (per tonne)	£2.00 (£2.00)
Climate Change Levy:	
Electricity	0.583p/kwh
Natural Gas	0.203p/kwh
LPG	1.304p/kg

Insurance Premium Tax:

Standard Rate	12%
Higher Rate (travel, appliances, some vehicles)	20%

HMRC interest rates

	Late Payment (%)	Repayment (%)
All taxes (since 21/11/17)	3.00	0.5
All taxes (since 23/8/16)	2.75	0.5
Average Official rate for 2018/19	2.5%	

(These rates change occasionally – see the HMRC website for details)

Tax credits:

Working tax credit

	£ per year
Basic element	1,960.00
Couple and lone parent element	2,010.00
30 hour element	810.00
Disability element	3,090.00
Severe disability element	1,330.00
Childcare element:	£ per week
Maximum eligible cost for 2 or more children	300.00
Maximum eligible cost for 1 child	175.00
Max. percent of eligible costs covered	70%

Child tax credit

	£ per year
Family element	545.00
Child element (each child)	2,780.00
Disabled child element	3,275.00
Severe disabled child element	4,600.00

Tapering

	£
Income thresholds & withdrawal rates	
First income threshold	6,420.00
First withdrawal rate	41%
First threshold for child tax credit entitlement only (where no WTC claimed)	16,105.00
Income rise disregard	2,500.00
Income fall disregard	2,500.00

Pension credit

	£
Standard Minimum income guarantee credit: (per week)	
Single	163.00
Couple	248.80
Capital:	
Amount disregard	10,000.00
Amount disregard – care homes	10,000.00
Deemed income:	
£1 per week for every £500 (or part thereof) in excess of these amounts	

Personal benefit rates

	2018/19 £	2017/18 £
Old State Pension (per week):		
– Single Person (based on own NIC)	125.95	122.30
– Single Person (based on spouse's NIC)	75.50	73.30
– Non-contributory (over 80 pension)	75.50	73.30
New State Pension	164.35	159.55
Child Benefit (per week):		
– First Eligible Child	20.70	20.70
– Each Extra Child	13.70	13.70
– Guardian allowance	17.20	16.70
Statutory Sick Pay (per week):		
– normally receive £116 per week or more	92.05	89.35
Statutory Maternity Pay (per week):		
Average Weekly Earnings of £116 or over		
– Higher Weekly Rate (first 6 weeks)	90% of weekly earnings	
– Standard Rate (remaining 33 weeks)	145.18	140.98
Statutory Paternity/Adoption Pay (per week)	145.18	140.98
Job Seekers Allowance (income based – per week):		
– Single Person (over 25)	73.10	73.10
– Married Couple (both over 18)	114.85	114.85
National Living/Minimum Wage (per hour):		
– ages 25 and over (from Apr 18)	£7.83	£7.50
– ages 21 to 24 (from Apr 18)	£7.38	£7.05
– ages 18 to 20 (Development rate – from Apr 18)	£5.90	£5.60
– ages <18 (Young worker rate – from Apr 18)	£4.20	£4.05
– Apprentice rate (under 19 or in first year)	£3.70	£3.50
Employment & Support Allowance (per week):		
– Single under 25 (first 13 weeks)	57.90	57.90
– Single 25 and over (first 13 weeks)	73.10	73.10
– Work related Activity Group (week 14+)	73.10	102.15
– Support Group (week 14+)	110.75	109.30
Universal Credit (per month):		
– Single under 25	251.77	251.77
– Single 25 and over	317.82	317.82
– Couple one at least over 25	498.89	498.89
– Child element:		
– First child	277.08	277.08
– Second/subsequent child	231.67	231.67
Benefit Cap (per annum) (inside Greater London totals in brackets)		
– Single (no children)	13,400.00 (15,410.00)	
– Single parent (children living with them)	20,000.00 (23,000.00)	
– Couple (with or without children)	20,000.00 (23,000.00)	

These rates are selected from a complex list of benefits available based on personal circumstances and therefore are provided in basic outline only. For a full list of benefits see the www.gov.uk website.

Duty rates

	Duty	Typical Item
Cigarettes	16.5% of retail price + £217.23 per thousand	packet of 20
Cigars	£270.96/kg	packet of 5
Hand rolling tobacco	£221.18/kg	30g
Beer	19.08p/litre	pint

8.42p for low strength or an extra 5.69p for high strength apply

Wine
>22% abv	£28.74/litre pure alcohol	
15%–22%abv	£3.8482/litre	75cl bottle
5.5%–15%abv	£2.8865/litre	
4%–5.5%abv	£1.2230/litre	
1.2%–4%abv	88.93p/litre	

Sparkling wine
5.5%–8.5%abv	£2.7946/litre	75cl bottle
8.5%–15%abv	£3.6972/litre	

Cider/Perry
Still
1.2%–7.5%abv	40.38p/litre	75cl bottle
7.5%–8.5%abv	61.04p/litre	

Sparkling
1.2%–5.5%abv	40.38p/litre	75cl bottle
5.5%–8.5%abv	£2.7946/litre	

Spirits
	£28.74/litre of pure alcohol	70cl bottle

Fuel Duties :

Unleaded/Heavy oil (Diesel)/Bio-diesel & bioethanol	57.95p/litre
Bio-diesel for non-road use	11.14p/litre
LPG	31.61p/kg
Other Natural gas (road fuel)	24.7p/kg
Fuel Oil	10.7p/litre
Aviation gasoline	37.7p/litre

B Appendix B

This appendix reviews recent UK budgets, and their associated Finance Bills and Acts to provide a summary of recent changes to the UK tax system.

The 2018 Budget and Finance Acts 2017 (No. 2) and 2018

As a result of the 2017 general election, several measures that were originally to be included in Finance Act 2017 were delayed and subsequently legislated in Finance Act (No. 2) 2017 which received royal assent on 16 November 2017.

The Act brought in corporate interest restriction rules and reform to corporate loss rules. The Act includes the removal of the capital gains tax indexation allowance for companies after December 2017 and an increase in the rate of research and development tax credit to 12%. A stamp duty relief for first home buyers was introduced for properties valued at less than £500,000.

The budget for 2018/19 was presented in Autumn 2017 to allow for longer period of consultation compared to the previous practice of a Spring Budget. Finance Act 2018 received royal assent on 15 March 2018. It was published as a Finance Bill on 1 December 2017. It contains measures announced in the Autumn 2017. The number of pages in Finance Act 2018 is the lowest since 1997. For income tax, the rates of tax remain the same, but the personal allowance is lifted to £11,850 and the basic rate threshold to £34,500. The VAT threshold is frozen at £85,000.

Previous Budgets: changes to the UK's tax system

The 2017 Budget and Finance Acts

Budget 17 was presented to Parliament on 8 March 2017 and contained a number of new measures including tax free childcare, the Lifetime ISA, the introduction of Making Tax Digital for businesses, an increase in the rate of NICs for self employed and the reduction of the tax free dividend allowance from £5,000 to £2,000. Previously announced changes that were due to be included in

Finance Act 2017 included the introduction of the new trading allowance and a property income allowance of £1,000 each (as proposed in Budget 2016), loss restriction rules for companies and reform of termination payment rules for employees.

In April, the Government called a snap election, some measures were delayed. Those that were enacted in Finance Act 2017 include an increase to the income tax personal allowance (now £11,500) and basic rate threshold (now £33,500) the introduction of the new Lifetime ISA and new rules for salary sacrifice arrangements. The capital gains tax annual exemption has been increased to £11,300 and for corporation tax, the rate has been reduced to 19%. The VAT registration threshold was increased to £85,000.

The 2016 Budget and Finance Acts

Budget 2016 was complex and contained a number of measures to take place in later years. The personal allowance was increased to £11,000. A major reform of the way dividends are treated in income tax computations saw the removal of the old dividend credit and replacement with a £5,000 tax free allowance, accompanied by a similar tax free allowance for savings income. From April 2017 a £1,000 tax free allowance was proposed for trading and property income, nicknamed the 'uberisation' allowance as it is designed for people who have minor 'trading' activities such as airb&b and ebay sales.

Capital gains tax rates were reduced from 28% and 18% to 20% and 10% respectively, except for chargeable gains on residential property.

A new business tax roadmap was published with the aim of levelling the playing field between small companies and large multinationals, which has been the source of some dissatisfaction recently.

The 2015 Budget and Finance Acts

In 2015 we saw two budgets, as a result of the General Election which took place in May 2015. The personal allowance was increased to £10,600 and capital gains tax annual exempt amount to £11,100. The annual investment allowance was due to revert to £25,000 at 1 January 2016, but the Chancellor announced that it would increase to £200,000 permanently instead.

The Government continues its campaign against tax avoidance by strengthening a number of existing measures such as the disclosure of tax avoidance (DOTAS) regime and the rules relating to promoters of tax avoidance schemes.

Probably the most controversial and innovative new legislation is the diverted profits tax, or 'Google tax', as discussed in Chapter 12.

The 2014 Budget and Finance Acts

The 2014 budget was clearly a pre-election budget containing few controversial measures. In the second reading of the Finance Bill in the House of Commons, Danny Alexander, Chief Secretary to the Treasurer, said "The Bill is certainly substantial – 602 pages, 295 clauses and 34 schedules – but it is packed with measures that will help British businesses invest and create jobs, help British households work and save, and help ensure that everyone in Britain pays their fair share of tax".

The basic personal allowance increased to £10,000. Business investment was supported by a temporary increase in the annual investment allowance to £500,000 from 1 April 2014 to 31 December 2015, at which time it will revert to £25,000.

The 2013 Budget and Finance Acts

The 2013 budget was a little less controversial than the previous, 2012 budget and contained some good news for businesses. The reduction in headline corporation tax rate to 21% in 2014/15 then 20% will mean that from 2015/16 the complexity of small profits relief will be removed and there will be no need for marginal relief. Increases to income tax personal allowances, capital gains tax AEA and VAT registration threshold were as expected.

Some innovative measures were introduced including a special employment allowance of £2,000, 'above the line' credit for large companies' research and development activity as well as the new cash basis for very small businesses. The new General Anti Abuse Rule (GAAR) was enacted following a long period of consultation and is estimated to raise approximately £50m annually.

The 2012 Budget and Finance Acts

The 2012 budget contained a few unexpected announcements, some of which were subsequently reversed following popular protest. The main rate of corporation tax was reduced by an additional 1% over what had been expected, becoming 24% for FY2012. For income tax payers, the personal allowance was increased to £8,105, although the higher rate band was reduced to £34,370 to keep the band the same as the previous year. A raft of modifications was announced to VAT rates to close loopholes and make the tax simpler. Some of these, e.g. the pasty tax, were reversed before coming into effect. For Stamp Duty Land Tax, a new rate of 7% was introduced for property over £2million.

The 2011 Budget and Finance Acts

Key changes in the 2011 budget included an increase by £1,000 of the personal allowance to £7,475, accompanied by a £2,400 reduction in the basic rate limit to £35,000. Corporation tax was reduced to 26% and will drop to 23% by 2014, while the small profits rate was reduced to 20%. Important changes to capital allowances were announced that will be effective from April 2012, including a reduction in annual investment allowance to £25,000 and writing down allowances to 18% and 8% for main rate and special rate pools respectively. The annual allowance for pensions reduces significantly from £255,000 to £50,000 from 6 April 2011 and the lifetime allowance will reduce from £1.8m to £1.5m from 1 April 2012.

The 2010 Budgets and Finance Acts

2010 was an unusual year in which there were two budgets and three Finance Acts as a result of the change of government. The first Budget and Finance Act was fairly uncontroversial, in the run-up to the election however, more radical changes followed in the Emergency Budget after the new Coalition Government came into power. Key changes included the increase of the annual investment allowance for capital allowances from £50,000 to £100,000 and an increase in the lifetime limit for CGT entrepreneurs' relief from £1m to £2m. Most tax bands and thresholds were frozen, although the VAT registration threshold was increased to £70,000 from £68,000.

2009 Budget and Finance Act

The 2009 Budget did not introduce any radical changes, although it was the latest budget on record to that point.

Several modest measures were introduced to ease the impact of the recession on business, including a new loss carry back provision and reintroduction of 40% first year allowances for plant and machinery. A new regime for capital allowances for cars, now based on CO_2 emissions, completed the Government's review of the treatment of cars under the tax system.

The new dividend exemption system for taxing foreign profits of companies was announced and took effect from July 2009

The new 45% personal tax rate announced in the November 2008 Pre Budget Report was lifted to 50% effective from April 2010. For corporation tax, the planned increase of the small companies' rate to 22% was deferred.

2008 Budget and Finance Act

The 2008 Budget contained a number of controversial measures. The abolition of the 10% starting rate of income tax for non-savings caused an outcry, despite being announced in the 2007 Budget. Another controversial issue was the new additional charge of £30,000 for non-domiciles who wish to continue to use the remittance basis for their UK tax liabilities.

Other key changes introduced by the 2008 Budget included the simplification of capital allowances and capital gains tax. For capital allowances, in addition to the reforms previously announced in 2007 (for example, the introduction of the new Annual Investment Allowance), Finance Act 2008 provided for the write off of small pools of expenditure of £1,000 or less.

Radical overhaul this year of capital gains tax for individuals (although not for companies) mean that taper relief and indexation were abolished and capital gains were taxed at a flat rate of 18%, from April 2008. Following concerns that this would adversely affect those whose retirement savings are tied up in businesses, a new Entrepreneurs' Relief has been introduced to reduce the capital gains tax rate to 10% where taxpayers dispose of all or part of their business.

For corporation tax, the changes announced in 2007 came into effect so that the small companies' rate increased to 21% and the full rate of corporation tax fell to 28%, a lower rate than most of the UK's competitors.

Summary of main reforms, 1979–2012

Personal income taxes	Basic rate 33% down to 20%
	Top rate 98% (unearned income), 83% (earnings) down to 40% then raised to 50%
	Lower rate 25% down to 10%
	Independent taxation introduced
	Married couple's allowance abolished, Children's Tax Credit introduced then abolished, child tax credit and working tax credit introduced.
	Mortgage interest tax relief abolished Life assurance premium relief abolished PEP, TESSA and ISA introduced
	Capital gains tax at income tax rates
	Car benefits in kind switched to a CO_2 emissions base rather than mileage.
National Insurance	Rate for employees increased from 6.5% to 12%
	Rate for employers reduced from 13.5% to 12.8%
	Ceiling abolished for employers
	Cuts for low earners

	Alignment of floor with income tax allowance
	Imposition of NI on benefits in kind
	1% increase in rates and removal of the zero rate beyond the UEL – 1% applies without limit.
VAT	Standard rate increased from 8% to 20%
	Higher rate of 12.5% abolished
	Reduced rate introduced on domestic fuel and other selected items
	Thresholds for various schemes (e.g. cash accounting) increased.
	Flat rate scheme introduced for small business.
Other indirect taxes	Large real rise in duties on road fuels
	Smaller increase in tobacco duties
	Slight real decrease in duties on beer, larger decline for spirits
	Small increase in real duties on wine
	Air passenger duty, landfill tax, climate change levy and aggregates levy introduced
Corporate income taxes	Main rate cut from 52% to 24%
	Small companies rate cut from 42% to 20%
	Starting rate introduced, cut to 1% then abolished.
	General 100% first-year allowance replaced by 20% writing-down allowance
	Reintroduction of FYA for small businesses on selected other capital expenditure
	100% ECA for energy saving plant and machinery.
	R&D credit introduced for SMEs, then extended to large business and the rate of credit increased.
	Advance corporation tax and refundable dividend tax credit abolished
Local tax	Domestic rates replaced by council tax (via poll tax)
	Locally varying non-domestic rates abolished, replaced by national non-domestic rates

(Source: originally based on 'A Survey of the UK Tax System',
IFS Briefing Notes No 9 by L. Chennells, A.Dilnot and N. Roback)
Latest version IFS Briefing Note BN09 by James Brown and Barra Roantree is available at:
http://www.ifs.org.uk/bns/bn09.pdf
For more fiscal facts about the UK tax system see
http://www.ifs.org.uk/tools_and_resources/fiscal_facts

 **Glossary**

Ability to pay

A system of taxation under which tax is levied on a taxpayer according to his economic ability to pay tax, or 'taxable capacity'. *See also* Benefit principle.

Accounting period

The interval for which corporation tax is assessed and charged on the profits arising during the interval.

Accruals basis

Under the accruals basis profits for an accounting period equal revenue earned in the period less expenses incurred in earning that revenue. This can be contrasted with a cash receipts basis which looks at the amount of cash received and paid during a period.

Accumulation and maintenance trust

A trust in which income is accumulated for minor children until they reach a specified age.

Ad valorem

varying according to value or price

Additional personal allowance (APA)

An allowance that was given to any single person with a child living with them (not available from 6 April 2000).

Additional rate of tax

Income tax rate payable on taxable total incomes exceeding £150,000.

Additional voluntary contributions

Payments made by an employee to increase retirement benefits due from the approved pension scheme run by his or her employer.

Advance corporation tax

A payment which was made to the Inland Revenue whenever a UK company paid a dividend (no longer part of the UK tax system).

AESP

All employee share-ownership plans that enable share ownership in their own companies to employees with tax advantages.

Age allowance

An allowance available to individuals over 65 years of age instead of the ordinary personal allowance.

Agricultural buildings allowance

An allowance, for income tax and corporation tax purposes, available for capital expenditure on farmhouses, farm buildings cottages, fences, drainage and similar works.

Agricultural property relief

Relief from inheritance tax available on the agricultural value of agricultural property in the UK, the Channel Islands or the Isle of Man.

Annual accounting scheme

A method of accounting for VAT which only requires the registered trader to complete one VAT return each year.

Annual exemption

The amount of capital gains that an individual may make each year that is not subjected to capital gains tax. Also the amount which an individual may transfer each year which is not subjected to inheritance tax.

Annual Investment Allowances

A special capital allowance that effectively relieves 100% of the first £500,000 of qualifying expenditure per annum.

Annual tax on enveloped dwellings (ATED)

Tax payable by companies ('non-natural entities') that own high value UK-based residential property. Previously known as Annual Residential Property Tax.

Annuity

An amount of money paid annually or at other regular intervals.

Arising basis

Income which is taxed as it arises regardless of whether or when it is remitted to the UK.

Arms length price

A price that would be struck between two unrelated parties, i.e. an open market price. Used in income and corporation tax where transactions are made between related individuals or companies.

Associated companies

Companies which are under common control or where one company controls the other. Used in corporation tax when deciding which rate of tax is applicable.

Associated disposal

One of a series of linked disposals of related assets to connected persons for capital gains tax purposes.

Associated operations

Two or more operations which are related are deemed to take place at the time of the last of the operations for inheritance tax purposes.

Average rate of tax

Equal to the total tax paid in the tax period, usually one year, divided by the value of the tax base.

Avoidance

The legal manipulation of a taxpayer's affairs in order to reduce the taxpayer's tax liability, although often against the sprit of the legislation.

Bad debt relief

Relief for VAT paid on a taxable supply made by a registered trader who has subsequently written off all or part of the debt in his accounts.

Badges of trade

The six elements which the Royal Commission identified as helping to determine whether or not trading is taking place for income tax and corporation tax purposes.

Balancing allowances and charges

For capital allowance purposes, relief for capital expenditure, or the claw back of relief already given, given in the year in which an asset is disposed of or the business ceases to trade.

Basic rate of tax

The main rate at which income and capital gains taxes are levied (see Rates and Allowances for current rate).

Basis period

The time period that determines which income or profits are taxed in a particular tax year.

Beneficial loan

A loan given to an employee who derived the benefit of the loan because of their employment.

Beneficiary

Individual who may derive benefit from a trust.

Benefit principle

In contrast to the ability to pay principle, under the benefit principle tax is raised by reference to the amount of benefit a taxpayer is deemed to receive from the public sector. *See also* Ability to pay.

Benefits in kind

A benefit received by an employee or members of his or her family or household due to their employment.

Blind person's allowance

An allowance given to taxpayers that are registered blind.

Bonus issue

An issue of additional shares in proportion to existing holdings to shareholders.

Budget

An annual statement by the Chancellor of the Exchequer setting out proposals for taxation and government expenditure in the following tax year.

Burden of tax

The amount by which a taxpayer's income or wealth is reduced because of taxation.

Business asset rollover relief

Relief from capital gains tax available if the proceeds from the disposal of certain classes of assets are reinvested in other qualifying assets within a specified period.

Business property relief

Relief from inheritance tax on transfers of relevant business property.

Capital allowances

Relief from income tax and corporation tax on capital expenditure on eligible assets. Similar to depreciation for accounting purposes.

Capital distribution

A repayment of capital by a company to its shareholders.

Capital gain

The increase in the value of an asset on its disposal by an individual or company.

Capital gains tax

The tax levied on capital gains. The liability to tax only arises when the asset is disposed of.

Capital transfer tax

A tax on the transfer of wealth between individuals. It was imposed in the UK between 1975 and 1986.

Capitalisation of future tax benefits

Future tax benefits are capitalised when the current value of an asset includes an allowance for the increased expected yield from the asset due to future tax benefits.

Cash accounting scheme
A method of accounting for VAT which depends on payments and receipts rather than invoices for identifying tax points.

Cash basis
Income and expenditure recognition basis which allows for inclusion in tax computation when each flow occurs.

Cash voucher
A voucher, stamp or similar document capable of being exchanged for a sum of money.

Cash-flow tax base
Under a cash-flow tax based system, cash flows rather than profits are taxed.

Chargeable asset
All assets are chargeable assets unless they are specifically exempted from capital gains tax.

Chargeable business asset
The whole or part of a business or assets used in a business until it ceases to trade, or shares or securities of a company.

Chargeable lifetime transfer
Under inheritance tax, a transfer of value made by an individual during their lifetime that is not an exempt or potentially exempt transfer. In practice, only transfers into a discretionary trust are chargeable lifetime transfers.

Chargeable transfer
A transfer of value made by an individual who intended to confer a gratuitous benefit that is not an exempt transfer.

Chattel
Tangible movable property, for example furniture.

Child Tax Credit
Tax credit introduced in April 2003 (replacing Children's tax credit). Sums paid based on core family element payment with additional payments based on the number of children in a family unit.

Class 1 national insurance contribution
Payments made by employees, primary contributions, and employers, secondary contributions.

Class 1A national insurance contribution
Payments made by employers when employees are provided with most benefits in kind.

Class 2 national insurance contribution
Flat rate payments made by the self- employed.

Class 3 national insurance contribution
Voluntary payments made to individuals in order to maintain rights to some state benefits.

Class 4 national insurance contribution
Payments made by the self-employed based on a percentage of taxable profits.

Close company
A UK resident company which is under the control of five or fewer participators or of participators who are directors.

Close investment-holding company
A close company which is a non-trading company.

Collector of taxes
Civil servants appointed by the former Board of Inland Revenue to collect the tax which is assessed to be payable.

Commissioners for Her Majesty's Revenue and Customs

Civil servants appointed by the Crown who are responsible for collecting and accounting for, and otherwise managing, the UK's Revenue and Customs laws and regulations. They appoint all the officers for Revenue and Customs who run HMRC on a day to day basis. Established by the Commissioners for Revenue and Customs Act 2005. They are responsible for all the tasks previously performed by the Commissioners of Inland Revenue and Commissioners of Customs and Excise.

Compliance costs

Costs which are incurred by taxpayers in order to enable them to comply with a specific tax or more generally with the tax system.

Components of income

The name given to the various sources of incomes that need to be aggregated together at step 1 of a personal tax computation - introduced by ITA 2007.

Composite supply

A taxable supply for VAT purposes made up of a mix of standard rated, zero rated or exempt supplies where it is not possible to apportion the value of the supply to each of the rates. One rate is applied to the whole of the supply.

Comprehensive income tax

A tax which is levied on an individual's comprehensive income. An individual's comprehensive income is the amount which an individual could consume without diminishing the value of their wealth. *See also* Economic income.

Connected persons

Persons who are defined as having a special relationship for tax purposes and transactions between them are sometimes accorded special treatment (see Chapter 8: *Gross proceeds on disposal* for list of connected persons).

Consortium

A group of companies in which one company is at least 75% owned by UK resident companies who are called members of the consortium.

Consortium relief

Allows trading losses to be surrendered from a member of a consortium to a consortium held company and vice versa for corporation tax purposes.

Consumer Prices Index

Index used as the default measure of inflation for annually adjusted thresholds and rates of direct taxes from April 2012.

Consumption taxes

Also called expenditure taxes, a consumption tax taxes the resources which an individual has consumed during a set period of time.

Contracting out

When employees leave the additional state pension and join a contracted out occupational pension or stakeholder pension instead, They eventually receive payments from the scheme rather than the State, and pay reduced national insurance contributions as a result.

Corporation tax

The tax that is levied on the profits of companies and unincorporated associations such as clubs and political associations but not partnerships.

Corrective taxes

A tax which is intended to affect the behaviour of taxpayers. Tax relief on pension contributions is intended to encourage individuals to provide for a private pension.

Crowding out

This is the effect which may occur when public expenditure increases and causes a reduction in size of the private sector, thus reducing the tax base.

Cum div

A quoted security which carries the right to an imminent dividend.

Cum int

A quoted security which carries the right to an imminent interest payment.

De minimis limit

Various taxes use a minimum value rule below which different rules from usual often apply. For example, expenditure on long life assets for single companies below £100,000 will not be subject to a writing down allowance of only 10%. They continue to receive allowances at 20%.

De-pooling

For capital allowance purposes, an election made by taxpayers for nominated items of plant and machinery with a short life to be maintained outside the pool so that balancing allowances may be claimed on their disposal.

Depreciating asset

For capital allowances purposes, an asset which is, or within the next ten years will become, a wasting asset. Wasting assets have a useful life of 50 years or less thus a depreciating asset has a useful life of less than 60 years

Deregistration

The process by which a registered trader voluntarily or otherwise ceases to be registered for VAT.

Diminution in value

The loss in value of an item, for example, of the donor's estate when a transfer of value for inheritance tax purposes occurs.

Direct tax

A tax which is levied on the taxpayer who is intended to bear the final burden of paying it. Examples include income tax and employee national insurance contributions.

Disabled person's tax credit

Benefit paid to person with illness or disability.

Discovery assessment

An assessment made by HMRC based on evidence they discover after a self-assessment return became final.

Discretionary trust

A trust in which no beneficiary has an absolute right to the income. The income is distributed at the discretion of the trustee.

Disincentive effect of taxation

Where a transaction, such as employment, is subject to tax there is a gap between the selling price and the purchase price which is equal to the tax levied. This gap may act as a disincentive to the transaction. For example an employee may be unwilling to undertake overtime at the rate offered if he is subject to a high marginal rate of tax.

Dispensation

Usually refers to an agreement between an employer and HMRC over expense reimbursements that results in them not needing to be separately disclosed to HMRC by both employer and employee.

Divisional registration

Registration by a company so that each division is registered separately for VAT purposes.

Domicile

The place that an individual thinks of as home. He or she may not live in the place of domicile but is likely to retain some links with it.

Duality test

When expenditure has both a business and a private purpose the expenditure is likely to fail the 'wholly and exclusively' test and be disallowable for tax purposes because of a duality of purpose.

Earnings basis

Income and expenditure recognition basis which allows for inclusion in tax computation on normal accounting accrual and realisation concepts.

Earnings cap

The upper limit on the earnings on which an approved pension scheme can be based.

Economic efficiency

A tax is economically efficient if it does not distort the economic decisions which are made by individuals or companies *See also* Fiscal Neutrality.

Economic income

The maximum value which an individual can consume during a period and still expect to be as well off at the end of the period as at the beginning. *See also* Comprehensive income tax.

Economic rent

The amount that a factor of production, such as land, earns over and above what could be earned if it was put to its next best use.

Effective incidence of tax

The effective incidence of tax falls on those individuals whose wealth is reduced by the tax. This may not be the same as the formal incidence of tax.

Eligible interest

Interest paid on loans to purchase annuities, or other qualifying loan interest payments. Used in Income Tax.

Emoluments

Income (not necessarily just money) from an office or employment.

Employee

An individual with a contract of services.

Employee share ownership plan (ESOP)

A trust into which a UK resident company transfers funds for the benefit of some or all of its employees.

Enhanced Capital Allowance Scheme

Government Scheme under which extra capital allowances are given to certain types of environmentally friendly plant and machinery.

Enhancement expenditure

Capital expenditure incurred to enhance the value of an asset.

Enterprise zone

An area designated as benefiting from tax and other incentives in order to encourage investment.

Entrepreneurs Relief

Introduced in 2008 to allow certain capital gains to be taxed at 10% instead of 18%.

Error or mistake relief

Relief for tax overstated due to some error or mistake on the part of the taxpayer.

Estate at death

The value of all the assets owned on the date of death together with any interest held as a joint tenant and capital held by a trust in which the deceased had an interest in possession.

Estate Duty

A wealth tax imposed on the transfer of property on death. In the UK estate duty was abolished in 1975 and replaced with Capital Transfer Tax

Evasion

The illegal manipulation of a taxpayer's affairs so as to reduce the taxpayer's tax liability.

Ex div

A quoted security which does not carry a right to the imminent dividend.

Ex Gratia

Done or given as a favour and not under any compulsion.

Ex int

A quoted security which does not carry a right to the imminent interest payment.

Excepted estate

An estate in respect of which it is not necessary to deliver an account of the property for inheritance tax purposes.

Excess burden of tax

Where a tax is not economically efficient the loss to the economy caused by the distortion is termed the excess burden of tax.

Excluded property

Property which is specifically excluded from an estate at death for the purposes of inheritance tax.

Exempt income

Income which is specifically exempt from income tax.

Exempt supply

A supply of goods or services which is specifically exempt from VAT.

Expenditure tax

A tax on the amount consumed by an individual in a given period of time.

Extra-statutory concession

A series of statements made by HMRC which give concessions to taxpayers over and above those allowed by legislation.

Factor of production

Resources used as inputs into a production activity to produce outputs such as goods and services. Typically include land, labour and capital. Some argue entrepreneurship should also be included in this list.

Fall in value relief

An inheritance tax relief available if assets are disposed of within a given period after death for less than their value at the date of death.

Finance Act

Usually an annual Act of Parliament which contains the fiscal legislation needed to implement the budget.

Financial year

The rate of corporation tax is set for financial years, which runs from 1st April to the following 31st March.

First year allowance

A special capital allowance which may be available in the year in which an asset is acquired and is at a higher rate than the normal writing down allowance..

Fiscal drag

An increase in tax revenues generated when a tax threshold is not increased in line with inflation

Fiscal neutrality

A fiscally neutral tax system does not discriminate between economic choices.

Fixed profit car scheme

Maximum allowance available to an employee for use of their own car on their employer's business. Expense payments in excess of this amount is a taxable benefit in kind. Scheme ceased to exist April 2002 when new approved rate scheme commenced.

Flat tax

An income tax system with only one rate of tax for all income levels and in which an income is taxed once and only once.

Foreign emoluments

The emoluments of a person, not domiciled in the UK, from an office or employment with an employer not resident in the UK.

Franked investment income (FII)

Dividends together with the related tax credit received by a UK company from another UK company which are not treated as group income.

Franked payment (FP)

Dividends together with the related tax credit paid by a UK company to another UK company which are not treated as group income.

Free estate

The value of all the assets owned outright by an individual at his death.

Free-standing additional voluntary contributions

Payments made by an employee who is a member of an occupational pension scheme in order to increase retirement benefits.

Functional test

A test to identify assets which are actively used in the business and thus are eligible for capital allowances as opposed to those which form part of the setting in which the business was carried on.

Furnished holiday lettings

Holiday lettings taxed under Property Income using the regulations for Trading Income. The income is treated as earned income for tax purposes.

Furnished letting

A letting of furnished property which is taxed under Property Income.

General Commissioners

Part time and unpaid individuals who used to hear taxpayers' appeals against the assessments of the inspectors before the introduction of the Tribunal System in April 2009.

Gift relief

A relief from capital gains tax when a qualifying asset is disposed of and both the transferor and transferee elect for the transferor's gain to be reduced to nil.

Gift with reservation

A gift from which the donor continues to receive some benefit e.g. a parent gifting the family home they own to their children, perhaps as part at attempt at inheritance tax planning, but continuing to live there

Gratuitous disposition

A disposal of an asset which was intended to confer some benefit to the recipient.

Gross amount of tax

The aggregate of the input tax and output tax included in the VAT return for a period.

Grossing up

The conversion of net receipts to gross receipts such as in tax computations. Use the formula 100/ (100 – tax rate).

Group charge

A charge paid under an election by one member of a 51% group to another without deduction of income tax.

Group

Two or more companies which are related for either corporation tax or capital gains tax purposes for transfer of losses and other payments.

Group income

Dividends paid under an election by one member of a 51% group to another member of the same group.

Group interest

Interest paid under an election by one member of a 51% group to another without deduction of income tax.

Group registration

Registration for VAT purposes by a group of companies under common control.

Group relief

Trading losses incurred by one member of a 75% group can be surrendered to another member of the same group.

Her Majesty's Revenue and Customs (HMRC)

Government department responsible for administering and collection of all UK revenue and customs laws and regulations. The combined responsibilities of the Inland Revenue and HM Customs & Excise were vested in this new body from 2005.

Higher rate tax

Taxable income of an individual in excess of a specified threshold is taxed at the higher rate of tax.

HM Customs and Excise

The Government department, responsible to the Treasury, which once administered VAT and all customs and duties. These tasks are now undertaken by HMRC.

Holdover relief

Relief from capital gains tax which can be claimed when a business asset is replaced by a depreciable asset.

Horizontal equity

A tax system displaying horizontal equity treats similar individuals, companies or situations in similar ways.

Hypothecated taxes

Taxes raised to fund specified benefits or Government spending.

Imputation system

A system under which shareholders in receipt of dividends are given a tax credit for the corporation tax paid by a company.

Incidence of taxation

The formal incidence of tax falls on those who must actually pay the tax while the effective incidence of tax falls on those whose wealth is reduced by the tax. *See also* Indirect taxes; Regressive taxes.

Incidental costs of acquisition

Specified costs incurred when an asset was acquired which are allowed when calculating a chargeable gain for capital gains tax purposes.

Incidental costs of disposal

Specified costs incurred when an asset was disposed of which are allowed when calculating a chargeable gain for capital gains tax purposes.

Incidental expenses

Small payments to employees to cover expenses.

Income tax

A tax levied on all income, earned and unearned, attributed to an individual in a given period.

Income taxed at source

Income paid net of tax, usually at the basic rate of income tax.

Income taxed by assessment

Income paid gross on which income tax is levied for example rental income.

Income

Valuable consideration received in exchange for the provision of goods or services.

Incorporation

Creation of a company to conduct an income earning activity, for example to operate a business previously run by a sole trader or partnership.

Independent taxation

The taxation of spouses as individuals rather than as a family unit.

Indexation allowance

An allowance intended to compensate for the effect of inflation on the value of capital assets when determining a capital gains tax liability.

Indirect tax

A tax which is ultimately borne by someone other than the taxpayer on whom it is levied. It is not always possible to identify the effective incidence of an indirect tax. VAT is an example of an indirect tax which is intended to be suffered by the final consumer. However, market forces might lead to manufacturers absorbing some of the VAT themselves, rather than passing it on to the final consumer. *See also* Incidence of taxation.

Individual Savings Account (ISA)

Savings product providing tax free income. Used to replace TESSAs and PEPs. See New ISA (NISA).

Industrial buildings allowances (IBA)

Capital allowance available on expenditure on industrial buildings and hotels. To be phased out by 2011.

Inheritance tax

Tax levied on certain lifetime transfers and estates on the death of individuals.

Inland Revenue

The government department that was, until 2005, responsible for income tax, corporation tax, capital gains tax and inheritance tax. Its responsibilities are now undertaken by HMRC.

Input VAT

VAT levied on the purchases of goods and services by a registered trader.

Inspector of taxes

Civil Servants who assessed individuals, companies and other organisations liability to tax in the former Inland Revenue.

Instalment option

Facility which allows some capital, gains tax and inheritance tax to be paid in instalments.

Intending trader registration

Registration for VAT by an individual or organisation which has not yet begun to trade.

Interest in possession trust

A trust in which the beneficiaries, the life tenants, have a right to receive the income from the trust for a period of time.

Interim payments

Payments of income tax on account on 31st January in the tax year and 31st July following the end of the tax year.

Intra-group transfer

A transfer of assets between two members of a company group which would in other circumstances give rise to a capital gains tax charge.

Irrecoverable VAT

VAT levied on the purchases of goods or services that cannot be recovered as input tax.

ISA

Savings product providing tax free income. Used to replace TESSAs and PEPs.

Job-related accommodation

Accommodation provided to an employee which is eligible for relief from being taxed as a benefit in kind.

Landlord repairing lease

A lease of property at a full rent. That is the rent paid under the lease is sufficient taking one year with another, to defray the cost to the lessor of any expenses subject to the lease which fall to be borne by him.

Large business

For tax purposes a large business would be one that exceeds two or more of the conditions necessary to be a medium sized business.

Lease

The granting of a right to the use of an asset for a specified period.

Lease premium

An initial payment made to the lessor (owner of the property) in return granting of a right to the use of an asset for a specified period.

Less detailed VAT invoice

May be issued by retailers when the VAT inclusive total is less than £100.

Letting exemption

Relief from capital gains tax available when part or all of a property, which was at some time the taxpayer's principal private residence, is let.

Life interest trust

A trust in which beneficiaries have an interest in possession throughout their life.

Life tenant

An individual who has a right to receive the income from a trust for a period of time.

Linked transactions

A series of transactions to connected persons where the disposal proceeds of each disposal are taken to be a proportion of the value of the aggregate of the assets transferred for capital gains tax purposes.

Long-life assets

For capital allowance purposes assets with useful lives of more than 25 years receive writing down allowances of 10% per annum.

Loss relief

Tax relief for trading or capital losses given by setting losses against taxable income or chargeable gains.

Lower rate of tax

The rate of tax which was levied on savings income and capital gains that fell into the basic rate band but was lower than the basic rate of tax.

Lump sum taxes

A fixed amount of tax paid by an individual regardless of his or her income.

Maintenance payments

Payments to a spouse, former spouse or children.

Management expenses

Expenses incurred in managing an investment company.

Marginal rate of tax

This is the rate at which a taxpayer would be taxed on the next unit of the tax base.

Marginal relief

Relief given to companies with taxable profits lying within given limits.

Marriage exemption

Relief from inheritance tax on gifts made in consideration of marriage.

Married couple's allowance

An allowance available to a married man whose wife lives with him (not available from 6th April 2000 unless aged over 65 as at that date).

Matching rules

The rules used to match acquisitions and disposals of quoted securities for capital gains tax purposes.

Medium-sized business

To be classed as medium-sized for tax purposes the business must be larger than a small business, have turnover of no more than €50 million or balance sheet total of not more than €43 million, and have not more than 250 employees.

Minor

An unmarried child under the age of 18.

MIRAS

The mechanism used to give individuals tax relief on the interest paid on their mortgages called Mortgage Interest Relief at Source (not available from 6th April 2000).

Mixed supply

A supply of goods and services by a registered trader which is made up of a separable mix of elements. The appropriate VAT rate to be applied to each part.

National insurance contributions

A tax paid by individuals and employers to secure certain benefits such as a state pension.

National Savings & Investments

A government owned bank in which individuals can invest in order to obtain interest.

National Savings Certificates

Certificates issued by the Government which offer tax-free returns.

Negligible value claim

A capital gains tax relief that can be claimed by a taxpayer when an asset becomes effectively worthless.

Net income

Line item in the personal tax computation resulting from deduction of tax reliefs from total income (before personal allowances are deducted to produce taxable income). Introduced by ITA 2007.

Net Relevant Earnings

Trading profits, employment income and income from furnished holiday lettings net of loss relief and excess of trade charges over other income.

New individual savings account (NISA)

New form of ISA from July 2014. All ISAs created prior to that date became NISAs automatically.

Nil rate band

The band of transfers for which the rate of inheritance tax is nil.

No gain/no loss transfer

Disposal of an asset without a gain or loss for capital gains tax purposes regardless of the actual costs and the value of any proceeds.

Nominal rent lease

A lease which is not expected to generate a profit over a number of years.

Non-cash voucher

A voucher which can only be exchanged for goods or services.

Non-natural entity

Legal entity that is not a human being. Typically a company or trust.

Non-savings income

Income other than interest and dividends. Includes employment income, business income and property income.

Normal expenditure out of income exemption

Exemption from inheritance tax where the gift or gifts are not so large that the donor's residual income is inadequate to maintain his or her usual standard of living.

Occupational pension scheme

Pension schemes available for employees set up by their employers.

OECD

Organisation for Economic Co-operation and Development. A grouping of the major economic world powers part of whose remit is to provide an international forum for tax issues (see http//www.oecd.org).

Ordinary residence

A taxpayer is ordinarily resident if the UK is a regular choice of abode which forms part of the regular order of an individual's life.

Output VAT

The VAT on supplies made by a registered trader or on the acquisition by a registered trader of goods from another member state.

Overlap losses

Losses incurred by a trader in a period which forms all or part of the basis period of more than one tax year.

Overlap profits

Profits earned by a trader in a period which forms all or part of the basis period of more than one tax year.

Part disposal

The disposal of part of an asset for capital gains tax purposes.

Partial exemption

Where a VAT registered trader makes some taxable supplies and some exempt supplies he or she may be unable to recover all of his input tax.

Participator

A person who has a share or interest in the capital or income of a close company.

Partnership

Two or more individuals carrying on a business together.

Pay and file

The system used to collect corporation tax before the introduction of corporation tax self assessment (CTSA).

Pay As You Earn (PAYE)

The system used to collect income tax and national insurance contributions from employees.

Payment basis

Charges are recognised for tax purposes when they are paid.

Payroll deduction scheme

Payments to charity from an employee's gross income under the PAYE scheme.

Period of account

The period for which a business prepares accounts.

Personal allowance

An amount of income that can be received tax free by an individual.

Personal company

A company is an individual's personal company if he exercises at least 5% of the voting rights in the company.

Personal equity plan (PEP)

A plan which enables individuals to invest in equities either directly or using unit trusts free of income tax or capital gains tax.

Personal pension scheme

A pension scheme which employees can invest in provided that they are not a member of their employer's occupational pension scheme.

Plant and machinery

Apparatus used by a business person for carrying on business not their own stock-in-trade which they buy or make for resale. Capital expenditure on plant and machinery may qualify for capital allowances.

Political accountability

Tax raising bodies should be accountable to those they raise taxes from. This usually takes the form of a requirement to obtain a mandate from the electorate in regular elections.

Potentially exempt transfer (PET)

A transfer of assets which may become liable to Inheritance Tax if the transferor dies with seven years of the transfer.

Premium

A payment in return for the granting of a lease on land or property.

Principal charge

A charge of 15% of the inheritance scale rate on the value of a discretionary trust every ten years.

Principal private residence

The main residence of an individual or a married couple, generally exempt from capital gains tax. An individual who owns more than one residence may nominate one as his or her main residence.

Profit sharing scheme

A scheme for employees which enables shares in their employer company to be distributed to them.

Profits chargeable to corporation tax (PCTCT)

Tax adjusted profits of a company excluding franked investment income after deducting charges and loss relief.

Profits for small companies rate purposes

Profits chargeable to corporation tax plus franked investment income.

Progressive tax

A tax is progressive if individuals with a larger taxable capacity pay proportionately more of their income in tax than individuals with a lower taxable capacity.

Proportional tax

A tax is proportional if tax paid is a fixed proportion of taxable capacity.

Qualifying corporate bond

A sterling bond which is a normal commercial loan which is exempt from capital gains tax for individuals (but not for companies).

Quarter days

25th March, 24th June, 29th September and 25th December. Often rents are due on the quarter days.

Quarter up rule

A valuation rule for quoted securities for capital gains tax purposes. The valuation is equal to the lower of the two prices quoted in the Daily Official List plus a quarter of the difference between the two prices.

Quarterly accounting

The system used by large companies to account for corporation tax under self-assessment.

Quick succession relief

Relief from inheritance tax when a chargeable transfer increased the value of a person's estate within the previous five years.

Ramsay principle

If an artificial scheme is used to avoid or delay a tax liability the courts can set aside the scheme and instead compare the position of the taxpayer in real terms at the start and finish of the scheme.

Rate applicable to trusts

The 40% (32.5% for dividends) rate for income tax and capital gains tax applied to discretionary trusts.

Rebasing

The procedure under which capital gains are calculated by assuming that assets owned on 31st March 1982 were bought on that date at their market value on that date.

Receipts basis

A way of allocating income to tax years on the basis of when it is received. Also known as cash basis.

Receivable basis

A way of allocating income to tax years on the basis of when it was due to be received. Also known as accruals basis.

Regressive taxes

A tax is regressive if the proportion of tax paid increases as income falls. *See also* Incidence of tax.

Reinvestment relief

Relief from capital gains tax available to individuals or trustees, but not companies, when some or all of the proceeds from the disposal of an asset or a material disposal of shares in a qualifying company are reinvested in a qualifying investment.

Relief

A reduction in tax allowed to a taxpayer.

Relevant supplies

Supplies to a non-taxable person in the UK from another EU member state. The supplier may be liable to register for VAT in the UK.

Remittance basis

A way of determining taxable income on the basis of amounts remitted to the UK.

Remoteness test

A test for determining whether an expense is deductible. An expense which is considered to be too remote from activities of the trade will generally not be deductible.

Renewals basis

An allowable deduction from income from furnished letting for the replacement of furniture.

Rent a room scheme

A scheme under which if an individual lets one or more furnished rooms in their main residence rents received up to £4,250 a year are exempt from tax under Schedule A.

Residence

An individual is deemed to be resident in the UK for a tax year if he or she spends more than 183 days in the UK during the tax year.

Retail prices index (RPI)

An index measuring inflation that is used to calculate the indexation allowance for capital gains tax purposes.

Retail schemes

Special schemes for accounting for VAT which are available to some retailers.

Retirement relief

Relief from capital gains tax is given in any case where a material disposal of business assets is made by an individual who, at the time of the disposal, has attained the age of 50 or has retired on the grounds of ill-health below the age of 50. This no longer applies for tax years after 2000/01.

Reverse charge

A system of accounting for VAT on supplies made to a UK resident registered trader by a person resident overseas.

Reversionary interest

An interest in a trust which will depend on the termination of another interest in the trust.

Rollover relief

See Business asset rollover relief.

Royalty

Payments made in consideration for the use of, or right to use, intellectual property (e.g. patents, copyrights, design plans, trademarks, business processes etc).

Savings income

Income source, primarily interest from banks and building societies.

Schedular system of taxation

All income was taxed under the schedular system in the UK until 2005/6 when a new scheme was introduced for individual taxpayers. Companies continued to use the schedular system until April 2009.

Secondhand goods scheme

A VAT scheme available to traders who buy second- hand goods from individuals who are not registered traders.

Self assessment

A system of administration of taxation in which taxpayers are responsible for assessing their own liability to tax. Applies to most UK taxes.

Self-employed person

An individual who has a contract for services. As compared to an employee who has a contract of service.

Self-supply

A supply of goods or services by a registered person which is used by themselves in the course of their business.

Settled property

Assets held within a trust.

Settlement

A trust.

Seven year cumulation

An inheritance tax computation depends on the transfers of value which have occurred in the seven years prior to the most recent transfer.

Share option scheme

A scheme open to employees and directors which grants them share options.

Short-life asset

Plant or machinery which is kept separate from the general pool for the purposes of calculating capital allowances.

Small Business

To be classed as a small business the entity must have a turnover or balance sheet value of less than €10 million, or fewer than 50 employees.

Small profits (previously companies') rate

The rate at which profits chargeable to corporation tax are taxed provided the profits for small companies rate purposes lie below a given limit.

Small gifts exemption

An inheritance tax exemption for gifts to the same person provided that they have a total value of less than £250 in the tax year.

Special Commissioners

Full-time paid individuals who had been legally qualified for at least ten years who used to hear complex appeals of taxpayers against the assessment of the inspectors before the introduction of the Tribunal System in April 2009.

Stakeholder Pension

Pension scheme available from 6 April 2001 to widen provision for own retirement income. Not tied to earnings and low cost.

Stamp duty

A tax on documents usually involving transfers of property (e.g. houses or shares).

Standard rated supply

Supply by a registered trader of goods or services which are not VAT exempt or zero rated.

Starting rate

Introductory rate of income and corporation taxation.

Statement of practice

A statement issued by HMRC in order to clarify the application of some aspect of the legislation.

Statutory total income

An individual's total income before deduction of allowances.

Structural reliefs

Tax allowances or reliefs considered to be integral to the design of the tax system (i.e. likely to last multiple years rather than undergo substantial changes year on ear).

Substitution effect of tax

A substitution distortion occurs when individuals consume one item rather than another because of the effect of taxation.

Surplus ACT

Used to arise when ACT was paid by a company that could not be set against its corporation tax liability for the period in which the ACT was paid (no longer a core part of the current UK tax system).

TAARS

Targeted anti-avoidance rules – used post Pre-Budget 2005 in relation to corporate tax avoidance.

Taper relief

Relief given to companies with taxable profits lying within given limits. Also called *marginal* relief. Also used to refer to relief given for capital gains from ownership of assets after April 1998 by individuals.

Tax additions

Relating to extra tax that might be included in personal tax computations at step 7 (introduced by ITA 2007).

Tax avoidance

The use of legal means to reduce tax liabilities, although often against the spirit of the legislation.

Tax base

The subject matter on which a tax is based. Tax may be levied on income, wealth or expenditure, making these the primary tax bases.

Tax borne

The tax on an individual's taxable income less tax relief on tax reducers other than those paid net.

Tax credit

A credit received with dividends from UK companies which is equal to the amount of tax deemed to have been suffered by the taxpayer. Also various schemes by which transfers are made to the needy such as working tax credit.

Tax evasion

The use of illegal means to reduce tax liabilities.

Tax expenditures

Tax allowances or reliefs given in place of direct Government subsidies; effectively tax foregone by the Government

Tax liability

Tax borne plus income tax retained on charges paid net.

Tax life

The deemed life of an industrial or agricultural building for the purposes of capital allowances.

Tax payable

Tax liability less tax already suffered and tax credits.

Tax point

The date on which a supply of goods or services is treated as taking place for VAT purposes.

Tax reducer

An allowance or relief which has the effect of reducing the tax due on taxable income. In the case of income tax these specifically relate to step 6 of the personal tax computation (ITA 2007).

Tax relief

The deduction allowed to reduce the amount that must be paid of a specific tax. In the case of income tax, these specifically refer to deductions allowable at step 2 of a personal tax computation to turn total income into net income (ITA 2007).

Tax system

The collection of specific taxes and tax rules that together describe how revenue is raised for a Government.

Tax wedges

In the case of an indirect tax the tax wedge is the difference between the marginal cost of producing a good or service and the marginal benefit of consumption.

Tax year

An income tax year for individuals which runs from 6th April until the following 5th April. A particular tax year is described using the two calendar years crossed by the tax year, e.g. tax year 2014/15 is the tax year starting 6th April 2014 and ending 5th April 2015. Used to be known as fiscal year.

Taxable capacity

This is the capacity of an individual to pay tax and may be measured by reference to the individual's income, expenditure, wealth or even ability to generate income. Not easy to compute with certainty.

Taxable income

Total income less allowances and reliefs.

Taxable person

A person who is, or should be, registered for VAT.

Taxable supply

A supply of goods or services by a registered trader which is not an exempt supply.

Taxable turnover

The turnover of a business which is subject to VAT at any rate.

Taxed income

Income received net of basic rate or lower rate tax.

Taxpayer's Charter

A statement setting out what a taxpayer is entitled to expect from HMRC.

Tenant's repairing lease

A lease where the tenant is obliged to maintain or repair the whole or substantially the whole, of the premises which are the subject of the lease.

Terminal loss relief

An income tax relief available to individuals for losses incurred in the final 12 months of trading.

Transfer of value

A disposition by an individual which reduces the value of their estate for inheritance tax purposes.

Treasury

The Government department responsible to the Chancellor of the Exchequer for the development of tax policy.

Trust

A trust is created when a settlor transfers assets to trustees who hold the assets for the benefit of one or more persons (beneficiaries).

Trustees

Hold assets within a trust for the benefit of one or more persons (beneficiaries).

Unfranked investment income (UFII)

Dividend income received by a UK resident company plus the associated tax credit.

Upper Accruals Point

Upper threshold level at which entitlement to state basic pension is capped. Affects national insurance contribution payments for contracted out employees.

Upper Earnings Limit (UEL)

A point at which the tax rate changes for national insurance contributions for employees and their employers.

Upper Profits Limit

A point at which the tax rate changes for national insurance contributions for business profits.

Value Added Tax (VAT)

An indirect or expenditure tax borne by the final consumer, charged whenever a taxable person makes a taxable supply of goods or services in the course of his or her business.

Value Added Tax Act 1994 (VATA 1994)

The Act containing the principal legislation for VAT.

VAT invoice

An invoice which must be supplied by registered traders to other registered traders.

VAT period

The period of time, usually three months, that is covered by a VAT return.

VAT return

Form VAT 199 which must be submitted to HM Customs and Excise together with any VAT payable within one month of the end of the VAT period.

Vertical equity

A tax system has vertical equity if those in differing economic circumstances are taxed differently, e.g. those on higher incomes pay more tax than those on lower incomes.

Vertical fiscal imbalance

Occurs when there is an imbalance between two levels of government in terms of revenue raising and spending obligations. For example in the UK, local government does not raise enough of its own revenue to fund its spending obligations and must rely on central government grants for funding.

Void period

A period in which there is no tenant leasing property and the property is not occupied by the owner.

Wasting asset

Assets with an estimated remaining useful life of 50 years or less.

Wealth taxes

A wealth tax is levied on a taxpayer's assets at a particular date. The primary difficulty with a wealth tax comes from valuing assets, especially intangibles like pension funds.

Wear and tear allowance

A deduction from the income from furnished lettings to give relief for the wear and tear of furniture and equipment provided.

Withholding taxes

Some income, such as debenture interest, has tax deducted at source regardless of the personal circumstances of the recipient. The tax so deducted is termed a withholding tax.

Work effort and taxes

There is a potentially complicated relationship between work effort and taxes. If marginal rates of tax are too high they may act as a disincentive to work.

Worldwide Debt Cap

Places a limit on the deductibility of interest payments under corporation tax for groups of companies with worldwide operations.

Working Tax Credit

Benefit available to families in which the parent (or parents) are currently working.

Writing down allowance

A capital allowance which is given as a deduction from profits to determine tax adjusted trading income for income tax or corporation tax..

Year of assessment

For income tax, a fiscal or tax year which runs from 6th April to the following 5th April.

Zero rated supply

A supply of goods or services made by a registered trader which is subjected to a nil rate of VAT

✓ Suggested solutions to questions

Chapter 4

Quick quiz answers

Answers provided below are not given using the full computation format. You are, however, advised to use the full computation in producing your answers before checking them here, at least initially, to ensure you have followed the necessary steps correctly and fully understand how these answers are arrived at.

1. Deirdre is entitled to a regular personal allowance (£11,850) to offset her total income for the year. Her income tax computation is therefore:

   total income = £36,700 – her personal allowance of £11,850 = £24,850.

   This would all be taxable at 20% as non-savings income as this only partly fills her basic rate tax band and so her tax liability = £4,970.
   As an employee she probably paid all of this via PAYE throughout the year. However, she should check this against her payslips or annual summary document form her employer (called a P60) to check this is the case.

2. Benson is entitled to a personal allowance of £11,850. His taxable income is (£28,650 + 1,500) – 11,850 = £18,300. The personal allowance should be deducted from his non-savings income making his taxable non-saving income £16,800 (i.e. £28,650 – £11,850)

Tax due:	£
Non-savings	
16,800 @ 20%	3,360.00
Savings	
1,000 PSA @ 0%	-
500 @ 20%	100.00
Tax liability	3,460.00

3. Candice has a taxable income comprising savings income of £18,850; dividend income of £2,500 less a personal allowance of £11,850 i.e. a total taxable income of £9,500. Remember the personal allowance can be offset in any order. As she has no non-savings income, it would benefit Candice to use her personal allowance first against savings income ahead of dividend income, so she will be

able to benefit from the Personal Savings Allowance and part of the Dividend Allowance.

Tax due:	£
Savings	
5,000 @ 0%	–
1,000 PSA @ 0%	–
1,000 @ 20%	200.00
7,000	
Dividends	
2,000 @ 0%	–
500 @ 7.5%	37.50
Tax payable	237.50

4. Taxable income comprises non-saving income of £23,850 less personal allowance of £11,850 and less the patent royalty (grossed up at 100/80) of £250 i.e. £11,750.

Tax due:	£
Non-savings:	
11,750 @ 20%	2,350.00
Add: Tax withheld patent royalty	
250 @ 20%	50.00
Tax liability	2,400.00

5. Dominic's taxable income comprises employment earnings of £21,215 less the personal allowance of £11,850 i.e. £9,365.

Tax due:	£
Non-savings:	
9,365 @ 20%	1,873.00

The charitable gift does not affect Dominic's calculation as he has paid sufficient basic rate tax to cover the repayment to the charity and is not a high rate taxpayer. Dominic will probably have paid this tax payable fully through the PAYE system as he is an employee.

6. Erica is entitled to a personal allowance of £11,850. Her taxable income is £12,350 less her personal allowance of £11,850 plus savings income of £500. Remember the personal allowance can be used to reduce the non-savings income first and the savings rate band available to Erica as her non-savings income is below £5,000.

Tax due:	£
Non-savings	
500 @ 20%	100.00
Savings	
500 @ 0%	–
Tax payable	100.00

7. Frank's taxable income comprises non-savings income of £33,350 less a personal allowance of £11,850 plus dividends of £3,000 i.e. a total taxable income of £24,500.

Tax due:	£
Non-savings	
21,500 @ 20%	4,300.00
Dividends	
2,000 @ 0%	–
1,000 @ 7.5%	75.00
Tax payable	4,375.00

National Insurance contributions: this is only due on his trading income (not dividend income) at Class 2 and Class 4:

Class 2:	£2.95 x 52 =	£153.40
Class 4:	(£33,350 – £8,424) x 9% =	£2,243.34

8. Geoffrey's taxable income comprises non-savings income of £110,500. His personal allowance of £11,850 will be reduced by ½ (£110,500 – £100,000) i.e. £5,250 so he has a taxable income of £103,900 (£110,500 – £6,600).

Tax due:	£
Non-savings	
34,500 @ 20%	6,900.00
69,400 @ 40%	27,760.00
Tax payable	34,660.00

9. Hillary's taxable income comprises non-savings income of £73,850 less a personal allowance of £11,850. She therefore has a taxable income of £62,000.

Tax due:	£	
Non-savings		
34,500 @ 20%	6,900.00	
27,500 @ 40%	11,000.00	
	17,900.00	
Less:		
Tax reducers		
EIS 30% x £50,000	(15,000.00)	
Tax payable	2,900.00	

If Hillary's investment had qualified for Seed EIS, then the tax reducer would have been 50% ie £25,000.

10. Ivan will have to pay class 2 NICs of £2.95 per week for 52 weeks ie £153.40. He will also have to pay Class 4 NICs at 9% on £46,000 – £8,424 ie £37,576 = £3,381.84.

11. Josephine will have to pay primary Class 1 NICs of £500 – £162 x 12% = £40.56.

12. Kamran does not have to pay primary Class 1 NICs on his benefit in kind. His employer will need to pay Class 1A NICs at the rate of 13.8% ie £55.20

Full questions

Question 1

Personal tax computation for Sam for 2018/19

	Non-savings £	Savings £	Dividends £	Total £
Employment earnings	26,850			26,850
Savings income:				
Building society interest		2,000		2,000
Dividend income			3,000	3,000
Net Income	26,850	2,000	3,000	31,500
Less personal allowance	(11,850)			(11,850)
Taxable income	15,000	2,000	3,000	20,000

Income tax due:	£
Non-savings income	
15,000 @ 20%	3,000.00
Savings	
1,000 PSA @ 0%	–
1,000 @ 20%	200.00
Dividend income	
2,000 @ 0%	–
1,000 @ 7.5%	75.00
Tax liability	3,275.00
Less: tax credits:	
PAYE	(3,080.00)
Tax payable	195.00

Note: The charitable donation does not affect the calculation as Sam has paid sufficient basic rate tax and is not a higher rate taxpayer.

Question 2

Personal tax computation for Jasper for 2018/19

	Non-savings £	Savings £	Dividends £	Total £
Employment earnings	67,500			67,500
Savings income:				
Bank interest		3,000		3,000
Dividend income			6,000	6,000
Net Income	67,500	3,000	6,000	76,500
Less personal allowance	(11,850)			(11,850)
Taxable income	55,650	3,000	6,000	64,650

Income tax due:	£
Non-savings income	
34,500 @ 20%	6,900.00
21,150 @ 40%	8,460.00
Savings	
500 PSA @ 0%	–
2,500 @ 40%	1,000.00
Dividend income	
2,000 @ 0%	–
4,000 @ 32.5%	1,300.00
Tax liability	17,660.00
Less: tax credits:	
PAYE	(15,000.00)
Tax payable	2,660.00

Question 3

Personal tax computation for Janet for 2018/19

		Non-Savings £	Savings £	Dividends £	Total £
Income:					
Employment earnings		35,850			35,850
Bonus		3,000			3,000
Savings income:					
Building society interest			5,375		5,375
Property income					
6/12 × £8,000	4,000				
Less expenses	(1,000)	3,000			3,000
Net income		41,850	5,375	0	47,225
Less personal allowance[1]		(6,975)	(4,875)		(11,850)
Taxable income		34,875	500	0	35,375
Tax due:					

Non-savings income	
34,500 @ 20%	6,900.00
375 @ 40%	150.00
Savings income	
500 PSA	–
35,375	
Tax liability	7,050.00
Less: tax credits	
PAYE	(6,500.00)
Tax payable	550.00

Note:

The premium bond winnings are exempt and therefore do not need to form part of Janet's tax computation. Do not forget that the property was only rented for half the year.

1   Janet is a higher rate taxpayer – you can see from the total column that £875 (£35,375 – £34,500) of her taxable income falls into the higher rate band. This means she is entitled to a £500 personal savings allowance. If we allocate all of the personal allowance to the non savings income, then £875 of the savings income will be taxed at 40%. However, by allocating enough of the personal allowance to the savings income to reduce it to £500, and the balance to non savings income, we can reduce the exposure to the higher rate band to £375. This saves Janet £100 tax (£500 x 20%).

Personal tax computation for Dave for 2018/19

	Non-Savings £	Savings £	Dividends £	Total £
Income:				
Employment earnings	34,000			34,000
Savings income:				
Bank deposit account		3,750		3,750
Dividend income:			8,760	8,760
Net income	34,000	3,750	8,760	46,510
Less personal allowances[1]	(11,850)			(11,850)
Taxable income	22,150	3,750	8,760	34,660

Tax due:	£
Non-savings	
22,150 @ 20%	4,430.00
Savings	
500 PSA	–
3,250 @ 20%	650.00

Dividends

2,000 @ 0%	–
6,600 [1] @ 7.5%	495.00
160 @ 32.5%	52.00
34,660	
Tax liability	5,627.00
Less: tax credits	
PAYE	(4,780.00)
Tax payable	847.00

1 Dave is also a higher rate taxpayer, but he has dividends which changes the way we think about allocating the personal allowance. Because the higher rate for dividends is only 32.5% compared to 40% for savings and non savings, it makes more sense to allocate the personal allowance to either savings or non savings. It doesn't actually matter which in this case because in total they are within the basic rate band. So, £34,500 - £22,150 - £3,750 - £2,000 = £6,600 of dividends falls into the basic rate band and £8,760 - £8,600 = £160 of dividends will be taxed at the higher rate.

Chapter 5

Quick quiz answers

1. Helena's bonus is taxable on the earliest of the time the payment is made or the time of entitlement. In this case, the entitlement arose on 31 March 2019, so the bonus will be taxed in the 2018/19 year.

2. Iain can fully reclaim the cost of business calls (£125) against his employment income - although he must keep detailed records of these calls to prove they were wholly, exclusively and necessarily for his employment. However, he won't be able to reclaim any of his line rental costs as these are not for a dedicated business line.

3. Julia's mileage allowance is exempt as it is less than 45p for the first 10,000 miles. She will actually be able to claim a deduction from her employment earnings for the shortfall of 3,000 miles @ (45p - 30p) = £450.

4. Assuming the house is not job related, Keith will be taxed on the annual value of the house of £10,200, plus the extra charge which arises because it is an expensive house of 2.5%× (£250,000 - £75,000) plus the value of the running costs of £2,500 i.e. a total of £17,075.

5. With this emission rating, Lorna will be taxed on £27,000 at the rate of 37% i.e. £9,990.

6. Michael cannot deduct the cost of the golf club subscription. Although he might be able to argue it is wholly and exclusively for his job, he would not be able to argue that it is *necessary*.

7. The annual value for the use of the DVD recorder is 20% x £1,500 = £300. For this year, however, the machine is only available for 6 months so the taxable benefit in kind is 6/12 x £300 = £150.

8. Pauline's use of the bicycle is an exempt benefit. When it is transferred to her, however, she will have a taxable benefit equivalent to the market value at the time, i.e. £500.

9. Quentin's removal expenses are an exempt benefit in kind because they are below the threshold of £8,000. Note, however, that if the new job is within a reasonable commuting distance from his old house, the exemption does not apply.

10. Ravi's employer making a parking space available does not give rise to a taxable benefit.

11. Sumo's tax liability will be:

Trading income	85,500
Personal allowance	(11,850)
Taxable income	73,650

The gross (£7,200 x 100/80) pension contribution will increase the basic rate band to £43,500.

43,500 @ 20%	8,700.00
30,150 @ 40%	12,060.00
73,650	
Tax liability	20,760.00

12. As an employee, Tiffany's contribution to the occupational pension scheme will simply be deducted from her gross salary. No further adjustment to her tax computation is needed as this will give her full tax deduction available at her marginal tax rate. The employer's contribution is not a taxable benefit to Tiffany. Her tax liability (before PAYE) will therefore be:

Employment income (30,850 – 5,000)	25,850
Personal allowance	(11,850)
Taxable income	14,000
Tax liability:	
14,000 @ 20%	2,800.00

Full questions

Question 1

Employment income for Serene Volley

	£
Salary	26,400
Pension contributions (£26,400 x 5%)	(1,320)
	25,080
Car benefit £16,400 @ 29%	4,756
(no fuel benefit arises)	
	29,836

Personal tax computation for Serene Volley for 2018/19

	Non-savings £	Total £
Earnings from employment	29,836	29,836
Interest is exempt		
Total income	29,836	29,836
Less personal allowance	(11,850)	(11,850)
Taxable income	17,986	17,986

Income tax due:	£
Non-savings	
17,986 @ 20%	3,597.20
Tax liability	3,597.20
Less Tax credits	
PAYE	(4,190.00)
Tax payable/(repayable)	(592.80)

Question 2

Employment income for Kim White

	£
Salary	21,600
Beneficial loan[1]	468
	22,068
Expense claim[2]	(4,625)
Employment income	17,443

Notes:

1 The taxable benefit from the beneficial loan is £468.75 (18,750 @ 2.5% x 10/12)

2 Ordinary commuting (travel between home and the permanent workplace) does not qualify for relief. The travel to a temporary workplace qualifies as it is for a period lasting less than 24 months. Kim can therefore make an expense claim based on 10,500 miles as follows:

$$
\begin{array}{lll}
\text{10,000 miles at 45p} & \text{£4,500} \\
\text{500 miles at 25p} & \text{£125}
\end{array}
$$

3   The loan interest paid of £140 is eligible for relief since the loan was used by Kim to finance expenditure for a relevant purpose. It is paid gross.

Personal tax computation for Kim White for 2018/19

	Non-savings £	Savings £	Dividends £	Total £
Earnings from employment	17,443			17,443
Building society interest		750	0	750
Total income	17,443	750	0	18,193
Interest paid[3]	(140)			(140)
	17,303			18,053
Less personal allowance	(11,850)			(11,850)
Taxable income	5,453	750	0	6,203

	£
Income tax due:	
Non-savings	
5,453 @ 20%	1,090.60
Savings (as basic rate PSA £1000)	
750 @ 0%	–
7,053	
Tax liability	1,090.60
Tax payable (before PAYE)	1,090.60

Question 3

(a) Personal tax computation for Domingo Gomez for 2018/19

	Non-savings £	Savings £	Dividends £	Total £
Pensions (6,082 + 3,480)	9,562			9,562
Building society interest		18,160	0	18,160
Total income	9,562	18,160	0	27,722
Less personal allowance	(9,562)	(2,288)		(11,850)
Taxable income	0	15,872	0	15,872

	£
Income tax due:	
Savings	
5,000 @ 0%	0.00
PSA 1,000 @ 0%	0.00
9,872 @ 20%	1,974.40
15,872	
Tax liability	1,974.40
Tax payable	1,974.40

Notes:

1. No tax relief is available in respect of the charity donations as they were not made under the gift aid scheme.

2. Interest from the savings certificate is exempt from income tax.

3. As there is no non-savings income left after his personal allowance Domingo gets the benefit of the full £5,000 savings nil rate band, and as his income falls into the basic rate tax band he receives £1,000 personal savings allowance.

Employment income for Erigo Gomez

	£
Salary	36,000
Pension contributions (36,000 x 6%)	(2,160)
Charitable payroll deductions (12 x 100)	(1,200)
	32,640
Relocation costs (Note 1)	3,400
Mileage allowance (Note 2)	(2,900)
	33,140

Personal tax computation for Erigo Gomez for 2018/19

	Non-savings £	Savings £	Dividends £	Total £
Earnings from employment	33,140	0	0	33,140
Total income	33,140	0	0	33,140
Less personal allowance	(11,850)			(11,850)
Taxable income	21,290	0	0	21,290

	£
Income tax due:	
Non-savings 21,290 @ 20%	4,528.00
Tax liability (before PAYE)	4,528.00

Notes:

1. Only £8,000 of the relocation costs are exempt, and so the taxable benefit is £11,400 – £8,000 = £3,400.

2. The mileage allowance received will be tax free, and Erigo can make the following expense claim:

10,000 miles at 45p	4,500
8,000 miles at 25p	2,000
	6,500
Mileage allowance (18,000 at 20p)	(3,600)
	2,900

(b) Tax returns

Unless the returns are issued late, the latest date that Domingo can file paper self-assessment returns for 2018/19 is 31 October 2019.

If Domingo completes a paper return by 31 October 2019, then HMRC will prepare a self-assessment computation on his behalf.

As Eric is willing to submit an electronic form he has until 31 January 2020 to do this.

(c) Record keeping

1. Domingo and Erigo were not in business during 2018/19, so their records must be retained until one year after 31 January following the tax year, which is 31 January 2021.

2. A failure to maintain records for 2018/19 could result in a penalty of up to £3,000. However, the maximum penalty will only be charged in serious cases.

Question 4

Employment income assessment for Edward King

	£
Director's remuneration	179,000
Pension contributions (£179,000 x 4%)	(7,160)
Charitable payroll deductions (12 x £200)	(2,400)
	169,440
Beneficial loan (£87,000 x 4/12 @ 2.5%)	725
Home entertainment system[1]	2,200
Mileage allowance[2]	(800)
Professional subscription	(240)
Employment income	171,325

Notes:

1. Edward will have been taxed on the use of the home entertainment system totalling £3,120 (£5,200 x 20% x 3) for the tax years 2015/16, 2016/17 and 2017/18. The benefit for the acquisition of the home entertainment system in 2018/19 is the market value at the date of the gift of £2,200, as this is greater than £2,080 (£5,200 – £3,120).

2.

	£
Mileage allowance received 12,000 @ 35p	4,200
Less 10,000 miles @ 45p + 2,000 miles @ 25p	(5,000)
	800

Personal tax computation for Edward King for 2018/19

	Non-savings £	Savings £	Dividends £	Total £
Earnings from employment	171,325	0	0	171,325
Total income	171,325			171,325
Less personal allowance	(nil)	0	0	(nil)
Taxable income	171,325	0	0	171,325

Income tax due:	£
Non-savings	
34,500[1] @ 20%	6,900.00
150,000 – 34,500 @ 40%	46,200.00
171,325 – 150,000 @ 45%	9,596.25
Tax liability	62,696.25
Less:	
PAYE	(62,600.00)
Tax payable	96.25

Note:

1. No extension to the basic rate band (or higher and additional rate bands) is needed for charity donations made by Edward as his gifts were made via the payroll deduction scheme. As such, full relief has already been provided for this in his salary deduction (see section 4.45)

Chapter 6

Quick quiz answers

1. The staff loan written off and the increase in general provision are not deductible for tax purposes and so Matthew must add back £400 in his adjustment of profits.

2. None of this £800 deduction would be allowed under the cash basis. The income would not have been recorded, as the sums have not been received.

3. We need to know the CO_2 emission levels. If they are more than 130g/km, then only 85% of the lease payments will be deductible, i.e. £3,570.

4. Both the T shirts and the Christmas party are fully deductible for tax purposes. Note, however, that as the cost of the Christmas party exceeds £150 per head, a benefit in kind may arise for Orlando's employees.

5. Pauline must add £115 to her profit for tax purposes (i.e. sales value not cost price must be added back).

6. Quentin's landlord will be taxed under the property income rules on £10,000 – (£10,000 × 14 × 2%) i.e. £7,200. Quentin can therefore deduct this amount over the term of the lease i.e. £480 (£7,200 ÷ 15) per annum.

7. The cost of debt collection is deductible. Both the acquisition of new premises and the patent registration are capital transactions and so on face value the fees associated with these are not deductible. However special provision allows the cost of patent registration to be deducted and so Rachel can claim £230.

8. Assuming Gerald does not own multiple properties that provide him with an income over £150,000 a year, HMRC will assume that Gerald will be using the cash basis for his computations of taxable property (unless he expressly opts otherwise to use the accruals basis). On that basis he will be assessed on actual income receive in the year ie 5/12×£8,400 + 7/12×£8,600 = £8,516. If he instead opted to be assessed under the accruals basis he would be assessed on 6/12×£8,400 + 6/12×£8,600 = £8,500.

9. Using the formula for short lease premiums, Heather will be assessed on: £48,000 – (48,000× (40 – 1) ×2%) = £10,560

Full questions

Question 1

The treatment of each of the items, for tax purposes, is as follows:

(a) *Reconstruction of the roof*
The expenditure was incurred to renovate an asset soon after it was acquired and the asset, a building, was not in a usable condition immediately after acquisition. Following the decision in *Law Shipping* the expenditure will be deemed to be capital and hence will be disallowable for tax purposes.

The expenditure on the roof should be added back to the net profit in order to determine the tax adjusted trading profit.

(b) *Embezzlement by the director*
Defalcations by directors are not allowable deductions for trading income purposes. Hence the expense should be added back to the net profit in order to determine the tax adjusted trading profit. (Embezzlement by a staff member (not a partner or director), however, is an allowable tax expense). All payments in connection with criminal offences (e.g. fines or bribes) are explicitly excluded as deductions.

(c) *Redundancy payment to a works manager*
Redundancy payments made wholly and exclusively for the purpose of trade are allowed without limit, provided that the business continues to trade. If Jones ceases to trade there is a limit on the amount of any redundancy payment of the statutory amount plus up to three times the statutory amount. In the case of the works manager the maximum deductible is £48,000

($£12,000 \times 3 + £12,000$). Since the actual payment is lower than this it will be an allowable expense even if Jones ceases to trade. Hence no adjustment needs to be made to determine the tax adjusted trading profit.

(d) *Salary of senior manager seconded to a charity*
Such a payment is specifically allowable for tax purposes and hence no adjustment needs to be made in order to determine the trading profit.

(e) *Costs of the crèche*
The construction costs are capital expenditure and as such are not allowable for tax purposes
The running costs of the crèche are incurred in order to provide a benefit in kind for employees and as such are allowable deductions for tax purposes. Hence the construction costs should be added back to the net profit in order to determine the tax adjusted trading profit while no adjustment is required for the running costs.

(f) *Receipt from insurance company*
The cost of repairing the asset is an allowable expense. The receipt from the insurance company will reduce the allowable expenditure by £18,000 because the business has been reimbursed for its costs.
The receipt of £6,000 in compensation for loss of profits is taxable. Since the business has already reduced the balance on the repairs account by £18,000 and increased the balance on the profits and loss account by £6,000 no adjustments in respect of these items are necessary.

(g) *Gain on the sale of investments*
Capital gains are not taxed under trading income rules. Hence the gain of £30,000 should be deducted in order to calculate the tax adjusted trading profits. We will see in Chapter 8 how capital gains are dealt with.

(h) *Sales to X Ltd*
Drawings in the form of goods or services made by sole traders or partners have to be dealt with at market prices. This includes selling goods to an associate for less than market value. The sales figure should therefore be increased by £30,000.

Question 2

Sam – trading profit for the year ended 5 April 2019

	£	£
Net profit		50,000
Add		
Depreciation	7,600	
Motor expenses (8,800 x 20%) (Note 1)	1,760	
Patent royalties (Note 2)	–	
Personal capital gains tax advice	320	
Gifts to customers (560 + 420) (Note 3)	980	
Own consumption	1,480	12,140

Less		
Use of office (5,120 x 1/8)	640	
Private telephone (1,600 x 25%)	400	
Capital allowances	6,100	(7,140)
Tax adjusted trading profit		55,000

Notes:

1. Of the 25,000 miles driven by Sam during the year ended 5 April 2019, (25,000 – 5,000 = 20,000) x 75%) = 15,000 were for U.K. business journeys. With the addition of the 5,000 miles driven for business in Europe, this means 20,000 of the 25,000 miles driven are for business. The business proportion is therefore 80% (20,000/25,000 x 100).

2. Patent royalties are allowed as a deduction when calculating the trading profit so no adjustment is required. Remember there is a requirement to withhold income tax on patent royalty payments, which is why they receive special mention here.

3. Gifts to customers are an allowable deduction if they cost less than £50 per recipient per year, are not of food, drink, tobacco or vouchers for exchangeable goods and carry a conspicuous advertisement for the business making the gift.

Question 3

a) *Tax-adjusted profits for year ended 31 January 2019 (using the accruals basis)*

	£	£
Surplus per cash book		8,412
Adjustments to get profit calculated on accruals basis:		
Accounts receivable and work done not invoiced		
(£2,900 + 1,300)	4,200	
Accrued costs (interest)	(74)	
		4,126
Profit per accounts (accruals basis)		12,538
Tax adjustments:		
Ben's wages	12,000	
Capital items [1]	7,227	
Entertaining	2,103	
Motor expenses [2]	212	
Lunch costs [5]	246	
Clothing [6]	680	
		22,468
Less: Capital Allowances [3]		(6,830)
Tax-adjusted trading profits – accruals basis [4]		28,176

Note:

1. Capital items comprise computer (£1,855), machinery (£4,122) and repairs to machinery before able to be used (Law Shipping) (£1,250).
2. Motoring expenses– only two-thirds of the costs are for business purposes therefore one third must be added back as is not a business expense.
3. Because you have not yet covered capital allowances, the question gives you this figure – a total of £6,830. Once you have studied capital allowances in Chapter 7, you will be able to see how this is worked out.
4. Because you are given the cash figures in the question, we should really take into account the VAT implications. However, because you haven't yet covered VAT, we have ignored it in this answer. To make the question complete, you would need to know the VAT payable on the purchases (input tax) and the VAT payable on the sales (output tax). The difference would then be removed to reach the profit figure and hence taxable figure, as for a registered company this excludes the VAT impact for recoverable transactions.
5. The food costs are not reclaimable at all as only meals related to overnight stays are allowable – even if he is incurring more costs when travelling on business than we would otherwise (see Caillebotte v Quinn [1975] 50 TC 222 and Watkins v Ashford, Sparkes and Harward [1985] 58 TC 468).
6. Even though the suits are used only for work, they are conventional (not special) clothing and therefore not deductible.

Tax-adjusted profits for year ended 31 January 2019 (using the cash basis)

	£	£
Surplus per cash book [1 and 2]		8,412
Tax adjustments [3]:		
Ben's wages	12,000	
Entertaining [4]	2,103	
Motor expenses [5]	212	
Lunch costs [6]	246	
Clothing [6]	680	
Interest deduction cap [7]	464	
		15,705
Tax-adjusted trading profit – cash basis [8]		24,117

1. No adjustments are made for accounts receivable and un-invoiced work as these are recorded under the cash basis only when they occur.
2. No adjustment is made for accrued expenses when using the cash basis.
3. Rent paid in advance at 11 months x £3,000 also deductible under the cash basis.

4. Entertaining costs are not allowable deductions for tax purposes under either basis.
5. The motor expenses will only be allowable for the business element. Ben may opt to use the fixed rates (i.e. 45p/25p for business miles driven) but the question says that he does not wish to use this.
6. Clothing and lunch costs are not allowable deductions for either basis.
7. Interest as a tax deduction is capped under the cash basis to £500. Therefore, we must disallow (£964 – £500) = £464.
8. Charges for capital items are only included under the cash basis in the periods in which purchases or disposals occur. Capital allowances will therefore not be allowed. All other items are deductible under the cash basis as legitimate expenses incurred and paid within the tax period.

It is often helpful to create a reconciliation to show how the differences arise between the two trading profit figures you have computed using the different bases:

		£
Tax-adjusted profit – accruals basis		28,176
Minus :	debtors and work done not invoiced	(4,200)
	Capital items (inc. capitalised repairs)	(7,227)
Add:	accrued interest costs	74
	capital allowances	6,830
	interest deduction cap	464
Tax-adjusted profit – cash basis		24,117

Chapter 7

Quick quiz answers

1. The car is a high emissions car and so must go into the special rate pool where it will receive an 8% writing down allowance. It does not qualify for either the AIA or FYA. There is no apportionment for the length of ownership within the accounting period and no private use reduction as it is used solely for business purposes.

2. Theresa can claim 100% of £15,000 as this is a low emission car (<75g/km).

3. In 2018/19 Umut would be entitled to the maximum level of AIA of £200,000. The excess over £200,000. i.e. £250,000. is transferred to the main rate pool and the writing down allowance will be @ 18%, i.e. £45,000. This gives Umut a total capital allowance entitlement of £245,000 for the year.

4. Vivian is entitled to a full capital allowance against this purchase using the AIA available for this part of the year. This maximum entitlement is £200,000. If Vivian has used up some or all her AIA for the year and she expects to sell the computer within eight years and realise a loss (i.e. if it is expected to fall in value faster than the 18% main pool capital allowance rate, both of which are quite likely) then it may be worth de-pooling the asset and keeping it separate as a short life asset so as to get the benefit of the balancing allowance that is expected as soon as possible.

5. Walter has sold the car for less than its tax written down value and so for tax purposes has a balancing allowance of £5,000. He can only claim 75% of this (£3,750), however, as he uses the car 75% for business purposes.

6.

Xanthe y/e 31.03.19	£	Main £	CAs £
Opening balance		15,000	
Disposals			
Plant *(lower of cost/proceeds)*		(14,200)	
		800	
WDA (small pool <£1,000)		(800)	800
WDV c/f		nil	
Total allowances			800

7. Yolande's accounts are for 3 months so she can claim 3/12 x £200,000 AIA, + 3/12 x 18% x 100,000 i.e. a total of £52,250.

8. Zeus For y/e 31.3.18:

	£
Trading profit	12,000
Property business income	250,000
	262,000
Less loss relief against general income	(77,500)
Net income	184,500

In 2017/18, the loss relief cap applies to relief against non-trading income ie 25% x £262,000 = £65,500. The relief against trading income is not capped, so the total relief available is £65,500 + £12,000 = £77,500.

Full questions

Question 1

For each new asset, we need to think about whether it qualifies for either ECA or the AIA.

Looking at the new assets acquired by Luke we can say:

- The new van (purchased 29/7/17) qualifies for AIA (remember vans are not treated the same as cars and do qualify for AIA).
- The car purchased 25/10/17 has CO_2 emissions of only 65g/km and so will qualify for enhanced capital allowances (i.e. 100% in year of purchase).
- The plant disposed of must be deducted from the relevant pool at the lower of cost or the value it is sold for. It will have been added to the main pool when acquired (pre AIA commencing) and so should be deducted from there.
- The new plant (purchased 1/05/18) qualifies for AIA.
- Cars don't qualify for AIA and so the second new car (purchased 15/5/18) is put into either the main or special rate pools depending on their CO_2 emission levels. Here the car is 180g/km, and so must go into the special rate pool.
- The new lift (purchased 30/5/18) is an integral feature that also qualifies for AIA.
- The additions all fall well within the AIA allowance for the period so can be fully claimed in tax year. The maximum AIA limit is £200,000 for the relevant period.
- No hybrid rates apply as the capital allowances rates did not change in this period and it is a 12 month accounting period

y/e 30/6/18	£	Main £	Sp rate £	CAs £
Opening balance		10,000		
Additions qualifying for ECA				
1st new car (25/10/17)	6,000			6,000
Additions qualifying for AIA:				
New van (29/7/17)	4,000			
New plant (1/5/18)	15,000			
New lift (30/5/18)	8,000			
AIA	27,000			27,000
Balance to main pool		nil		
Other Additions				
2nd new car (15/5/18)			20,000	

Disposals

Plant	(7,000)		
	3,000	20,000	
WDA (18%)	(540)		540
WDA (8%)		(1,600)	1,600
WDV c/f	2,460	18,400	
Total allowances			35,140

Question 2

	£
Net loss as per accounts	(56,400)
Add back accounting depreciation	12,340
Less capital allowances (see below)	(384)
Tax adjusted trading loss	(44,444)

	Main pool	Short life Asset	Special rate pool	CAs
	£	£	£	£
WDV b/f	21,600	8,800		
Additions				
Car			11,800	
Disposals				
Short life asset		(11,700)		
Lorry	(8,600)			
	13,000		11,800	
Balancing charge		(2,900)		(2,900)
WDA (18%/8%)	(2,340)		(944)	3,284
WDV c/f	10,660	nil	10,856	
Total allowances				384

The new Ford Focus car must go into a special rate pool as it is a high emissions car (CO_2 emissions exceed 130g/km).

The net loss from Jogger can be dealt with in a number of ways as he uses the accruals basis. Phil can use it to reduce his current year's income, i.e. offset it against other income sources he may have for the year such as property income or savings income. He can carry it back to the previous year, or he can carry it forward to future years. If he carries it forward to future years, it can only then be offset against subsequent 'Jogger' profits.

Question 3

	Main £	Special £	Mercedes £	CAs £
Balance brought forward	59,400	14,200	26,300	
Additions qualifying for ECAs				
Solar panels	27,000			
ECA 100% (Note 1)	(27,000)			27,000
Additions qualifying for AIA:				
Air conditioning	28,000			
Sewing machines	15,000			
AIA (Note 2)	(43,000)			43,000
Disposals (5 x £250)	(1,250)			
	58,150	14,200	26,300	
Writing down allowance (18%)	(10,467)			10,467
Writing down allowance (8%)		(1,136)	(2,104)x50%	2,188
Written down value c/f	47,683	13,064	24,196	
Allowances for the accounting period				82,655

Notes:

1. The value used for the solar panels is the net value, after deducting the government grant.
2. The AIA maximum limit for the year is £200,000. As the AIA cap did not change in the period, no transitional rate needs to be applied.
3. The Mercedes should normally be placed in the relevant pool – in this case it would be the special rate pool as it has emissions exceeding 130g/km. However, as also has private use, it must be given its own pool, and the special pool rate be used for the WDA (i.e. 8%), with a restriction (at 50% in this case) for the allowable part of the capital allowance. Note that if it was an employee of the business (not the owner) using it then no private usage would be deducted. Instead the employee would be taxed on the company car as a benefit in kind.
4. As the capital allowance rates did not change in this period, no hybrid rates need to be applied.

Chapter 8

Quick quiz answers

1. Andrew will have a chargeable gain as follows:

	£
Disposal proceeds	5,000
Cost	(1,700)
Chargeable gain	3,300

He will have to add this gain to any others in the year to see if he has to pay any CGT on this transaction. If he has no other gains he'll not have to pay CGT on this as it comes under his AEA for 2018/19.

2. A hearse may be exempt from capital gains tax as a motor vehicle, however, the exemption is for passenger vehicles and arguably a hearse is not constructed to carry passengers (of the kind implied by the rule anyway). However, assuming Barbara is not carrying on a business as an undertaker, the hearse will be exempt as a wasting chattel (estimated life less than 50 years) and so Barbara will not pay capital gains tax on the profit.

3. A painting is a chattel and since it was sold for less than £6,000, it will be exempt from capital gains tax.

4. As Davina's gain of £450,000 is fully available for entrepreneurs' relief, it will simply be subject to a 10% charge after deducting the AEA.

5. Eddie will be able to claim a loss of £6,950 based on deemed disposal proceeds of £50.

6. When part of an asset is sold, the formula A ÷ (A+B) is used to determine how much of the cost is attributable to the part of the asset that has been sold. In this case 200,000 ÷ (860,000 + 200,000) of the original cost is attributed to the part sold i.e. £94,340 and so the gain is £105,660. This is then reduced by the AEA of £11,700. Because Felicity is a higher rate taxpayer, her capital gains tax liability is therefore £93,960 x 20% = £18,792.00.

7. Gregory must acquire the new asset between August 2017 and August 2021 in order to qualify for rollover relief, unless HMRC allows an extension. HMRC will do this if he can show a firm intention to acquire a new asset within the time limit, but was prevented from doing so by circumstances beyond his control, and that he acquired the new asset as soon as he reasonably could.

8. The part of the gain attributable to the consideration in shares is £50,000 x £80,000/£100,000 = £40,000. This is the part of the gain that can be deferred using incorporation relief. The cost of the shares for any future disposal will therefore be £80,000, reduced by the deferred gain of £40,000 i.e. a cost base of £40,000. Helen may be liable to tax on the balance of the gain of £10,000 for the year 2018/19, depending on how much of her AEA is available to reduce the gain.

9. The £12,200 capital loss generated in 2018/19 must first be set against the £24,800 capital gain in 2018/19. The capital loss brought forward will then be set against the £12,600 net 2018/19 gain, but the loss relief can be restricted to protect the £11,700 2018/19 annual exemption so only £900 of the brought forward loss will be used in 2018/19 (£12,600 – £11,700). This leaves £6,200 capital loss to carry forward to the next tax year.

10. £143,000. The proceeds of the old warehouse exceeds the investment in the new warehouse by more than the value of the chargeable gain, so there can be no rollover in this case and all of the chargeable gain will be taxable.

Full questions

Question 1

Net chargeable gains for 2018/19 are:

	£
Antique table [1]	6,500
Cottage [2]	0
Plot of land [3]	1,357
Ryft plc shares [4]	0
PK plc shares [5]	2,125
	9,982

Because this is below the AEA, no capital gains tax will be payable.

1 – The table is a chattel whose proceeds and cost both exceed £6,000.

	£
Net sales proceeds (£35,000 – £3,500)	31,500
Less: cost	(25,000)
Gain	6,500

2 – Holiday cottage – disposed of to a connected person and therefore deemed proceeds of market value used. The loss arising can only be used against gains on disposals to the same person and is computed as follows:

	£
Proceeds – market value	45,000
Less: incidental costs of disposal	(1,100)
	43,900
Less cost	(47,500)
Loss – only use against gains on disposals to the same person	(3,600)

3 – Plot of land

	£
Proceeds	13,000
Less: incidental costs of disposal	(500)
	12,500
Less: Cost	
£24,000 x (£13,000/ (£13,000 + £15,000))	(11,143)
Gain	1,357

4 – Ryft plc shares – exempt as sold within an ISA.

5 – PK plc shares – sale proceeds must be matched with cost of shares purchased within the following 30 days.

	£
Proceeds	8,500
Less: cost – £8,500 x 1,200/1,600	(6,375)
Gain	2,125

Question 2

Jointly owned property

(a) Cars are exempt from capital gains tax

(b) The chargeable gain on the house is calculated as follows:

	£
Disposal proceeds	381,900
Cost	(86,000)
	295,900
Principal private residence exemption (PPR)	(265,638)
	30,262

David and Angela are assessed on half the gain each – and remember that the rate applicable to residential property remains at the 2015/16 rate of 18% or 28%.

The total period of ownership of the house is 264 months (237 + 27) of which 237 months qualify for exemption as follows:

	Exempt	Chargeable
1/10/96 – 31/3/00 (occupied)	42	
1/4/00 – 31/12/03 (working in UK)	45	
1/1/03 – 31/12/15 (occupied)	132	
1/1/16 – 31/03/17 (unoccupied)		27
1/4/17 – 30/9/19 (final 18 months)	18	
	237	27

The exemption is therefore £265,638 (295,900 x 237/264).

David Brook

(a) The antique table is a non-wasting chattel, but is exempt from capital gains tax because the gross sale proceeds were less than £6,000.

(b) The transfer of 20,000 £1 ordinary shares in Bend Ltd to Angela does not give rise to any gain or loss, because it is a transfer between spouses.

(c) Ordinary shares in Galatico plc

Deemed proceeds (15,000 x £2.95)	44,250
Cost (15,000 x £1.96)	(29,400)
	14,850

Using the quarter up method (see section 8.4 under Gross Disposal Proceeds) to determine the market value, the shares in Galatico plc are valued at £2.95 (£2.90 + ¼ (3.10 – 2.90)

Using weighted average, the cost of the shares disposed of is £1.96 per share (£39,200/20,000)

	£	£
Capital gains tax liability:		
House (30,262/2)	15,131	
Annual exemption*	(11,700)	
	3,431	
Capital gains tax at 18%		617.58
Galatico plc shares	14,850	
Annual exemption (all used on the House sale)	(0)	
	14,850	
Capital gains tax at 10%		1,485.00
Total Capital Gains Tax due		2,102.58

* You are allowed to apply the annual exemption in whatever way best suites the taxpayer. It will be better here to assign it to the house sale first as that incurs CGT at a higher rate.

Angela Brook

(a) The antique cabinet is a non-wasting chattel. The gain is restricted to £2,000 (7,200 – 6,000 = 1,200 x 5/3) as this is less than £3,500 (7,200 – 3,700).

(b) Bend Ltd shares

Disposal proceeds	62,400
Cost (48,000 x 15,000/20,000)	(36,000)
	26,400

David's original cost is used in calculating the capital gain on the disposal of shares in Bend Ltd.

	£	£
Capital gains tax liability:		
House (30,262/2)	15,131	
Annual exemption*	(11,700)	
	3,431	
Capital gains tax at 28%		960.68
Antique cabinet	2,000	
Ordinary shares in Bend Ltd	26,400	
Chargeable gains	28,400	
Annual exemption (all used on the House sale)	(0)	
	28,400	
Capital gains tax @ 20%		5,680.00
Total Capital Gains Tax due		6,640.68
Due 31 January 2020		

*Again, the annual exemption should be applied to the house sale for Angela as this gives her the lower CGT bill.

Question 3

(a) Freehold office building

	£
Disposal proceeds	246,000
Cost	(104,000)
Potential Chargeable gain	142,000
Less amount not reinvested (£246,000 – £136,000)	(110,000)
Gain eligible to be rolled over	32,000

The chargeable gain is £110,000 as this is the amount not re-invested and is lower than the gain calculated.

(b) Retail business: Goodwill

	£
Disposal proceeds	120,000
Cost	nil
	120,000
Rollover relief (120,000 – 36,000)	(84,000)
Chargeable gain	36,000

Note:

The proportion of the gain relating to the cash consideration cannot be rolled over, so £36,000 (120,000 x 60,000/200,000) of the gain is immediately chargeable to capital gains tax.

(c) Ordinary shares in Gandua Ltd

	£
Deemed proceeds	220,000
Cost	(112,000)
	108,000
Gift relief	(90,000)
Chargeable gain	18,000

Note:

Gift relief is restricted to £90,000 (£108,000 x £150,000/£180,000) being the proportion of chargeable business assets to chargeable assets.

(d) Antique vase

The insurance proceeds of £68,000 received by Wilson have been fully reinvested in a replacement antique vase. The disposal is therefore on a 'no gain, no loss' basis, with the capital gain of £19,000 (insurance proceeds of

£68,000 less original cost of £49,000) being set against the cost of the replacement antique vase.

(e) **Land**

	£
Disposal proceeds	85,000
Cost	(68,000)
	17,000

Note:
The cost relating to the ten acres of land sold is £68,000 (120,000 x 85,000/150,000 (85,000 + 65,000)).

Chapter 9

Quick quiz answers

1. Grotius Ltd will have two accounting periods for tax purposes, the year ended 31 August, 2018 and the four months ended 31 December, 2018.

2. The dividends do not form part of taxable total profits and so are not taxed as part of Helvetius' income.

3. Isocrates Ltd can claim 4% per annum as a deduction in calculating trade profits, as this exceeds the rate used for accounting purposes which is 3%.

4. Justinian Ltd must include £4,875 in its total taxable profits under trade profits (£3,900 × 100 ÷80). The income tax withheld on the patent royalties by the payer of £975 (£4,875 – £3,900) can be offset against any income tax withheld on payments made by the company, and any surplus can be reclaimed against the corporation tax liability.

5. Lychophron Ltd is a large company for instalment payment purposes as its profits exceed the relevant threshold (£1.5m x 5/12 = £625,000). As such it will have instalments due on 14 July, 2018 and 14 September, 2018 for this short period.

6. The non-trading loan relationship profit will be £7,000 – (£5,650 + £1,200) = £150. The loan to purchase plant is a trading loan relationship, not a non-trading loan relationship.

7. New Money Ltd's research costs are deductible so no adjustment is required to the accounting profit for the £11,000. The special R&D deduction for tax purposes gives an *additional* deduction of £11,000 x 130% i.e. £14,300. At a corporation tax rate of 19% this will mean a reduction in corporation tax of £2,717.

8. Origami Ltd has total taxable profits of £11m for the year ended 30 June 2018. After deducting the £5m allowance, the remaining £6m is multiplied by 50% i.e. £3m. This means £5m – £3m = £8m can be offset this year, leaving £2m to be carried forward to the next year.

9.

Proceeds	14,600
Cost	(5,000)
Unindexed gain	9,600
Indexation allowance	
$\dfrac{278.1 - 179.3}{179.3}$ 0.551 × 5,000	(2,755)
Indexed gain	6,845

10. When Quay Ltd pays corporation tax for the year ended for the accounting period ended 31 July 2018 the company can recover 50% of the penalty tax, as 50% of the loan has been repaid, i.e. £4,875. The remaining penalty tax can be recovered if the shareholder repays more of the remaining loan, or if the company writes the remaining loan off.

11. Because Ranch Ltd is a close company and a benefit has been provided to a non-director, non-employee participator, the company cannot deduct any costs, including capital allowances in respect of the car. Billy is taxed on the value of the benefit as if it were a dividend.

12. Time, Verity and Wallace are associated companies for the purposes of the corporation tax rate bands. Only Time and Wallace can exchange losses since they are the only companies with the required 75% ownership relationship. These two companies can also form a capital gains group.

Full questions

Question 1

Ultimate Upholsterers Ltd, Corporation Tax computation for the 12 months to 31 March 2019

		£
Trading Profit (Note 1)		324,960
Non-trade loan relationships:		
Loan interest receivable	12,000	
Less Debenture Interest payable	(10,000)	
		2,000
Chargeable gain (Note 2)		7,410
Taxable total profits		334,370
Corporation tax: £334,370 × 19%		63,530.30

Note 1: calculation of trade profits

In order to calculate the trade profits we need to calculate the capital allowances. The writing down allowance is given in the question. Capital allowances are not available on buildings. However, tax relief will be available for the lease premium paid. The landlord will be assessed on £26,000 i.e.

£50,000 – £24,000   (£50,000 × (25 – 1) ×2%).

Ultimate Upholsterers will be able to claim relief of £1,040 (£26,000 ÷ 25).

Adjustment of Profits:	£
Trading profit	375,000
Less Capital Allowances:	
Plant and machinery	(49,000)
Less relief on lease premium paid	(1,040)
Adjusted trade profits	324,960

Note 2: calculation of chargeable gain on land

	£
Proceeds	47,410
Less cost	(10,000)
Unindexed gain	37,410
Less indexation allowance:	
$\dfrac{278.1 - 90.87}{90.87}$	
£10,000 × 2.060	(20,600)
Indexed gain	16,810

Question 2

With two associated companies the applicable limit is £750,000 (£1.5m ÷ 2). With augmented profit of £1.2million ABC Ltd and a tax liability over £10,000, the company is required to make instalment payments of their tax liability.

a) Instalment dates will be

1st instalment	31 Oct 2017 + 6 months + 14 days	14 May 2018
2nd instalment	14 May 2018 + 3 months	14 Aug 2018
3rd instalment	14 Aug 2018 + 3 months	14 Nov 2018
Final instalment	14 Nov 2018 + 3 months	14 Feb 2019

Amounts due on each date above:

$$\frac{3 \times 228,000}{12} = £57,000$$

b) Instalment dates

1st instalment	31 Oct 2018 + 6 months+ 14 days		14 May 2018
2nd instalment	14 May 2018 + 3 months		14 Aug 2018
3rd instalment	(not due as falls beyond final instalment date)		
Final instalment 30 Jun 2018 + 3 months + 14 days			14 Oct 2018

Amounts due each instalment

$$\frac{3 \times 228,000}{8} = £85,500$$

Balance due in final instalment £57,000.

Question 3

In order to answer this question, first we must perform a trading profit adjustment. As part of this process, we will need to compute the capital allowances that are available to the company.

1 Capital allowances

Plant and machinery		Main pool	Allowances
Additions eligible for AIA:			
31/1/19 Plant	10,500		
AIA	(10,500)		10,500
31/1/19 Low emission car			
(private use n/a)	13,000		
ECA 100%	(13,000)		13,000
Writing down allowance			
1/4/18 Balance brought forward		263,504	
Disposal 1/8/18		(9,400)	
		254,104	
WDA @ 18%		(45,738)	45,738
WDV c/f		208,366	
Total allowances			69,238

2 Trade profits

Net profit as per accounts		127,663
Add back:		
Depreciation (not deductible)	43,150	
Non trading loan interest payable (reclassify)	700	
Entertaining (not deductible)	730	
Charitable donation (reclassify)	5,000	
Trade expenses disallowable:		
Gifts of alcohol	280	
Legal expenses for non-trading loan (reclassify)	500	50,360
		178,023

Less

Debenture interest (reclassify)	1,200	
Building society interest (reclassify)	759	
Capital allowances	<u>69,238</u>	<u>(71,197)</u>
Adjusted Trade profits		<u>106,826</u>

Corporation Tax computation

Trade Profits		106,826
Non trading loan relationships:		
Debenture interest	1,200	
Building society interest	759	
Less non trading loan interest	(700)	
Legal costs re non trading loan	<u>(500)</u>	<u>759</u>
		107,585
Less charitable donation		<u>(5,000)</u>
Taxable Total Profits		<u>102,585</u>

Corporation tax

£102,585 @ 19%   £19,491.15

Payable 1/1/20

Chapter 10

Quick quiz answers

1. Yes, Kieran will have to register for VAT as his turnover exceeds the threshold which is £85,000 with effect from 1 April 2018.

2. The value of the supply is £500 so the VAT is £100.00. From 1 April 2015, a settlement discount is only taken into account when the customer actually takes advantage of it.

3. Maurice does not have to register as his taxable supplies are less than the threshold. He could, however, register voluntarily so that he can reclaim his input tax.

4. The input tax attributable to taxable supplies is £50,000. Nigella can also recover a portion of the unattributable input tax i.e. 80%, since 80% of her supplies are taxable ((£500,000–£100,000)÷£500,000). This means that a total of £53,200 is recoverable and the balance of £5,800 is not recoverable. Do not forget the de minimus test though, £5,800 spread over the whole year is £483 per month which is less than the de minimus of £625 and so Nigella can in fact recover all of her input tax.

5. The basic tax point is 20 August as this is when the goods are made available to the customer. Do not forget though that this basic tax point can be altered if an invoice has been issued within 14 days of the basic tax point. That is the case here, and so the actual tax point will be 30 August, the date of issue of the invoice, even though the customer did not pay until 13 September.

6. Under cash accounting we are only concerned about cash received and paid, not invoices issued. Portia has received £5,525 from her debtors, so we can use the VAT fraction of 1/6 to work out the VAT i.e. £920.83. She has paid £4,000 to suppliers before VAT and so the tax on that is @20% i.e. £800.00. Portia must therefore pay HMRC the difference between these two figures i.e. £920.83 minus £800.00 which is £120.83.

7. The earliest quarterly return in which relief can be claimed for the impaired debt is the quarter ended 30 June 2019, i.e. the quarter in which the debt has been outstanding for six months (10 April 2019).

8. Roxanne can recover £333 i.e. all the tax on the repairs @ 1/6 x £2,000. Input tax is not recoverable on the car itself because it is partly used for private purposes.

9. Goods acquired within 4 years prior to registration and held on registration date, services supplied within six months prior to registration qualify for input tax recovery. Suzanne can therefore recover £550 (accountancy fees and spare parts).

10. Deductible input tax – quarter ended 31 October, 2018

	£
Input tax attributable to taxable supplies	18,000
Proportion of remaining input tax	
£88,400 ÷ £100,000 = 89% (rounded)	
89% × (£24,000 – £18,000 – £1,500)	4,005
	22,005

(Non deductible of £1,995 exceeds *de minimus* of £625 per month.)

Full questions

Question 1

A person who makes taxable supplies becomes liable to be registered for VAT:

- at the end of any month, if the value of his or her taxable supplies in the period of one year then ending has exceeded £85,000, or
- at any time, if there are reasonable grounds for believing that the value of his or her taxable supplies in the period of thirty days then beginning will exceed £85,000.

Taxable supplies are made up of both standard rated and zero rated supplies. Since the trader's taxable supplies of £87,000 (£78,000 + £9,000) exceeds the annual limit of £85,000, the trader is liable to register for VAT. The trader must notify HMRC within 30 days of the end of the month in which the limits were exceeded. The trader will then be registered from the first day of the following month.

Had the trader voluntarily registered from the beginning of the accounting period his VAT position would have been:

	£
Output tax:	
Standard-rated supplies £9,000 × 20%	1,800
Less input tax:	
(9,000 + 4,000) × 1/6	(2,166)
VAT recoverable	(366)

Question 2

VAT for the year ended 31 March 2019

	£	£
Output VAT		
Standard rated sales (£115,200 x 20/120)		19,200
Zero rated sales		0
Input VAT		
Impairment losses (£1,440 x 20/120)	240	
Standard rated purchases (£43,200 x 20/120)	7,200	
Zero rated purchases	0	
Rent (£1,200 x 13 x 20/120)	2,600	
Telephone (£2,600 x 60% x 20/120)	260	
Entertaining UK customers	0	
Entertaining overseas customers (£240 x 20/120)	40	(10,340)
VAT payable		8,860

Question 3

(a) VAT Return Quarter ended 30 November 2018

	£	£
Output VAT		
Cash sales (28,000 x 20%)		5,600
Credit sales		2,292
Input VAT		
Purchases and expenses (11,200 x 20%)	2,240	
Impairment loss (800 x 20%) [2]	160	(2,400)
		5,492

The VAT return for the quarter ended 30 November 2018 should be submitted by 31 December 2018, being one month after the end of the VAT period.

Note:

1. The calculation of output VAT on the credit sales takes into account the discount for prompt payment, but only for the customers who took it:

   90% x £12,000 x 95% x 20% = £2,052

   10% x £12,000 x 100% x 20% = £240

2. Relief for an impairment loss is not given until six months from the time that payment is due. Therefore, relief can only be claimed in respect of the invoice due for payment on 10 April 2018. Relief is based on the amount of output VAT that would have originally been paid.

(b) Anne can use the cash accounting scheme if her expected taxable turnover for the next 12 months does not exceed £1,350,000. In addition, Anne must be up to date with her VAT returns and VAT payments. Output VAT on most credit sales will be accounted for up to one month later than at present, since the scheme will result in the tax point becoming the date that payment is received from her customers. However, the recovery of input VAT will be delayed by two months. The scheme will provide automatic bad debt relief should a credit sale customer default on the payment of the debt.

(c) (i) Sale of assets on a piecemeal basis: upon cessation of trading, Anne will cease to make taxable supplies, so her VAT registration will be cancelled on the date of cessation or an agreed later date. Output VAT will be due in respect of the fixed assets at the date of de-registration on which VAT has been claimed (although output VAT is not due if it totals less than £1,000).

(c) (ii) Sale of business as a going concern: Since the purchaser is already registered for VAT, Anne's registration will be cancelled as above. A sale of a business as a going concern is outside the scope of VAT and therefore output VAT will not be due.

Chapter 11

Question 1

Without a salary sacrifice, Zainab has a gross pension contribution of £100 per month, because the incentive system to encourage pension contributions adds basic rate tax (currently 20%) to the pension contribution, so her £80 net pay contribution becomes a gross contribution of £100. Assuming she is a basic rate taxpayer, Zainab could sacrifice £119 of gross (before tax and NIC) pay each month, which would be worth £80 of net pay after deduction of basic rate tax and national insurance (80 x 100/100−(20+12.8). The employer contributes this sacrificed salary of £119 to Zainab's pension, so pension contribution increases by £19 compared to the previous arrangement. Zainab's net (take home) pay is the same, but she has now put more each month into her pension. Her employer saves £16.42 in national insurance contributions (£119 x 13.8%).

Question 2

(a)

- Andrew is under the control of Slick Productions Ltd
- Andrew is not taking any financial risk
- Andrew works a set number of hours, is paid by the hour and is paid for overtime
- Andrew cannot profit from sound management
- Andrew is required to do the work personally
- There is an obligation to accept the work that is offered
- Andrew does not provide his own equipment.

Chapter 12

Question 1

Petra's income will be subject to UK tax as follows:

i. Bank Interest − not taxable as not remitted to the UK;
ii. Employment income − taxable, since it was paid by a UK employer for work performed in the UK and would get relevant personal allowances for this income.

As a non-domiciled but resident and ordinarily resident taxpayer, Petra will also have to pay the relevant annual remittance based charge to keep her remittance basis of assessment − unless she has foreign income of less than £2,000 or has not been in the UK as a non-domicile for seven of the last ten years. The size of this charge may mean it is more tax effective for her to give up this tax status and instead be taxed on her worldwide income as if she was domiciled in the UK (with relief then potentially available for foreign taxes paid).

Question 2

Even though Andromeda is incorporated in France, its central management and control is located in the UK, because most of the directors live here and this is where the board meetings are held. This means that Andromeda must pay UK corporation tax. If France also treats Andromeda as a resident company for tax purposes, then the double tax treaty between them will determine which country has priority, usually the country where the effective management is carried out, in this case probably the UK.

Question 3

The under-pricing of goods exported by Zanzibar to Zeus means that the UK profits of Zanzibar will be understated, and this will attract the operation of the transfer pricing rules. These require Zanzibar to use arm's length prices to compute its UK profit for tax purposes. The company will have to look to the OECD guidelines to determine which method best fits its situation, and be prepared to justify the choice to HMRC, which includes keeping documentation to show how the arm's length price was calculated.

Question 4

	Non-savings £	Savings £	Dividends £	Total £
Income:				
Employment Income	42,000			42,000
Overseas rental income	7,000			7,000
Total Income	49,000			49,000
Less Personal Allowance	(11,850)			(11,850)
Total Taxable Income	37,150			37,150

Tax Due:				
Non-savings income	34,500	@ 20%	6,900.00
	2,650	@ 40%	1,060.00
Tax Borne			7,960.00
Less:			
Double tax relief ([1])			(1,930.00)
UK Tax Payable			6,030.00

Notes:

1. The double tax relief is the lower of the overseas tax paid and the UK tax on the overseas income.

The rents are taxed at a higher rate overseas than the UK tax. We need to calculate the amount of UK tax attributable to the rent.

Without the rental income, Gerald's taxable income would be £30,150 and the UK tax at 20% would be £6,030.00. Therefore, the UK tax on rents is £7,960.00 – £6,030.00 = £1,930.00. This is lower than the £3,150 overseas tax paid, so is all the UK income tax liability is reduced by.

(b)

Treated as an employee:

	£
Employment income	50,000
Personal allowance	(11,850)
Taxable income	38,150

Income tax	
34,500 @ 20%	6,900.00
3,650 @ 40%	1,460.00
Income tax liability	8,360.00

Class 1 NIC will be (using annual thresholds):
(46,350 – 8,424) @ 12% + (50,000 – 46,350) @ 2% = 4,551.12 + 73.00 = £4,624.12

Treated as self-employed:
Andrew's trading profit for 2018/19 will be £50,000 so his income tax liability will be unchanged at £8,360.00.

Class 2 NIC will be £153.40 (£2.95 x 52)
Class 4 NIC will be (46,350 – 8,424) = 37,926 @ 9% + (50,000 – 46,350) = 3,650 @ 2% = £3,413.34 + 73.00 = £3,486.34.

Index

Index of cases

Subject index

Notes:

App A/B = See Appendix A or B
G = Defined in Glossary
W = See Website for more details
Supp = see online supplement for more details